HIDING MAN

HIDING MAN

A BIOGRAPHY OF DONALD BARTHELME

TRACY DAUGHERTY

ST. MARTIN'S PRESS ❊ NEW YORK

The quotation from *Donald Barthelme: Genesis of a Cool Sound,* by Helen Moore Barthelme, is reprinted with the permission of Texas A & M University Press.

www.stmartins.com

Book design by Mspace/Maura Fadden Rosenthal

Library of Congress Cataloging-in-Publication Data
Daugherty, Tracy.
    Hiding man : a biography of Donald Barthelme / Tracy Daugherty.—1st ed.
        p. cm.
    Includes bibliographical references.
    ISBN-13:   978-0-312-37868-4
    ISBN-10:   0-312-37868-8
  1. Barthelme, Donald.   2. Authors, American—20th century—Biography.
3. Postmodernism (Literature)—United States.   I. Title.
    PS3552.A76Z66 2009
    813'.54—dc22
    [B]

                                                            2008029881

First Edition: February 2009

10   9   8   7   6   5   4   3   2   1

For my mother, my father, and my sister

CONTENTS

Try to be a man about whom nothing is known.
                    —Donald Barthelme, *Snow White*

I loved idiot paintings, tops of doors, decors, saltimbanques, canvases,
signboards, popular engravings, obsolete literature, church Latin,
badly-spelled pornographic works, novels by our grandmothers, fairy
tales, little children's books, old operas, folk refrains, popular rhythms.
                    —Rimbaud, "A Season in Hell"

... the author ... historically died of a mortal disease but poetically died
of longing for eternity.
                    —Kierkegaard, *The Point of View for My Work as an Author*

THE LOST TEACHER

The assignment was simple: Find a copy of John Ashbery's *Three Poems,* read it, buy a bottle of wine, go home, sit in front of the typewriter, drink the wine, don't sleep, and produce, by dawn, twelve pages of Ashbery imitation.

A dutiful student, I walked to the Brazos Bookstore, a few blocks from my apartment, and purchased a paperback edition of the book (nobody walks in Houston, so this was more dutiful than it sounds). Next I made my way to Weingarten's to pick up a bottle of red. I didn't drink much, and didn't know one wine from another. Then I went home.

I lived in an efficiency apartment in a slightly fixed-up, but not fixed up enough, old building near a freeway underpass southwest of downtown. Always, when I unlocked my door, I was greeted by loud scurrying. The bugs were so big, I felt sure I'd return someday to find them pulling books from my shelves, rearranging the space more to their liking. The apartment was close to where my teacher lived when he was a young man, writing and publishing his first short stories. I didn't know this then, and if I had, it would have made me more self-conscious than I already was about my work.

Thus the assignment. I was in my first year of a Ph.D. program, but really I was just stalling for time while trying to write a novel. My fellow students, talented and confident, intimidated me. Determined

INTRODUCTION

to meet their standards and to perform perfectly, I wasn't performing at all. I edited in my head long before my hands scooched near a keyboard. My pages remained pristinely, sadly blank.

My teacher's solution: Ashbery, sleeplessness, and alcohol. He didn't tell me I needed to loosen up, but we both knew that this was the case. I fed the stray cats in the weeds behind my building so they wouldn't mew all night, then settled at the card table where I ate and tried to write each evening. I switched on my Smith Corona electric typewriter. This was in the days before Microsoft Word or WordPerfect. The only mouse in my place had four legs and a tail. I opened the book:

> At this time of life whatever being there is is doing a lot of listening, as though to the feeling of the wind before it starts. . . .

What the hell was this? I rubbed my neck and tried again:

> From the outset it was apparent that someone had played a colossal trick on something.

A colossal trick. Right. Well, my task was not to analyze or understand *Three Poems,* but to respond to its rhythms, take its music into my body, and come up with a similar score. I finished reading, only half-concentrating. My front window was busted, and mosquitoes invited themselves in and out of the room. I had tried covering the window with a sheet, but the sheet flapped raggedly in a breeze. The night before, my upstairs neighbor, another student, had shattered the pane by trying to climb the wall. He had come home drunk around midnight and discovered that he'd lost his key, so he shimmied up the rainspout to reach his window. He slipped. His foot crashed through my glass, startling me awake.

I fiddled with the sheet. Through the window I glimpsed a streetwalker standing beside a light pole on the corner. She wore a long blue dress and flicked a Bic lighter off and on. The vice squad had chased hookers from one end of my neighborhood to another. Soon, the women would be driven from my street, too, but for now their presence charged the block with an undercurrent of danger and morbid titillation.

This was my life in Houston, in the grad-student boondocks of the area known as Montrose. I had come here because I wanted to be a writer.

And now, because I wanted to be a writer, I was stuck with Ashbery. I started to open the wine and realized I didn't own a corkscrew. Another walk to the store, keeping my head down as I passed the hooker. "Evening, sugar," she said. I nodded and sped up. Back in my apartment, I poured a little wine into a Dixie cup. I sat down and started to type.

By one o'clock, my flesh had served as an all-you-can-eat smorgasbord for the mosquitoes. I was bleary, yawning, and tipsy. A third of the bottle remained. My shirtsleeves sagged with sweat. I had filled four pages with abstract nonsense. I poured more wine and hit the keyboard again. "All fall, my father held a trouble light beneath the car," I wrote. "My family was not on the move."

Two more hours passed. Just after 3:00 A.M., the phone rang. I jumped, tipping the cup. Someone's dead, I thought. A car crash, a stroke. I picked up.

"How's it coming?" said Donald Barthelme.

"Fine," I croaked. "I think."

"Good. Twelve pages, on my desk. In five hours." He clicked off.

Fast-forward twenty years, to the early winter of 2001. I'm attending the "Andy Warhol: Photography" exhibit at the International Center of Photography in Manhattan. The show displays many of Warhol's photo-booth portraits of writers, artists, and celebrities from the 1960s, including a picture entitled *Man with Newspaper: He Is a She, ca. 1963,* featuring a shorthaired man in black glasses reading a tabloid. The tabloid's front-page headline, all about a sex-change operation, says HE IS A SHE! The photograph's interest lies in the contrast between the cheesy newspaper and the man's impeccable appearance. He's well groomed and cleanly shaved, in a dark suit and fashionably thin tie. He peruses the paper with raised eyebrows and a tight mouth, just this side of shocked, just this close to lasciviousness—campy, funny, an assured performance. The picture is rare in the Warhol collection in that its subject is not identified by name.

I recognize the man as the late Donald Barthelme, whose short stories, appearing regularly in *The New Yorker* and in ten books between 1964 and 1987, along with his four novels, substantially expanded the range of American fiction for those who were paying attention. In the 1960s, the whole culture, it seemed, paid heed—absurdities and social disruptions appeared to leap off his pages, weekly, and into the streets of our cities. His *New Yorker* pieces read like dispatches from the front lines. He had "managed to place himself in the center of modern consciousness," William Gass wrote. Barthelme knockoffs glutted the lit mags, and he even had to disown a few stories, penned by a canny imposter, that popped up in various publications. He wasn't just influencing other writers; apparently, his mischievous spirit inhabited some of them.

In the late 1970s, his influence waned. The nation's psychedelic fiesta wound down and the culture sobered up (or so goes the official line). Straightforward narrative storytelling reasserted its grip on American literature, buttressed by the reverence surrounding Raymond Carver and other new "realists." Following Don's death from throat cancer in 1989, his books, with few exceptions, drifted out of print and out of reach—a situation that has only recently begun to change as Dave Eggers, Donald Antrim, George Saunders, and other prominent young writers now claim Don as an influence on their work. For a while, Amazon's Web site noted the "unfortunate discontinuance" of many of Don's titles.

Asked, once, about critics' responses to his work, he replied, "Oh, I think they want me to go away and stop doing what I'm doing."

"Neglect is useful," he mused in 1960, before fully launching his literary career. One of our "traditional obligations in our role as the public [is] the obligation to neglect artists, writers, creators of every kind." In this way, he said, a "Starving Opposition is created, and the possibility of criticism of our culture is provided for." As far as he could see, at that time, neglect was "proceeding at appropriate levels."

Since the 1960s, neglect has become a growth industry, merging with historical revisionism to wipe out the competition—that is, anything that doesn't hew to the official line. For the past three decades, most of the quality fiction published in the United States has been doggedly representational, respectful of a narrow literary and cultural tradition, as though all Americans agree on what's valuable, what's true; as though the social upheavals of the fifties, sixties, and seventies—Vietnam, the sexual revolution, the civil rights and women's movements, the proliferation of nuclear arms—never happened; as though certain imaginative responses to these events—in abstract art and Pop Art, the Berkeley Free Speech Movement, the 1967 attempt to "exorcise" the Pentagon, the protests of May 1968 in Paris, and fiction that questioned all authority, including that of language—never happened.

They happened. Straightforward narrative storytelling is only one way to measure the results of these seismic shifts, but you wouldn't know that, poking through most bookstores.

Neglect is useful if we are mindful of why and how it occurs—thus the possibility for a cultural critique. In part, Don's "unfortunate discontinuance" was a result of officialdom's widespread desire to bury the troubled 1960s. Also, with the exception of a few, he has suffered at the hands of younger writers, many of whom see him as dated as "groovy," "make love not war," and the rest of hippie lingo. Others dismiss him as a writer who wrote only about writing, a troublemaker like Marcel Duchamp scribbling a mustache on a print of the *Mona Lisa*—a perpetual adolescent gleefully trashing classical art.

In fact, Don stressed that he didn't like fiction about fiction. And though the specific events that chiseled his sensibility have passed, he was right, I think, to insist that the "problems" they pointed to—among them, the need to refresh language continually, to keep it free of "political and social contamination," safe from co-optation by commercial interests—are "durable ones."

One of authority's tools in creating a Book of Neglect is to suggest that opposition to dominant cultural currents occurs only in moments of extreme crisis, when society is strained—world wars, the Great Depression, the 1960s. A signal value in reconsidering the life and work of Donald Barthelme now is seeing that opposition is *built into* the dominant culture: It has always carried the seeds of its own unraveling. Like a plant that blooms only every few decades, oppositional art erupts into the open now and then, as it did in the 1960s; while its flowering may seem an isolated event, if we trace its roots, we realize its perennial nature.

In 1990, Lois Zamora, one of Don's Houston colleagues, wrote that the relationship of his fiction "to political writing needs critical repositioning. As time passes, and 'postmodernism' and other current ideologies come increasingly into focus, we will identify and appreciate ambiguities in his work that have as yet been barely noticed or discussed by the critics." The time has come for this "critical repositioning."

Just before his fatal illness, Don said he believed that the latest generation of American writers held "lowered expectations in terms of life. My generation, perhaps foolishly, expected, even demanded, that life be wonderful and magical and then tried to make it so by writing in a rather complex way. It seems now quite an eccentric demand."

In the mid-1980s, he would sit in his Houston duplex, across the street from the Edgar Allan Poe Elementary School, and tell me he had "done his little thing" in fiction. His moment had passed. The "postmodern" writing with which he'd been linked had been forced to retreat into a small arrondissement in the American literary landscape, surrounded by General Carver and his troops. In writing classes, Don quoted his old philosophy teacher, Maurice Natanson: "It is a mistake to regard literature as a graveyard of dead systems." Privately, he didn't sound so sure.

Years have passed, now, since I listened to his rueful talk, and gradually I've come to see it's wrong to think of Don as a *victim* of neglect. He was, rather, a *connoisseur* of it. Often, his stories are built on obscure foundations. Just as often, they celebrate the long lost, the hopeless, the never was. Like the lonely clowns beating their drums on empty streets in the late lithographs of Daumier (one of Don's heroes) or Baudelaire's "pitiful" acrobats "illumined" in the shadows of alleys "by burned-down candles, dripping and smoking," Don's characters proceed by marginal means.

In other words, I believe he *designed* his stories—and his teaching—to fall into dormancy, only to bloom again unexpectedly. His personal anguish bumped up against his awareness that he was chasing the impossible, and his choice to pursue an aesthetics of uncertainty—what he called "needful obscurity." "Art is not difficult because it wishes to be difficult," he said, "but because it wishes to be art."

One of Don's men in the shadows laments, "The point of my career is perhaps how little I achieved. We speak of someone as having had a 'long career' and that's usually taken to be admiring, but what if it's thirty-five years of persistence in error? I don't know what value to place on what I've done, perhaps none at all is right." This melancholy was not new in Don's work. From the beginning, *failure* is a primary theme of his fiction. "[W]hat an artist does is fail," he writes. "The actualization fails to meet, equal, the intuition . . . there is no such thing as a 'successful artist.' "

By the late eighties, this concern seemed intensely personal in Don's writing—as it did in Daumier's last efforts—and burdened even his lightest sentences. His gestures carried the weight of all this, too. His walk was a shamble. His shoulders drooped. Frequently, he blotted sweat from his forehead with the back of his sleeve.

One afternoon, I arrived at his university office for an appointment. He sat at his desk with a copy of his latest collection, *Overnight to Many Distant Cities,* which had just been published. He picked up the book and balanced it on the tips of his fingers. "Looks a little slender, don't you think?" he asked me. Then he shrugged, the profoundest, weariest shrug I had ever seen. It seemed to take about a minute.

On the morning I was to turn in my Ashbery assignment, I was dragging from exhaustion and a hangover. He looked as bad as I felt. I decided to drop the assignment on his desk and leave him alone, but he told me to sit down. He skimmed my first few pages, chuckled the way I'd heard him laugh over a jazz riff whenever he'd put on a record in his home. He grinned at me. "Congratulations," he said. "Now you can get some rest."

"It's junk," I said.

"It's an imitation. It's *supposed* to be junk."

"But what's the point? I can't do anything with it."

"What do you think you've achieved?"

"I don't know. That's what I mean," I said. "I didn't understand a word of the Ashbery. I don't understand a word of what *I've* written."

"In that case," he said, "you've just composed your first important draft."

It took me weeks, months to understand that Don didn't mean writing should make no sense. He meant it shouldn't be so overdetermined, it falls dead on the page. The process requires a pinch of uncertainty so the energy of discovery can be built into the work.

The "irruption of accident" can produce "estimable results," Don wrote. And: "What is magical [about art] is that it at once invites and resists interpretation . . . it remains, after interpretation, vital—no interpretation or cardiopulmonary push-pull can exhaust or empty it."

Don's teaching had this quality. At the university, grad students used to fret about their futures, between classes, in a musty lounge on the second floor of the English Department building. Here, Don dropped a few of his pedagogical hints, like scattering bread among the hungry and lost. The school gave him a discretionary fund to spend on the creative writing program. Often, he aided struggling students with their personal expenses. And he furnished the lounge with texts. I had the impression that, given more money, he would have hung a sign above the door—CABARET VOLTAIRE—decked the place out with French paintings, and hired starving poets to crawl around the lounge shouting "Umbah-umbah!" in healthy Dadaist fashion for our entertainment and edification.

A tossed-off remark, a question in passing, a note in the margins of a story, a book he'd offer . . . we'd feel his little prods now and then, the merest touch, with no context or follow-up. But later—who knows why—they'd suddenly make enormous sense. He was planting seeds in his students that might not grow for years. In the two decades since the night I cribbed *Three Poems* and the day I discovered Don in the Warhol exhibit, I'd startled dozens of times at the unexpected movement of these new/old kernels in my mind.

And his stories: Silently now, as title after title is suspended, rescued, suspended again, they wait to be rediscovered. That they wait without much expectation is one of the most beautiful and melancholy aspects of his art.

After Don died, his colleague Phillip Lopate wrote of him, "It [is not] easy to conjure up a man who, for all his commanding presence, had something of the ghost about him even in his lifetime."

Don once dismissed the possibility that his biography would clarify his stories and novels. In a 1981 *Paris Review* interview with J. D. O'Hara, he said, "There's not a strong autobiographical strain in my fiction. A few bits of fact here and there . . . which illuminate . . . not very much." As with his stories, he rigorously edited the interview, cutting much of the biographical content so only a smidgen remains on the page. In the raw transcript of his conversations with O' Hara, he said, "I will never write an autobiography, or possibly I've already done so, in the stories," thereby suggesting a stronger personal strain in the fiction than he was willing to admit publicly. And though he insisted that his life story would not "sustain a person's attention for a moment," his main objection to a literary biography was this: It would indicate "your life is over, a thing that might make a boy a shade self-conscious." I like to think he wouldn't mind, so much, this book's appearance now. He admitted to O'Hara that "biography is always interesting. Even the Beckett biography [by Deidre Bair], which is not very good, is fascinating." He also said that his work had "not perhaps [been] adequately" commented upon; this is the "kind of thing that comes with time."

On another occasion, he said, "Time works on fiction as it does on us." And time is pitiless—another reason for telling this story now. "I remember Donald well . . . or as well as I remember anything these days," said Roger Angell, the venerable *New Yorker* editor, when he and I chatted about Don. "I'm patchy, I mean." Kirk Sale, Don's downstairs neighbor for nearly twenty years, kept telling me his memory was lousy, but he urged me to prod him, because, he said, "I don't mind trying" to remember Don. He even sent me a little poem:

> *When I reflect how many cells*
> *Remain in what my brain's become,*
> *I take my comfort from the thought,*
> Cogito, ergo *some.*

George Christian, with whom Don began to write as a professional journalist, would have had much to say about Don's early career. Christian died a few years ago from Parkinson's disease. Time has worked on Don's fiction, and it has worked on those who knew him. It's necessary to gather what we can *while* we can.

Finally, it comes down to this: I still want to know Don better so as to know better the world *he* knew. Though some of the details have changed over time, the world he knew is, of course, our world. He still has lessons to teach us.

PART ONE

BAUDELAIRE
AND BEYOND

TOOLS

The America that Don knew as a boy and as a teenager, in the 1930s and 1940s, was a nation whose structures were beginning to be formed with messianic fervor. Or so his father believed. His father, Donald Barthelme, was born in Galveston, Texas, in 1907, the son of a lumber dealer. He learned, early, to calculate board feet, negotiate timber rights, and distinguish loblolly from other sorts of pine trees. These skills led him to a pragmatic view of building and of problem solving in general, a view his eldest son would inherit.

During the elder Barthelme's childhood, Galveston was dominated by singular personalities who left indelible imprints on the city's finances, institutions, environment, and cultural life. William Lewis Moody, Jr., the son of a cotton magnate, owned controlling interest in the city's national bank; in 1923, he purchased the *Galveston News,* Texas's oldest continuously running newspaper; in 1927, he formed the National Hotel Corporation, and subsequently built two of the city's landmark inns; he organized what became the biggest insurance company in Texas, and bought a printing outfit and several ranches, though he had little interest in raising cattle. He used the land for duck hunting and fishing. A Gulf Coast Citizen Kane, he managed the city's money and information, and shaped much of the public space. In 1974, Don would publish a story called "I Bought a Little City" about a Moody-like man who, otherwise bored with his life, establishes an amiable but unimaginative empire in Galveston, and presides over the city's decline.

The other major figure in town, prior to World War I, was N. J. Clayton, a supremely confident architect with a love of high Victorian style. Even today, the generous loft spaces in many of Galveston's commercial buildings bear his mark. He favored bold massing and articulate composition, and was fond of Gothic detail. That one man's sensibility, if pushed aggressively, could fashion a city's looks was a lesson absorbed, and cherished, by Barthelme senior. It was an example of idealism, optimism, and hard work that he impressed on his children.

Always short for his age, with red hair, fair skin, and fat glasses from the time he was three, the elder Barthelme felt as a boy that if he was going to get anywhere in life, he "wasn't going to be able to just stand there." "I had to walk into a room with a swagger, and talk loud, and tell 'em I was there," he said. In their memoir, *Double Down,* his sons Rick and Steve said that, early on, their father adopted the attitude, perhaps modeled on men like Moody, that the "world was a place that needed fixing and he was just the man to fix it."

By the time he reached high school, he was an assured and popular young man, always tweaking authority to win his friends' loyalty, practiced at the swagger he'd affected, a hell-raiser.

As a college freshman, he enrolled in the Rice Institute, in Houston, but was asked to leave "for some indiscretion in the school newspaper, which he edited," Rick and Steve recounted, "an indiscretion that wasn't his, as it turned out, but some fellow student's for whom Father was taking the fall."

The elder Barthelme's father approached school administrators on his behalf but found them unbending. Instead of waiting twelve months to reenroll, when his suspension would expire, Barthelme transferred to the University of Pennsylvania. There, he studied architecture with Paul Philippe Cret, and he met Helen Bechtold, whom he would marry in June 1930. They were introduced on a blind date when he went with a buddy to Helen's sorority house. As Helen and a friend approached the boys in the house's foyer, Helen whispered that she hoped she would get the "tall, dark, and handsome one." Instead, her date was the "short, red-headed one."

"He was a fortunate man," Rick and Steve wrote in *Double Down.* "[Mother was] a prize that took some winning, according to the family lore, for while Mother was smart, talented, stylish, attractive, and sought after, our father was only smart and talented." Away from school, Helen lived in Philadelphia with her mother and sister. Her father had died when she was twelve, leaving his family financially secure, but Helen wanted a teaching career and even made what she once described as an "abortive attempt" at writing. She was interested in acting at the time she met Barthelme.

On April 7, 1931, Don was born (he would later write, "What else happened in 1931? . . . Creation of countless surrealist objects"). In December of 1932, his sister, Joan, arrived. Helen Bechtold Barthelme abandoned her teaching, writing, and acting dreams; she hunkered down to become the "beloved mother" of a family that would eventually total five children, all of whom, swayed by their mother's love of reading and drama, excelled at writing.

After graduating from Penn, Donald Barthelme, Sr., worked as a draftsman for Cret and for the firm of Zantzinger, Borie, & Medary (where he helped design the U.S. Department of Justice building in Washington, D.C.), but he was unable to find lasting work in Philadelphia. In 1932—just before Joan was born—the family moved to Galveston, where Barthelme joined his father's lumber business. The company was best known for building a magnificent roller coaster near the seawall at the beach. Barthelme's father, Fred, a New York transplant, was a prominent and successful member of Galveston society.

Barthelme was restless working for the old man and living in a garage apartment behind his parents' house. He worked briefly for the Dallas architect Roscoe DeWitt, then, in 1937, moved his family to Houston, where he joined the firm of John F. Staub. In 1940, he branched out on his own.

At Penn, his course of study had stressed traditional architecture and conventional building techniques. On his own, he studied the Bauhaus movement in Europe and pored over Frank Lloyd Wright's published plans; still, he didn't chafe against Penn's established pedagogy. He admitted his perplexity at the Philadelphia Savings Fund Society building, designed by Howe and Lescaze—this was one of most prominent modern buildings erected in the United States in the 1930s, and Barthelme didn't *get* its austerity.

In Philadelphia, he encountered, once more, powerful personalities. In class one day, evaluating one of Barthelme's designs, Cret asked, "Where did you get this idea?" "Oh," Barthelme said, "I got it out of my head, Mr. Cret." "It's good that it is out," his teacher replied. Temporarily, Barthelme worked for Cret in a Philadelphia firm that employed Louis Kahn. At night, Kahn would go around the office and leave critiques on his coworkers' designs, including those of his bosses. People "laughed at him," Barthelme said. "But he was teaching himself."

Little by little, Barthelme taught himself modern architecture. He would pass his enthusiasm for learning on to Don. Though Don's chosen pursuit would differ from his father's, the idea of *the modern* and the aesthetic principles of modern architecture form the background of Don's writing. A broad familiarity with what was at stake in his father's world is essential to understanding what mattered to Don in his work.

Paul Philippe Cret, Barthelme's mentor at Penn, accepted a teaching position at the university in 1903, which he held until his retirement in 1937. He studied at the Ecole des Beaux-Arts in Paris, one of Europe's oldest centers of art and architectural education, dating back in various forms to 1671. The

Beaux-Arts basic design principles stressed symmetry, simple volumes, and lucid progression through a series of exterior and interior spaces; the outside was a rational extension of the inside. Beaux-Arts urbanism relied on visual axes with clearly marked meeting points as its prime ordering device; its most celebrated examples were Georges-Eugène Haussmann's schemes for the reorganization of Paris in the mid-nineteenth century. The Beaux-Arts approach was not seriously challenged in American academia until the late 1930s, when a second wave of Europeans came to the States, who were advocates of the International Style, and assumed positions of power.

As Cret's career progressed, he absorbed elements of the International Style and began a process of simplification, minimizing the ornamentation of his designs. He reduced the number of moldings, which served to highlight the planar and volumetric quality of his work. Many of his earlier designs, such as the one for the Indianapolis Library, used Doric colonnades. By the early thirties, when he conceived the Folger Shakespeare Library in Washington, D.C., he had replaced the colonnades with abstract fluted piers.

At a time when university architecture departments felt the first ripples of a change, when, more than ever, competing ideologies dominated the field, Barthelme was excited to find a man like Cret, who bridged the gap between tradition and innovation. Cret was not bullying or domineering, but he was unflappable and firm. These qualities enabled him to perform the architect's trickiest task smoothly: appeasing prickly clients and warring constituencies. He could "cut through" the politics, bad histories, "complexities and ambiguities" of a situation, wrote Elizabeth Greenwell Grossman, and "offer a design that seemed by its simplicity to reveal the immediate character of [an] institution."

Initially, Barthelme followed this example to good effect, but calm, compromise, and diplomacy were not attributes he could sustain. Eventually, he would topple into the "excesses" of his profession, the "heroics and mock-heroics" exhibited by architects in general, as Don later reflected.

What came to be called the International Style of modern architecture, in the years between the first and second world wars, valued lightweight materials, open interior spaces, smooth machinelike surfaces, and exposed structural components, airily clad in collaged metal sheeting or glass curtain walls. It was a craft test-driven in the Bauhaus workshops in Germany in the 1920s under the direction of Walter Gropius, who championed austerity and performance in the steel windows and door frames of the houses he designed, in exposed metal radiators, exposed electric lightbulbs, and elemental furniture. He believed that materials and forms should be celebrated for their independent, asymmetrical structures, rather than for their compatibility and relative invisibility in an overall design.

In the Bauhaus vision, all the arts joined to shape a splendid future. "Together let us conceive and create the new building . . . which will embrace architecture and sculpture and painting . . . and which will rise one day toward heaven from the hands of a million workers like the crystal symbol of a new faith," said the group's 1919 proclamation. Beneath the document's socialist zeal, one can still hear the trauma of war, and an uncertainty about whether any social order can survive the erosions of time and the violence of men.

The Parisian architect Le Corbusier expanded the Bauhaus model, promoting "house machines," "healthy (and morally so too) and beautiful," he said, "in the same way that the working tools and instruments which accompany our existence are beautiful." Mies van der Rohe, who began his career in Berlin, expounded a skin and bones architecture in the office buildings he designed. "The maximum effect with the minimum expenditure of means," his projects proclaimed.

The schools of modern architecture were not uniform, nor were their practitioners always in agreement, but the field's leading figures shared a belief that architecture should boldly reflect its time. Convictions about the character of the time conflicted wildly, but this did not blunt the energy with which Gropius, Le Corbusier, Mies, and others set out to convert the world to their aesthetic aims. They were on a crusade. As large-scale turmoil scarred Europe more and more in the first half of the century, the tenor of the time, and appropriate responses to it, became harder to parse. One could argue that the only sane response to the Holocaust was emptiness and silence—not to build at all. But Europe's upheavals had another effect: the flow of brilliant architects to the safety and relative openness of the United States, which Le Corbusier called the "country of timid people."

If U.S. institutions were slow to accept the new architecture, young architects in the nation's finest programs, schools, and firms were not at all timid about embracing change. A "tendency toward Oedipal overthrow" has always been "rampant in [the] profession," says the architecture critic Herbert Muschamp. To survive, one must cultivate a strong personality.

During this pivotal migration of genius, Donald Barthelme, Sr., started his practice. Since childhood, he had worked to overcome timidity, to prove himself by staking out fresh directions. Later in life, he recalled meeting, early in his career, Mies van der Rohe, and criticizing one of the master's buildings for its lack of human scale. "Mr. Barthelme, I find that I can make things beautiful, and that is enough for me," Mies replied.

• • •

Barthelme's first major projects straddled the battle zone between the future and the past. Zantzinger, Borie, & Medary's design for the U.S. Department of Justice building, which Barthelme had a say in (though, as a junior member of the team, not a very large one), combined classical style with Art Deco detailing and an unusual use of aluminum for features commonly cast in bronze, such as interior stair railings, grilles, and door trim.

After his return to Texas, Barthelme inherited a project begun by Frank Lloyd Wright, which struck an early modernist blow in Dallas. The entrepreneur Stanley Marcus had commissioned Wright to build a house on six and a half acres of north Texas prairie. Marcus recalled:

> We had told Mr. Wright that we could only afford to spend $25,000, which was a lot of money in the Depression year of 1934, but which he assured us was quite feasible. We invited him to come to Dallas. . . . He arrived on January 1, with the temperature at seventy degrees. He concluded that this was typical winter weather for Dallas, and nothing we could tell him about the normal January ice storms could ever convince him that we didn't live in a perpetually balmy climate. When his first preliminary sketches arrived, we noticed that there were no bedrooms, just cubicles in which to sleep when the weather was inclement. Otherwise, ninety percent of the time we would sleep outdoors on the deck. We protested that solution on the grounds that I was subject to colds and sinus trouble. He dismissed this objection in his typical manner, as though brushing a bit of lint from his jacket. . . .

Additionally, Wright provided "little or no closet space, commenting that closets were only useful for accumulating things you didn't need." Frustrated, Marcus enlisted Roscoe DeWitt to serve as a local associate for Wright, who had returned to Taliesin, and to be an on-the-ground interpreter of Wright's plans. Marcus clashed again with the great man when he asked DeWitt to be on guard against inadequate flashing specifications—Wright's buildings were notoriously leak-prone, but he deeply resented this precaution.

Bad feelings got worse, cost estimates spiraled, and, eventually, Marcus turned everything over to DeWitt and his young designer, Donald Barthelme. "I couldn't understand [Wright's] plans," Barthelme said. "He had a column that was in the shape of a star, and he had marked a little note that said, 'stock column.' So far as I knew there was no such stock column. He also had six panes of glass about six feet wide each that were slipped into adjacent tracks with no frame around the end. I can just imagine trying to slide those doors open."

Ultimately, the house, completed in 1937, bore no resemblance to Wright's initial design. Barthelme designed a long, low-lying structure with cross-ventilation and open living and dining rooms. Pronounced overhangs sheltered the windows. The result was too conventional to be a notable piece of architecture, Marcus said later, though it was unconventional enough to be "highly controversial" in Dallas at the time. "It proved to be a home which met our living requirements better than the Wright house would have done."

That same year, for the Texas centennial celebration in Dallas's Fair Park, Barthelme designed the Hall of State, which remains among the most monumental structures in Texas, and was then, at $1.2 million, the most expensive building per square foot ever constructed in the state. Originally, a consortium of ten Dallas firms had been hired to create the hall, but they failed to produce a plan acceptable to the State Board of Control. Barthelme synthesized their ideas and added his own. Faced with Texas limestone, with bronze doors and blue tile (the color of the bluebonnet, Texas's state flower), the building is an inverted T—a structure in which Paul Cret's influence is apparent.

Barthelme assembled a team of regional, national, and international artists to add Art Deco touches to the Hall of State. He conceived a symbolic seal of Texas to hang above the entrance, depicting a female figure, the "Lady of Texas," gripping a shield and the state flag. Beside her, an owl, representing wisdom, perches on the Key of Prosperity and Progress. On the frieze around the building, near its top, the names of fifty-nine legendary Texans are carved. The first letters of the first eight names, reading left to right—Burleson, Archer, Rusk, Travis, Higg, Ellis, Lamar, and Milam—spell the architect's name, minus only the final *e*. A playful touch, a buried secret: These would become hallmarks of his eldest son's art, as well.

John Staub, for whom Barthelme worked from 1937 to 1939, was Houston's most eclectic architect. He made his career designing houses in a variety of architectural styles for the city's elite. His houses were among the first in Houston to accommodate air-conditioning. While working for Staub, on a commission from the Humble Oil and Refining Company, Barthelme designed the company's prototype super service station—an attempt to lure customers by making gas stations look dynamic and progressive.

Barthelme organized his own practice in Houston in 1940. "I told [Staub] I just didn't like the fact that he didn't change anything," Barthelme said. "I didn't mind his traditionalism, but I thought he should improve on it, use it as a taking-off place. I just can't understand why you take something and slavishly copy it." That year, Barthelme won eighth place in a national competition sponsored by *Architectural Forum* magazine for a house, "the qualifications of which," according to contest rules, "should be the provision of a livable area so enclosed and organized by the materials used as to relate the elements of the building to one another, to the building as a whole, and to the land." Barthelme's nondoctrinaire design, emphasizing spaciousness and light, was a personal exploration of modern materials and environmental sensitivity. He had now fully clothed himself in the modern.

In 1939, when Don was eight years old, his father conceived a house for the family in the newly platted West Oaks subdivision off Post Oak Road in what was then the extreme suburban fringe of Houston, well beyond the city limits. Completed in 1941, at 11 North Wynden Drive, the Barthelme house was unlike any the city had ever seen. A low-lying, dark-colored, flat-roofed rectangle with irregular projecting volumes and open interior spaces, it was "wonderful to live in but strange to see on the Texas prairie," Don said. "On Sundays people used to park their cars out on the street and stare. We had a routine, the family, on Sundays. We used to get up from Sunday dinner, if enough cars had parked, and run out in front of the house in a sort of chorus line, doing high kicks."

His youngest brother, Steve, recalls, "The furniture . . . wasn't like other people's furniture. It was architect furniture, a lot of swoopy Scandinavian stuff"—Alvar Aalto and Eero Saarinen—"with large side helpings of Eames, the kind of furniture that pretty much stands up to announce, in a deep, rich chrome or molded-plywood voice, 'Hi. I'm the chair.'"

Before getting the go-ahead on his house, Barthelme had to wheedle the builder and the bank's loan officer. Among other things, they were concerned about the master bedroom's door. There wasn't one. There was a screen behind the wall, say Rick and Steve, for "those non-architectural moments."

One of the interior walls was brick. The others were made of redwood. A circular stairway led to a boxy room, which first served as Barthelme's studio but then became Don's bedroom as more children were born. Peter had arrived in 1939. Then Frederick was born in 1943, and Steven in 1947. "The atmosphere of the house was peculiar," Don said. There were "very large architectural books around and the considerations were: What was Mies doing, what was Aalto doing, what was Neutra up to, what about Wright? My father's concerns, in other words, were to say the least somewhat different from those of the other people we knew." In addition, he said, his mother had a wicked wit, which kept the kids hopping. She was their own "Lady of Texas," a playful but formidable figure.

Perhaps this hothouse ambience accounts in part for the kids' later achievements. Joan became the first woman named corporate vice president in the male-dominated Pennzoil Company; Peter, a successful advertising man, published a series of sophisticated mystery novels; Rick and Steve, English professors at the University of Southern Mississippi, pursue literary fiction, both with great success. The "sheer literary talent and output of the Barthelme family has never, I think, been sufficiently recognized," wrote the literary critic Don Graham. "Perhaps only the James family—Henry, William, Henry senior—surpasses them in this regard."

Barthelme was never happy with the house. He changed it constantly, taking saws to the furniture, rearranging the space, covering the floors—first with tatami mats, then tiles, then different tiles, then rugs. The kids came to see their house—"a cigar box with a cracker box on top," they said—as a perpetual work in progress, always subject to revision. The old man had "an ever-ready work force" in his children, Steve recalls. "He was prone to handing each of us a hammer and saying, 'Tear out that wall there.'"

Along one side of the house, bamboo served as a privacy shield. Its roots kept sneaking into the plumbing, requiring frequent repair. At one point, Barthelme covered the exterior wood with copper, believing that the copper, when coated with an acid compound, would discolor attractively. It simply turned brown, leaving him dissatisfied, though his kids liked the warps and ripples in it, the feel of the wood's runnels underneath, and the soft light variations caused by reflections from swelling Gulf Coast clouds.

With its sharp corners and adjustable pathways, the house could be tricky terrain for a normally active child. Don had a further complication, which he discussed with J. D. O'Hara in their preparatory conversations for the *Paris Review* interview:

> There was one thing that . . . affect[ed] my childhood, which is that I was subject to fits. I don't quite want to say that it was petit mal. It was some sort of fits I had as a child, between eight and twelve or six and twelve, and I used to black out and fall, and it seems to have affected me. My family took me to a doctor to have me inspected by a neurologist who was then thought to be the best there was, and I had to take medication and so on. But it's something that comes on you very suddenly, and you fall down and you go away, black out, and you come to . . . and this was really the main thing I remember about that period, the first dozen years, is that I was subject to this. And then, quite mysteriously, it stopped.

O'Hara asked him if the spells were "impressive for Dostoyevskian reasons." Don replied, "No, it's the loss of control. I mean, when you fall down without any warning, black out, it teaches you something. It had nothing to do with ecstasy, I'll tell you, it had to do with somebody or something that could take away your consciousness at its volition rather than yours."

He concluded, "Since it went away and has never come back, I think it probably manifests itself now only in dreams. Certainly dream correlations to this kind of feeling have endured into [my] mature life."

Don deleted this exchange from the interview and never again spoke publicly of his "fits." In the 1970s, he told a friend, Karen Kennerly, that his first memory of childhood was of having a seizure. His narrator in "See the Moon?" (1966) speaks of being "moonstruck," a word once used as a euphemism for epilepsy, and in his third novel, *Paradise* (1986), the main character, Simon, responds to his doctor's question, "Ever been subject to epilepsy?" by saying, "I had seizures when I was a child. They stopped. I think it was petit mal."

If Don's memory of taking medications is correct, it's likely that he was among the first children in this country to be given the anticonvulsant phenytoin, more commonly known as Dilantin, which came into widespread use in 1938. As an adult, he frequently spoke of being "nervous in the world," a lingering effect, perhaps, of the "fits." In any case, the abrupt blackouts sometimes made his father's house, ever-changing in the elder Barthelme's search for perfection, a challenge to negotiate.

"Modernist architecture was a crusade, a religion, and the faithful couldn't just go out and buy a rug like other folks," Steve says. Once, Barthelme decided he had to design a rug, which meant the family had to make one. "It took a month or so. About twelve feet by fifteen, assembled from three carpets, cut into long strips. It was a nice-looking thing once we finally got it finished and down, at one end of the big open living area, lying over the ghosts of those ornery tatami mats . . . which had the annoying habit of continually getting torn or disarranged."

For better or worse, Barthelme's "crusade" kept the family in a perpetual state of excitement. On the back porch, he kept his handsaws and rasps, his coffee cans full of nails. When Barthelme senior's father died in the early 1950s, the lumberman's tools came to live there, too. It was a "magical" part of the house, Steve says.

For Don and his siblings, the principles, methods, and means of architecture, as embodied in the house in which they came of age, gave life a mythic dimension. Their father taught them that all activity—sitting in a chair, eating dinner, hammering a nail, crawling into bed—bristled with artistic content. He taught them that nothing is set in stone, not even stone. And he taught them the power of an aggressive personality—"a designer is responsible for what he can do to people," he used to say. He convinced them that "everything good ever done was done by people who followed their own ideas." He told them, "Walk alone, if necessary. Don't walk the beaten path."

THE EDUCATIONAL EXPERIENCE

South of Houston, rice paddies bake in the sun, and oil fields often sit idle. Migrant families move seasonally through fields, picking cotton. Frequently, children drop out of school before reaching the higher grades. Here, in the unlikely spot of Brazoria County, one of the poorest regions of Texas, Donald Barthelme, Sr., brought his vision of the future. It was a vision with powerful implications for the way he would raise his children.

West Columbia Elementary School was crowded to more than twice its capacity with the kids of low-wage workers. In the 1940s, Brazoria County got a boost from war-related petrochemical industries, but the public infrastructure remained sorely underfunded. The surrounding landscape, and the architecture, was bleak. The school district came to Barthelme for help, expecting little more than a few new classrooms.

The pressing need was not just for room but also for an environment that would stimulate students and teachers. Barthelme saw this; he set out to build a "half school and half circus," and it earned him national acclaim.

Architectural Forum noted that "Barthelme [has] made a lot out of a little—esthetically, educationally, and in sheer space—by practicing economy in its most fundamental sense: almost every feature of his school is made to earn its keep several times over." The exposed structural elements were pleasing to the eye and took the place of conventional ornaments now banished; light diffusers doubled as heat diffusers; corridors were sized to be de facto play areas. Barthelme designed a jaunty arcuated canopy of reinforced concrete—the iconic material of the modern movement, exotic because it was so rarely used in this country. The canopy stood free of the steel-framed single-story school building, which was clad with a glass and marble curtain wall. Barthelme juxtaposed glass and open bar joists, redwood and marble. He achieved vibrant color with patterns of tackboards, windows, orange tiles. "The exposed joists require frequent repainting to combat rust," the magazine pointed out. "While this is a maintenance handicap, it guarantees a certain permanence of gaiety."

Barthelme used top lighting—desirable because it is "out of the normal cone of vision"—and filtered the sun with east-west louvers. The building's steel frame "was so light, it looked as if it didn't have the gumption to hold itself together," Barthelme said. About the marble curtain wall: "[I] slipped [it] in like a deck of cards."

Classrooms branched away from a central activities hub, creating separate but adjacent "neighborhoods." These areas drew traffic out of the hub, relieving congestion. "People just don't seem to notice that corridors are missing," Barthelme said, proud of his cost-cutting moves. "Nobody comments on it." He aimed the classrooms toward one another, treating them as sheltered extensions of open courts, which promoted a communal feel.

"Barthelme is a liberated man," *Architectural Forum* concluded. Completed in 1951, West Columbia Elementary School was, for him, the culmination of a decade of hard work, and it cemented his reputation as a brilliant designer of modest yet lyrical public buildings. At a cost of just over $229,000, the project was stunningly economical, as well. The architect's fee totaled a mere eighteen thousand dollars.

He bought and sold stocks, devised elaborate budgets—and yet he was only a moderately successful investor.

The kids earned small allowances for their chores and cleaning around the house. As they grew older, their father would sometimes say to them, "Go get me my wallet from the bedroom." He kept it on a shelf in his closet. He would take out a twenty-dollar bill, hand it to the kids, and say, "Go have some fun."

In addition to books, he liked to spend his money on photographic equipment, Leica cameras, enlargers, and developing fluid, as well as eight-millimeter movie projectors. From the mid-thirties to the late fifties, he often documented his family on film, posing the kids in the oyster-shell driveway, encouraging them to act out little plots for the Bell & Howell.

In one home movie, Barthelme chases Don and Joan around a statue of a horse on the Rice campus. They won't sit still for him. In another movie, this one made by the boys, the Barthelme brothers play private eyes. Their mother shows up as a drunken barmaid. She smokes a pipe and wears a beret. In a photo from around 1952, she sits in a wooden chair, holding a glass of what appears to be lemonade. Her fingers look like wooden ornaments—some kind of intricate furniture design. Rick and Steve, shirtless little boys, stand behind her, gazing at their father's camera.

Helen threw herself into housework and child rearing, cooking casseroles heavy with margarine and salt, baking potatoes, and making chicken or roast beef sandwiches. Or she sat and encouraged the kids to read. Rafael Sabatini's *Captain Blood* was a favorite among the boys: swashbuckling and mayhem at sea. In one adventure after another, Blood faked his way through trouble, confidently, the way their father did.

The elder Barthelme drove a Lincoln Zephyr handed down from his father, and later, white Corvette convertibles with red seats. On weekends, he packed up the family and took them to Stewart Beach in Galveston, or to his parents' place on Avenue I, or to his father's ranch on the Guadalupe River near San Antonio. Bob Wills and His Texas Playboys kicked a swing beat through the car's speakers, a stark contrast to the symphonic music that was played in the house. Clouds rose like the tops of Stetsons as the family cruised down Highway 6, past Arcola, Alvin . . .

Don called his grandparents "Mr. Bart" and "Mamie." He loved to sit in the ranch house's big inner room, with its "stack of saddles in a corner" and "rifles on pegs over the doors," listening to Mr. Bart's stories about being a semipro baseball player and barnstorming in the east—free of conventional ties—before becoming a lumberman. Mamie, short and plump, was a schoolteacher. Like Helen, she encouraged the kids to read and to listen to music.

The ranch was a "wonderful place to ride and hunt, talk to the catfish and try to make the windmill run backward," Don said. In an autobiographical story called "Bishop," composed in the early 1980s, he wrote about a man who recalls sitting with his grandparents on the veranda of a ranch house or walking along "terrain studded with caliche like half-buried skulls, a dirty white, past a salt lick and the windmill and then another salt lick."

> [H]is grandfather points out the place where his aunt had been knocked off a horse by a low-lying tree branch. His grandmother is busy burning toast and then scraping it (the way they like it) and is at the same time reading the newspaper . . . something about the Stewart girl, you remember who she is, getting married to that fellow who, you remember, got in all the trouble . . .

The story ends with the character imagining "walking in the water, the shallow river, at the edge of the ranch, looking for minnows in the water under the overhanging trees, skipping rocks across the river, intent . . ."

On the return to Houston from Galveston or Mr. Bart's ranch near Kerrville late at night, the kids sank sleepily into the car's backseat, lulled by the darkness and the humming of the engine, while all around them, especially along the coast, a sulfurous smell rose from the reeds and refinery lights burned like candle flames.

The Barthelme children learned from their father that anything was possible if they put enough thought into it, and put it into words; intensity of feeling was crucial, but showing their emotions left them vulnerable to humiliation by others.

Irony, self-consciousness, feigned indifference: These formed a holy trinity on North Wynden Drive.

Barthelme encouraged, in his kids, unconventional thought *outside the home* but expected obedience to his rules. If he requested a particular tool from the back porch and a child brought him too small a hammer or the wrong set of pliers, he gave the child a look of immense disappointment.

Most of all, wrote Rick and Steve, what the kids learned in the Barthelme home was the "skill of editing—what our father was always doing with the house."

His work on schools got Barthelme thinking about the relationship of space to thought, on the effect of the built environment on the development of children's minds—concerns that found their way into his home.

In October 1959, he was invited to address a gathering of the Educational Facilities Laboratories at the University of Michigan in Ann Arbor. Only nine other architects received invitations to the event. The EFL was sponsored by the Ford Foundation to promote better use and design of school facilities. The gathering had been called to debate a report issued by J. Lloyd Trump, an educational reformer who proposed eliminating traditional high school schedules in favor of varied classes dictated by students' needs. He promoted large lecture sessions and private study booths where pupils could work alone.

The architects had been asked to mull the structural implications of Trump's ideas. Most said the proposals would have little impact on conventional school design. But when it was Barthelme's turn to speak, he said, "Dr. Trump . . . has pushed a door ajar, and without apology we have a truck to drive through it."

He provided rough sketches of a School of Tomorrow, built to mold young minds in the ways that he saw fit. "The Barthelme scheme recognizes no compromises," *Architectural Forum* reported. Above all, it emphasized group work. Barthelme favored a "drafting room" atmosphere where students could study individually at single workstations, but in an open space under a wide-span dome, surrounded by others, where spontaneous collaborations could erupt. The aim was to facilitate leaps from isolation back into teamwork and to "put learning . . . into the context of use."

"I never understood why it was a good idea to learn things in fragments," Barthelme said. "Few of us have ever met a past participle socially, or passed a quiet evening curled up with a good algebraic equation. We rarely encounter these things isolated from the particular situations in which they are meaningful. What we use in business, or with the family, or with students, is the whole language."

Barthelme insisted that the best education takes place when people work alone en masse: a lonely crowd. He hearkened back to the Beaux-Arts tradition in suggesting that students be given individual problems to solve at their own pace. Each student "programs his direction and develops his solution," he said. "Along the way he is led into diverse fields, gets information *with* or *without* theory, but *at the time he needs it.* Theory is not taught until the time the student asks 'Why?' and has developed an acute interest in the matter."

He conceded that voluminous "preparation of source material, correlation of subject matter, vertical and horizontal organization, insight, and knowledge" would be required of the staff. These demands would raise their level of professionalism.

Some of the educators in Ann Arbor worried that Barthelme's model required too much maturity from students. In reply, Barthelme said, "Whereas previously it was the teacher's problem to get the information *into* the student, it was now the pupil's problem . . . to the get the information *out* of the teacher." The stage, he said, "is set for learning."

In 1981, when asked what effect his father's career had on his own outlook and ambitions, Don said:

> It was an attitude toward his work. [In school he received] very fine training, but it had nothing to do with what was really going on in architecture. So he went through a complete reversal . . . his task was to do an entirely new thing, which was contrary to his training in important ways. And he did it with great enthusiasm, with great zest, and he did it very, very well.

Here, Don cast his father as a hero, rebirthing himself, bringing a whole new vision to the world, rather than—as was closer to the truth—gradually absorbing fresh ideas and deciding which ones excited him and fitted his skills. The mythic imagination had been encouraged in the house on North Wynden Drive, and the "new" would remain a touchstone for Don. Even in rebellion against his father's world, Don would not stray too far from its resources.

Finding copies of *Architectural Forum* around the house with his father's name—*his* name—printed inside naturally piqued his curiosity. Some of Don's early stories are built around graphics, collages, or investigations of perspective similar to the plans or illustrations in architectural journals. Even Don's sense of language stressed plasticity, the ability of words and phrases to be rearranged in the interest of shaping and design. When he became a teacher, he likened the revision process to house remodeling.

He spent ten years in parochial schools in Houston, first at St. Anne's Elementary, then at St. Thomas Catholic High School. Sister Huberta Gallatin, his seventh-grade teacher, recalled that Don was intensely attentive. "I was aware that he was studying me when there was a little flare up of some kind," she said. "He would peer over his glasses at me with a wry little smile. I remember that because he never fit into the rank and file, and he got my attention as unobtrusive as he was."

He respected the teaching sisters. Still, he always regarded his father (sometimes in anger) as his primary mentor, the home as the seat of knowledge. The elder Barthelme was a nonstop talker, exhausting his wife and kids in debates about the house, the arts, the future of the world. Karl Killian, founder of Houston's Brazos Bookstore, recalls the family as a race of giants who "actually talked to each other—genuine discussions." The house, an intense learning space on which Barthelme tested new designs to stimulate the mind, provided "a very volatile atmosphere."

With the furniture on display, and the supper talk a series of seminars, it's safe to say that every new book in the house became a topic. In 1941, Sigfried Giedion published a landmark volume, *Space, Time and Architecture,* whose thrust was that modern architecture was an inevitable historical development. It became a bible for American architects, and Barthelme absorbed its ideas.

Space, Time and Architecture insists that specialization is the death of the imagination. The architect must be aware of developments in *all* the arts. Giedion made a distinction between *transitory facts,* which "in their dash and glitter often succeed in taking over the center of the stage," and *constituent facts,* "tendencies [in any given art] which, when they are suppressed, inevitably reappear." Giedion then noted, "Their recurrence makes us aware that these are elements which, all together, are producing a *new tradition.*"

Novelty for its own sake, as opposed to fresh variations on the old: This was a distinction, favoring the latter, that Barthelme fiercely impressed on Don. In other words, here was a dialectic—in Barthelme's case, between the worldview and work ethic of the Beaux-Arts and the tropes of modern design.

For Giedion, modern architecture was the world's moral beacon, essential to a positive cultural reformation. Don would come to feel this way about fiction.

If the books in the house were part of the father's power, inevitably the sons would take them up or put them down, always aware of their capacity for betrayal. In the early 1980s, Don related to one of his students a dream he'd had. He was in an open room lined with bookshelves that were filled with the story collections he'd written. His father stood beside him, examining one of the books. Barthelme turned, walked over to his son, and hit him in the head with it. He said, "Why don't you get a real job, Don?"

And the mother? She cherished books, too, which made them all right. She may have relinquished her dreams of writing, teaching, and acting, but for Don and his brothers and sister, she became a larger-than-life heroine, someone "no one could not love," a buffer against the father, a princess straight out of a book. In the family, "a number of men [were] competing for the attention of a single woman," Don said. It was like the "Snow White myth," which, "naturally," became "meaningful to me."

SOUL

Along with lessons learned from his dad, Don's early schooling was shaped by an educational philosophy developed by the Basilian religious order. Formed in France, the Basilian Order dedicated itself to the marginalized, and to spreading "education within the [Catholic] church's mission of evangelism." In 1899, members of the group traveled to Texas and settled there on the coast. In an abandoned resort hotel in La Porte, near Galveston, Father James T. Player taught a dozen or so students. Around this time, the order moved into the countryside, to minister to Mexican cotton pickers and other indigent populations. It founded St. Thomas Catholic High School in Houston in 1900, and in 1928 took control of St. Anne's Elementary, which had been floundering financially.

In the 1930s, Father John O' Loane oversaw the Houston schools, using principles laid down by Francis Forster, one of the Basilian's first Superior Generals. "Catholic boys cannot be built into good, staunch Catholic men unless in their school days they are subjected to discipline," Forster had declared. "It is a religious heresy to hold that a member of a community must be left to work out his own salvation."

In his end-of-year report in 1933, Father O' Loane boasted that, under his hand, the rule of order "has been well observed by all members" of the schools, and the "fraternal spirit has been commendable."

The Barthelmes attended St. Anne's Church. In 1937, Don started classes at St. Anne's, and he remained there through the eighth grade. His sister, Joan, was two years behind him in school. They were a close pair, Joan a pretty curly-haired blonde and Don a quiet, friendly boy with thick glasses. The family called him "Bo."

In the 1930s, the corner of Westheimer and Shepherd, home of the church and the school, formed part of a free-for-all zone in a city known for its lack of urban planning. West of downtown, the area was fast becoming a commercial clot, dotted with gas stations, small businesses, and restaurants, growing by random distension and infilling.

On the other hand, River Oaks, Houston's wealthiest residential neighborhood, was located just west of the church. The desire to connect this enclave to downtown led to beautifully landscaped corridors along Buffalo Bayou, which meandered between River Oaks and Main Street. Parks and open spaces, modeled on the Olmstead Brothers' designs, bordered the mercantile explosion. Driven back and forth to school from their house on the nearly treeless "prairie," Don and Joan saw the madness and marvels of city life. On Westheimer, near their school, they thrilled to the lights of Houston's first large neighborhood movie theater, the Tower, built in 1936. It sported a flamboyant modernist facade.

From the school itself, Don experienced the same restlessness he felt at home; during his time there, the building underwent constant change. Architect Maurice J. Sullivan built it in stages between 1930 and 1953, along with the church, which he completed in 1940: a distinctive collage of styles, with a Spanish exterior and a Byzantine chapel finished with an exposed concrete mosaic.

In this environment, Don pursued his formal education. "Teachers enjoy bright students, the deep thinkers, who tend to surprise them. Don was certainly one of these," said Sister Huberta Gallatin. "This was a student who loved to write, something special in my experience. Always I was eager to read his compositions . . . amazed that a boy so young had such insights and was able to articulate them so well." She recalled that "[e]very once in a while he would pen some philosophical observation, roll it up and when he passed by my desk he would toss it to me. Dignified teacher that I was, I dared not read it until I was in the clear. I had to maintain discipline! I wish I had kept those tidbits because now I cannot remember the contents except that I was delighted. . . ."

"We were schooled in guilt," Rick and Steve wrote of their parochial school experience. "The Catholics were good at their jobs. You're eight, maybe, and you go into your older sister's room and take a new yellow pencil away from her desk and erase some drawing you have been working on, and suddenly you think: *This is a sin. I'm stealing.* What you're stealing is eraser. But that's not the best part. The best part comes next, when the eight-year-old thinks: *No, this is prideful worry. Worrying too much about sins is a sin. It's 'scrupulousness.'*" They added, "Catholic education can accustom a soul to a high level of stimulation, and if you get too comfortable later in life, you miss it."

Outside of Houston, the Basilian Fathers built "mission congregations" to feed, clothe, and shelter Mexican field-workers, whose living conditions, harsh to begin with, had worsened as the Depression's misery spread. "Christian justice" and its relationship to "social justice" were central to Basilian thought, and were etched into the mission statements of the schools Don attended: "Members of [our] community share the responsibility of actually bearing the Christian message to the society at large. Promotion of social justice and service to those in need stand at [our] core."

Trained at home to revere design and abjure provincialism, and taught to see art as a lived-in space, its beauty as functional, Don learned at church and school to embrace social differences. He was told that beauty could change the world, and that changing the world is life's highest aim.

Don's father practiced "social justice" in his architecture, not only in his school designs but also in his ideas for housing defense-industry workers. In the late thirties and forties, many American architects engaged in government projects. The nation's Defense Housing Coordinator estimated that 300,000 defense-industry laborers needed houses in 1940; in fiscal year 1940-1941, Congress appropriated $420 million for military personnel and their families, and $150 million for the accompanying public services. In 1942, an extra 525,000 houses were needed right away, only some of which private enterprise could provide. Few of the nation's communities were prepared to meet this demand.

Defense housing proved to be a crucial test for supporters of modern architecture: Their vision of enlightening the world through art collided with a need for immediate low-cost shelter. More often than not, expediency won the day.

In 1941, Barthelme, working with Richard Neutra, Roscoe DeWitt, and David R. Williams, designed Avion Village, a three-hundred-unit complex for airplane-factory workers near Dallas. It was not terribly modernist in design, but in its attention to detail—porches placed to catch the prevailing southeast breezes, flexible sliding walls—it showed that care could marry haste. It put the human body and the body's needs at the center of its plan, dignifying the lives of the workers and their families.

In addition to its impact on his father's work, the war caught Don's attention in the March of Time newsreels he saw in movie houses before the main features; in photos of President Roosevelt in the newspapers, alongside his vice president, a Texan, John Nance Garner; and in Edward R. Murrow's nightly radio broadcasts. "This is London," Murrow began, and reported on the German blitzkrieg, the fall of France, Dunkirk, the Battle of Britain, and other wartime events.

In his final novel, *The King,* published posthumously, Don drew on his memories of wartime broadcasts. Radio propaganda fills the book, including that of Ezra Pound: " 'Good evening, fellow Englishmen,' the radio said. 'This is Germany calling.' "

Don didn't fully understand the war's horrors until more than a dozen years after Murrow's era. With the 1960 publication of William Shirer's *The Rise and Fall of the Third Reich,* Don got his first comprehensive account of the Nazi death camps. The book depressed him severely. How could such terror have stippled the globe while he and other children were tucked away in comfort, prosperity, and idealism? Such a world *shouldn't be. . . .*

A central oil and cotton port, Houston survived the Depression better than most American cities. During the war, it began to boom. Its new Municipal Airport, finished in 1940, opened just in time to handle war traffic and reap hefty profits. Perhaps at John Nance Garner's urging—and with support from Lyndon Johnson—the federal government asked Brown & Root, a local construction outfit, to build a naval base near Corpus Christi, Texas; by war's end, Brown & Root was one of the nation's largest firms, and was tapped to rebuild U.S. military installations on Guam. In this prosperous atmosphere, Houston's cultural institutions flourished. The day Pearl Harbor was attacked, the major headline in the *Houston Chronicle* was WORKS OF MASTERS OF MANY AGES TO MAKE CITY GREAT ART CENTER. A philanthropic New York couple, Mr. and Mrs. Percy S. Straus, had donated their collection of paintings, "one of the most extraordinary and complete in its field," to Houston's Museum of Fine Arts. The couple's son lived in Houston, and they liked the idea of refining the provinces.

Movie stars crossed the country promoting the sale of war bonds (and Hollywood glamour). Houston's Music Hall and City Auditorium sponsored regular events featuring Jimmy Stewart, Nancy Kelly, Mischa Auer, Tyrone Power, Henry Fonda, and Olivia de Havilland. Sometimes, the stars flew into town on Howard Hughes's private plane.

This was the Houston to which Donald Barthelme's prairie house belonged: an energetic, culturally vibrant place, that embraced the modern; the Houston that attracted Margo Jones, who founded the Community Players, using a cleaned-up incinerator building as a theater, and staged, as her first production, Oscar Wilde's *The Importance of Being Earnest;* the Houston that, in 1938, was the "champion parking meter city in the world," with 3,700 meters; the Houston that, in 1937—the year Don started school—had

84,272 telephones, "more connections than any other city in the state or in the South," according to the *Houston Post.* (Years later, Don would write a story called "Return," about a man who moves to Houston and goes about "getting connected . . . long lines binding me once again into the community." The character says, "It felt fine, being connected.")

Houston was forward-looking, and flush. In 1935, when a boy's shirt cost about thirty-nine cents and eight pennies bought a loaf of bread, the city passed a $2.1 million bond for new public schools, including Mirabeau B. Lamar High School, which Don would attend his senior year. M. D. Anderson, who had made his fortune in the international cotton business, bequeathed twenty million dollars "to go to the establishment and support and maintenance of hospitals, homes, and institutions for the care of the sick," an endowment that would make possible one of the world's premier cancer-research centers in Houston. Hugh Roy Cullen, an independent oil man, would jumpstart the University of Houston, giving money in memory of his son, who had died in the collapse of a drilling rig. The names Schlumberger and de Menil, which would later signal the nexus of money and cultural expansion in Houston, began to be known around town toward the end of the Depression and the start of the 1940s.

Though all of these developments would acutely affect Don's life, he was barely aware of them at the time. He was busy going to movies, catching crayfish in the bayou, sitting by a river with his grandpa, reading, and listening to his father.

"A verbal bully," Peter Barthelme once called his dad—and as the oldest child, Don caught the brunt of the attacks.

In his early adolescence, Don developed an uncontrollable twitch in his upper lip. The malady would strike him randomly, causing him tremendous embarrassment, particularly since the ability to put things into words, and to speak clearly, was valued so highly in the Barthelme home. The twitch disappeared only after Don underwent a series of medical tests, including aptitude and psychological profiles. As he recalled later, doctors told his parents he was a verbal genius and they should "let him be."

The narrator of "See the Moon?" tells his son, who remembers taking a lot of pills as a kid, "You had some kind of a nervous disorder, for a while. . . . We never found out what it was. It went away. . . . Your mouth trembled. . . . You couldn't control it." It was "nothing so fancy" as epilepsy, he says.

Shortly after the twitch disappeared, Don willed himself into becoming a superb public speaker. He would "distance" himself from his listeners "with a formal, slightly autocratic manner and [he'd] shape . . . his lips to pronounce each word with great care," says Helen Moore, the woman who would become his second wife. It's possible that at some point Don took speech lessons.

The "slightly autocratic manner" he developed could make him seem arrogant to people who didn't know him well. As a teenager, he wouldn't tolerate phoniness. In this, he followed his father. Joe Maranto, a pal in later years, said that Don was "fully formed" very early, "precocious, but rare in that he was sort of born with a vision and a gift; like some people can play basketball, he had that unique ability to [write]. Don did not have to work hard learning it; he worked hard at what he did."

His writing was so good that, in his junior year at St. Thomas, one of his teachers accused him of plagiarism. The papers he turned in were too accomplished for a high school boy, said his instructor, a stern and stubborn priest. This incident was a factor in Don's break with Catholic schooling.

HIGH AND LOW

"[My father] gave me, when I was fourteen or fifteen, a copy of Marcel Raymond's *From Baudelaire to Surrealism*," Don told an interviewer for *The Paris Review*. Raymond's volume didn't appear in English until 1950, so Don's memory was running ahead of itself here. He couldn't have read the book until he was nineteen—and fighting fiercely with his father.

In the meantime, the curriculum at St. Thomas Catholic High School required him to study Thomas Aquinas and Dante, whose philosophies and writings would echo throughout his work. For example, in the eighteenth canto of Dante's *Paradiso,* the souls of just and temperate rulers arrange themselves as lights in the air above Jupiter to spell the words *DILIGITE IUSTITIAM QUI IUDICATIS TERRAM,* meaning "Love righteousness, ye that are judges of the earth." Dante wrote, "In five times seven vowels and consonants / they showed themselves, and I grasped every part / as if those lights had given it utterance."

Contemporary readers—accustomed to billboards, marquees, electronics, computer graphics, and special effects in the movies—have little trouble imagining such a scene, but in the early fourteenth century, this was a remarkable image, almost an "anti-image," says the distinguished Dante scholar John Frecerro. It is a representation of a representation, "leading nowhere beyond itself."

Frecerro's description anticipates literary postmodernism, and dovetails with some of Don's mature interests. In an untitled interchapter in his 1983 collection, *Overnight to Many Distant Cities,* Don imagines a utopian metropolis whose form, when seen from the air, spells the word *FASTIGIUM,* not the "name of the city," the narrator tells us, "simply a set of letters selected for the elegance of the script." A fastigium is the apex of a structure; it is also an infinite sequence—in language, a list progressing alphabetically, letter by letter: *absentees, absenting, absolutes, absolving,* and so on. World without end. If Don's city is not the Empyrean, it is nevertheless a slice of eternity, a place, we're told, where a "girl dead behind . . . rosebushes" can come back to life, much as Beatrice's soul will live forever among the petals of the Mystic Rose in Paradise.

Paradiso was one of Western literature's earliest attempts to "represent that which is . . . beyond representation," Frecerro says. Given this, Dante is a natural literary father for Don, who always told his students, "What we are after is the unsayable." In 1986, just three years after imagining FASTIGIUM, he published a novel called *Paradise.*

Thomas Aquinas also whispers in Don's sentences, in Don's obsession with possibility. In the *Summa,* Aquinas defines God as pure actuality, manifested only in acts, without potentiality. Don turns this equation around and meditates on *shouldness* (what should be, rather than what exists in the world).

On December 6, 1273, a few months before his death, Aquinas reportedly dropped his pen and vowed not to write again. "I can do no more," he said. "Such secrets have been revealed to me that all I have written now appears to be of little value." One of Don's last characters, a writer on the island of St. Thomas, says, "I don't know what value to place on what I've done, perhaps none at all is right."

Like millions of Catholic boys in the 1940s, Don carried a little green book around school: the *Baltimore Catechism,* a manual of Catholic teaching first published in 1885, which contained hundreds of questions and answers. The bishops of America had compiled this English version of the *Roman Catechism,* written in Latin in the sixteenth century, in Baltimore in 1885. In subsequent editions, the *Baltimore Catechism* grew fatter and contained many more questions.

The Q & A form is traditional for philosophical investigation, but Don's deepest acquaintance with it would certainly have been through the *Baltimore Catechism.* It "is to be hoped" that the format will "be read with more pleasure" than a book of dry instructions, wrote the Reverend Thomas L. Kinkead in his 1891 preface to *An Explanation of the Baltimore Catechism.*

Q. What is man?
A. Man is a creature composed of body and soul, and made to the image and likeness of God.

Q. Why do many marriages prove unhappy?
A. Many marriages prove unhappy because they are entered into hastily and without worthy motives.

The *Explanation* addressed these and other questions. It argued that "much time is wasted" in schools. "Many teachers do little more than mark the attendance . . . and the children have no interest in the study." Young minds need to know that the "truths of their Catechism are constantly coming up in the performance of their everyday duties."

To a wry sensibility like Don's, the simplistic logic and awkward wording of the explanations were an endless source of mirth. For example, one "explanation"—a gloss on the phrase "To know," as in "To know God"—begins: "A poor savage in Africa never longs to be at a game or contest going on in America because he does not know it and therefore cannot love it." Don could not resist mocking such language, both as a schoolboy and later as a mature writer. The Q & A format would become one of his signature styles, in stories like "The Explanation," "Kierkegaard Unfair to Schlegel," "Basil from Her Garden," and others.

After a day of classes at the high school, Don read his father's magazines at home—the architectural journals and design catalogs as well as *The New Yorker.* Founded as a humor magazine just six years before Don was born, *The New Yorker* became a major literary showcase. In *About Town,* a history of the publication, Ben Yagoda quotes book critic John Leonard: *The New Yorker* was the "weekly magazine most educated Americans grew up on" (Leonard is roughly contemporary with Don). "Whether we read it or refused to read it—which depended, of course, on the sort of people we wanted to be—it was as much a part of our class conditioning as clean fingernails, college, a checking account, and good intentions. For better or worse, it probably created our sense of humor." Yagoda adds that the magazine created " 'our' sense of what was proper English prose and what was not, what was in good taste and what was not, what was the appropriate attitude to take, in print, toward personal and global happenings."

In the mid-1940s, when Don began reading *The New Yorker,* Howard Brubaker ran a column in it called "Of All Things," featuring quick, lighthearted satire of world events, like this quip from May 1, 1943: "Sweden announces that German warships found violating her waters will be fired upon. This is in accord with the well-known Swedish doctrine, 'I want to be alone.'" Or this: "Meat and poultry are again scarce in the New York area. Some of our citizens have practically nothing for dinner now but interesting conversation." The clever tone—distanced, charmingly snide—the wordplay, the mixture of public and private registers, and, above all, the swift pacing had natural appeal for an adolescent. Brubaker's jokes were verbal equivalents of *New Yorker* cartoons, another attraction for a smart young reader. The cartoons delivered fast punch lines and absurd imagery, as well as cultural comment.

Early threads of Don's style appear in James Thurber's contributions to the magazine during this period. Often, it's not clear whether Thurber was writing fiction or nonfiction; if he was mounting a parody, and if so, of what. In a piece called "1776—And All That," his narrator begins: "Everybody must know by this time that the freshmen in our colleges and universities do not know anything about the history or geography of the United States." From this documentary premise, Thurber moved swiftly into a fantasy about how people learned of the students' shocking ignorance: "It all began when the publisher of the *Times,* in a depressed mood, scribbled a memo to his editors. 'Have idea nobody knows anything. Find out.' The well-oiled machinery of the great newspaper began to move." From here, Thurber's narrator becomes an active character, designing educational aids. He proposes a "new kind of map of the United States . . . the exact shape and size of a goldfish. When the student [opens] his geography, the map [will] pop up. The textbook . . . [will] also . . . contain pop-ups of the Presidents." Eventually, the narrator abandons his idea: College freshmen will not "be interested in the Presidents even if they did pop up." The piece—idea-driven—never takes off as a story; its imaginative flights never rise very high. It appears to want to satirize something—but what? College students? Newspaper publishers? Textbook makers? In fact, the first sentence is just a convenient wedge, prying open the floodgates to a torrent of absurd observations, situations, and details.

Compare this to Don's "Swallowing," first published on the op-ed page of *The New York Times* on November 4, 1972, and reprinted in Don's nonfiction book, *Guilty Pleasures.* It begins:

> The American people have swallowed a lot in the last four years. A lot of swallowing has been done. We have swallowed electric bugs, laundered money, quite a handsome amount of grain moving about in mysterious ways, a war more shameful than can be imagined, much else. There are

even people who believe that the President does not invariably tell us the truth about himself or ourselves—he tells us *something,* we swallow that.

The piece then swerves into a riotous fantasy, in no sense nonfiction (nor is it recognizably an editorial on presidential policies): "In the history of swallowing, the disposition of the enormous cheese—six feet thick, twenty feet in diameter, four thousand pounds—which had been Wisconsin's principal contribution to the New York World's Fair of 1964-65, is perhaps instructive." Like Howard Brubaker preparing a punch line, Don twisted the word *swallowing* from its metaphoric to its literal meaning; then, like Thurber, he shifted tone, from essay into story. After an elaborate string of events, a poet, "starving as all poets are," eats the giant cheese. Later, "his best-known" poem is "*I Can't Believe I Ate the Whole Thing*"—a line in a popular antacid commercial in the early 1970s.

Don concludes: "The American people have swallowed quite a lot in the last four years, but as the poet cited goes on to say, there are remedies."

A comment on the Nixon administration? A fairy tale? A parody of world's fairs, poets, TV commercials? A fable on the transformative power of art? Though built around a more extreme premise than "1776—And All That," "Swallowing" lifts its moves from Thurber.

Yagoda says that the "little man" is "Thurber's contribution to *The New Yorker* and to American literature." The prime example is the beleaguered and hapless middle-class hero of "The Secret Life of Walter Mitty" (1939). With an almost throwaway line—Mitty experiences a "distressing scene with his wife"—Thurber began an "exhaustive, merciless, and meticulous three-decade chronicle of the war between men and women, especially between husbands and wives." Yagoda says that Thurber's "little man" blazed the trail for John Updike's suburban wanderers, and prefigured Don's work by "matter-of-factly positing an absurd but resonant premise and doggedly pursuing its logical consequences. It is a Kafka sort of method, and it can be seen as representing *The New Yorker*'s first brush with literary modernism of any kind."

In many of the magazine's unsigned "Talk of the Town" pieces (most of them written by E. B. White), the "little man" was abstracted into an anonymous speaker, a faceless "we," floating from scene to scene, making ironic comment. A column from April 13, 1946, begins: "A man must have some reading matter with him in the subway." Our man has brought with him Article 28 of the UN Charter. He ("we") is headed for a "crisis meeting of the Council, scheduled for eleven." The commentator then notes: "It struck us, as we put our nickel in, that no crisis worthy of the name can possibly occur at exactly eleven o'clock in the morning, crises, real ones, must occur earlier than eleven (say at 7:20, before a nation has shaved)."

The incongruities, shifting perceptions, and leaps of illogic were tricks that Don would master. He'd pick up the timing, too, in the comic precision of oddly qualified phrases like "crises, real ones."

In the 1940s, Edmund Wilson was a regular book reviewer for *The New Yorker,* tackling popular and serious literature, the high and the low, in a conversational mode that made book discussions sound as natural as talk about the weather. Of one well-known novel, Wilson said, "I hope I am not being stupid about this book, which has left me feeling rather cheated." His bluntness and passion, offered casually, provided an effective, enticing model for a budding young intellectual.

But of all the *New Yorker* writing that Don devoured as a teenager, none entered his bones as deeply as S. J. Perelman's work. A high school pal, Pat Goeters, recalled that Perelman was the "first writer Don imitated." For this reason, Goeters felt Don would never make a splash—he was more interested in "humorists" than in "serious writers and great ideas."

"Perelman . . . could do . . . amazing things in prose," Don told Larry Mc-Caffery in a 1980 interview. "[He] was the first true American surrealist—of a rank in the world surrealist movement with the best."

The New Yorker didn't cotton to Perelman at first. Harold Ross found his writing "dizzy," attempting to "burlesque too many things at once." In a rejection letter written in 1933, Ross told Perelman, "I think you ought to decide when you write a piece whether it is going to be a parody, or a satire, or nonsense. These are not very successfully mixed in short stuff; that has been my experience. You have some funny lines [here] . . . but on the whole it is just bewildering. . . ."

By 1937, though, the magazine's editors had come to see that Perelman had a knack for blurring genres, styles, and tones (or else he simply wore them down), and they signed him up for an annual number of pieces.

A nameless, nervous narrator—a manic version of Thurber's "little man"—anchors Perelman's stories, a persona that Woody Allen, as well as Don, would borrow. He employs high diction about low matters ("What pitchforked me into this imbroglio was a full-page advertisement"), jargon ("we're tops in the nuisance field"), archaisms ("he liked to linger abed"), and exaggerated whimsy ("the text . . . buttonhole[d] me and exud[ed] an opulent aroma of Drambuie and Corona Coronas").

A Perelman story will shift, without warning, into a play with stage directions and bare-bones dialogue. Or a piece will begin with material plucked from somewhere else, a magazine quote or a quote from someone else's story. Puns, obscure references, references to popular culture, comic horror, and double entendres make up Perelman's paragraphs. Perhaps the strategy that most intrigued Don was the merging of one world into another.

For instance, in a piece called "Strictly from Mars, or, How to Philander in Five Easy Colors" (October 26, 1946), comic books, pre-Columbian sculptures, and the Jupiter Symphony nestle together in a mad, allusion-filled collage.

One other *New Yorker* regular is notable for his influence on Don's formal experiments. Frank Sullivan, a former *New York Herald* reporter and a member in the early 1920s of the Algonquin Round Table with Dorothy Parker, Alexander Woollcott, and James Thurber, began contributing to the magazine in 1926. In 1932, he inaugurated the "Greetings, Friends!" Christmas poem, and wrote an annual year-end verse until 1974, when Roger Angell, Don's editor at the magazine, took over for him. Sullivan's other signature was his character Mr. Arbuthnot, the "Cliché Expert." In dozens of pieces throughout the thirties and forties, Mr. Arbuthnot expounded on subjects as varied as love, politics, alcohol, movies, war, and crime. His reflections took the form of "testimonies" and were presented in Q & A fashion:

> **A—** . . . You realize, of course, what the dropping of that test bomb in the stillness of the New Mexico night did.
>
> **Q— What did it do?**
> **A—** It ushered in the atomic age, that's what it did. You know what kind of discovery this is?
>
> **Q— What kind?**
> **A—** A tremendous scientific discovery.
>
> **Q— Could the atomic age have arrived by means of any other verb than "usher"?**
> **A—** No. "Usher" has the priority.
>
> **Q— Mr. Arbuthnot, what will never be the same?**
> **A—** The world.
>
> **Q— Are you pleased?**
> **A—** I don't know.

For Don, these pieces were unintentional parodies of the *Baltimore Catechism.* They were also appealing for their skewering of overused language, their wrenching of familiar phrases into new and humorous contexts, and their light treatment of grave subjects.

• • •

By eventually accepting cross-genre pieces, and stories of increasing complexity and range, *The New Yorker* stretched readers' perceptions, first of humor, then of cultural dialogue. It cemented its widening reputation as a serious magazine in August 1946 with the publication of John Hersey's "Hiroshima," a devastating account of nuclear destruction. Harold Ross knew that *The New Yorker* had turned a corner at that point. "I started to get out a light magazine that wouldn't concern itself with the weighty problems of the universe, and now look at me," he wrote Howard Brubaker.

The magazine's array of light and sober prose, cartoons, and glittering ads would serve as Don's template of stylish absurdity mixed with serious intent until his father gave him Marcel Raymond's book. Even after he'd read *From Baudelaire to Surrealism, The New Yorker*'s pull proved irresistible to him.

"Style is not much a matter of choice," Don said. And he maintained that childhood reading thrills never really fade. He also claimed that Rafael Sabatini's adventure stories were a lifelong presence in his work.

The novel *Captain Blood: His Odyssey* was published in 1922, followed in 1930 by a story collection, *Captain Blood Returns,* and finally by a book of novellas, *The Fortunes of Captain Blood,* in 1936. Errol Flynn played the pirate hero in a movie in 1935, one of the first films Don ever saw.

At first blush, Blood seems an entirely different rascal from Thurber's "little man," but the figures do share some traits, and both add a pinch to Don's typical literary persona. Like Walter Mitty, Blood is fiercely imaginative and intelligent. While not hapless, he does harbor hidden longings— particularly for his secret love, Arabella Bishop. And like Mitty, he is frequently misunderstood. Both men hope to do right but are regularly thwarted by circumstance.

"Peter Blood, bachelor of medicine and several other things besides, smoked a pipe and tended the geraniums boxed on the sill of his window above Water Lane in the town of Bridgewater," Sabatini's novel begins. Don's imagination seized upon the teasing phrase "and several other things"; often, he employed similar vague wording to add humor to his work or to parody traditional descriptions: "Kevin said a lot more garbage to Clem," or, "The countryside. Flowers."

Sabatini plays complex narrative games. In the novel, his nameless teller steals accounts of Blood's tales from a second source, which has been plundered by a third writer, who attributes Blood's deeds to a different hero altogether.

In *Overnight to Many Distant Cities,* Don's love of Sabatini finally came clean in a pastiche of the pirate's sagas. In reading "[*my*] Captain Blood," you "are reminded, I hope, of the pleasure Sabatini gives you or has given you," Don said. "The piece is in no sense a parody, rather it's very much an *hommage.* An attempt to present, or recall, the essence of Sabatini."

Like the original, Don's Blood is a sad, solitary figure, quick with rapier and wit, and given to aesthetic rapture. He imagines throwing captured women into the sea, "fitted with life jackets under their dresses," so he can delight in the patterns they would make "floating on the surface of the water, in the moonlight, a cerise gown, a silver gown . . ."

At story's end, Blood paces his ship's foredeck alone, worrying. We're told: "The favorite dance of Captain Blood is the grave and haunting Catalonian *sardana,* in which the participants join hands facing each other to form a ring which gradually becomes larger, then smaller, then larger again. It is danced without smiling, for the most part. He frequently dances this with his men, in the middle of the ocean, after lunch, to the music of a single silver trumpet."

Always, Don insisted that humor was his only mode of seriousness. Sabatini first showed him this trick, smuggling social jibes into his work beneath the action or the jokes. Take, for example, Don's "*sardana*" reference: In Spain, under Franco's repressive regime, all traces of Catalonian identity, including the dance, were banned, but the *sardana* often erupted in the streets of Barcelona, an assertion of freedom and justice. In Don's story, the dance carries serious weight in an otherwise lighthearted list of details.

When he was asked in a *Paris Review* interview to name his influences, Don slipped in Errol Flynn. "Why Errol Flynn?" J. D. O'Hara asked him. "Because he's part of my memory of Sabatini," Don replied. "Sabatini fleshed out. He was in the film version of 'Captain Blood,' and 'The Sea Hawk.' He should have done 'Scaramouche,' but Stewart Granger did it instead, as I recall." Don's quibbling reveals how important the pirate movies were to him, how much delight he took, as a child, in Captain Blood. When he said he hoped his swashbuckler would remind readers of the "pleasure Sabatini gives you or *has* given you" (italics added), he recalled another of Sabatini's charms: his wistfulness. Don bared his *own* nostalgia here, reaching back for an elusive childhood joy, but the quality is present in Sabatini. At the end of *Captain Blood,* the adventurer's strongest desire (aside from securing his lover) is to return to the simple beauty of his past. He will not be able to do so. "I had counted upon going home, so I had," he says, sighing. "I am hungry for the green lanes of England. There will be apple-blossoms in the orchards of Somerset."

The final scene of *The King,* Don's last book—on one level, a sword-flashing adventure fantasy; on another, an elegy for vanished innocence—echoes Sabatini. The noble knight Launcelot lies beneath a tree, dreaming of his love, and of quiet, intimate pleasures, joys the reader knows he will never again grasp. Two onlookers, who can somehow see into the dream, marvel:

"What a matchless dream!"

"Under an apple tree . . ."

Writing his final novel, Don tried to erase the decades, and cushion himself once more in his earliest reading delights.

If *New Yorker* stories offered one set of models for a writer, Hemingway supplied another. He "taught us all," Don said. To O'Hara, he admitted that Perelman and Hemingway were paired in his mind, suggesting that he discovered them around the same time, in the 1940s; more than this, he could see that Hemingway's writing affirmed the "amazing things" in Perelman's prose, obviously not with the same intent, but in musical terms. From Hemingway, one learned "wonderful things about . . . sentence rhythms," Don said, "and wonderful things about precision, and wonderful things about being concise. His example is very, very strong."

Attuned to structural matters from his father's architectural practice, Don could see that music was storytelling's skeleton, connecting writers as apparently diverse as Hemingway and Perelman. Don absorbed a lot about music during this period, listening to jazz records, taking up drumming. A good sentence needed a beat or a variation from a beat, just as a musical phrase did. Hemingway's music was inescapable:

> *It was getting hot, the sun hot on the back of his neck.*
> *Nick had one good trout. He did not care about getting many trout. Now the stream was shallow and wide.*

The repetition of plosive sounds—*t*'s, *d*'s, and *k*'s—in "getting," "hot," "trout," "neck," "Nick," and so on, does the time keeping; variations save the phrasing from dullness and emphasize Nick's experiences. The line "getting hot, the sun hot" bores down on the reader, the recurring "hot" as relentless as the sun; the hammering beat of "one good trout" underscores the solidity of Nick's achievement. At the end, the rolling *l*'s and long vowel sounds of "shallow" open the passage up—a widening river—particularly after the regular rhythm of the preceding sentence. The final *d* in "wide" circles us back to where we began, with the plosives, as though impelled by an eddying stream.

As a high school student, Don followed Hemingway's example on the page and off. For a while, Hemingway worked as a journalist, so Don pursued journalism by working on the staff of the St. Thomas *Eagle.* He appears in a photo of the group, dated 1947, with a piece of tape stuck comically to his face. The editorship rotated among students. Just as Don was set to take his turn, the priests who oversaw the publication passed him over without explanation. He was reminded of the incident that got his father expelled from the Rice Institute. The priests considered Don too irreverent, too iconoclastic, to be trusted with the school's staid paper. What made the snub even worse was that Don's talent was undeniable: He had recently received Honorable Mention, Junior Division, for a short story (now lost) in a *Scholastic Magazine* competition.

The *Eagle* disappointment, and his teacher's charge of plagiarism, infuriated Don. He looked around his school—a place "surrounded by oak trees, almost on the banks of Buffalo Bayou," says his friend Pat Goeters. "The bayou was the habitat of turtles, water moccasins and occasionally skinny-dipping boys who wanted to have the rep of being tough guys." Don saw weary instructors mired in routine, boys worrying about their acne.

One day at a bus stop, on his way to school, he met a Lamar High School student named Beverly Arnold (*née* Bintliff). Her father was involved with real estate and had developed a tony new residential neighborhood in northwest Houston. "I started dating Don," Arnold recalls. "I was going to First Methodist Church. He was a good Catholic, but he would accompany me on some Sunday afternoons when I went to the teenage activities at church. He was the first boy to kiss me, there at the bus stop. When you're fifteen, you know, everything's romantic.

"Don was brilliant even then. His vocabulary was overwhelming," she says. "He wrote me a love letter that said, 'Someday I want to grow up to be a musician or a writer.' And he said, 'I will always love you but I will also always want to be a writer.'"

Another letter he sent her, along with a dozen Easter roses, reads:

> *Baby:*
> *This note is a summary of how I feel about you. If I ever want to back down, which isn't likely, you got it in writing.*
>
> *You're a good kid. I like the way you stand up for me, whether I need it or not. I like the way you look. You are pretty, did you know?*
>
> *I think about you more than I should; its bad for my hard, cynical journalists mind, which I hope to have some day. I like to be with you, which is bad for the don'-give-a-darn attitude I want too.*
>
> *To use a broken down expression—you get the idea.*
>
> *I feel real good about you. I have felt that way for the last couple of weeks; perfectly content. Everything in the world changes, they say. I hope we can keep this. If it is up to me, we will.*
>
> *And remember, you have all my love.*
>
> *Don*

Pictures of Don at the time show a tall, long-faced boy, laughing uproariously, or squinting wryly even in serious moments. At school he wore a bow tie, a pressed white shirt, and wool pants. In one photo of a teenage swimming party, he looks casually assured, easy in his body.

Arnold introduced him to her friend Alafair Kane (*née* Benbow). "We ran around in a little crowd," Kane says. "Don would have parties at his house. He liked to dance—always a lot of fun, very friendly, a very happy personality."

Arnold and Kane recall that he played a horn of some sort—trumpet, perhaps. "I never heard him play the drums," Arnold says, "but Alafair's family had a trap set in their playroom, and he'd go over and perform for them."

Pat Goeters, a year ahead of Don at St. Thomas, and editor of the *Eagle,* met Kane and fell in love with her, he says. Through her brother Sam he met Don, and that's how Don came to write for the paper. "Recruiting writers among a school full of testosterone-crazed boys wasn't all that easy, but compared to actually getting their copy on deadline it was a snap," Goeters says. He asked Don to contribute a column, "Around and About." At the time, Don's style was a "Damon Runyan ripoff," Goeters says. He and Sam considered themselves the serious writers, and Don a bit of a "lightweight," but Don's column was funny and entertained their classmates.

Another friend, Carter Rochelle, met "Bo—that's what we called him back then—[because] his family lived across the street from my cousin, Mac Caldwell. I spent quite a lot of time in Don's home. He had his own upstairs room—his 'garret'—and even had his own phone extension and portable typewriter, pretty big stuff in those days. We passed many an evening there with other friends, making up story lines, talking endlessly about writing (he had already decided that he would be a writer for *The New Yorker*), listening to jazz on his record player. He was already very well informed about jazz and was an early admirer of Charlie Parker, Miles Davis, and Stan Kenton. It seems to me that Mrs. Barthelme usually had to break up our klatches in his room or we would have gone on all night."

Rochelle says the "Barthelme family was comfortably situated and solidly cohesive." Rochelle's mother and father had both passed away, so he lived on his own in an apartment, and worked after school. "Twice that I recall, Don ran away from home and holed up in my place," he says. Eventually, "his father came and pulled him out."

Don nursed his grievance against the priests for denying him the *Eagle* editorship. One day in February 1948, Pat Goeters went looking for Don. "I found him slouched against the pale green glazed tile wall in the steamy hall outside his home room. I was there to pick up Don's monthly column," Goeters says.

The boys exchanged their usual greeting. "Wh'say, Brer Pat?" Don said.

"Wh'say, Brer Don?"

"What tar-baby say?"

"Tar-baby ain't sayin' nothin'."

"We both wore white, oxford-cloth button-down dress shirts with cuffs turned twice, faded jeans with no belt, white socks and run-down brown penny loafers," Goeters says. "If they had made this the school uniform only about three students would have had to partially modify the way they dressed. Don wore horn-rimmed glasses which he frequently adjusted on his nose and a perpetual sardonic smile."

Don said to Goeters, "Thinking about going to Mexico. Wanna come?"

Goeters wasn't terribly close to Don at this point, but the idea appealed to him. He shared Don's frustration with the school's tight views of literary expression. Besides, he didn't really believe Don was serious. "But if it was a dare, I wasn't going to be left out," he says. He asked Don, "How'd we get there?"

"Hitchhike, I guess." He "sounded impatient," Goeters says.

Don insisted that they stop at a drugstore on Shepard Drive to buy pencils and notebooks. Then he left a note for his folks: "We've gone to Mexico to make our fortune." He was two months shy of his seventeenth birthday.

Goeters says that Alafair Benbow was the only person to whom they bothered to say good-bye. She doesn't remember this.

Between them, the boys had thirty dollars. A trucker took them from Houston to San Antonio, where they spent the night in a downtown Y. The next day, they hitched a ride to Laredo, on the Texas-Mexico border. The driver took the car through customs; as he did, the boys, and the other passengers from the car, walked across the international bridge. On the other side, Don and Goeters hooked up again with the driver. In Mexico City, the man sheltered the boys while they looked for work. A passage from Don's story "Overnight to Many Distant Cities" (an earlier version of which appears in a piece called "Departures") recounts—mostly accurately—the whole affair:

> *In Mexico City we lay with the gorgeous daughter of the American ambassador by a clear, cold mountain stream.* Well, that was the plan, it didn't work out that way. We were around sixteen and had run away from home, in the great tradition, hitched various long rides with various sinister folk, and there we were in the great city with about two t-shirts to our names. My friend Herman [Goeters's first name] found us jobs in a jukebox factory. Our assignment was to file the slots in American jukeboxes so that they would accept the big, thick Mexican coins. All day long. No gloves.
>
> After about a week of this we were walking one day on the street where the Hotel Reforma is to be found and there were my father and

grandfather, smiling. "The boys have run away," my father had told my grandfather, and my grandfather had said, "Hot damn, let's go get 'em." I have rarely seen two grown men enjoying themselves so much.

Details from "Departures" suggest that the driver who helped the boys clear the final checkpoint may have been a black jazz drummer, steering a big Hudson. He was traveling with a white songwriter and his Hawaiian wife. Don described what happened at the border: "My friend Herman and I changed all the money we had into one-peso notes with a fifty-peso note on the outside of the wad. We showed the wad to the border officials demonstrating that we would not become a burden upon the State. We had learned this device from the movies."

He went on: "After the second border checkpoint had been passed, the car stopped at a house and everybody got out to change the tires. The drummer and the songwriter pried the tires off the rims. Herman and I helped. Copper wire, hundreds of feet of it, was wound round each of the rims. Our friends were smuggling copper wire, a scarce item during the War. The benefits of leaving home were borne in on us. We had never met any absolutely genuine smugglers before."

"Don insisted that we should visit the *Mexico City Herald,* the English language newspaper, and try for a job as staff writers," Goeters recalls, but nothing came of this attempt. The boys sent telegrams to their families, saying they were fine.

Don's father and his dad flew to Mexico City to find the boys. Once there, they engaged all the street photographers they could find. The photographers made their living taking pictures of tourists, but apparently none of them had snapped the boys. The Barthelmes checked into the Hotel Reforma and waited until Saturday night, when the kids, if they were here, would probably head downtown, looking for action. Sure enough, Barthelme spotted them right away. "Bo! We're sure as hell glad to see you boys!" he called across the crowd. "Hi, Pops," Don said sheepishly. Goeters had never met Don's family, so he worried when Don "was willing to talk to these two older men and go back to their hotel with them." The men had "obviously been drinking." Though Don called one of them "Pops," this was a "term he often used in imitation of jazz musicians to refer to almost any male."

Eventually, Goeters grasped the situation and followed Don and the "two weaving Americanos" back to their hotel for a "strained reunion."

The following morning, the men flew home, with the runaways in tow. Ultimately, the Mexico adventure turned out to be "more just the end of childhood than the beginning of something," Goeters says. He felt Don was "ready to be found and brought back home."

Despite this and the cheery spin Don put on the incident in his stories, this episode increased the tension with his father. Goeters returned to St. Thomas to finish the term so he could graduate (having lost both the *Eagle* and Alafair Benbow), but Don refused to submit again to the priests' authority. His parents finally agreed to let him transfer to Lamar High School, a public facility near the affluent River Oaks neighborhood.

THE NEW MUSIC

"I do believe this was my idea," Don said of becoming a writer. "I can't blame anybody else for it."

In his senior year at Mirabeau B. Lamar High School, away for the first time from the sisters and priests who had been his teachers, he tested his idea. In the 1949 issue of *Sequoyha,* the high school's literary magazine, he published a parody of *Pilgrim's Progress.* It was called "Rover Boys' Retrogression." His choice of targets, and the changes he worked on the original, revealed his state of mind and—remarkably—set the pattern for much of his future work. Not only did parody remain a central impulse throughout his career but, more important, he was already developing strategies for transforming personal material into allegory, fantasy, or absurd imagery.

His father's influence appears, in this earliest locatable work, in two ways: Form is the foremost concern, not for its own sake, but for the way it embodies, economically, the ideas behind it; and an intensity of feeling is conveyed without revealing its sources. The story's core remains safe from ridicule. These are weighty matters for a comic piece by a seventeen-year-old.

John Bunyan wrote *Pilgrim's Progress,* "an Allegory . . . [about] the way to Glory," in 1678. It traces the soul's journey from the City of Destruction to the Celestial City, detailing along the way the pitfalls of the Slough of Despond and the Valley of Humiliation. *The New Yorker*'s breezy style was in Don's mind, as was "Hemingway as parodist," when he decided to lampoon Bunyan. Whereas the magazine's wits tackled news items, and Hemingway, in *Torrents of Spring,* aimed his arrows at the American naturalists, Don chose—in his first year away from Catholic teaching—a sacred text. Reportedly, Bunyan wrote *Pilgrim's Progress* in jail, while being punished for conducting religious services that did not conform to the dictates of the Church of England. In rebellion against conformity and spiritual discipline, Don built his first published work around a pointed literary source.

"Rover Boys' Retrogression" follows two characters, Half-Asleep and Not-Quite-Awake, as they journey to the River of Respect Due. There, they fail to worship properly an "impressive array of state barges carrying great quantities of Personages, Dignitaries, Golden Calves, Sacred Cows, Cabbages, Kings, and Members of the School Board." Eventually, they reach Expulsion.

A preface accompanies the piece, in which Don explained:

> a parody, to be completely effective *as a parody,* must be a complete reversal of attitude, set in the form of the work being parodied. As "Pilgrim's Progress" is highly moral, the ensuing "Rover Boys' Retrogression" is not. It has been written as the antithesis of Bunyan's book, not because the writer feels any perverse delight in caricaturing things as they are, but purely from an altruistic effort to respect the integrity of the parody form, as he sees it.

"Disingenuous though it is, the disclaimer allowed the story to escape whatever censorship existed," says Robert Murray Davis, the first scholar to track Don's juvenilia. Don's trouble with the St. Thomas *Eagle* gave him a tactic for smuggling heresy into print. The preface is noteworthy for another reason. Like his father, Don sought to educate his audience, to mount a crusade for his art. Many of Don's later fictions are also, implicitly, forms of literary criticism.

In fleeing the "School Board," and heading for Expulsion, Half-Asleep and Not-Quite-Awake parallel Don and Pat Goeters on their flight to Mexico. Nearly thirty years would pass before Don wrote plainly of the incident, in "Departures," and even then he mixed the material into a collage, instead of constructing a narrative or a memoir from it. From the beginning, stories and characterizations based on the conventions of literary realism failed to engage him; he was energized by the fusion of parody and myth, the high and the low, and by the alchemy of turning experience into a stylized essence.

He satirized the sacred, but gently—Bunyan was an iconoclast, one whom Don must have admired on some level. Don razzed the authorities and

praised freedom—nothing surprising for an adolescent, except for the sophistication of its style. What *is* surprising is the complex layering already
evident in Don's work. Aside from the *Pilgrim's* parody and the buried personal references, a second literary source comes in for scrutiny: The Rover
Boys Series for Young Americans.

Edward Stratemeyer, writing under the pseudonym Arthur M. Winfield,
published the first Rover Boys book, *The Rover Boys at School, or The Cadets
at Putnam Hall,* in 1899. Whitman Publishers reprinted this volume in a
handsome edition in the 1930s. The Rover Boys, Dick, Tom, and Sam, are
among the most obnoxious heroes in children's literature, haughty, cruel, violent. The series kicks off with a disingenuous preface. Stratemeyer wrote,
" 'The Rover Boys at School' has been written that those of you who have
never been at an American military academy for boys may gain some insight
into the workings of such an institution." The story is longer on high jinks
than on insight. Stratemeyer referred to his characters as those "lively, wide-
awake"—as opposed to Half-Asleep or Not-Quite-Awake—"fun-loving Rover
brothers."

"Rover Boys' Retrogression" is not just a rebellious parody of a classic
text; it is an homage to a book *about* rebellion, and a disguised travelogue of
Don's escape from home. He took a theme—refusal of authority—and fashioned a collage around it. In so doing, he emphasized the piece's structural
principles. Significantly, he also found a way to get it into print, refusing to
stay at a school where his work was not appreciated.

"Rover Boys' Retrogression" signals one other uprising: Here, Don followed his father in embracing an art form and approaching it with serious
playfulness, but it was his mother's art (or the art she sacrificed for the
family) that he chose to pursue. It was her dream that he would animate, and
to succeed at it, he would do whatever he had to, whether his father liked it
or not.

Don and Goeters were buddies now, after their Mexico adventure, and they
did their best to stir excitement at home. They competed for girls, a friendly
rivalry that Goeters usually won. He was tall, blond, and handsome. Don
was a little gawky, with big horn-rimmed glasses. He, Goeters, and Carter
Rochelle practiced journalism together. "In the fall of 1948, Don and I drew
up a detailed plan for an entire page especially for teenagers to run every
Saturday in our local morning daily, the *Houston Post,*" Rochelle recalls.
"That September we borrowed his dad's 1948 Studebaker and drove over to
the newspaper's headquarters, went into the city room and asked to see the
editor. Amazingly, we were granted an audience. We presented our idea. The
city editor, Harry Johnston, said he thought it was a great idea—which is why

they had just started [a teen page]. Even so, he let us unfold our plan in detail, and it turned out that he liked our thinking better than what they were doing. We got to meet the managing editor, who also listened to our proposal and promised to consider it. A week later, the city editor offered me a job as a cub reporter. Don wasn't hired, presumably because he was still seventeen while I was eighteen going on nineteen. When I initiated the teen page, I brought Don in as its record critic. Each week he'd review all the new LP records (LPs had just come in, the previous year)." Don filed pieces on Stan Kenton's band-leading skills, and the odd syncopations in the music of Thelonius Monk and Dizzy Gillespie. His work stood out among traditional articles on school activities and sports events. His reviewing lasted "about six months, until he and I had a couple of disagreements over editing and he gave it up," Rochelle says.

Often, Pat Goeters would take his mother's car after school, and he and Don would go joyriding. Once again, late in his career, Don felt comfortable enough—personally and professionally—to write straightforwardly about his youth. In an autobiographical piece called "Chablis," he recounted:

> I remember the time, thirty years ago, when I put Herman's mother's Buick into a cornfield, on the Beaumont highway. There was another car in my lane, and I didn't hit it, and it didn't hit me. I remember veering to the right and down into the ditch and up through the fence and coming to rest in the cornfield and then getting out to wake Herman and the two of us going to see what the happy drunks in the other car had come to, in the ditch on the other side of the road.

Goeters says this passage "refers to the time Don got me to take him to Galveston so he could drive past the house of a girlfriend who had recently dumped him. He wanted to drive by without stopping in order to ignore her. He told me that would serve her right. Then he insisted on driving on the return trip and drunkenly missed a turn, went off the road and bounced us across a field, tearing up the bottom of the car."

Don's youngest brother recalled that when he was a teenager, he wasn't allowed to drive his father's car because "my older brothers had raced and wrecked the three earlier Corvettes my father owned until he had gotten fed up." In "Chablis," Don wrote, "There were five children in my family and the males rotated the position of black sheep for a while while he was in his DWI period or whatever and then getting grayer as he maybe got a job or was in the service and then finally becoming a white sheep when he got married and had a grandchild. My sister was never a black sheep because she was a girl."

In "Grandmother's House," a late dialogue piece, two of Don's speakers reflect:

—Seventeen is a wild age.

—Seventeen is anarchy.

—I was atrocious when I was seventeen. Absolutely atrocious.

—Likewise.

—Drunk driving was the least of it.

—When you think about it now you turn pale.

As the Barthelme children grew, the dynamic shifted on North Wynden Drive. "Though we felt a fierce tribal loyalty with Don and Joan, an engagement with their exploits and opinions, they were young adults," Rick and Steve wrote in *Double Down.* To some extent, Peter, too, felt stuck in the second Barthelme family—the ur-family being Mom and Dad, Don, and Joan. By the time Peter, Rick, and Steve were adolescents, their father had "for the most part excused himself from the child-rearing business to spend his energies on buildings he was designing and clients who needed endless care and persuasion."

In his late teens, Don was headstrong and stubborn like his father, emotionally guarded, furiously protective of the things that mattered to him— his mother, his writing, his friends. He looked "very much like his mother," his cousin, Elise, recalls. "Their mouth and jaws cupped into mischevious grins, conveying a bond between them that was innate and made stronger by mutual love and respect." The "Barthelme characteristics" included "expressive eyes and lithe body movements." Don had his mother's "wry humor" and "kept his own counsel."

His father's busy schedule gave Don more time, more room, to break away, race the car, drink and smoke, read, listen to music, and hone his writing, for which he received more and more attention. In the spring of 1949, his story "Integrity Cycle" (now lost) tied for fourth place in a *Scholastic Magazine* contest, and he won the Texas Poet Laureate Award for a poem entitled "Inertia." The high school newspaper, the *Lamar Lancer,* said the poem addressed the "subject of world cooperation."

It would have been small consolation for the elder Barthelme to know that his son still carried the Basilian Order's reverence for social diversity wherever he went, or that Don pursued even his leisure activities with the passion of someone searching for meaningful principles. During his late adolescence, this passion led Don into Houston's jazz clubs. Nietzsche's assertion that "without music the world would be a mistake" became his new spiritual dogma.

Don's interest in jazz had developed early. In his upstairs bedroom, his father's former study, he played the drums day and night, until the family could take no more. He moved his trap set outside, into the space his father had once intended as a garage. The neighbors began to complain. Don arranged with them that he would play whenever they were gone. A picture, taken by his father sometime in the mid-forties, shows Don dressed in white shirt and pants, looking very serious behind a huge bass drum and a snare. A hi-hat, a crash, and a ride cymbal round out the set. Don's hair is slicked back and his thick glasses shine. He props his hands on his drumsticks, which are propped on his right thigh. His fingers are graceful and long, nimble, an extension of the sticks. When he played, he'd keep time with his right hand on the ride cymbal while his left roamed over the snare, the bell of the crash, the hi-hat, diddling, filling, breaking, catching the beat off guard, switching tempos: steady rhythm, startling tangents. Sometimes he wrote musical scores, none of which survive, and he may have fiddled with horns, but the drums were the only instrument he learned to play well.

Pat Goeters recalls visiting Don "in his aerie" and listening to "New Orleans jazz on the radio (WWL in New Orleans–'Moonglow with Martin'). As it got late, Papa Barthelme would come to the bottom of the stairs and yell, 'What'sa matter, ain't Goeters got a home?'"

Don's senior year in high school, he, Goeters, Carter Rochelle, and other friends went to "black clubs," Don said, "to hear people like Erskine Hawkins who were touring—us poor little pale little white boys were offered a generous sufferance, tucked away in a small space behind the bandstand with an enormous black cop posted at the door. In other places you could hear the pianist Peck Kelly, a truly legendary figure, or Lionel Hampton, or once in a great while Louis Armstrong or Woody Herman. I was sort of drenched in all this." Houston was generally more relaxed about racial matters than most American cities. In few other metropolitan areas in the South in the 1940s would he and his "pale little" pals have enjoyed the freedom to enter such clubs.

From jazz, Don learned "something about making a statement," he said, "about placing emphases within a statement or introducing variations . . . [taking] a tired old tune . . . [and] literally [making] it new. The interest and the drama were in the formal manipulation of the rather slight material. And [the musicians] were heroic figures, you know, very romantic."

The local jazz was heavily inflected with Texas swing and rhythm and blues, called "race music" in those days. It was guitar-heavy, drum-heavy, with a four-beat, twelve-bar base. Don listened to the two black radio stations in town, KCOH and KYOK, both now defunct, whose DJs gave themselves monikers like "Mister El Toro" and "Daddy Deepthroat." The largest clubs, all southeast of downtown, were the Eldorado, at the corner of Elgin and Dowling streets ("it was strictly an African-American establishment," Rochelle recalls, "and we were underage as well, but they let us sneak in the back because we knew some of the people there"); the Club Ebony, at Rosewood and Dowling; the Club Savoy on Wheeler; and Shady's Playhouse, at Elgin and Ennis.

In addition to jazz greats, Houston's clubs featured talents like Lightnin' Hopkins, Albert "Ice Man" Collins, Johnny Ace, Bobby "Blue" Bland, and T-Bone Walker, whose R & B electric guitar stylings helped define what was later called "West Coast jazz." In 1949, Don Robey, a Houston businessman and reputed gambler, founded Peacock Records to promote Clarence "Gatemouth" Brown, a regular in Robey's Bronze Peacock Club. The record label thrived, putting Houston on the jazz map, along with Oklahoma City and Kansas City. It was a thrilling scene in which to be immersed.

In the various jazz styles that developed during this period, drummers were major innovators. The slightest variation in rhythm could violate or purify the music (depending on how one heard it). For example, Jo Jones, who got his start in the thirties playing with the Blue Devils in Oklahoma City (a band revered by the young Ralph Ellison), would often abandon the beat to play rhythmic variations on his band mates' solos, using the hi-hat as the focal point. This untethered the tune, gave it flight. Known for his delicate brushwork, he also shifted the beat away from the bass drum and tom-toms and moved it to the cymbals—in effect, lifting the rhythm from the bottom to the top, lightening the sound. Jones was part of a generation of musicians that included Chick Webb, Gene Krupa, Baby Dodds, Buddy Rich, and Sid Catlett. They streamlined jazz drumming, dropping the bells, whistles, and rattles that had characterized big-band percussion in the tens and twenties. They introduced subtle polyrhythmic playing and syncopation to expand swing and encourage improvisation. Webb was one of the first drummers to tune his drums melodically—he keyed his bass drum to the stand-up bass's G string. "Some say drums have no part of the melody," Catlett once said. "They just provide the rhythm. I look at it like this: swing is my idea of how a melody should go. Now I ask you, what is swing without the drums?" Using swishes, crashes, strokes, thunderous rim shots to choke off a phrase, or accenting a piano's bass line with snare taps to drive it into the forefront of a tune, these stickmen redefined jazz in their time, and Don paid close attention.

In the *Paris Review* interview with J. D. O'Hara, Don lists as one of his strongest influences "Big Sid Catlett." Versatility distinguished Big Sid—his ability to move from big bands to small combos, from swing to bebop. He was Louis Armstrong's favorite drummer; Satchmo used him from 1938 to 1942, and again from 1947 to 1949. In between, Catlett hooked up with Dizzy Gillespie and Charlie Parker for some of the earliest bop recordings. Don admired him for his capacity, and his willingness, to be a transitional figure, to carry the old into the new, to play the new *against* the old in ways that enriched the traditions *and* the innovations he pioneered. The depth of this achievement—and the fierce resistance to it, intially—is reflected in a Buddy Rich interview from 1956, in which Rich expressed his suspicions of change, praising the old big-band styles and excoriating bebop. "Whereas in the days when it was necessary to swing a band, when a drummer had to be a powerhouse, today more or less the 'cool school' has taken over," Rich said, "and I don't believe there's such a thing as a 'cool drummer.' You either swing a band or you don't swing a band and that's what's lacking today. There aren't any guys who get back there and play with any kind of guts. And I like a heavyweight."

Catlett made no such distinctions. He was a team player, serving the music. With the Teddy Wilson Quartet, in the 1940s, he could be completely self-effacing, showcasing his band mates. With Benny Goodman's orchestra, he could rein in the large group and drive them relentlessly toward a single destination. With Armstrong's All-Stars, he could provide individual rhythms for each soloist, leading them to the grooves that best suited their particular strengths. He could make swing bop, and bop swing. He was playful and serious, high and low. He was Perelman and Hemingway.

After graduating from Lamar High School in the spring of 1949, Don wanted to hit the road with a small band. His father did not approve, and they argued. Eventually, Don defied his dad, packed up his drums, and did a series of engagements in southeast Texas. It's impossible to know where he played, but in those days the Last Concert Café, a Mexican restaurant and dance hall on Nance Street in Houston, regularly hosted amateur jazz bands, as did the Tin Hall Dancehall and Saloon in Cypress, Texas, the oldest roadhouse in Harris County, and the Starlight Barber Shop and Pool Hall in Crockett. These were likely venues for a local group, catering to mostly middle-class, and some mixed-race, crowds. The tour seems to have soured quickly. By September, Don had enrolled at the University of Houston, once again frustrating his father, who had hoped he would go to an Ivy League school.

FROM BAUDELAIRE TO ROSENBERG

Apparently worried that Don was frittering away his talents, his father seems to have tried to rein him in. Sometime during Don's first, or perhaps at the start of his second, year in college, he gave his son the Marcel Raymond book. He also slipped Don a copy of Rabelais's *Gargantua and Pantagruel,* with the counsel, "If you imitate a writer's style, always choose the best."

These gestures were generous and shrewd. Just as Don was starting his university education, his father reasserted his role as primary mentor. He made sensitive choices: Both books suited Don's interests and tastes, while appealing to his wit and verbal skills. They also insisted on the wisdom of heeding one's elders. Gargantua is Pantagruel's father. He laments his "advanced age" and the generational changes he has witnessed. He admits, ruefully, "I see the robbers, hangmen [and] freebooters . . . of today more learned than the theologians and preachers of my day. What can I say?" He implies that fathers have always sacrificed to give their children every advantage.

Raymond's *From Baudelaire to Surrealism* holds that progress must be based on tradition. It traces a consistent artistic line rooted in romanticism, noting the fruitful meanders and the dead ends facing young writers. Mallarmé was an especially heroic figure to Raymond, who wrote that for the poet, "[T]he word with its vowels and diphthongs represents a kind of flesh" animated by the spirit of an "ideal world." By wrenching words from their habitual contexts, freeing them from common usage and cliché, Mallarmé sought to "restore the integrity and primordial innocence of things that have been bastardized and disfigured."

Don would have recognized here a Christian allegory: language's fall from grace and the writer's attempt to save it. He would also have seen that a writer like Perelman, despite his humbler materials, was not so different from Mallarmé. Inadvertently, in trying to steer Don in a more serious direction, his father gave him a map for the road he was already on. Still, in bestowing these books, the elder Barthelme implicitly embraced, or at least sanctioned, his son's desire to become a writer (better that than the itinerant life of a jazz drummer).

"Did you ever realize that if you took all the wonderful things in the world and put them on city blocks one after the other, you would run like a rabbit from it?" This was the kind of question Don's father asked his students when he started teaching at the University of Houston in 1946. By the time Don enrolled in the school in the fall of 1949, his father was a fixture in the architecture department—its first professor. Barthelme's practice still flourished, though his reputation as a "son of a bitch" caused him more and more headaches with contractors. Additionally, though his projects had drawn the attention of other architects, none of them had made the kind of splash that changes the face of a city. Other modernists were making more visible marks in Houston. Herman Lloyd designed the city's first International Style skyscraper. Completed in 1952, the twenty-one story Melrose Building on Walker Avenue was distinguished by turquoise spandrels and horizontal brise-soleils. Drivers in the north-south traffic on the Gulf Freeway, which led in and out of town, couldn't miss it. Barthelme had been a local pioneer, but starting in the late forties, others began stealing the spotlight. When the University of Houston approached him, he was delighted to take up a new challenge.

The UH campus, southeast of downtown, had been a busy work in progress since the twenties. Flat, white, surrounded here and there by skinny new trees, the quadrangles and buildings, made of shell limestone, felt to students cold and imposing. The school was isolated from the rest of the city. World War II veterans crowded the campus; many of them lived in a haphazard trailer village on-site, while those with families occupied wooden barracks nearby. As Barthelme organized the architecture school, the noise and activity of fresh construction made classroom focus difficult. Nevertheless, he managed with what he had.

Eventually, he designed a course called Concepts, and later expanded it to a two-year requirement, with a second half named Human Studies. "I invited guests from all disciplines each week," he said. "The subjects of these courses included space, enclosure, change. . . . I went wherever the subject led. Our criterion: Did it make sense?"

He remembered the one "important" nugget he'd gotten from Frank Lloyd Wright during the fight over the Stanley Marcus house. "You shouldn't enclose space," Wright said. "Human beings appreciate and enjoy everything about space," Barthelme observed. "Space in which to breathe, space in which to move. When you take space away from them, you deprive them. But what do we do? We live in boxes." This conundrum vexed him as he led his students in the classroom. While lecturing, he "realized that all architecture was enclosure—even the open squares are an enclosing form. All architecture based on a single concept!"

Teaching, as well as exposure to young people's enthusiasms, renewed Barthelme's energy. He continued to receive commissions and did some of his most innovative work during this period, including the West Columbia Elementary School and the first modern church in Houston. He also ran increasingly afoul of workers and contractors, making what many of them considered excessive demands and insisting on perfection. On one project, he made the contractors "rip [everything] out and buy new glass" when the glass didn't meet his window specifications. Stories like this formed Barthelme's suppertable talk, and reveal the heroic picture he presented to his children. (In *Paradise,* Don writes of an architect who had "been working on transforming an old armory into a school and had just ordered the contractor to rip out and replace six thousand square feet of expensive casement windows. Probably the man's profit on the job." Later, the architect suspects the furious contractor of wiring a pipe bomb to his car.)

Barthelme's woes with manufacturers and bosses made it harder for him to get good prices on materials; eventually, he turned to teaching full-time. Years later, he admitted, "I really quit practicing because I could not get competitive bids."

Between classes at the University of Houston, Don studied Marcel Raymond's book. He may not have reacted to the volume the way his father had hoped—by turning away from popular writing—but the elder Barthelme had certainly known how to reach him. Many years later, *From Baudelaire to Surrealism* still informed Don's aesthetic views. For Raymond, the point of writing was not to represent the world as it is, but to engender startling new revelations. He called this activity "forc[ing] . . . the gates of Paradise." It happens, he said, when words "are no longer signs; [when] they participate in the objects . . . they evoke."

Fourteen years after reading this sentence, Don would write, "[A] mysterious shift . . . takes place as soon as one says that art is not about something but *is* something . . . the literary text becomes an object in the world rather than a text or commentary upon the world."

Raymond said that "obscurity" is an "indispensable element in a poetics" that hopes to rescue language from shopworn uses. Don revived Raymond's point in his 1982 essay, "Not-Knowing": "However much the writer might long to be, in his work, simple, honest, and straightforward, these virtues are no longer available to him. He discovers that in being simple, honest, and straightforward, nothing much happens: he speaks the speakable, whereas what we are looking for is the as-yet-unspeakable, the as-yet-unspoken." Then he quoted Raymond on Mallarmé: The poet's style is a "whisper . . . close to silence."

From Raymond, Don learned to value language that captured or created *immediate experience.* A writer approached this goal by combining forms (phrases, imagery) in a way that triggered mental agitation, instead of melting the forms together so their properties vanished in an illusion of "reality."

In the end, Raymond admitted that Baudelaire, Mallarmé, and Rimbaud "failed" in their desire to create a "new sensibility." Their downfall and the defeat of anyone who heeds them was and would continue to be inevitable. Still, they could be likened to "Icarus or Prometheus," adventurous souls "illuminating the virgin lands into which others have ventured after them."

He concluded, "[S]ince romanticism . . . the poet has often performed the function of the look-out aboard ship. It is true that this poetry has few readers, and that it sometimes discourages readers; nevertheless, it registers the slightest changes in the atmosphere, it makes the gesture that others will imitate and develop (in writings that will be read and rewarded), and it is first to utter the long awaited word."

In Raymond, Don discovered the excitement and the sanction of a visionary literary tradition. At the same time, he caught an inkling of the difficulties involved, of the loneliness and misunderstandings likely in the life of such an artist—all of which would have seemed, to a nineteen-year-old, far more romantic than miserable.

Don's copy of *From Baudelaire to Surrealism* contained an introduction by Harold Rosenberg, a Brooklyn-born art critic who, along with William Phillips, Philip Rahv, Granville Hicks, and others writing in *Partisan Review* and *New Masses,* had sparked the 1930s debates about proletarian literature, art, and politics.

Rosenberg's introduction forcefully affected Don. It begins: "The best French poetry since Baudelaire has been enlisted in a siege against the cliché. This has not been by any means merely a question of taste. It has been more a matter of life and death." In "Not-Knowing," Don would echo almost

word for word Rosenberg's argument that the "Frenchman has so much tradition he can easily say anything, except what he wants to say . . . he must restore freshness to his language." The ultimate goal, Rosenberg said (a line
Don quotes in his essay), is the "silencing of the existing rhetoric."

Rosenberg argued that American writing must stop the "cultural clatter"
that threatened to obscure the nation's romantic spirit. Following World
War I, Williams, Cummings, Stein, Pound, Moore, Eliot, and Stevens became
"enthusiastically frenchified." "They learned from Paris what it meant to
find a word that was free . . . or that stuck out . . . at an angle." Then a "depressing series of events took place . . . a new generation of American poets
started out to invent themselves and found they had a philosophy, marxism." In the proletarian literature of the thirties the "cliché was restored to a
premium," Rosenberg wrote. Young writers now had to reverse this trend.
They had to understand that "verbal substance" equals "living substance,"
and "lift . . . up" their words in startling phrases that bring readers "face to
face with existence." The "acid of poetry" will turn the commonplace to dust
as it "burns each word away from the old links."

Thirty-two years after first reading Rosenberg, Don still followed his
lead. That he depended so heavily on Raymond's and Rosenberg's remarks in
composing "Not-Knowing" is revealing in many ways. It speaks of the consistency of Don's beliefs, and of his loyalty to his literary mentors.

It's also important to recall where he got the book.

In the 1980s, after living away from Texas for nearly twenty years, Don
returned to Houston. He assumed a teaching position at the University of
Houston. In returning to his father's enclave, partaking of his father's identity at the very same institution, and revisiting, for a crucial essay on writing, his father's long-ago gift, Don seemed finally to accept the old man's
world. And yet the aesthetic he championed was one of which the elder
Barthelme never approved. In the 1950s, Don's attachment to Rosenberg's
vision signaled a break from his father, even though the latter had offered
him the book. In the early 1960s, Don would work for Rosenberg in New
York, learning fresh ways of thinking about abstract art and Pop Art, and
moving far beyond his father's concerns.

BARDLEY

"It was a bright shy white new university on the Gulf Coast. Gulls and oleanders and quick howling hurricanes." These lines from Don's "See the Moon?" remain an apt description of the core campus of the University of Houston. "The teachers [were] brown burly men with power boats and beer cans."

Initially a junior college established in the 1920s, the university got a boost from the financial contributions of Hugh Roy Cullen. His money, earned in cotton and oil, went almost entirely into the campus infrastructure. These physical improvements helped the institution secure university status, but Cullen's generosity did not extend to the curricula or to research funding. Nor did the school attract top-notch personnel. By the time Don enrolled as a student in 1949, the faculty was a motley assemblage of former public school teachers and instructors lured from more established universities around the country. In Don's first year there, the school's vision of itself changed from ambitions of greatness to a more practical and hardheaded approach, serving returning soldiers, and trying to expand its financial base by attracting as many students as possible. The architecture school was in its infancy; there was, as yet, no law school, and other professional programs were rare. The College of Technology was essentially a trade school.

On-site housing was scarce, except for the temporary barracks

set up for married ex-servicemen. It was an urban campus, full of com-
muters and students from various social backgrounds, many of whom
couldn't afford more expensive schools. In 1949, construction on what would
become the main administration building, Ezekiel Cullen, had just begun.
Its shell-limestone facing (its "bright shy white" look), relief sculptures, and
aluminum detailing would set the standard for future campus buildings, but
at the time, the campus had no real center, no quads to speak of, no paths
with any logical orientation. Like the house in which Don had been raised,
the school underwent constant revision. Near the new administration building sat an oval reflecting basin. It had been there since 1939, intended to
serve as a central gathering spot, but it was too small and spare a space to
draw many students, and it wouldn't be effective as a plaza until it was completely redesigned and fountains were added in the 1970s. In the late forties,
Don's father and a new colleague of his named Howard Barnstone were
teaching in barnlike metal structures, which would serve as the architecture
school for nearly forty years, until Philip Johnson designed a building for
the school that was modeled on plans for a never-made eighteenth-century
palace.

Don had a strongly developed sense of citizenship, a loyalty to his city and
its institutions, including the school, and a pride in helping improve his local
surroundings (a pride he'd learned from his father). Don's acquaintances in
his first semesters at UH describe him as a buoyant, eager young man, full of
energy and projecting a confidence he may not always have felt. Joe Maranto,
who edited the school's newspaper, the *Daily Cougar,* said that Don attracted
people "like a magnet." He was slender and tall, with light brown, slightly red-
dish hair. When he smiled, the corners of his mouth curled up, and he would
raise his eyebrows mischievously, making his companions feel they were
in on a joke with him. One day in the fall of 1949, he showed up in the Department of Journalism, ostensibly to make an appointment with a faculty
adviser. Helen Moore, who was working for the department on a student fellowship, was struck by his "striding, almost jaunty walk," his pride and self-
assurance, his "deep and rich voice and the way that he spoke with a
distinctly sharp enunciation" (having overcome his lip twitch of a few years
before). When he looked at her, she said, "his blue eyes were serious and intense," and he listened to her closely.

That afternoon, returning home, Don told his mother that he had met a
"handsome girl" at the University of Houston. Years later, he confessed to
Helen Moore that he had ducked into the journalism office on the pretext of
needing advice because he had seen her sitting there. He enjoyed spreading
his wings on campus. Exposed at home to a wider world of culture than most
of his classmates, he could dazzle people with his erudition. And the times
were heady. The war was over. Jackson Pollock was making waves, Miles

Davis had just recorded *The Birth of the Cool,* John Cage had recently written and performed his Sonatas and Interludes for Prepared Piano, and transistor radios and portable tape recorders were popular.

Maranto, a World War II veteran, had noticed Don's column about Stan Kenton on the *Houston Post*'s "Teen Page" when Don was still in high school. When he met Don at UH, Maranto, a fellow jazz lover, recruited this fine young talent for the *Cougar.* More than ever, Don was immersed in *The New Yorker*'s style of humor. He "would quote Dorothy Parker, always in an appropriate way, at the right moment when it fit," Maranto recalled. He saw Don's potential to become a new Benchley or Perelman, both of whom were "getting kind of tired about that time," but he also noted Don's creative restlessness, and couldn't predict which direction his work might take. "[W]riters like Steinbeck and Hemingway always got into the characters of people," Maranto said, but it didn't appear that Don would emulate them because on some level, it seemed, he didn't "really like people all that much."

Don typed quickly with only two fingers. In the cramped *Cougar* office, he "pecked away, usually writing a little something against one of the university departments, just having a ball," Maranto said. He would "break himself up writing those things; he was a joy to be around." Don was much more at home at the newspaper than in the classroom. Most of his teachers let him down. As he wrote in "See the Moon?" they seemed more interested in "burning beef in their backyards, [these] brown burly men with power boats and beer cans," than in keeping up with the latest intellectual developments. The creative writing curriculum was minimal. He was so disillusioned that by spring term, he had stopped taking classes.

Just as advocates of modern architecture fought with Beaux-Arts proponents in America's architecture departments in the 1920s and 1930s, university English departments were split between philologists, who espoused the study of grammar and a historical approach to literature, and a diverse group of young professors (critics) who promoted the close reading of texts. The critics maintained that philological study merely cataloged—and thereby deadened—poetry and prose. Marxist critics felt that texts should be analyzed in an economic context, while the so-called New Critics believed that stories and poems should be studied as ideal formal constructs.

It was not until the 1930s that anything resembling a course of study in creative writing appeared on a university campus and it coincided with the rise of the New Criticism. In the 1920s, Allen Tate, one of the founders of the New Criticism, said that "we study literature today as if nobody ever again intended to write any more of it. The official academic point of view is that all the literature has been written, and it is now a branch of history . . . the young writer is not going to find out how to study the poem; he will only know how to study its historical background."

Tate and his comrades—John Crowe Ransom, Robert Penn Warren, Cleanth Brooks—argued that a text's "quality" could be separated from its historical context and other circumstances of its production. Ultimately, quality lay in a text's language. Writers from different periods could share formal properties. For example, Baudelaire and T. S. Eliot were spiritual kin, Tate said; they had in common the qualities of "irony, humility, introspection, reverence."

Don felt ambivalent about the New Criticism. He was already a good, close reader of texts, and he shared a number of the New Critics' beliefs. He was sympathetic to the argument that a dry, grammatical study of literature divorced thought from feeling. He appreciated subtlety and irony, key qualities in the canon of the New Criticism. He was also beginning to read and appreciate the modernists.

But he was powerfully swayed by Marcel Raymond's historical awareness, Raymond's tracing of a consistent literary tradition, and the implication that a writer must choose to ally himself with one tradition or another. This choice, Raymond felt, was essential to the *kind* of text a writer would produce.

As Don explained years later, a writer becomes a writer "by selecting fathers. In the beginning, you know, I thought Hemingway was as far as writing could go. . . . I didn't even know there was a Heinrich von Kleist. . . . I didn't know anything about Kafka at that point, and how can you write without at least knowing that Kafka exists? . . . [A]s one reads more and more and more you get more fathers in your hierarchy of fathers. And then, after summoning twenty or thirty fathers, perhaps *you* are born. . . ."

Maranto had exaggerated when he said that Don didn't like people; nevertheless, it was true that love of literature, not of individuals, would animate Don's fiction. Maranto was right that Don would not get into characters the way Steinbeck and Hemingway did. Instead, he would get into the *nature of literary form.* The psychological drama in his work does not lie in the tension between personalities, but in the conflicts between traditions, sensibilities, generations, and the tyrannies that time works on human efforts.

Agreeing, then, with many tenets of the New Criticism, Don remained convinced that its approach was limited. Most of all, he was uncomfortable with its social biases and their broader implications. Its founders were southerners, rooted in the heavy paternalism of the old Confederacy. They weren't nostalgic for slavery (though in early essays, which he later repudiated, Robert Penn Warren argued for continued segregation), but they adhered to a rigidly hierarchical social system.

How does this civic view get translated into a program of close reading? Listen to Robert Penn Warren: "Poetry wants to be pure," he claimed, but inevitably the elements of a poem are uneven, poems "mar themselves with cacophonies, jagged rhythms, ugly words and ugly thoughts." In his view, the poet was the benevolent overseer, trying to hold these tatters together. The reader's task was to analyze how well, or poorly, the master succeeded.

The longing for purity appealed to Don; he had absorbed his father's notion of *what should be.* Yet anything that smacked of paternalism was bound to make him wary. And it was unsettling to imagine *any* single authority—a father, a priest, an architect, a crusading literary critic—telling people what purity looked like.

Besides, tatters could be pretty.

"If any one person is to be singled out for having begun a tradition of creative writing" at the University of Houston, "it's Miss Ruth Pennybacker," says Lee Pryor. Pryor taught in the university's English department for over forty years. Pennybacker, who never published a word of fiction, graduated from Vassar and arrived in Houston in 1935. According to Pryor, she taught freshman composition, and gradually developed courses in story and poetry writing. She served as the major adviser for the school's literary magazine, *Harvest.* Don took a turn editing the magazine. "Miss Pennybacker," as she insisted on being called, was the only creative writing teacher he ever had.

In 1949, Don wasn't pursuing an academic track. He wanted to be a writer, not a teacher of writing, which is what creative writing programs seemed destined to produce. Though drawn to Miss Pennybacker, and her passion for art, he romanticized the Hemingway model. "[Because] Hemingway had been a newspaperman, I sought and got a newspaper job with the idea that this had something to do with writing," he said.

In June 1950, though no longer enrolled in classes, he began contributing unsigned book reviews to the *Daily Cougar,* starting with a savage account of Speed Lamkin's novel *Tiger in the Garden.* Lamkin, now largely forgotten, wrote potboilers as well as Broadway plays and television scripts for *Playhouse 90.* Paul West has said that "*Tiger in the Garden* [was] once regarded as the cream of the writing in the Gothic seminars of the deep South."

Don did not share this view. Lamkin's prose is "as emotion-charged as a telephone's dial tone," he wrote. The plot characterizes the city of Houston as a "crazed Negro," holding the "population of Hardtimes plantation at bay with a bread knife." Don's review appeared in the *Cougar* on June 16.

He supplied the paper with three more book reviews that summer, on Jan Valtin's *Wintertime,* Frederick Buechner's *A Long Day's Dying,* and Joyce Cary's *The Horse's Mouth* ("Barmaids, Walls and Models Enrich Tale of Frustration"). Additionally, he published a "news item," cast in the form of a drama, on the university's Home Ec Department. The piece was set in an alchemy lab. There, a character named Pitkin turns up, the first of many appearances in Don's *Cougar* columns by members of the fictional Pitkin family. The name is snitched from Nathanael West's 1934 novel, *A Cool Million,* in which Lemuel Pitkin, duped and physically dismembered by a series of con men, serves as an ironic witness to the American Dream.

Maggie Stubblefield Maranto, the wife of Joe Maranto, recalls that at about this time, Don's friend Pat Goeters "created [a] homely" character named Maud Alice Pitkin, whom he often talked about at parties. "Yes, I'll take credit for the Pitkins," Goeters says. "Sometimes Don would come to my house and we'd engage in a kind of 'battle of the bands' write-off," trying to top each other's literary efforts. "It was during one of those times that I wrote some fable about Lindberg Pitkin. In my friendship with Don, almost every mildly enjoyable event became something of a ritual or, in Don's case, a tale to be told, enhanced and bejeweled."

On August 18, Don published his first signed piece in the *Cougar,* "Author Hits Cokes for Distinct Gain," about stealing redeemable soda bottles.

By September he had reenrolled in classes. No doubt he bowed to family pressure. Perhaps he didn't know what else to do with himself. What's clear is that his main interest at the time was his work on the paper. Returning to the university as a full-time student was the only way to continue legitimately working at the *Cougar.*

Joe Maranto made Don the amusements editor ("Scribe Turns to Culture, Wincing," Don announced in the paper). He would cover books, music, and local stage productions. He would also contribute a regular features column. Soon he was signing these columns "Bardley," a play on the Bard of Avon, Melville's Bartleby the Scrivener, and his own name.

The Pitkin family became part of the university community. Sabatini Pitkin, and his brother Rathbone, "interviewed" in one article, complained that soon everyone in America would be teaching art instead of creating it. Another brother, Ron L., was listed as the author of a book called *Your Mind: Hell or Haven?* This was Don's parody of L. Ron Hubbard's *Dianetics,* the founding text of Scientology. The parody presages "The Teachings of Don B.," Don's 1973 satire of the Carlos Castaneda books.

In October, Clyde Rainwater, a student journalist at Yale, wrote a review of the nation's school newspapers. He said that Don seemed to think he was Wolcott Gibbs, a *New Yorker* humorist. The remark's accuracy must have stung Don. Rainwater dismissed Texas as lacking culture and insisted that "there's nowhere else in life but New York." In a little over a decade, Don would come to agree; for now, he acidly thanked Rainwater for showing him "how they do it in the East."

Occasionally, Don wrote a serious editorial, one of which shows how unsophisticated his political thinking was at the time. "Probe Where Probe Is Due, Sans Spotlight" (May 4, 1951) scolds the "headline-seeking" zeal of the House Committee on Un-American Activities. While investigating Communists in the movie industry, congressmen were paying too much attention to actors, Don said. The pols were dazzled by celebrity. Nevertheless, Don supported the committee's mandate, and urged exposure of producers and directors with ties to the Communist party. Years later, he was appalled at himself for having written such a thing.

As months passed, Bardley became increasingly playful and bizarre. He declared "total war" on television because he had been refused admission to a local channel's party. He lambasted a radio station for not broadcasting "Confederate propaganda." He said all Americans should take a course on "turning things off," especially radios. Don was using the *Cougar* to create his own imaginative world, and to experiment with a variety of styles.

In one piece entitled "Grimm Revisited," dated July 13, 1951, a witch named Jane appears:

> Jane was one of the younger wicked old witches in the community. She was electric, vital, a leader. When it came time to dun the villagers for contributions to the Community Chest or the Milk Fund, Jane padded from humble door to humble door, morning till night. Everyone said she was one of the nicest wicked old witches they had ever known.
>
> But according to the union rules Jane had some witchly duties to perform. One of these was stealing away little children, and in exercising this function Jane met Oliver [Birdsong].
>
> It was a momentous meeting.

Jane botches things. She phones a sister witch, Hazel, for "professional advice." Hazel is annoyed to be disturbed; she says that "any woman who had spent the day reciting incantations over a bubbling cauldron deserved a good night's sleep." She offers no help. Eventually, Oliver escapes from Jane and she is driven out of the witches' union.

Over a decade later, in *Snow White,* Don's first novel, Jane would resurface, along with Don's strategy of exploring social movements—feminism, communal living—in fairy-tale form.

In a 1984 television interview with George Plimpton, aired on Houston's public broadcasting station, Don said, "I originally began writing in rather traditional, ersatz Hemingway fashion, and it was really terrible, it was truly terrible. It was in reaction to my own inability to satisfy myself with traditional forms that I sort of began throwing things on the floor and looking to see what sorts of patterns they made."

"Rover Boys' Retrogression" and the *Cougar* pieces make clear that Don was never *seriously* drawn to traditional forms, except as backgrounds to play against. He dashed off many of the newspaper pieces; they're certainly not literary (though a number of them are *fictional*). Nevertheless, his obsessions and signature styles are already apparent. His strategies would become less sophomoric, more refined, and stunningly varied, but his identity as a writer remained remarkably consistent from his first published piece to his last.

What accounts for his resistance to traditional forms? His father taught him to notice structure, to understand its origins, to appreciate variations on it, and to value innovation. Don began as a critic, one with a historical inclination. Form was not a given; it was not something to take for granted; it could wear out with time. Its manipulation—more than the content of a piece—was what distinguished one artwork from another. In his father's home, stalking art with this critical attitude was as natural as breathing the air.

In April 1951, Joe Maranto left the *Cougar* to become a church reporter for the *Houston Post.* Many years later, Don commemorated his friend's good fortune in fiction. In his story "January," a writer gets his start covering religion for a Knight-Ridder paper, an experience that teaches him to "think of religion in a much more practical sense than . . . before, what the church offered or could offer to people, what people got from the church in a day-to-day sense." The character adds, "I came to theoretical concerns by way of very practical ones"—Don's view of *his* education as a journalist.

In "See the Moon?" Don mentions a "Cardinal Maranto," another nod to his friend's *Post* assignment.

Maranto's new job was an important development for Don: In his buddy's absence, Don became the *Cougar*'s editor in chief. On April 20, the *Cougar* announced that "[Barthelme], a 20-year-old sophomore journalism major, is the youngest student in the COUGAR'S history to hold the position of editor."

A month earlier, he had also begun writing for the university's news service, a position that put him in touch again with Helen Moore, who directed the service. If she was aware of his attraction to her, she didn't let on. She was engaged to another journalism student, Peter Gilpin, and she later recalled that "Don seemed so young" (she was three years his senior). She "thought little" of him except as a talented writer whose skills she was glad to exploit. He covered fine arts at the university and campus productions at the Attic Theatre. "As he wrote his articles, Don was thoughtful and meticulous," she said. He "sometimes erased to make changes, but he often started over on a clean sheet of newsprint."

Between articles, he pursued more expressive forms of writing, penning the music for a campus play, writing short stories and poems for Miss Penny-backer. Maranto, and another pal, George Christian, who worked at the *Post,* brought Don's writing to the attention of the editors there, and on July 15, Don went to work for the paper, reviewing movies, concerts, and plays. On September 20, "Stage Business," the first installment of his regular Sunday column on local drama, appeared in the *Post.* He was not yet twenty-one, but he was already following Hemingway's path, earning a living as a newspaperman.

LET'S TAKE A WALK

For decades, the *Houston Post* had enjoyed the reputation of opinion maker in the greater Southwest. Under the bellicose management of Rienzi M. Johnston, who came to Houston in 1885 after serving the *Post* as a political correspondent in Austin, the paper solidified its standing as a promoter of real estate development and progress, framing public debate within business and politics. Johnston turned the paper into a family affair, hiring his daughter Hallie as a columnist and grooming his son, Harry, to one day assume the editorship (in the 1950s, shortly after Don worked with him, Harry became chief of the Atlanta bureau of *Time* magazine). Johnston's granddaughter, Mary Elizabeth, became a *Post* reporter and eventually joined the editorial board of *Fortune.*

In October 1895, Johnston hired, at fifteen dollars a week, a young gadabout named William Sidney Porter—former ranch hand, bank teller, land office clerk, magazine editor—and gave him a regular column, "Tales About Town" (later called "Some Postscripts"). At first, the column, occasionally accompanied by Porter's cartoons, contained society items, standard newspaper fare, but it soon expanded to include vivid character sketches of street people, store clerks, and local artists. It became the *Post*'s liveliest feature, and Porter was Texas's most celebrated writer.

Porter befriended a sixteen-year-old named Will Hobby, who had quit high school to take an eight-dollar-a-week job in the *Post*'s circulation department. He fetched Porter sandwiches and listened to his tall tales. One day in June 1896, a man came looking for Porter, who had stepped out of the office. Proudly, Hobby pointed to the famous writer's desk. The man identified himself as a police officer. He had a summons for Porter's arrest. The charge was embezzlement. Though Porter wound up fleeing Houston, he eventually served a prison term.

Will Hobby grew up to become governor of Texas. After leaving jail, Porter adopted the pen name O. Henry and, building on many of the stories he had published in the *Post*, crafted a highly successful literary career. While at the paper, Porter was a staff favorite, and over fifty years later, he was still a topic in the newsroom. Hubert Roussel, the amusements editor, and Don's immediate supervisor, kidded Don that his desk had belonged to O. Henry. Don joked that he could see O. Henry's initials carved into the wood. In "Return," a piece commissioned by the Houston Festival Committee and published in the *Post* in 1984, Don wrote:

> [A]s a raw youth, I had worked for the . . . newspaper . . . When I was hired they showed me my desk, and they told me that it had been O. Henry's desk. . . . I could see the place where O. Henry had savagely stabbed the desk with his pen in pursuit of a slimy adjective just out of reach, and a kind of bashed-in-looking place where O. Henry had beaten his poor genius head on the desk in frustration over not being able to capture that noun leaping like a fawn just out of reach. . . . So I sat down at the desk and I too began to chase those devils, the dancy nouns and come-hither adjectives, what joy.

In the office, Don established himself as a literary expert fully versed on Porter, Damon Runyan, and Ambrose Bierce. Sly references to these writers spiced his columns. It's intriguing to note that Porter's last, and most well-known, piece for the *Post,* "An Aquatint," published on June 22, 1896, features a repulsive tramp dressed in a "burlesque" of a "prince" who saves a child from drowning. "Well, thank you, sir," the child's mother tells him. A similar situation ends Don's 1968 story, "Robert Kennedy Saved from Drowning." Kennedy is the one wrapped in princely regalia here, and though the narrator is not described, the story's title is a clear allusion to Jean Renoir's 1932 film, *Boudu Sauvé des Eaux* (*Boudu Saved from Drowning*), in which a lower-class Parisian—a Porter-like tramp—is fished out of the Seine. "Thank you," Kennedy says, simply, at the end of Don's tale.

Eventually, the Ambrose Bierce jokes got out of hand, as Don, Joe Maranto, and George Christian kept slipping his name into news items. Finally, Maranto, about to leave for a job at the *Houston Chronicle,* signed a column,

"Ambrose Bierce, Editor." Harry Johnston, city editor at the time, shrugged it off, but the managing editor, Arthur Laroe, demanded to know what this Bierce business was all about, and stopped all the fooling around.

"[N]ewspaper work didn't teach me all that much about writing," Don said later, "but it taught me a lot of other things. It taught me what a union was, for example, which I had known only in the abstract." The narrator of his 1970 story "Brain Damage" confesses, "I worked for newspapers at a time when I was not competent to do so. I reported inaccurately. I failed to get all the facts. . . . I put lies in the paper. I put private jokes in the paper. I wrote headlines containing double entendres. I wrote stories while drunk. I abused copy boys."

"Brain Damage" may be true to the spirit of Don's newspaper days, but the story is also highly literary. The sentences echo Dostoevsky's *Notes from Underground:* "I used to be in the government service . . . I was a spiteful official. I was rude and took pleasure in being so."

Dostoevsky's man says, "I know nothing at all about my disease, and do not know for certain what ails me." Don wrote, "I could describe [brain damage] better if I weren't afflicted with it. . . ."

This is not precisely *making reference* to another writer's work, but folding one's experience, emotion, and playfulness into a preexisting form, a necessary skill for smuggling private jokes into the paper while the soft, steady lights shine above you, and the editor's scrutiny burns your back.

"George is editing my copy," Don complained to Joe Maranto one day. Don considered George Christian his peer—their desks sat side by side. But Christian had worked at the paper longer. Maranto pointed this out to Don, who insisted, "He should not be editing my copy."

Don "always wanted to write tight, short sentences, except when he wanted to write a long one to impress you and he thought you'd know that's what he was doing," Maranto says. When Hubert Roussel wasn't happy with an article, he'd punch a buzzer in his office. It rang in the outer room—one buzz for Christian, two for Don. The offending party would scurry into the editor's office for a harsh scolding—Roussel was a no-nonsense perfectionist. "The newspaper building was populated with terrifying city editors whose gaze could cut brass, and ferocious copy desk men whose contempt could make a boy of twenty wish that his mother and father had never met," Don wrote in "Return." "I loved working there."

A photograph from the time shows Christian and Don at their desks, both wearing white shirts with the sleeves rolled nearly to the elbows and thin dark ties. They sport very short haircuts. The room is stark and white, with unadorned walls; it looks airless. The desks are wooden, massive, with square recesses for the typewriters, and long telephone cords curl around the desk's squatty legs. The wooden chairs are straight-backed and stiff. Christian seems serious, almost ponderous. Don appears to be smirking as he types.

Frequently, the boys worked late at night, as the *Post* was a morning paper. Often at dawn, they'd stagger out of the office, catch the first of the sun's rays topping the downtown buildings, raise their arms, and shout, "Back, back!" (In an untitled interchapter in *Overnight to Many Distant Cities,* Don imagines a chamber orchestra forming in a newsroom, and playing Haydn until the sun comes up.) Don didn't own a car, so he walked home from work, past Buffalo Bayou, where William Porter may have witnessed—or more likely imagined—the drowning child saved by the tramp.

During the late mornings and afternoons, Don attended classes at the university, a schedule he maintained throughout 1951 and 1952. He also continued his Bardley columns for the *Cougar;* they gave him more freedom than his work at the *Post,* where he was assigned standard movie, concert, and drama reviews. Week after week, he sat in the dark in the city's major theaters—the Majestic, Loew's, the Met—watching Doris Day, Bette Davis, Spencer Tracy, Robert Ryan, Greer Garson, Martin and Lewis, Jeff Chandler, James Cagney, Clark Gable, Burt Lancaster, and others.

In addition to his journalism, Don continued to write for Miss Pennybacker's creative writing classes. In the 1952 issue of *Harvest,* he published a poem entitled "Shrunken Clocks for Small Hours," whose brittle imagery comes right out of "The Love Song of J. Alfred Prufrock" ("We crouch in empty cups / And wonder"). It is harder to tell if the speaker's despair is also a lift from Eliot, or whether Don, an undergraduate, was already genuinely world-weary.

If Texas was hard on budding writers—offering few first-class professional outlets—it was, as the old saying has it, "hell on horses and women."

Larry McMurtry quibbles with this chestnut: Most "horses are considered valuable" in the Lone Star State, he says, "and are treated well." McMurtry's essay, "Eros in Archer County," published in 1968, offers a scorching look at Texas's sexual mores—attitudes that helped shape Don. The essay focuses on rural areas and small towns in the 1940s and 1950s, but much of what McMurtry says also held true for cities. Men and women were "mutually frightened and inhibited," he writes, and they "suffered the emotional crises that people probably always suffer in periods of rapid transition. Men who were quite content with the nineteenth century were suddenly having to cope with women who had begun to take an interest in the twentieth." From the political to-do of their elders, women had learned that "they were supposed to have orgasms too, after which there was generally confusion and distress. How is the female to switch in one generation from an orientation which sees the act of love as a duty to one which sees it as a pleasure?"

The forties saw a general rise in affluence. McMurtry writes:

> Until the forties, a great many Texans *had* been poor all their lives, and when they began to come into the money it was natural that they should over-rate it and expect the wrong things of it. They had imagined it would make them happier with one another, and they resented one another all the more when it didn't. Men made money and women spent it. If one spent unstintingly, sexual poverty might be disguised. Spending might accomplish what fucking hadn't. . . .

Sports offered further distractions from domestic distress, or "compensation" for sexual insecurity.

This was the erotic legacy Don's generation inherited from its forebears (compounded, in Don's case, by a strict religious education). "His demeanor, especially with women, was polite and attentive," recalled Helen Moore Barthelme. "And he was a good listener, whether you were a man or a woman, an appealing trait to women in the 1950s. Women were expected to defer to men, especially in discussing ideas, but one did not have to do this with Don."

On the other hand: "If you were a female person, it's perfectly true that he'd often meet you with a sort of attentive bossiness which is the southern male's ingrained behavior with women," Grace Paley said years later. "It was really an awful pain in the neck. A regional problem and serious."

Maggie Stubblefield Maranto, who was dating Joe Maranto at the time, says that when she first met Don, he was "going with" a young woman from Galveston named Anne Hamilton. "Poor Don. She threw him over because she wanted to be an actress—I have never subsequently heard of her, so that was a mistake. I did think she was foolish to let him go. I have always felt she set a pattern of Don being jilted that really affected him."

Don was drawn to Helen Moore, but she was older, already engaged. At first, she did not return his attention. He seems to have adopted a courtly manner toward romance, and to have developed—perhaps from witnessing his mother's forbearance with his father—a strong sense of propriety. Mary Blount, a journalism major at the university, and later a well-known children's book writer, recalled that in her freshman year she began dating Don's office mate at the *Post,* George Christian (whom she eventually married). One day, before her engagement, she accepted an invitation from another man to go to a prom. Don sought her out in the *Cougar* office and said she should "take a walk" with him. Around the reflecting basin in front of the new Ezekiel Cullen Building, Don admonished Blount to "call this fellow and cancel your date with him." That's what George wants, he said. Blount laughed at him but *did* call off her date. All his life, Don showed a keen interest in gossip, and in working behind the scenes to arrange social affairs.

Christian introduced Don to his first cousin, Marilyn Marrs. They started dating. Don took her to many of the performances he had to review for the paper. Marilyn, whom Don called "Magnolia" or "Maggie," was a senior at the Rice Institute, majoring in French. At the time, there was no women's housing at Rice; she lived off campus with her aunt and uncle. She was tall and thin, with a long face and large eyes, dark, slightly curly hair, and a wary smile. "Miss Maggie was a sexy creature," said Herman Gollob, "but she suffered from a deadly case of intellectual snobbery."

During this period, Don had an argument with his father that was serious enough to drive Don from the house. Pat Goeters, Don's old running buddy in Mexico, along with Joe Maranto and another friend, Henry Buckley, an architecture student, rented a dilapidated house with Don on Leek Street, near the university and close to Cullen Boulevard and the Gulf Freeway. The house sat near scrapyards and decaying industrial warehouses; a drive-in burger joint, right across the street, blared loud music late into the evenings. Students gathered to eat and drink in their cars. Young women in short skirts hurried around the parking lot, ferrying fries and Cokes on metal trays. Often, in the early mornings, walking home from the *Post*—about a two-mile trek—Don would stop at an all-night restaurant that served grilled cheese sandwiches and black-bottom pie, a "custard affair with chocolate on the bottom half and light custard on the top," says Maggie Maranto. The restaurant was a couple of blocks from Don's house, in a crime-ridden neighborhood, but it was run by a friendly Austrian called "Papa Kurt," who looked after his customers.

Maggie was engaged to Maranto by now, and she spent a lot of time with him on Leek Street. None of the housemates had much money, she says. Don was "existing on the pittance he earned as a reporter." Her memories suggest that Don's dad had cut him off, but their split wasn't so dire that Don didn't invite his father to see the house once he and the others fixed it up. Goeters's mother owned a paper factory. She gave him foot-square black-and-white sheets, with which he fashioned a checkerboard pattern on the living room wall. Maranto brought home newspapers from the *Post*'s overrun archives, with front-page banner headlines declaring the end of the Spanish-American War and World War I. With these, the boys papered the ancient walls next to the stairs to the second floor, where Don and Goeters had their bedrooms. The housemates glued record album covers to the ceilings, filling the gaps with the black-and-white paper. They painted the living room black.

Buckley bought an Eames lounge chair—the one solid piece of furniture in the place. Maranto had rescued a table from the trailer he'd lived in at the University of Houston. Don took the table and whittled down the legs so it sat at a comfortable height for him to work at his typewriter.

He had never learned to cook. "I used to go over once a week and cook a huge pot of spaghetti sauce or a big batch of vegetable soup and leave it for them," Maggie Maranto says. Or they would eat at the drive-in, listening through its tinny speakers to Johnnie Ray and Rosemary Clooney.

"The guys shared fantastic conversations and much wit and laughter," Maggie recalls. She adds, "Don was a man's man, who got on extremely well with other men, especially those with similar intellectual capacities." Goeters remembers conversations in the house as drunken and endless.

In leaving the house on North Wynden Drive, Don said good-bye to a dynamic place that had enclosed him and freed him to dream. Occasionally, the "peculiar atmosphere" created by his father may have inclined him to feel inadequate; at other moments, it made him feel there was nothing he couldn't do. His parents remained in the house until 1977, by which time condos and high-rise office buildings blanketed the Post Oak area so densely that they cast the old houses into shadow. When George Herbert Walker Bush left the White House, he built his Houston residence in a neighborhood next to the once-startling Barthelme place. In the sixties and seventies, Don frequently returned to the family home to see his folks (developers demolished the house in 2001 to make room for four town houses), but from now on he would merely be a visitor in the world his father had built.

FEVERISH

Shortly after taking the Leek Street house with Don and the others, Joe Maranto married Maggie Stubblefield and moved into a nearby apartment. This could have meant disaster for the boys, but Maggie took pity on them and continued to cook for the group. "One or more of them would drop by our apartment, oddly enough just at dinner time, and join us for a meal," she says.

Don, Goeters, and Buckley pooled their resources and bought the couple a plastic Eames chair and a bottle of champagne for the wedding reception. A photo of the event shows Don sitting with Pat Goeters, another friend, Harry Vitemb, and the newlyweds. Goeters, tall, light-haired, strikingly handsome, leans toward the camera, commanding attention. He had brought a date to the wedding, a woman known to the others only as "Hot Martha," which may account for the look on his face. Maranto and Maggie, she in a ballooning white wedding gown, appear to be calm, patient, bemused, as if putting up with children. Don's eyebrows arch skeptically above his glasses. He wears a dark suit, white socks, and penny loafers. His smile, cocky, sly, seems to signal that he knows the gang is just playing at being grown-up.

The city condemned the Leek Street house a few months after Maranto's wedding. Don, Goeters, and Buckley moved into an apartment on Cullen Boulevard, closer to campus. Buckley was studying architecture, and Goeters, who had once entertained the idea of becoming a priest, began frequenting the UH architecture barn. Goeters was "eccentric and individualistic, and I can remember him at times suddenly deciding he wanted to be elsewhere, and off he would go," Maggie Maranto says. "One time he took off in his car on a whirlwind trip to Canada to see a girlfriend he decided he was in love with. He drove almost day and night to get there, and found to his chagrin that she wasn't in love with him. He returned via Chicago and registered to attend architecture school there." He also studied with Marshall McLuhan, who told him to read Ezra Pound's *The ABC of Reading* and to write like T. S. Eliot. He began crafting short pieces full of literary references, the kind of stuff "one needed a decoder ring to read and understand," Goeters says.

Back in Houston, Goeters signed up for architecture courses. Don's dad became his mentor. "He was brutally critical and tore at my psyche, but he was always highly supportive," Goeters says. Don must have felt betrayed. This friend, with whom he had once fled his father, had now developed an intimate relationship with the man. Often, the elder Barthelme praised Goeters's talent and promise. Don and Goeters had always pretended to be rivals—over women (he "did try to hit on my sister the night before she left for the convent," Goeters says), over literary accomplishment—but now their competitiveness turned edgy. "I shared with him what were to me life-changing experiences. As a friend my feelings ran to extremes," Goeters says, reflecting on his conflicts with Don.

Besides his mother, the woman with whom Don had been closest—his sister, Joan—had also left North Wynden Drive. She was earning a journalism degree at the University of Colorado.

Her absence (Don's younger brothers remained in a childhood world of their own), Maranto's marriage, and Goeters's drift toward Don's dad, left young Bardley feeling isolated. He enjoyed his independence, but the family huddle would always be essential to him. As for romance, this was not yet the era, as people later said of the 1960s, when everybody slept in everybody else's bed—especially not for an ex-Catholic whose lapse had occurred, largely, from an excess of idealism.

In September 1952, when he was twenty-one years old, Don married Marilyn Marrs. They drove to Dallas, where Marrs's parents lived, for the wedding. Except for Joe Maranto, none of Don's friends attended. This suggests an early tension between Don and his bride: Did she not want his pals around, or did he feel his friends did not approve of her? ("They weren't getting married in a church and my narrow-minded Catholicism wouldn't credit the marriage," says Pat Goeters, who refused to serve as Don's best man.)

Don was an intensely romantic young man, with a genuine love of women. If he appeared to some as autocratic, Marilyn seems to have struck people as downright haughty. Don's family and friends regarded her as imperious and unapproachable. "Joe and I were not impressed with her," Maggie Maranto says flatly. "She loved herself a lot more than she loved Don." Don was drawn to "her intellect," but she was "very cold."

To Marilyn, it was Don's circle that was chilly. "When I'd go out with my Rice friends, we all talked a lot, there was a lot of give and take, and we'd be silly together," she recalls. "When I'd go out with Don and his friends on a Saturday night, say—with Pat [Goeters], George [Christian], and the Marantos—they'd all be sitting around waiting for someone to say something clever. There was a kind of self-consciousness that was inhibiting. Even though they were all best friends and really liked each other, it was not entirely comfortable. I was pretty young, but I found it strange."

The couple moved into an apartment just west of Main Street, downtown. They carried on with their classes, Don at UH, Marilyn at Rice. She was now pursuing a master's degree in French. She became obsessed with Mallarmé. "At the time, very few people in this country were reading Mallarmé, and I'm sure Donald was wondering why I was so interested in him," she says (of course, Don knew Mallarmé from Marcel Raymond's book). "Donald didn't know French, but he was intellectually curious. I mean, we were in our twenties—how could you not be intellectually curious? Later, in his writing, he developed a sort of collage approach like Mallarmé's. As it turned out, this fit in well with postmodernism, but it was something personal to Don, and not just something he developed for the work, or because it happened to be in the zeitgeist."

"We didn't see much of [Don and Marilyn]," Maggie Maranto says. "I remember we once went over and Marilyn cooked dinner for us. She wasn't very good at that sort of thing, being an intellectual and definitely *not* the housewifely sort."

Whether or not Don's wife was "cold," it seems clear that she had a more serious demeanor than most of his friends, and this set her apart from them. Her absorption in her studies appears to have prevented her from fully appreciating his literary abilities; it also appears to have been a form of self-protection against his professional ambitions (which, at this time, meant he worked odd hours and for low pay).

Helen Moore Barthelme recalls "hear[ing] about Don occasionally from Mary Blount, who later married George [Christian]," but she seldom saw him "except at a play or musical event" that she attended with her new husband, Peter Gilpin. Blount remembers how poor Don was. One evening, she strolled with him past the reflecting pool in front of the administration building on the UH campus. They discovered a ten-dollar bill on the sidewalk and agreed to share it. Blount was still living at home with her parents; Don needed the money more than she did, so he took eight dollars and she got two.

Around this time, the Catalina Lounge downtown became the most popular new nightspot for jazz, so Don took Marilyn there whenever he could afford to. Given their busy schedules, their social life revolved around the events the paper asked Don to cover (the downside was, after an evening performance, he had to return to the office and work until dawn). "[Hubert] Roussel went to all of the interesting shows, and assigned George and Don the second-rate performances to review—whatever was left on the list," Marilyn says. "Occasionally I went to a floor show at the Shamrock with Don. There were free dinners there. We were poor, and a free dinner was not to be turned down. But I had a lot of work to do on my thesis, so Don mostly went to things without me."

In 1952, the young medium of television, along with the increasing sophistication of sound and film technologies, spread popular culture faster than ever before. At the same time, more people than ever were aware of a split between high and low culture—an awareness made possible, in part, by the access to higher education provided by the G.I. Bill, and by the success of paperback-book publishing, which made classics, as well as pulp, more readily available. Around this time, Willem de Kooning began his *Woman* series of paintings, marrying abstraction to figurative representation; Ralph Ellison published his modernist masterpiece, *Invisible Man,* a book Don devoured with relish; but much of the country spent the evenings staring at *I Love Lucy* and *The Adventures of Ozzie and Harriet* on the small screen, or listening to dance records. In 1952, RCA introduced the first three-speed record player for 33s, 45s, and 78s. This came as a blessing. The new president, Dwight Eisenhower, threatened to commit more American troops, and possibly nuclear weapons, to the conflict in Korea. The public, still war-weary, craved distractions, and the entertainment industry was happy to oblige.

In the first seven months of his marriage, Don, in his capacity as an arts reviewer, could offer his wife a wide array of cultural excitement (whenever he could get her out)—from an evening of Mozart piano sonatas performed by Paul Badura-Skoda, fresh from the Viennese Conservatory, to the Latin singing of Joaquin Garay, best known as the voice of Panchito in Disney's *The Three Caballeros* ("Disney's horniest animated feature," according to one reviewer). Frequently, Don covered events in the Empire Room at the Rice Hotel, on Texas Street downtown. Here, and at the Shamrock Hotel, which sported an elegant performance space, Don and Marilyn attended shows by Betty Jane Watson, an original member of the London cast of *Oklahoma!*; by Paddy Wing, billed as a "Chinese tap dancer"; and by Eddie Peabody, the "King of the Banjo." Peabody, tall and thin, with corn-colored hair, performed in a checked coat and a bow tie. Sometimes he played three banjos at once, and he invented the banjoline, a cross between an electric six-string Hawaiian guitar and a standard plectrum banjo.

One of Don's favorite shows that winter was by the Dixieland clarinetist Ted Lewis, at the Shamrock. Lewis wore a black suit and a battered top hat, and was known as the "High-Hatted Tragedian of Jazz." His band mates wore white harlequin costumes with Shriner-like caps. His signature song was "Dip Your Brush in the Sunshine."

Don's mature fiction is characterized by deliberate anachronisms, wild juxtapositions, and references to high and low culture. Perelman's work influenced him in this regard. But so did these early newspaper days: the blurring of styles, of serious and silly entertainments he witnessed night after night, and in venues like the Rice Hotel, whose old-fashioned ornamentation contrasted sharply with the contemporary structures rising around it.

In September, the *Cougar* solicited a new article from Bardley, welcoming back, after a short absence, his "nastiness." Don wrote a piece whose sole purpose was to allow him to print, in bold letters at the bottom of the page, "REPENT." More and more, Korea dominated the news. At the *Post,* Joe Maranto had run a mail-exchange newsletter for soldiers and their families back home. In November, Don was assigned to interview Michele Condrey, a Houston actress who had just returned from a USO tour. She shared with readers her positive impressions of troop morale. In the meantime, the movies: Gary Cooper, Ray Milland, Lillian Ross, Francis the Talking Mule . . .

By themselves, Don's movie reviews for the *Post* are of little interest, but when placed in the context of the budding counterculture, and Don's relation to it, his immersion in Hollywood films is noteworthy.

Don didn't read French, so at best he could only have been dimly aware of the Parisian journal *Cahiers du Cinéma.* The journal offered exciting new criticism by Jean-Luc Godard and François Truffaut. Both would become innovative filmmakers, and Godard in particular would turn out to be essential to Don, but in 1952 they were defining a film aesthetic in provocative essays for *Cahiers,* based largely on an appreciation of mainstream American movies.

The French New Wave, which erupted in the late fifties, had its beginnings around the time Don was born, when Henri Langlois, a Turkish immigrant to France, established the Cinémathèque in Paris to salvage classic silent movies, already in danger of being lost, misplaced, or destroyed. Langlois was especially drawn to the films of Louis Feuillade, which included such features as *Fantômas* and *Les Vampires.* "I am persuaded that Surrealism first existed in the cinema," Langlois said. "You've only got to look at 'Les Vampires' to understand that the cinema, because it was the expression of the twentieth century and the universal unconscious, carried Surrealism within it." At the same time, he championed Howard Hawks, John Ford, and other American directors, whose simplicity and naturalness, he said, augured film's future.

He showed movies at a ciné-club called the Cercle du Cinéma. Reportedly, James Joyce and André Breton were patrons. Later, when the Cinémathèque acquired larger screening rooms in the avenue de Messine, then on the rue d'Ulm, young cinephiles like André Bazin, one of the founders of *Cahiers*, Truffaut, and Godard found the hub around which to build their lives.

Prominent critics disparaged the group's favorite films—Feuillade's wild fantasies and American adventure tales. But in Hollywood's slick treatment of genre, mixed with the possibilities of Surrealism, the ciné-club boys saw new directions for the eye and the mind. Langlois's preference for pairing unlikely works (a Chaplin short followed by an anti-Russian German film) also broke boundaries of subject and style, and prompted new thinking about visual structures.

In 1945, Bazin wrote a seminal essay entitled "The Ontology of the Photographic Image," which established *Cahiers du Cinéma*'s critical framework and influenced the way Don's generation of moviegoers viewed films and their effect on other arts. For Bazin, realism in art was a struggle against death. As examples of this, he offered Egyptian tombs, icons, and mummies—"arts" designed to arrest the movement of time. Similarly, the conventions of realism in literature and film sought to freeze life before us. This impulse conflicted with the artist's desire to explore possibilities of color, form, sound: Art's true vocation being the fulfillment of its own medium. Bazin argued that the discovery of perspective in painting sidetracked it into a misguided effort to represent the world. Photography and film, with their ability to render the world directly, had now freed painting to return to its proper concerns: shape, color, texture, the flatness of the canvas. (In America, Clement Greenberg was making the same argument with regard to Abstract Expressionist painting.)

Like a painter, a filmmaker must focus on the primary materials of the medium, which include *filmed reality.* To argue whether footage is staged or candid, fact or fiction, is beside the point. It is *all* a record of the reality in front of the camera at that moment. The filmmaker's responsibility is to render reality's contradictions, not to try to force reality into a predetermined model.

One of Godard's earliest essays, "Towards a Political Cinema," written in 1950, when he was nineteen, takes Bazin's theories a step further, and argues that cinema is part of the reality it is creating. To improve cinema, then, is to improve the world itself—a utopianism, it turns out, consistent with the doctrines of modern architecture.

Inherent in this view of filmmaking is the notion that the director is an artist, shaping the medium's most basic elements. With this vision, Godard and Truffaut celebrated Howard Hawks, Alfred Hitchcock, and other American directors, whom most French intellectuals rejected as banal. The directors' brilliance lay not in the genres they plied—horror, comedy, Westerns, etc.—but in the variations they worked on conventions, often quite subtly, through camera angles, editing, and lighting. As in a jazz improvisation, the style of the pictures became a commentary on the subject, and revealed the hand of an "author."

Godard and Truffaut had the lucky support of intellectual comrades, and a fertile establishment within which to develop their ideas. In Houston, Don had to educate himself with whatever was there. What was there in 1952 was the *Houston Post,* a far cry from *Cahiers du Cinéma.* If his movie reviews were restricted to plot summaries and evaluations of actors, he was nevertheless developing an eye for the visual language of film, so that, less than a decade later, when he *did* become aware of Truffaut and Godard, he was already their aesthetic brother.

Occasionally, in Don's newspaper pieces, it's possible to glimpse him straining against his editor's strict standards. Mostly, he could only get away with prankishness—an unexpected climax to a sentence, say: The movie *Painting the Clouds with Sunshine* is "packed with color, spectacle and glamour, and is a pretty dreary business," he wrote. *Take Care of My Little Girl* "cracks the fraternity-sorority question wide open," he quipped, "with beautiful Jeanne Crain used as a maul." It ends up "more rhinestone than brimstone."

On May 25, 1952, Don's colleague W. D. Bedell reviewed, for the *Post,* Charles Mills's novel, *The Alexandrians.* The headline ran A DEEPLY DISTURBING NOVEL OF THE SOUTH. *The Alexandrians* traces the rise and fall of a small Georgia town, from its settlement in 1839 to the 1930s, and documents the decline of the plantation economy, touching along the way on the social effects of slavery and religious intolerance. In the October 10, 1952, issue of the *Cougar,* Don, still in the first flush of his marriage, offered "Chapter One" of *Amanda Feverish,* "a deeply disturbing novel of the South . . . [the] only four-chapter novel in the entire world." Subsequent chapters, entitled "Panic," "Visitation," and "Finale," appeared throughout the month of October.

Don began his tenure with the *Cougar* with a review of Speed Lamkin's novel of the South, and now he would end it with a parody of a Southern novel . . . or was it a parody of Bedell's review, or, as the style suggests, of Faulkner, the granddaddy of Southern novelists?

Amanda Feverish follows the protagonist's efforts to get a drink. She dispatches several suitors to fetch her a draught of "Old Illusion." The first, St. Clair Pitkin, a "moody, star-crossed scion of a fine old Southern family," overdoses on morphine and fails to return. The second, Pierre-Jean Louis Maurois Ennui, a "handsome if decadent French poet living on love and peach brandy in a shack in the middle of Amanda's peach orchard," falls victim to his own home brew, which is laced with insecticide. Amanda's disquiet grows.

> A fine pink haze, composed of gin and magnolia blossoms in equal parts, hovered over the Feverish plantation. It was dusk, the magic hour when the overpowering fragrance of the old slave quarters suffused every part of the grounds, even the south forty, where Amanda Feverish, windblown, wildeyed, sat under a juniper bush, pulling the wings off a giant, green-gold dragonfly.

Finally, Erskine Scaldwell, hoping to breathe the Old South's "wine-like if decaying atmosphere," calls on Amanda. She draws "an immense hogleg from her garter," shoots him, then herself. Old Josh, "her aged, faithful Sioux butler," is left emitting the "soft patter of tears . . . peeling onions in the kitchen." As Robert Murray Davis wryly noted, "Less than three months after [*Amanda Feverish*] was published, [Don] was drafted, but there was probably no connection."

PART TWO

AFTER PAPA'S WAR

BASIC TRAINING

Draftees were given one month to put their affairs in order before reporting for basic training. Don cleaned out his desk at the *Post,* probably in the sad light of dawn after one of his nightly shifts. Naked of his things, the desktop showed its scars, the ones Don had left as well as the ones that didn't quite date to O. Henry. Maggie decided to remain at Rice to pursue her French degree. His friends threw him a farewell party; Helen Moore sought him out to wish him luck.

One morning at the beginning of April 1953, Don boarded a bus to Louisiana. At a military reception center at Camp Polk, he and the other recruits were told to shuck their clothes for a medical inspection. They were each handed two cardboard tags with a letter and a number, designating their company and position. One tag stayed with the men; the other was tied to their suitcases. Eventually, the recruits were fingerprinted, fitted for shoes, given mess kits, canteens, and khaki and denim uniforms.

Don was assigned to Company M, 145th Infantry Regiment, 37th Infantry Division—the "Buckeye Division," mostly composed of members of the Ohio National Guard. Camp Polk, established in 1941, covers over 198,000 acres of the Kisatchie National Forest, eight miles southwest of Leesville. During World War II, Louisiana was one of the busiest sites of domestic military training; all around Camp Polk, truckloads of soldiers pitched tents in the woods and

conducted maneuvers. Kids crowded the roads near the camp, selling candy and Cokes to the young recruits. Gen. Mark Clark, whose name figures prominently in one of Don's best stories, "The Indian Uprising," spent time at Camp Polk.

After the war, the camp served as a POW holding station. Eventually, it was inactivated and put on a standby basis. It came back to life in September 1950, just three months after North Korean troops moved south past the thirty-eighth parallel with the goal of uniting the Korean peninsula.

After his initial round of medical tests, Don and his fellow recruits shuffled into a dark room for the first of several film screenings—a grim parody of Don's civilian moviegoing: short films on administering first aid, removing wounded soldiers from a battle zone, and treating frostbite. Afterward, at the rec center, Don drank weak beer and wrote postcards to his family. He made arrangements to send his civilian clothes home.

The next morning, reveille came at 5:30. The wooden barracks were drafty and cold, so it was a relief to step into the sunshine. Many young soldiers, including Don, got their first taste of domesticity in the army. They each took a turn at KP duty, twelve uninterrupted hours of gouging the eyes out of potatoes and taking out the trash. The men worked, ate, slept, and marched in alphabetical order.

Don was assigned a rifle, a .03, weighing about nine pounds. He was told to memorize its serial number and to treat it as part of his body. Rifle drills were aimed at getting the men comfortable with their weapons, shifting the rifles from shoulder to shoulder, lifting them into the air, placing their butts on the ground, all in precise order. Assembly, disassembly.

The cry of "Let's go, let's go!" started each day as a bugle brayed in the background. The men lined up for roll call in front of the barracks, breakfasted at 6:15 (cereal, a half-pint bottle of milk): 250 soldiers in a vast room, 10 to a table, none talking. Afterward came calisthenics, then close-order marching in formation, 120 steps per minute while gripping the rifle. Extended order drill followed the march: learning to "drop," hitting the rifle butt on the ground, then your knees, then your left side. Roll over, and you're ready to shoot. On some days, the officers required that the enlisted men take a five-mile hike. Lunch, called "dinner," was at 12:30, then more films. The movies were produced by the Army Signal Corps and featured army actors demonstrating training procedures. Occasionally, a B-grade Hollywood actor would show up in one of the films (Don knew every one of these hacks) playing a stern doctor concerned about sexually transmitted diseases. The men would recognize him from the movies screened on base as evening entertainment and whoop with derision.

Bayonet practice followed the training films. At 5:25 P.M., the camp colors were lowered and the men would retreat in formation to their barracks.

They would shower and shave, then meet for supper. After that, they were free to hang out at the PX, go to a movie (for which they had to pay—usually a dumb war drama), write letters, clean their rifles, do their laundry. Lights-out was at nine o'clock. With a pass, they could catch a bus to a small Grey-hound station on Third Street in Leesville and drink in the nearby bars.

On April 6, Don wrote to Joe Maranto, explaining that he had planned to return to Houston on Easter break, but a "lieutenant [or] some other higher animal inspected the barracks and said everything was filthy you could have eaten off the floor actually had you anything to eat but he wore some special glasses with built-in dirt and the whole outfit was restricted. . . ."

Don went on to say that "Geeters," his nickname for Pat Goeters, had writ-ten to him, expressing his disgust with the difficulties of architecture school. "i maintain i could teach him a few things about disgust," Don wrote. He ended:

> *two guys from this company are awol right now and if they don't start feeding me and letting me have a little sleep say fifteen minutes every other day i might very well join them except for the fact that after this couple of years is up i'll never join anything again. . . .*
>
> *bardley*

Like all draftees, Don received several pounds of junk mail at the camp, solicitations from Democratic and Republican fund-raisers (who apparently hoped that a boy's induction would have sparked a growing political con-science), subscription ads from book clubs, as well as from *Time, Life, Look,* and other magazines. Since World War I, the military had boasted that sol-diers were more bookish than the average American citizen. A former chair-man of the War and Navy Department's Commission on Training Camp Activities wrote, "In the number of books circulated [among recruits], fic-tion holds the first place. That is natural. A good story helps tide over the unoccupied moments, when the stoutest heart is apt to sink."

Don asked his wife, Maggie, to mail him the latest issues of *The New Yorker.*

During the latter half of his training at Camp Polk, he gained slow- and rapid-fire skills on the rifle range, experience with "snooping and pooping," the soldiers' terms for scouting and patrolling, hiding in the bushes while insects crawled all over him, and dry-run experience, going on maneuvers fully equipped with automatic and semiautomatic rifles, pistols, and ma-chine guns, but without ammunition.

He learned to handle "night problems." He was ordered to practice walk-ing silently in the dark, without smoking or eating, to pitch a pup tent with-out light, and to stay alert for suspicious sounds. Members of another platoon circled Don's group, clicking rifle bolts, sneezing, striking matches, and making all sorts of racket to steel everyone's nerves. Don was supposed to sit quietly, undetected. Suddenly, a flare would fill the sky; the recruits had been trained to flatten themselves or freeze, so the enemy couldn't see them in the flare light. Anyone who startled was "dead."

On certain "route step marches" during the day, officers told the soldiers they could move in any rhythm they wanted so long as they stayed reasonably together. They could talk and even sing. Don always loved to sing, and he knew a lot of show tunes from the performances he had covered for the *Post.* On many a long trek, his deep, sonorous voice carried throughout the Kisatchie National Forest.

Just before lights-out each night, or on Saturday and Sunday afternoons when he didn't have KP duty, he wrote, sitting on his bed, balancing paper on his knees, without benefit of a light. He had to learn to concentrate as several radios droned in the bunks around him.

In June, he finished his basic training. He turned in his rifle and bayonet: an amputation. He returned to Houston for a while; during this hiatus, he spent most of his time explaining to family and friends the various insignia on his uniform—the brass buttons and lapel ornaments, the crossed-rifle pin, indicating infantry, the blue piping on his cap, and the regimental colors. He had had to buy the insignia (army regulations), and he purchased an extra as a gift for Maggie, the way frat boys pinned their girls or couples exchanged rings. He gave Maggie a list of the books and magazines he'd need in the coming months. She told him how happy she was in graduate school.

At the end of training, he received no diploma, no mark of completion or achievement, just the certainty that he'd have to do it all again. He had no idea where he'd be shipped. His *physical* location did not match the army's sense of his place. He was leading alternate lives; though the bureaucratic one lacked immediacy, it controlled his future.

Within a few weeks, he got assigned to Fort Lewis, near Tacoma, Washington, and the cycle started again. In July and August of 1950, the Second Division was the first to embark from the United States for fighting in Korea. It was to this division, as a member of its Second Replacement Company, that Don was assigned.

He found the terrain more amenable than the sweltering Louisiana forests. The temperatures ranged from the low eighties during the days to the forties at night, which made long marches, and sleeping outside, more pleasant, though new arrivals were told to watch for poison ivy. Scotch broom sweetened the air. Ivy and sumac rioted over low-rolling hills. The barracks buildings, two-story wooden structures painted white, with dark green trim, seemed more solid than their Southern counterparts, less weathered and bug-eaten.

Don had plenty of time to write and read. Fighting in Korea ebbed and flowed during June and July, and the military's plans kept changing. For now, Don's division stayed put. Kim Il Sung, the North Korean leader, and Syngman Rhee, the right-wing U.S. ally who controlled South Korea, jockeyed for advantage while conducting armistice talks. One day, North Korea (shaken by the recent death of Stalin) appeared to agree to the United States' terms; the next, Rhee had forced all non-Korean prisoners of war into hard labor or into service in the South Korean army, angering the Chinese, who had hoped to extradite their former POWs.

One day, the war appeared to be ending; the next, the conflict flared again.

In his free time, Don learned about America's nuclear West: the Hanford Reach, with its growing atomic research; the tricity area of Richland, Pasco, and Kennewick, Washington, where the army employed much of the local population to work at Hanford or at nearby weapons storage bunkers, underground facilities in the high desert. Don's short story "Game" (1965) would draw on this knowledge.

Finally, in mid-July, he was sent on what he called the "grand cruise" across the Pacific, precise destination still unknown. On the troopship, he must have been mindful of Hemingway's war reporting, the battle passages in *A Farewell to Arms* and *For Whom the Bell Tolls.* "You could write for a week and not give everyone credit for what he did on [the] front," Hemingway had written about D day. "The beach had been defended as stubbornly and intelligently as any troops could defend it."

Don hoped to record similar heroics, but it wasn't to be. He soon realized that Korea was not like Papa's wars.

THE THIRTY-EIGHTH PARALLEL

I've crossed . . . the Pacific twice, on troopships. . . . You stand out there, at the rail, at dusk, and the sea is limitless, water in every direction, never-ending, you think *water forever,* the movement of the ship seems slow but also seems inexorable, you feel you will be moving this way forever, the Pacific is about seventy million square miles, about one-third of the earth's surface, the ship might be making twenty knots, I'm eating oranges because that's all I can keep down, twelve days of it with young soldiers all around, half of them seasick—

This passage from *Paradise* amplifies a scene from "See the Moon?": "[I sailed] over the pearly Pacific in a great vessel decorated with oranges. A trail of orange peel on the plangent surface."

The woozy troops thought they would dock first in Japan and wait to be assigned, but they were shipped straight to Korea, arriving the day the truce was signed, July 27, 1953. The war's official end left the troops in limbo. Don's outfit was reshuffled to Sasebo, Japan, where the soldiers set up a tent city. They were ordered to paint latrines at Pusan. While on shift there as perimeter guard, Don got his first sustained look at the "grimy hills of Korea."

Finally, on a Sunday in late August, traveling on what he called a "toy train," he and his fellows arrived at Second Division headquarters

11

in the Chorwon Valley, just north of the thirty-eighth parallel. "Walking down the road wearing green clothes," he writes in "See the Moon?" "Korea green and black and silent. . . . I had a carbine to carry. . . . We whitewashed rocks to enhance our area. . . . Mine the whitest rocks."

For a while, the army considered sending Don to bakers school; this struck him as hilarious, given how hungry and helpless he had been in the kitchen on Leek Street. He insisted to his superiors that his "weapon was a typewriter"; tenacious and persuasive, he eventually landed a spot in the division's Public Information Office. Only eight men out of twenty thousand were so assigned. Most of the time, he wrote news releases and articles for the division's publication, the *Indianhead.* Once, while on assignment in Tokyo, he saw the names of Buck Pvt. Harold Ross and Sgt. Alexander Woollcott on the masthead of a 1918 Paris edition of the army's newspaper, *Stars and Stripes.* Like these *New Yorker* icons, he hoped to get some bylines in the paper, and he almost did, but time ran out on his tour: one more missed opportunity that made *his* war a pale copy of Papa's—not that he ached to see action, and he certainly didn't want to remain in the service any longer than he had to. But as another Korea veteran, the writer James Brady, suggests, it's a "sour" feeling to put in your time and then be forced to admit, "It ain't much but it's the only war we got."

Three years before Don arrived in-country, W. H. Lawrence of *The New York Times* wrote of the enthusiastic greeting U.S. troops received at Pusan Harbor, with schoolchildren "waving Korean, American, and United Nations flags, lined up . . . singing the Korean national anthem." GIs snapped pictures and gave the kids candy. Pusan itself, Lawrence said, consisted of "thatched shack after shack amid dirt and squalor which would make any pineboard shack in the Hoovervilles of 1932 look like the Waldorf-Astoria." But by the summer of 1953, even the shacks were gone. Don's outfit saw very few civilians; they'd been routed from their land and evacuated to the south, out of the battle zone. Only the grimy hills remained, punctured with shell craters.

The historian Callum A. MacDonald wrote:

> At 10:00 p.m. on 27 July [1953] a sullen silence fell over the front. The opposing armies disengaged and fell back on their main defense lines behind the DMZ. The outposts in No Man's Land were left "deserted and quiet except for the rats." There was little rejoicing. For the first time in its modern history, the U.S. had failed to win. [Things] had ended in a draw . . . [the] "sour little war" was finally over.

Nevertheless, dangers remained in this once-fertile wasteland. Don and his fellow newcomers were warned to watch for land mines. On the narrow road that twisted out of the harbor to Pusan, heavy American vehicles hauling weapons and equipment kicked up dust and caused traffic snarls; daredevil drivers swerved swiftly around one another on the edges of twelve-foot embankments, provoking accidents. The weather was harsh, diseases easy to catch. The soldiers heard rumors that Korean dust was full of parasites that fed infections. And of course no one knew if the truce would continue to hold.

Second Division headquarters sat in a bare valley, near the bombed-out town of Chorwon, bounded by distant red-soil hills. Soldiers named the area's American outposts "T-Bone," "Alligator Jaw," "Spud," "Little Gibraltar," "Norti," "Old Baldy," and "Pork Chop."

Don and his coworkers in the Public Information Office pulled light duty. They worked from seven to five, making reveille in "an offhand way." They suffered no inspections, no guard duty. Their showers spit hot water, and they kept cases of warm Asahi beer in the office. A Korean houseboy washed their clothes, cleaned their rifles, and heated water so they could shave in the mornings. The army employed several young Koreans—the kids called themselves "Number One Boys"—to carry and organize equipment. The soldiers referred to them, collectively, as the "gook train."

For all the comparative ease of the assignment, Don was "not, of course, deliriously happy," he wrote Joe Maranto. "[F]eel that everything is going to pot, can't write worth a damn (tho well enough to show these people)." He said, "we run into a lot of stories . . . that we can't write [for the *Indianhead*]—had half-a-dozen of EM [enlisted men] attempting to blow off their officers' heads in the last month. Despite sunny pictures being painted in Stateside publications, morale is lousy. In indoctrination classes they're asking us to report anybody who bitches about the army or expresses a desire to go home. . . . Remember [Orwell's] 1984."

Don's fellows in the PIO included a "Master from Columbia and a Master from Wisconsin, the latter with a degree in drama," he said. "[A]lso a Southern Cal type and a Kansas U. type, and one from Minnesota and one from Pitt. We're getting a new one from CCNY this morning; he's a lawyer and looks to be pretty much of a bomb." For the first time in his life, outside his father's house, Don wasn't the best-educated person in his group. He felt this deficiency keenly, and wrote his family for books, books, and more books: Dylan Thomas, Ezra Pound, Saul Bellow. He asked his wife to send, along with *The New Yorker,* the *Partisan Review* and *Theatre Arts.*

In October, he wrote to Maranto that a television crew from Seoul "comes up here to the front and films things if we do the scripts. Needless to say, this is marvelous experience." He was looking forward to a Thanksgiving party at a nearby Dutch compound: "[A] whole gang of bigwigs are flying in from the Netherlands and there is a promise of much liquor."

Francis Cardinal Spellman "choppered in on Christmas day to say mass," Don wrote. Later, someone passed around a couple bottles of "vin terrible from somewhere, and the Thais chipped in with a bottle of Mekhong, a whiskey that is peculiarly their own and tastes remotely like anti-freeze. Not that anti-freeze of whatever kind isn't welcome at the moment—it's been snowing (I had a WHITE CHRISTMAS!)." In fact, the temperature hovered around nine degrees.

Don informed Maranto that he had begun "pedagogging two nights a week" at an army education center: "English (on a very elementary level), about 15 students, $1.25 an hour. One of my students is an aged Negro M/Sgt. who hasn't been inside a classroom since 1930 and 5." This was Don's first teaching experience.

The army had not prepared or properly equipped its troops to face the killing cold of Korea's valley winters. By January, temperatures shot to sixty below zero. The shell holes filled with ice. A hard, frozen coat encased the area's remaining spruce and pine trees and the untidy concertina-wire fences on the headquarters' perimeter. Don slept in his uniform, keeping handy his web belt and canteen. Beside his bunk, an oil stove reeked poisonously, but it kept him relatively warm at night. During the day, soldiers sat on logs or sooty sandbags, shivering inside wet ponchos, crumbling cocoa cakes into boiling water. Sometimes they peed on their rifles to unfreeze them. Otherwise, they used ammo tubes as urinals in the snow. Deep fog drifted off the Sea of Japan and seeped into the folds of their clothes.

Stilled by the punishing weather, and with no imminent threat of combat, the men grew bored, lazy, careless. It was easy to make a mistake with the equipment, to trip over something—a jerrican full of water, a sleeping bag—and sustain a serious injury. The men shaved several times a day, just to have something to do.

The sun began to sink around 2:30 every afternoon, and a fierce Siberian wind tumbled over the hills. The soldiers waited for the gook train to bring them their mail, then retreated to their tents to clean their rifles, count their grenades, and hunch over lukewarm suppers of lima beans and chewy ham. Food arrived from the army's rear flanks by way of jeep trailers; it came in insulated thermal containers, but nearly always, the last men served found their meals frozen solid.

By 4:30, the light was gone. In the dark, the lonely tinkling of the tin cans with which the men had decorated the concertina wire made everyone feel a few degrees colder. Heading out to the latrine, you had to make sure your toilet paper wasn't a block of ice.

Sometime in December or January, Don wrote his father that he had taken R and R in Seoul. There, he had seen *From Here to Eternity.* Though the filmmakers "emasculated half the characters," the movie "nevertheless had some wonderful moments." Don went on to describe a "multi-million luxury hotel S. Rhee is building in Seoul with American gold." Don had met one of the architects. He "is not really an architect at all but an artist who used to design sets for the 'Kukla, Fran and Ollie' TV show and is a PFC belonging to our 9th Regiment." The "main architect is equally not a real architect but some kind of a bastard designer who went to MIT and parades around in Seoul looking weirdly out of place in Ivy League uniform." Together, these men were building a "14-story Babel in which the interiors are all very chi-chi in . . . what they fondly believe to be the modern manner. They are being very arty about the whole thing and that's quite a trick because it's almost impossible to be arty in Seoul since the city is all bombed-out ruins and poverty."

The letter shows an attempt to connect with his father, and reveals Don's aesthetic development. He saw that it didn't make sense for an architect, standing among ruins, to insist on the "modern manner." It was a case of ego over need, of forcing the *wrong design.*

In March 1954, Don described for Joe Maranto Marilyn Monroe's trip to entertain the troops: "Just before the show I was backstage and the door to her dressing room was open . . . we watched her warming up for the show, complete with bumps & grinds and wiggles in tune to the music being played on the stage, and she was winking & blinking at us and smiling a more or less girlish smile and in fine giving the damnedest pre-show show you've ever seen."

His letters mention few friendships with other soldiers, but he did become close to a young man name Sutchai Thangpew, from the Royal Thai Battalion, a group of around one thousand elite soldiers attached to the American division. The battalion was famous for its bayonet skills. Thangpew, a lieutenant, was engaged to a woman in Bangkok. Like Don, he was a talented writer; he had been assigned to record his battalion's history. Someday he hoped to become prime minister of Thailand, and Don believed he would succeed. Thangpew was tall and handsome, gentle and intelligent, with a kindly smile. Don once traveled with him to Tokyo, where they visited the national theater, and saw a ballet and a Kabuki show. Later, when Thangpew married, Don sent him a wedding gift. For years afterward, Don scanned the newspapers for word of his friend's rise in politics, but he never saw anything about him.

Increasingly, Don felt left out of the lives of his Houston friends. Maranto sent Don some of the book reviews he had written. Don replied, "To pay your . . . reviews the highest compliment of which I am capable, they remind me of me. There is a certain intensity, plus a reaching for the word that is not merely the mot juste but also has a cluster of overtones; in fine, they are very, very good. As is my custom, I say not that they *seem* good to me, but flatly that they are good." Despite his confident tone, he must have felt that Maranto was passing him by. Now and then he admitted in his letters that he wasn't pleased with his own writing.

He grumbled about the paucity of "good music" in Korea, though "strangely enough the most consistent source of good serious music our Zenith can pick up is Radio Moscow, which sometimes gives us Tschaikowsky [*sic*], sometimes propaganda in English." In another letter to Maranto, he mentioned that he had heard from Pat Goeters. "Goeters is still writing the obscurantist prose he was writing when I left. I am pervertedly happy that such things remain constant." Maybe he wouldn't be *entirely* at sea when he got back home.

Like dust in the hills around the Chorwon Valley, Korea sprinkles Don's fiction, in stories such as "See the Moon?" and "Visitors" and "Overnight to Many Distant Cities." The most extended mention of his tour appears in "Thailand," collected in *Sixty Stories* in 1981. Here, Don splits himself into two personalities, one a droning old veteran recounting his service in the "Krian war," the other an impatient young man ready to "consign" the vet "to history." It's as though, in his late forties (when he wrote the piece) Don had accepted the fall from Papa's perch: There are no Hemingway hero tales, just a boring old man and his clichéd reminiscences. His memories are of no use to a new generation—or so the story's *form* suggests. In fact, the vet's recollections are anything *but* dull, and come, nearly whole cloth, from Don's prowls along the thirty-eighth parallel:

> . . . there was this Thai second john who was a personal friend of mine, named Sutchai. Tall fellow, thin, he was an exception to the rule. We were right tight, even went on R & R together, you're too young to know what that is, it's Rest and Recreation where you zip off to Tokyo and sample the delights of that city for a week. . . .
>
> This time I'm talking about . . . we were on the side of a hill, they held this hill which sort of anchored the MLR—that's Main Line of Resistance—at that point, pretty good-sized hill I forget what the designation was, and it was a feast day, some Thai feast, a big holiday, and the skies were sunny, sunny. They had set out thirty-seven washtubs full of curry I never saw anything like it. Thirty-seven washtubs full of curry and a different curry in every one. They even had eel curry. . . .
>
> It was a golden revel. . . . Beef curry, chicken curry, the delicate Thai worm curry, all your various fish curries and vegetable curries . . . toward

evening they were firing off tracer bursts from the quad-fifities to make fireworks and it was just festive, very festive. They had fighting with wooden swords at which the Thais excel, it's like a ballet dance, and the whole battalion was putting away the Mekhong and beer pretty good. . . .

As the veteran talks, his bored young listener tells himself, "*I cannot believe* I am sitting here listening to this demento carry on about eel curry." Finally, the young man thinks, "*Requiescat in pace*" (a play on Montresor's words at the end of Edgar Allan Poe's "The Cask of Amontillado"). "I close, forever, the book [on you]."

"Thailand" shows that Don never closed the book on his past. Still, he refused to address his experiences *directly*—after all, his father had taught him that if you reveal too much of yourself, you'll be open to ridicule. In "Thailand," Don preempted any censure he might get for writing a straightforward narrative (what could be more familiar than a *war story*?). Nevertheless, the young man's impatience with old-fashioned stories makes him appear shallow, and the narrator, a veteran of a much more varied world than his companion has known, enjoys the last laugh: "They don't really have worm curry. . . . I just made that up to fool you."

When spring came, with its rains, the roads in the Chorwon Valley became deep red swamps; on hikes, the men sank to their ankles in mud. The Number One Boys stayed busy scraping and shining the GIs' boots. The soldiers would fill their rucksacks with peaches, sugar, coffee, pork and beans, and toilet paper, then walk into the hills, amazed at how much light the stars cast. As the weather warmed, fat flies gathered around mess kits and piss tubes. As the men sat reading—letters, manuals, Mickey Spillane novels—they swatted at their ears.

For his twenty-third birthday, Don asked Marilyn to send him Erich Auerbach's *Mimesis. Mimesis* examines several major works—the authors ranging from Homer to Proust—and argues that a writer's grammar, syntax, and diction can't help but absorb the "style of the age." Auerbach claimed that Dante's vernacular, a combination of lyricism, historicism, science, and philosophy, led to the realism of Balzac and Flaubert.

Don also requested Suzanne Langer's *Philosophy in a New Key,* a study of semantics and symbols. He was particularly keen on Langer's notion that words loosed from their familiar contexts or meanings (as in the poetry of Mallarmé) retain their roots. A whiff of past associations clings to language, even when it is put to odd new uses.

Marilyn's enthusiasm for her French classes encouraged Don to read French poetry and to try to pick up some idioms, while stationed in Korea.

He read novels by Gide and Stendhal, Faulkner, Huxley, and Moravia. He read Shakespeare and a study of Socrates. He wrote his mother that he had found Truman Capote's *The Grass Harp* "wanting Capote's earlier magic." He devoured Eisenstein on film and Lionel Trilling on the liberal imagination, Max Beerbohm on the theater and Edmund Wilson on the novel. He admitted in a letter to Joe Maranto that he felt a "mammoth inferiority thing" from having a poor education.

A pair of photos taken by fellow soldiers—one in the Second Division camp, the other in a Tokyo garden—shows Don to be comfortable with himself in spite of his unhappiness. He is tall and rangy, relaxed in his uniform, grinning in front of the "grimy hills" or deadpanning next to a fake stork in a fountain. His letters make it clear, though, that he was impatient, biding his time until he could get back home. "Perhaps the army has given me something," he wrote to Maranto, "but if it has I don't know what it is, except that it has kept me earthy and close to the soil all right. . . .

"But . . . is that a virtue?"

NO BUTTERFLY

While on the thirty-eighth parallel, Don tried to write "THE GREAT AMERICAN NOVEL." His letters to Joe Maranto provide the first direct record of his ambition to write serious fiction. On December 29, 1953, he said, "[the novel] is moving forward steadily. Two chapters, about 12,000 words have been written, and an addition[al] 1400-word beginning for Chapter the Third. It's hard work, especially as all I can tell about it right now is that certain portions are terribly bad."

He read Ezra Pound, Saul Bellow, and Dylan Thomas as he made his way through these early chapters.

In January, he told Maranto he'd made corporal, and that he'd drafted a fifth chapter. "When the sixth is done I will go back and make drastic revisions on it and the preceding chapters, which will comprise the first half of the book and run to about 36,000 words. It's a very peculiar book to date; it keeps changing its form."

His accurate daily word count indicates Hemingway's influence on his working methods. To his parents, he wrote that his project was not a "deeply disturbing novel of the south"—despite his admiration for Faulkner and Carson McCullers—nor was it a "persecuted artist-type thing, or the record of somebody's miserabboble adolescence." It was "an unlove story, like the unbirthdays in Disney's 'Alice in Wonderland.' "

A few months later, he told Maranto:

> *No I am not satisfied with [the novel], not by a couple of miles, but I have*
> *seven and a half long chapters on paper now and am nearing 50,000*
> *words and that's more words than I've ever laid end to end before in my*
> *life on one subject. I fear it is a terribly bad novel but hope to do a rewrite*
> *that will correct the most glaring faults. I haven't tried to write the thing*
> *paragraph by polished paragraph, and make each paragraph a jewel as I*
> *tried to do with the pieces for the* Post. *I would never have gotten more*
> *than a few gilded pages on paper if I had.*
>
> *As it stands the thing has a million rough edges and I will never get all*
> *of them smoothed out but perhaps it's better that way.*

He sounded more optimistic with his wife's parents. "[I] am working on a major fiction project that may turn out well enough to publish," he wrote Mr. and Mrs. Marrs in February 1954. "I have written about 30,000 words . . . and so far it doesn't seem too bad."

Writing time was hard to find. "[W]e're short-handed and over-loaded here," Don told Maggie's parents, "and it's getting to the point where there is very nearly no such thing as off-duty hours. . . . Next week I have to take our tape recorder out and record some tank noises for the Psychological Warfare people, who will then transcribe the tape on disks and in the event of a resumption of the fighting play the records over an amplifier to confuse the enemy and make him believe there are tanks where no tanks actually exist."

On R and R in Tokyo, Don laid the novel aside. He purchased paperback copies of Camus's *The Plague,* Gide's *Strait Is the Gate,* Orwell's *Down and Out in Paris and London,* Eisenstein's *The Film Sense,* the "Hortense Powdermaker study of Hollywood . . . [and] a lot of stuff by the various Sitwell's [sic], including the *Canticle of the Rose.*" He saw the movies *The Robe* and *The Moon Is Blue.*

Finally, on April 22, 1954, he announced to Maranto: "The first draft of the novel is finished and I have launched a radical campaign of revision. It is a new attack which could conceiveably [sic] erase the major difficulties. It will in any case likely go into a third draft. Right now it's just under 50,000 words, and that's kind of slight for what I want."

R and R gave Don a break from soldiering and writing, and at least one of his Tokyo excursions had implications for his marriage and future sexual affairs. Years later, he told Helen Moore about an incident that eventually appeared in "Visitors": "[In] Tokyo . . . [h]e was once in bed with a Japanese girl during a mild earthquake, and he's never forgotten the feeling of the floor falling out from underneath him, or the woman's terror. He suddenly remembers her name, Michiko. 'You no butterfly on me?' she had asked. . . . He was astonished to learn that 'butterfly' meant, in the patois of the time, 'abandon.' "

As "Don described the experience later," Helen says, the girl's "skin 'turned white' with terror when the tremors began. Spending the night with [her] posed a moral dilemma for Don as well as for a fellow soldier who had made the trip with him. They discussed whether when you were married but forcibly separated like this, it was immoral to be with another woman. It was a dilemma that Don seemed not to have resolved when he told me the story a few years later."

The incident stayed with him. In 1979, he reviewed the Dutch war film *Soldier of Orange* for *The New Yorker.* In describing the movie's skill at depicting sudden horror, he wrote, "The transformation of everyday reality into unprecedented ghastliness is like being in bed in an earthquake, the bed falling beneath you."

On R and R, Don abandoned his khaki field uniform for a more comfortable cotton poplin shirt and an olive-drab tie, an M-1950 garrison cap, softly cocked above his right ear, and the army's new "Mickey Mouse" boots (so called because they resembled Mickey's big feet). The boots were rubber-lined inside, which helped in the soggy hills, though they were too hot for town.

Don's favorite spot in Tokyo was the Imperial Hotel—he admired it "more than any other building." Designed by Frank Lloyd Wright in 1916, the hotel was demolished in 1968, despite worldwide pleas for its preservation—the owners said it had become expensive to repair.

When commissioned, the hotel was meant to symbolize Japan's relationship to the West as well as to announce the emergence of Japan as a modern nation. Wright planned a thoroughly up-to-date building that managed to respect the "worthy tradition" of Japanese aesthetics. He followed the "principle of flexibility instead of rigidity"—a far cry from the "luxury hotel" Don had seen in Seoul, which forced its "artiness" onto a landscape of poverty and ruin.

Don spent hours wandering the Imperial's halls, delighted by their unpredictable curves, admiring—with his father's eye—the way Wright had designed the floors to be supported by centered joists, like a waiter balancing a tray on his fingertips, so earth tremors wouldn't yank down the walls.

"There were little terraces and little courts [in the building], infinitely narrow passages suddenly opening into large two- or three-storey spaces. . . . And there were many different levels," wrote the critic Peter Blake. Famously, the Imperial had survived the Great Kanto Earthquake of 1923 (as well as the bombings of 1945)–another reason Don liked to spend time there. He admired the walls' low center of gravity, wide at the base, thin at the top, with small windows in the first two stories and more abundant spacings on the third.

Like Don's father, in the best of his work, Wright made the most of minimal units, marrying practicality and pleasure. To travel over eight thousand miles from home, and to see these familiar principles at work, reassured Don, and convinced him of the wisdom of modern design.

At the same time, he saw how unique the Imperial was. Most of Tokyo's modern buildings were top-heavy—foolish in a quake-prone region, further examples of "arty" designers forcing their will on a place, rather than learning from it. Don was beginning to see the flaws in modernist zeal.

At dusk, the Imperial's lovely Oya stone (an easily carved lava) caught light from the reflecting pool out front. Don walked past the water and headed for the Tennessee Tea Room or the Roppongi district's bars, with their wide-open doors, loud music, and drooping banners declaring YOU MUST BE DRINKING HERE TO REMAIN INSIDE. He went in search of jazz.

American jazz had been popular in Japan starting in the 1920s; it was banned from the airwaves during the rabid nationalism of World War II, and began to make a comeback in the fifties. Still, American performers rarely appeared in Tokyo. The 293rd Army Band played at service clubs near the Roppongi district and in Hibiya Hall, frequented by Gen. Mark Clark. Don may have caught the band there, but he would have preferred a less regimented sound. It's possible he saw the trumpeter Webster Young and the pianist Hampton Hawes, both of whom served in the military in Asia.

A pair of Japanese jazz drummers drew rave notices in Tokyo at the time, and Don would have found them. Oguchi Daihachi, who had been a POW in China in the forties, returned to his home in Nagoya after the war, and decided to pursue a music career. He learned about taiko drumming, an ancient Japanese art, featuring large bass drums and hypnotic rhythms. Building on this tradition, he added small drums to the taiko core, and scored jazz-based multirhythmic pieces to create a new style of music. At the same moment, in and around Tokyo *kissas* (cafés), the drummer Joji Kawaguchi and his Big Four band were making a name for themselves by taking current pop tunes and jazzing them up with long, percussion-centered improvs.

In "The King of Jazz" (1978), Don honored the players he listened to in Tokyo. In the story, a trombone player named Hideo Yamaguchi challenges the top "bone man," Hokie Mokie, for the title "King of Jazz." "Tell me, is the Tennessee Tea Room still the top jazz place in Tokyo?" Hokie asks Hideo. "No," Hideo replies, "the top jazz place in Tokyo is the Square Box now."

The story's title comes from a 1930 movie, *The King of Jazz,* directed by John Murray Anderson and featuring the Paul Whiteman Orchestra, whose most popular tune was "Japanese Sandman."

After a night of music and drink, Don might have walked to the Hardy Barracks in central Tokyo, a large American military installation with an NCO club, ten-cent movies, a swimming pool, a library, and—most important—cots to crash in. The compound was constructed around a white stone building with trim rectangular windows; just outside its gates, laundry, grocery, and tailor shops vied for the GIs' dollars. Several blocks to the west, the Shinjuku neighborhood, with its tiny bars, overpriced liquor, and available girls, beckoned. It's likely that Shinjuku is where Don met "Michiko." The area was known among American soldiers for its "love hotels." Shinjuku stank of cigarettes, sugar, and burning stovetop oils. The streets were sticky with spilled drinks and greasy food wrappers. The neighborhood had come to life in the mid-twenties because it was one of the few areas of Tokyo to survive, intact, the Kanto earthquake. It "only concerned [itself] with customers' yen," says Leonard Anderson, a Korean vet. In bed there, a boy could fall and fall.

Don's grandfather, Mr. Bart, died while Don was overseas, a sadness he never overcame. In a tent on the side of a grimy hill, or in a noisy Tokyo *kissa,* he recalled the saddles on the walls of his grandfather's ranch, the creaking windmills, and the creek. He remembered the lumberman's tools, their faint metallic smells; baseball; the odor of pine; the joy on the old man's face when he spotted Don and Pat Goeters in front of the Reforma Hotel in the heart of Mexico City. Don recalled the world he had known, and he knew he could not now return to it, not to the way it had been.

As Don's tour of duty neared its end, he wondered what to do with himself. His wife had been awarded a teaching assistantship in the French department at Rice. She would need at least two more years to finish her degree. If he returned to the *Houston Post,* he would work nights and he and Maggie would rarely see each other. On the other hand, "for better or worse," he wrote to Joe Maranto, he could not "imagine anything" other than being a journalist, since he could not live off "literature." The sloppy work of the wire-service reporters he had met—their lack of investigative acumen, their parroting of military press releases—disenchanted him, but he liked the access to celebrities and dignitaries that journalism provided him. His friend Sutchai Thangpew had made him curious about Thailand. The U.S. Military Advisory Group was expanding its operations there; Hanoi was about to fall, and America planned to double its Southeast Asia advisory contingent. For a while, Don flirted with the idea of applying for duty in Thailand, to cover "straight news," but he never followed up on it. His hope of joining the Tokyo staff of *Stars and Stripes* was thwarted by a grumpy first lieutenant, who refused to let him leave the Second Division. Then Don's tour was up.

Meanwhile, he reported to Maranto that the "current novel is better than anything I've ever done but not finished and I can't get a typewriter after hours to nurse it on here and so will have to wait until I get home. I don't think I'll want to publish it when it's finished, but I do want to finish it and see how it comes out. It's been tremendously good exercise and has taught me much."

When he did get back to Houston, he refused to show the manuscript to any of his friends. It has never surfaced. His remark that it was an "unlove story" like the "unbirthdays" in Disney's *Alice in Wonderland* suggests its unconventional nature. When Don *did* publish a novel, *Snow White,* over ten years later, it, too, echoed Disney.

As the Second Division prepared to ship out, the *Indianhead* planned a farewell edition. Don wrote a story for it, describing life in the trenches for the Thirty-eighth Regiment as the cease-fire took hold. He interviewed soldiers who had been there that day, and reported:

> At 2200 hours, men of the division were told, the ceasefire was to go into effect.
>
> After that time, they were instructed not to fire unless attacked.
>
> The Communists opposite the 38th Regt's sector wanted to slug it out until the final bell. Round after round came into the 38th trenches. The fire was returned.
>
> At 2154 hours, regiment ordered all shooting stopped.
>
> At 2200, despite many warnings, men dashed from their bunks, shed their flak jackets, and stood in little groups on the edge of a no-man's land that was suddenly safe.
>
> On the opposite side of the line, the Chinese poured out of their bunkers and caves by the hundreds. They waved and shouted unintelligible English words and phrases. Many wore peculiar dead-white garments. Many sat out in the open and began to eat.
>
> Men got the feeling that something, or a part of something, was finished.

Despite the boxing imagery and the repetition, Hemingway this wasn't. Not only was the report a final piece for the *Indianhead,* it was Don's last, halfhearted attempt to be Papa (or else it's a parody). His own novel may have dissatisfied him, but it signaled the direction he was commited to, *away* from strict realism—as did his layout for the paper's last issue.

He outranked his young editor, and put the man through the "most nerve shattering experience he ever had" by "jumping design"—providing sixteen pages of staggered headlines, articles beginning above and below the fold, photographs arranged asymmetrically: all, now, standard newspaper design, but radical at the time, especially in military culture. It "shook up the printers" who thought "in terms of straight newspaper makeup," "scared [everybody] to death," and convinced them that Don had "gone ape." He wasn't even supposed to produce the issue, but he took over by pulling rank and "browbeating the poor devil [his editor] to the point of madness."

His determination sprang from an earlier episode, when a lieutenant who objected to a story Don had written asked him to change the piece. Don refused, until the man gave him a direct order. Don's implacability—and his frustrations—with the *Indianhead* presage the conflicts he would face in just a few years as editor of the University of Houston's *Forum.*

Any "rumors of new newspaper or mag ventures [in Houston] that sound remunerative?" Don asked Joe Maranto. Maranto said no, and admitted he was getting tired of the low pay and odd hours of newspaper writing. He considered jumping to an ad agency. This horrified Don. "Your present lick is no good," Don wrote back, "but at least it's better than the cess pool." Advertising is "DISASTER," he insisted. Then he quoted the Duke Ellington song, saying, "DO NOTHING TILL YOU HEAR FROM ME."

"I am still dreaming this old dream . . . of starting a weekly mag a la Harold Ross," he wrote Maranto, or of founding something like the *Allied Arts Review,* "but sans any quality of hope; it can only be created in despair."

In March 1954, he wrote Maranto, "I have no juice, no fire. Banality . . . I'm damn near done for. I think perhaps a high opinion of yourself and your talents is a condition of the kind of writing I used to do . . . probably something that I'll never do again. You see from all this that I'm desperately conscious of my inadequacies. Novel begun as a defense against this, among other things. I just threw the first two chapters of the draft away, by the way, and am trying to concentrate on the refurbishing of the rest."

Members of the Second Infantry Division sailed out of Korea in shifts; briefly, in late September, Don was reassigned to the Public Information Office in Seoul. There, he continued to read: Mark Twain's *Life on the Mississippi,* Oscar Wilde's *The Picture of Dorian Gray,* Will Durant's *The Story of Philosophy,* a biography of Emerson, plays by August Strindberg, Jean Cocteau, and Gerhart Hauptmann.

On September 28, Don told Maranto that he was "resettled in a relatively plush little berth [in Seoul] with the Korea Civil Assistance Command, which administers the flow of US aid to Korea, as an information specialist. . . . I will be here for another 60 days and then I will come HOME." He said his new strategy was to finish up at the "so-called University." After Maggie completed her studies at Rice, he intended to consolidate my gains and head for Stanford, an MA and a job with the *San Francisco Examiner* or *Chronicle,* which is my next objective, newspaper-wise. The plan is to spend two years in that area and then whip off to the Yale Drama School for two more years, say, and a Boston or Philadelphia paper, at which time I'll be ready to take a crack at NEW YORK. This is my five year plan, anyhow, at the finish of which I hope to have an MA in English and a lot of related work in drama and the cinema (perhaps a year at the CCNY Film Institute could be worked in, or at the Southern Cal equivalent) and nine years' experience in journalism. The latter would break down as two years on the *Post* pre army, two years in army writing jobs, another year on the *Post* or some allied job in Houston, two years on a Bay area paper and two years on a Boston or Philly paper.

This master plan is of course subject to being screwed up by a number of things: recall into the army, for one, a third world war, fall of the H bomb, divorce, anything. But it has a lovely sound and it is one of these lines that I'll be working. All this time, incidentally, I would concurrently be working in fiction, like Glenn Miller in that awful picture, searching for a cool sound.

In December, he boarded a troopship for California, from where he'd settle at Fort Lewis for a short reorientation period. On the ship, Don hunkered into his berth, his back against white-painted steel, enjoying the pillow and the clean sheets, the electric lights by which to read. He would be home by Christmas. The rivets in the ship's hull looked like snowman's buttons.

"[I sat] in the bow fifty miles out of San Francisco, listening to the Stateside disc jockeys chattering cha cha cha. Ready to grab my spot at the top," he wrote.

To Joe Maranto, he had written, "Whatever you can say about the army you can't say that it doesn't take something away from you. . . . It will take me six months to get back in shape at least. Maybe something is permanently gone. I don't know. I'm afraid to look."

COCKYPAP

It's impossible to arrive in Houston for the first time ready for its physical challenges, and equally hard to return to it, prepared, after a long period away. The intense humidity and the heat—even in winter—along with the swampy odors rising from Buffalo Bayou (the city's "cunty" smell, according to Larry McMurtry) give the air a solid, flinty feel.

On a warm December day, Don came back to Houston with a well-worn manuscript in his duffel—pages he would soon throw away—and tried to catch his breath. He had been released from the army on reserve status; six more years would pass before he'd receive his official discharge. Fears of being recalled into the service made his homecoming dicey—no fanfares, bands, or parades, no rituals to mark an end. Oscar Cortes, another Korea veteran from south Texas, says, "I got a card from the Apache Distributing Company that distributes beer. They sent me a card for me to go by and pick up a free case of beer. That's the only thing I got." It was more recognition than most vets received.

Christmas helped. Don's family had always set up a tree (in a corner, near a window, or in the middle of the living room, depending on the placement of the furniture and/or the walls that year). Joan was home from school, Don's younger brothers were excited by the presents, and Maggie made a holiday effort to enjoy the family.

Don's father photographed his son's "veteran face, f.6 at 300," Don wrote. In fact, the elder Barthelme snapped the whole clan: Don's mother, her hair beginning to gray, her posture slightly droopy; Joan, more poised than ever, wary around her dad; Pete, a strapping adolescent; Rick, practicing tough-guy looks, wearing his wide-collared shirts rumpled and loose; Steve, the baby, blissful, tender, doted on.

Then there was the old man: face as blocky as his chest. Was he proud of his eldest son? Not so you'd know.

Maggie was a dream—and as *distant* as a dream—dark hair pulled back with a bow, eyes roving and alert. The noise, the bustle—preparing for Christmas, recovering from it later—prevented prolonged intimacy with Maggie, a mercy, perhaps, in these first awkward days at home. Don sat in his father's house, knee touching his wife's knee almost shyly, wondering why he'd worn a gaudy Asian shirt with a leaf motif. It was so out of place. "My clothes looked old and wrong," he wrote later.

His arm circled Maggie's waist as they watched the kids rip into their gifts. (Had he bought the right things? What did one get for kids these days?) As Maggie laughed at the children's delight, she rested a hand uneasily on Don's thigh.

After "[my] pause at Pusan," the "city looked new with tall buildings raised while my back was turned," says the narrator of "See the Moon?"

"There just wasn't much to Houston" in the early 1950s, Philip Johnson once said. "I couldn't understand how anyone lived there, but that was before the personality of the place came through to me: I found out those people weren't afraid to try *anything!*"

Stephen Fox, an architectural historian, once wrote that Houston's view of growth has always been "What is coming will be of more value than what is here already." The city's "yearning" for a "new start" had begun in earnest while Don was gone. Fresh structures would eclipse the old Houston: the Melrose Building on Walker Avenue, a conventional U plan decked out like a sleek steel skeleton; the Texas National Bank Building, in progress on Main, with a green curtain wall and rooftop terraces; the First Unitarian Church, built in the style of Eero Saarinen, around a courtyard on Fannin Street; and, most impressively, Mies van der Rohe's plan for a new addition to the Museum of Fine Arts, slated for completion in 1959. The design for this addition called for a double-volume space made mostly of glass, "full of the 'nothing' to which Mies . . . aspired to reduce architecture."

In Don's absence, the city, afloat on oil money, had stepped up to announce itself as an architectural center. Don's father supplied much of the energy behind this move. In Tokyo and Seoul, Don had seen the triumph—for better *and* worse—of modern architecture. Now, with Houston's rapid development, he saw his father's old religion catching on. The narrator in "See the Moon?" describes his father as a "cheerleader." "We have to have cheerleaders"—they help promote the possible. And the possible *was* possible in Houston. Don never doubted that.

But he had to get to know the place again, starting with the theaters. He spent long afternoons in the familiar old seats, hiding inside the Majestic, Loew's, the River Oaks, watching shoot-'em-ups, gangsters, and eating buttered popcorn.

There was the El Patio Restaurant on Kirby Street: a sea of melted cheese, chili peppers, good cold beer. Downtown was Guy's Newsstand, next to—amazing!—a block of new Korean shops. Guy's offered over three thousand magazines on every subject from stock tips to tits, including German rags and French newspapers. At Guy's, you could buy Churchill cigars, marked down because their wrappers were flawed. An old woman, Mary Thompson, ran the place—she called it an "emporium"—having inherited it from her late husband, who had established the newsstand with winnings from the racetrack.

Slowly, by drifting back to his haunts, Don convinced himself he hadn't gone missing in action.

All his friends—Maranto, Goeters, Christian—were married now, or about to be married. They threw plenty of couples parties, but Maggie was always studying or grading papers, and she rarely went to gatherings with Don. In January 1955, he enrolled in spring classes at the University of Houston. He returned to the arts beat, and his old night shift, at the *Post*. As he'd predicted, he rarely saw his wife.

His first new piece for the paper, on January 18, was a review of Jean-Paul Sartre's *The Flies* at the Alley Theatre: a "respectable" production, Don said. Though movie notes took most of his time once more, his writings for the *Post* from January to October 1955 show him battling his editors to broaden his range, covering such subjects as city planning (a speech by Richard Neutra), sacred music (a French organ recital at the First Presbyterian Church), screenwriting (a discussion with William Inge about *Bus Stop*), contemporary fiction (a review of Joyce Cary's latest novel, *Not Honour More*). Obliged to include trivia in his columns—for example, "Tiny Diva Warms Shamrock," about the dancer and baton twirler Maureen Cannon—Don nevertheless filled the entertainment pages with more and more references to high art: a stage production of *Macbeth*, Elia Kazan films. After his reading binge in Korea, he was desperate to believe he hadn't backslid. "John Wayne Goes to the Bottom" read the title of his impatient review of the movie *The Sea Chase.*

Occasionally, the paper let him out of his box to cover some of the "straight news" he'd gotten a nose for in Korea. Sometimes he worked the police beat, an experience recalled in "The Sandman" (1972):

> ... the cops decided to show ... four black kids [they'd arrested] at a press conference to demonstrate that they weren't ... beat all to rags, and that took place at four in the afternoon. I went and the kids looked OK, except for one whose teeth were out and who the cops said had fallen down the stairs. Well, we all know the falling-down-the-stairs story. . . . There weren't any TV pictures because the newspaper people always pulled out the plugs of the TV people, at important moments, in those days—it was a standard thing.

Helen Moore later recalled seeing Don at arts events and parties throughout that spring. She was married at that time to Peter Gilpin, a staffer at the *Houston Chronicle.* "[Pete and I] were always together when I saw Don," she said. "Don's wife Marilyn was never there." Helen still worked in the news and public relations department at the University of Houston, and did some teaching in the journalism school. Don took to dropping by her office, and asking her to coffee at the Cougar Den, a snack bar in the student union. He found her prettier than ever, with her hair short, casually combed. She smiled easily, a smile that barely stifled laughter. She had dark eyebrows and a slender nose.

"I began to realize he was an attractive man," she admitted later. "He not only looked older [than before], but his demeanor was also more somber."

In July, Don showed up in Helen's office and told her he was interested in a day job so he could leave the *Post.* He asked if there were any full-time positions on her staff. She informed him that she had just given notice to the university president; she was taking a job with a private advertising firm. Don drooped (to him, advertising was a "cess pool"). "Talk to Farris Block," Helen told him. Block, a former journalist, would be her replacement in the PR pool. Don said he didn't want to work for anyone else at the school, and that he'd miss his afternoon coffees with her.

Eventually, he changed his mind and *did* talk to Block. Like Don, the narrator of "See the Moon?" applies for a job at his "old school" and presents a "career plan on neatly typed pages with wide margins." The interviewer says, "You seem married, mature, malleable," then adds, "We have a spot for a poppycock man, to write the [university president's] speeches. Have you ever done poppycock?"

"I said no but maybe I could fake it. . . . [So] I wrote poppycock, sometimes cockypap." Which Don did, beginning in the fall of 1955 (though his pieces for the *Post* continued through October 2). He also became the editor of *Acta Diurna,* a weekly faculty newsletter.

Now his social circle widened to include university staff members, administrators, and teachers. Maggie still wouldn't go with him to parties. His interests dovetailed with very few of the people he met. "At four o'clock the faculty hoisted the cocktail flag. We drank daiquiris," he wrote. His colleagues nudged him in the ribs, nodded at music pounding from the hi-fi speakers, and said, " 'Listen to that bass. That's sixty watts' worth of bass, boy,' " or told him, " '[You get] a ten-percent discount on tickets for all home games.' " But Don didn't belong with these folks. Not really. He didn't listen to them. Dreaming, he withdrew and "stared at the moon's pale daytime presence."

As he would write years later, "I had never . . . [worked] in the daytime before, how was I to know how things were done in the daytime?"

That fall, in a Restoration Drama course, he met Herman Gollob, an affable fellow Texan, a Korea vet, with a passion for literature and the theater. "I'd read his [movie] reviews . . . and thought they were exceptionally trenchant and witty and graceful," Gollob recalls. "I introduced myself to him, told him I'd been a fan, and then proceeded to argue with what I recalled as his mocking assessment of *The Man from Laramie,* a western starring James Stewart."

Don hated the class they shared. Gollob liked the professor, a man who told "little whimsical jokes" and spoke of his father's love of George Bernard Shaw. Don "reviled" Gollob for his excitement in the class, and for turning his work in on time. Gollob didn't take any of this personally—Don was "unwilling to suffer fools," but he wasn't "mean-spirited."

The two friends started going to movies together, and they went to hear jazz. Gollob credits Don with teaching him about music. Always, Don kept his eyes on the drummers, gauging how much energy they expended or reserved. He raved about Sid Catlett. Catlett refused pyrotechnics. He barely moved, sitting straight on his throne. Listen, Don told Gollob. Catlett's four-bar solos, his triplets and ruffs, weren't just fills, they were *expansion* and *analysis,* linking musical themes. Style was the answer to life's stress, Don said. Style was something *clean.*

Don was "very much the glass of fashion, very Ivy League . . . the first person I'd known who wore button-down blue oxford shirts, rep ties, and tweed jackets," Gollob says. He was a "courtly guy. Always opened doors for women and walked on the outside of the street. Gentlemanly." Around this time, Don began driving an MG. "He'd bought it secondhand off some guy on campus," Gollob recalls. "It was bad-looking but I loved tooling around with him in it."

In the afternoons, after classes at UH, they'd retire to Stubby's Lounge, across the street from the campus, "a windowless concrete blockhouse with the best jukebox in town." From there, they'd make their way to the rental house Don shared with Maggie. Gollob remembers:

> ... we spent many an evening in [Don's] living room killing a fifth of Black and White, listening to Shelly Manne and Shorty Rogers and Bud Shanks and André Previn (a fantastic jazz pianist back then) and Dave Brubeck and Gerry Mulligan, descanting and descanting again on life and art (the latest Salinger story in the *New Yorker,* Robert Aldrich's scorching movie version of Odet's ... *The Big Knife*), while in the bedroom Maggie analyzed the genius of Mallarmé and Baudelaire, emerging occasionally to ask us, in a voice taut with controlled animosity, to turn down the music and lower our voices.

A few years later, in "For I'm the Boy Whose Only Joy Is Loving You" (1964), Don took a swipe at Maggie. In mock-Joycean brogue, a husband and wife banter: "Ah Martha coom now to bed there's a darlin' gul. Hump off blatherer I've no yet read me Mallarmé for this evenin'. Ooo Martha dear canna we noo let the dear lad rest this night? When th' telly's already shut doon an' th' man o' the hoose 'as a 'ard on? Don't be comin' round wit yer lewd proposals on a Tuesday night when ye know better. But Martha dear where is yer love for me . . ."

"I've never been a good drinker," Maggie says, looking back on her marriage to Don. "It's not about principles. I just can't digest alcohol very well." At the parties Don took her to, "which I have to say weren't very wild, I was the only sober person left after the first two hours, which isn't very fun. It was difficult."

"She wasn't relaxed or natural," Gollob says of Maggie. "*We* couldn't have been *more* relaxed. I will say, she was sultry-looking, had a great body and great mind. . . ."

As for alcohol: "We were all drinking," Gollob says. "Partly it was a Texas thing. Don was a bitter drinker. He drank when he was sad and it added to his gloom. When he was drunk, he could be a cold motherfucker. You did not approach him frivolously. He'd freeze you out quickly."

Gollob began dating a Rice undergraduate who happened to be one of Maggie's students. One night, in Stubby's Lounge, he admitted to the girl that he thought Maggie was a "snobbish bitch" and that it must be awful to have her for a teacher. A few days later, Gollob dropped by Don's office at UH to take him to lunch at their favorite barbecue place. "I understand you think my wife is a snobbish bitch," Don said. "My date had ratted on me, possibly because I'd had the poor taste to take her to Stubby's, not one of Houston's chic watering spots," Gollob says. Fearing a freeze-out from Don, he decided it was best to confess. "Yes, I do think she's a snobbish bitch," he replied. "Rising, [Don] patted me on the arm and said, 'So do I. In fact, I'm getting a divorce. I'll have to look for an apartment right away. Why don't we share one?' "

Despite Don's flippancy with Gollob, the decision to split from Maggie wasn't easy or made without regret. Later, he told Helen Moore he had gone to her office seeking work a few months back hoping a day job would save his marriage. He told her it was Maggie who "no longer wanted to be married."

"By the time Don came back from Korea, it was evident that our paths had diverged seriously, and we never got it back together again," Maggie explains. "I was very much into my schoolwork and the thesis.

"I think Donald always wanted two things that were incompatible, and he spent a lot of time and effort trying to reconcile the two," she says. "He wanted a bourgeois family life, like the one he'd grown up with, and at the same time he wanted a swinging bohemian life. That's one of the reasons I knew the marriage wasn't going to work. I didn't want either of those things. I wanted to go out and see the world. You know, in the fifties, most people just wanted to settle in the suburbs with two kids. In 1956, I went to France, to the University of Paris, and got a doctoral degree. I left Donald my car. In 1959, I saw him in Houston, to get the car back." She laughs as she recalls the quirky charm that drew her to Don in the first place. "He told me the car had needed two things: It needed to be painted and it needed new brakes. He couldn't afford both. So he'd gotten it repainted."

Gollob was eager to move out of his parents' place, so he and Don, along with Henry Buckley and Maurice Sumner, both graduates of the UH architecture school, rented a dilapidated Victorian-style house on Burlington near Hawthorne, just west of Main Street downtown. It was a "gothic dwelling to gladden the heart of Charles Addams," Gollob says. The guys were "too scared to unboard" the door to the attic, and "fantasized all these horrible things that were up [there]." Finally, they "made a pact that no one could leave anybody else in the house alone. It was terrifying." In retrospect, it was also like the "ultimate Barthelme story . . . funny, but dark and unknown too." Later, when city planners ran the Southwest Freeway through midtown, the house came down.

Gollob remembers Don working on a novel in the gloomy old rooms. Don told him he had already tossed two complete drafts of the project, so this was likely an evolution of the "unlove" manuscript. Gollob assumed it was "autobiographical and rich in Maggie-inspired angst." He suggested that Don had been too "extreme" in rejecting the earlier drafts. "Maybe you're too harsh a critic of your own work," he said. "Maybe you could have benefited from someone else's perspective."

"[Don] hit me with the kind of look that Hamlet must have given Claudius [when Claudius] advised him to stop mourning because it was unmanly," Gollob recalls. Don said, "Thanks so much. I'll remember that when I'm throwing this third draft into the toilet. I can see that it's full of the same self-pitying shit that smelled up the others."

From Korea, Don had written to Joe Maranto that he would probably take the novel into a third draft; that he wanted to finish it even though it wasn't likely he'd publish it. He stuck to his plan. He was teaching himself discipline, self-editing.

Otherwise, goofiness prevailed. Don entertained his housemates by acting out movies. *The Man with the Golden Arm* was one of his favorites, Gollob says—an indication, along with Don's review of *The Flies,* that he was developing an interest in existentialist fiction. Based on a Nelson Algren novel, Otto Preminger's film starred Frank Sinatra as Frankie Machine, a former card dealer and heroin addict struggling to reintegrate into society and find a new livelihood—subjects of interest to Don after his service in the army. Though he cracked up his housemates with parodies of Sinatra's anguish, it was the restraint of Sinatra's performance that impressed Don. Kim Novak's role in the movie also intrigued him: a sympathetic female, woman as savior.

Within a few months, Gollob moved out of the Burlington Street house and went to California to enroll in a fine arts program at the Pasadena Playhouse. "Don always loved Houston," Gollob says. "I never did—couldn't wait to get out of the goddamned place."

Don, with whom he stayed in touch, was "as close to a Hamlet figure as anyone I've ever known," Gollob recalls. "Hamlet's soliloquies and speeches could have sprung directly from [Don's] soul, not just the pain, the bitterness, the scorn of 'I have of late . . . lost all my mirth' . . . but the antic wit and humor of Hamlet the punster, the jiber—he had among his other talents a prodigious gift for laughter and a love of plays and players."

"[You] go to college, and if you run through one or two or three very good teachers, you're extremely lucky," Don said. He had been disappointed in the faculty at the University of Houston; he continued to take classes because he was unable to imagine anything else. Finally, in Maurice Natanson, a philosophy professor, Don found a sympathetic soul and an engaging mentor. Natanson's enthusiasms were Kierkegaard, Sartre, Husserl, and phenomenology in modern literature. He was a "wonderful guy, an excellent teacher, and I took everything," Don said. "[Because of Natanson,] what I mostly did, at school, was study philosophy."

Natanson's long career included teaching stints at the universities of Nebraska, Houston, North Carolina, and California—Santa Cruz, as well as at

Yale (he died in 1996). Eileen Pollock, a young novelist who studied with him many years after Don did, says that Natanson's knowledge of Kafka, Beckett, and Thomas Mann made him the perfect philosophy teacher for budding writers. "He was a lovely man," she recalls. In addition to sharing his love of literature, "he had a nicely old-fashioned way of making a sophomore or junior feel as if studying philosophy actually had something to do with figuring out how to live one's life"—a powerful appeal for Don after his sojourn in the army. "He had a warm, charismatic presence," Pollock says, "very rabbinical, with a full white beard, crinkly, lively eyes, and an impish smile. He spoke in this hypnotically odd cadence, drawing out some syllables, accenting others, while stroking his beard. He had a wry sense of the absurd. He took his subject seriously—and yet he didn't, perhaps because the subject itself seemed to indicate that nothing had a solid foundation beneath it."

Don was already familiar with existentialism, but Natanson excited him about it. Kierkegaard became a guiding spirit for Don. In the course of his career, he would make half a dozen direct or indirect references to Kierkegaard in his work, as well as numerous echoes of phrases, images, and ideas from Kierkegaard's writings. "Purity of heart is to will one thing," says a character in Don's story "The Leap." "No," his companion replies. "Here I differ with Kierkegaard. Purity of heart is, rather, to will several things, and not know which is the better, truer thing, and to worry about this, forever." Timidly, the first speaker asks, "Is it *permitted* to differ with Kierkegaard?" His companion replies, "Not only permitted but necessary. If you love him."

Don and his sister Joan with their
parents, Helen and Donald Sr.,
at the Texas State Fair,
Dallas, 1936. *Barthelme Estate*

Don, Houston, 1947. *Barthelme Estate*

Don, Houston, 1947. *Courtesy Beverly Arnold*

Don with his drums in the Barthelme house,
Houston, 1947. *Barthelme Estate*

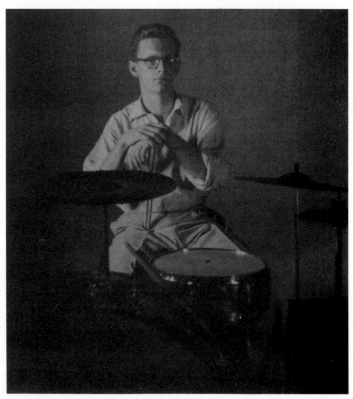

Don in the Barthelme house, Houston, 1950. *Barthelme Estate*

Don reading in the Barthelme house, Houston 1952.
Barthelme Estate

Don and his brothers—Steven in the foreground, Peter and Frederick standing behind Don—Houston, 1952. *Barthelme Estate*

Interior of the Barthelme house at North Wynden Drive, Peter reading in the foreground, Steven in the background, Houston, 1951. *Barthelme Estate*

George Christian and Don in their office at *The Houston Post*, 1952.
Barthelme Estate

Don and his father, Houston, 1952.
Barthelme Estate

Don with his first wife, Marilyn Marrs, Houston, 1952. *Barthelme Estate*

Don in Korea, 1953. *Courtesy Marilyn Gillet*

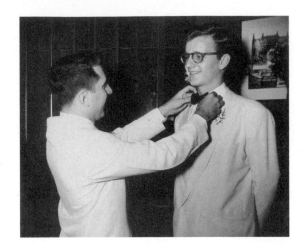

Joe Maranto helping
Don prepare for his first
wedding, Dallas, 1952.
Courtesy Marilyn Gillet

Barthelme family portrait—foreground: Steven and Frederick; second row: Joan, Marilyn
Marrs, Don, and Helen; back row: Peter and Donald Sr., Houston, 1954. *Barthelme Estate*

Don's second wife, Helen Moore,
Houston, early 1950s. *Barthelme Estate*

Don, Houston, 1958. *Barthelme Estate*

THE OBJECT

Despite her writing, editing, and teaching experience at the University of Houston, Helen Moore was earning, when she left the institution, less than Farris Block offered Don as a new hire with little PR experience. When she told the school's president, A. D. Bruce, that she planned to take a job with the Boone and Cummings advertising firm, he made a tepid counteroffer in an attempt to keep her. She informed him that his figures fell far short of her new salary—nearly twice what she'd made at UH. "But that's more than some of our *male* faculty members earn!" he said.

She had tried to get a job with the newspapers, but for most women in the 1950s, journalism was a closed shop. The city's dailies, and the smaller papers, were boys' clubs. Helen's husband, Peter Gilpin, a staffer at the *Chronicle,* took long lunches with his comrades once they'd met the hectic morning deadlines. Alcohol oiled their talk of wives and kids. Women were rarely allowed at the table. Over at the *Post,* Don, George Christian, and an all-male crew had always worked at night, getting home at dawn, a routine Don was grateful to leave behind.

Television newsrooms were as unfriendly to women as the papers. In 1953, Helen had helped the university launch the nation's first educational TV station, KUHT. She had written much of its PR

14

material. But the school's radio and television department was all male, as were the station's news writers and on-air personalities.

Because of television, advertising was booming. The big firms needed talent, so their doors were open to women, and the salaries were competitive. Helen joined Boone and Cummings. Shortly thereafter, she moved into an apartment with one if its executives, Betty Jane Mitchell. Helen's marriage to Gilpin had foundered because of his drinking. "I felt quite alone in my marriage," Helen says. The new job and her friendship with Mitchell were gifts.

Meanwhile, Don had taken charge of the faculty newsletter she had edited at the university. In her memoir, Helen claims that she started the newsletter. Lee Pryor, a UH English professor, says *he* founded it. In any case, the publication did not become significant until Don took the reins. Right away, he set out to broaden the newsletter's range and widen its readership. On February 27, 1956, he sent a memo to Douglas McClaury in University Development, arguing that *Acta Diurna*'s format should be revised so it was not just an "internal news organ," but, rather, was a "p. r. medium for outside distribution." He wanted to change the layout and make it standard magazine size. The cost of the new *Acta* would be about $77.50 per week, as opposed to the old budget of $47.50, because of better paper, an increased press run, and more mailings. The administration was slow to respond. Don kept pushing. A month later, he wrote to Pat Nicholson in the Office of Development: "As to material used [in the proposed new *Acta*], articles written by members of the faculty on subjects of wide general interest could supplement regular news and feature stories. Publication in this format might be an especially valuable method of presenting our faculty to the community and to their colleagues."

While *Acta* had been a small newsletter about staff activities on campus, Don envisioned his editorship as an opportunity to become Harold Ross. He hoped to learn from the pieces he edited, to advance his education, and to make contacts in publishing, academia, and other fields. Within a few months, his tenacity had convinced the university to take a chance on a multidisciplinary journal. In a PR statement, he announced that in September 1956, the University of Houston planned to publish "as part of our public relations program the first issue of a monthly magazine which will run from 16 to 24 pages." He solicited articles on and off campus. He convinced Maurice Natanson to contribute a piece on self-understanding, and he wrote Dr. Richard A. Younger, of the Harris County Historical Association, requesting permission to publish Younger's talk "The Grand Jury on the Frontier," which he had delivered in Houston. "The level of readership we are aiming at will be roughly that of *Harper's* or the *Atlantic*," Don said.

• • •

"Kierkegaard is Hegel's punishment," Natanson might say to start a class. Or: "Philosophy, for Husserl, is the search for radical certitude." As Natanson presented them, philosophers were romantic figures, just like the jazzmen Don heard on Dowling Street. "[After] Sartre . . . there are few philosophers alive today who qualify for a magisterial role. The elders are not being replaced," Natanson said. "Instead, there is a profusion of professors. Whatever esteem philosophy may have had in earlier times has been eclipsed by the demands of immediacy: the realms of politics, economics, and history. . . ."

Natanson's wistfulness—his longing for philosophy on a grand scale—appealed to Don; it matched his feeling that previous generations had chewed up the landscape, leaving scraps for their followers to harvest. Something vital had leaked from the world. Papa's wars had been spectacular; in their wake, only minor skirmishes remained. "Although it has always been known that philosophy bakes no bread, it was assumed that it could occasionally supply a little yeast," Natanson said, adding that philosophy was virtually invisible now in Western Europe and America.

Stubbornly, Don attached himself to the discipline's marginal status, the way he'd embraced Baudelaire, Mallarmé, and a literary tradition with limited public appeal. Like Kierkegaard, he disdained the "untruths" of crowds. At the same time, a sweet optimism—a pinch of his father's crusading spirit—encouraged him to believe that intellectually rigorous art could improve *everyone's* lives. Natanson kindled this fire in him.

Prior to Kierkegaard, the "story of . . . philosophy is the story of the loss of individuality," Natanson taught. By contrast, Kierkegaard's "burden" is the "exploration of the Self." He went on to explain: "By the Self Kierkegaard means the 'inwardness' of the individual, that unique aspect of each of us [that balances] freedom and necessity." (English translations of Kierkegaard's works were still fresh in the fifties; Walter Lowrie had begun issuing his versions in the late 1930s.) "Paradox is the booby-trap into which we plunge [with Kierkegaard], just as Alice went down the rabbit hole," said Natanson. Kierkegaard's writings contain "odd inner ironies" and fantastic "humor" that celebrates the Self's contradictions: "One does not know for sure at any point whose side the laugh is on."

In Kafka, "Kierkegaard found his novelist." Kafka gave narrative shape to the horror of feeling "condemned" in a godless world. Prior to Kafka, Dostoevsky had located life's meaninglessness in consciousness. "I was conscious every moment of so many elements in myself," says the unnamed narrator of *Notes from Underground*. "I felt them simply swarming in me." Worse, every thought he has, every phrase he utters, he has stolen from

some other source; the ubiquity of language, its overuse, leaves him skepti-
cal of ideas. Urgencies (the world is never still), endless possibilities, and
the Self's confusions necessitate action *in the moment,* though what to do
remains a mystery.

For Natanson, it was Edmund Husserl, born in 1859 in what is now the
Czech Republic, who best expressed the weight of the moment. At every instant, Husserl said, consciousness remakes the world. Consider a chair. A
chair can be a place to sit, or a surface on which to stack books, or it can be
torn apart, rearranged, and turned into a sculpture. Or it can be made into a
sculpture by virtue of our agreeing to call it one. Depending on our *inten-
tion,* the chair has several possibilities, and its actualization here, now, in
one shape, serving one particular function, is merely one choice among
many. When we turn to an object, we're aware of our awareness of it. Whatever we make of a thing, our choice reveals our intentionality. By studying
objects, consciousness discovers its *form.* It haunts the world as the spirit of
what the world might be, or what it might still become.

In class, Natanson pointed out that *fiction* is an object in the world, made
of words. What *is* fiction, he said, but an invitation to consider the real by
way of the unreal, to examine possibility for a clearer grasp of the actual.
This is fiction's strategy. "What if *this* happened?" it asks. "Or *that*?"

Just as we can seize a chair and remake it, fiction seizes *us.* The object of
fiction's intentionality is human nature, human experience.

Following Husserl's example, Sartre used fiction to trace consciousness:
In Sartre's work, the "chain of thought [that was] stated with agonizing force
by Kierkegaard," and was echoed in Dostoevsky and Kafka, "comes to artistic fruition," Natanson said.

What did he mean by this? In his biography of Sartre, Ronald Hayman reported that Sartre sought a "means of blending philosophical reflection
with the direct transcription . . . of personal experience," a literary form that
would bypass the "familiar opposition between realism and idealism, af-
firming both the supremacy of reason and the reality of the visible world."
Sartre wanted to be able to sit in a sidewalk café, contemplate a chair or the
drink in front of him, and call it "philosophy." Husserl's phenomenological
method was a revelation to him. So was Hemingway's prose. Papa made "insignificant-seeming details significant" without relying on subjectivity,
Hayman wrote. "Objects in his narratives were conspicuously solid, though
he offered no more than would have been apparent to the character he was
presenting."

For example, in "A Clean, Well-Lighted Place," Hemingway's lack of metaphors and similes forces the story's objects to emerge as themselves, in and
of themselves, in all their raw *thingness*: ". . . the leaves of the tree made
[shadows] against the electric light" and "The waiter poured on into the

glass so that the brandy slopped over and ran down the stem into the top saucer on the pile."

A phenomenological impulse lies behind Hemingway's celebrated prose style—an obsessive focus on objects, stripped of mental baggage—and Hemingway elevated it to a literary aesthetic.

Sartre extended Hemingway's method. In *Nausea* (1938), his narrator, Roquentin, says of a chestnut tree, its presence "pressed itself against my eyes." Usually, "existence hides itself," but now "existence had unveiled itself" to him. "It had lost the harmless look of an abstract category: it was the very paste of things, this [tree] root was kneaded into existence."

Seeing to the "very paste of things" and choosing an immediate response to it is an assertion of value, an assumption of responsibility for one's self and one's fellows, Natanson said.

"A man is involved in life, leaves his impress on it, and outside of that there is nothing," Sartre wrote. Therefore, *everything* is at stake in every moment. What Natanson made his students read, from Kierkegaard to Sartre, was a literature of moments. Don absorbed it all: Kierkegaard's hidden narrators, his ironies and fragments, Dostoevsky's self-consciousness, Kafka's paradoxes, Sartre's *things*. These writers were not interested in characterization, setting, or the development of action. Rather, they built word objects that engaged consciousness directly, so that consciousness could engage itself.

Busy with the magazine, Natanson's classes, and speechwriting for the school president, Don didn't spend much time at the house on Burlington Street, especially after Herman Gollob left for California. In the evenings, he'd go to movies or plays or to an occasional dinner party. One night in March 1956, he ran into Helen Moore at a dinner given by a couple they knew from the university. In the living room, after the meal, they withdrew into a corner and caught up with each other. Don had heard from mutual friends that Helen had separated from Pete Gilpin, and she knew of his split from Maggie. He asked Helen if she had any hope for reconciliation with her husband. She told him she only wanted to be free. "With scarcely a pause in our conversation, Don startled me by asking if I would marry him in the event I should get a divorce," Helen says. "He was quite serious. At the moment, I had not the least doubt about his seriousness. . . . I was not at all prepared for such a proposal. I could only reply that I felt he was too young for me—as in fact I did. Then addressing me as 'old girl' for the rest of the evening, Don . . . set about to persuade me that he was indeed as mature as I."

Don had been attracted to Helen for some time. Is it a stretch to think that talk of *the moment,* making a choice, in Natanson's classes, affected his behavior with her at the dinner that night, particularly as he had felt the need of a "master plan" after Korea, and had seen that plan vanish?

In any event, the morning after the party, Don phoned Helen at her office and asked her out to a restaurant that night. She accepted. "I never imagined falling in love with him," she says. "I had not yet made a decision about my marriage even though I had been distraught over it for a long time. This was the 1950s, and divorce was a difficult alternative to an unhappy marriage. At the same time, I had made a big career change the previous year and until that week would not have taken seriously the possibility of leaving one marriage and beginning another."

Don spun her around town in his new Austin-Healey sports convertible, treated her to "romantic and often expensive" restaurants, took walks with her at night down tree-lined avenues near the Rice campus. The apartment she lived in with Betty Jane Mitchell, on Harold Street, was close to his place on Burlington. It was in a big house that had been converted into flats; the tenants shared a swimming pool out back. Often, Don strolled over to see Helen. He would sit with her on the terrace by the pool, recounting his overseas experiences, speaking of his desire to return to Japan someday, of his dreams of being a writer. She got the impression he was "excited and happy" about the challenge of turning *Acta Diurna* into a respectable magazine.

One evening, she and Don invited friends from the UH news service to an all-night swim party. On other occasions, they went to dinner parties with Helen's sister, Margo Vandruff and her husband, Roy, or they ate with George Christian and Mary Blount, who were engaged to be married. They saw Joe and Maggie Maranto. Don told Helen he felt envious of "Georgia and Pat Goeters [, who] sat close to each other when they were in [a] car and . . . held hands in public. He wanted that, too. He was as demonstrative as he could be without causing us embarrassment," Helen says.

Pat Goeters "liked Helen a lot" and Maggie Maranto thought of her as an "earth mother" for Don, though she fretted that he had latched on to her on the "rebound" from Maggie Marrs. On visits to town, Herman Gollob found Helen to be a "good, intelligent person"; though not "inspired," she was "wonderful, warm, outgoing."

Throughout the spring and summer of 1956, Don courted Helen. They attended concerts by the Houston Symphony in the Miller Outdoor Theatre in Hermann Park, went to movies and plays, or spent evenings in friends' apartments discussing performances they'd seen or books they'd read. Helen loved the intimacy of these evenings, so different from the "lavish social events that were popular with many of the journalists" in town. "Perhaps as important as anything else, no one was particularly interested in talking about sports," an immense relief to her.

Don had found an object of adoration. He focused on her with phenomenological (not to say *phenomenal*) fervor. He studied her carefully, cherish-
ing her good sense, her humor and beauty, gauging her mysteries and
potentials. Helen felt "uneasy" with his unreal expectations about the "possibility of perfection" in marriage. Still, "being with Don was so intensely romantic," she says, "I soon believed that the life he imagined for us was
indeed possible."

THE MANY FACES OF LOVE

Then wear the gold hat, if that will move her;
    If you can bounce high, bounce for her too,
Till she cry, "Lover, gold-hatted, high-bouncing lover,
    I must have you!"

Don was fond of quoting *The Great Gatsby*'s epigraph to Helen, perhaps for the literary game in it as much as for its sentiments. Fitzgerald attributed the lines to Thomas Parke D'Invilliers, a fictional character, a campus wit in Fitzgerald's first novel, *This Side of Paradise.* D'Invilliers publishes densely layered poems in the college literary journal that puzzle his classmates. "What the hell is [this poem] all about?" Amory Blaine complains. "I swear I don't get him at all, and I'm a literary bird myself."

In one of the novel's funniest scenes, D'Invilliers disparages American writers. "[They're] not producing among 'em one story or novel that will last ten years," he says. "Every author ought to write every book as if he were going to be beheaded the day he finished it." In short, D'Invilliers is Bardley. (Fitzgerald based D'Invilliers on his friend, the poet John Peale Bishop, whom he found to be "exquisite, anachronistic, and decadent." Bardley to a tee.)

Helen recalls that, along with *The Great Gatsby,* Don read at the height of their courtship a book called *The Many Faces of Love,* by

Hubert Benoit, a psychiatrist strongly influenced by Zen Buddhism. Perhaps because of the time American soldiers spent in Asia, and their exposure to new ideas, Eastern religions were getting a lot of Western press—a trend that would continue into the 1960s—and Zen, in particular, attracted those who saw in its stoicism affinities with existentialism.

Moving from a failed marriage into a hopeful new romance, Don sought certainty in what he would later call the "incredibly delicate and dangerous business" of love. "[He] desired both the beauty of the mythic Helen and the promise of his own 'Daisy' [Buchanan]," Helen says. "The 'mystery' of a girl became a recurring theme for Don, but I'm not certain that he ever fully accepted the notion that in marriage it would be impossible for her to retain the mystery for which he yearned."

Benoit lingered on love's mysteries. Words are "snares and often lead us into error," he wrote: Above all, the "word 'love' is one that conceals the most dangerous pitfalls." His skepticism, and his sense of language as a tricky sign system, appealed to Don, as did the book's format. It takes the shape of a conversation among The Author, a Young Woman, and a Young Man. Its exploration of love, sex, and marriage in Q & A form recalled the *Baltimore Catechism,* but without the punitive overtones. It also resembled Kierkegaard's *Either/Or,* a dialectic on marriage written shortly after Kierkegaard's failed engagement.

Benoit echoed Kierkegaard in a chapter called "The Fear of Loving," which Don underlined extensively. "As soon as I am in erotic love," Benoit wrote, I become aware of "my temporal self," aware of " 'existing' in time, the time in which [I] will have to die." This "great central question, of existence or non-existence, of being affirmed or denied by existence, arises particularly and intensely in erotic love, concerned as it is with man's highest organic function, that of sex."

A person of great imagination, for whom awareness of death is keen, will have difficulty satisfying his desires "without coming into collision" with an almost paralyzing fear, Benoit contended, tying language to the fear of death. Words may be "snares," but they are our only means of giving "intellectual recognition" to our needs. If we are conflicted or frightened, we may *refuse* "plain language." We are likely to express ourselves indirectly so as not to expose—to ourselves and others—what we really want, or fear.

Either/Or, Kierkegaard's tortured meditation on marriage, is a prime example of a refusal of "plain language." He published it under a pseudonym and stocked it with voices speaking indirectly through allusions and aesthetic references. Don was reading *Either/Or* with Maurice Natanson around the time he read *The Many Faces of Love,* and it became a seminal book for him. "By bypassing" a subject in writing, "you are able to present it in a much stronger way than if you confronted it directly," Don once said, indicating what he had learned from Kierkegaard. "I mean there are some things that have to be done by backing into them . . . indirection is a way of presenting the thing that somehow works more strongly."

Later, in Kierkegaardian spirit, Don called one of his earliest successful stories "Hiding Man." The title remained an apt description of most of his narrators.

The Many Faces of Love was part of Don's enormous personal library. Natanson's classes added new volumes to his shelves, but in the spring and summer of 1956, he sold hundreds of books to used-book stores to pay for his "romantic" meals with Helen. "He really wanted nothing less than an ideal relationship," she said.

"I was startled one day when [Don] said that we 'should have met and married when we were nineteen . . . we missed a lot by not having those years together,' " Helen said. He would have liked to "erase our earlier marriages, especially mine. He wanted to recover the past, what he thought of as our 'innocent years.' "

Helen remained uncertain. Don pressed hard for a marriage date, even though neither of their divorces was final. One August night, on the terrace by the pool at Helen's place, she agreed to mid-October.

Since returning from Korea, Don had rushed to align his life just so, like a man desperate to repair something shattered. But whatever image he held of an "ideal relationship," it did not involve adjustment, falling in line, or caution.

An interest in pop culture, antiauthoritarian sentiments, and sexual liberation was stirring in America. In 1956, Allen Ginsberg's *Howl* was published. Elvis Presley's pelvis caused a buzz. The previous year, *Blackboard Jungle* and *Rebel Without a Cause* hit movie theaters. Jasper Johns painted the American flag as if it were an advertising logo. Less noticed—but noted by Don—was the publication a few years later of Grace Paley's short story collection *The Little Disturbances of Man,* which celebrated the overlooked lives of mothers and wives.

Don wasn't wild about the Beats; in any case, the Beats were not yet a coherent cultural force. Rock and roll was trifling next to jazz. No youth movement existed, no specific battle cry against traditional values. But Don's vast reading, and his experience as a journalist, had taught him to notice signs of change.

He wasn't alone. In 1955, Pauline Kael, who would one day join Don as a *New Yorker* writer, published an essay entitled "The Glamour of Delinquency," in which she excoriated the "prosperous, empty, uninspiring uniformity" of American life. The modernist dream of improving society through better surroundings had failed to erase the routine of "a dull job, a dull life, television, freezers, babies and baby sitters, a guaranteed annual wage, taxes, social security, hospitalization insurance, and death." What tipped Kael off to rising middle-class misery? The movies. "When the delinquent becomes the hero in our films," she wrote, "it is because the image of instinctive rebellion expresses something in many people that they don't dare express." She didn't fully endorse *On the Waterfront, East of Eden,* or *The Blackboard Jungle,* but she understood their importance. Ultimately, the pictures failed for her in not plumbing the issues they raised: "It's a social lie to pretend that these kids are only in conflict with themselves or that they merely need love and under-standing. Instinctively, the audience knows better."

As a journalist, Don had reviewed enough movies to appreciate the undigested longings buried in Hollywood formulas. What characterizes much of his fiction, and art that critics would later call "postmodern," is a tendency to view culture as a series of signs—guideposts to the nation's hidden roads—and to suggest possible (but not authoritative) readings of the messages written there. The signs are incomplete, hastily made, and they could be wrong.

One afternoon in August, Don dropped by Guy's Newsstand at the corner of Main and Blodgett. The place smelled of newspaper ink, car exhaust, and sweet cigar smoke. Among German and French cinema journals, Don found a copy of *Theatre Arts.* In it was *Waiting for Godot.* He stood there and read the whole thing.

That evening, when he took Helen out to dinner, he brought the magazine with him. She had already read the play. "I found it exciting but did not foresee the implications for Don," she says. "He was deeply moved and ecstatic about the language. . . . Each time we were in a bookstore after this, Don looked for work by Beckett and immediately read whatever he found. It seemed that from the day he discovered *Godot,* Don believed he could write the fiction he imagined." It would be heavily ironic, and he could "use his wit and intellect in a way that would satisfy him."

Of course, Don's breakthrough wasn't that easy. "The problem is . . . to do something that's credible after Beckett, as Beckett had to do something that was credible after Joyce," he said years later.

Initially, though, the *excitement*! *Waiting for Godot* showed Don that philosophy could become drama, almost directly, without the interference of plot, setting, and so on. By stripping away fiction's stock devices, Beckett focused on consciousness. He could animate the intentionality at the heart of awareness. "Nothing to be done," Gogo says. Standing around, vainly anticipating some purpose, is "awful," yet, as Pozzo says, we "don't seem to be able to depart"—that is, to get out of our chattering heads. When nothing matters, and nothing's to be done, consciousness will find something to do anyway in order to keep itself busy.

Gogo and Didi, bored senseless, argue for no apparent reason. "That's the idea, let's contradict each other!" Gogo says. "It will pass the time."

The audience waits with Didi and Gogo; then the cycle of waiting repeats, an interminable expectation of—what? We don't know any more than the characters do. The play wraps us in the boredom of routine, then unexpectedly shifts to reveal objects and bodies *as they are,* stripped of our trained perceptions of them. They stand starkly in all their wonder and terror—the "essential," Beckett wrote, "the extra-temporal."

Friends of Beckett said that the dialogues between Didi and Gogo resembled the exchanges Beckett had with his wife:

> I sometimes wonder if we wouldn't have been better off alone, each one for himself. We weren't made for the same road.
>> It's not certain.
>> No, nothing is certain.
>> We can still part, if you think it would be better.
>> It's not worth while now.
>> No, it's not worth while now.

Two more of the many faces of love.

FORUM

Don wasn't writing much, but his discovery of Beckett and his philosophical studies were guiding him away from vague attempts at an "unlove" story. He was forming a firmer aesthetic. He grounded his magazine editing in philosophy, too, especially in existentialism as it evolved under Jean-Paul Sartre.

Sartre's influence in America is hard to measure. In the forties and fifties, *Time* and *Harper's Bazaar* ran pieces on existentialism. The word "today refers to faddism," Maurice Natanson complained. But when Sartre and Simone de Beauvoir visited New York City in the 1940s, the intellectuals there, led by Hannah Arendt, gave them a cool reception. Sartre had declared himself an atheist, but Arendt and her circle traced his ideas to Kierkegaard's apolitical Christianity. In addition, Arendt saw Sartre as an apologist for the Soviet Union.

In Manhattan, Sartre sought the nitty-gritty of American culture: the vitality of jazz, Harlem, popular movies, novels by James M. Cain, John Steinbeck, and Richard Wright—raw, passionate writers, to whom the New York intellectuals felt vastly superior. What Sartre interpreted as bold American energy, the Old Left regarded as lowbrow, and they questioned his taste.

If existentialism didn't take with Arendt's crowd, or with most American academics, it had a stronger and longer-lasting effect on American fiction. Among others, Saul Bellow, Richard Wright, and

Ralph Ellison were intrigued by Sartre's thinking. So was Harold Rosenberg, though he never used the word *existential* in any of his art criticism. Rosenberg would exert a strong personal influence on Don. But already, in the mid-1950s, Don was mapping a steady route.

The first issue of the new *Acta Diurna*–renamed *Forum*–appeared in September 1956 "in spite of every imaginable obstacle–a scarcity of money, faculty indifference, and very little editorial talent other than [Don's] own," Helen says. Don's desire to make the journal interdisciplinary ruffled the university's bureaucrats. Even more outrageously, he wanted to solicit articles from nonacademic writers.

The debut–made up mostly of contributions from UH faculty–fell short of Don's hopes. Natanson's piece, "Defining the Two Worlds of Man," on the relationship of philosophy to science (accompanied by a Ben Shahn sketch of a man holding his head in his hands), was exemplary, but on the whole, the articles were disappointing. Still, they covered a remarkably wide range of subjects–photography, television, engineering, music, art, and history.

As he laid out the issue, Don wrestled with the fear that his wife would not grant a divorce in time for him to marry Helen when he'd planned. Maggie had received a Fulbright Fellowship. She suggested postponing the divorce until after she returned from France. Finally, though, after much back-and-forth, she agreed to move ahead. Helen's divorce from Peter Gilpin was finalized on October 5. "Don was concerned that his mother should understand that we both had grounds for divorce, reasons acceptable to her, although not to the Catholic church," Helen said later. More than anything, "Don seemed to want . . . to live as if neither of us had been previously married." He insisted that she drop the name Gilpin and restore her surname to Moore. "I had no doubt that he was trying to change the past."

On October 12, at the First Unitarian Church, Don and Helen were married. The timing, so soon after their divorces, convinced them to downplay the event. George Christian and Helen's youngest sister, Odell Pauline Moore, were the attendants. Otherwise, only family filled the seats.

That night, the couple stayed in Don's apartment on Hawthorne Street, listening to jazz and drinking champagne. Helen recalled:

> Don had filled the entire apartment with flowers. There were huge bouquets wherever I looked, on the tables, on the floor, upstairs as well as downstairs. On the previous weekend, Don had painted some of the rooms, and then on the day of our wedding he spent hours cleaning the house and making other preparations. Later, I found [his] list of things to do that day.

The next morning ... we drove to New Orleans for our honeymoon. Before we left, Don gathered up all the flowers and took them next door to our neighbor, an attractive young woman and the mother of two small children.

In the French Quarter, the couple listened to jazz at Pete Fountain's, and to the Preservation Band (though Preservation Hall had not yet been opened as a venue for musicians). They drank hurricanes at Pat O'Brien's, ate lunch at the Court of Two Sisters, had dinner at Antoine's, and beignets at the French Market. They sat in Jackson Square, watching people and pigeons flock around St. Louis Cathedral. Even in the 1950s, these pastimes were standard tourist fare, and they were the kinds of things Don tended to mock. Many years later, he disparaged New Orleans jazz as the worst sort of treacle.

Within a few days, Don and Helen returned to Houston, and Don was back on the job. He insisted they live off his university salary, and asked Helen not to look for work. When, after several months at home, she became restless, he urged her to develop a newspaper column that might be syndicated, something that would muster her "authority" and "clear ... distinct ideas." For three months, she tried, halfheartedly, to compile material for a column, but she decided she was "not interested in writing anything that [would] appeal to a broad newspaper audience."

Meanwhile, "Don's writing consisted almost solely of the work that he was doing for the university," she said. "Although he usually had some kind of manuscript in progress, he had very little time for writing fiction and seldom worked on it. He kept this manuscript and anything else creative ... in a single letter-size file folder that he sometimes carried back and forth to the office."

Bored, Helen enrolled in philosophy and art classes at UH. She fantasized with Don about attending an Ivy League school where he could concentrate on philosophy and she could earn a doctorate in literature, but neither of them looked into the possibility. Between classes, she shopped and tried to become a gourmet cook. Don designed their living space. He painted the apartment white, with the exception of one wall, which he covered in redwood paneling. He bought a chest of drawers for the bedroom and finished it with walnut stain; for the living room, he purchased a Danish walnut couch and chair. He built redwood bookshelves. "Don had no desire to own possessions for the sake of possessions," Helen wrote. Unlike his father, "he was not compelled to add or change anything" once a place was furnished. "[In] creating a comfortable, handsome ... space, Don thought only of the present. If we did not have enough room or there was some other reason to give up unnecessary furnishings ... he would give up whatever seemed appropriate, even recordings and books [including Helen's Steinbeck collection.]" Helen said he "did so with little sense of loss."

Helen wished for more furniture, "even a little clutter," but Don had a "clearly defined notion of what a room or house should look like." She deferred to his austerity. At his suggestion, she took up sewing, though the idea was foreign to her; she discovered it was easy to make bedspreads and curtains.

Most of all, Don was adamant that she jettison items she had shared with Peter Gilpin.

During the week, they ate at home, where Helen cooked the meals. Don cleaned up afterward and generally straightened the apartment. After dinner, they'd listen to Maria Callas or bebop on their hi-fi, lying on a rug near the speakers. Don would tell Helen who played the instruments on every jazz recording. On the weekends, they went for lunch at Alfred's Delicatessen on Rice Boulevard or the El Patio Mexican Restaurant on Kirby Drive. They went to movies, plays, concerts. Saturday afternoons were for browsing the bookshops—Guy's, Brown's, Rita Cobler's. On Sundays, they'd eat a late breakfast, listen to Bach, especially the Concertos for Two Harpsichords, or Gregorian chants. In the early afternoon, they drove to Don's parents' house. "At first, I found these visits uncomfortable," Helen admitted later, "chiefly because of harsh arguments between Don and his father." Usually, the get-togethers began pleasantly enough, "with Don laughing at his father's adventures"—battles with university administrators or clients, including Bud Adams, later the owner of the Houston Oilers (Barthelme designed Adams's Petroleum Center). Don would talk about *Forum.* Helen said that although "these conversations were largely between Don and his father . . . I was struck by the repartee . . . among the entire family, including Peter, who was in his last year at St. Thomas High School in 1956 and planning to enter Cornell University the following year." In describing the family, Helen wrote, "Rick [was] a handsome youth whose rebellious years were just beginning. Joan's wit, like Don's, was sharp and sometimes biting when directed at her father. Don's mother . . . an especially attractive woman . . . was articulate and witty but always kind." Steve was nine in 1956, and treated with "special affection" by the family.

Always at some point just before dinner, during a brief "cocktail hour," as a soft symphony unfolded on the record player, Don and his dad "began to disagree about something." They argued over "ideas or writers"; his father "disapproved of Don's interest in the 'new' literature, and was not interested in reading the avant-garde work with which Don could identify." They also differed on "how to rear the younger sons. Don felt his father was too rigid in the rules he set for Pete and Frederick. [He] believed that his father's continual disapproval [was] harmful."

Despite her discomfort, Helen saw that the "brilliant, witty afternoons and evenings" at the Barthelme home "gave Don's life a dimension that he could not find anywhere else." His disagreements with his father "emerged from the forthrightness of their relationship." From his father, he had inherited an "inflexible will and [the] ability to challenge anyone at all."

On the couple's first Thanksgiving together, Helen baked a turkey and they invited Henry Buckley, one of Don's old roommates, to eat with them. Right after Christmas, they threw their first party. Over a hundred people—from the university, the *Post,* the advertising world—jammed their apartment. They were ready "to boast" of their marriage.

Their friends included the Marantos, George and Mary Christian, Pat Goeters and his wife, Georgia, who had their first son by now, Helen's sister Margo and her husband, Roy, and new acquaintances they'd made in the local art world: Jim Love, a sculptor working with found materials, Robert Morris and Guy Johnson, painters who mixed straightforward landscapes with irrealism. Johnson taught art classes at Lee College in Baytown, an oil-refining center on the Gulf Coast. Often, Don and Helen drove down to dinner with Johnson and his wife, Nancy. "It was at their home that we first heard a recording of Kurt Weill and Bertolt Brecht's *The Rise and Fall of the City of Mahagonny,*" Helen recalled. They bought two of Johnson's paintings, their first art purchases together. One featured a solitary guitar player sitting on a desolate coastal shoreline.

At the heart of these friendships was a yearning for cultural excitement. Houston wasn't New York, but it wasn't a backwater, either. It was brash and fast, and there was plenty of money in Houston. Sometimes at work, Don and his friends suffered isolation (Beckett? Brecht? What the hell are you talking about?), but they had each other, and they felt a powerful sense of possibility.

Don was especially happy that Helen got along so well with his dad, who amused her. She wasn't intimidated by him. One of his favorite pastimes, during family visits, was showing his slides. One Sunday afternoon, he slipped in a picture of Don's first wife. Helen didn't blink. By staying calm, she seems to have passed a test, and he moved on without comment. Later, at her request, he designed, free of charge, a building for her friend Betty Jane Mitchell's ad agency. Don was flabbergasted. The old man never worked without a commission. "He likes you," Don concluded.

Don wrote to small businesses, larger companies, and arts organizations, soliciting ads for *Forum.* In the spring of 1957, he claimed that *Forum* had "at present a circulation of 3,000."

On March 13, he contacted Dr. William J. Handy at the University of Texas, seeking an article. The letter served as a template for his requests.

"The magazine is, in a sense, experimental in character, in that the audience for which it is published differs somewhat from that of most university quarterlies," he said. "The people we are trying to reach are, largely, graduates of colleges, in responsible positions, who have allowed their intellectual ties with the universities to lapse or become crusted over, but at the same time are eager for the kind of special knowledge and insight to be found in the scholarly community. This group, numerically large, represents an audience and a need that the scholarly community cannot easily ignore." He added, "Unfortunately, we cannot compete with other journals in terms of compensation."

Pat Goeters and Henry Buckley, now working as architects, designed covers for the first two issues. Most of the contents still came from University of Houston professors: a piece on "alienation" in the novels of William Faulkner, a study of rattlesnake venom, a discussion of "social motivation analysis." Don contributed an essay called a "A Note on Elia Kazan," in which he argued that the unfettered emotions in Kazan's films were a response to the "crucial problem posed for imaginative literature . . . by the widespread public acceptance of the 'new sciences' of sociology and psychology." He quipped that "sound [psychological] motivation is now required even for song cues in musical comedy." While noting that Method acting and Marlon Brando were somehow "right . . . for this time," he stated that "Method actors do not fare well . . . in high comedy or expressionistic drama, where manner is valued above psychological realism."

While generally lauding Kazan's craft, Don concluded that the "wordlessness and frustration" in his actors' performances "seem overwhelmingly images of helplessness, a universal lostness in the face of an existence that is complex and unforgiving."

Steeped in existentialism—and moving far beyond film reviewing—Don established terms here that would define his fiction: the recognition that form is not a given, that it is buffeted by social developments, that it is time-dependent and that it can lose its power. He believed that style and manner are more central to art's effects than content.

He read widely in popular and academic journals, seeking writers and subjects for *Forum.* He had always prided himself on being a quick study; when he started at the *Post,* he and George Christian had joked that "given forty-five minutes, they could master anything."

He wrote to Leslie Fiedler, then teaching at the University of Montana, to solicit an article on J. D. Salinger. And he noticed the work of a young writer named Walker Percy. On March 12, 1957, he wrote to Percy, "Your recent articles in *Partisan Review* and *Commonweal* . . . especially 'The Man on the Train,' represent the kind of thing in which we are particularly interested." "The Man on the Train" explored existentialist themes in American landscapes. Along with his letter, Don sent Percy copies of the first two issues of *Forum.* Percy responded on March 26: "*Forum* is most attractive—and original (Rattle snakes and existentialism!). Liked articles on Kazan and consumer behavior. Would like to see more—to get a better feel of what you're trying to do."

Don felt an immediate link with Percy: Both men had been raised as Catholics, both were immersed in Kierkegaard, and both looked to popular culture for signs of the nation's health. But many weeks would pass before Don got back to Percy. Helen had discovered she was pregnant.

One day in March, she was home alone and began to hemorrhage. She tried to phone her doctor, but without success. She reached Don at the university; he called one of their neighbors and asked her to look after Helen until he could get home. By now, Helen was dangerously weak. She later recalled that "in Houston, a city ordinance prohibited ambulances from carrying a pregnant woman to the hospital. A pregnancy or miscarriage did not qualify as an emergency."

Don phoned his father, whose architectural offices on Brazos Street were near the apartment. He got to Helen right away. Her neighbor had a friend who pulled some strings and managed to lure an ambulance. Don arrived in time to help the attendants carry his wife down the apartment steps on a stretcher. On the way to St. Joseph's Hospital, she began to lose consciousness. Don pleaded with the driver to go faster, but he refused to break city rules and turn on the siren. Dutifully, he stopped at all the traffic lights. Helen arrived at St. Joseph's with a frighteningly low pulse, but she recovered quickly under the doctors' care. Don implored her not to worry about the miscarriage, saying they would have plenty of chances to have children.

THE PSYCHOLOGY OF ANGELS

Soon after Helen's miscarriage, Don moved her into a new apartment inside an old house remodeled to accommodate several flats. It was on Richmond Avenue, near Montrose, a rapidly developing area of town. Oaks, cicada-riddled willows, and imported palm trees shaded the neighborhood. Don threw himself into erasing the couple's loss. Despite Helen's claim that he'd fix a place up and leave it alone, the open-ended environments he'd known at home and at school had given him a spatial restlessness. He bought a black table for the new living room and spent several days lacquering it. Dissatisfied, he took the table to a professional finisher. Don filled the apartment with houseplants and flowers. On weekends, he and Helen haunted junk shops and cut-rate antique stores. They bought a walnut breakfast table. At a place called Trash 'n Treasure on Westheimer Road, they found a nineteenth-century oak table for their dining room. The owner thought it an "old piece of junk," but Don refinished it and it made a handsome addition to their home. He bought an Alvar Aalto lounge chair, a Bertoia set, and a set of Prague side chairs. From the Museum of Fine Arts he bought a Chagall poster for the living room wall. He enjoyed working with his hands, arranging and rearranging things.

Meanwhile, Don continued his correspondence with Walker

Percy. On May 20, 1957, he told Percy he would like to have a five-thousand word essay for the summer issue of *Forum.* In July, he nudged Percy again, saying the "issue would be closed out by the end of the month and appear sometime in August." Percy responded with an article that he hoped would "interest both the scientifically minded and the literarily minded." He added, "[D]on't hesitate to send it back."

Originally entitled "Symbol and Sign," the essay ran in *Forum*'s summer issue under the title "The Act of Naming." In it, Percy argued that, because of language, man is "that being in the world whose calling it is to find a name for Being, to give testimony to it, and to provide for it a clearing."

On October 2, Percy wrote to say he'd received his copy of the issue. A "very good-looking job," he said, "striking format. I, for one, am proud to be part of it. Thanks also for your skillful editing which helped my piece not a little." He praised Don's choice of contributors, including James Collins, a "first-class philosopher . . . [and] writer" who had recently published a book called *The Mind of Kierkegaard.*

In the fall of 1957, Maurice Natanson left Houston for a job at the University of North Carolina. Don felt "academically stranded." He and Helen talked again about moving east, perhaps to Brandeis or the New School in Manhattan, but once more they failed to follow up on it. Helen had gone back to work (*her* way of coping with the miscarriage). Her friend Betty Jane Mitchell was faring better now with her ad agency, after handling the account of the popular patent medicine Hadacol. Helen served as as an account executive for the firm.

With Natanson gone, "Don was more isolated than ever," Helen recalled. He stayed in touch with Natanson, seeking topics for *Forum,* and he kept the books he'd bought for Natanson's courses, including a copy of Tolstoy's *The Death of Ivan Ilyich.*

At the ad agency, Betty Jane Mitchell assigned Helen to represent Dominican College, a four-year Catholic school for girls in Houston. She met the school's dean, who invited her to teach a few courses in journalism and literature. She had missed teaching, and happily accepted the offer. Occasionally, she asked Don to give a guest lecture. He looked forward to these sessions, reading aloud from a poem or novel, and kidding the "sweet nuns."

One day, he soothed a young woman dismayed by the portrayal of the alcoholic priest in Graham Greene's *The Power and the Glory.* Don explained that the church's hierarchy was humane and effective, with young priests standing ready to correct their elders' missteps.

These classroom visits gave Don his second taste of teaching (after the tutoring in Korea). He was conscientious and thorough in his lectures. His tone was polite, even when discussing religious themes. He revealed, Helen said later, "nothing of his own withdrawal from the church."

Early in the summer of 1957, Helen learned that she was pregnant again. In spite of her recent miscarriage, and the loss of a premature child with Peter Gilpin, she did not want to cut her hours at the ad agency or change her daily routines.

She and Don continued to walk in the evenings, and to go to movies and plays. On the weekends, they made their regular trek to the Barthelme house. Steve showed them snakes and frogs he'd found in the woods or in the bayou. Don's mom bragged about Steve's school assignments.

At the end of October, Helen lost the child: a boy weighing less than two pounds. She never saw him. When she awoke from the anesthesia, Don asked her how she'd feel about donating the baby's body to the hospital for medical research. "He thought this was the best thing for us to do and I agreed at once. The child I lost in my first marriage was buried in our family cemetery plot in Houston, and I did not want to face that experience again."

She returned to work and stayed active so as not to dwell on the loss. In quick succession, she and Don attended events at the Contemporary Arts Museum, Joan Crystal's Louisiana Gallery, and the New Arts Gallery. One evening at a reception in the Museum of Fine Arts, she noticed how often people introduced Don as the "son of the architect." Over and over, he affirmed that he was "indeed the son of the great man"; then he "withdrew into a kind of aloofness." For the first time, she realized how difficult these evenings were for Don.

On another occasion, at a surrealism exhibit, Don saw a "small egg-shaped object covered in fur, the inspiration for what became [his] favorite line in his fiction," Helen recalled. Most likely, she was thinking of Meret Oppenheim's fur-covered teacup (1936), one of surrealism's icons. In "Florence Green Is 81," Don's narrator claims that the "aim of literature . . . is the creation of a strange object covered with fur which breaks your heart."

Every night, Don brought home proofs from the magazine. Sometimes, Helen helped him read them. She found the time spent on type fonts, illustrations, and the placement of page numbers tedious. He'd spread everything on a rug and spend "hours moving type around." For him, "every element was part of the design." He was "never entirely satisfied."

In the mornings, "he would walk over to the university's press to help with headlines and other display type that was set by hand." He wrote constantly to designers and typographers, requesting special fonts. "He kept a file of clippings of miscellaneous art," Helen wrote, "mostly out-of-copyright art, that he could use as illustrations, a practice he had begun as a reporter at the *Post.*"

His whimsical eye is apparent in *Forum*'s Fall 1957 issue. To accompany Maurice Natanson's article on the tension between "Philosophy and the Social Sciences," Don chose drawings of Tweedledee and Tweedledum sidling up to each other. Loose caps cover their eyes.

He never lost the "guilty pleasure" of playing with clip art, and illustrated many of his early stories. A number of his letters to Roger Angell, and to book editors, concern the appearance of his stories on the page once they had gone to the printer.

On October 17, 1957, Don wrote to Natanson that he had "evolved a new type dress and a very Bauhaus layout scheme." He had a strong sense of what he wanted visually. In an exchange with New York photographer Gene Gaines, he asked for a portfolio of the Dancers of India, a troupe traveling in the United States under the auspices of the Indian government. "Our idea . . . [is to] . . . catch the dancers at the height of their various movements, silhouette these shots and superimpose them on shots of the ancient Indian statues from which they are supposed to derive their inspiration," he said.

That fall, the famed sociologist David Riesman wrote to Don. In 1950, Riesman had published *The Lonely Crowd,* a study of the insular American character. He was tinkering now with fiction. On November 8, Don replied that *Forum* didn't publish fiction: The editorial board wouldn't allow it. "It is difficult to know where to publish short stories that are not formula or run-of-the mill," Don said. He suggested *Southwest Review* at Southern Methodist University. They have "run a good deal of distinguished fiction."

Scarce funding continued to plague him. The board pressured him to cut costs. On April 17, 1958, he wrote Wayne Taylor of the UH Printing Department, "[W]e would . . . like to pay not more than $16.00 per page for [the next] issue, which will run forty pages." He proposed that "margins will be, for this issue, restrained to more conventional proportions," that "there will be no full-page, four-way bleed cuts," that the "amount of handset type will be drastically reduced," and that "no changes will be made (except for typos) in pages that are already made up." This is *confession* more than *plan,* revealing Don's previous layout practices. He concluded, "The undersigned will stay out of your way as much as possible."

His agony is even more palpable in his letters to writers. Percy had asked him, "[H]ow come a U. of Houston publication isn't paying about a dollar a word?" After all, Houston was an oil town; the university was famous for the generous endowment it had gotten from Hugh Roy Cullen. But the Cullen money had been used for capital expenditures, not for daily operations or faculty salaries. The Cullen myth kept other potential donors away. The university would soon become part of the state system, but at that time it was still a private institution.

Don explained all this to Percy, who never again mentioned money. Other writers were not as understanding. In the summer of 1957, Don had written to Thomas A. Bledsoe, director of Beacon Press in Boston, hoping to excerpt chapters from some of Beacon's books in *Forum*. Initially, Don was interested in Lewis A. Coser and Irving Howe's *The American Communist Party: A Critical History*. Coser and Howe were amenable, but Bledsoe wrote what Don considered a "very nasty letter," insisting that oil-soaked Houston ought to be able to pay reprint fees.

Alfred Kazin, whom Don hoped would move the magazine's literary studies beyond "pale new critic[ism]," wrote to say that he appreciated Don's interest in his work, but couldn't understand why *Forum* didn't pay. Perhaps feeling he had nothing to lose, Don responded:

> You are absolutely right but if I sent you . . . money I would have to cut exactly 16 pages out of the magazine. If I sent $300 each to three more contributors there would be no magazine. This perhaps would be no great loss but I must believe otherwise. The magazine is produced at absolute minimum cost. The University has an annual deficit of close to $600,000 a year. All of Cullen's money went into grandiose buildings with nothing left to keep the radiators burning. The magazine is printed in our own makeshift campus printing plant where the question of whether or not we should spend $15 for a new roller is gravely debated. The printers, about half of whom are students, are suitably underpaid. I set a good deal of the display type myself and do a number of other things which you probably wouldn't believe to save money. We bought the good paper in quantity at a distress sale. The handsome typefaces were begged by me from the manufacturers. If I send a telegram I have to pay for it out of my own pocket (I'm not a professor either, by the way). The faculty feels that it's too esoteric: what is all this Dada business anyhow? Because the magazine is produced here, all hands are pretty sure that it can't be much good.
>
> All of this is irrelevant. The answer to your question is that the printer shouldn't be paid when the writer is not. But the printer is invariably adamant whereas the writer is sometimes willing to be victimized. This difference between printers and writers is what makes possible marginal journals like our own, which have no real (economic) right to exist. Whether all this effort on the part of writers, printers, and editors is worthwhile—whether the magazine itself is a good magazine, or is meaningful in any way—is another question. We are, of course, visited

from time to time by the thought that we are merely deluding ourselves
about the worth of the whole project. . . . But this is my problem, not yours.

Don was all alone in endeavoring to create a first-class publication. The writers he rejected didn't always respond with grace. A journalist named James Boyer May submitted an article entitled "I'm an Old Anti-Sartrean." Don turned it down, citing his affinities with Sartre. May wrote back, "As to your sympathy with the 'existential-phenomenological movement' (to me no more definable than the non-existent 'beat movement' I've . . . wasted time in analyzing for CBS)—every editor is undoubtedly entitled to promote his views [but this one is] narrow . . . self-defeating . . ."

Clearly, Don considered himself an editorial *artist*. Early in his marriage to Helen, he told her that the two of them "should be committed to becoming part of the intellectual and artistic elite rather than the wealthy elite." He "believed his mother was disheartened over having a less affluent lifestyle than any of her friends, the kind of life that one could have expected from an architect as famous as his father," Helen recalled. "Several of their early friends were now quite wealthy, but it was not a world that Don envied."

Still, he did not want to be part of the "carriage trade." Growing up, Don had never had to worry about money. He told Helen they "should buy whatever [they] needed and then find the money to cover [their] expenses." She wrote, "This was a new approach to budgeting for me." She oversaw their joint bank account. Don never kept track of his spending. Each month, despite Helen's efforts, several checks came back marked "insufficient funds." Don simply wrote new checks to replace the returns.

In the spring of 1958, Helen suggested they move in order to economize. They took a tiny flat on Emerson Street. Shortly after settling, they invited Don's dad to dinner—he was alone for a few days while the rest of the family visited Don's aunt in Pennsylvania. Helen asked her father-in-law what he thought of the apartment. He looked around. It's "ingratiating," he said dryly.

Soon, Helen became pregnant again. Though she and Don had lived in the apartment less than six months, they began to look for a larger space. They wound up moving across the street, to a 1920s house owned by Linn and Celestine Linnstaedter. Linn was a colleague of Don's dad in the UH architecture department; Celestine practiced psychiatry in Houston's VA Hospital.

Don was not happy with the new place. He partitioned the big central room with a Japanese rice-paper screen, which he built to hang from the ceiling. He converted one of the bedrooms to a living room. Despite his dissatisfaction, he enjoyed the Linnstaedters, who lived next door.

He asked Helen if she would still love him after the baby was born. She assured him she would. She worked as hard as ever at the advertising agency. In the early fall, she lost the child, another boy. Again, she and Don donated the body to the hospital for research, but Helen wrote that she regretted this later and was always haunted by "images" of the "two infants." She remained convinced that Don had felt the same way. In her book, she cited a passage from his 1973 story "One Hundred Ten West Sixty-First Street":

> Paul and Eugenie went to a film. Their baby had just died and they were trying not to think about it. The film left them slightly depressed. The child's body had been given to the hospital for medical experimentation. "But what about life after death?" Eugenie's mother had asked. "There isn't any," Eugenie said. "Are you positive?" her mother asked. "No," Eugenie said. "How can I be positive? But that's my opinion."

"I have no doubt that Eugenie was speaking for Don," Helen wrote. "Don knew that the Catholic church would not have approved of what we did, and he later told me that his mother talked to him about it. Giving the bodies to the medical school . . . was, I believe, an attempt to leave the experience in the past. The presence of two tiny graves would not let us do this. And as always, he was driven by an implacable will to make decisions independent of all authority, in this instance both the church and his mother."

Fighting *Forum*'s editorial board was like "working in a vacuum," Don said, but still he plowed ahead. He secured articles from Leslie Fiedler ("The Secret Life of James Fenimore Cooper"), Walter Kaufmann (from his forthcoming book *From Shakespeare to Existentialism*), Hugh Kenner (discussions of T. S. Eliot and Samuel Beckett), James Collins ("Art and the Philosopher"), Richard Evans (interviews with Carl Jung and Freud biographer Ernest Jones), Peter Yates (on West Coast music), Parker Tyler, the editor of *Art-News* (on contemporary American film), William Carlos Williams (from *I Wanted to Write a Poem*), and Norman Mailer (an excerpt from *Advertisements for Myself*). Walker Percy submitted a new piece, "The Loss of the Creature," which dealt with the gaps between perceptions and reality.

Though they were not paid, these writers were eager to be part of a journal composed with the care, seriousness, and range of curiosity Don brought to his work. In the spring of 1958, he published a translation of Jean-Paul Sartre's essay "Algeria," which analyzed the torture techniques of French soldiers. Sartre noted it was a bitter irony that Frenchmen had become torturers in Africa so soon after the French had suffered at the hands of German troops.

The piece had first appeared in Europe (it was banned in France); Malcolm

McCorquodale, a Houstonian who worked for the arts patron Dominique de Menil, saw the essay while traveling and brought it to Don's attention.

Without hesitating—and without university approval—Don phoned Sartre in Paris to ask his permission to print McCorquodale's translation of the piece. Sartre eagerly agreed. Several follow-up calls were needed to finalize arrangements. When Don's boss, Farris Block, saw the phone bill, he exploded. The magazine did not have the budget to cover such expenses. Don replied, "I'll pay for it." Block knew Don didn't have the cash, and he dropped the argument. Helen recalled that the couple's home phone bill was a nightmare of magazine-related charges.

Don kept pressing his luck with Block and the editorial board. At his own discretion, he solicited work from writers all over the country and beyond: Randall Jarrell, E. B. White, Erwin Panofsky, Ronnie Dugger, Kenneth Tynan, Cyril Connolly, the editors of *Dissent,* Diana Trilling ("I've been reading and enjoying your *Partisan* pieces for some time . . ."). One of his favorite contributors to *Forum* was Joseph Lyons, a research psychologist with the Veterans Administration Hospital in Lexington, Kentucky. In the Summer 1958 issue, Lyons's essay "The Psychology of Angels" appeared. Parts of the piece resurfaced in Don's 1969 story "On Angels."

By July 1958, in a general fund-raising letter, Don could accurately boast, "The response from our readers has far exceeded our expectations; and some of the nation's most distinguished scholars have informed us that *Forum* has filled a major gap in the field of scholarly publishing."

Then the bad news: "We are now . . . at a point where certain difficulties must be resolved if the magazine is to make the fullest use of its opportunities. The University of Houston, as you may know, is suffering heavily from lack of funds. . . ."

Once more, Helen became pregnant, and once again she lost the baby. "I assumed that with Don's Catholic background, we would eventually have children," she later said, "[but] I now had ambivalent feelings about [it]." Just before the latest pregnancy, her gynecologist, Dr. Charles Bancroft, had recommended medical testing; nothing suggested that either she or Don had any reproductive problems. "It was apparent that Don detested having to undergo . . . tests and seemed to feel that somehow it tainted the idea of having a child. I was struck by the depth of his need for 'mystery' and spontaneity. It was becoming clear that Don's sensibilities made it difficult for him to confront the realities of being a father." Helen wrote that in the 1950s, "pregnancy was an event that women faced pretty much alone," and she admitted that after the latest miscarriage, "I . . . had no desire whatsoever to become pregnant again."

Typically, Don wanted to move on and put the past behind him. He told Helen he was always seeking a spot where "everything is different." He found a two-story apartment that he liked on Kipling Street, and placed a deposit on it. Designed by Burdette Keeland, a colleague of his father, it had white brick exteriors, redbrick interior floors, and a glass wall overlooking a garden out back. Don added texture to the living room by covering one wall with natural burlap.

Linn and Celestine Linnstaedter had been very kind to the couple, both as friends and landlords; Don dreaded telling them that he and Helen had found a new place to live. He informed them one evening in their yard. Before they could respond, Don, apparently self-conscious about Celestine's psychiatric training, told her in a "sharp, accusatory tone that he knew what she was thinking about the psychological implications" of his frequent desire to move. "Celestine was visibly stunned," Helen recalled. Don seems to have mounted an attack to ward off criticism—or to deflect the guilt he was feeling.

THE MECHANICAL BRIDE

In 1959, without alerting his editorial board, Don decided *Forum* would publish fiction. He was preparing to take his own fiction from the back burner; fitfully, he had been working on a story he'd eventually call "Hiding Man."

On September 25, he wrote to Martha Foley, a Columbia University professor and editor of the annual *Best American Short Stories* anthology. He asked her if she could "recommend some young fiction writers . . . who might be interested in contributing fiction or poetry to our quarterly. We have only recently decided to add fiction and poetry to the magazine, and this letter is an exploratory gesture." There is no record of a reply. No doubt, Don was exploring the possibility of advancing his own efforts while expanding *Forum*'s scope.

In a letter signed "Earl Long," Walker Percy told Don he had been "wrassling with a piece of fiction and not doing too well." Don phoned him and asked to see what he was up to. Percy hesitated; he was not yet comfortable enough to show Don the "curious adventures of my ingenious young moviegoer."

To encourage him, Don phoned his old friend Herman Gollob, now working as an acquisitions editor for Little, Brown in Boston. He mentioned Percy's novel. Gollob made some calls and discovered that Knopf had already bought it. Don contacted Percy, who admitted, "Yes, Knopf did option my book, paid me a small sum, then

shot it back with the suggestion that I rewrite it. Since then I've been sitting here . . . of no mind to do anything . . . [but] soon . . . [I'll] give you any part you might want."

True to his word, Percy mailed the book's second chapter to Don, who wasted no time setting it into type. To shape it as a stand-alone story, Don deleted most of the last twelve pages of the manuscript. Percy didn't mind. "Glad you wish to use as much as you do. You are welcome to it. Your reaction to the last section will probably be of great value to me. There's my weakness . . . Platonizing . . . and it may be fatal."

The excerpt, entitled "Carnival in Gentilly," appeared in the Summer 1960 issue, a year before Percy published the novel.

Don fought hard to land another story in *Forum,* by a young author named Bruce Brooks. John Allred, chair of *Forum*'s editorial board, objected to the story's homosexual theme and nixed it without submitting it to the other board members. Furious, Don wrote to him, "[N]ot publishing this story (or the next one) is a certain way to kill *Forum.* The magazine is dead just as soon as we are governed by other people's anticipated reactions to what we print. We have killed it ourselves." He went on to say "Joyce, Pound, Eliot, Lawrence, Stein etc. etc. were all greeted with exactly this kind of outraged alarm when they first appeared. They were redeemed by time. Ought we to content ourselves with 'safe' writers or writers for whom other people have already taken the risks? To argue that ours is a special situation is no argument. Our situation is precisely what we make of it."

Don's relationship with the board, uneasy from the start, began to crumble. He initiated another editorial brawl when he accepted an essay by William Gass, a relatively unpublished young professor then teaching at Purdue. "The Case of the Obliging Stranger" opens with an elaborate description of a man bound and trussed and baked in an electric oven. Gass wrote:

> Any ethics that does not roundly condemn [baking the man] is vicious. . . .
>
> This is really all I have to say, but I shall not stop on that account. Indeed, I shall begin again.

Several paragraphs follow, in which Gass argues that the task of ethics is to "elicit distinctions from a recalcitrant language." Meanwhile, the man "is overbaked. I wonder whether this is bad or not. . . ."

Forum's board did not know what to make of Gass's playfulness and erudition—early hallmarks of his later, much-celebrated essays. On October 30, 1959, board member Howard F. McGraw sent Don a formal letter: "I . . . undoubtedly . . . have [a] different audience in mind for *Forum.* I myself conjure up, as the typical reader, a busy layman of better-than-average curiosity and intelligence. . . . [M]y guess is that at least nine out of ten readers would give up [on Gass's essay] after a page or two."

At the bottom, in different typescript, McGraw added informally:

> *Don,*
>
> *If, at this point, you'd be embarrassed to reject the piece, go ahead and run it . . . but I do feel strongly about this matter. I think you . . . assume too much interest, background, and mental acuteness on the part of* Forum's *readers.*

Don published Gass's essay in the spring of 1960.

Maggie Marrs returned to Houston to retrieve the car she'd left with Don when she flew to France. She noticed a new gravity in him. "I wouldn't say it was sadness," she says. "We were young. Sadness is something you learn later. I learned sadness over time, on subsequent trips to Paris because it's so old, with the ancient stones on the bridges. . . . Don probably learned sadness in New York." But he had visibly matured since she'd seen him last.

Around this time, Maurice Natanson made a brief return to Houston, for a guest lecture sponsored by the Contemporary Arts Association. Don was pleased to see him, but the visit reminded him how dry his intellectual environment had become since his former teacher's departure. Ever the existentialist, Natanson urged Don to act to dispel his gloom about *Forum's* future, but Don's actions had been thwarted at every turn. He had proposed a "Conference of Editors of American Literary and Intellectual Journals" to be held in Houston, but the university refused to fund it. He submitted a grant application to the Ford Foundation, but it was rejected.

Don also felt isolated in his personal life. The Marantos had moved to Dallas; Joe had joined the PR wing of the Mobil Oil Corporation. Pat Goeters was busy establishing his architectural practice and producing documentaries for Houston's public television station. Don and Helen had made many friends among those active in the local art scene, but few of them could discuss writing and philosophy. Helen was only peripherally part of Don's intellectual world. She worked full-time in advertising, a field Don disdained, no matter how supportive he wished to be of his wife. After a series of medical tests and miscarriages, the marriage no longer held the mystery, romance, and spontaneity Don thought he could sustain with Helen. As with the magazine, his idealism had vanished. It was an increasing burden to maintain creativity at home and at work, and to keep a high level of interest. And he wasn't writing much.

"I could see and feel an abating of his exuberance for life," Helen recalled. A few months after her most recent miscarriage, Don read William Shirer's *The Rise and Fall of the Third Reich.* Shirer's accounts of Nazi atrocities so wrenched him, Helen "became apprehensive that he might commit suicide." He seemed now to "live with an intense consciousness of the world as evil."

If there had been hints of a persistent melancholy in Don—in his clashes with his father, his lip twitch, his defensive irony, his fear that something might be "permanently gone" after the army—this period, in 1959 and 1960, just before his breakthrough into important literary work, provides the first glimpse of a depression that would hound him all his life.

He retained enough Catholicism and stoic pride to rule out killing himself. Even in the pit of his misery, he told Helen he believed that a person "had a responsibility to live out his life, whatever the circumstances." In later years, he liked to paraphrase Nietzsche: The thought of suicide had often consoled him, Don said, and gotten him through many a bad night.

Natanson's visit unnerved him. He worried that isolation had changed his personality. One night, half-jokingly, Natanson "alluded to Don's penchant for fast cars, a reference to his Austin-Healey," Helen wrote. After that, Don "seemed to feel guilty that we were indulging ourselves." Though he "insisted on a beautiful place in which to live and work," he had a horror of seeming phony. He bristled when a friend kidded him about his fancy Bertoia chairs, and when another acquaintance told him he and Helen made a "chic" couple. He talked disparagingly of "driving a Jaguar," his shorthand for wealthy elitism. In years to come, many of his critics dismissed him as chic—in part, Don believed, because his stories appeared in *The New Yorker* next to glittering ads for watches, jewelry, fashion, and Jaguars.

Following Natanson's visit, Helen and Don talked again of Don leaving the university in order to write. "Don saw it as the need to confront the choice between a career with money and the lifestyle it could provide . . . or a wholehearted commitment to writing," Helen said later. At the end of 1959, she had started her own ad agency. She continued to teach at Dominican College. Despite her earnings, the couple remained in debt because of Don's reckless spending. He wasn't "indulging" himself so much as failing to keep track of finances in any organized way.

Helen feared he'd want to move again to ease his restiveness. She was happy on Kipling Street, and tired of constant change. Sure enough, one day Don complained to her—after they had lived on Kipling little more than a year—that the apartment was "inappropriate for a serious writing career."

That Don stayed with *Forum* as long as he did, despite his frustrations, suggests he knew what he had accomplished, even if few others did. Simply put, for a brief time he edited one of the nation's most serious and innovative intellectual journals—and at an out-of-the-way place with little funding and a conservative editorial board. The "strange and beautiful" pieces he published pleased him immensely, as evidenced by their echoes in his fiction.

The American College Public Relations Association gave *Forum* its highest award, in recognition of its distinction, in 1958. In a testimonial for the journal, Norman Mailer noted, "It looks as if I might receive better than full value for my subscription." Tirelessly, Don explored funding schemes. He sent a copy of the magazine to Ima Hogg, the wealthy daughter of Texas's former governor, with a note saying, "[We] thought you might be interested." When McNeil Lowry of the Ford Foundation came to Houston to talk to the directors of the Alley Theatre, Don notified the UH Development Office that they ought to pitch the magazine to him. The "drudge work" and his "numerous petty tasks" must have been "more deadening for him than anyone knew," Helen wrote.

At the same time, he delighted in the journal's growing body of work: a massive collage. In January 1959, he wrote Patrick J. Nicholson of the university's Development Office: "Because *Forum* has now published a total of ten issues, and because its future is now being debated" (in light of budget constraints), "it seems appropriate to offer at this time some facts about it which may serve to enrich the discussion." He composed an eclectic list, a precursor of the playful catalogs that would appear in his fiction. With great exuberance, he noted the wide range of subjects represented in the pieces that *Forum* had published:

> Educational television, engineering education, sea animals, H. H. Bancroft's histories, opera, Faulkner, the new Germany, the director Elia Kazan, consumer research, anthropology, radiation in venom tests, the natural numbers in mathematics, home design, the French playwright Jean Giraudoux, the "new critics," pottery, Niccolo Machiavelli, the idea of progress, semantics, the Suez crisis, the separation of church and state, Ernest Jones, freedom as an idea, Coleridge, the relation between philosophy and the social sciences, Stalinism, contemporary music, the Algerian question, logical positivism, angels, academic freedom, psychology and ancient religions, scientism, movies and art, C. G. Jung, architectural literature, recognition of China, the fantastic, the Organization Man, nihilism, disarmament, magic, Eliot's verse plays, the Welfare State, destiny, the Affluent Society, the new French fiction, modern composers, Freud, dictators, the contemporary theatre, the suburbs, the neo-Dada movement, *Fortune* magazine, and James Fenimore Cooper.

Don thrilled at this woolly mix, at the fur that flew when worlds collided. He continued to attract top talent: Robbe-Grillet, Gregory Bateson, Roger

Caillois, and Marshall McLuhan. Pat Goeters had studied with McLuhan in Toronto; he had talked with Don about McLuhan's vision of a new kind of writing for the electronic age.

Don solicited a piece from McLuhan. For *Forum*'s Summer 1960 issue, McLuhan submitted a copy of a speech he had written, entitled "The Medium Is the Message." Soon, this phrase would ring throughout the "global village."

McLuhan analyzed the way power structures—government, media—"get inside the . . . collective mind" through propaganda, advertising, and electronic imagery to ensure a "condition of public helplessness." Individuals exist in a storm of information and stimuli, he said, and the way to survive it is to ride the waves, just like Edgar Allan Poe's main character in the story "A Descent into the Maelstrom." "Poe's sailor saved himself by studying the action of the whirlpool and by cooperating with it," McLuhan wrote in a book entitled *The Mechanical Bride,* first published in 1951.

McLuhan's version of riding the maelstrom was to forget what we *think* we know—about newspapers, laundry detergents, magazine ads, movies, clothing—and study objects as they really are (a phenomenological approach); so, for example, the front page of *The New York Times* is not just a summary of the news but also a series of discontinuous columns of pictures and print, collaged together in a frenzied fashion that recalls Cubist paintings, Joyce's novels, and modern theories of physics. *Something* about the present conjures chaos, and it is changing the way we process thought, the way we act and consort with one another.

Trivia, cultural products, and social behavior are signs, McLuhan said. These signs don't always match the meaning of a thing (a Cadillac and a clunker both "mean" transportation, but they signal different values: wealth and class *versus* tastelessness and poverty). Power creates and repeats certain signs (Cadillac equals class) to control mass behavior.

Poe's sailor, locked in the whirlpool, dodging debris, says, "I must have been delirious, for I even sought *amusement* in speculating" upon the objects sinking and flying around. For McLuhan, the sailor's surrender to chaos, and his playfulness, provided a guide to the future.

Notably, in France, Roland Barthes was writing essays similar to McLuhan's for the left-wing magazine *Les Lettres Nouvelles.* Eventually, Barthes's pieces were gathered in a collection called *Mythologies:* discourses on Greta Garbo's face, food photos in magazines, laundry detergents, popular wrestling, tabloid profiles of space aliens. Like McLuhan, Barthes argued that the trivia of everyday life was packed with meanings that were often at odds with their functions. We inhabit a world of signs; they claim to be "natural," but, in fact, they mask power's real motives.

Don adopted this outlook in writing his first successful short story, "Me and Miss Mandible," in October 1960. "We read signs as promises," his narrator says. "I believed that because I had obtained a wife who was made up of wife-signs (beauty, charm, softness, perfume, cookery) I had found love. . . .

"All of us . . . still believe that the American flag betokens a kind of general righteousness. But I say . . . that signs are signs and some of them are lies."

In a later story, "Brain Damage" (1970), Don echoed "A Descent into the Maelstrom." Like Poe's sailor, discovering entertainment in chaos, Don's narrator goes "*[s]kiing along on the soft surface of brain damage, never to sink, because [I] don't understand the danger—*"

In his *Forum* essay, McLuhan sketched themes he would expand in books (*The Gutenberg Galaxy, Understanding Media, The Medium Is the Massage, Counterblast, Through the Vanishing Point*): Electric light is pure information; electronic media have created a global village that connects people through transmitted images (the modern equivalent of tribal drums); in the past, print technology isolated individuals, enforcing private instead of public experiences; electricity has made us tribal again, postliterate, yoked together in a seamless electronic web; the real "message" of television is the subtle mutation of our sensory patterns; and literature must change to reflect the fragmented, instantaneous nature of our age.

The best writing now, according to McLuhan, is *inclusive:* elliptical, indeterminate, open-ended, forcing readers to participate in extracting meanings from texts.

McLuhan provided some of the earliest, most cogent dissections of the "information age." Don saw something else in his work—a kind of media theology. As Andreas Huyssen has written, ". . . try an experiment in reading [McLuhan]: for electricity substitute the Holy Spirit, for medium read God, and for the global village of the screen understand the planet united under Rome. . . . God is the ultimate aim of [the electronic] implosion. . . ."

Years later, McLuhan's "theology" appeared in Don's story "At the End of the Mechanical Age" (1973). A couple meets over kitchen soaps in a supermarket—"RUB and FAB and TUB and suchlike." The pair "huddle[s] and cling[s]" as the "mechanical age" comes to a close. Meanwhile, "God . . . stand[s] in the basement reading the meters to see how much grace had been used up. . . . Grace is electricity, science has found, it is not *like* electricity, it *is* electricity . . ."

After work each day, Don huddled with Helen on Kipling Street, trying to keep his restlessness at bay. Finally, he insisted on moving again. They drove around for hours in the evenings and on weekends, often at night. Helen later explained that "Don wanted to 'see the interior and the lighting—we can learn more about the house at night,' [he said]." Eventually, they found a duplex on the corner of Harold and Roseland streets, near a number of art galleries and the University of St. Thomas, a Basilian school. The duplex owner was a commercial artist; the apartment, built between 1910 and 1920, opened onto a yard next to his office building. Don converted the screened sleeping porch into a study. It overlooked Chinese elms, oaks, and magnolias. Awnings draped the windows. Next door, a rooming house sheltered transients. Nearby, other old homes were being converted into architectural offices, galleries, or advertising firms. When Helen first saw the new place, its shabbiness and darkness depressed her. Within a couple of weeks, Don, his brother Pete, and Henry Buckley had painted the interior a bright white, with an ocher accent in the living room.

"After we moved [in], I became unusually nervous," Helen wrote. "Not only was I still recovering from the emotional loss of the two little boys but I was also physically exhausted." Don wasn't soothed by the change, either. A few months earlier, he had decided to see a psychiatrist, a prominent Houston doctor named Spencer Bayles.

How could Don afford him? Clearly, he and Helen were living beyond their means, and turning to Don's family for help—a situation that kept him dependent on his father.

With Bayles, Don shared his frustrations with the *Forum* board, his feelings of aloneness, his difficulty finding time to write, his concern over Helen's uneasiness. He didn't discuss these sessions with her, but she understood how unhappy he was; three years earlier, he had talked her out of psychoanalysis, ridiculing its uselessness. It was a sign of his desperation that he was willing to see a doctor now.

In "The Sandman," an unusually autobiographical story, Don's narrator recalls his analysis with a doctor "down in Texas"—"a tall thin man who never said anything much. If you could get a 'What comes to mind?' out of him you were doing splendidly." The doctor urges his patients to act, but never does anything himself. The experience leaves the narrator a "little sour."

In "Florence Green Is 81," Don compares story writing to a psychiatric appointment, with the reader as the doctor, bored, "washing . . . hands between hours," and the writer as the "nervous dreary patient."

It's likely that Don considered himself smarter than Dr. Bayles—at the very least, he was quicker with words. The heavy emotional masking in his writing, his aloofness in public encounters, his cutting irony—all suggest the self-consciousness and defensiveness a doctor would have had to negotiate to make any headway with Don. Bayles wasn't up to the task—or so Don felt. In the 1980s, he told his UH colleague, the poet Cynthia Macdonald, that as a young man he had seen a therapist who advised him it was time to get out of Houston. The therapist said "that when he had achieved certain things in life and in himself"—presumably, literary success and peace with his father—"he could return." Don already knew these things. As he would write years later in "Return," any "ordinary shrink could have said to me, 'Why are you being so hard on yourself?' and many have, I was disappointed."

Disappointments aside, Don didn't completely dismiss psychoanalysis (his fiction is enriched by his broad reading in the subject). In the spring of 1959, he published in *Forum* a piece called "The Psychology of Destiny," by Henri F. Ellenberger, which argued that the individual is free to choose from among the traits he has inherited from his family to shape an *elected destiny.*

In that same issue of *Forum,* Don elected to publish a short story he had written, "Pages from the Annual Report." The byline read "David Reiner."

In the story, Baskerville, a worker stuck in a drab office among piles of paper, "some of them four feet tall," laments being lost in a bureaucratic dead end along with his partner, a man named De Vinne. Baskerville "likes things a little more exciting than they are," but he can't change anything. He can't locate the corporate "headquarters." His aimless exchanges with De Vinne read like dialogues from *Waiting for Godot.*

At one point, a "girl from the mimeograph room" barges into the office. Baskerville wants her to give "headquarters" a message from him. The scene mimics Didi's talks with the mysterious boy in *Godot.*

Eventually, Baskerville reveals to De Vinne that the papers on their desks contain the "substance of human lives." The office holds together "the meaningless lives of hundreds and hundreds of people." Baskerville asks, "You're aware that there's nothing on the paper?"

"[W]hy has our own organization . . . turned on us?" De Vinne inquires.

"Because it knows we're thinking."

In this early attempt to translate Beckett and Kafka to an American setting, Don overburdens a slender conception with broad jokes and existential torpor. But the rhythm is tight—a fine balance, learned from Beckett, between melancholy and humor. The fiction ends with a fiction—a contributor's note affixed to the bottom of the page, in which Don's longing is palpable: "David Reiner lives in New York City. He is now at work on a novel."

In the fall of 1959, Don printed Harold Rosenberg's "The Audience as Subject." It thrilled him to publish this man whose views had galvanized him from the moment his father gave him Marcel Raymond's *From Baudelaire to Surrealism.* Don's correspondence with Rosenberg had begun when Houston's Contemporary Arts Museum planned a show entitled "Out of the Ordinary," featuring works by Joseph Cornell, Robert Rauschenberg, Leon Golub, Francis Picabia, Joan Miró, Yves Tanguy, Jim Love, and Guy Johnson. Don was friends with Love and Johnson; he had become active in the Contemporary Arts Association, which supported the museum. He had helped the museum's director, Robert C. Morris, enlist Rosenberg to write the show's catalog introduction. In the course of their exchanges, Don courted Rosenberg for a contribution to *Forum.* Soon thereafter, "The Audience as Subject" arrived in the mail. In it, Rosenberg wrote of Robert Rauschenberg, "his work has sought out the clutter of souvenirs and legacies to which the common heart is attached."

Don would remember that line. In "See the Moon?" his narrator says of the elements that compose his story, "It's my hope that these ... souvenirs ... will someday merge, blur—cohere is the word, maybe—into something meaningful. A grand word, meaningful. What do I look for? A work of art, I'll not accept anything less."

Like Marcel Raymond, Rosenberg insists that the *authentically* new is a variation on tradition, not a thing randomly conceived for novelty. He concludes that the "new" is "full of pep in having found out how to make materials talk back in unexpected ways to the civilization that is producing them."

Among the last pieces Don published in *Forum* was "Sartre and Literature," by Maurice Natanson. The writer of fiction, Natanson said, must plunge into the "world of objects" and return to " 'the things themselves' " in human experience. It is impossible to *speak* of consciousness, or to *represent* its movement, without emphasizing the objects of its awareness.

Natanson believed this fact had profound implications for the concept of character in fiction.

If a writer merely depicts a character in a setting, a "false dualism" gets established. The setting is presented as "out there," separate from the character. Natanson insisted that, in life, "[any object I perceive is] not at a distance from me, it does not subsist over there." Rather, "[it is] an integral part of my awareness." To be true to the nature of awareness, a writer must render the "world unbetrayed by sensibility or understanding." This, Sartre did in his fiction. He "erased the distance between consciousness and the world."

In "existential literature," we are "presented with reality as the ... product of consciousness situated in the world." Writers can best represent the *activity* of consciousness by simultaneously offering and interrogating the "given." This creates "an internal questioning of the literary work." Ideal forms for "self-interrogation" are the "confession, the diary, the embattled monologue," in which "each fragment of experience takes on multiple possibilities for interpretation."

In an existential novel, the characters "cause the world to be," Natanson stated; every scene's "particulars ... are exploded by consciousness into a kind of shrapnel."

The "central achievement" of this kind of fiction is the "uncovering of the imaginary as the informing structure of the literary microcosm." To denigrate writers like Sartre for insufficient realism, undeveloped characters, and missing action (as some critics did, and do) is to condemn them for not doing what they never intended to do in the first place.

Don's editorial choices—and his stubbornness—continued to upset *Forum's* editorial board. When John Allred received Don's response to his rejection of the Bruce Brooks story, he called a meeting to review manuscript procedure. According to policy, if two board members vetoed a manuscript, it would be dropped. For nearly four years, Don had slipped his choices past the majority of the board, because most members didn't bother to read any one piece.

The meeting took place on March 23, 1960. Don didn't attend. The board decided it would assume complete editorial control. On March 30, Don informed the board, "[T]here is apparently a fundamental disagreement about what kind of a magazine *Forum* should be. [I have] been attempting to publish a serious journal, comparable to other university-sponsored journals." In truth, *Forum* existed in a league of its own. Don did not feel that "there was sufficient support for [his] objective." He offered his resignation.

In a letter to his old friend Herman Gollob, he admitted that his plans were "very nebulous" and joked, "Probably, I'll reenlist." More seriously, he said, "I'm ... toying with the idea of going to Iowa for a sort of combined study/vacation at their summer writing program. It would be a couple of months and although I dislike the idea of this kind of thing, it might spur me to get more work done." He didn't pursue this avenue.

When Don threatened to quit the magazine, he was in the midst of preparing the Summer 1960 issue. He agreed to stay on until it had gone to print. On September 9, with his obligations met, he wrote another letter of resignation; he left the job on October 1.

DARLING DUCKLING

"This is your big chance. The Lord has sent me here only to introduce you to the literary world. Dash off a few brilliant short stories and I'll try to peddle them for you." Herman Gollob had made this offer to Don in January 1958, shortly after joining the William Morris Agency in New York. After leaving Houston, Gollob studied acting at the Pasadena Playhouse. Then he went to work for MCA Artists, a talent agency for actors. Finally, he landed at William Morris.

Throughout his final months as editor of *Forum,* Don had worked on a story called "Hiding Man," set in a nearly empty movie theater devoted to horror films. Here, a disguised priest tracks down a young man, a lapsed Catholic, and hopes to snatch him back to the fold. Hovering between fantasy and realism, the story is indebted to Kafka. Gollob didn't know what to do with it. It wasn't the kind of thing he thought he could sell. In December 1959, he sent an apologetic letter to Don, who set the story aside.

In early October, after resigning from *Forum,* Don established a rigorous writing routine. By and large, he stuck to the schedule for the rest of his life. He rose at dawn, dressed neatly in corduroy or khaki slacks, and settled at his Remington typewriter on the screened-in back porch. By 8:30 or 9:00 A.M., Helen prepared a

breakfast of bacon or ham with fruit juice and toast. She'd take it to him and then retire to the dining room to work on her ad accounts or lectures for her classes at Dominican College.

The clacking of Don's typewriter shot through the porch screens and startled early morning passersby on the sidewalks. He revised each sentence several times, often tearing the paper from the roller and tossing it into the trash. He'd lean back in his chair, light a cigarette, and read his words aloud. Sometimes he'd call to Helen, "asking her how spell" a certain word? Or he'd say, "How does this phrase strike you?"

On his way to the kitchen for a second cup of coffee, he'd stop to give her a kiss. Or he'd quote Eliot: "I grow old . . . I grow old . . . I shall wear the bottoms of my trousers rolled." Or to make her laugh, he'd balance a pencil on the tip of his nose.

Occasionally, he'd read a passage to her and seek her reaction, or he'd pace the house, repeating his sentences aloud. Flaubert, he said, used to walk into the woods and shout his words to the tops of the trees.

If a paragraph proved especially troublesome, Don strolled around the neighborhood, past the art galleries, the artists' studios, and the historic houses of the Montrose area, many of which were being renovated to serve as apartments or offices for architects and lawyers. After a half hour or so, he'd return to his Remington.

By noon or one o'clock, he'd knock off for the day. The wastebasket bulged with paper, thirty or forty sheets at a time. Most of them contained just a sentence or two. What he kept, after a morning session, ranged from nothing at all to maybe two pages. Very carefully, he carried his ashtray to the kitchen, and emptied it into the trash. "[D]uring these first years of writing, he was irresistibly happy," Helen recalled.

Shortly before Don quit his job to write full-time, the *Houston Post* printed an interview with his father entitled "Construction and Conformity." Portions of it gave Don fertile material for his first successful short story.

By now, Donald Barthelme, Sr., was a veteran of Houston's architectural scene, and a teacher at the University of Houston as well as at the Rice Institute. In the interview, he comes across as brash and uncompromising. The years had not softened him. "The customer is never right in architecture," he claimed. "He operates from a very limited background."

He applauded iconoclasts: "We depend upon . . . people who refuse to conform to move us into new paths, to find for us new aspects of things which add new enlightenment." But then, perhaps inadvertently revealing worry over his eldest son, a budding nonconformist, Barthelme qualified his thought: "On the other hand, it's practically impossible for those people to exist unless they are provided with private sources of income and are armored against all sorts of pressures from their friends and other[s]. The penalty of non-conformance is so great as to even endanger your life, if nothing else by the slow process of starvation."

School design, one of Barthelme's favorite topics, dominated the conversation. "Did you ever notice the similarity between school . . . and canning tomatoes?" Barthelme asked the reporter. "You put things in both can and child, test both, label both." Then he railed against traditional learning arrangements:

> People don't come in grades. As a matter of fact, you go into any elementary school, you'll find that there are three sizes of chairs in that room . . . because there are three sizes of children, and they can't all use the same chairs.
>
> . . . no two people are alike. Their rates of learning are not alike. There's nothing at all about them that is alike. Yet we must cram them into some sort of grades. . . .

In the months following his father's interview, Don drafted a story about a thirty-five-year-old man named Joseph who has been, through clerical error, "officially" declared "a child" and sent back to Horace Greeley Elementary School. "I . . . sit in this too-small seat with the desktop cramping my thighs . . . in the no-nonsense ugliness of this steel and glass building," he says. Like Don's father, Joseph discovers that age is not an accurate predictor of development. "The distinction between children and adults, while probably useful for some purposes, is at bottom a specious one, I feel," Joseph says. "There are only individual egos, crazy for love."

Eventually, it dawns on him that he has not been forced here by accident, after all. "A ruined marriage, a ruined . . . career, a grim interlude in the Army when I was almost not a person. This is the sum of my existence to date, a dismal total," he says. "Small wonder that re-education seemed my only hope. It is clear even to me that I need reworking in some fundamental way. How efficient is the society that provides thus for the salvage of its clinkers!" He will sit in the wrong-size desk, reliving his early schooling, until he learns to conform.

Like "Pages from the Annual Report" and the aborted drafts of "Hiding Man," "The Darling Duckling at School" proceeds from a Kafka-like vision—an all-knowing and secretive system controls everyone's lives—but the story succeeds, where the others did not, because it is animated by more than its premise. Personal anguish (a "ruined marriage," a "ruined career") and Don's wry admiration for his father's views lift the piece beyond its clever conception and into pathos.

Joseph has "misread" society's signs. In his "former existence" as an insurance-claims adjustor, he "read the company motto ('Here to Help in Time of Need') as a description of the duty of the adjustor, drastically mislocating the company's deepest concerns," which are to earn a hefty profit and please its investors. This failure to heed cultural "clues"—a concern raised by Walker Percy and Marshall McLuhan in their *Forum* pieces—spirals Joseph into a Nietzschean repetition. The teacher's name, Mandible (a fearsome, man-eating creature?), suggests another reason for Joseph's regression.

Yet in Don's hands, the situation is not a nightmare. Joseph wonders at the life around him, enjoying the "furnace of love, love, love" in the sixth-grade classroom. In his former job, he had been compelled to spend time "amid the debris of our civilization: rumpled fenders, roofless sheds, gutted warehouses, smashed arms and legs." He admits, "After ten years of this one has a tendency to see the world as a vast junkyard, looking at a man and seeing only his (potentially) mangled arms, entering a house only to trace the path of the inevitable fire." Still, Joseph marvels at the world, combing through its trash with the interest of an artist, plucking castoffs to make a collage. A sweet optimism fills the story, despite Joseph's disastrous fate. He fulfills the teacher sexually ("She knows now that everything she has been told about life, about America, is true") and they get caught.

When Don had finished a satisfactory draft of the story, he walked into the dining room and said to Helen, "Well, Babe, are you ready for this?" Helen later wrote, "I turned ... and saw Don standing there holding a typescript. [He] spoke in a serious, challenging tone, but underlying it was a kind of gaiety that characterized his mood as he worked. We moved into the living room, and I sat on the sofa while he stood facing me and read. ... His voice was rich and deep, every word precisely enunciated. I was astonished— I had heard nothing like it before, yet in it I could hear the Don that I knew and loved, his incisive wit and his satirical humor, the matter-of-fact tone and the ironies it created."

Don sent the story to an ambitious new West Coast journal called *Contact.* Each morning, he eagerly anticipated the postman's arrival, leaving his desk and waiting on the front porch to take the mail. Within weeks, *Contact* responded positively.

The magazine's history is worth reviewing, since Don believed his work belonged in its pages. One of its editors was Evan S. Connell, who would write the brilliant novels *Mrs. Bridge* and *Mr. Bridge*, and several other distinguished books. *Contact* had enjoyed two previous incarnations before it was revived in 1958. In 1920, William Carlos Williams cofounded the journal, with the aim of presenting writing that was "stark" and "fearlessly obscene," literature that would "speak to the present." He chose the name because he believed, erroneously, airplane pilots said "Contact" when they touched ground after a flight. The word suggested earthiness as well as the ability to soar, and it had a modern ring.

From 1920 to 1923, *Contact* published Ezra Pound, Kenneth Burke, H.D., Marianne Moore, and Wallace Stevens, among others. After that, the magazine suspended publication, as Williams busied himself with his own writing. In 1931, the year of Don's birth, Williams was ready to try the journal again, and he chose as his coeditor Nathanael West.

At the time, West was flirting with Surrealism. On the dust jacket of his novel *The Dream Life of Balso Snell,* he described himself as "much like Guillaume Apollinaire, Jarry, Ribemont-Dessaignes, Raymond Roussel, and certain of the surrealists" in his "use of the violently disassociated, the dehumanized marvelous." West's sensibility seemed antithetical to Williams's longing for a spare, natively American realism. But in 1931, when Surrealism made its American debut at the Wadsworth Athenaeum in Hartford, Connecticut, in a show that featured Picasso, Max Ernst, and De Chirico, curators translated the word *Surrealism* as "Super-Realism." Like Surrealist painters, the writers West admired were not content to define Surrealism as dream imagery and unconscious impulses. The unconscious, they said, was filled with clichés, trivia, and debris from popular culture—hence, Duchamp's ready-mades, cultural objects, like his urinal, that become art because we *call* them art, and see them with fresh vision. Williams's famous "red wheelbarrow" is just such an object.

Here was the point of contact between Williams and West, between Surrealism and Super-Realism. The men were united in their desire to translate Surrealism to an American landscape. Among the writers they sought to publish were Hemingway, Faulkner, Edward Dahlberg, Hart Crane, and Harold Rosenberg.

In a decade when naturalism dominated American literature (*Studs Lonigan, The Grapes of Wrath*), *Contact* chose the path of nonconformance. West, who explored the malevolence of American jingoism through his character Lemuel Pitkin, was writing almost entirely in clichés—deliberately so, as he understood the power of banality to shape public experience. His deadpan delivery, use of worn-out phrases, and the dumbing down of therapeutic approaches—eventually, Don would seize and refine each of these stylistic strategies. Given *Contact*'s colorful past, it's not surprising he chose the journal as the first place to send his work.

On the cover of the issue in which Don's story appeared (February 1961), a street worker, gripping his hard hat, leans against a wheelbarrow—an homage to Williams's poem. Williams is listed as a contributing editor, along with Nelson Algren, Wallace Stegner, Walter Van Tilburg Clark, and S. I. Hayakawa.

In payment for his story, Don received "12 Shares of Class A Capital Stock of Angel Island Publications, Inc."

"Don observed that he felt a bit like he was starting a new life, that he felt a little strange," Helen recalled. After a morning of writing, he would sometimes help Helen compose ad copy or design a print ad. "[He] did not enjoy writing such material, especially anything in which humor was inappropriate," she said. "For print media advertising, he was much more interested in art and design than in copy. I worked with several commercial artists, but Don designed most of the ads during the first year of my agency."

In the afternoons, he helped Helen organize her lectures for Dominican College. For a course she was teaching on the short story, he wrote the following notes: "In a work of literature form and content are so beautifully welded together that it is difficult to separate them. . . . Form may be said to be the arrangement of parts so that a preconceived effect is successfully achieved. In a successful work of literature, *Form* is used to state or establish *Meaning* . . . [the] task of the writer in general is to give form to the raw material of experience—to say what it means."

He once told Helen he thought formal experimentation could lead him to other dimensions of experience besides that of time-bound realism, to a place where "everything is different." The world as it is disappointed him, as it had disappointed his father. Accepted wisdom and the accepted *forms* of things had gone stale. He insisted, "What I write has to be in the present. I cannot understand how anyone can be interested in the past."

He returned to "Hiding Man."

Helen wrote that the story's theme may "have been suggested by an article that had appeared in *Time* magazine in which Marcel Camus is quoted as saying, 'The cinema has replaced the church, and people seek truth at movies instead of the Mass.'" At the time, Camus was a relatively unknown French film director who had just completed his first feature, *Black Orpheus,* a translation of the Orpheus myth to the barrios and hills of contemporary Brazil.

In its issue of November 16, 1959, *Time* ran an article on *Black Orpheus* and the French New Wave. Camus, quoted extensively, did not mention film in connection with the church, but an unnamed critic said movie directors now "speak of cinema as of a religion."

Whether or not Don was thinking of this article, he clearly had in mind Walker Percy's *The Moviegoer* as he began reworking "The Hiding Man." Don's story is less about movies than about popular entertainment and church rituals as sign systems. It is a McLuhan-like exercise in reading American culture for clues to concealed realities.

In the story the theater's movies—*Attack of the Puppet People, She Gods of Shark Reef, Night of the Blood Beast*—recall movies Don reviewed for the *Houston Post.* "People think these things are jokes," the narrator, Burlingame, says of the films. "[B]ut they are wrong, it is dangerous to ignore a vision. . . ."

Like Ralph Ellison's protagonist in *Invisible Man,* Burlingame has freed himself from the received ideas of society and church. He has learned to interpret the culture, and he has gone underground. "Most people don't have the wit to be afraid," he says. "[M]ost view television, smoke cigars, fondle wives, have children, vote . . . never confront *Screaming Skull, Teenage Werewolf, Beast with a Thousand Eyes,* no conception of what lies beneath the surface, no faith in any manifestation not certified by hierarchy."

Just two years after Don published "Hiding Man" in the Spring-Summer 1961 issue of *First Person,* America was stunned by a man who tried to hide in a nearly empty movie theater. When Lee Harvey Oswald ducked into the Texas Theatre in Dallas shortly after President Kennedy was shot, two genre movies were playing, *War Is Hell* and *Cry of Battle.* As Burligame says, "it is dangerous to ignore a vision," especially a nation's violent image of itself, neatly packaged in its popular entertainments. "People think these things are jokes, but they are wrong."

In her memoir, Helen said:

> As Don wrote his first stories, trying to do something that no other writer had yet attempted, I did not find his work strange. Nor was it puzzling. . . . The idea of creating fantasies or incongruous situations, of combining the real with the unreal, was emerging as a new way of interpreting the world. . . .
>
> In the literature of the post-World War II period, and with the continuing dominance of New Criticism, the story as an object mattered; it was a work of art that the writer created. And the most powerful influence of all continued to be what the Modernists, especially Pound and Eliot, had given us: the necessity of creating something "new."
>
> A reader did not ask what a story or poem meant. . . . What you talked about was "form and content." This phrase seems hackneyed today, out-of-date and overworked. But it was real then, and what is more important, it was at the heart of Don's creativity.

Maggie Maranto offers a slightly different perspective:

> Though Don was an essentially post-Word War II product, he was really just about the last of a long line of wonderfully inventive, trenchant, but

lighthearted humorists who filled the pages of newspapers, magazines, and books dating back to the late 1800s. A number of popular magazines were being published in the early years of the twentieth century, leading to a proliferation of fiction writers, since they could actually make a living from their contributions. There was, for example, Jerome K. Jerome, P. G. Wodehouse, Booth Tarkington, James Thurber, Dorothy Parker, Ring Lardner, and S. J. Perelman. All of them catalyzed Don's thinking and his view of life, and inspired him to put his own special, unique wit to paper.

These summaries, insightful as they are, suggest a more uniform literary setting than existed in America. Don's struggles with *Forum* show how limited taste could be, even in (maybe *especially* in) an academic environment. As Don began to write in earnest, Nabokov's *Lolita* still faced bookstore bans, nearly five years after it had first been published in the United States. *Time* magazine wrote of Samuel Beckett, "[his] vision is too ghastly to be borne in the long run . . . [he] has conjured it up about as many times as most readers will be able to stand" (ten years later, he won the Nobel Prize).

Yet news weeklies discussed complex writers such as Albert Camus and Max Frisch. In October 1960, as Don started writing every morning, *Time* reviewed a translation of Heinrich von Kleist's *The Marquise of O,* which became one of Don's favorite books. In spite of moral, legal, and financial challenges, in spite of the stubbornness of old-fashioned tastes, literary possibilities seemed to be expanding, and finding popular acceptance.

Nathanael West's darkness, in *Miss Lonelyhearts* and *A Cool Million,* flowered in the black humor of the 1950s and early 1960s. Some observers felt nihilism and absurd laughter were inevitable reactions to the war in Korea or McCarthyism. Unsparing novels by ex-soldiers such as James Jones and Norman Mailer posit the shock of World War II as the center of a cynical worldview that offered laughter as the best response to nuclear threats and Nazi atrocities.

If we take a still longer view, we see West extending a tradition of grotesque humor traceable to Hawthorne, Poe, Melville, and Twain. But in the 1950s and 1960s, many American writers—among them, Mailer, J. D. Salinger, Ken Kesey, John Barth, Kurt Vonnegut, and Terry Southern—used wicked comedy in a particularly self-conscious manner. Joseph Heller's *Catch-22* holds pride of place on the period's Shelf of Alienated Laughter. In 1969, Bruce Jay Friedman edited a widely reviewed anthology called *Black Humor.* By 1969, black humor had begun to fade as a publishing trend; Friedman admitted that very little bound the writers he had picked for the book. Yet he insisted that "if you are alive today, and stick your head out of doors now and then, you know that there is a nervousness, a tempo, a near-hysterical new beat in the air, a punishing isolation and loneliness of a strange, frenzied new kind. It is in the music and the talk and the films and the theater and it is in the prose style" of American writers.

A vague claim, but hard to dispute at the time. A nervous frenzy invaded the homes of middle-class Americans every evening via their television screens. Images of mushroom clouds nestled among commercials for hair spray and canned peas. Sitcom characters mocked civic values. Stand-up comedians—Mike Nichols and Elaine May, Mort Sahl, Lenny Bruce—edged their performances toward political satire. The daily newspaper was Sahl's comic prop. The "*New York Times* . . . is the source and fountain and bible of black humor," Friedman wrote.

It was not only the content but also the *style* of humor that felt quicker, harder, meaner. Spontaneity and improvisation became commonplace in stand-up comedy—a jazz influence. Several comics served as warm-up acts in nightclubs, and romanticized the musicians. "Lenny Bruce seems concerned [only] with . . . making the band laugh," a newspaper reviewer wrote. It was a jazzman, Philly Joe Jones, Miles Davis's drummer, who got Bruce work in the early days, and spread the word about his talent.

"Abstraction" was the "direction in which I was going," Bruce once said. "Musicians, jazz musicians especially, appreciate art forms that are *extensions* of realism, as opposed to realism in a representational form."

Bruce's routines, said a reviewer, are "clearly the equivalents of the brief but corny 'quotes' from another tune and the sardonic, deadpan mockery with which a jazzman can approach a very square set of chord changes."

Nathanael West worked such changes in his black-humor masterpiece, *A Cool Million,* from which Don pinched the name Pitkin for his *Daily Cougar* columns. West "quoted" Horatio Alger again and again in a merciless parody of the American Dream. The typical Alger hero saves damsels in distress. Poor Pitkin gets beaten and the girl gets raped. West related these disasters in Alger's cheerful style, sometimes stealing whole scenes from Alger's novels and altering only a word or two.

Most of all, literary black humor shared with the popular comedy of the 1950s and 1960s a cynicism toward the *language* of the status quo. As Bruce said, as West's novels demonstrated, and as Don clearly saw, "[H]umor [lay in] distinguishing between the *moral* differences of words and their connotations."

THE UGLY SHOW

Composing a great or even near-great bookshop is as exacting a task as composing a novel [says Larry McMurtry]. One has to be done word by word . . . the other volume by volume. . . . Booksellers who manage . . . to keep their shelves filled with interesting books will rarely be the most successful financially. The world, by and large, is well content to buy the conventional standards—the sort of books that make safe gifts to god-children. But the booksellers who have interesting books will always have . . . respect. . . .

In Houston, in 1960, as Don started to write his first important stories, the great book store was the Brown Book Shop, on San Jacinto Street, near Buffalo Bayou, downtown. The bayou meanders through Houston, only a few feet deep in spots, and in other places filled with family discards: old shoes, busted toasters, empty picture frames. In the sixties, San Jacinto Street was a flat, nondescript business corridor. The bookshop's proprietor, Ted Brown, was highly pragmatic. He knew that Houston bobbed on a sea of oil, and he stocked his shelves with books on petroleum, geology, and drilling technology. But he was also "elegant," according to McMurtry, a bit of a dandy: His "heart, all along, was in literature, and he kept a wall . . . of sets, first editions, travel literature, press books."

After a morning of writing, Don drove to Brown's store to browse

through the Grove paperback editions, the Evergreen books featuring European playwrights and American experimental novelists. He bought copies of the *Tulane Drama Review,* which excerpted one-act plays and essays associated with the Theatre of the Absurd. He bought plays by Edward Albee, Bertolt Brecht, and Arthur Kopit. He thumbed through Ionesco's *The Bald Soprano,* Robbe-Grillet's *The Voyeur,* and Arrabal's *The Automobile Graveyard.* He snatched up Max Frisch's novel *I'm Not Stiller.* And always, he prowled around for Beckett.

Houston was blessed with several secondhand bookshops, as well as junk stores overflowing with jazz 78s and yellowed volumes of the classics. There was Joe Petty's, downtown, and rows of antique stores along Washington Avenue. McMurtry recalled:

> My book hunting seldom turned up anything of much value, but it kept me in reading matter and also gave me a knowledge of the funkier reaches of Houston that has stayed with me to this day. I came to love the city, particularly its steamy, shoddy, falling-down sections. Houston as a city was a series of crumbling, half-silted-over neighborhoods. You could still come upon little drugstores that looked as if they had been free-framed by a *Life* photographer in the thirties. Once, in a district not far from the slum that's called the Bottoms, I came upon a vast wooden boat, so weedy and overgrown with vines and creepers that it was hard to even guess what period it dated from. It sat in the middle of a large, neglected lot, visited only by winos and grackles. Sam Houston could have ridden in that boat, or Cabeza de Vaca.

Don knew Houston's funky reaches, too; like McMurtry, he had discovered them while searching for books, records, live jazz, and old furniture. In "Return," Don imagined motoring along the bayou on a raft "powered by eight mighty Weed-Eaters." He wrote:

> I saw many strange and wonderful things. I saw an egret and then another egret and a turtle and a refrigerator without a door on it and a heron and a possum and an upside-down '52 Pontiac. And I said to myself, this blessed stream contains many strange and wonderful things. It was getting dark now, and the moon had risen, and I saw a wise old owl sitting in a tree. So I throttled back my eight powerful Weed-Eaters and spoke to the owl, saying, "How's by you, boychick?"
>
> And then I looked closely and saw that it wasn't a wise old owl at all, it was Philip Johnson, out hunting for new clients, by the light of the moon.

• • •

When he wasn't lingering in Brown's, or following the bayou's trickle to some hidden treasure, Don spent his afternoons with artist friends, folks active in the city's Contemporary Arts Association. He was close to Jack Boynton, a painter who combined abstraction with whimsical Texas imagery. Boynton's best-known painting is *Amarillo Boot,* a colorful cowboy boot embossed with the word *ART.*

Don lunched with Jim Love, a sculptor who worked with detritus salvaged from the bayou. He made birds out of hammers, dogs with garden spades.

Love and Boynton knew that Don was writing stories, but Don didn't discuss his fiction with them. "You sure are an illiterate bastard," he kidded Boynton. It was true that Boynton didn't read much. His wife, Ann, was severely depressed. She had given up painting to raise her two daughters, and she worried about money. Don and Boynton's conversations revolved around Ann's troubles, and the difficulties artists faced in the marketplace.

Among Don's other friends, only Joe Maranto expressed an interest in Don's writing, but the Marantos had moved back east. Joe was doing PR work for Mobil Oil in New York. Don stayed in touch with Herman Gollob, who had moved to Boston to work for Little, Brown, but for now, Don didn't send him any more fiction.

George Christian, Don's former colleague at the *Houston Post,* was barely aware of Don's writing. Don felt Christian wouldn't appreciate the absurdist direction his fiction was taking. Pat Goeters had established his own architectural firm. Most of his discussions with Don centered on the arts. Don "worked in even greater isolation than when he edited *Forum,*" Helen recalled. "There was no other writer with whom he could talk about his work. . . . There was simply no one at all."

Early in 1960, at the urging of Pat Goeters, Don joined the board of the Contemporary Arts Association. The CAA had begun in 1948 as an alliance of artists, business leaders, and architects who felt that the Museum of Fine Arts' traditional programming needed to be balanced with exhibits of contemporary work. The charter established the association as a nonprofit organization to be staffed by volunteers and supported by membership dues. Its first exhibition, held in two gallery spaces in the Museum of Fine Arts, opened in October 1948. It was called "This Is Contemporary Art," less a proclamation than an invitation to Houstonians: Come in. This stuff won't bite.

In 1949, the architectural firm of MacKie and Kamrath designed a museum building and erected it, for five thousand dollars, on a downtown site owned by a family named Detering (who would later open Houston's premier rare-book shop). The Contemporary Arts Association paid a dollar a year for its museum lease. In time, the Deterings felt they could no longer afford to be so generous. In 1954, the owners of the Prudential Insurance Company lot, near the corner of Fannin and Holcombe, extended a charitable hand to the CAA.

In its new spot, the museum, a small triangular building of glass and steel, sat in the shadow of the eighteen-story Prudential Building. An azalea forecourt and an elaborate fountain, placed between the museum and the skyscraper's entrance, welcomed visitors into a pleasant open space.

The CAA's success began to strain its volunteers. It needed more resources, firmer support. Accounts vary as to when Jean and Dominique de Menil got involved, though Jean *was* elected to the first board of directors. In 1955, the Menils came up with the money to hire the Contemporary Arts Museum's first salaried director, Jermayne MacAgy.

Houston's cultural life is impossible to imagine without the Menils. Even those, like Don, who tried to avoid their reach were dependent on them for the vibrancy and rapid development of Houston's arts scene. Jean de Menil came from an aristocratic French family. In World War II, he worked for the Resistance, "traveling through Europe on 'business trips,' conducting cloakand-dagger missions for the underground," wrote Frank Welch, a Texas architect. Dominique was the daughter of Conrad Schlumberger, the man who developed *the* system for discovering subsurface oil; petroleum companies adopted it worldwide. Dominique was heir to a vast fortune. She was energetic and intellectually curious, eventually studying math and science at the Sorbonne. She met Jean at a ball in Versailles. A devout Catholic, Dominique fell under the sway of a Dominican priest in Paris, Father Marie-Alain Couturier, a follower of modern art. He introduced the Menils to the Cubist paintings of Picasso and Braque, and sparked in them a lifelong passion for collecting.

The Menils fled Paris just ahead of the Nazis, and arrived in Houston in the late 1940s. Jean went to work for the Schlumberger Oil Company. He "just loved things American and *Texan!*" recalls an acquaintance. Dominique adapted quickly to her new home, but noted disapprovingly that "Houstonians [think] nothing about spending thousands on a prize bull but [draw] the line at buying art."

On one of their many trips to New York, the couple met Philip Johnson. They invited him to Houston to design their house—the beginning of Johnson's long relationship with the city. The local architectural establishment felt snubbed. "[Jean] and Dominique wanted to set an example" of improving the city's culture, recalled their friend, Marguerite Barnes. "Out of town" professionals had more mystique than the local boys, and Jean sought "cachet . . . with the New York culturati." "They really had the thought that if they brought someone like Philip Johnson to Houston and he designed a nice house, it would lead to better architecture in the city," Barnes said. They "wanted to improve the climate."

Johnson designed for them a 5,600-square-foot wood-frame house on San Felipe Road, in the River Oaks neighborhood, with a glass entry and a facade of salmon-colored brick. Completed in 1950, it was the first International Style house built in Houston.

In 1955, the Menils lured Jermayne MacAgy from San Francisco's Palace of the Legion of Honor to direct Houston's Contemporary Arts Museum. In addition to arranging shows of individual artists, such as Mondrian and Rothko, MacAgy organized thematic exhibits that placed contemporary art in a historical context. She mounted a Surrealist retrospective and a show on art and technology; in 1959, she curated "Totems Not Taboo: An Exhibition of Primitive Art," which featured over two hundred rare pieces from across the world.

In mid-1959, the CAA board voted not to renew MacAgy's contract. Frank Welch has said there was "controversy over . . . MacAgy's radical ideas." The more likely explanation is that the "Menil grip" had proved too tight for the board. "I know that Don thought that Dominique was dominating and somewhat imperious," Marion Barthelme says. He "was not interested in getting trapped in her powerful web." The CAA board probably felt the same (even to her friends, Dominique was known as the "Iron Butterfly").

After MacAgy's dismissal by the CAA, Don's friend Robert Morris assumed the directorship of the Contemporary Arts Museum, and he and Don set about organizing the "Out of the Ordinary" show, which ran from November 26 to December 27, 1959.

Morris left shortly after that to take a job at the University of Bridgeport, in Connecticut. The CAA board scrambled to distribute responsibilities among volunteers. Each board member agreed to arrange a show for the coming year, and to work with others to schedule special events. Given the board's varied interests, film, theater, music, and architecture became as visible as painting and sculpture.

In April 1960, the museum presented, in the new Cullinan Hall at the Museum of Fine Arts, a show entitled "Architectural Graphics." Don wrote the catalog introduction. "The city . . . may be seen as a texture of signs which must be correctly read if they are to yield their secrets," Don said. "Many of these [signs] are necessary: we are all familiar with the anarchy which obtains when a traffic light breaks down. Others are gratuitous, a gift from the makers of, say, Wunda Cola, and hardly essential to survival. Both kinds of messages claim space in the visual landscape."

From an "oversupply of information" in the culture, "we must constantly select that which is relevant, that which is true," Don wrote. "Some messages are contradictory; others are disguised." Further, "we live in secondhand

worlds . . . between the human consciousness and experience there is inter-
posed a screen of communications, designs, patterns, and values which instruct us in what we are experiencing, and sometimes, have the experience
for us."

Don realized that these cultural pressures posed severe challenges to
artists, including writers. The "traditional alphabet is staggering under the
tremendous variety of functions we are asking it to serve," he wrote.

> Words are not suited to electronic computers, which utilize the language
> of mathematics, nor to such emerging phenomena as the post office's
> new letter-sorting devices, which reduce the old alphabet to clusters of
> horizontals and verticals. The inadequacy of our present system is also il-
> lustrated by the thousands of special symbols developed to handle spe-
> cial problems, those of printers, map makers, electrical engineers,
> chemists, biologists, and so on.
>
> Thus the vocabulary of [the artist] is further strained. In this welter of
> competing interests, he must find a solution that is acceptable to all and
> is, if possible, beautiful. The problem . . . that our experience is struc-
> tured by the very devices we use to clarify it, places a considerable re-
> sponsibility on the man who is sending the message.

In the fiction he had started to write, he was probing this responsibility.
Already he was pushing, playing with, and shattering physical texts on the
page, using his sensual awareness of typography. As his narrator (a sort of
off-kilter museum director) would say in "The Flight of Pigeons from the
Palace":

> The public demands new wonders piled on new wonders.
>   Often we don't know where our next marvel is coming from.
>   The supply of strange ideas is not endless.
>   The development of new wonders is not like the production of canned
> goods.
>   Some things appear to be wonders in the beginning, but when you be-
> come familiar with them, are not wonderful at all.

For his exhibition in the CAM's gallery space, Don mounted "New American
Artifacts: The Ugly Show." Excited by Duchamp's ready-mades, and Harold
Rosenberg's "anxious object"—a constructed piece that doesn't know if it's a
work of art or a pile of junk—Don collected from pawnshops, antique stores,
and the banks of Buffalo Bayou "cultural artifacts of ambivalent status." Fellow board members complained that things like brass knuckles didn't belong

in a museum, but that was Don's point. When stripped of its usual function, and placed in an aesthetic context, a pair of brass knuckles can be seen in an entirely new light—as an intriguingly shaped object, ugly or not. At the same time, the object does not lose its former connotations; rather, those meanings get smuggled into a new realm of experience.

Don's list of the show's "wonders" reads like the verbal collages that would spice his fiction:

> A baby blue styrofoam chrysanthemum. An auto hubcap, brand unrecognizable. A hideous jukebox. Paint-by-number pictures of lambs, sans paint. An unbelievably ugly plastic chair. A giant-size vaseline jar. An imitation shrunken head. A plaster "flamenco." *Reader's Digest. Official Detective. Ricky Nelson Magazine.* A TV antenna. A whiskey decanter disguised as a Greek vase. Bunny rabbit decals. *Big Bonus* stamps. A gilded baby shoe coin bank. *Klutch* denture adhesive. Plastic-bright artificial fruit. *Tiki Joe's Luau Kit.* A plastic red rose in pseudo crystal vase. Three (bad) reproductions of Gainsborough's *Blue Boy.* An "obscene" ashtray. A large Coke bottle. A box of *All.* Half-ceramic, half-wood totem poles. A toy machine gun. A plastic soldier's helmet. "A roseate and gaudily commercialized" badly-printed stuffed head of Christ. A copy of the American flag printed out of register on flimsy plastic.

Right away, Prudential received a complaint from a museum visitor: How could these last two "objectionable" items be displayed on property owned by the insurance company? A few days later, Don told a newspaper reporter that the head of Christ and the plastic American flag "belong in the show and I don't agree that their removal was necessary. We took them down, however, because Prudential requested it." His pique at the company may have inclined him to mock insurance firms in "The Darling Duckling at School." The narrator's habit of seeing the world as a massive field of litter belongs to the kind of sensibility that created "The Ugly Show." The exhibition ran from June 17 to July 19, 1960. Always, Don looked back on it with fondness and pride.

DANGLING MAN

As he began to write in earnest, Don had his eye on visual art, theater, film, and music. He also thought about what it meant to be a
Texan. Two of his short essays, published in the spring of 1960, de-
cipher Texas "signs," and suggest that the Lone Star State left him
hanging.

"Culture, Etc.," published in the *Texas Observer* on March 25,
explored the "myth that every Texan is in some sense a cowboy, or
capable of being one, or should possess the cowboy virtues." This
myth, Don said, is "received from the media" and enforces "provincialism." It produces exquisite ironies:

. . . we have the moneyed cowboy whose money proceeds not from cattle
but from a nice little plastics plant. To complicate the picture insanely,
let us say that he is also, in his rough-hewn way, a patron of the arts. Note
that the drama here is generated by the delicious incongruity he
presents—and savors—in his role of the cultured cowboy: "I died with my
boots on in the Art Museum." When we remember that he is not a cowboy
at all but a plastics engineer, the multiple level of the charade is revealed,
the lostness of the leading actor established.

Frequently, Don encountered such "schizophrenics" in Houston's art circles. He felt the pressure, familiar to every Texas male,

to adopt a laconic God-and-football swagger. The "ritual demands of the [cowboy] role" sever "certain important areas of thought and feeling" from anyone who tries it on, Don wrote.

One afternoon, in the Texana section of the Brown Book Shop, he discovered a curious, slender novel self-published by H. L. Hunt. It was called *Alpaca,* and it took place in a "tiny, vaguely Southern American republic." Hunt was a Dallas millionaire who fit the stereotype of the Texas oil tycoon. His novel was a radical proposal for changing the U.S. Constitution, disguised as a utopian fantasy: The "establishment of a perfect state where the number of votes a man has bears some resemblance to his financial status." As Don notes, one of Hunt's characters claims, "[W]hat is good for the possessor of the greatest wealth in the Nation is good for the poorest citizen."

Don reviewed the book in the *Reporter* on April 14 and mocked the "modesty" of men like Hunt: "One of the disadvantages of being the richest man in the country (or the second or fourth) must be a profound sense of political frustration," he wrote. "No matter how many billions you command, you are given under the Constitution only one vote. The insult is personal; in the voting booth, you are brought at a stroke to the level of the poorest citizen. . . . H. L. Hunt of Dallas sets out to correct this gross equity."

In the fall of 1960, around the time he began drafting "The Darling Duckling at School," Don negotiated with the New York producers of Beckett's *Krapp's Last Tape* and Edward Albee's *The Zoo Story* to bring the shows to Houston, under the auspices of the Contemporary Arts Association. An off-Broadway cast from the Cricket Theatre had performed both plays in Manhattan, and Don arranged for a double-bill performance in the University of Houston's Cullen Auditorium on January 30 and 31.

Shortly afterward, he persuaded a local actor, Tom Toner of the Alley Theatre, to give a staged reading from Dostoevsky's *Notes from Underground.* Mack McCormick, a Houston folklorist, wrote a musical based on the song "Hang Down Your Head, Tom Dooley," and Don staged it at the Contemporary Arts Museum. McCormick had recently seen the once-legendary blues singer Lightnin' Hopkins playing to small crowds in Dowling Street dance halls. With Don's help, he arranged a Hopkins concert at the museum.

Don's energy, his creativity, and his ability to get things done impressed his fellow board members. They urged him to consider filling the vacancy left by Bob Morris. Don was writing now; he did not want a full-time job. He asked if a part-time director would satisfy the board. They responded enthusiastically.

On March 12, 1961, Don submitted his formal application to the CAA.

"Don relished the challenge of it," Helen recalled. Upon receiving the board's approval, he "began a schedule in which he wrote for at least four, sometimes five hours, after which he turned his attention to the museum. It was an ideal schedule for Don."

His first initiative was to arrange a lecture by Harold Rosenberg. "Every year something almost takes me to Texas but I never quite make it," Rosenberg replied to Don's query. "The minumum fee would be $250. Perhaps this is more than you had in mind, so that once again I shall have almost visited Texas. It was pleasant to hear from you again."

While Don courted Rosenberg, *The New Yorker* ran two long articles, in back-to-back issues, on "The Super-American State" of Texas. Don feared Rosenberg would see them and *never* want to visit Houston. The writer, John Bainbridge, offered old chestnuts: "The life-style in Texas is marked by bravado, zest, optimism, ebullience." He was seduced by clichés: the "so-called American Dream . . . come[s] true . . . in Texas. Novels and movies about Texas sometimes give the impression that the native millionaires travel in nothing but four-engine airplanes complete with bar [and] galley. . . . As a matter of fact, some years ago [oilman] Glenn McCarthy did own a Boeing Stratocruiser. . . ."

Don was particularly incensed by the magzine's dismissal of Texas's cultural treasures. John Graves, one of the best writers in the state, got only a passing nod in the piece; instead, Bainbridge lingered over purple-prosers like Mary Lasswell and Mrs. Perry Wampler Nichols (who wrote, "Visitors stepping into this land of bluebonnets and endless skies find weaving about their hearts, like webs spun by giant spiders, the love of something friendly and great"). Houston's Contemporary Arts Museum, one of the country's most innovative institutions of its kind, was not mentioned.

"What is the biographer going to do for a region that has so few men of distinction?" the historian Walter Prescott Webb once asked about Texas. The question, Bainbridge said, still awaited an answer.

On April 13, Don wrote Rosenberg, "It's cheering to find that you're not intimidated by all that nonsense in the *New Yorker*." His citizen's pride had been hurt; worse, he knew he could have done a better job for the magazine.

He agreed to Rosenberg's fee. "I'm pleased at the idea of having you on our cultural vaudeville series," he said. As to the potential crowd size, he said, "I can only suggest that we have had audiences ranging from one to three or four hundreds for these things. Some of them will be very knowledgeable, some won't."

Rosenberg arrived in Houston on May 10, and stayed for three days. Don put him up in the Warwick, one of the city's finest hotels, near the Museum of Fine Arts and the Rice Institute. Rosenberg drew a moderate crowd for his lecture, which was on the "subject of continuity and novelty in contemporary painting."

John Bainbridge's pat view of Texas would have collapsed if he'd learned that the director of an arts museum in Houston, who staged Beckett plays and Lightnin' Hopkins concerts, was writing short stories like "Florence Green Is 81," in which the narrator, a writer named Baskerville, "free associat[es], brilliantly, brilliantly," to "put" the reader into the center of his consciousness.

Baskerville, an ex-Catholic and an admirer of Edmund Husserl, edits with his "left hand a small magazine, very scholarly, very brilliant, called *The Journal of Tension Reduction* (social-psychological studies, learned disputation, letters-to-the-editor, anxiety in rats)." The range of references in his thought stream reflects the articles he has edited: lentils, Siberia, Quemoy and Matsu, the population of Santa Ana, California, the Sea of Okhotsk. The story takes place at a dinner party in the home of Florence Green, a wealthy arts patron. Baskerville, working to secure funding for his magazine, flirts unsuccessfully with an attractive young woman across the table, drinks too much, and admires Florence Green's desire to go someplace "where *everything is different.*"

Two years later, when the story appeared in *Harper's Bazaar,* "several prominent Houstonians"—including Dominique de Menil—"believed the character of Florence was based on each of them," Helen recalled.

At about the time Don took charge at the museum, he was working on two other stories, "The Big Broadcast of 1938" and "The Viennese Opera Ball," both of which would appear in literary journals in 1962 ("Broadcast" in *New World Writing* and the "Opera Ball" in *Contact*). "The Viennese Opera Ball" presents a rush of cocktail-party chatter—a language collage. "The Big Broadcast of 1938" tells the story of Bloomsbury, a man recently divorced from his wife, Martha. Somehow, in exchange for giving Martha the house he had shared with her, he has acquired a radio station: "Bloomsbury could now play 'The Star-Spangled Banner,' which he had always admired immoderately, on account of its finality, as often as he liked. It meant, to him, that everything was finished. Therefore he played it daily, 60 times between 6 and 10 a.m., 120 times between 12 noon and 7 p.m., and the whole night long except when, as was sometimes the case, he was talking."

His "talking" consists of repeating a word—*nevertheless,* say—over and over for a quarter of an hour, during which the "word would frequently disclose new properties, [and] unsuspected qualities." Despite its absurd premise, the story is genuinely moving, as Bloomsbury, a man alone in the middle of the night, talks to his distant ex, who is probably not even listening. He broadcasts his oddly evocative words until the electric company, whose bill he hasn't paid, shuts him down.

In May of 1961, after he had directed the Contemporary Arts Museum for less than two months, Don learned of a writer's conference sponsored by Wagner College on Staten Island. Saul Bellow, Robert Lowell, and Edward Albee would be the writers in residence. Sterling Lord, a powerful literary agent, was scheduled to give a lecture on publishing. Only fifteen fiction writers would be selected to have their work critiqued by Bellow. Don was interested in the opportunity; he was also excited about the possibility of seeing New York City for the first time.

He mailed off a personal bio along with "The Darling Duckling at School" and "The Big Broadcast of 1938," which he had just sold to *New World Writing*. Right away, the conference organizers accepted his application.

On July 9, he and Helen flew into Newark and then took a shuttle bus to Manhattan's East Side. They knew nothing of New York except that Grand Central Terminal was conveniently located and that it was near the Mobil Oil offices, where Joe Maranto worked. "[Our] hotel and its setting were bleak," Helen recalled.

The couple spent the weekend with Joe and Maggie Maranto. They walked to Central Park, to the Museum of Modern Art, and to the Met. It was a "treat" to stop in randomly at galleries. Mostly, though, they were overwhelmed by all there was to see in so short a time.

On Monday morning, they walked through Battery Park to Manhattan's southern tip. The ferries for Ellis Island and the Statue of Liberty left from there; Castle Garden (now called Clinton Castle), an old fort that had once protected the harbor, drew crowds with its fast-food stands and coin-operated binoculars offering views of the water. At one time, Castle Garden had processed immigrants. On this pleasant summer morning, Don and Helen were immigrants in a new world, and they shared the excitement of the people around them.

They walked past the waterfront's perpendicular piers (the "miserable . . . slipshod, shambling piers of New York," Herman Melville once said of them). At the Staten Island Ferry terminal, shabby and crowded with pizza shops, Don bought a pair of tickets.

After crossing the water, the couple caught a cab to Wagner College. The conference was scheduled for ten days and would consist of class sessions, individual meetings with the writers in residence, readings, and lectures. Don and Helen shared a dorm room and ate in a campus dining hall. Among the other students at the conference were Susan Dworkin, only nineteen (she would become an accomplished playwright), Arno Karlen, a promising short story writer whom Don had published in *Forum,* Buzz Farber, who would end up acting in Norman Mailer's films, and Sarah Dabney, an instructor at Smith College. "This was Don's first intimate contact with other accomplished writers and the first important critical acknowledgement he received," Helen wrote. Still, he was "uncomfortable in the role of student. Since his teen years, he had been at the center of any creative group in which he took part."

Saul Bellow was a notoriously poor teacher. His "heart wasn't in it," says his biographer, James Atlas. Bellow had come to Wagner that summer expecting "leisurely days and idle nights." Instead, he told a friend, he had wound up "sweating over papers and talking 12 hours a day til my mouth was like an ashpit." The temperature hovered at around "106 degrees, like a stokehold."

The Adventures of Augie March had made him famous. Don "saw him as the major American novelist of our time," Helen recalled. Dworkin wrote, "[T]hat summer, no one in the world mattered more than Saul Bellow." The great man was uncomfortable, carrying the weight of the world. His students' " 'ego-stricken needs' unnerved him." Dworkin said he "sat and listened to us read our work in class. He sat with his thumb pressed to his temple, like a man rehearsing suicide. Sometimes he gazed into space—and when he was forced to look at us, it was with *fear.* Why this brilliant writer should be afraid of us, I could not understand. I felt sorry for him . . . I felt guilty in his presence, as though I personally had done whatever it was that had been done to Saul Bellow and was personally trying to destroy him."

In class, Bellow rambled about his marriages and the alimony he paid his former wives. "For the most part, Bellow said very little about our work," Dworkin recalled. "He seemed reluctant to make judgments or give too much guidance."

Nevertheless, he was brutal to the young men in class. Karlen submitted a chapter from a novel that read a lot like *Augie March. Augie*'s author ignored it. Farber read a story that seemed to Bellow to romanticize poverty. "I've lived in dirt, and when you've lived in dirt, there's nothing interesting about it," Bellow said.

" 'The Big Broadcast' and Don's reading of it [in class] clearly intrigued other students," Helen recalled, "but Bellow was much less enthusiastic about what Don was doing than the younger people were. I believe he . . . thought that Don's fictional world was too restricted."

"Do you really believe it's that hard for people to talk to each other?" was all Bellow said when Don had finished reading.

Don didn't respond.

After the conference, Karlen sent Bellow a letter complaining about the way he had handled the class. Bellow replied candidly, admitting that he felt competitive with other writers, especially men. "I myself have often been in-dignant with older writers, and I know how you must have felt," he wrote. He said that when he looked at Karlen, "I saw my own pale face twenty years ago . . . and no doubt I said the wrong thing[s]."

Generally, Bellow was less harsh, though less engaged, with the work of his female students. He told Dworkin, "You'll be a good writer." "I couldn't re-member ever having been so happy," she wrote. Later in the week, at a party, she overheard Bellow confess to someone that he frequently told young writ-ers they were good. "He hadn't the heart to do otherwise. They needed en-couragement so much, much more than they needed hard criticism; he was scared by the need in their faces; he remembered his own need when he was young."

"I cried and cried," Dworkin recalled. "For weeks after [that] at home, I cried. My family didn't know what to do."

One day in class, a woman named Bette Howland (who would later pub-lish many books) presented a story about an abortion. The heat in the room and the student pressure finally cracked Bellow's composure. He blurted that he couldn't stand women writers who "wore their ovaries on their sleeves."

In the afternoons, craft sessions brought together all the fiction-writing students. The discussions bored Don. They centered on characterization and scene setting—conventions that Don had worked past in his writing.

One day, a student criticized Bellow for writing *Henderson the Rain King* when he'd never been to Africa. Don couldn't believe this was even a topic of conversation; imagination was the whole point of fiction, wasn't it?

Edward Albee was the writer with whom "Don might have had [the most] rapport, but he was concerned only with the students in drama," Helen re-called. "Don was excited about having produced Albee's play for the Contem-porary Arts Association, [but] he appeared uncomfortable that Albee was the 'writer' and he was the 'pupil.' Albee had not read any of Don's stories and knew nothing of what Don was attempting to do. Don spoke with him just once briefly and that conversation concerned the Houston production of *The Zoo Story.*"

Generally, though, Albee was congenial—"thin, in large sweaters" was Dworkin's description of him. He hung around students in the evenings, whereas Bellow returned to Manhattan at the end of the day. Lowell seemed "filled with anguish," Helen wrote later. He had a "movingly sad look." "I commented to Don that I thought Lowell should not have been there—it ap-peared too difficult for him."

The students bonded—under Bellow's gaze, they shared a siege mentality—and that justified the conference to Don. One of the participants "got drunk one night and ran around the dorms with a toilet seat over his

head, shouting," Dworkin says. Another student, Ed McClanahan, an English instructor at Oregon State College, told stories about Bernard Malamud, who had taught at Oregon State, and whose latest novel, *A New Life,*
based on the school, had scandalized some of the locals. Don was "[w]ry—
drunk a lot," Dworkin recalled. He laughed at people from "behind his ice
cubes." "He didn't care what Saul Bellow thought of his work. He had
brought his wife along, and she was drinking too, and they were having a
fine, quiet time at the conference."

Don was not as sanguine as Dworkin thought he was. "I saw Don as more
insecure with [Bellow, Albee, and Lowell] than I thought he would be," Helen
said, though she admitted his insecurity came more "from his desire to have
his talent recognized than from any doubt about what he was attempting to
write. He knew that he was already an accomplished writer and wanted to be
taken more seriously."

One evening, Don and Helen were strolling across campus, when they ran
into Bellow. Helen said that Bellow "alluded to our marriage . . . [he] mentioned that there were obviously good things in Don's life that he ought to include in his work, so that his writing would encompass the whole world."
Don, she recalled, "was friendly, but . . . he did not reply to Bellow's advice;
instead, he just responded by nodding pleasantly."

On another night, Sterling Lord gave a talk about the book business. "I
don't believe Sterling . . . met Donald personally" at the conference, says
Lynn Nesbit, who would soon become Don's agent. However, Helen later insisted that Arno Karlen "recommended Don to . . . Lord," who was Karlen's
agent at the time.

In any case, Nesbit says she "had just been promoted by Sterling to be a
junior agent when he went to the . . . conference and brought back a sheaf of
stories and threw them on my desk." One of them was "The Big Broadcast of
1938." "I found [it] completely compelling and original. Sterling had told me
I should contact any of the writers whose stories impressed me and ask if
they were interested in representation. As I recall, the only one I wrote to
was Donald."

Nesbit wasn't alone in countering Bellow's dismissal of "The Big Broadcast of 1938." Herman Gollob read it when Don and Helen came to visit him
in Boston soon after the conference. "I was awed by the controlled madness . . . [the] exuberant quirkiness . . . [the] comic flair," he says. "Most of
all, I think, I marveled at the unforced precision of the language, the seemingly effortless colloquial tone, traceable I felt to Don's newspaper days."

Once more, Don challenged him to "summon up the courage to publish
'the most brilliant work of our time.'"

Gollob was newly married, still green at Little, Brown. He didn't want to
make mistakes or push his luck too fast. His earlier muted reaction to "The

Hiding Man" was based on his perception of its limited commercial appeal. He was beginning to appreciate what Don was up to, and he felt heartened by the responses of editors at *Contact, New World Writing,* and *First Person.* Gollob encouraged Don to keep up this "radically different approach to fiction." A few more stories, a few more publications, and . . . well, we'll see, he said.

Don asked his friend if he knew of any magazine-editing jobs on the East Coast. Gollob promised to keep his ear to the ground.

Susan Dworkin's remark that Don was "drunk a lot" during the conference raises the issue of Don's alcoholism. In her memoir, Helen said Don's drinking did not become a problem until sometime after he moved to New York City in 1963. Dworkin's observation that Don's wife "was drinking too" may suggest that Helen was being circumspect about her own consumption. On the other hand, Dworkin said the gathering was not a staid affair. In a letter to Elizabeth Bishop, Robert Lowell complained about the "sounds of intimacy, outrage and drinking" every night at the conference.

Some of Don's late stories ("Chablis," "Grandmother's House"), written with a personal candor new to his work at the time, make it clear that, at least on occasion, he drank heavily while in high school. Pat Goeters says that, from an early age, Don had an "alcoholic's attention span." He recalled, "In Houston, Don and I were like alcoholics-in-training. We would go out to local clubs, listen to jazz and drink beer. In those days, only beer and wine could be purchased in bars. Our 'adventures' had a distinct *Catcher in the Rye* flavor—young men poking at life from the sidelines while hungry to be in on the action. We were both alcoholics by the time he left Houston for New York, but it was in New York that he began to drink every day."

Don's first wife, Maggie, thinks Don had alcoholic "tendencies" early on, but she believes his drinking was not "serious" until he moved to New York and "had more possibilities to do what he wanted, which made life easier for him in some ways, and more difficult in others." Herman Gollob recalled that Don, in his mid-twenties, "was addicted, as was I, to West Coast jazz and to Scotch," but it's unclear how literally he meant "addicted." Helen noted, persuasively, that while Don edited *Forum,* he worked meticulously each night on his proofing chores and the magazine's layout. Later, as the museum director, he maintained a rigorous schedule, and pursued his writing and museum duties with astonishing energy. The only certainty is: If he was alcoholic at this point, he was functioning at a remarkably high level.

As they sat suspended over Texas, waiting for their plane to land, Helen and Don felt powerful emotional tugs. To nineteen-year-old Susan Dworkin, Don had seemed impudently confident, but Helen knew he had been bruised

by Bellow's brush-off. The East Coast appeared to him elitist and strange.
Still, he felt he had to "crack" it. Manhattan shocked Helen. She had found
the city "bleak" and overwhelming. And yet she had gotten some "insight
into the New York literary world . . . a world in which there was a genuine conviction that if you mattered as a writer, then you lived in New York." She later
wrote, "I could see that [Don] had to be there for his writing." As the plane began its descent, this realization settled uneasily into her stomach.

THE EMERGING FIGURE

Before leaving for the conference, Don had composed a catalog introduction for a show called "The Emerging Figure." The show ran at the Contemporary Arts Museum from May 31 through June 21, 1961. It featured one of Willem de Kooning's *Woman* paintings, and work by Richard Diebenkorn, Alex Katz, Lester Johnson, James Weeks, and others. Don's introduction traced the return of human figures "in the work of the children of the de Kooning generation." Against the grain of fashionable criticism led by Clement Greenberg, a supporter of pure abstraction, Don argued that figures were always implicit in Abstract Expressionism. He quoted Thomas Hess: The figure, Hess said, is one of abstraction's "lineal continuities."

Hess was a friend of Harold Rosenberg. Together, they fought Greenberg over the *meaning* of the avant-garde. To Greenberg, reference to the world was "literary" (that is, it belonged to the *verbal* arts) and was to be expunged from "pure" painting. To reach its highest possibilities, painting must concentrate on the materiality of paint and the flatness of the canvas. For Rosenberg and Hess, "pure" painting, devoid of social implications, was arid and inhuman. They preferred messier works of art. The "action" of painting—traces of the artist's movements in the brush strokes on the canvas—revealed the artist's emotions, social status, and cultural context, and these were more important than the medium's pedigree.

Don's catalog piece placed him squarely in the Hess/Rosenberg camp. In years to come, the tensions between Greenberg and Rosenberg would grow, and the avant-garde would split even wider apart.

In his introduction, Don stressed that the "current interest in the figure" was not a turning away from abstraction; it was, rather, an "attempt to explore and consolidate the victory of the new style." In other words, there was no going back to traditional portraiture. From now on, portraiture would include gestures learned from abstraction: The visual territory has expanded. The new figurative paintings were not "about" people—they were "enriched by anonymous human presences."

Already, Don was approaching fictional characters in this manner. He believed that in painting *and* in writing, the "direct, unmistakable, and unclouded recapitulation of some aspect of human experience ('LOOK MA, I'M DANCING')" was "self-defeating." "We cannot rid ourselves of the feeling that such an account has been won too easily," Don wrote. Surprise and insight were possible now only through indirection, masking—saying and seeing things "slant," as Emily Dickinson put it.

In truth, the figure had emerged in avant-garde painting almost a decade before Don's catalog comments. De Kooning displayed his paintings of women in New York's Sidney Janis Gallery in March 1953. Mark Stevens and Annalyn Swan, de Kooning's biographers, call *Woman I* the "barbaric yawp of American painting"—it is, they say, "personally, socially, culturally, and artistically fraught with uncertainty."

The frank ugliness of the figure flies in the face of the Great Master heritage, traducing one of the oldest painterly traditions, the worship of the female form. But de Kooning also violated Abstract Expressionism by reintroducing the human form within a storm of brush strokes.

In a not-so-subtle swipe at Clement Greenberg, Don wrote in his introduction, "It is just as arbitrary to insist that a painting cannot own a reference to a human form as to insist on ideological [and] theological . . . grounds that it contain one."

In 1953, de Kooning had thumbed his nose at *everyone.* By 1961, the heroics of his gesture—the new territory it seized, enlarging ideas of figuration as well as abstraction—were more apparent than ever.

Don's catalog piece ends with a line that he would echo over twenty years later in "Not-Knowing": "It is not that we prize difficulty [in art] for the sake of difficulty, only that we hope to know . . . that the experience is genuine."

If figures were emerging in abstract painting, consumer goods were disappearing in magazine and newspaper ads. Four months after the "Emerging Figure" show, Don made his first appearance in a major national publication, with "The Case of the Vanishing Product," a commentary on advertising, in the October 1961 issue of *Harper's*. "A remarkable number of advertisements give not so much as a clue to what is being advertised," Don wrote—a fact he'd gleaned working with Helen on her ad accounts. Instead, many ads are filled with objects—"keys, clocks, corkscrews, kiosks, balloons, musical instruments, stones . . . none of [which] is being offered for sale. Instead they are the means by which we are to conceive of other things which *are* being offered for sale—typically nowhere in sight. The very high level of abstraction in contemporary advertising both confers a new freedom upon designers and increases the possibility of ambiguity in its use."

With one eye on the art world and the other on his wife's advertising business, Don could see the culture's growing visual awareness, and the emerging social consequences. "It is not . . . surprising that, living in a land of plenty within a circle of poverty and near or actual starvation, Americans should be self-conscious about their fabulous consumption, and that advertisers should be cautious in reminding us of it," he said.

As director of the Contemporary Arts Museum, he "flew by the seat of [his] pants, pulling together exhibitions, but [he] loved that kind of spontaneous, creative effort," says Marion Barthelme, recalling stories Don told her about his museum days. "He and Jim [Love] went down to Matagorda where Forest Bess had a studio, for instance, and just took everything off his walls for one show." Bess, the son of an oil worker from Bay City, painted small abstractions filled with geometric symbols reminiscent of Kandinsky or Klee. He held his first show in the lobby of a Bay City hotel in 1936, but by the mid-forties Meyer Shapiro and Betty Parsons backed him. Don showed his work in April 1962.

Don arranged stagings of innovative theater, such as Edward Albee's *The American Dream,* Jules Feiffer's *Crawling Arnold* (about a businessman who reverts to childhood), and Fernando Arrabal's *The Automobile Graveyard.* The crowds, especially for the Arrabal production, were gratifyingly large, but Don clashed with the director, an aggressive Brooklynite named Ned Bobkoff, over the setting designs. Hubert Roussel panned the plays in the *Post.* On February 2, 1962, he wrote that Albee's drama was a "structural katzenjammer which makes its points 20 times over with lamentably amateur enthusiasm and winds up as a greatly pretentious bore."

Don knew that his short stories would provoke similar reactions from Roussel and his old newspaper buddies, so he kept the stories to himself. No one at the museum took a strong interest in his writing.

In the fall of 1961, Don arranged for the John Coltrane Quartet to perform in Houston. The day before the concert, Hurricane Carla threatened from the

Gulf. The musicians exercised the cancellation clause in their contract, took the performance fee but did not show up. If they had, they would have received a mixed reaction anyway. One of Don's greatest frustrations with Houston audiences was their lack of musical sophistication. In September, he scheduled a performance of Elliott Carter's music. Carter was one of America's most original modern classical composers. Only fifty people showed up for the concert. The newspapers didn't cover it. Don fumed.

He felt better on September 30, when a respectable crowd gathered in Jones Hall to hear Peter Yates, a musicologist, speak on experimental music and lead a performance of a computer-composed string piece by members of the Houston Symphony Orchestra. Later that week, Don arranged a modern staging by Harry Partch of Euripides' *The Bacchae;* called *Revelation in the Courthouse Park,* Partch's work was a music-theater piece. The music was played on large glass tubes.

Don oversaw the museum's literary events, as well as short courses taught by visiting artists. In November 1961, he put together a poetry festival featuring W. D. Snodgrass, Robert Bly, and Kenneth Koch. "Don had a nice bunch of friends, sort of artistic exiles in the wild wastes of Houston, and he introduced me to them," Koch recalled. "[At my reading] I got a surprising . . . reaction to my poem 'Lunch' . . . someone in the audience asked me why I didn't make up my own language and write poems in that. I think the idea was that if I was going to be so obscure I should take it all the way. Don was good-humored about and pleased by me (and my poetry) as some odd sort of event he was bringing to his native city—like its first air balloon or TV set. He was smiling almost all the time. Of course, I liked him a lot. . . . He was very pleasant, genial, ironic. He was very funny. Irony and all, he seemed mild compared to the people I knew in New York."

Ever since the Wagner College trip, Helen had worried about Don's restlessness. He didn't obviously display his discomfort. In fact, most of his friends thought he was content in Houston. To Herman Gollob, however, he had written, "This job at the museum is sapping my will to live, never great to begin with."

Helen was most aware of Don's unhappiness when his reactions to people differed sharply from her own. A breach was growing between them. For example, during the poetry festival, she gravitated to Robert Bly. He was "serious, older, and [he] told us that he was soon to be a father," Helen recalled. His "demeanor and actions were . . . dignified, whereas Koch, who spent a lot of time with a young woman poet, was more lighthearted about his visit." Koch's jokey behavior embarrassed her (and Bly), yet it was Koch whom Don appreciated. "[Don and I] spent a lot of time in the car," Koch says. "He explained drinking in Texas to me. The dry and wet rules were complicated and I don't remember them. But people kept a bottle in the glove compartment. Just in case. Beer was drunk during the daytime to provide a 'base' for the whiskey to be drunk later. Actually we didn't drink very much." Still, Helen fretted when Don disappeared with Koch for a couple of hours each day before dinner.

She was also more and more troubled by Don's spending. He paid out of pocket for museum meals and events. She borrowed against her ad agency's income to keep their personal finances afloat. "[We] were severely strained . . . in part from our trip to New York the previous summer and in part from the cost of entertaining for the museum," Helen wrote. "Don continued to write checks whether we had funds or not. . . . I was growing increasingly alarmed about our company's debt. And even with the extra money I was borrowing from the agency, it had become difficult just to pay our personal bills."

On the first night of the festival, she and Don took their guests to La Louisiane, a French restaurant on Main Street. The group toasted Houston's "wildness" and laughed about the restaurant's wall paintings of satyrs and nymphs with flapper haircuts. At the end of the meal, Don refused the poets' money and paid the tab. Two nights later, at Ye Olde College Inn across the street from Rice, Don announced that it was the *poets'* turn to "pick up the check." Helen was shocked. She was relieved not to shell out more cash, but she thought Don rude. Later, he explained to her that the CAA was "paying [the poets] enough that he thought they could share the costs." "Don and Kenneth seemed to get along so well that [Kenneth] probably regarded it with humor," Helen says. "But I doubt that Bly thought it was funny."

As they said good night outside the Warwick Hotel, Bly and Koch kissed Helen's cheek. In the car on the way home, Don said, "Now you have something you can tell our grandchildren, the night when you were kissed by two famous poets."

The following spring, Harold Rosenberg recommended Elaine de Kooning for a short course on painting at the museum. "The E. de Kooning idea sounds fine and I will put it to the board," Don wrote back. "I'd like, though, to have an alternative, a man, to propose—somebody who's both a good painter and a good teacher. So, who?" Don's preference for a man indicates his attitude, common in the art world at the time, that women weren't to be taken seriously as painters.

In any case, Elaine de Kooning arrived in June for a two-week course. "Congenial and a good teacher, she became friends with Don and with the artists active in musuem affairs," Helen wrote—a notable understatement, given others' accounts of Elaine's energy and personality. "Elaine was vivacious: she loved a party and craved attention," say Willem de Kooning's biographers. She was in "perpetual motion."

By 1962, Elaine was a serious alcoholic, desperate for money. At the Cedar Tavern in Manhattan, where the Abstract Expressionists boozed away their nights, she had experienced firsthand the art world's indifference to female painters, and she had learned that the only way to overcome it was to act as manly as the men. She could outdrink and outtalk most of the guys, and she took as many lovers as they did, among them Harold Rosenberg and—less casually—Thomas Hess.

Though she and Willem never divorced, she had separated from him in the 1940s. In the late fifties, she began to travel the country as an itinerant teacher, doing stints at Pratt Institute and Parsons School of Design, and at universities in New Mexico and California. Everywhere she went, she "partied hard with . . . students and faculty," according to Stevens and Swan. Though she "sometimes looked like a boorish drunk who spilled drinks and scattered cigarette ashes . . . she usually had a marvelous sparkle around her. She seemed to enlarge life." She was also an excellent mentor, and she knew her Kierkegaard (she used to read him aloud to Willem as he painted). She and Don hit it off right away. To promote her course, Don created a broadside, "Elaine de Kooning Paints a Picture," with a photo of Elaine at work.

"I love Texans," Elaine said later. "They just do everything in a natural and big way. An easy way. They drink big and drive fast in big cars. I think it has to do with all of that space, and all of that frontier energy that's still there. In Texas, everything is possible. And Texans are open to new ideas and to art. New things just make sense to Texans."

When *The New Yorker* published such trite generalizations, Don couldn't abide them. Coming from Elaine's mouth, they were charming.

In 1961, Jorge Luis Borges shared the International Publishers Prize with Samuel Beckett, Joseph Heller's *Catch-22* was published, and Stanley Kramer released *Judgment at Nuremberg.* Early in 1962, Nabokov's *Pale Fire* emerged, Albee's *Who's Afraid of Virginia Woolf?* was produced on Broadway, and Andy Warhol did the first of his Marilyn Monroe portraits. The world seemed edgy and at risk—the Berlin Wall had just gone up, and Cuba was a tinderbox—but the arts were dizzy with energy (*fueled,* perhaps, by planetary anxieties). In the "wild wastes" of Houston, far from the creative pivot of New York, Don felt he was missing out.

On his visit to Houston, Harold Rosenberg had mentioned that he and Thomas Hess were thinking of starting a literary/arts journal in New York, with funding from the Longview Foundation, a philanthropic organization based in New Orleans. Rosenberg and Hess served on Longview's board. In her memoir, Helen said that it was not until the summer and fall of 1962 that

Rosenberg began to court Don to be the journal's managing editor, but a letter from Don, dated March 28, 1962, indicates that the discussion was well advanced before Helen knew about it. He told Rosenberg, "In regard to working on the Longview magazine, there ain't anything I'd rather do. It would take I think around $9000 for us to live in N. Y.—which may be more than the foundation would want to pay. Let me know what you think. We can be packed in about 30 minutes."

Despite its debts, Helen's ad agency had expanded. Her sister Odell Pauline Moore came aboard to handle the books, leaving Helen more time to write copy and attend to the creative side of the business. Helen leased space in a building Pat Goeters owned near the Museum of Fine Arts. Don's brother Pete joined the firm as a writer. Pete had married a woman he'd known since elementary school, and her father's medical offices were across the street from Helen's company. Daily, Don was reminded how rooted he was among family, friends, and Houston's upper-middle-class community.

Helen worked hard to establish herself; Don had earned a position that provided him plenty of aesthetic challenges. It was an awkward time to suggest a risky change.

Sister Mary Antoinette, the president of Dominican College, liked Helen, and she had noticed Don's success at the Contemporary Arts Museum. She asked Helen if Don would consider becoming the college's development director. Helen passed along the idea. The job didn't interest him, but an offer from the college would give him a bargaining chip with the Contemporary Arts Association. He stipulated a hefty salary, with mornings free to write. To his surprise, Sister Antoinette agreed to his terms. Still waiting to hear from Rosenberg, Don told the college he couldn't make a decision until the fall.

In the meantime, Sister Antoinette urged Don and Helen to attend a meeting of the American College Public Relations Association at the Greenbrier Resort in West Virginia. This would give them a chance to talk to development personnel from other schools around the country. Don could imagine nothing duller, but Helen was eager to go, and if Dominican College paid for part of the trip, it would be possible to take a train to New York without too much additional expense.

In late July, Don and Helen flew to White Sulphur Springs. The resort was expansive and spectacular, overlooking the Allegheny Mountains. The baroque interiors were dark and warm. Croquet lawns, golf courses, trout streams, and spas ringed the buildings. One wing of the resort was closed for remodeling; unbeknownst to the guests, the U.S. government was preparing it to be a secret bunker for Congress in the event of nuclear war.

Don rented a typewriter and spent his mornings working on "Florence Green Is 81" (he mentions the resort in the story). Each day, Helen attended sessions on university development. Don skipped them. She "found his absence disquieting." People kept asking her where her husband was. She didn't know what to tell them.

The tension between Don and Helen mounted, a week later, when they went to Manhattan. Helen didn't like New York any better now than she had the first time. Rosenberg had invited them to his flat in a brownstone on East Tenth Street. It was his office and a temporary residence whenever he came into the city (he and his wife, May, shared a house on Long Island). On the appointed afternoon, Don and Helen arrived early and waited on the steps. Soon, Rosenberg came limping up the walk. "How good you look against a New York background," he said as he greeted Helen.

The apartment "was not inviting; it was dark, almost oppressive," Helen recalled. She tried to "imagine living there" but couldn't. Artwork cluttered the rooms. Paintings were "stacked on the table, in chairs, and leaning against the walls." Hastily, Rosenberg straightened the covers on his Murphy bed, then mixed them all drinks. He mentioned the magazine. "He wanted my assurance that moving to New York was what I wanted to do . . . and then he added that as soon as plans were more concrete he would contact Don," Helen said. "Although he was restrained in showing how he felt, Don was elated."

That evening, Elaine de Kooning invited the couple to visit her loft on Broadway, near Union Square. It was up a long flight of stairs. Her painting studio occupied the front of the loft; at the other end, she'd arranged a kitchen, a bed, and a serving bar. Magazine clippings plastered the walls. Elaine loved to tell the story of how, walking home late one night, she had been attacked by a mugger outside her door. When he pulled a knife, she invited him upstairs for coffee. After that, they became fast friends.

"Elaine was cheerful and generous, but I found her a little intense," Helen admitted later. Elaine asked a number of acquaintances to drop by and meet Helen and Don, "including several younger artists who seemed to be around most of the time." Elaine showed off her latest paintings, large portraits of people without faces. "I found [them] strange," Helen wrote. "They were not abstract; details of the figures were realistic so that the blank faces made them resemble unfinished paintings."

At this point, Helen could feel Don pulling away from her, excited by the promise of New York, a place that seemed to her dirty, odd—anything but inviting. She feared losing her own identity. In her memoir, she said:

> Uncertain of our future, we returned to Houston. During the weeks of August and early September, Don discussed both the CAA and Dominican

College with his parents, and they both urged him to accept the position with the college . . . he did not discuss New York as a real option. He did not mention it to Pat Goeters or anyone else at the museum. Don faced difficult choices; he was happy at the museum, and I did not believe that he could be satisfied in college development. There was no doubt that he was considering the appointment only because it put him in a negotiating position with the CAA.

Don kept secret his longing for New York because it meant leaving his family, leaving his friends, and committing to a literary life, when all he had to show were four stories in obscure journals—stories, he felt sure, his comrades would not appreciate.

It's possible that he recontacted Spencer Bayles—the psychiatrist he'd once seen—to hash out his feelings. At some point, Bayles told him "it was time to get out of town."

Don *did* tell Pat Goeters about the Dominican College offer. Goeters was chair of the CAA board, and he discussed the situation with the other members. Funding was tight, and the board was reluctant to match the college's offer, but Goeters fought hard for his old friend. The board conceded to a pay hike and agreed to let Don keep his mornings free for writing.

Right away, Rosenberg called. He offered Don the position of managing editorship of *Location* magazine. "I'll need you in New York by the first of October," he said. "Don accepted with almost no hesitation," Helen recalled. "This meant that we had a very short time in which to radically alter our lives."

Goeters was furious. He thought Don had played him for a fool, threatening to jump to the Dominicans, when all along he meant to go to New York. Ironically, Goeters's wife, Georgia, had recently organized a panel discussion at the museum "with about seven prominent creative types—painter, musician, playwright, etc.—titled 'Why Creative People Leave Houston.'" One by one, as individual board members learned of Don's decision, they boiled.

Don's family accepted the news warily—except for Don's dad, who didn't accept it at all. He said that Don was making a major blunder in not taking the college job, and he lectured his son on financial responsibility. Helen didn't lecture, but she realized with horror that they couldn't afford to move. "I don't believe [Don] ever understood the seriousness of our financial plight," she said later. Whenever she voiced her fears, he brushed them off. "We'll take care of it," he'd say.

She saw no way to "take care of it." Further, she was "uneasy about walking away from [her] responsibilities . . . at the advertising agency," especially now that she'd involved her sister in the business. "I would be walking away from a company that was in debt almost exclusively from my excessive withdrawals," she wrote in her memoir.

Finally, she suggested to Don that he go on to New York. She'd stay in Houston for a few months to try to stabilize the agency. Don didn't like the plan, but he was persuaded of its wisdom.

One Sunday, toward the end of September, he and Helen drove to Galveston to say good-bye to Don's grandmother, Mamie. They took her to lunch at John's Seafood Restaurant, at the edge of the causeway to the mainland. Don was uncomfortable and ate little. Mamie told the couple they were making a mistake. It was a terrible idea to live apart, even for a short while, she said. She had never been separated from her husband, Bart, except for the week he'd gone to Mexico to look for Don and Pat Goeters.

George Christian was the only person in town who expressed honest sympathy for Don. He still worked as an amusements editor at the *Post;* he knew that, culturally, Houston couldn't hold a candle to New York, and he understood how much Don needed to write.

One day, Helen drove Don to Cypress, a community northwest of Houston, so he could say good-bye to her sister Margo Vandruff and Margo's husband. Margo and Roy lived in a modernist home designed by Pat Goeters. On the grounds outside the house, Don turned to Helen and asked her if she wanted to "stay [in Houston] and build a home like this." Helen would have liked nothing better, but she knew how devastated Don would be if she told him the truth. She said she was sure about leaving.

Helen made plans to live with her mother until she could join Don in Manhattan. The couple stored most of their possessions in the attic of the Harold Street house, then sublet the place to Don's brother Pete and his wife, Lillian.

In his last few days at the museum, Don arranged a new show, "Ways and Means," featuring recent work by John Chamberlain, James Weeks, and Frank Stella. He prepared the museum's annual report. He stuck to his schedule and didn't allow the board's anger to deter him from wrapping up his business.

Despite his note to Herman Gollob, in which he disparaged his duties, Helen has expressed the belief that the museum was a "rich" experience for Don. "When he recalled his work [there] a few years later, it was with a touching sense of loss," she wrote in her memoir. "He called it 'the best job' he had ever had." Marion Barthelme agrees. "I know Don thought that working as the CAM director was one of the happiest periods of his life," she says. Helen has gone so far as to say, "I don't think he felt as good about himself and his work again until he returned to the University of Houston to teach in the 1980s."

A few days before Don left Houston, Pat and Bill Colville, CAA board members, gave him a going-away party. His friends were civil, congratulatory, full of good wishes. Still, the occasion was stiff. Don had always "compartmentalize[d] the people he knew," Helen wrote. "I don't think it occurred to him to include George and Mary [Christian] or other . . . newspaper friends in the social life of the art community."

He was scheduled to fly out of Houston's Municipal Airport on a Sunday afternoon. Beforehand, he and Helen lunched with his parents. His mother spoke enthusiastically about Don's opportunities in New York and the exciting things he would see. Even his father seemed sanguine. He wished Don well. But then, as the meal came to an end, he turned to his son and said, "Be prepared for failure."

The remark stunned Helen. Don, she recalled, "did not appear to be disheartened . . . nothing could dampen [his] high spirits." He was leaving a real, provincial museum for what André Malraux had called the "imaginary museum" of the age—painting, music, literature, and the arts.

Donald Barthelme, the writer, was about to emerge. Armed, Helen recalled, with an "extraordinary ability to challenge another person, to oppose someone else's will with his own"—strengths he had acquired from his father—he was on his way to becoming the nation's finest prose stylist, and in the process he would change the shape of the American short story.

PART THREE

HERE IN THE VILLAGE

LOCATION

October 12, 1962, was Don and Helen's sixth wedding anniversary. They spent it apart. Don was thirty-one. He had rented a room in a small midtown hotel. From there, he walked every morning to the *Location* office at 16 East 23rd Street. In Houston, Helen stayed with her mother and worked late each night to pull her ad firm out of the red. On the morning of the twelfth, Don sent Helen a telegram: "On this worst of anniversaries love and hope for many better."

The *Location* office was small and drab, outfitted with only a desk, a typewriter, a few chairs, and a smattering of file cabinets overflowing already with paperwork and submissions for the magazine. Don, always design-conscious, must have felt ill at ease there; on the other hand, the working conditions were not markedly different from those he had known at the *Post.* The dirty windows overlooked Broadway. At lunch, or in the late afternoon, Don left the building, walking through the dreary lobby—almost always empty, except for the elevator man—and strolled up the street to Madison Square Park, where Melville used to walk his granddaughter. The park was also the setting for some of O. Henry's stories of New York society.

Leaving work, Don walked west on Twenty-third, past the Flatiron Building on Fifth, past Edith Wharton's birthplace—an old

Anglo-Italian brownstone—and the Chelsea Hotel, the home, at various times, of William Dean Howells, Mark Twain, O. Henry, Dylan Thomas, and Vladimir Nabokov. Though he wasn't writing much new fiction, Don carried a single file folder containing notes and partial rough drafts everywhere he went.

Occasionally, he stopped by the headquarters of the Longview Foundation, which funded *Location,* in the Lincoln Building at 60 East 42nd Street. The building had been erected in 1929—the pinnacle of Art Deco New York—and was hailed by architects for bringing airiness and light into downtown office spaces. After signing Foundation forms, usually in a vain attempt to get more money for the magazine, Don would walk a couple of blocks to the New York Public Library, or stroll through Bryant Park, past the statues of Goethe and Gertrude Stein. In Ralph Ellison's *Invisible Man,* the park is the backdrop for a shooting that sets off a race riot. The novel's modernist take on New York—hallucinatory, fragmented—remained vivid in his mind.

In the evenings, he often met Joe Maranto at Grand Central Station; they'd eat oysters in the basement restaurant there, or catch a local to some eatery and then to a series of jazz clubs. In October 1962, the jazz world buzzed about Charles Mingus at Birdland; he appeared there on the nineteenth and the twenty-sixth. The famous old venue, on Broadway and Fifty-second, was on its last legs, weakened by the rock-and-roll craze. It would close its doors in 1965 (a new incarnation would open later in a different location), but for now, Mingus, with Dannie Richmond on drums, revived the place with tunes like "Eat That Chicken," "Monk, Funk, or Vice Versa," and "O. P." Around this time, Bill Evans, Paul Motian, and Chuck Israels played the Village Vanguard. McCoy Tyner appeared there, as did John Coltrane with Eric Dolphy and, on drums, the great Elvin Jones. At the corner of Bleecker and Thompson streets, the Village Gate still offered evening jazz. In the basement there, the month before, a twenty-one-year-old folk singer named Robert Allen Zimmerman had written a song called "A Hard Rain's A-Gonna Fall." Calling himself Bob Dylan, he had just begun performing in the Café Wha?, Gerde's Folk City, the Gaslight—formerly a Beat poets' hangout—and other hole-in-the-wall coffee shops around the Village. Don was a Woody Guthrie fan, but he was too busy soaking up jazz to catch much of the folk scene on MacDougal Street.

The number of clubs where he could hear his favorite music live almost every night was overwhelming. It was like stepping from the black-and-white world of the 1950s into the Technicolor sixties.

He also filled his evenings with art parties. "Once, Don took Joe to a party at the apartment of Willem de Kooning," Maggie Maranto recalls. "Elaine de Kooning was separated from Willem, but they were still great friends." Willem was preparing to leave the city for his new home in the Springs, a section of East Hampton, New York; a month before, he had taken a loan to begin building his country studio on Long Island. "Don and Joe collected Elaine from her place, and while the three of them walked over to Willem's, the two guys kept her in stitches with their quips, flinging them back and forth at one another," Maggie says. "Elaine thought they were the funniest people she'd ever met."

Elaine had embarked on a series of portraits—of Fairfield Porter, Michel Sonnabend, Al Lazar, and, most famously, of John F. Kennedy: faceless men (as Elaine depicted them) sitting with their legs apart. Frequently, on impulse, Elaine invited Don and others to her studio on Broadway and talked for hours, gesturing at her paintings with her cigarette (spraying the furniture with ashes), pouring whiskey until the empty bottles piled up along the floorboards. Earlier that year, JFK had posed for Elaine in West Palm Beach; she praised his courtliness and humor, and the fine figure he had cut in his sailing clothes. She would show her guests the charcoal sketches she had made of the president. She confessed she was a "teeny" bit in love with this handsome man who was leading the country. Sometimes, after listening to Elaine go on, Don didn't get back to his hotel until just before dawn.

Still, he managed to maintain his writing schedule, working in the mornings in the dull *Location* office, then editing manuscripts in the afternoon. At lunch, he would meet Rosenberg and Thomas Hess to discuss the magazine. "I spent the first several years of our friendship listening to Tom and Harold tell these ferocious, man-eating, illuminating jokes, art-jokes and politics-jokes and literature-jokes, usually at lunch," Don said. "I was astounded by the ferocity of their enthusiasms, both positive and negative. The vehicle was always a remarkable wit."

Hess and Rosenberg "were not worried about putting the magazine out on time and certainly never put any pressure on me," Don said. "We waited until we had enough decent stuff for a good issue. That experience was a great pleasure—listening to Tom and Harold talk." Hess's favorite refrain was, "The only adequate criticism of a work of art is another work of art," a mantra Don made his own.

Often, John Canaday and Clement Greenberg were topics of conversation (and scorn) at these lunches. Canaday was the art editor of *The New York Times.* In a much-discussed article, he had recently condemned the "frauds, freaks, charlatans, and worse" of Abstract Expressionism. Likewise, Greenberg had turned away from de Kooning's paintings toward the imagist work of Morris Louis and Kenneth Noland. Don had arrived in New York, and in the midst of the Abstract Expressionist crowd, at a time when Abstract Expressionism was losing its clout in the art world.

H. Harvard Arnason had mounted a recent show at the Guggenheim that featured Louis and Noland, a gesture seen as supportive of Greenberg and dismissive of the loyalty that Rosenberg and Hess felt for de Kooning. A year earlier, de Kooning and Greenberg had scuffled in a bar called Dillon's, near the Cedar Tavern. Greenberg was there one day with Kenneth Noland. De Kooning walked in and said to Greenberg, "I heard you were talking at the Guggenheim and said that I'd had it, that I was finished." "Well, yeah. I had said that," Greenberg admitted. "Sure. I meant it too." De Kooning claimed that Thomas Hess had "ridden his back" as Greenberg had ridden Jackson Pollock's, to advance their careers. The yelling degenerated into punching and the men had to be separated. "I'm not scared of you. I'm not scared of you," de Kooning shouted as several people pulled him off of Greenberg.

This was heady stuff for Don. He was now among people for whom art was a serious matter, something worth fighting over. At almost the instant he'd hit town, *Art International* published Greenberg's "After Abstract Expressionism"—the text of his remarks at the Guggenheim that had so enraged de Kooning. To be sure, this piece was the subject of many "man-eating jokes" at Don's first lunches with Rosenberg and Hess. Morris Louis had just died of lung cancer. Rosenberg delighted in (and tortured himself with) the nasty gossip that Louis's death was a stroke of luck for Greenberg. Many in the art world believed that Greenberg sang Louis's praises to raise the artist's prices. Greenberg had stretched several of Louis's canvases, and he helped the artist's widow sell the paintings, sometimes keeping profits for himself after an exhibition. It may have dawned on Don that his new friends saw *Location* as a weapon with which to attack Greenberg and his crowd.

At the heart of these lunch conversations was the modernist conviction, dimmed perhaps but not extinguished, that art could change the world—that art *must* change the world or the world would be doomed. Among New York intellectuals, the Eichmann trial and continuing revelations of Nazi atrocities were obsessive subjects. Rosenberg had just published a long piece in *Commentary* comparing Eichmann to the "abstract . . . officer in Kafka's *The Penal Colony* who throws himself into the lethal machine out of fidelity to his idea." If the Nazi story was not told effectively—if there was not the art to interpret it properly—then telling it over and over, Rosenberg argued, would be "inadequate and even absurd." An edgy combination of optimism (faith in art) and pessimism (recognition of humanity's evils) shaped the spirit behind the art and literature in the pages of *Location*.

"[The] situation has changed, almost reversed itself since the 10's and 20's in regard to the use of magazines: then, it seemed, what was needed was a place for poems to *appear*—not enough was published. Now *too much* is published—you know that, good lord, there is a magazine under every stamp. But what is needed now is *ideas*. Nobody can understand anything."

This was Robert Alexander's response to Harold Rosenberg in 1961, when Rosenberg began to plan *Location*. Walter Lowenfels, a politically radical poet who had made his name in the 1920s, wrote: "Dear Harold: Hear you are committing the final sin—editing a magazine." But Lowenfels was eager to appear in its pages.

Rosenberg proposed to the board of the Longview Foundation a journal that would present "expression and thinking in art and literature that is relevant to and in continuity with the significant trends of our time." The magazine's aim would be to "overcome the intellectual isolation of the arts in America, the growing parochialism and professionalist inbreeding that goes hand in hand with their separation from one another and from thought in general—and to further their creative inter-communication."

The Longview Foundation conducted the Creative Arts Program of one of the nation's largest philanthropic organizations. In 1921, Edith Rosenwald, daughter of the head of Sears, Roebuck and Company, married a prominent New Orleans businessman named Edgar Bloom Stern. From their joint fortune came the Longview Foundation. At various times, Saul Bellow, Louise Bogan, Alfred Kazin, Meyer Shapiro, Adolph Gottlieb, and Hans Hofmann served on its arts panels. Bellow and Kazin were especially excited about *Location*.

Rosenberg felt that the ideal magazine should "endeavor to maintain a continuous dialogue" within the arts and "across their borders. In addition, it would be alert to fields of thought outside the arts by which the arts are being influenced." These aspirations matched the work that Don had done with *Forum;* Don was the perfect choice for managing editor.

In his initial budget for the magazine, for the period of October through December 1962, Rosenberg projected $1,370.14 for office equipment, $890 for travel and entertainment expenses, and only $300 for Don's position (at $1.50 per hour). For the long term—covering a year, or eight issues—Rosenberg suggested that the "Editorial Assistant," working twenty hours a week, get a monthly check of $1,440—slightly more than the $9,000 per year Don had asked for.

The magazine would never make it to eight issues, and Don would see only a fraction of his budgeted salary.

His first shock came when he saw the word *assistant* in his title. He had assumed he would have full editorial control. Clearly, Rosenberg and Hess had firm ideas about the magazine's contents and direction. It should be a journal "of persons not of *pieces*," Rosenberg said. "We oughtn't to distinguish between artists and writers." They should all be thought of as "collaborators."

Among the people he said he would not be "unhappy" working with were Willem de Kooning, Larry Rivers, Hans Hofmann, Barnett Newman, Kenneth Burke, Kenneth Koch, Robert Bly, Saul Bellow, Philip Guston, Robert Rauschenberg, and Elaine de Kooning.

Rosenberg wanted to see articles about Larry Rivers in "action situations— [he is a] hunter . . . of underwear, [an] actor," he said. He wanted to capture the fast talk of the sculptor Reuben Nakian: "If his words are sappy what of it, so long as his line is divine."

Kenneth Burke "has turned himself . . . into a meat-grinder on the edge of the linguistic counter," Rosenberg said, and suggested *Location* run a profile of him. Allen Ginsberg, he said, "should be disassociated" from the "beat idea and mob. His habits are his own business." Rudy Burckhardt's "photos are no good. . . . There's Rudy in 'em." Bob Bly is one of the "very few 'new' people I have a positive feeling about. . . . Let's give him space."

Don did not agree with all of these assessments, but he deferred to his employers. Still, he didn't hesitate to assert himself when he could. Though he spent most of his early days on the job soliciting ads from publishers and art galleries, he also made editorial decisions on his own, causing some friction with Rosenberg. At one point, Meyer Liben, a longtime contributor to *Commentary,* complained to Rosenberg that "a stranger" had rejected his manuscript (which Rosenberg had solicited). "[The magazine's] attitude was unfriendly, cavalier, not to say puzzling," Liben wrote. Rosenberg apologized to him on Don's behalf.

Don *did* share Rosenberg's view of contemporary American fiction. "[In] vigor and originality painting and sculpture stand at present in the lead among the arts of America," Rosenberg had written in his proposal for the magazine. The "experience of painters and sculptors can be of great value in helping current American literature to reestablish contact with modern developments in form, method and thought." *Location* would be an organ for reinspiriting modern fiction, he said. It would be American fiction's salvation.

Immediately after Don's arrival in New York, the Sidney Janis Gallery opened its "New Realists" exhibit of Pop Art. "The art world thronged to the opening, staged in an ample ground-floor space on Fifty-seventh Street that Janis rented especially for the occasion," wrote Mark Stevens and Annalyn Swan. "The show was a sensation and the talk of the town. De Kooning went to Fifty-seventh Street, but, observing the scene within, would not enter the gallery." The times they were a'changin'.

Accustomed to Houston's car dependency, Don loved to roam the streets on foot, alone or with friends, popping into one gallery after another. New York "is a collage," he said. "The point of collage is that unlike things are stuck together . . . to make a new reality."

Manhattan's other great charm for Don was "all the filth on the streets." It reminded him of Kurt Schwitters, he said. "Schwitters used to hang around printing plants and fish things out of waste barrels, stuff that had been overprinted or used during make-ready, and he'd employ this rich accidental material in his collages."

Don followed Schwitters's example, filching observations from the streets. Walking, he would pass a store that had mounted on a sidewalk stand an Olivetti typewriter. A piece of paper in the machine invited passersby to leave messages, and "you'd go to see what crazy things people had written on the Olivetti today."

In "A Shower of Gold," one of the first stories he worked on in New York, Don used the Olivetti and other observations from his daily walks. His character, Peterson, says:

> Yesterday in the typewriter in front of the Olivetti showroom on Fifth Avenue, I found a recipe for Ten Ingredient Soup that included a stone from a toad's head. And while I stood there marveling a nice old lady pasted on the elbow of my best Haspel suit a little blue sticker reading THIS INDIVIDUAL IS A PART OF THE COMMUNIST CONSPIRACY FOR GLOBAL DOMINATION OF THE ENTIRE GLOBE. Coming home I passed a sign that said in ten-foot letters COWARD SHOES and heard a man singing "Golden Earrings" in a horrible voice. . . .

This passage shares the ecstatic spirit of E. B. White's elegiac songs of the city (a city ever changing, always vanishing), which appeared regularly in *The New Yorker*—reportage made semisurreal by collage, and offered without judgment. What in later years some reviewers and critics would call Don's "absurdity" was simply alertness and wonder on the streets.

His eager tasting of the city did not come cheaply, especially on the pittance Rosenberg paid him. Helen had supplied Don with sufficient cash to pay his expenses for at least a month, but within a week he asked her to wire additional funds. "After that, it was every two or three days," she recalled, "so that within a short time I had sent him a considerable sum and had to finally explain that we simply could not continue spending this much money.

"At that point Don called his father for financial help. He was spending every evening enjoying New York."

He frequented the Blue Note, Trudy Heller's, Arthur's Tavern, the Kettle of Fish, the White Horse, where the drunken ballads of Irish immigrants sounded remarkably like the story songs emerging now from the doorways of Village coffeehouses. Don did not see much of his hotel.

Changing times are characterized by equal amounts of excitement and sadness. Frequently, new singers, like the older ones, find themselves offering elegies. E. B. White was by no means the first writer to lament the loss of old New York—nor was Henry James, though his *The American Scene,* published in 1907, is perhaps the most famous of the city's many eulogies. After a twenty-year sojourn in Europe, James returned to New York, to find its "Gothic" pride "caged and dishonoured" by "buildings grossly tall and grossly ugly." Some of these were the Beaux-Arts beauties White found charming in the 1920s and 1930s, but for James, they were filled with too many windows, a "condition never to be reconciled with any grace of building."

Don and E. B. White shared James's deepest uneasiness. James wrote, "The precious stretch of space between Washington Square and Fourteenth Street [once] had a melancholy glamour," which he found difficult to render now "for new and heedless generations." The writer's difficult task—that of rendering life accurately—was made even harder by the speed and mutability of the modern city. The city's changes were violently at odds with James's memories and his inner life. His real lament, White's lament, and Don's challenge in 1962 were all about words—about the impossibility of *rendering* what is beyond our absorption.

James wrote, "New York . . . languishes and palpitates, or vibrates," a line Don echoed in "City Life" (1969): "This muck heaves and palpitates." In the midst of massive tremors, the writer, James said, can't help but wonder if his "impressions" have any "real relation" to life as it is lived.

Don agreed, and his detractors always mistook his intent in tracing city life in fragments. He did not particularly welcome the fragmentation, the "hardness and brightness" White decried; he was trying to solve James's old dilemma, attempting to find fresh and effective ways to render for a "new and heedless" generation what he saw.

Right before moving to New York, Don finished "The Viennese Opera Ball." It takes place in the Waldorf-Astoria Hotel. The Waldorf-Astoria is the centerpiece of the most extended passage in *The American Scene.* For James, the hotel's "illusions about itself"—its "wealth and variety," its superficiality—were synonyms for American civilization. Social affairs like the Viennese Opera Ball (one of the hotel's annual events) fused business and play, and lubricated the nation's "general machinery."

In these remarks, Don found a theme for his story.

He took several other cues from James. At a hotel party, James said, he encountered "violence in . . . communication" and was "transported to conditions of extraordinary complexity and brilliancy." The whole thing "remains for me . . . a gorgeous golden blur."

From *these* remarks, Don fashioned his story's form, its fresh style for "new and heedless" readers.

He wrote: "Carola Mitt, brown-haired, brown-eyed and just nineteen, was born in Berlin (real name: Mittenstein), left Germany five years ago. In her senior year at the Convent of the Sacred Heart in Greenwich, Conn., Carola went to the Viennese Opera Ball at the Waldorf-Astoria, was spotted by a *Glamour* editor."

The story then mixes fashion-industry talk with talk by academics, wealthy doctors, and other guests at the ball (a series of "violent communications"). The effect is to undercut the glittering surface, and to suggest the hypocrisy at the core of the nation's "machinery." The narrative points out that the fashion world's marketing of female beauty has serious consequences for sexual behavior and pregnancy rates. One result is that abortion has become a financial boon to the medical community (in the story, abortion is the doctors' main topic of conversation). Art, history, and people have become products churned out in America's lubricious whirl.

As it turned out, Henry James was not Don's only source for the story. In its December 22, 1961, issue, *Time* magazine ran an article on fashion models entitled "The Bones Have Names." The piece profiled the latest "leaders in the new wave" of modeling: Dolores Wettach, Isabella Albonico, Dorothea McGowan—and Marola Witt. "Marola Witt, brown-haired, brown-eyed and just 19, was born in Berlin (real name: Wittenstein), left Germany five years ago," the article says. "In her senior year at the Convent of the Sacred Heart in Greenwich, Conn., Marola went to the Viennese Opera Ball at the Waldorf-Astoria, was spotted by a *Glamour* editor."

A gleeful collagist, Don lifted whole paragraphs from the *Time* piece, pasted them against the background of James's remarks about the Waldorf-Astoria (which Don assumed any sophisticated reader—the kind of reader *he* was after—would know), and produced a tiny, potent meditation on American culture. He saw how the fashion article illustrated James's theme—how, more than ever, James's theme was current. Rather than *commenting* on this, Don produced a collage that *demonstrated* it. The result is a far more effective snapshot of contemporary America—with links to the nation's past—than any direct presentation of weighty material.

Toward the end of the story, a character quotes Emile Meyerson, in French. In English, the line would read: "Man practices metaphysics just as he breathes, without thinking about it." Even in the shallowest situations, the human soul—however we define it—is at issue.

In "Florence Green Is 81," Don had quoted Oscar Wilde's remark that "Mr. Henry James writes fiction as though it were a painful duty"—a comment on James's *style,* although not on his content, for which Don had the greatest admiration. America's style had changed; New York's style had changed, wholesale, at least twice over since James had first observed it. Don knew that for old truths to emerge refreshed, they would have to be clothed in yet another style, for yet another generation. His chosen duty was to find that style, to join the community of writers he admired—makers of books, window signs, *New Yorker* stories—and add his contribution. His duty was to celebrate the city and lament its sorrowful wounds.

LOVELY OLD PICTURESQUE
DIRTY BUILDINGS

In Houston, Don had "learned to impersonate a Texan well enough," he said. For better or worse, his "sensibility was pretty well put together" before he came to New York. Still, "New York is . . . our Paris; you go to have your corners knocked off."

Night after night now, often at parties in Elaine de Kooning's studio, he got his corners shaved. "I was one night congratulated by a prominent poet on my 'rural irony'; being from Texas, you're a natural target," Don said.

Meanwhile, in Texas, Helen was miserable. Every other day, she spoke to Don on the phone. "I could hear [his] loneliness as well," she recalled. By late October, after sitting alone on her wedding anniversary, she'd had enough. She told her sister Odell to manage the ad agency, at least temporarily. Helen was going to New York.

As soon as she told Don she was ready to join him, he began to search for an apartment. He "walked around for days," he wrote Helen. He looked at, he said:

lovely old picturesque dirty apartment buildings in filthy and fine neighborhoods, bits of old Village, up to 36th Street (Murray Hill district) and as far up as the sixties where the rents are really high but everything is double-picturesque. On the Lower East Side the rents are lower but the place is filled with bums (an estimated 45,000) whereas

on the Upper East Side the rents are higher but the place is filled with . . .
homosexuals . . . (an estimated 100,000). On the West Side the place is
filled with Puerto Ricans and Americans who will, it is said, cut your
throat for a nickel.

He settled on a flat in the Mayfair Fifth Building at Fifteenth Street and
Fifth Avenue, about eight blocks north of Washington Square. He sent Helen
a sketch of the floor plan; the sleeping alcove was "like the dining room part
of a living room–dining combination rather than a bedroom." There was a
"handsome parquet floor." He assured Helen that "the neighborhood is quite
good"–the building had a "24-hour doorman." The rent was $163 a month. He
suggested that Helen recruit his brothers to help her ship the couple's furniture. "Sweetheart, I look forward eagerly to your goddamn arrival," he told
her, and signed the letter with "every kind of love."

"I really had no idea how we would get our agency through this crisis,"
Helen recalled. Despite an upturn in business (largely by representing beer
and wine interests in the city), "I knew that I was leaving Odell with a serious indebtedness."

Don met Helen at Newark's airport. They took an airport bus into Manhattan, then caught a cab to their new apartment. Helen's reaction to New York
was just as muted as during her previous visits. The apartment was "really . . .
an efficiency," mostly bare of furniture, she wrote later. "Directly across
from us on 15th Street there was a garment manufacturing shop. We could
look into a room crowded with sewing machines, racks of clothes, and the
workers–all women–bent over them."

Don was eager to show her around the city, and also determined, perhaps,
to keep her from dwelling on the apartment's small size, so he fed her a
quick lunch and took her to the magazine office. "It was dark and dismal,"
Helen slated flatly in her memoir. Don was frustrated that she didn't share
his excitement about the romance of New York. Their apartment building
had once housed the publication offices of *Il Martello,* Carlo Tresca's anar-
chist newspaper. Delmonico's once stood across the street–Charles Dickens
had been honored there on his lecture tours in America. Don pointed out to
Helen the site of the old Triangle Shirtwaist fire, which happened to be near
Henry James's childhood home. None of this impressed her.

On Sunday evening, Don took her to Kenneth Koch's apartment in the
West Village. Koch had promised Don a piece for the first issue of *Location,*
and Don wanted to discuss it with him. "The apartment . . . was extremely
depressing," Helen recalled. It "was in an older building that needed remodeling. The paint was flaking and peeling everywhere, and there were water
stains on the wallpaper and other signs of decay. When I saw the bathroom,
I immediately thought of *Baby Doll,* a 1950s film with Karl Malden. The film

became famous in part for a notorious scene in which Carroll Baker is bathing in an old enamel tub in a run-down farmhouse."

Koch's wife had set up a table with a typewriter in the kitchen so she could work on her dissertation. Helen mentioned that she might enroll in graduate school, and Koch promised to help her find part-time teaching at the New School for Social Research. Don sat down with Koch and his manuscript, Koch's wife resumed her typing, and Helen was left with little to do for two hours but contemplate the apartment's dreariness. She had not liked Koch on his visit to Houston. Though she saw a "more serious dimension" of him now, as he and Don discussed writing, Helen was "extremely uncomfortable" throughout the visit. "I was . . . relieved when we left the building," she said. "Don said he thought Kenneth's apartment could be comfortable as a home, but I could not take [him] seriously."

On Monday after breakfast, Don went to work at the *Location* office. Helen didn't want to sit around the nearly empty apartment, so she walked all morning, trying to find grocery stores and cleaners. Don came home for lunch, and in the afternoon Helen walked up Fifth Avenue to the museums. She carried with her Joseph Heller's *Catch-22,* which had been published the previous year and was gaining cult status among serious readers. Now and then she'd find a bench in a park where she could sit and read the book or a newspaper. A week earlier, President Kennedy had announced that Soviet missiles had been discovered in Cuba. The world appeared to be on the brink of a nuclear confrontation; it was hard to know how seriously to take the threat, but New York was busy stocking its fallout shelters with food and water.

On Monday evening, Don and Joe Maranto took Helen to a spaghetti house near Grand Central Station. They noticed Dwight Macdonald eating at a corner table—recently, Don had read Macdonald's *Against the American Grain.* He loved the fact that he could walk around town and run into writers he admired. After dinner, Don, Helen, and Joe headed to the Village Gate to catch a Miles Davis set, then to another bar to hear Sonny Rollins.

Don was especially thrilled to see Rollins perform. Rollins had just released his landmark bop album, *The Bridge.* Early in his first set, Helen began to complain that she was exhausted. She asked Don if they could take a taxi home. "Don was unhappy at giving up the evening so early," Helen recalled. Once again, she had failed to grasp the romance of the city and its music, which had so captivated Don. "For the very first time, I became unreasonably angry with him and we were soon having an explosive and devastating argument," Helen said. They "had spoken harshly to each other only two or perhaps three times" during their six years of marriage, but now their underlying worries—Helen's fears about her business, Don's anxiety about succeeding as a writer—lay bare the tensions between them. Helen accused him of ignoring his responsibilities. Her debts were his debts. She had sacrificed to make it possible for him to come to New York, and here he was, spending all their money in jazz clubs. For his part, he no longer felt he could "take care" of her the way she wanted to be taken care of and still pursue his literary dream.

Underneath all this was his clear delight in New York and her equally obvious disgust with most of what she had seen of the city. The argument got so bad, Don finally said that he had agonized over their separation at first, but now he had begun to enjoy his independence. He wanted to "live alone and date other girls."

"I was shattered by this admission, even though I too had begun to enjoy the freedom of being without the daily responsibility of marriage," Helen wrote. "I told him that I 'understood' and had certainly found other men attractive but that I could not fathom giving up our marriage.

"By the end of the evening," she said, "I had decided that I should just return to Houston."

The following morning, they agreed to wait a few weeks before deciding anything. Don insisted on sticking to his daily routine. He went to the *Location* office, and he met Helen for lunch at the Museum of Modern Art. He had arranged to meet Jack Kroll there. Don had been introduced to Kroll at a party—a bear of a man, a veteran of the Korean war, a former jazz drummer, now a writer with a love of high and popular culture, he understood Don and looked past Don's "rural irony." In 1963, Kroll would join the staff of *Newsweek* and become the magazine's premier arts and entertainment critic, but for now "he seemed a bit lost," Helen recalled. "Don told me that Jack's friends wanted to help him, but it was not clear what he wanted."

Kroll had "troubles" with women, and he was behind on alimony payments to his ex-wife; his friends knew him as a world-class procrastinator who could never decide what to write about. He was six years older than Don and he knew the city well—Don watched him closely to see how he handled the "mess" he was in.

In any case, Helen liked Kroll. The witty lunch conversation kept her from stewing. Still, she continued to feel like an outsider in the city. "Jack . . . [was] sometimes difficult to follow in his stream of erudite conversation," she recalled, "allusions to people, events, and ideas that were then part of the New York scene." But the day was brilliantly sunny. Khrushchev had just agreed to dismantle Russia's Cuban missiles; the world crisis seemed to be over and the public relief was palpable. Don invited Kroll to come over sometime for fried chicken—one of Don's favorite meals, "but one that I seldom cooked," Helen wrote. Nevertheless, the invitation suggested steadiness, and she left the museum feeling better.

For the next couple of weeks, Helen relaxed a little. She found Manhattan to be "an adventure every day. Walking around it was an exhilarating experience. We could walk everywhere—to restaurants, theaters, museums, art galleries, and even produce markets, grocery stores, and the laundry. Even though our future together was still undecided, [Don and I] spent hours looking at furnishings for our apartment."

Then depression set in again: "There were so many shops . . . that the search for new or exciting designs was exhausting and made the effort less an aesthetic experience than we had known" together in Houston, she recalled.

Every day, Helen phoned her sister. They discussed the ad agency's accounts and once or twice a week Helen would go with Don to the *Location* office. There, she'd write copy to send to Odell. Don had always cordoned off his worlds: He kept his interests far from his father so his father couldn't mock them; he kept his journalist friends away from his art pals so conflicts wouldn't arise between them; he had kept his fiction hidden from most of the Houston crowd. Now Helen was bringing ad accounts into his New York office—smuggling Houston, a world he had tried to leave, into Gotham. Don's discomfort grew as Helen—despite her efforts to enjoy the city—failed to adjust to her surroundings.

Her worries about the agency prompted her to press him for a decision about their future. His response was mixed—evidence of genuine anguish. "During these few weeks in Manhattan, Don was more passionate than ever but unyielding in asking for a separation," Helen recalled. "He thought that the life we had shared was 'too pretty,' that the 'real world is not like that.'"

In his youth, in a city struggling for respectability in the arts, he had idealized women. Now, in this world-class metropolis, he saw sophisticated men and women—people like Jack Kroll—moving casually in and out of romantic "messes."

In Houston, Don had had to accept being the "great man's son." Here in New York, he found himself a "target"—the naïve Texan full of "rural irony" in an art world rent by petty jealousies. He chafed against these saddles. For all his love of romance—and his efforts to keep it alive—he did not want to be hoodwinked by "pretty" ideals. He wanted to see the "real world." He wanted to be his *own* Donald Barthelme.

Even if Texas had shaped his sensibility, he didn't have to deny his limitations or stop trying to overcome them. The world was *not* filled with eccentric prairie homes; it was crowded with dirty apartment buildings, and he would seize the world.

When Helen confronted him about his confusing behavior, he blurted that he "hated the idea of having a child." This sentiment seemed apropos of nothing, but it was consistent with his new obsession with the "real." More than anything else, Helen's miscarriages had eroded the romance of marriage for him. Now, he insisted on facing what he saw as the truths about women and men.

At the same time, he refused to sacrifice romance and mystery. He wanted passion. He wanted separation. "I had known that Don was repelled by the physical realities of pregnancy, a reaction I certainly shared," Helen wrote in her memoir. Don's impulse to shut the past behind him played a role here, too. He and Helen had never confronted their grief over the lost babies, or their decisions to donate the bodies for medical research. It was a grief that haunted their intimacy together.

Eventually, Helen understood that "Don did not want to give up our marriage but wanted to change the conditions of it." She yearned for a "happy and pleasant relationship." He longed for a "passionate" one. If they lived apart, Don reasoned, they could retrieve—and preserve—the mystery and excitement they had once shared together. To Helen, this was just one more crazy New York idea.

"After arriving in New York, I realized immediately that Don was now drinking excessively," Helen recounted. "In Manhattan, there were endless reasons for drinking, among them the jazz clubs, where he could indulge his passion for music." Though she could not imagine "that alcoholism would eventually become a serious problem" for him, she began to worry about the frequent "social affairs to which he was invited each week, including those at Elaine [de Kooning's] home."

"Pop art was flowering" in the art world, "but the agon of Pollock and de Kooning was still in the air," says Phillip Lopate. Since the early 1950s, hard drinking and casual affairs had been part of the Cedar crowd's ambience—and Don had landed in its midst.

It "was just assumed" that everyone got "drunk at the Club," remarked one of the people who had frequented the artists' old meeting place on Eighth Street. In recalling those days, Elaine said, "We used to drink until all of the booze was gone. . . . If there was one bottle, we drank that. If there were ten bottles, we emptied them."

At the Cedar, many of the painters—flush now with money from their growing celebrity—switched from beer to scotch. "Openings in galleries had bars. Pretty soon, artists went to the openings and drank the bars dry," said a friend of the de Koonings. "Bill sort of went along at first. And then, he was a real drinker." Harold Rosenberg had a prodigious capacity for liquor. He never seemed to get tipsy, "no matter how much he drank," Elaine said. Friends joked that his bum leg was hollow and alcohol drained straight into it. By the early sixties, Elaine was "darkening, becoming a sloppy drunk," write Stevens and Swan, Willem de Kooning's biographers. "Increasingly, she seemed to need an audience of young people—often gay men—to admire and fawn over her. She was growing mannered, some thought, trying too hard to be marvelous." An acquaintance of hers said, "She absolutely insisted on being the center of attention every minute and on wrecking all social situations until she passed out."

Sociability aside, each individual had his or her own reasons for drinking. Willem de Kooning sipped whiskey at night to steady his racing heart when he couldn't sleep, worrying over a painting. Franz Kline used scotch to loosen his tongue; a little high, he could entertain people with witty stories. Many artists believed alcohol weakened their superegos and gave them access to the unconscious. And, of course, sexual inhibitions dropped away.

Pollock "would glower into his drink, greet men with 'Fuck you' and women with 'Wanna fuck?'" say Stevens and Swan. Don was a courtly Texan, and he never would have spoken that way, but Pollock's attitudes lingered in Don's new world. Elaine drank to be one of the guys. After a few belts, she talked as raunchily as the boys. One night, at the Cedar, she referred to Helen Frankenthaler, who painted in light, wispy colors, as "that tampon painter."

In the mid-fifties, Rosenberg, who was genuinely fond of de Kooning, took to stopping by the painter's studio to talk about his work. He always carried a bottle of whiskey with him. At first, Rosenberg drank most of what he'd brought. Eventually, de Kooning shared more of the liquor. Elaine believed it was the frequent gallery openings, "together with Rosenberg's habit of stopping by the studio . . . that tipped the crowd-shy de Kooning into alcoholism."

What might get missed, at a distance, is the degree to which these artists and writers believed alcohol helped them *think.* Rosenberg loved all-night conversations about art, aesthetics, politics—always with a bottle to fuel him. Don's "wicked lunches" with him were a version of this. If Don had addictive tendencies early in life, his lunches with Rosenberg and Hess, and his nights at Elaine's studio and in jazz clubs, appear to have tipped him over the edge.

Elaine invited Don and Helen to a party about a week after Helen arrived in New York. Willem de Kooning was there—an "extremely appealing" man, Helen recalled. "Gray haired and very handsome, he was easy to talk to . . . he told me a story about returning home to Europe for a visit after the war. Whenever he had found himself homesick for the United States, he would go to see American westerns, especially films directed by John Ford."

Franz Kline had died a few months earlier, and de Kooning was grieving for his friend. Frightened by Kline's untimely passing, he "seemed not to fit into the frantic atmosphere" of Elaine's studio, Helen said.

In her memoir, she is characteristically restrained in describing Elaine's parties. Elaine's friend Lee Hall says that Elaine's studio had become a "loony command center in the art world, a hurly-burly of activity [and] ambition" filled with "art world hang-abouts, spongers, drunks, and punks." Helen said only that "Elaine drank heavily" and that her portraits of faceless men on the walls were "disconcerting." Helen's reserve hides the profound discomfort she felt among gay men, among hard-core drinkers, and amid such open sexuality.

Harold Rosenberg went around parties "acting like a stallion," commented one woman who attended these gatherings. He would "flar[e] his nostrils and glar[e] in what I suppose he thought was a sexy and a little dangerous way. But Harold was not much—a lot of promise with too much wifey in the background and too much drink." And he was Don's new mentor—another source of Helen's anguish.

Elaine was unusually charismatic and completely uninhibited with men. In the early 1960s, according to Lee Hall, Elaine "seemed to flaunt with renewed vigor her sexual promiscuity." She would pace in front of a man in whom she was interested, wearing platform-heeled shoes, one arm crossing her breasts as she cupped her right elbow in her left hand. One of Elaine's young lovers at the time spoke of her later to Hall: "She was this kind of daredevil, and she was fun. A lot of fun." She "just came on really hard," he said, an "amazing force . . . infusing energy" into everyone around her. "She found everything amusing." He remembered the way she would say that word: "A-muuusiing. Sort of extending it over a long breath."

Don was clearly beguiled by her, an older artist trained, like his father, in the Beaux-Arts drafting tradition.

"Despite the immediacy and the vivacity, I felt that Elaine was always holding something back, that there was some secret that she couldn't impart," commented John Ashbery. He said she was eaten up with "despair." Her melancholy touched the hiding man in Don: In her, he saw himself.

Elaine found Don amusing, and her conversations with him dissolved much of his anxiety about plunging into a literary life. "Just take care of the luxuries," Elaine once told a lover, quoting her mother, "the necessities will take care of themselves."

Helen did not share this outlook. But Don was listening to Elaine now, and Helen was becoming more and more unhappy. At night, she would walk the city with him, past Times Square, which was getting increasingly seedy. Martin J. Hodas, the "King of the Peeps," had set up pornographic nickelodeons all over the area. Neon signs for Canadian Club, Admiral televisions, BOA, and Coca-Cola flashed above the streets, and in the garish red-and-yellow light Helen despaired of her future with Don. Back in the Village, he tried once more to inflame her imagination with the lure of the place. He pointed out an abandoned umbrella on a window ledge and said it looked surreal—like Lautréamont's famous bumbershoot next to a sewing machine on a dissecting table. Walking on MacDougal Street, he pointed out the Café Bizarre on West Third and told her it had once been Aaron Burr's livery stable. But Helen was too locked on the present to care about the past.

During the day, she walked to the New School and to NYU, collecting graduate catalogs and information about various programs. Don continued to insist on a separation. Don felt she would need a job in order to rent her own place. Each morning, over breakfast, he spread the classified section of *The New York Times* on the table and circled available advertising positions in Manhattan. After managing her own firm in Houston, Helen was determined not to start at the bottom with some new outfit. She wanted to go back to school and prepare to teach full-time. Don's fiddling with the ads "annoyed" her. He "wanted . . . me to stay in New York but to have an income independent of his," she wrote. "Such an arrangement would free him of concern for my financial well-being."

Finally, Don forced her hand, saying "if I decided to remain in New York, I could stay in this apartment and he would look for another for himself. I had seen Don use this kind of coercion to obtain what he wanted with other people, but never before had he used it to impose his will on me," Helen recalled. "Don . . . was adamant. I was equally unyielding about not searching for a job that I did not want."

After a few more days of arguments and tears, Helen, "numb with grief, but unwilling to stay in Manhattan under the conditions that Don demanded," returned to Houston.

UP, ALOFT IN THE AIR

In early December 1962, Don wrote to Helen that she should not fly back to New York on the nineteenth, as she had planned. "[T]he fact is that I want to live alone and have wanted to for a long time," he said. "I can give you what you want only by pretending to feel otherwise than I do feel . . . it is better to hate myself than to hate you, and I am afraid, if a reunion is forced rather than natural it would come to that."

He decided that he and Helen should "remain apart for now, being miserable in our separate ways: everything feels so temporary to me I don't know what's happening."

Helen recalled that in her frequent phone calls to Don, she heard the anguish in his voice, but he was also thrilled to have landed in a stimulating world teeming with intelligent, creative people—a world Helen, despite her ambitions and gifts, had resisted. In keeping with Don's tendency to isolate areas of his life, he insisted on a clean break with his former existence in Houston; Helen's attachments to the Bayou City remained firm, and threatened to sink him. Furthermore, there was something romantic in the sophisticated messes Don's new friends were making of their lives. He wrote to Helen that Kenneth Koch "came over the other night and declared that everything is going to hell around him," which, he added, "seems to be true." Jack Kroll continued to flounder.

Don did not aspire to be in a mess, but he admired what he saw as the courage and sacrifice necessary to survive as a writer in Manhattan. The romantic image of the struggling artist did not have much space in it for domestic responsibilities. And though Don was working hard, he was also roaming the jazz clubs every night.

He told Helen he was discouraged about his writing. "[N]o other stories have been sold, or for that matter written," he said. The evidence contradicts this; he seems to have been making a sad face for Helen in order to soften her pain. Lynn Nesbit had taken him on as a client. Almost immediately, she sold "Florence Green Is 81" to *Harper's Bazaar* for three hundred dollars—the story would appear in the magazine's April 1963 issue. Don wrote every morning in the *Location* office, revising stories he had drafted, or started to draft, in Houston: "The Piano Player," "For I'm the Boy Whose Only Joy Is Loving You," and "The Ohio Quadrilogy," which he would retitle "Up, Aloft in the Air." Around the time Don told Helen he wasn't writing, he began a new story, "Carl," which he would eventually call "Margins." He sent his father some dialogue from the story and said the piece "further extends the line of attack originally announced in my stories 'The Joker's Greatest Triumph' and 'The Ohio Quadrilogy' "—that is, a lack of linear narrative and a flattening of emotional content. Neither of these stories had yet been published; it seems Don had been sending drafts of his work to his father, whose responses, if any, have been lost.

Nesbit was pleased that her new client was so disciplined and prolific. A small, energetic woman with a wide, thin smile, she was "easy ... to approach," combining "brains and beauty," wrote the editor Michael Korda. She lived on Barrow Street in a garden duplex, and in later years she gave the only book parties in town that weren't "dull and stiff," according to Korda. "She was elegant, witty, and to all appearances self-assured," he said, and always impatient to get her business done.

"Donald and I had instant chemistry," Nesbit says. When she met him, she was surprised that he "wasn't a crazy bohemian. He liked good living, good food. He had bourgeois values." They became a couple, though Nesbit says it was clear "he was restless in his personal life. Loyal but not steadfast." Occasionally, on weekends, she and Don stayed with Joe Maranto in Stamford. "They'd go to the beach and have a good time in the country while I was in Texas with the kids, visiting my parents," Maggie Maranto recalls.

Nesbit encouraged Don to keep after Herman Gollob. Don told his old friend that "a really courageous book publisher" would grab his work. "[My stories are] brilliant, they're better than anyone else's, so why don't you have a little courage." Don's letters were "swaggering," Gollob recalls, "but ingratiating as well as engaging." The confidence was "part of Don's posture, not much of a posture actually, but I never saw Don suffer much about the quality of his work."

In the meantime, Don continued to assert his editorial muscle at *Location,* often at cross-purposes with Rosenberg and Hess. He wrote Helen:

> [Robert] Bly reacted so violently to the . . . editing job I did on his thing that our relations deteriorated rapidly from an impasse to a shambles, with the result that he picked up his marbles and went home. He told me that he'd shown the edited version to his friends Louis Simpson and John Logan (both Poets), who agreed with him that it was the worst single job of editing a manuscript seen in the Western World since the invention of movable type. Luckily, Harold didn't agree.

Still, Rosenberg was miffed at Don for alienating Bly, who did not relent and would not resubmit work to the magazine. Don felt the first issue of *Location* was shaping up to be an "uneasy collection of good things which don't seem to cohere in any meaningful synthesis. Maybe they will with a little more tinkering and shifting about." He was proud to get a piece from Marshall McLuhan as well as four "brief chapters" from Kenneth Koch's novel *The Red Robins.* The rest of the material he wasn't crazy about (a Kenneth Burke poem, solicited by Rosenberg, was "fantastically poor," Don said), and he especially disliked Larry Rivers's cover design, a charcoal drawing of the Hudson, as well as Rivers's layout ideas, which Don had worked to develop with Rivers at a Southampton retreat. Rosenberg and Hess were pleased with the artist's work, so Don backed off, as he did when Rosenberg accepted an excerpt of Saul Bellow's *Herzog.* Don agreed that Bellow's work was good, but he still resented the elder writer's treatment of him on Staten Island, and he was not keen to publish the old master.

Helen always objected whenever Don used her name in a story, as he did in "The Ohio Quadrilogy," a piece about a man named Buck, who flies around Ohio conducting sexual affairs while his wife, Helen, sits at home in Texas.

When Helen complained about the story, Don changed "Helen" to "Hérodiade," from a Mallarmé poem about the search for ideal beauty. Don revised the piece as he and Helen grew apart, and she developed fresh routines in Houston. "In 1963, I made new friends and became interested in activities that were a change from my former life with Don," Helen wrote in her memoir. "I . . . attended sports car races, and along with a young biology professor who was a colleague at Dominican College, I learned to fly a Cessna 150."

In recoil from the drinking and casual affairs of the writers and artists she had met in New York, she seems to have courted straight-ahead adventurers. Flying made Don nervous, and he didn't like it that Helen was taking lessons. "Tell [the pilots] . . . when they crash . . . [to] turn off . . . the ignition," he wrote at the end of "Up, Aloft in the Air."

By late January 1963, Don had completed most of the stories that would form his first book. He had recently finished a new story, "To London and Rome," and sent it to the *Evergreen Review.* The magazine rejected it, but it would appear in the Fall 1963 issue of *Genesis West,* edited by Gordon Lish. *Contact* had already published "The Darling Duckling at School" and "The Viennese Opera Ball"; "Hiding Man" had appeared in *First Person,* and *New World Writing* had taken "The Big Broadcast of 1938." "Florence Green Is 81" would soon surface in *Harper's Bazaar,* and Don was working on a couple of new stories to round out the collection. *Esquire, Noble Savage,* and *The Paris Review* were among the magazines that had not responded favorably to his work. He had not yet tried *The New Yorker.*

In late January, Helen made one last try to salvage a marriage that was clearly in a tailspin. She returned to New York without telling Don she was coming. When she arrived, a "girl was there with him" in his apartment, she recalled. "I discreetly waited downstairs until he had escorted her out."

"We were glad to see each other, and [Don] was so . . . happy . . . that I was not angry at first," Helen claimed. "In fact, we hugged, laughed, and talked for several minutes. About the girl, Don said simply that 'she was not anyone who mattered.'" He had leapt eagerly into the sophisticated mess of the art world (whose sexual attitudes were considerably loosened by the growing use of birth-control pills).

Once more, Helen was swept into the whirl of art-world parties—most of them held in Elaine de Kooning's studio. One evening, Helen remarked dryly that there were an awful lot of parties in art circles, and Don replied, "[N]o one else works as hard as we did [in Houston]."

"Before long, [Don] became as passionate as ever," Helen recalled. But after finding him with another woman, "it was impossible for me to respond to his gestures of love. I was affectionate but . . . felt nothing more."

Almost immediately, Don insisted that they live in different places. He offered to let her stay in the Fifteenth Street apartment while he looked for another spot. Discouraged, Helen "decided there was nothing for [her] to do." She returned to Houston and moved in with her mother.

Don's affair with Lynn Nesbit hastened the end of things. "Helen would have hung on forever," Herman Gollob says.

She resumed her work at the ad agency and began teaching again at Dominican College. "[W]ithin a short time," she said, "I started a new social life without Don." She was soaring above the mess.

Don felt restless on Fifteenth Street now—he associated the apartment with Helen—and he hoped to find a less expensive place. An acquaintance told him about an empty rent-controlled flat on West Eleventh Street, near Sixth

Avenue. Don checked it out, and in the spring of 1963, he moved into what would become his permanent home in Manhattan.

West Eleventh Street is in the heart of the West Village, famous for its bohemian past, when rents were low and rooms were widely available, before Sixth and Seventh avenues cut through the small, winding streets. Among those who have called the Village home are John Reed, Max Eastman, Theodore Dreiser, Upton Sinclair, Woody Guthrie, Bob Dylan . . . "these nuts that call[ed] themselves artists," as one old-timer put it, "not even bothering to close [their] blinds."

In 1917, Marcel Duchamp climbed the arch in Washington Square Park and declared the "Independent Republic of Greenwich Village." When Eastman helped found *The Masses* in 1910, he meant to harness the neighborhood's literary talent to publish "what is too naked or true for a money-making press," a tradition carried on by *The Partisan Review* and *The Village Voice.* Don had landed in a literary haven (though, in the 1960s, bohemianism shifted somewhat to the East Village). The ghosts of some of America's greatest writers whispered on the street corners here. The Village, with its angled, curving lanes, was intoxicated with itself. Don felt right at home. (In one sense, Houston had prepared him for life here: the Bayou City's lack of zoning led to long stretches resembling the mixed-use neighborhoods Don found so appealing in the Village.)

His apartment was one block west of the building where James Thurber had lived in the 1920s, and across the street from a brownstone once occupied by S. J. Perelman. Grace Paley lived with her husband, Jess, and their two children across the street in the Unadilla Apartments, a few doors from the Greenwich Village School. Grace would become one of Don's closest friends.

In 1963, Don paid around $125 a month for his railroad apartment on the building's second floor. Three central windows, the middle one given over to a small air conditioner, faced south, toward the school across the street. The apartment's walls were old and painted yellow. The kitchen was placed toward the back, overlooking a tiny yard below. Just off the living room, Don set up his desk and typewriter.

The rest of the space remained empty for a while—Helen had asked Don to send their furniture back to Houston. "What about when you return to New York?" Don asked her. "I was puzzled and frustrated," Helen recalled, "but when I asked if he were ready for me to come back, his answer was 'not yet.' And so within a few days, the moving truck arrived [in Houston] and I established my own home once again."

On West Eleventh, Don wrote most of the stories that made him famous. In *The Death and Life of Great American Cities,* published a year before Don arrived in the Village, Jane Jacobs cited the neighborhoods around West Eleventh as models of good city life—short, lively streets that promoted "frequent contact with a wide circle of people" and provided opportunities for "humble" self-government by concerned neighbors. Don would celebrate these qualities in such stories as "The Balloon," "City Life," "The Glass Mountain," and in the novel *Paradise.* And as Grace Paley once pointed out, living across the street from a school meant that Don was one of the few American men writing in the mid-twentieth century who paid vivid attention to children.

"[O]nce in a while when I was low on cash I'd write something for certain strange magazines—the names I don't even remember. Names like *Dasher* and *Thug,*" Don once told an interviewer. "I do remember picking up five hundred bucks or something per piece. I did that a few times. Kind of gory, or even Gorey, fiction" that will never resurface. One such story was "The Ontological Basis of Two," published in the June 1963 issue of *Cavalier* (a cutrate *Playboy*) under the pseudonym Michael Houston. Don carried a copy of the magazine with him to Texas when he returned for two weeks right before Christmas.

A fanciful seduction tale, and a parody of B. F. Skinner's behavioral theories, the story is most notable for what it reveals of Don's preoccupations at the time. One character wears a "Ford Foundation overcoat"; another burns with a "Guggenheim-applicant feeling."

When Don saw Helen, he handed her the copy of the magazine. He told her that *Playboy* had turned the story down, killing his "hopes of a warm winter."

He "wanted to avoid the places that had been part of our weekly ritual since 1956," Helen recalled. "I could see that he was cautious and unwilling to risk anything that might threaten his self-control." He told her he still wanted to live alone but that he "had not given up on a later reconciliation." She didn't respond; she simply told him about her new life and adventures. He asked her if the pilots who gave her flying lessons "were tall and blond and wore long white scarves." She invited him to the airfield—the Collier Airport in northwest Houston—but the thought of the place terrified him.

"[F]or me, the worst was past," Helen wrote in her memoir. "I had grieved for an entire year and could no longer feel . . . sorrow. My pride and my own expectations [made it] impossible for me to propose any kind of compromise." The night before Don returned to New York, he reiterated that for now he needed to be alone, to pursue his career. "As we walked to his car, I looked up at him and saw that tears were streaming down his face," Helen said. "It was the first and only time that I ever saw him cry."

FOR I'M THE BOY

The first issue of *Location*—with a circulation of about five thousand copies—arrived in the nation's literary bookstores in May 1963. In addition to the Bellow, Koch, and McLuhan pieces, it featured photographs of Robert Rauschenberg's studio taken by Rudy Burckhardt, excerpts from an interview with Willem de Kooning by David Sylvester, a series of Saul Steinberg drawings, an excerpt of a Larry Rivers memoir, an essay on modern music by Peter Yates, and photographs of sculptures by Reuben Nakian, Mark di Suvero, David Smith, and Barnett Newman.

Don was not happy with the issue. Individual pieces pleased him, but he felt that the magazine lacked a coherent theme and that it wasn't sufficiently critical of the current state of the arts. In introductory notes, Rosenberg and Hess tried to explain the focus of the magazine—it would explore "certain aspects of [an] artist's work that will reflect something of the logic and direction of his enterprise," Hess said. It would concentrate one at a time on "single [art] objects" to indicate "something" of the object's "variety." Rosenberg suggested that the journal's aim was to overcome specialization in the arts, which had become fields of academic study in order to find niches in a culture that didn't care for them—" 'At last there is a place for the Artist in America,' sighed the poet as he was sworn in."

Rosenberg railed against the sorry state of American literature:

"For twenty years poetry and fiction have had their goals set by a tradition-alist imagination in harmony with the formal conservatism of the mass media. The result has been an incredible naiveté in regard to the process of composition.... The conditions of psychic self-enslavement and joyless-ness under which most current literary works are produced makes reading difficult for anyone but a sadist." Literary innovation depends "on criticism," Rosenberg said. Every writer must react "against the insufficiency of what he admires most."

It should be noted that Rosenberg's literary sensibility, and his hopes for *Location,* had been shaped by an earlier magazine, the *Partisan Review,* founded by William Phillips and Philip Rahv in a Greenwich Village loft in 1934. Its first issues coincided with the rise of the John Reed Club. Phillips, the child of Jewish immigrants in East Harlem, and Rahv, a Russian trans-plant, were pressured by the club to express Soviet ideology in the magazine, in the style of socialist realism. Phillips and Rahv were Marxists, but they were modernists in their literary tastes, and eventually they broke with the club. This political/literary push-pull, with multiple contradictions and a strong polemical edge, continued to define Rosenberg's judgments about art and his editorial style.

Visually, *Location* celebrated collage—not only in the photographs of sculptures, paintings, and drawings but also in the variety of layouts and typefaces (courtesy of Don).

Edges, placement, shapes: These formal concerns are echoed in each of the texts. In the magazine's attention to "objects" and "acts," an existential outlook is apparent. In its interest in "Random Order," a desire to wrest freshness from tradition and spark a cultural revolution is just as plain.

Despite his dissatisfaction with the issue, Don felt proud of certain things. In preparing the Rauschenberg article, he had accompanied Rudy Burckhardt to Rauschenberg's studio and "noticed that the windows over-looking Broadway were dark gray with . . . good New York grime. Rauschen-berg was then working on some of the earliest of his black-and-white silkscreen paintings, and the tonality of the paintings was very much that of the windows. We ran a shot of the windows alongside photographs of the paintings . . . instant art history."

Writers, editors, and publishers pressured *Location* to respond to the era's tumultuous events. In July 1963, Rosenberg received a note from Barney Rosset of Grove Press asking him to use the magazine to rally support for Henry Miller: "[The] New York State Court of Appeals has just banned *Tropic of Cancer* in the entire state of New York."

A few months later, the editorial staff of Basic Books solicited the magazine's help in rounding up tributes to John F. Kennedy. "The *New York Times* . . . received an unprecedented number of poems" about the assassination, the letter said. "Most of them were expressions of profound grief. A young President had been murdered, and with him, it seemed, died a new hope that he had generated for the world. But for the most part these poems were notable for their sincerity rather than for their poetry." Basic Books wanted to publish an anthology of worthy responses, and it felt the magazine was in a position to assist.

Rosenberg, Hess, and Don resisted the temptation to be topical, and they tried harder for thematic cohesiveness in the second issue, which appeared in the summer of 1964. They continued to champion formal experimentation: The issue featured a story by William Gass, poems by John Ashbery, photos of Ray Johnson's letter collages and of a retrospective of William Baziotes's work, and reproductions of new paintings by Willem de Kooning. The issue's most striking images were of de Kooning's studio: coffee cups half-filled with paint atop a paint-encrusted table resembling a coastal landscape; newspaper clippings, gloves, pamphlets pinned to a wall.

In a lead editorial piece entitled "Form and Despair," Rosenberg blasted literature's concern with "social and historical happenings" and urged writing to "examine its own practices," the way recent painting had done. The failure of American writers to consider form amounted to a "lack of seriousness," he said.

On the pages immediately following, Saul Bellow rebutted these remarks. "A literature which is exclusively about itself?" he cried. "Intolerable!" There was good reason, he said, why the "modern novel is predominantly realistic," and that was because "realism is based upon our common life." Therefore, content—the "social" and the "historical"—was far more crucial than form, in his view.

Don weighed in on this debate, contributing an essay entitled "After Joyce"—his first formal statement of literary values (and only one of two essays on writing he would ever publish). He noted that a "mysterious shift . . . takes place as soon as one says that art is not about something but *is* something"—that is, when a literary text "becomes an object in the world rather than a commentary upon the world." He went on to say: "Interrogating older [literary] works, the question is: what do they say about the world and being in the world? But the literary object is itself 'world' and the theoretical advantage is that in asking it questions you are asking questions of the world directly."

Instead of "listening to an authoritative account of the world delivered by an expert (Faulkner on Mississippi, Hemingway on the corrida)," the reader bumps into "something that is *there*, like a rock or a refrigerator." *Finnegans Wake* remains "always *there,* like the landscape surrounding the reader's home or the buildings bounding the reader's apartment. The book remains problematic, unexhausted."

Twice in "After Joyce," Don harkened back to the first fiction he had ever published, in his high school literary magazine. *Pilgrim's Progress,* which he had parodied in "Rover Boys' Retrogression," is an "object," just as *Finnegans Wake* is an object, but John Bunyan did not *intend* this "special placement" for his work, so he failed to reap any metaphysical benefits. Don pointed to Kenneth Koch's *The Red Robins* as an intentional literary object. "Koch's strategy is to re-enter the history of the novel and fix upon a particular kind of American sub-literature, that of the Rover Boys [and] Tom Swift. . . . These books, sentimental, ingenuous, and trivial, furnish a ground of positions, attitudes and allusions against which" Koch enacts his "search for poetry."

Don insisted that art can change the world: "I do not think it fanciful . . . to say that Governor Rockefeller, standing among his Mirós and de Koonings, is worked upon by them, and if they do not make a Democrat or a Socialist of him they at least alter the character of his Republicanism." At a minimum, a literary object forces a reader to consider: "*What do you think of a society in which these things are seen as art?*"

Don admitted he was promoting cultural terrorism, smuggling "Hostile Object[s]" into readers' hands with the aim of reviving "outmoded forms" and "celebrating life." The traditional novel, he said, was a "doomed tower."

Location did not make it to a third number. The magazine cost nearly thirty thousand dollars per issue to produce, and it didn't sell well in stores. Subscriptions were slow to accumulate. More to the point, tensions grew between Don and *Location*'s founders, Hess and Rosenberg. They remained friends, but friendship was easier if they didn't work together. Like Don's father, Rosenberg and Hess were formidable intellectual figures. Don needed distance from them.

"[H]e was a talker, he *had* to talk . . . [a]s he went on, he was more salty, scandalous, he was murderous," Saul Bellow once said of Rosenberg in a thinly disguised fictional portrait. "Reputations were destroyed when he got going, and people torn to bits." He "lived for ideas," and he could carry his listeners into "utterly foreign spheres of speculation." Don thrilled at all of this, but he had his own ideas, and felt, as he had felt in his father's house, that his thoughts couldn't grow in the shadow of the great man.

If Don disagreed with Rosenberg, he was made to feel he had missed something, and never allowed to forget it.

In an undated "Memorandum on *Location* Prospectus and Prospects," apparently addressed to Rosenberg and Hess between the first and second issues, Don said, "Let me confess now that my own idea for the magazine hasn't worked out." The memorandum is worth quoting at length because it reads like an aesthetic manifesto—even more so than "After Joyce."

Don said he was embarrassed at "being inside the establishment," forced to praise rather than critique great figures such as Willem de Kooning and Reuben Nakian. In his view, the establishment position had "fatal consequences":

> We are heavily committed to the leading figures of an achieved revolution. Most literary-art magazines come into being as the organs of revolutionary parties and see their missions in terms of promulgation of a radical doctrine, destruction of the existing order, and establishment of a new regime. *Location* enters as an apologist for an existing order. We are not defending a stockade but guarding a bank.

Speaking of American literature, he expressed the opinion that "we all seem radically bored" with it. "This is probably literature's fault rather than our own, but we have not found a way to make this radical boredom a principle which operates to the advantage of the magazine."

Don's solution? The magazine must stop "walking softly and carrying a big bouquet." Instead of interviewing artists and respectfully repeating their "ideas," *Location* should "think up a net for trapping" *unspoken* ideas and "establish a factory for extracting the oil from them." Perhaps creating a "lexicon of key ideas" would be a place to start, he said. Maybe this "would [give us a] way of seeing what these ideas do, where they take the holder of the idea."

Then there was the "literary problem":

> Instead of having Bellow write about form in the novel, why can't we come out and say (if we believe it; I do) that American literature is best and most clearly seen in the extremes represented by Bellow on the one hand and William Burroughs on the other, and that neither of them can deliver a thoroughly satisfactory art-experience. . . . In other words, we have to take a radical position with regard to American literature, admit its minor virtues and announce that it lacks necessity and point out its immense shortcomings.

Very few writers were "capable of supplying" pieces of the caliber Don sought. The only remedy he could see was a "more active role in the *writing* of the magazine on the part of the editors."

• • •

"For I'm the Boy" appeared in *Location*'s second issue. The story was Don's surest means to date of staking out a "radical position" on American literature. In its formal concerns, it was literary criticism masked as fiction.

Don meant the story to stand on its own, but he was mindful that it would appear in *Location* among certain other pieces, and he tweaked it accordingly. In the magazine, it came after Saul Bellow's dismissal of formal experimentation and Don's "After Joyce." "For I'm the Boy" rebuts Bellow and exemplifies the kind of fiction Don extolled in his essay. Its placement created the kind of fission Don hoped *Location* would model.

"For I'm the Boy" concerns a man named Bloomsbury, who has just watched his wife fly away at an airport. She has left him after his repeated flirtations with another woman. Bloomsbury has brought to the airport two "friends of the family," Huber and Whittle. Their presence prevents an intimate good-bye, and turns the couple's parting into an awkward public ritual. As the men drive home, Huber and Whittle ply Bloomsbury for details about his marriage—they want a story—but Bloomsbury refuses them.

Now and then, his mind drifts into reveries about his wife and the "bicycle girl" he has courted: memories presented in mock-Joycean brogue, in contrast to the Jamesian formality of the narrative.

Formally, the story is a war of styles: rigorous content-based paragraphs versus freer-form passages in stream-of-consciousness mode. This stylistic war continues the debate begun in the magazine's essays.

Don furnishes a "ground of positions, attitudes and allusions"—a "cluster of associations"—against which to enact the "search for his own poetry." Some of the allusions, such as the Joycean dialect and the name Bloomsbury, with its literary echoes, are obvious.

The story's title is a line from the old Irish ballad "Bold O'Donahue":

> *For I'm the boy to squeeze her, and I'm the boy to tease her*
> *I'm the boy that can please her, ach, and I'll tell you what I'll do*
> *I'll court her like an Irishman*
> *Wi' me brogue and blarney too is me plan*
> *With the holligan, rolligan, swolligan, molligan Bold O'Donahue.*

Bloomsbury courts the bicycle girl "like an Irishman"—but he and the girl are merely sites of linguistic clustering, drawing together high and low art, a popular old ballad and Joyce's *Ulysses*. Art emerges as the story's central concern.

Of course, a gathering of allusions (Bloom buried) does not a story make. More is at stake here.

On closer reading, we discover that Kierkegaard provides one of the story's foundations. In Part Two of *Repetition,* a young man, devastated over a broken love affair, says no words can capture his "soul anguish." The young man can only use *others'* words to approximate his feelings: snippets of poems and quotations.

Then he recalls the biblical story of Job's trials, and the torment caused by his friends, who demand explanations of his anguish.

Bloomsbury is a contemporary version of Job *and* of Kierkegaard's young man. He recalls his broken love affairs in a pastiche of others' words (the Irish ballad, traces of Joyce). And like Job, he resists the "friends of the family," who seek an accounting of his failures.

Bloomsbury knows that words cannot "explain" feeling. As Sartre wrote, responding to Kierkegaard, "The only way to determine the value" of a feeling "is, precisely, to perform an act which confirms and defines it . . . a mock feeling and a true feeling are almost indistinguishable."

"*Give us the feeling,*" Bloomsbury's friends demand. He refuses, saying, "We can . . . discuss the meaning but not the feeling."

Here, the story's center is revealed: the key to the particular allusions its author had gathered. Why the name Bloomsbury? Virginia Woolf's husband, Leonard, published the first British edition of T. S. Eliot's *The Waste Land*, the second section of which, "A Game of Chess," is strongly echoed in Don's story in the domestic tension and the playful language.

Duncan Grant, a Bloomsbury artist, once said, "The artist must . . . above all retain his private vision." The character Bloomsbury seeks to do this, against mounting pressure from his friends. Once feelings are put into words, the feelings are betrayed; they have assumed a ritual posture for public consumption.

Which brings us to art, our most refined public expression of what is private, unreachable, unsayable. Finally, it fails—words cannot do the trick—but it is the best we have: a snippet here, a snippet there.

Rather than *content*—an explanation of something—art's value lies in the fact that it offers *forms* for our experiences.

And yet we live in a world that demands explanations. Frustrated (and shaken by their own romantic failings), Bloomsbury's friends beat him with fists, a bottle, and a tire iron until "at length the hidden feeling emerged, in the form of salt from [Bloomsbury's] eyes and black blood from his ears, and from his mouth, all sorts of words."

As he had done in "The Darling Duckling at School," Don mined his private life to give the story emotional depth. The average reader does not know, and does not need to know, that Don was thinking of his first wife when Bloomsbury's wife rebuffs him with Mallarmé. Nor does the average reader know, or need to know, that Don's second marriage was failing as he wrote the story. Helen had taken up flying. Bloomsbury muses, "[A]fter so many years one could still be surprised by a flyaway wife."

Still, these hidden "clusters" lend the story pathos, darkening its tone.

Finally, Don's quarrel with Saul Bellow energizes the piece. Don had in mind not only Bellow's essay in *Location* but also a much-discussed article from five years earlier, "Deep Readers of the World, Beware," published in *The New York Times Book Review.* In the article, Bellow mocked existential novelists (taking a swipe at Joyce along the way). He said that in their attempts to be "deep," existentialist writers "contrive somehow to avoid" feelings in their work. They prefer "meaning to feeling."

When Bloomsbury tells his friends, "We can . . . discuss the meaning but not the feeling," Don offered Bellow his response.

In the end, "For I'm the Boy" does not settle at the level of literary debate. Its author celebrates life, as Beckett does, with humor and odd moments of joy: "Once in a movie house Bloomsbury recalled Tuesday Weld had suddenly turned on the screen, looked him full in the face, and said: You are a good man. You are good, good, good." Though this memory does not help him escape his friends' violence, he recalls that the "situation [was] dear to him," and that he had "walked out of the theater, gratification singing in his heart." In Don's fiction, a fine line always exists between irony and genuine sentiment ("a mock feeling and a true feeling are almost indistinguishable"), but the ambiguity, too, is one of life's deep pleasures.

"For I'm the Boy"—so far, Don's most complex demonstration of a radical new fiction—found freshness in paths Joyce had scouted, and showed writers where they might go after Joyce. Nothing like it had ever appeared in American literature.

COME BACK, DR. CALIGARI

Since childhood, and as a newspaper arts reviewer, Don had been an inveterate moviegoer. Manhattan was movie theater–rich: Among them were the Thalia on the Upper West Side, with its repertory program; the Paris, in Midtown, with lush blue velvet walls; Cinema 1 and 2, across the street from Bloomingdale's; the Beekman, with sleek curtains that opened in a whisper before each feature; the Bleecker Street Cinema, with its resident cat, Breathless, named after the Godard film; and in the Village, the 8th Street Playhouse, located next to the Electric Ladyland recording studios, where Jimi Hendrix did his thing.

In 1929, F. W. Murnau's *Nosferatu* had its American premiere at the 8th Street Playhouse, although the theater was then called the Film Guild Cinema. In the early sixties, the vampire classic and other gems of the silent era, surrealist masterpieces such as *The Cabinet of Dr. Caligari,* played regularly in Chelsea basements on rickety Bell & Howell projectors, too bright and prone to overheating, rented by impromptu film clubs. The old movies were also screened at the 92nd Street Y, but Don did not have to go there or seek out-of-the-way cubbyholes to watch amazing films. The French New Wave had hit, and New York's screens celebrated the precocious auteurs. As Phillip Lopate has written, "To be young and in love with films in the early 1960s was to participate in what felt

like an international youth movement. We in New York were following and, in a sense, mimicking the café arguments in Paris, London and Rome, where the cinema had moved, for a brief historical moment, to the center of intellectual discourse, in the twilight of existentialism and before the onslaught of structuralism."

Unique rituals characterized New York's rather insular cinema society. Rudy Franchi, former program director of the Bleecker Street Cinema, remembers that Breathless, the house cat, "a jet black smallish creature," would often "escape from the office area and start to climb the movie screen." He says, "I would sometimes get a buzz on the house phone from the projection booth with the terse message 'cat's on the screen.'" The audience cheered for Breathless to make it to the top, but he never got there before Franchi pulled him down.

The theater sold copies of *Cahiers du Cinéma* and was "fanatical about proper projection and proper screen ratio," Franchi says.

For Don, an added draw of the art-house theaters was their architecture. The tilted glass facade, horizontal orientation, and ribboned windows of the Beekman gave it a touch of the International Style. The auditorium of the Thalia, which was located on West Ninety-fifth Street, sloped *upward* toward the screen. The novelty of this wore off when a tall person sat in front of you.

In the early 1960s, one of the pleasures of many foreign films was their naughtiness, as appealing to cinema buffs as what Lopate has called the movies' "existential self-pity." ("Unless I am mistaken," he wrote, "suicide was in the air, in the cinematic culture of the early sixties.") Films like *Boccaccio '70,* in which a voluptuous woman on a poster comes to life and seduces a puritanical soul (a story sure to lure pale, solitary moviegoers) stirred controversy among those who also worked to ban books such as Henry Miller's *Tropic of Cancer.*

Scandals were fun, but the richest pleasure was finding a film before it got much press; a private discovery—best seen during an afternoon matinee in a nearly empty auditorium.

Many writers indulged in the guilty joy of sneaking off during the day to catch a flick. Arthur Miller lived just three blocks from the Beekman. George Plimpton also lived nearby, editing *The Paris Review* in his apartment. Sometimes the two could be seen, each sitting alone, watching an early-bird show.

In his first two years in New York, Don saw premieres of films by Fellini, Truffaut, Godard, Jean Renoir, and Michelangelo Antonioni. Antonioni's breakthrough feature, *L'Avventura,* opened at the Beekman the year before Don arrived in Manhattan. In September 1963, the first New York Film Festival was held in Lincoln Center's Philharmonic Hall. Among other films, the festival screened Yasujiro Ozu's *An Autumn Afternoon,* Luis Buñuel's *The Exterminating Angel,* and Roman Polanski's *Knife in the Water.*

But it was Antonioni whom everyone kept talking about. More than any-one else at the time (at least on a commercial scale), he took advantage of what his medium had to offer, much the way Jackson Pollock had privileged the drip and de Kooning the brush stroke on canvas. Antonioni's films did what *only* films could do. He had a "way of following characters with a pan shot, letting them exit and keeping the camera on the depopulated land-scape," Lopate wrote. "With his detachment from the human drama and his tactful spying on objects and backgrounds, he forced [viewers] to disengage as well, and to concentrate on the purity of his technique."

He was also in tune with existentialist fashion (or the part of existential-ism that wallowed in grim cupidity).

Happily for Don, the explosion of foreign movies in Manhattan coincided with a growing American film underground led by Stan Brakhage, Jonas Mekas, and Andy Warhol. In 1963, at the Factory on Forty-seventh Street, Warhol produced his first film, *Sleep,* a six-hour tour of a slumbering man's body. This was followed a year later by *Empire,* an eight-hour still-camera view of the Empire State Building. "The themes of [Warhol's] films were un-speakably banal," wrote film historian Klaus Honnef. Yet the movies' "clum-siness" made them "strikingly immediate and fresh":

> If the cinemagoer really concentrated and became involved in these films, they had an incredibly forceful effect. Offering utterly meaning-less trivia, they took an attentive audience out of the real world of pur-pose and constraint and induced a mood bordering on the ecstatic.... [Warhol's] films would be unthinkable without the traditional film to hold them up against; they are shaped by their deliberate contrast to the Hollywood approach....

If Honnef's assessment sounds strained now, it's a sign of Warhol's suc-cess at exposing Hollywood formulas. It's also a sign that the passions of New York's 1960s film culture are long gone, as are many of the theaters in which that culture thrived. The 8th Street Playhouse, where Don used to walk from his apartment, has closed. The Bleecker Street Cinema fell into financial ruin, ended its days as a porno house, and was gutted for retail space. The Thalia was boarded up in 1987, and in the spring of 2005 the Beekman, which made an appearance in *Annie Hall,* Woody Allen's Oscar-winning paean to the city, shut its doors.

Since the 1920s, contributors to *The New Yorker* had written for urban ro-mantics, the type of people who would frequent sophisticated films and pop-ular culture. Fittingly, the magazine's offices, at 25 West 43rd Street, in a

Beaux-Arts building beloved of E. B. White, were near Aeolian Hall, where Gershwin debuted *Rhapsody in Blue* in February 1924. No matter the era, the "old" New York was always vanishing, always assuming a brittle, nostalgic glow—a wonderful elegance. The magazine's awareness of this was part of its appeal; at times, it was a measure of its stodginess.

Harold Ross, born in Colorado and raised there and in Utah, had come to the city, as Don would, with a western swagger and a lot of newspaper experience. He knew what he wanted when he founded the magazine: a mixture of humor, sophistication, and romance. Within a year of its first appearance on newsstands, "the look, the editorial and graphic components, and the feel of the magazine would be more or less in place," wrote Ben Yagoda. After that, "virtually any alteration or innovation would be made *within* those constraints," he added.

And yet nothing was ever good enough for Ross. Robert Coates, an early "Talk of the Town" writer, has noted that in the magazine's early days, "not only partitions" in the office "but editors and just about everything else came and went or were shifted about almost constantly. We used to joke about it at the time [as evidence] of Ross's restlessness, but as I see it now, something deeper was involved. . . . Ross's sudden changes of plan and direction were like the chargings-about of a man in a canebrake, trying blindly to get through to the clearer ground he is certain must lie beyond."

This desperate desire for clarity stamped itself on the magazine's prose style—take, for example, the strict rules about serial commas. E. B. White once quipped that "commas in the *New Yorker* fall with the precision of knives in a circus act, outlining the victim." (In 1984, Don would tell George Plimpton that he had waged a "twenty year" war with Ross's successor, William Shawn, who always "stippled" Don's stories with commas, interfering with the "freer style of punctuation" Don preferred.)

Shawn, the Chicago-born son of a cutlery-shop owner, had come to New York in 1932, hoping to be a composer. He went to work as a fact-checker at *The New Yorker.* He appealed to Ross because he "fully comprehended . . . the magazine's commitment to a rhetoric and even a poetry of facts," Yagoda wrote. When Ross died of throat cancer in 1951, Shawn took charge of the magazine. He seemed even more frantic than his predecessor to find clear verbal ground. Over time, the magazine's articles grew longer, qualifier-laden, as though the sentences could never find their cores. Shawn's editorial style was indirect; he would let his writers know he was dissatisfied, and he would stand firm, but he would rarely come out and say what he wanted. Harold Brodkey said that Shawn "combined the best qualities of Napoleon and St. Francis of Assisi." His manner left many of his writers confused and paralyzed, locked in endless bouts of rewrites that often led nowhere. In the early 1960s, John Cheever, one of *The New Yorker*'s most celebrated fiction writers, complained that Shawn, and by extension the whole magazine, was "hobbled" and "capricious."

Joseph Mitchell had gone silent, as had J. D. Salinger. Renata Adler, who joined the staff of the magazine in 1963 as a manuscript screener, said that Shawn's "inhibition[s]" led to an "ethic of silence":

> There began to be a feeling [at the magazine] that it was vulgar, perhaps morally wrong to write. Turning in a piece, of course, put Mr. Shawn in the predicament of having to decide whether to publish it. If he rejected it, there had to be one kind of painful conversation. If he accepted it, he was put under the pressure of publishing it. . . . This hesitation was not only explicit in his conversation. The aversion to personal publicity for editors and writers, the increasing respect for the privacy of subjects were turning into a reluctance to publish at all. . . .

The "physical structure of the office" appeared to "externalize writer's block," Adler added. "Wherever there was space sufficiently wide for people to gather in a corridor for a chat, whole rooms would be built . . . in such a way as to take up what had been the entire gathering space. . . ."

Ved Mehta, another *New Yorker* staffer, concurred. "The *New Yorker* had an air of complete privacy," he said:

> The offices of editors, writers, artists, and other people connected with it were all mixed together and there was no way of telling who was to be found where. None of the offices had names on them. Most were little more than cubicles, each with an individual window and outfitted with a desk, a chair, a typewriter, and, in some cases, a divan bed, which would always be piled high with books, manuscripts, and old newspapers. The monoton[ous] . . . dusty hallways and dingy walls gave the place a bleak atmosphere, as though the *New Yorker* were making a conscious statement that writers and artists should be above worrying about their surroundings.

Certain staff writers, "under the pressureless pressures of being left alone to do whatever they liked . . . fell apart," Mehta recalled. They "had nervous breakdowns, or developed writer's block, which sometimes lasted for years."

"I've always felt that there was a connection between *The New Yorker* and depression. Depression as an aesthetic," Phillip Lopate says. "There's the recessive quality of the first-person pronoun in much *New Yorker* writing. It's genteel, not in your face. Reserved. Taking in the world and being reflective without getting too excited, too parvenu. It's a depressive stance, and it's a mark of a certain social status. You know, it's not a working-class disease."

Often, the magazine's short stories reflected this tamped-down mood. By the early sixties, staleness had crusted over much *New Yorker* fiction. Always, the stylistic precision was high, but for years the magazine had published the quiet suburban sketches of Cheever, John O'Hara, and John Updike, while rejecting more forceful work such as Philip Roth's novella *Goodbye, Columbus.*

In January 1963, amid the roughly 250 fiction submissions a week—most of them, according to Adler, "amazingly bad," and some of them "obscene and extremely violent," some with photographs—an unusual piece surfaced, making its way around the office partitions, past the piled-up newspapers on the ugly gray shelves of the eighteenth floor, past the drone of rock music from behind a closed door, cigarette smoke in the hallways, and the faint witch-hazel scent of William Shawn's aftershave, which lingered in corridors. The story landed on the desk of Roger Angell, a fiction editor. A parody of the films of Michelangelo Antonioni, it was called "L'Lapse." The writer was Donald Barthelme.

"At the time I didn't have an agent," Don told George Plimpton in 1984. "We sent [the story] agented only by a stamp." He was misremembering. Lynn Nesbit had submitted the story to Angell, who returned it with praise and an offer to consider it again if Don revised it. On January 25, Angell contacted Nesbit: "Donald Barthelme has rewritten 'L'Lapse' " and the magazine will "buy it," he said. "I have already told him the good news."

"L'Lapse" is less a story than what Roger Angell would refer to as a "casual," a straight humor piece, capturing the excitement and silliness of the Antonioni craze. The timing was terrific. *La Notte,* Antonioni's follow-up to *L'Avventura* had opened in New York the previous year. A long, slow study of ennui, it featured Jeanne Moreau, Marcello Mastroianni, and Monica Vitti. The camera constantly pulled away from the actors, and the script avoided any engagement among the characters. "Eroticism is the disease of the age," Antonioni had pronounced to a newspaper reporter. Long lines of movie buffs had waited to see *La Notte,* and rumors now spread that *L'Avventura* might be scheduled to play at the Film Festival in September.

In "L'Lapse," composed as a script, a "wealthy film critic" named Marcello tries to instruct his lover and protégée, Anna, in the art of film reviewing. Anna is a "lengthy, elegant beauty, blond, whose extreme nervousness is exteriorized in thumb-sucking." The couple sits in "the plaza in front of the Plaza" while "shabby-looking pigeons wheel about meaningfully but in slow motion." Anna's reviews suffer from forced enthusiasm. She depends on phrases such as "penetratingly different." Marcello ("*wealthy, bored*") complains, "If I'm going to teach you the business, *cara,* you gotta learn not to make adverbs out of words like 'penetrating.' " Anna's heart is not in her work:

ANNA (*removes thumb*): But, Marcello, I didn't *like* the picture. I was bored.

MARCELLO: Look, sweets, it doesn't matter you were bored. The point is, you were bored *in a certain way.* Like brilliantly.

The script indicates the camera is to pull away from them as they talk: "*Shot of nail kegs at construction site. Camera peers into keg, counts nails. Shot of bus disappearing around corner. Shot of I.R.T. breaking down.*"

Frustrated, Anna spits at Marcello, "Critic!"—a lift from *Waiting for Godot.* Then she says, timidly, "Last night when we were talking about pure cinema, and I called for a transvaluation of all values, and you said that light was the absence of light—we weren't communicating then, were we? It was just jargon, wasn't it? Just noise?"

Marcello, "*facing the truth,*" says, "No, Anna, I'm afraid we *were* communicating. On a rather low level." Anna ("*frenzied, all thumbs*") cries that she wants her life to be "*really* meaningless," filled with "febrile elegance!" Marcello admits, "Meaninglessness like that is not for everybody. Not for you and me, *cara.*" The camera pans to a man on a nearby bench, who stares back at the camera inquiringly. "*Shot of cement bags. Shot of leaf floating in gutter; leaf floats down drain. Camera waits four minutes to see if leaf will reappear. It does not reappear. Shot of traffic light; it is stuck.*"

Don's piece appeared in the March 2, 1963, issue of *The New Yorker,* just before a long Cheever story and an excerpt from Hannah Arendt's *Eichmann in Jerusalem.* If it didn't quite signal a sea change in *New Yorker* fiction, it distinguished itself by its energy. As in the best of Perelman, its parody was so deadpan and earnest, the reader felt disoriented. Anna's movie reviews ("penetratingly different") were similar to the magazine's capsule reviews. For example, in "Goings on About Town" for March 2, the magazine called the film version of *West Side Story* "inhumanly overproduced." *Cara!*

Ever since his teens, Don had longed to see his name printed in *The New Yorker*'s famous Caslon typeface. Now he had succeeded.

On March 5, Angell wrote to Don, addressing him as "Mr. Barthelme":

> [The novelist] Niccolo Tucci asked me to convey my congratulations to you. He told me that he had been asked by Mr. Antonioni, who is a friend of his, to write a screenplay. Tucci didn't want to, but he didn't know how to say this to Antonioni. So when he read your casual, he translated it into Italian and sent it off to Antonioni, saying it had expressed his own feelings exactly.
> And now, when are you going to send us another casual?

• • •

Roger Angell was forty-two years old at the time. Later that year, he would be divorced from his first wife, by whom he had two daughters, and would marry Carol Rogge, who had worked as a secretary in *The New Yorker*'s fiction department. Angell was the son of Katharine Angell, who had joined the magazine in 1925 as a manuscript reader and become indispensable to Harold Ross. When she married E. B. White in 1929, she was the magazine's chief literary editor.

It is not surprising, then, that from an early age Roger's pursuits were literary. In 1938, when he was eighteen, he asked his stepfather to give him a book of A. E. Housman poems, a bottle of Amontillado, and a top hat for Christmas. "I can only assume that he is going to sit around in the hat, drinking the sherry, reading the poems, and dreaming the long long dreams of youth," White wrote a friend.

While in the service in the early forties, Angell was stationed at Hickam Field in Hawaii. There, he became the editor of *TIG Brief,* an Air Force magazine. In 1943, White recommended his stepson to Harold Ross for editorial work at *The New Yorker.* "Although he is a member of the family I have little hesitancy in recommending him," White said. "He lacks practical experience but he has the goods." He told Ross, "When my wife was editing the *New Yorker Short Story Book,* Roger turned out to have a pretty sound knowledge of that kind of stuff and helped her with opinions and recommendations, practically all of which made a good deal of sense."

Eventually, Angell moved into his mother's old office, and according to Renata Adler, he "established an overt, superficially jocular state of war with the rest of the magazine." As Adler explained the situation: "The fiction editors themselves wrote fiction, a conflict of interest which did not exist in other departments."

William Shawn recognized the politics of the fiction department, but he did nothing to ease tensions or restructure practices. Staffers assumed that Angell aspired to the general editorship, but Ved Mehta thought of him as "cold and irascible," lacking the nurturing qualities that were "a *sine qua non* for the job of the *New Yorker*'s editor."

If Shawn was a remote father figure to Don, Angell would become a big brother, a man with business authority, but someone who also (according to Mehta) lacked confidence: Angell was drawn to Don's swagger. The men shared military experience, editing, and the trauma of divorce. In time, Angell said, Don became "my lifeline to the literary world and I became his lifeline to an everyday life."

But first Don had to prove he was capable of negotiating *The New Yorker*'s quirks. He attempted a parody of a *Playboy* interview, but the satire seemed "vague and obscure" to Angell, and he warned Don away from the Q & A format, so reminiscent of Frank Sullivan's "Mr. Arbuthnot" pieces.

Don suggested several ideas for parodies, including a Broadway treatment of William Burroughs ("Lunchtime!"); Angell encouraged him, but none of the pieces went anywhere. In early April, Lynn Nesbit submitted Don's story "Carl" (an early draft of "Margins"). Angell replied, "This strikes us as being highly artificial and entirely unconvincing. . . . I'm certain he can do something better than this little sermon."

On May 6, in a letter rejecting another parody, Angell told Don, "I do hope that you will not be discouraged by these setbacks. Your eye and ear for parody are unblemished, and I think you should have full confidence in them. . . . I am quite sure, also, that you need not confine yourself exclusively to parody. We will continue to look forward anxiously to anything you send us."

Angell was impressed by Don's tenacity—and also by his humor and brevity, two of the magazine's mainstays, at least in fiction. Though nothing had succeeded since "L'Lapse," Angell was certain that Don had the goods.

Meanwhile, Herman Gollob, noting that his old pal had now published six short stories (in March and April alone, he had placed pieces in *The New Yorker* and *Harper's Bazaar*), felt ready to take a chance with Don at Little, Brown. "I showed the stories to my boss, Ned Bradford, the shrewd, dapper, silver-haired editor in chief," Gollob wrote later. "For the next hour or so I could hear him roaring with laughter in his office. . . . Emerging at last, he said, 'This bastard is either crazy or a genius. Probably both.'"

Short story collections didn't "fly off the shelves," Bradford said, and Don was so "esoteric," no one would know what to do with him. Still, Bradford felt he "might turn out to be an American Kafka or Joyce" and said that they couldn't "pass up a chance to publish someone" like that. "[O]ne of these days he might write a novel that more than ten people want to read," he told Gollob. "Sign him up," Bradford said.

"I told Don the amazing news, and it instantly galvanized him into action," Gollob recalled. "He wrote two stories in three days—'Marie, Marie, Hold on Tight' and 'A Shower of Gold.'"

Don had drafted a version of "A Shower of Gold" in Houston, but he changed it substantially once he moved to New York. He completed it at the Gollobs' house on Martha's Vineyard, in a room overlooking the ocean.

To seal the book deal with Little, Brown's editorial board (once he'd got the go-ahead from Bradford), Gollob showed up at the sales conference in a pair of dark glasses and recited a monologue from "A Shower of Gold." "That did the trick," Gollob says. "They upped the print run from one to eight copies." It wasn't the "Joycean shit" that impressed the board. It was the fact that Don's work was "screamingly funny."

In midsummer, Don submitted to Roger Angell a new draft of "The Piano Player" (later, a reviewer tagged the story "John Cheever in a fun-house mirror"). Angell was so taken with the piece, he not only bought it but also offered to pay Don an additional fee for any new work of his the magazine purchased, on the condition he be shown it first. On July 22, Angell wrote to Nesbit: "[Mr. Barthelme] seemed most interested in the offer . . . in return for a first look at all of Mr. Barthelme's work that falls in the category of fiction, humor, reminiscence, we will pay an additional 25% to the basic price for any works we purchase from him. There are secondary benefits as well."

What this amounted to in hard figures was never very clear. *The New Yorker*'s financial agreements with writers were variable and murky—sometimes, it seems, even to the accountants. But Don and Nesbit saw nothing to lose. The offer was extraordinary, given that Angell had accepted only two pieces so far. Don's writing was "breathtaking," Angell thought, even in the stories that didn't work. Here was a special and singular talent. So Angell took a chance—perhaps seizing an opportunity to intensify his little "war" with the rest of the magazine.

Soon after "The Piano Player" appeared in the August 31 issue, William Maxwell, another fiction editor, a fine writer, and a man of genteel tastes, told Angell the piece had "baffled" many staffers. Other editors—Rachel MacKenzie, Robert Henderson—groused about Don's work. Angell was delighted.

Curiously enough, the ever-hesitant William Shawn "was on to Barthelme before anyone else," Angell recalled. "[H]e told me that the key to Barthelme wasn't to read him like fiction, but like poetry.

"I enthusiastically admired what Don was and what he became, but none of that would have meant much and little of it would have happened were it not for Shawn's daring and intuitive understanding of what sort of artist had turned up when Don began submitting his amazing early pieces," Angell says. "In the small flood of books about Shawn that appeared after he died, there was little mention of his genius as a fiction editor, which was held to be secondary to his other gifts and not an integral part of his influence over the writing and thinking of that time."

As for "suggesting that Don move in a particular direction, I couldn't," Angell says. He had urged Don to expand beyond parody, but apart from that, "I didn't know where he would go. Nobody in the world had seen writing like this."

Sometime in the late spring of 1963, Don met Andy Warhol in Times Square for a photo shoot. Without speaking much, the men arranged scenarios in a tacky Fotomat: Don reading a tabloid or sitting primly in a suit and tie.

In its June issue, *Harper's Bazaar* ran two of the pictures. In one, Don sits grinning. The magazine's upper edge cuts off his head. In the other, Don lunges toward the camera as though about to vomit. The photo is blurry; his mouth is tight, his eyes half-closed. The pictures appeared with shots of other young talents making news around New York—the painter Larry Poons, the dancer Edward Villella. The magazine announced, "Donald Barthelme's book of short stories will be published by Little, Brown."

Don was working at a blinding clip now. Immediately after signing the agreement with *The New Yorker,* he submitted his latest draft of "The Ohio Quadrilogy," now called "To Cleveland Then I Came." Angell turned it down. "It is almost impossible, of course, to explain acceptances and rejections of this kind of story," Angell said to Don, "but the events here did not seem to contribute to an area of comprehension, and all the changes and switches were often more exasperating than illuminating."

Better news came in September, with the acceptance of "Marie, Marie, Hold on Tight." Angell told Nesbit this was the "best story of his that we have seen." Don instigated his comma war with Shawn. On September 3, Angell wrote:

> *Dear Don:*
> *(Do people call you Don? Is it all right for me to call you Don?)*
> *Shawn would be happy if you could add just a little more punctuation to this piece. . . .*

The story ran in the October 12 issue. Angell added a "cost of living adjustment" to Don's payments for the "quarter"—a matter of a few thousand dollars. On October 14, Angell wrote to Nesbit, accepting "A Shower of Gold" and sending a "15% quantity bonus for SHOWER and the three others" ("L'Lapse," "The Piano Player," and "Marie, Marie, Hold on Tight"). He said, "[Don] certainly is one of the happiest events of the year for us."

In mid-October, Angell asked Don to come see him at the office. He wanted to meet this brilliant young writer, and prepare "A Shower of Gold" for its appearance in the magazine. The men hit it off. Angell's wedding was approaching. He was cheerful and buoyant, with a round, boyish face and a prim mustache. Books lined a wooden cabinet to the right of his desk, but the desk was remarkably clear. A bulky white typewriter sat atop a metal stand in the middle of the floor. Angell wore a tie and neatly pressed pants. Don, clean-shaven, grinned as slyly as he had in the Warhol photos.

Together, they discussed Don's paragraphing in "A Shower of Gold," which Angell found long and confusing. He would soon urge Don toward "more customary" paragraphs and dialogue formats, to which Don was amenable.

Not long after their meeting, Angell mailed him "a good-sized bundle of insults." The magazine had received them in droves, in response to "The Piano Player." "I can't remember when the readers were more stirred up," Angell said. "The people who liked it didn't write—they never do. I hope your agent told you about the fat checks we sent you. Write for the *New Yorker* and own a Jaguar! P. S. Please don't think you have to anser [*sic*] all these cranks. They have all received non-placating letters from the *New Yorker.*"

By the end of the year, Angell had bought two more stories (he referred to them as "casuals"): "Margins," a rewrite of "Carl," and "Down the Line with the Annual," a parody of *Consumer Bulletin.* The stories were scheduled to run early in 1964. Don was learning that Angell responded well to satire or a version of E. B. White's "reportorial fabulism"—stories with a recognizable New York setting tweaked into mild absurdity.

The "new purchase[s]" entitled Don to an "additional bonus," Angell explained to Nesbit. He would receive 20 percent over and above the previous 15 percent "quantity bonus." Angell advised Don not to try to fathom the financial arrangement. "[I]t just adds up to a nice bundle of extra bread," he wrote.

Don got it: The more he produced, and at a faster pace, the more he could rack up bonuses. His journalistic training, working swiftly, meeting deadlines, served him well.

As 1963 drew to a close, Don no longer considered himself an immigrant to the island. He was a New Yorker now. He had planted roots in the literary world.

At Christmas, he flew to Houston, after talking Angell into a four-hundred-dollar advance on "A Shower of Gold" (in exchange, he offered Angell a "startling and perfect" Christmas gift; Angell does not now remember what it was). Over a year earlier, Don's father had told him to be "prepared for failure" in New York. Now, Don returned to Texas in triumph, though his mother grieved over his moribund marriage. While in Houston, Don had no contact with Helen.

In the new year, as it became clearer that *Location* was sinking, Don pestered Angell for advances against future work. Along with the advances, Angell obliged him with a "COLA" payment (a cost of living adjustment) and a new 35 percent quantity bonus for Don's "current bonus cycle." The lure of extra money for additional work within a certain time frame began to be addictive—the kind of "pressureless pressure" that paralyzed many *New*

Yorker writers, who found they couldn't handle the pace. Don *could* handle it, for the most part, though even with all the bonuses, he wound up owing the magazine money. At the end of January, he was indebted to *The New Yorker* to the tune of eight hundred dollars. By June, another five hundred had been added to the total. Angell wrote to him, "[P]lease don't start worrying about this; you are well within our limits on advances, and I don't want this small indebtedness to interfere with your work in any way."

The grip of addiction tightened. Don't worry. Keep working. But Don was doing what he loved, and he was finally being recognized for it in a widely circulated weekly magazine.

On June 28, Angell bought a new story, "The President" ("a mighty strange and disturbing piece"), for $776.00. In effect, this money was already spent. Meanwhile, the final issue of *Location* had appeared, featuring "For I'm the Boy." Don had also published "Will You Tell Me?" in *Art and Literature,* a new journal edited by John Ashbery. "Will You Tell Me?" was a subtle collage, too formally extreme for *The New Yorker.* Don didn't even try interesting the magazine in it. But he *had* begun a campaign to educate, cajole, and nudge Angell to take larger risks. In August, Don sent him two versions of a story called "Then": a regularly paginated manuscript (which Angell rejected) and a cut-up version, modeled after the cut-and-paste experiments of William Burroughs and Brion Gysin. Angell replied, "I spent a happy fifteen minutes arranging [the lines of the story] in my own manner and came up with another text." He was learning.

Come Back, Dr. Caligari was published on April 1, 1964. In addition to the standard bound galleys, Little, Brown provided reviewers with what it called a rare "Advance Preview" of the book (a sign of the editors' pride and/or nervousness). It was presented in an elegant red box containing two of the stories, "Me and Miss Mandible" and "Florence Green Is 81," in loose manuscript form, with Don's neat Smith Corona typeface. Accompanying the stories was a letter from Herman Gollob, identified as "Associate Editor":

> *Dear Reader:*
> *You are about to discover one of the most exciting, uniquely gifted new writers of the past decade: Donald Barthelme . . .*
> *We feel that this will be the most dazzling—and daring—literary debut since the emergence of John Updike, and when you've finished these two samples, we think you'll know why.*
> *Mr. Barthelme's bizarre vision of life may terrify you, confound you, infuriate you, or just plain amuse you, but we guarantee that it will not leave you indifferent.*

The book jacket, designed by Milton Glaser, featured a pair of purple sunglasses and a false-face beard: a ghostly clown. In his author photo, on the back flap, Don looks puffy and tired, with dark circles under his eyes. The picture appears to have been taken at night, against the brick wall of a jazz club.

The collection contained a dizzying array of references: to Husserl, Eliot, J. D. Ratcliff (a *Reader's Digest* writer), Pamela Hansford Johnson (an English literary critic), Kenneth Burke, I. A. Richards, Le Corbusier, Mandrake the Magician, Batman and Robin, Cyril Connolly, Gertrude Stein, Joyce, popular jazz, Futurist manifestos, Oscar Wilde, *Parsifal,* Edmund Wilson, Coriolanus, the Third Reich, Beckett, Shakespeare, Conrad Veidt, *Glamour* magazine, movie tabloids, Kierkegaard, Lawrence Durrell, Buber, and Sartre.

Each story came densely layered: collages, fragments, palimpsests. At every turn, language was challenged, poked, and prodded.

More than half the stories were written or first drafted in Houston. It is tempting to look for tonal changes between these pieces and the stories written in New York. For example, "Hiding Man," composed entirely in Texas, offers a claustrophobic setting, a character in flight from everyone around him. An expression of Don's isolation in Houston? "Marie, Marie, Hold on Tight," written in New York, is an exhilarated shout, a declaration of intellectual interests. There appears to be a movement, between the stories, from alienation to comradeship, from despair to exuberant irony.

But this is reductive. Texas held many intellectual pleasures for Don. And "Marie, Marie, Hold on Tight" stands as an early example of the emotional displacement that would mark much of Don's fiction. The narrator is blurry, subsumed within a communal "we." In New York, as well as Houston, Don lived as a hiding man.

What Manhattan *did* bring to his fiction was a wider range of urban references, experiences, and detail. "Marie, Marie, Hold on Tight" had its genesis in the activities of a young man named Henry Flynt, who was making waves in New York art circles when Don landed in the city. Flynt called for an *end* to art, which, according to him, had become a cheapened commodity, mere "entertainment" whose "function" was to "regiment . . . people." Flynt urged citizens to pursue aesthetic fulfillment by shunning commercial art and doing whatever they liked to do, whatever "is not physiologically necessary (or harmful), [and] is not for the satisfaction of a social demand."

Flynt hung around George Maciunas, Yoko Ono, and the Velvet Underground (and turned bitter when, in his view, they sold out for successful careers). In February 1963, he printed flyers, posters, and a press release advertising a lecture he'd planned in Walter De Maria's loft. The publicity material said "Demolish Serious Culture!"; "No More Art!"; "Demolish Lincoln Center!"

Whether or not Don attended Flynt's talk, he was certainly aware of the man. Flynt noticed that Don parodied his press release in "Marie, Marie, Hold on Tight" when the story appeared in *The New Yorker*.

"Marie" is a mirror image of "Hiding Man": instead of a lone fellow escaping the church, we have a band of comrades picketing St. John the Precursor. Their placards (in "Kierkegaardian spirit") say, "MAN DIES! / THE BODY IS DISGUST! / COGITO ERGO NOTHING!" Their flyers ask, *"Why does it have to be that way?"* and "What is To Be Done?" Other signs read:

NO MORE
ART
CULTURE
LOVE
REMEMBER YOU ARE DUST!

Flynt's crusade provided raw material for a witty philosophical meditation—and gave Don a structure for combining metaphysical ideas with a New York happening. Finally, he burnished the story with his usual layers. The title is a line from *The Waste Land* and evokes an elegiac longing for love and faith. Mentally, Don's narrator addresses a woman named Marie, who is apparently watching the demonstration on television at home. He remembers once buying Marie a "cerise" bathing suit—the color of the hyacinths in *The Waste Land*.

Marie is Don's sister's middle name. The three demonstrators could be seen to parallel Don's three brothers. On a personal level, this very New York piece appears to be a postcard home.

The stories in *Come Back, Dr. Caligari* are jazz on the page. If, on the surface, their range of subjects seems too varied and light to suggest a coherent worldview, a deeper reading reveals a remarkable consistency of thought. Art, humor, philosophy, and music offer important, if limited, escapes from despair, despair born of Western culture's attempts to exploit and direct people's desires. This exploitation takes the form of false "signs"—"wife-signs" (beauty, charm), company mottoes ("Here to Help in Time of Need"), modernist architecture (built for our betterment), and bloody national symbols honoring "righteousness." Cultural hollowness litters the world with fractured marriages, spiritually hungry individuals, and mass devastation (whispers of Nazi horrors haunt the stories).

The only alternative to material greed and social climbing is self-creation. At the end of "A Shower of Gold," Peterson, a "minor artist" appearing on a game show to earn money, tells a television audience, "In this kind of world . . . absurd if you will, possibilities nevertheless proliferate and escalate all around us and there are opportunities for beginning again. Turn off your television sets, cash in your life insurance, indulge in a mindless optimism. Visit girls at dusk. Play the guitar. How can you be alienated without first having been connected?"

In a scene reminiscent of Ralph Ellison's "King of the Bingo Game," the television producers try to shut Peterson up, but he refuses to be silenced. In the existential moment, he performs an act of self-transformation. Identity, he says, is not based on received images or social roles; it is an ongoing process. Borrowing from the myth of Perseus and from *Hamlet,* he declares, "My mother was a royal virgin . . . and my father a shower of gold. . . . As a young man I was noble in reason, infinite in faculty, in form express and admirable. . . ."

"Peterson went on and on," the narrator says, "and although he was, in a sense, lying, in a sense he was not."

OLD FOGEY

Caligari enjoyed wide notice, a distinct achievement for an "eso-teric" book dropped into America's dense cultural life. The Kennedy assassination continued to top the news. Two months before Don's book appeared in stores, the Beatles played *The Ed Sullivan Show.* In New York, dinner conversations revolved around Con Ed's new nuclear-powered electric station on the Hudson River, which was proving to be inefficient and possibly unsafe.

In 1963, the year prior to the publication of Don's first book, many significant events occurred in New York. *The New York Review of Books* debuted—spearheaded by Robert Lowell, Elizabeth Hardwick, Robert Silvers, and Barbara and Jason Epstein—during a lengthy newspaper strike in the city. The Pace Gallery opened, having relocated from Boston. Andy Warhol unveiled his Jackie Kennedy silk screens. Two members of the Pulitzer Prize drama committee re-signed in protest after Edward Albee's *Who's Afraid of Virginia Woolf?* failed to garner the prize. James Baldwin's *The Fire Next Time* was published, Thomas Pynchon's *V.* appeared, Mary McCarthy came out with *The Group,* and Susan Sontag earned praise and puzzled re-sponses for her first novel, *The Benefactor.*

In the wake of all this, mention of *Caligari* slipped into the pages of *The New Yorker, Newsweek, The New Republic, The Nation, Library Journal, The New York Times Book Review, The Saturday*

Review, and *The New York Review of Books.* It didn't hurt that Don had supporters at *The New Yorker*—William Shawn assigned Renata Adler to write a
short piece on Don, whom she called a "very talented young writer . . . [who]
can write extremely well in any number of incongruously mixed styles."
Don's pal Jack Kroll was now book editor at *Newsweek.* His unsigned review
called Don's literary terrain the "cratered landscape of the broken heart."
Kroll wrote, "His prose bales together, like a junkyard compressor, as many
fragments of deracination and regret as a jazz-quick, free-association technique can gather."

In *The New York Times Book Review,* R. V. Cassill said Don might turn
"existentialism [into] as popular an American institution as pizza pie."
Robert M. Adams, writing in *The New York Review of Books,* claimed that
the American short story was an exhausted genre but that Don might revive
it. His praise for *Caligari* came at the expense of John Cheever and Joyce
Carol Oates, whose latest offerings he singled out for scorn.

Granville Hicks, in an article in *The Saturday Review,* resurrected proletarian rhetoric from *The New Masses,* calling Don "a member of the advance
guard . . . very far out indeed" and saying that his "controlled craziness may
be showing literature a new path to follow."

On balance, the most thoughtful assessment of *Caligari* (until literary
quarterlies, working at a slower pace, began to examine it in depth a year or
two later) appeared in *The New Republic.* There, Hilary Corke proposed that
"Mr. Barthelme has regarded each construction [in the book] as a unique
problem demanding a unique solution." Each piece presented a "once-only
technique" appropriate to its theme but "inappropriate to another theme,"
she said. "The term 'short story' is more than usually inadequate to such a
piece of prose," Corke argued. "It partakes much more of the nature of
poetry—a construct whose form is an essential part of its meaning. (It shares
the multiple meaning of poetry too.)" In sum, she concluded that Don's work
was "vastly more interesting than the tame successes of almost anybody I
can think of."

Caligari "sold well enough to earn out its modest advance," wrote Herman
Gollob. Don didn't pause to enjoy his success. Throughout the spring and
summer of 1964, he peppered Roger Angell with submissions. When he
pushed Angell to be more daring, Angell countered by warning Don not to be
"so personal and so elusive that the surface devices dominate the stor[ies]
and become irritating in their accumulative effect." In their dance together,
each man gave ground, and each learned from the other.

"With *The New Yorker,* Don found himself playing in the big leagues,"
Phillip Lopate says. "He was taken into the Establishment at a very high

level. Other avant-garde writers, like Mark Mirsky and Jonathan Baumbach, wound up in academia, creating little niches for themselves. Don's career could have taken that turn, early, but it didn't because of *The New Yorker.*"

"What helped Don the most hurt him the most: *The New Yorker,*" says the writer Jerome Charyn. Don's "best stuff didn't always appear" in the magazine and "they probably published him for the wrong reasons"—solely for his humor.

"There's not another writer of his quality I've seen in *The New Yorker,* where the language just sings," Charyn says. "He was a contemporary Jonathan Swift. *The New Yorker* helped him financially, and helped him find an audience, but over time he didn't expand the way he might have. He took *The New Yorker* too seriously. For someone so bright . . . I don't know why he treated them with such respect. Perhaps it was from a kind of insecurity."

Kurt Vonnegut agreed. "Barthelme was a good example of how a magazine like the *New Yorker* confines one's growth," he told the literary critic Jerome Klinkowitz. "Once you have such membership in a group, it's like you'll do anything not to be excluded. And the group itself of course has a very narrow definition of what fits."

Angell is highly sensitive to such criticism. People suggest that Don "sold out by publishing in *The New Yorker.* That's nonsense," he says. "Don was thrilled to publish with us. And of course we didn't pay him all that much."

Beyond the obvious—money, middle-class approval—why *did The New Yorker* mean so much to Don? After all, he had told Harold Rosenberg and Thomas Hess he was embarrassed at "being inside the establishment." He lauded "revolutionary" magazines and said he did not want to be an "apologist for an existing order."

At the same time, he had always dreamed of publishing in *The New Yorker.* "Don was very aware of celebrity," Lopate says. Two things suggest themselves when confronting this paradox.

First, Don learned from watching his father practice architecture that art's goal is the health and betterment of the community. Without compromising, one works to change the world—and this means moving, when you can, within spheres of power. As a museum director, Don had gotten a taste of the civic arena, and he used his position there to educate the public.

Second, even though he was never satisfied with the results, Don's dad remained optimistic about art's efficacy, an optimism Don shared as he started his career.

Possibly, Don changed *The New Yorker* more than *The New Yorker* changed Don. Consider his Q & A stories. In Frank Sullivan's hands, the Q & A form never rose above word games. Don pushed the form to metaphysical extremes ("Q. Is purity quantifiable? A. Purity is not quantifiable. It *is* inflatable").

There are many ways to achieve a revolution. Don *knew* the magazine, perhaps better than any reader of his generation: He'd parsed it since child-hood. "Don perfectly matched *The New Yorker* tradition," Lopate concedes. "He was a sort of flaneur in his writing; he was not confessional. He was like Joseph Mitchell, whom the magazine used to publish all the time, funny but not too disclosing, very much the man about town. The magazine's history was one that allowed for pastiche and parody." So Don got inside it, wearing talk-of-the-town clothing, and proceeded to explode its values from within—not to destroy the magazine, but to expand its scope. It is hard to imagine another writer pulling this off.

The following exchange from Don's interview with J. D. O'Hara in *The Paris Review* reveals his stealthy approach:

> BARTHELME: [The popular] notion of an avant-garde is a bit off. The function of the advance guard in military terms is exactly that of the rear guard, to protect the main body, which translates as the status quo.
> O'HARA: Well, you've established yourself as an old fogey.
> BARTHELME: So be it.

Among avant-garde critics of *The New Yorker,* one senses (understand-ably, perhaps) bitterness and jealousy, a personal animosity. Mark Mirsky, who worked with Don and Jerome Charyn on *Fiction* magazine in the early 1970s, seems astonished that Don embraced Roger Angell as a mentor. "Roger was (and still is) the quintessential Harvard man of a certain period, hair meticulously combed, suit and tie with the touch of modesty that be-speaks the glass of fashion," Mirsky says. And Angell disdained much exper-imental writing.

But Angell always encouraged Don, even when rejecting him. *The New Yorker* may have been a troubled family, but it *was* a family, and it stirred powerful loyalties in Don. Still, he feared too much comfort. By the end of the summer, he felt restless, fearful of becoming complacent. He knew *Cali-gari* should be followed by a bigger book (Gollob was pressuring him to write a novel). He was ready to stretch, to see new things, and to raise the stakes in his writing.

COPENHAGEN

"Can We Talk," an unusually personal story, offers a day in Don's life toward the end of 1964. In the morning, he'd go to the bank to "get [his] money for the day." He'd go shopping for new clothes or run to the Laundromat. He taught himself to cook, starting with salads and soups. He saw friends in the city (Kenneth Koch, Jack Kroll) or went to visit Herman Gollob in his house on Martha's Vineyard.

He reread Gertrude Stein. Her descriptions of artichokes and lettuce in *Tender Buttons* appear glancingly in "Can We Talk."

He wrote early in the mornings, and spent his afternoons and evenings with women. "Can We Talk" details an affair ("I . . . decided to make us miserable") in which the woman suffers deep ambivalence. "When I leaned out of your high window in my shorts, did you think *why me?*" the narrator asks. He suspects his lover wants to be rid of him; her coolness fans his longing. "After you sent me home," he says, "you came down in your elevator to be kissed. You knew I would be sitting on the steps."

Often, late at night after the jazz clubs closed, Don confessed to Lynn Nesbit that his literary career felt precarious to him, or he'd reminisce about Korea, recalling with particular warmth his old friend Sutchai Thangpew. Nesbit tried to reassure him about his

writing, and to clarify her relationship with him. "Now I would know better, but I was young and at the time it didn't strike me as odd to get involved with a client," she says. "He was unlike anyone I had ever met. To his credit, he liked women. Very few men do."

She was drawn to his "quirky charm. Sometimes things he said didn't quite track, but later they made a kind of sense," she says. "He'd get inside your mind. He really opened my eyes about contemporary art." On the page and off, it was his voice that especially engaged her. "I had gone to Northwestern. I was a drama major, specializing in oral interpretation of literature, looking at short stories and novels from the point of view of dramatizing them, studying aspects of the narrators," Nesbit says. "One of the things that makes good fiction is voice, and Don's was absolutely amazing."

From Nesbit, Don learned that Renata Adler had written *The New Yorker*'s review of *Come Back, Dr. Caligari,* as well as a positive piece on him in *Harper's Bazaar.* "He called and invited me for a drink," Adler wrote. He "had brought me a book. He said I must read it if we were going to be friends. It was Doris Lessing's *The Golden Notebook.* A few days later, he called and asked whether I had read it. I said I had. He asked what I thought of it. I said I thought it was wonderful, even great, but that I didn't think things were as bad as that."

Don saw Adler regularly. "He came to visit me at my . . . apartment, a small studio in a brownstone on East Ninety-second Street, and I would visit him in his apartment . . . in the Village," she recalled. "Either he would cook, or we would go out to dinner, but basically what we did was drink, also talk, mainly drink."

The art parties continued in Elaine de Kooning's Broadway loft, but they were grim occasions now. JFK's murder paralyzed her. She took the assassination personally, since she had met the man. Bill de Kooning had left the city for his new studio in the Springs, and Elaine felt unsupported. Nothing Don said soothed her.

A pair of stories, written around this time, suggest that, in spite of Don's love of the city, New York was not unremittingly romantic for him. Perhaps in response to the president's death, an apocalyptic breeze blows through "The Police Band" and "A Picture History of the War."

In "The Police Band," an idealistic police commissioner forms a musical group whose performances are meant to "triumph" over violence and crime. The group's "grateful cheer" will bathe city crowds with "new and true emotion." "That was the idea," says one of the musicians once the initiative fails. "The . . . Commissioner's *musical* ideas were not very interesting, because after all he was a cop, right? But his police ideas were interesting."

Art fails to make a dent in this mean, mad metropolis. For his poor leadership, the commissioner gets sacked. Neighborhoods deteriorate. Still, the narrator remains somewhat hopeful. "I thought it might be good if you knew the Department still has us," he says. "We have a good group. We still have emotion to be used. We're still here."

Formally and tonally, "A Picture History of the War" anticipates "The Indian Uprising" and *The Dead Father.* A man named Kellerman, "gigantic with gin," runs through Manhattan carrying his naked old father under his arm. The father is a war hero, disappointed that his boy does not march in his bootsteps. Kellerman admits his failings, hoping to foster closeness and understanding with his dad, but the old vet, locked inside patriotic rhetoric, does not share a common language with his son. Desperately, Kellerman longs for guidance—"Who is fit for marriage? What is the art of love? What physical or mental ailments can be hereditary? Is our culture sick?"—but his father's silence roars down the streets. Finally, Kellerman rushes up to a fireman with his questions. Still no answers.

The father is a floating metaphor, the way the Dead Father will be. He is priestlike, a remote paternal authority. He has seen action in every major war. His nakedness and his weight signal Kellerman's psychological burden. Literary associations cling to him: Aeneas hauled his father, Anchises, out of Troy as it burned; in *The Making of Americans,* Gertrude Stein wrote of "an angry man dragg[ing] his father along the ground"; and in Beckett's *Endgame,* Hamm is unable to discard his father, despite trying to store the old fellow in an ash can.

In "Picture History," as in "The Police Band," New York is tearing itself apart: "There are sirens, there is a fire. The huge pieces of apparatus clog the streets. Hoses are run this way and that. Hundreds of firemen stand about, looking at each other, asking each other questions. There is a fire somewhere, but the firemen do not know where it is." The modern city, where Kellerman writes books, swigs gin, and reads *Commentary,* parallels the battlefields his father recalls with nostalgia . . . the "bones of the slain" scattered about.

"A Picture History of the War" appeared in the June 20 issue of *The New Yorker.* Its poetic structure, allusions, and layered imagery asked a lot of the magazine's readers—more than they were accustomed to giving. Soon, Angell would gather a new "bundle" of subscribers' "insults" to send Don's way.

Significantly, in its quieter moments, the story offered glimpses of community life. In years to come, as Don settled into his neighborhood, "community" would appear more and more often in his fiction. As Kellerman dashes about the city, he sees mothers in the parks: "[D]eliriously pretty and sexy mothers in brawny Chanel tweeds." Mothers worrying about children and old men. Mothers talking to and hugging each other. Admiringly, Kellerman notes, "That is love."

On August 26, Angell wrote to Don, apologizing for the commas that "tiptoed into 'The Police Band'" when it appeared in the magazine on August 22. "I don't know how that happened, and I'll try to avert any such sneakiness" next time, he said. He wrote that he was mailing Don a one-thousand-dollar advance "against future work," and explained, "this gets sent to you instead of your agent, since it is a separate deal. There's no hesitation whatsoever about letting you have this, but it does depress me to realize that this means you really are departing next week." He promised he'd come by Don's place on Tuesday "with a jar of Mothersill's as a going-away present."

This is the first indication of Don's plans to leave New York on an extended trip. Helen Moore Barthelme claimed in her memoir that Lynn Nesbit had urged Don to "travel because he 'had not been anywhere.'" The truth is, he left to "get away from Lynn, who wanted to marry him," Angell says. "I was ready to have children," Nesbit admits. Don (who was still not divorced from Helen) wanted the excitement of an affair, not the commitment of another marriage. "He would say to me, not just once but over and over, 'Astonish me,'" Nesbit says. "That's a pretty big burden to lay on a twenty-four-year old." Also, Don was pressuring himself to produce a second book, a novel, and this caused tension between the two; Nesbit realized she needed to separate business from her personal relationship with Don.

"I had a friend and I introduced her to one of my clients, Per Laursen from Denmark," Nesbit says. "Per was in America, traveling through the South, and he would have written the first book about civil rights—before any of us really knew what civil rights was—but he got terrible writer's block.

"Anyway, he and my friend Carol married in Maine, and Donald and I were the best whatevers at the wedding. Then they went to Denmark. Donald said, 'I'll go to Denmark with Carol and Per and you can come over in six months and we'll see where we are.' I think he thought it would reassure me if he went to Denmark with my friends, rather than going off to Paris or something. You know, he'd just be working. That sort of thing."

Don asked Nesbit to look after his apartment while he was away. Eventually, she sublet the place to Tom Wolfe (whom Don had encouraged her to read). In the first week of September, Don left the States with a little *New Yorker* money in his coat. He had discussed with Herman Gollob the possibility of turning "A Shower of Gold" into a novel. This was to be his overseas project. "The President" had just appeared in *The New Yorker*, and it pleased Don to see people reading the magazine on the plane.

He intended to visit his family in Houston at Christmas, and return to New York around the first of the year. He felt the change of scenery would free him of his tensions. He also hoped that, away from the jazz clubs and the art parties, he'd drink less.

Years later, Don's eldest daughter, Anne (pronounced *Anna*), heard the story of his travels this way: "He was vacationing in Europe with some other gentlemen. I don't know who they were. I think he had been to Barcelona and Paris, and they had gone to Scandinavia." In letters to Helen, Don never mentioned the Laursens. He said he had gone directly to Copenhagen—the home of Søren Kierkegaard. He told Helen he had rented a "small but pleasant flat for five weeks at the end of which I'll have to get out and hustle up another." He intended to write, not sightsee, but the "truth of the matter is that I haven't been doing as much Serious Thinking as I should be doing, but I hope to remedy that shortly. But first I have to stop and write a new story as I'm getting to the point where I'll need some money." He had decided that "A Shower of Gold" was too self-contained to be developed any further. He said he was "still groping for a handle" on a novel; "[I have] a fair idea of what I ought to be doing, if not precisely how to do it."

The city, he said, was "very beautiful and old-worldish with cobblestones instead of good sound asphalt and no building taller than six stories." Cigarettes were seventy-five cents a pack, and Scotch was "ten dollars a bottle."

For fifty-two cents, he could get a "seat in the last row of the top balcony" at the Copenhagen Ballet. He saw a Balanchine performance and, on another occasion, *Cavalleria Rusticana.* One night in the theater, he sat next to an eighty-year-old man who "spoke . . . about the wickedness of old New York, thumping me in the ribs from time to time. He had lived there as a boy, heh heh."

He informed Helen he had gone to "an old church and sat in the royal box. And the organist was practicing. And then into the graveyard next to the church. Here lies Anna Pederson, a good woman. I threw a mushroom on the grave. Bach streaming from the church windows. I felt like Old Werther." The graveyard would find a place in the next story he'd write, "The Indian Uprising."

Of course, he visited Kierkegaard's grave. It was a fourteen-minute bus ride from the center of town, in Assistens, a former churchyard-cum-park. The monument was triple-tiered (aside from Søren, the grave held his mother and father and other family members) and topped with a thick stone cross. A low wrought-iron fence surrounded it. Nearby, on the park lawn, in the dappled shade of palm trees, women in bikinis sunbathed in the unseasonably warm weather, reading paperbacks, propping their purses and bags against moss-covered tombstones.

In the late afternoons, Don strolled past the outdoor cafés along the Ny-

havn Canal. He smelled the fresh fish unloaded from wooden schooners, listened to seagulls and to waves licking the boats' hulls. Square stone buildings with pitched red roofs lined the bank. The buildings were painted
yellow, orange, blue, and pink. The cafés served overpriced salads and beer.
Men and women sitting at the tables flirted with one another. Here and
there, along the canal, day laborers, just off shift, dangled their feet in the
water and munched fat falafel sandwiches.

He went to the street market for food. Next to the bins of fruits and vegetables, jewelry and candle sellers set up flimsy wooden booths. Hashish—
illegal but quite plentiful and cheap—could be purchased in thick, broken
chunks.

Don wrote to his parents that he had gone on a date one night with a
"beautiful blonde Communist." She took him to a "café where there were a
great number of depressed-looking young men sitting around being depressed." Later, in the woman's place, he made the mistake of "chuckling
about some aspect or other of the Hungarian Revolution." In a huff, the
woman said, "You are a fool. Get oudt uf my room."

Wherever Don went, he was pestered with questions about the Kennedy
assassination and America's role in Vietnam. On August 7, just three weeks
before Don had left the States, the U.S. Congress passed the Gulf of Tonkin
Resolution. Don was desperate for English-language newspapers. Not only
was Johnson deploying more American troops to Southeast Asia but China,
North Vietnam's neighbor and ally, had just successfully tested an atomic
bomb.

Don assured his folks that his public encounters weren't *all* awkward. He
had "met a girl named Birgit who seems a little less doctrinaire" than the
blond Communist, he said.

According to Anne, her father wrote to his grandmother, "I've met this
crazy Danish lady."

Anne says, "My dad was with some other men. They were looking for a
bar and they stopped this woman on the street and asked her for directions.
Then they asked her to join them and she did. They were all wooing her, apparently. My father didn't want to lie to her, but he didn't think it sounded all
that impressive, being a writer, so he told her, 'I'm a typewriter repairman.' "

Birgit Egelund-Peterson was the daughter of a university science professor. "During the Second World War, her father smuggled Danish Jews to
Sweden," Anne explains. "When he told me he had worked in the Underground, I thought he'd built a tunnel. My grandmother was a nurse. They
had four kids. My grandmother had Huntington's disease, and spent the last
ten years of her life bedridden in a hospital. My mother watched her own
mother die horribly."

Birgit was "ethereal, she was beautiful, detached, a scary-fairy woman,"

Anne says. "She was as brilliant as my dad was. That was their attraction. But she was not as together as he was. She spoke Russian, French, German, English, Danish. She read Kierkegaard like it was *Dick and Jane.* But there was just something that didn't connect with her. She couldn't keep a job in Copenhagen."

Seeking steadiness, Birgit latched onto Don. Almost immediately, she moved into his flat. Don's plans changed. He canceled his flight back to Houston, having decided to stay longer in Denmark. "I got letters from him and I could tell something was going on, but I didn't know what it was," Nesbit says. On December 24, Don exchanged Christmas telegrams with Helen. He didn't mention Birgit. Shortly after that, he wrote Helen and suggested that they get a divorce.

UPRISINGS

"Edward put his hands on Pia's breasts. The nipples were the largest he had ever seen. Then he counted his money. He had two hundred and forty crowns. He would have to get some more money from somewhere." These lines from Don's "Edward and Pia" neatly summarize the way Don spent 1965: living with Birgit and fretting over cash.

When he sent the story to Roger Angell in May, Angell assumed it was autobiographical. In a subsequent letter, Don warned his editor, "Please do not confuse my fiction with my life, my life." But the story was the most straightforward Don had written, and its details matched his "life and times."

Angell told Don, "I plan to fight for . . . Pia's nipples, but I have not yet discussed them with Shawn." (The nipples *did* grace the magazine.)

Birgit tended to be as restless as Don. Together, they traveled to the Netherlands, Germany, France, and England. Don wrote Helen that London was "gray and dismal." He said "hordes of Indians and Frenchmen and Italians cruis[ed] the streets in cheap overcoats and too much hair and nothing-to-do (a lumpen-proletariat if ever there was one; what hope, what felicity for these troops?) and a general air of having settled for much, much less than any minimal

idea of human possibility known to me or thee—cities are deadly, the Japanese in Tokyo in 1953 looked more human than this."

Everywhere, people stared at Birgit, a stunning beauty who dressed fashionably, if sometimes oddly. She wore white plastic boots and plastic hats, green velvet skirts, many, many rings, and handmade necklaces with glass and wooden beads. She also wore heavy black mascara.

Her family owned a small farm in Sweden, just outside of Markaryd. She and Don stayed there off and on, returning every so often to Copenhagen and Don's rented flat. At the farm, Don chopped wood—most of the time the logs were too wet to catch in the fireplace. He tried to control his drinking (he was heavily into gin at this point). Frequently, he made himself dry vermouths with onions on the rocks. He cooked fried chicken for Birgit. He had trouble breathing the sharp, cold air and felt minor pains in his chest. To Birgit's dismay, he wouldn't go to a doctor; eventually, the pains went away.

The farm was remote from shopping areas. Don and Birgit would take a bus into Markaryd and stock up on household supplies for the week. Local children cheered them as they hauled their overflowing bundles onto the bus.

He found little in English to read: a few Ross Macdonald mysteries, *The Penguin English Dictionary,* infrequent copies of *Time, Newsweek,* and *Life* (the big story in America in late 1964 was the most recent James Bond movie, *Goldfinger—Life* splashed a gold-painted lady across one of its covers).

Back in the Copenhagen flat, Don and Birgit entertained a stream of visitors, including several of Birgit's friends. The visitors lounged about the flat, drinking tea or cheap wine, strumming Joan Baez songs on guitars, and testing Don's responses to their increasingly anti-American attitudes. In "Edward and Pia," he wrote, "Edward talked to a Swede. 'You want to know who killed Kennedy?' the Swede said. '*You* killed Kennedy.' 'No,' Edward said. 'I did not.'" Lyndon Johnson had just authorized Operation Rolling Thunder, a bombing campaign against North Vietnam's transport system. Birgit's friends peppered Don with questions about the war in Southeast Asia, and he grew weary of having to say he didn't support America's foreign policies.

Early in 1965, Don's mother fell ill. It's not clear what was wrong with her, but she spent two days in a Houston hospital. She regained her strength quickly, and urged Don not to make plans to hurry home. To cheer her up, he wrote her a lengthy, fanciful letter about his landlord, who, he said, had "soft-footed in" and taken away the sixty-watt lightbulb above Don's writing desk: "Cunning Landlord. He thinks I will not Notice, But I have counted the Watts and having a very good Grammar School Education by the Nuns, I Noticed that a few Watts were gone."

Don also told his mother that he went to a bar where people were "talking in a Strange Language. After a time it came to me that they were speaking English. And I said to myself what a beautiful language! I would like to hear more of it." He mentioned a trip to the Copenhagen zoo, where the giraffes wore "Neck Sweaters." Like "the rest of Denmark, [the zoo] was not Heated Properly." He had "no other Intelligence of moment except that I have thrown away a lot of bad Prose that I made myself. And that I am still Endeavoring to complete a new Work with which to Finance my future Life, if any." As in his letters to Helen, he failed to mention he was living with Birgit.

In the mornings he wrote fiction. He felt adrift from his friends and fellow writers. Eagerly, he awaited the arrival of red-and-blue air mail envelopes through the gold mail slot in the door of his flat. He sent Angell anxious notes: "Are you there or are you gone?"

He found a jazz club in Copenhagen, the Montmartre, and spent a happy evening there listening to the trumpeter Don Cherry, backed by a Scandinavian rhythm section featuring a young Alex Riel on drums. As in the States, jazz halls in Europe were giving way to "Big Beat" clubs. The Danish press called rock "*pigtrad*"–that is, barbed-wire–music. Don ignored it for the cooler sounds of the Montmartre.

With Birgit, he took long walks through Copenhagen. One night, she pointed out a street corner where she had been knocked off her bicycle by a car when she was a child. She pointed out the Botanical Gardens near the Round Tower, where she was once assaulted by a man. Her history in the city, and her mother's early death from Huntington's, made her wary.

Don took Birgit for boat rides, on tourist cruises in the harbor. He walked her past Tivoli Gardens, past the Old Stock Exchange building, with its oxidized copper roof and statues of dragons, past the Royal Library's sleek black glass facade, past iron railings in front of shops gilded with faces and figures. The city's whimsical architecture gave whole sections of town a giddy, fairy-tale air–but the air was darkened by Birgit's expectations of violence around every corner.

> *Dear Roger:*
> *Here is THE INDIAN UPRISING . . .*
> *I have also sent you a purple-and-yellow Christmas card.*
> *Best,*
> *D.*

With this note, sent near the end of 1964, Don began the most intense correspondence he ever had with Angell over one of his stories, an "endless transatlantic seminar on punctuation and the uses of the English sentence," Angell said. Don submitted the story in early December. On the fifteenth,

Angell sent Don a telegram care of American Express in Copenhagen: "Indian Uprising victorious. Palefaces routed. Shawn scalped. In short, yes. Congratulations. Do you wish a fast advance? Will write you shortly." Two days later, he sent five hundred dollars to Lynn Nesbit. By the end of the month, Angell had sent Nesbit the "balance of the payment—I think it came to a further $761." She took her small cut and sent the money to Don.

Sentence by sentence, "The Indian Uprising" remains one of the most challenging and beautiful stories written by an American. Angell knew it was something special. "We want to run this story because it is a rare and brilliant one," he wrote Don. "We know that it will confuse and distress a good many readers and we know that it will infuriate others, but we are ignoring these considerations because they are far less important than what you are doing here. Because you are serious about your writing, we have agreed to drop almost all of our own preferences in style, punctuation, and construction; we have done so in spite of the fact that we . . . don't really agree with you about the effectiveness and usefulness of some of your stylistic devices. [What] Shawn does *not* want is to have readers (and other writers) think that we have simply stopped caring or to think that we have, in the course of printing a 'different' kind of fiction, stopped proofing for grammar, consistency, and clarity."

As ever, the struggle started with commas. Don wanted very few in the story because he wished the "tone in certain places to be a drone, to get the feeling of the language pushing ahead but uninflected." Angell countered that Shawn's "preference for the comma" was a "stoutly-held belief of his, and not a compulsion." Nevertheless, Don insisted that "we should try it without horrible commas clotting up everything and demolishing the rhythm of ugly, scrawled sentences. . . . Yes it is true that I am a miserable, shabby, bewildered, compulsive, witless and pathetic little fellow but please Roger keep them commas out of the story!!!!!!!"

In certain paragraphs, Don skipped verbs and conjunctions to get the "pushing ahead" feeling he wanted. Angell and Shawn objected to these omissions—Shawn feared they would give the magazine "black eyes." Defending a particular sentence, Don said it "must not have an 'and,' I think. This construction [a long list lacking conjunctions] has parallels all through the thing and zee additional conjunction would be like most regrettable, sad & und undfortunate."

He explained his position: "When the sentences suddenly explode or go to hell . . . it contributes materially I think to the air of fear etc etc hanging over the story." Of another grammatical lapse, Don said, "I think it is beautiful, if you'll forgive me. I mean like it also exists for its own sweet sake. . . . The whole damned [story] is a tissue of whispers, hints and echoes and for that reason most annoying but I can't help that."

Over weeks of arguments about grammar and what Angell called "unnecessary misdirections" in the story, the men reassured each other of their mutual respect. Angell knew his letters were bullying, and he regretted it: "[P]lease don't get me wrong: I'm for this story most enthusiastically, and all [my criticisms are] meant to be helpful, not merely annoying."

For his part, Don wavered between fear that his story was being stomped by Shawn's stodginess and absolute faith in Angell. The latest galley "proof covered with little marks scared the hell out of me," he confessed at one point. "But I trust that you will protect this beautiful story with your last dying breath there on West 43rd Street."

Writer and editor cemented their bond and defined their relationship—Don pushing, Angell resisting, both giving ground—over "The Indian Uprising." By the end of the process, Don had agreed to more conventional forms of paragraphing, particularly when it came to dialogue, and to the addition of most of the commas Angell asked for. Angell began trolling for commas to *delete,* just to please Don. He tempered Shawn's worries that certain imagery in the story was "too wild."

For all the stylistic compromises, enough disagreements remained by the end of January that Angell nearly took the story "off the schedule." Remarkably, the editors were still quibbling with Don over commas. "[T]he difficult thing is that if even just one or two sneak back in the effect here, which must be that of a rush, confusion, hectic excitement, falling down stairs, etc, is vitiated. So I depend upon you, Roger, to not let this happen," Don wrote.

Seeking a "hushed" and "stuttering" quality in other sections of the story, Don *did* ask for a comma or two. Shawn would not "give way" on this point. Angell explained that readers would think the addition of the commas was "sheer carelessness on your part and on our part," and he said, "It looks like sloppiness and it makes both you and the magazine look bad." He apologized for sounding "pompous" and reiterated, "I think there is enough respect and admiration all around for an eventual solution, and I don't want to go on pushing you or annoying you. . . ."

Don replied, "Pardon me for taking my self so seriously." Shortly thereafter, he wrote, "I understand, dear friend, that you and Mr. Shawn and the magazine are treating my little nightmare most kindly (in fact, I'm amazed that your patience didn't depart about two letters back)." He ended another note by saying, "The main thing is to preserve the tone, and what is essential is **562%% choke! gasp! can't go on . . . commas . . . quirk . . . water. . . ."

Finally, in mid-February, Angell was able to write Lynn Nesbit that the "long struggles with THE INDIAN UPRISING have now been resolved, and the story is scheduled for the issue of March 6th." To Don, he wrote, "Thanks a million for your final compromise (or abject surrender)." He also addressed financial matters:

> *Another issue for you to resolve—a much more pleasant one. You now have the sum of $1048.35 coming to you, due to something we call "cola readjustment." Don't worry about what it means—I think it's simply a further slicing of last year's melon—but we would like to know what part of this sum, if any, you would like to have applied against your debt here. You are entirely at liberty to take the entire sum and to leave the balance outstanding of $1000 on the books. Or we can knock off as little or as much of the debt as would suit your convenience.*

Don took all but two hundred dollars. He noted ruefully that his agent's commission was "guarded by the alert Miss Nesbit who is privy to my every move (or almost)." "Miss Nesbit" still didn't know about Birgit, though she suspected that Don was having an affair.

Don told Angell that "Copenhagen is beginning to pall; has palled, in fact." Nevertheless, unexpected events would keep him from returning to the States for another several months.

"The Indian Uprising" was an "emotionally important" story to Don. "It was in part . . . a response to the Vietnam war," he said in an interview and a "political comment on the fact that we allow the heroin traffic in our country to exist." It was also a "response to certain things that were going on in my personal life at the time, and a whole lot of other things came together in that story." He said he couldn't sort it out for readers any "more clearly than that."

His letters to Angell offer further glimpses into the story's core. He said he wanted to limn the "secret places" of the "body" and the "spirit." He also wanted to "get" readers "to the problems of art and the resistance of the [artistic] medium. (Sculptors hacking away at blocks of granite etc relating back to all the hacking up of people in the story.)"

His "illegitimate" grammatical "maneuver[s]" were meant to produce a "very sharp effect of alienation" on the reader: Any tidying up of the story's style "would be disastrous for my liver," he said. The piece had to maintain its "discord" and "unpleasantness."

"The Indian Uprising" begins, "We defended the city as best we could"—a city that doesn't know what it has done to "deserve baldness, errors, infidelity." Fighting engulfs the streets, barricades are mounted, savages threaten the calm, ordered life of ordinary citizens whose luxuries include "apples, books, long-playing records." Drugs flood urban ghettos. Apparently, in the midst of all this action, a movie is being shot—or perhaps the violence is part of the film, scenes of comic mayhem reminiscent of Jean-Luc Godard (he is mentioned, in passing, in the story). At the end, "helicopters and rockets" kill children and destroy places "where there are children preparing to live."

The writing is dense, swift, packed with referents, and unspecific as to character and setting—a heady, frightening storm, like much of urban America in the 1960s.

Filled with parodic Parisian street names (as in Edgar Allan Poe's "The Murders in the Rue Morgue"), the piece is an eerie prophecy of May 1968 in France.

Various critics have seen the story as a satire on American film Westerns, "civilization" fighting "savages" to secure the country for its values. The story *does* tie America's Indian wars to U.S. violence in Vietnam, but it's far too easy to say that murdering Indians was wrong, and Don was never content to say the obvious.

Other critics read the story as a Freudian allegory of sexual unease. The narrator repeats, "I sat there getting drunker and drunker and more in love and more in love." The Indians' "short ugly lances with fur at the throat" suggest phallic fear.

As to his later comment about the story's being a "response" to his private life: We know of Don's separation from Helen at the time, his fraught relationship with Lynn Nesbit, his whirlwind affair with Birgit. The "hordes of Indians and Frenchmen and Italians" he had seen in London had struck him as a thwarting of "human possibility." This impression, coupled with his domestic turmoil, touched the story and added to its hectic "unpleasantness."

Other readers have noted the range of modernist references in the piece—to T. S. Eliot, Thomas Mann, Frank Wedekind—and suggest that Don is mocking Western literary tradition.

But none of these readings quite add up. They fail to explain why these specific materials are mixed here, or to fully convey the story's brilliance, mystery, and complexity.

So let's return to the street names. The narrator tells us that barricades are going up on "Rue Chester Nimitz" and "George C. Marshall Allée." Other avenues are named after American military commanders, but with a French twist—we are in an unreal urban landscape, neither New York nor Paris, but with echoes of both (Manhattan, we recall, was purchased from Indians). "Zouaves and cabdrivers" form battalions in the streets. Zouaves was a name for those fighting in the French Foreign Legion, whose fighting reputation was made in the Crimean War. They enjoyed enormous popularity in America just before our own Civil War.

Prior to 1968, barricades appeared in Paris during the revolutions of

1830, 1848, and in the days of the Commune in 1871. Manet painted them. So did Delacroix, Courbet, and Millet (when he wasn't drawing American Indians, figures inspired by the novels of James Fenimore Cooper). Daumier's lithograph *The Uprising,* like Don's story, blurs background and foreground in portraying anarchy.

In each of the French revolutions, social classes clashed, vying for power and justice; order and disorder fought for dominance, as they did in the United States during the 1960s, perhaps the closest our country has come to a second civil war, with rioting and political assassinations.

What Don has accomplished here is an overlay of French history on American experience, one time period on another, the way Robert Rauschenberg's silk screens show one image bleeding through to another. Once, in discussing Rauschenberg's methods, Don noted that "orphaned objects" come together—like stacks of detritus made to build a barricade.

Where does all this take us?

If we compare the various French revolutions, we see they all occurred at moments when leaders tried to tighten economic and political control, when economic systems shifted and narrowed, destroying old patterns of work and communal life. The barricades went up as people tried to retain their domestic and working lives, their living quarters, and their sense of justice. And of course, in the nineteenth century, the Paris of the barricades was the Paris of modernist art. They—city, barricades, and art—are cobbled together from the same sources.

In the 1850s, Napoléon III ordered Baron Georges-Eugène Haussmann, his prefect of the Seine, to redesign Paris. Haussmann proclaimed that redoing Paris "meant . . . disembowelling" the old city, the "*quartier* of uprisings and barricades"—and, not incidentally, the bohemian neighborhoods where Courbet, Manet, Baudelaire, Daumier, and later Rimbaud gathered. There, these artists lived in the gaps between the bourgeoisie and the laborers, and in the side streets populated by artisans' guilds, where Daumier's father once worked. There, they celebrated the "primitive" sensuality of life, as embodied in the archetypal noble savage. "The Savages of Cooper [are] right in Paris!" Paul Féval wrote in 1863. "Are not the great squares as mysterious as forests in the New World?" Baudelaire called Indians the New World equivalents of devil-may-care dandies, and Dumas wrote *The Mohicans of Paris,* his novel about urban "natives."

Haussmann's redesign displaced them all. He uprooted over 350,000 people in the inner city—roughly one-third of Paris's population at the time, most of it working-class—and widened and straightened the boulevards so they'd be harder to blockade. This made them, as one journalist observed, paths "without turnings, without chance perspectives"—the imaginative perspectives Manet and others fought for in their art. The barricades and modernist aesthetics were weapons in a war against the rigid ordering of daily life, the absolute control by economic forces of every aspect of experience.

One hundred years after Haussmannization, the United States was the best expression of the vision that had sparked fighting in the streets of Paris, and that touched off violence, now, in American cities. As Rimbaud, Marx, and others pointed out, Haussmann's project depended on cheap labor, on colonizing others, spreading the "poisonous breath of civilization" to poorer, darker-skinned peoples.

In Southeast Asia, a century later, America extended and modernized this tradition (assuming France's role in Vietnam). Indian uprisings indeed.

Street names like "Rue Chester Nimitz" and "George C. Marshall Allée" don't just combine one history and another; they suggest, like a silk-screen overlay, the culmination of a process: the surface as the latest incarnation of what lies beneath it—in this case, America as a perfected manifestation of Haussmann's "disembowelling."

As Don's narrator tries to sort out where he stands, he studies a map marked with blue and green, a hopeless attempt to locate opposing sides. Street gutters run with "yellowish" muck, like the fog in the streets of "Prufrock." These hues also recall the color schemes in Rimbaud's poems about the Paris Commune, most notably in "Chant de Guerre Parisien," "Les Incendiaires," and "Mauvais Sang." In Rimbaud's visions of the uprising, yellow dawns shade bloody streets, green-lipped corpses sprawl across paving stones, and cheap wine makes blue stains on the tablecloths of the poor (*vin bleu* was popular in a communard fight song).

"The white men are landing!" Rimbaud wrote. They intend to corrupt the barbarians. The battle is on.

Like Courbet, Daumier, and others, Rimbaud celebrated the 1871 revolt as a poets' rebellion. As he saw it, it was an attempt by artists and workers to shake off Haussmann's order, to take back their living quarters, and to refuse the exorbitant prices pinching their daily lives. It was an assertion of sexual and creative freedom—a carnival in the streets ("Oh that clown band. Oh its sweet strains") as much as a brief economic liberation: a political and libidinal Bill of Rights—again, as in the United States in the 1960s.

Along with Kafka, Joyce, and Beckett, Rimbaud was at the top of Don's reading list for young writers (a list he composed, years later, when he became a teacher). What did he learn from the Frenchman?

Consider the following description of a street barricade, written by Gustave Paul Cluseret, the Commune's first delegate of war. The barricades were makeshift constructions, he says, composed of "overturned carriages, doors torn off their hinges, furniture thrown out of windows, cobblestones where these are available, beams, barrels, etc." They are intended to "prevent enemy forces from circulating, to bring them to a halt."

Rimbaud's rebellion poems "make conscious the unconscious tendencies" of the revolution, according to critic Kristin Ross. In refusing logical expression and linearity, in recycling clichés, blurring referents (Which side are you on?), shoring up fragments of discourse—and dropping commas—he builds a language barricade.

Don's narrator fashions a similar bricolage: "I analyzed the composition of the barricade nearest me and found two ashtrays, ceramic, one dark brown and one dark brown with an orange blur at the lip, a tin frying pan, two-liter bottles of red wine, three quarter-liter bottles of Black & White . . . a hollow-core door in birch veneer. . . ."

All are "Prufrock"-worthy objects. Echoing Eliot still further, the narrator concludes, "I decided I knew nothing." Temporarily, he is brought to a halt. He can no longer circulate. "Turnings" and "chance perspectives" are necessary for him to proceed.

As we read, something else in "The Indian Uprising" nags at us, or should. Where have we heard before about redskins and palefaces skirmishing in the field of art?

In 1939, Philip Rahv wrote that American literature was divided into two camps: the "drawing-room fictions" of writers like Henry James, who strain for the European refinement of Marcel Proust and Thomas Mann, versus the "open-air" work of writers like Walt Whitman. "The paleface is a 'highbrow,' " Rahv wrote, "though his mentality . . . is often the kind that excludes and repels general ideas." And the "redskin deserves the epithet 'lowbrow' . . . because his reactions are primarily emotional, spontaneous, and lacking in personal culture."

In the twentieth century, the redskins overthrew the palefaces, Rahv stated. They were presently "in command of the situation, and the literary life in America has seldom been so deficient in intellectual power."

Rahv's literary Western was based on arguments about the merits of proletarian and modernist literature dating back to the 1930s.

In the 1970s, Don would make a visual collage titled "Henry James, Chief." He took an old photo of James and placed an orange strip across his forehead. Two white strips waver like feathers behind it. Don placed a small black triangle beneath James's eye: war paint, resembling a tear or silly clown makeup. By feathering James, Don played a Duchamp prank. More to the point, he turned the most famous paleface into a redskin.

In "The Indian Uprising," a captured Comanche says his name is Gustave Aschenbach: a redskin paleface.

In both instances, Don canceled Rahv's categories, rejecting a rigid view of American literature. At the same time, by playing with Rahv's metaphors, he joined the literary debate. (Harold Rosenberg may have reminded Don of Rahv's essay in his introductory remarks to the first issue of *Location:* in the past, the "vanguard writer" in America has been "surrounded by the Indians of the press and the professoriat," Rosenberg wrote. Today, the "age of the Indian wars is by no means closed.")

The controlled craziness of "The Indian Uprising" mounts a barricade against reductive views of politics, art, and personal engagements. Don mixed the high and the low (literary categories first distinguished during the Paris uprisings, which produced bushels of instant journalism, thoughtful poems, and memoirs). He also mixed the private and the public, the graphic and the comic, achieving what Rahv claimed American fiction could not manage: a volatile blend of emotion and intellect. More important, Don raised the level of the political debate, placing Rahv's argument in a much wider context. And he did all this while providing up-to-the-minute dispatches.

Given the vision of "The Indian Uprising," Don's grammatical battles with Angell and Shawn assume a metaphysical dimension—and explain why the comma war was so intense. It would be easy to reprove Shawn and Angell for their stylistic timidity, their caution in the face of a radical new fiction. But it was only natural that they would want to protect *The New Yorker*'s standards of precision. And they must be lauded for publishing the piece at all. Nothing like it had appeared—or has appeared since, aside from Don's *own* fiction—in the pages of a mainstream American magazine.

Don and Birgit moved restlessly from one address to another, to Spain and back, to Sweden. Angell could barely keep up with their wanderings, and he suspected something was wrong. In a letter, he tried to nudge Don into the open: "When am I going to hear about your fascinating life—your literary, culinary, linguistic, and military triumphs? When are we going to see your exhausted neo-Jamesian phiz again?"

And in another note, he wrote:

> *I have worked out a theory about all your sudden changes of plans, your hitherings and thitherings: the CIA has finally begun to swing and has hired you as the 007 of the Central European literary scene. You are on the track of an implacable Commie-rat plagiarist who is engaged in a desperate plot to inflate the world [James] Baldwin-market. Now he has doubled back to Denmark, you are closing in, and any day now . . .*

"I had a very gloomy call from Lynn [Nesbit] the other day," he said on another occasion. "[She] is very worried about you."

Don continued to write at an astonishing pace, and Angell's letters to him contain a cautious mixture of encouragement and rejection. The magazine declined two pieces, "The Affront" (which would later appear in *Harper's Bazaar* and turn up as part of *Snow White*) and "The Short Life of Henry" (which Don seems to have scrapped altogether). "God knows I am not asking for a formal, well-made story," Angell said regarding "The Affront," "but only some sense of arrival or completion near the end, instead of this trailing off. . . ."

Always, Angell tried to cheer Don up: "I think it is true that original, nervy writing like yours is a riskier process than everyday fiction. I mean, a story . . . that strikes us as not *quite* right is perhaps more apt to be turned down than a safe-and-sound story that is faintly second-rate. You dare more, you are higher above the ground, and there are more lights on you, so that the faintest slip is instantly visible and probably fatal. It doesn't seem fair, somehow, but I don't know what to do about it. [The] big thing is that you are writing so much and writing so well. I'm delighted. Lynn is delighted. Shawn is delighted. Now *you* be delighted. Congratulations."

His support was more effective wrapped in money. Angell asked Don to renew his earlier agreement at a rate of "20-10 cents a word *minimum*," with "25% extra for first reading" and unspecified "COLA" adjustments. He advanced Don $250 against future work.

"[T]hanks for the new advance. Which was needed," Don replied. "Living off the fat of my head as I do I appreciate such things in scanty times."

Later, Angell wrote, "Our corporate mattress was getting a little lumpy from all the cash stuffed under it, and . . . we are increasing the size of our payments to you and to all our contract writers. It simply means that that dangling carrot has grown a little longer and I hope you will respond shortly to this subtle enticement." He added, "I ran into your friend Tom Hess the other day, who told me how miserable it made you to appear in The NewYorker. I told him to grind his little ax on somebody else. Now you can be ten percent more unhappy."

"I know no better way to start the day than to wake up $1000 richer than when you went to bed," Don responded. "And unexpected monies are much more beautiful than expected monies."

In April, Tom Wolfe published "Tiny Mummies! The True Story of the Ruler of 43rd Street's Land of the Walking Dead!" and a sequel, "Lost in the Whichy Thickets: *The New Yorker*," in the *New York Herald-Tribune.* The articles attacked *The New Yorker*'s stuffiness and William Shawn's tentative editorial style. Don was appalled: "I thought it was pretty goddamn nasty, just flat nasty. Vicious is I suppose the word," he told Angell.

Wolfe praised Don as *The New Yorker*'s only "promising young writer." "I would rather have been cut up along with the rest of the troops," Don said to Angell. "Anyhow, the whole thing was sickeningly personal, I thought; and I hope you weren't angered to the point of challenging Tom Wolfe to zipguns in the park."

Don felt slightly sheepish, as Wolfe was now subletting his New York apartment.

Apparently, Wolfe failed to water Don's elm tree. When Don heard this news, he told Angell his "erstwhile tenant . . . killed my tree in the front of 113 W. 11 with either a burst of rhetoric or a single burning glance."

Angell rejected another of Don's stories, "Seven Garlic Tales," which *The Paris Review* picked up. Eventually, it, too, got folded into *Snow White.* But Angell bought "Edward and Pia" as well as "Game," Don's grimly funny take on missile silos, underground military bunkers, and soldiers who are asked to unleash nuclear weapons in case of an international catastrophe. "I am not well," the narrator complains. He has been stuck in a bunker with a fellow soldier for 133 days "owing to" a bureaucratic "oversight":

> Shotwell and I watch the console. Shotwell and I live under the ground and watch the console. If certain events take place upon the console, we are to insert our keys in the appropriate locks and turn our keys. Shotwell has a key and I have a key. If we turn our keys simultaneously the bird flies, certain switches are activated and the bird flies. But the bird never flies. In one hundred and thirty-three days the bird has not flown.

Each soldier has been ordered to shoot his partner if the partner starts to behave strangely. "Is [Shotwell's] behavior strange? I do not know," the narrator says. "I am not well."

"A really curious thing happened here about this story," Angell wrote Don:

> *We were on the point of turning this one down—an admiring rejection on the grounds that the situation of the not-quite-sane men watching the ICBM console, watching each other, and watching the Button, all in a system that had perhaps begun to go slightly and fatally haywire, was a familiar one. I mean familiar in literary terms. We sensed overtones of "Dr. Strangelove," remembered scenes from a couple of recent topical revues*

like the Second City, and noticed resemblances to Pinter. Nothing exact, no real imitation or exact echo, but there was this feeling that we had all encountered this situation before, so we thought, well, not quite right and too bad for old Don. What swung us over, after a day's further reflection, is the plain fact that all the writing here is just too good to miss—the story is terrifying and, to use the word honestly for once, unforgettable—and the even plainer fact that ICBM silos, console-watchers, sane or lunatic, are real, and that almost unbelievable fact is far more important than the weight of their previous appearance in fiction or drama. I think this is by far the best writing yet to appear on this theme, and we are damned lucky to have it. Thank you, buddy.

The story ran in the July 31 issue. On September 1, Angell informed Don, "I must tell you that you have a band of admirers in the Pentagon":

A few days ago, I was lifting a glass Down East with a friend-of-a-friend, who turned out to be an Assistant Secretary of Defense and he astonished me by asking all kinds of questions about you. At first, I thought he must be checking up on your draft status, but no—he was a reader. He said that GAME had knocked them all for a loop in the Pentagon, and I asked was it because it was true, for God's sake, and he said no, heh, heh, but it was, er, saying something that needed saying. But then he went on and talked about THE INDIAN UPRISING and A PICTURE HISTORY . . . and wrote down the name of your book, so I concluded he was a real fan. I will leave it up to you to decide if it is a Good Thing for us to have Defense tycoons who dig your stuff.

Despite this amusing news, "troubles" plagued Don. He admitted to Angell that he had thrown a "rented typewriter on the floor and broke its back." What could trigger such frustration? Angell shared personal updates, hoping Don would reciprocate. On June 14, he wrote Don:

Saturday I watched my older daughter graduate from school. Beautiful girls and beautiful boys with their clean American hair shining and white dresses moving in and out of the shadows of giant summer trees and Elgar and faculty babies playing on the lawn during the very serious commencement remarks delivered by a serious and nervous bald father (me) and the diplomas and the kissing and the wind blowing and just a small glistening of almost tears in everyone's eyes all followed by pineapple punch and chicken salad on paper plates and goodbye and

goodbye. I could hardly stand it. Anyway, it's full summer again, and . . .
the city is out of water, and you have been away much too long.

Angell's wistful tone and the pleasant American scene must have deepened Don's homesickness, but three more months would pass before he returned to Manhattan. He had many arrangements to make, much deciding to do. Birgit was pregnant.

A VILLAGE HOMECOMING

The "lease is up on the apartment [in New York] and my hair is falling out at an ever-accelerating rate and I haven't written a word of the novel that's supposed to be delivered in September. But none of these things is faintly as important as the problem of the divorce has suddenly become," Don wrote Helen on June 10, 1965. He came clean about Birgit and the pregnancy. Birgit had a "rather tragic history," he said; he was going to marry her and be a proper father to the child, and he wanted the baby to be an American citizen. If the divorce did not come through immediately, freeing Don to marry Birgit, and if the child arrived before the couple left Copenhagen, then they would have to "keep moving from country to country." Don would be like the Flying Dutchman.

The "immigration business" is "suitably Kafkaesque and hideous," he said. He hoped everyone in Houston was "prospering, as much as one can prosper in this evil world."

Helen thought Don was probably in love with Birgit, but she did not believe he wanted to be married again right now. She showed the letter to her sister Odell, who cursed Don as though he could hear her overseas. Helen had learned that a judge could grant a divorce within sixty days. Odell agreed that, under the circumstances, it was best to give Don what he wanted. Helen wrote him, insisting

that what they were about to do was "wrong, wrong, wrong." We "cannot end love with a divorce," she said.

Don answered on July 5, asking her to go ahead with the divorce "without paying the lawyer's fees . . . for the time is growing short." Since January, he had been borrowing money to "buy bread and booze," but he promised to send some cash to Helen soon. He thanked her for her "magnanimity in this meaty matter."

As soon as she filed for divorce, a court record would appear in the daily papers, she reasoned. She didn't want Don's mother to learn the news that way, so she called Mrs. Barthelme. "I don't think you have to do this," Don's mother told her. The anguish in her voice made it difficult for Helen to speak. She told Mrs. Barthelme to talk to her son and that everything would be clear to her then.

Don had not been honest with Helen about his work. He wanted as much of her sympathy as he could get. He was well along now on *Snow White.* For a while, after turning from "A Shower of Gold," he had toyed with the idea of expanding "The Indian Uprising." He told Angell, "I am tired of tiny stories however beautiful. . . . Some day I will write a great long story like other writers write, many-paged, full of words, resplendent."

"The Indian Uprising" resisted changes—it was as tight as a box—but soon Don had ideas for *Snow White.*

Meanwhile, Herman Gollob had left Little, Brown and was now an editor at Atheneum. He advised Don not to divorce Helen. "I told him to get rid of the kid, get an abortion, and come home. Always felt a little guilty about that, later, every time I saw that wonderful kid. He had to do the honorable thing, you know."

By now, Don had confessed his troubles to Angell. "We are now in a three-way snit over a) divorce papers, b) getting married, c) visa," he wrote. "Everything is under control, as far as I can see, but the timing is tight. We hope to be home the first part of October but can't count on it."

Angell didn't try to tell him what to do. He said, simply, "I am going to be 45 [soon]—an age when one likes to have one's friends nearby."

Despite the "snit" he was in, Don was writing plenty—new stories as well as *Snow White.* Over the summer, Angell bought "Snap Snap"—a parody of *Time*'s and *Newsweek*'s breathless journalistic styles.

"You are writing so much and so well that I haven't got time to do any writing myself," Angell told Don. "I just spend all my time sneaking commas into your manuscripts and sending you money. Actually, I am delighted by all of this fecundity and brilliance."

In August, Angell went on vacation, leaving the final editorial details on "Snap Snap" to William Maxwell. Maxwell's letters to Don were blunt, all business. Don's approach to revision unnerved him. "If you don't like the laparotomy," Don told him at one point, referring to a line in the story, "you may choose some other operation ending in 'omy.'" Maxwell didn't reply.

The moment Angell returned, he sent Lynn Nesbit $750 for Don "against future work," as if to reassure Don that, Maxwell aside, *The New Yorker* still loved him. Angell told Nesbit, "[Don's] indebtedness here now stands at $1750."

Birgit was sick now almost every morning, and she rarely felt like making love. Don bought her antinausea pills at the drugstore. He tried to make her laugh (she didn't understand his culturally specific jokes). Occasionally, an American movie played in Copenhagen and Don would coax Birgit out of the flat to see it. Some nights, he drank too much; when he did, his homesickness emerged in the form of discussions about movie trivia. He argued with her over actors and film titles. Sometimes he got heated over practically nothing. At such moments, his verbal abusiveness could equal that of his father's, but he was never physically violent. In later years, Helen learned from friends that Birgit's "manner was like that of a child" and "Don treated her like one." He would tell *his* friends that, at any given moment, Birgit "may suddenly step into the street to cross in front of a bus." She exhausted him.

Don once told Helen that before he met Birgit, "'something' happened to her in Denmark." "He was vague, referring to an incident that affected her life." In "Edward and Pia," Pia tells Edward that a man "raptured" her: "Edward walked out of the room. Pia looked after him placidly. Edward reentered the room. 'How would you like to have some Southern fried chicken?' he asked. 'It's the most marvelous-tasting thing in the world. Tomorrow I'll make some. Don't say "rapture." In English it's "rape." What did you do about it?' 'Nothing,' Pia said."

Don always wondered if Birgit would begin to suffer someday from Huntington's (she would be diagnosed with the disease in 1975). It was hereditary and its symptoms—ranging from clumsiness and involuntary movements to slurred speech, depression, apathy, severe irritability, and memory lapses—usually appeared before the age of forty. Birgit's inability to grasp simple actions (following directions, opening a bottle of pills), and her helplessness, frightened Don.

"You don't look happy," Birgit would say to him. "You don't look happy, either," he'd reply.

Things were rotten in Denmark. But on some days an air mail envelope would slip through the mail slot with a check from Roger Angell. Sometimes Birgit *would* laugh at Don's jokes.

Don asked his father for extra money so he could take Birgit back to the States. His mother objected to his "cavalier" attitude toward the circumstances. He responded by mail, saying, "I am sorry that I did not treat the announcement of new domestic arrangements seriously enough, or that I somehow did it in the wrong way, or that I am somehow wrong, wrong, wrong, probably fundamentally. You have to remember that for me levity is a mode of seriousness, my only mode of seriousness."

Don said he was "thinking of coming home to Texas where [the baby] can be had in a WARM, CHEERFUL, LOVING atmosphere . . . rather than a cold New York atmosphere." He asked his father to design a house in Houston for his "cuties." However in a follow-up letter, he said a "house is out of the question, really." He had no money. Jack Kroll planned to take an extended leave from magazine work, and he offered Don *Newsweek*'s book-reviewing spot, but the pay was "low, low," Don wrote his dad. "I think I could do better sitting at home staring at the typewriter."

To Lynn Nesbit, he wrote:

> *I feel [happy] about nothing. No confident expectation. I have a hope, which is that I can raise the baby without ruining it. The relations between Birgit and myself are peculiar. There is love but no confidence, apparently not on either side. She is a remarkable girl but we are all remarkable and that is no guarantee of anything. I suspect that I will be able to make her happy for a time, probably happier than she will make me. But what can make me happy? My little ego is so constituted that the most enormous outpourings of love and attention are not, apparently, enough for it.*

As regards his personal relationship with Nesbit—and responding to her rueful analysis of what had happened between them—he said, "I don't think you played wife when you should have played lover. I think that you played lover in a way congenial to you and me, which involved the laundromat as an additional but not crucial dimension. You are wonderful, sweet Lynn; it's me who is in difficulties, who am the difficulty."

In late October, just before leaving Denmark, Don renewed the lease at 113 West 11th Street. Birgit was almost nine months pregnant. Don booked a flight for the two of them—the *three* of them—on Icelandic Airlines, now more nervous than ever about flying.

As soon as they landed, Don drove Birgit to the house of his old friend Robert Morris in Connecticut (as per the sublet arrangement, Tom Wolfe still had a few days left in Don's apartment). Don phoned Helen and thanked her again for granting the divorce. He wanted to explain why he had been so rushed and why he might have seemed callous. He said he wanted the baby to have his name when it was born. "Otherwise I will have to adopt it later and it would always be an adopted child," he said. "Nor did I want to have to go to Mexico for a divorce."

Helen didn't want to talk about these things. The topic of children was intensely painful for her. Instead, she spoke about Don's Houston friends, and of recent shows at the Contemporary Arts Museum. "We both were reluctant to end our conversation," she says. "[W]hen we at last said goodbye, I felt very sad, for Don as well as for myself."

Don phoned Herman Gollob about the novel he was drafting. "You'll see that it's not *Indian Uprising,*" he said. "But I don't think you'll hate it."

Gollob helped him arrange a hasty private wedding in Montpelier, New Jersey. "Birgit was about to pop," Gollob recalled. Right before the ceremony, she had to see a doctor, "this eighty-year-old guy who lectured Don and Birgit about sex." Gollob and his wife, Barbara, were the only witnesses at the wedding. At first, the priest, a "strict Italian-American," misunderstood: He assumed Gollob and his wife were the bride and groom. When he realized the truth, he was "devastated" and balked at performing the ceremony for a pregnant woman. Don talked him into going ahead. Still, the priest confused Barbara's and Birgit's names: "Do you, Barbara, take this—"

"I gave him the honorarium in an envelope—all fifty dollars of it," Gollob said. "Next day it came back to me in the mail. He didn't want that money."

The Manhattan to which Don returned was more vibrant and edgy than ever. By late 1965, antiwar rallies had grown larger and more frequent. On October 15, four hundred demonstrators showed up outside an army induction center at 39 Whitehall Street. Passersby jeered at the protestors. One young man burned his draft card in front of federal agents. Events might have ended there despite incitements by the SDS, the Socialist Workers party, and other groups—except that the New York Supreme Court refused to overrule the Parks Commission's denial of a demonstration permit to the ACLU. In defiance of the court, six hundred City College students and faculty members held a four-hour silent vigil in Central Park, followed by a two-hour rally. The next day, a crowd of between ten and twenty thousand people, many of them middle-aged and middle-class, marched down Fifth Avenue from Ninety-fourth Street to Sixty-ninth.

Roger Angell and his wife, Carol, watched the march from the window of their apartment on Ninety-fourth between Fifth and Madison. His "quiet block" became "one of the forming-up side streets for marchers heading down Fifth," he wrote. "Somewhere a band was playing 'I-Feel-Like-I'm-Fixin'-to-Die-Rag,' the Country Joe and the Fish classic." He described the scene: "The gigantic skulls and caricatures of the Bread and Puppet Theatre tottered and swayed at the top of the block, and we waited while the various group banners—S.D.S and others—went slowly past, until our own bunch, Veterans for Peace (I was a veteran), came along and we went downstairs and out into the sunshine and marched away, too."

Two weeks later, demonstrators in support of the war—"cops and firemen and union guys, all waving American flags"—followed the same path up Fifth. With a felt-tip pen, Angell scrawled "Stop the Bombing!" on an old shirt cardboard and stuck it in his window. Someone threw a beer can at it; the can pinged off the glass. It was followed by more cans and a few eggs. Angell's landlady rang his bell and demanded to know what he'd done. "Whatever it is, stop." Angell removed the sign and shot a finger at the crowd. "My face was a mirror of theirs by now: the American look," he said. "The war had come home."

On the brighter side of the ledger, the city had erected several stunning new buildings while Don was gone: Eero Saarinen's "Black Rock"—the thirty-eight-story CBS Building on Sixth Avenue at Fifty-second; Edward Durell Stone's Huntington Hartford Gallery of Modern Art, a contemporary palazzo at Columbus Circle; and the International Style building at 277 Park Avenue, between Forty-seventh and Forty-eighth streets, designed by Emery Roth and Sons (whom Don had singled out in "The Indian Uprising" as purveyors of a lifestyle now under siege).

Andy Warhol was everywhere. His *Campbell's Tomato Soup Can* and *'65 Liz* were reproduced in magazines and on posters and billboards. With the help of Billy Klüver, a former Bell Labs engineer, he was preparing a new exhibit for the Leo Castelli Gallery. The exhibit would feature silver Mylar balloons filled with helium—just enough so they'd float in midair. Metal weights placed inside the balloons would incline them to careen haphazardly as gallerygoers walked among them and nudged, pushed, or bumped them around the room.

How to explain such a wondrous world to a child? Just before his daughter arrived, Don wrote "See the Moon?" "When a child is born, the locus of one's hopes . . . shifts, slightly," the narrator says. "Not altogether, not all at once. But you feel it, this displacement. You speak up, strike attitudes. . . . Drunk with possibility once more."

The story is a sort of traveler's report, "pieced together from the reports of [other] travellers." Only from such "fragments" can we know the world. "Look at my wall, it's all there," the narrator tells his unborn child. He points to scraps, newspaper clippings, and other souvenirs he has gathered for study. "That's a leaf . . . stuck up with Scotch tape," he explains to the baby. "No no, the Scotch tape is the shiny transparent stuff, the leaf the veined irregularly shaped . . ."

He wonders what he can do for his child: "I can get him into A. A., I have influence. And make sure no harsh moonlight falls on his soft new head." The moon—the bringer of lunacy, light-mindedness, fits, spells, and occasionally dark enlightenment—"hates" humans. It itches to afflict us. Nevertheless, drunk with "possibility," the father-to-be says to his kid, "We hope you'll be very happy here."

Angell thought this a "lovely" story and offered Don few editorial suggestions. The rough drafts indicate that Don wrote it quickly and made only minor changes to it later. At one point, the narrator studies a Catholic cardinal to grasp his serenity. This section gave Don the most trouble. Its relative length suggests that spiritual yearning is the heart of the story. The narrator says, "[M]aybe I was trying on the [cardinal's] role," in anticipation of becoming a father.

He treats his wife gingerly. "Dear Ann . . . I'm going to keep her ghostly. Just the odd bit of dialogue . . ." As in *Paradiso,* where Dante leaves mostly "unsaid" his experience of Beatrice (for speech would only sully her), Don's narrator admits the woman's greater power, and his own lack of promise.

Anne Barthelme was born on November 4, 1965, at St. Vincent's Hospital, just down the block from Don's apartment. A few days later, the city's lights went out. The two events linked up in his mind.

Later, Marshall McLuhan said that if the blackout had lasted six months longer, "there would be no doubt how electric technology shapes, works over, alters—massages—every instant of our lives." Billy Klüver said the power failure "could have been an artist's idea—to make us aware of something." Failure is a special skill of artists, exposing cracks in the status quo, he said.

Eventually, Don wrote "City Life," in which a woman is impregnated by the "fused glance" of her community's "desirous eye": "The pupil enlarged to admit more light: more me," she says. In light and darkness, the city's inhabitants are locked together—a village, a tribe—in an "exquisite mysterious muck":

> What a happy time that was, when all the electricity went away [the woman thinks]. If only we could recreate that paradise! By, for instance, all forgetting to pay our electric bills at the same time. All nine million of us . . . The same thought drifts across the furrowed surface of nine million minds. We wink at each other, through the walls.

She gives birth to her child: an unexpected development that may open, for her, the gates of paradise. In any case, she thinks of the birth as a communal "invitation" she had no choice but to accept.

A father—at last—Don felt a visceral attachment to his community. But as the street marches indicated, New York was a particularly *messy* paradise. "The more you create village conditions, the more discontinuity and division and diversity [there will be]," McLuhan said.

At the same time, Robert Lowell predicted that, in retrospect, this period would seem a "golden time of freedom" just before a "reign of piety and iron."

On Thanksgiving Day, 1965, Don invited Roger Angell and his wife to 113 West 11th Street to meet Birgit and Anne. "You have a lovely baby," Angell told Don. The couples shared good food and drink. They swapped the blackout stories they'd heard (people stuck on subways, in elevators—already folks were predicting that nine months hence Manhattan would see a baby boom). Anne slept quietly through dinner.

Before the year was out, Don's latest story, "The Balloon," would delight Angell. He bought it for the magazine and scheduled it to run early the next year. Don worked to finish his first novel.

He was thirty-four years old, with a new wife and child, a world of experience behind him, and a place now in the New York literary establishment. Warily but happily, he settled into the Village, preparing for the great days ahead.

PART FOUR
GREAT DAYS

SNOW WHITE AND THE SUMMER OF LOVE

Today's readers will find the February 18, 1967, issue of *The New Yorker* remarkably familiar. In the ads, the clothing, the women's hairstyles, and the car bodies appear antiquated, but the layouts are as recognizable now as they were forty years ago. "The Continental Life is never out of date," says a Lincoln Continental endorsement just inside the front cover. Turn the page and there's a Tiffany diamond ad: the look of love.

In the "Goings On About Town" section, the names have changed but not the forms of entertainment.

None of which suggests that time hasn't worked its effects. Note the volume of *print*—so much more in 1967 than now. Like most publications these days, *The New Yorker* attempts to resemble a television screen or a computer monitor rather than a book.

Which indicates, precisely, why the one item in the February 18, 1967, issue of *The New Yorker* that looks as odd now as it did then, as strangely out of place—and harder to read because we have become poorer readers—is Donald Barthelme's *Snow White:*

She is a tall dark beauty containing a great many beauty spots: one above the breast, one above the belly, one above the knee, one above the ankle, one above the buttock, one above the back of the neck. All of these are on the left side, more or less in a row, as you go up and down:

                    *
                    *
                    *
                    *
                    *
                    *

The hair is black as ebony, the skin white as snow.

We feel vaguely at home with this material—but tonally it's *off.* Cool. Snide. This is not *quite* the Snow White we thought we knew. (And in which form do we know her?—the Grimm brothers' version, which was told to us by our parents when we were little, or the Disney animated version? Already, confusion is king). And why are we reading about her now, in contemporary language, in a sophisticated magazine? Fleetingly, our minds register the phrase "containing a great many beauty spots," as though this maiden were an artificial vessel, a suspicion reinforced by the illustration of her physical features: The *text* contains the spots. Snow White as a storm of words, marks on a page . . .

Surely this is parody. But of what? The children's tale? The Disney movie? Romance? As though fitted with the wrong slippers, we stumble, off-kilter, our footing unsure.

As she walked around the Village, Birgit felt as wary as she had in Copenhagen. She clung to Don wherever they went—Sutter's Bakery for breakfast rolls; Balducci's for groceries (sometimes uptown to Zabar's because Don liked their colorful new shopping bags); Gene's, just down the block, for Italian food; Lamanna's liquor store over on Sixth. The Women's House of Detention, near the Jefferson Market Courthouse, chilled Birgit—all the trapped, miserable women inside, some separated from their children—but she felt comforted amid the mossy stones in the Second Cemetery of the Spanish and Portuguese Synagogue. Birgit found solace with the ghosts of fellow immigrants who had settled in this peaceful, shady garden tucked between brownstones.

Whenever she met new people with Don—at the Eighth Street Bookshop; the new Cedar Tavern, which was now located on University Place; or Nikos Magazine & Smoke Shop—she stayed silent, dreamy. She doted on her baby at home. She had shed most of the weight from her pregnancy but had retained enough pounds to lose her former waifishness. In Denmark, her face had been long and pale; it was rounder now. Sleeplessness lined her eyes, a result of Anne's late-night feedings. She first knew Manhattan in winter. She took to wearing a long black overcoat, buttoned tight around the neck.

Don flirted with a beard, liked it, hated it, shaved it off, grew it back—a full beard, a goatee, something in between. His hair had softened and thinned. It was a beautiful light red. He tried horn-rimmed glasses, perfectly round glasses, no glasses at all (when he wasn't working). He was often cold, no matter the weather, and preferred several layers of clothing, a T-shirt, a shirt, and a pullover sweater. Together, he and Birgit and Anne (with spiky brown hair that later lightened in color) were the very picture of a chic young Village family, strolling beneath the stately plane trees of West Eleventh.

The city felt livelier than it had when Don left more than a year ago. Its handsome new mayor, John Lindsay, promised broad political reforms. He had the charisma to convince nearly everybody he was a miracle machine. Even stodgy old Governor Rockefeller seemed to be loosening up. In 1966, he would approve the first major revision of New York's divorce law since 1787, making it easier for a couple to split.

The Marine Midland Bank would soon issue something called Master Charge, promising New Yorkers they no longer needed cash or checks to buy restaurant meals, rent hotel rooms, or purchase airline tickets. As he walked the streets, past the old wrought-iron lampposts that spoke of another era, past Oscar Wilde's former apartment or the building where Sara and Gerald Murphy once lived, Don felt the pleasure of worlds colliding: the genteel cultural past and the pulsing present, which seemed to be pulling the future toward it.

At home, he and Birgit tried to settle. He still liked to write early in the mornings, but Anne had something to say about that. Birgit got restless sitting around the sparsely furnished apartment, but she wouldn't go out on her own, and she'd needle Don to please stop typing, help her on with her coat, go with her down to the store.

Sunday night was garbage night on West Eleventh; the sounds of clattering cans could be heard in the dark. And on Monday morning, trash lay piled as high as your shoulders all along the walks, emitting the smells of rotting cabbage, chicken, and fish. Buses sighed and squealed to a stop each morning at seven o'clock in front of P.S. 41 across the street, the children laughing, shouting, crying. From around the corner, sirens brayed day and night, the high, healthy notes of a prosperous hospital.

Don shopped for Anne's clothing and toys, and always rose with Birgit in the odd hours to care for the baby. On the rare quiet evenings when Anne slept, Don and Birgit liked to read together. They'd tease out the meaning of a Kierkegaard passage—they were particularly drawn to *The Concept of Irony* and to the argument that irony, in stating as true that which is not true, has the power to (conceptually) obliterate all of existence.

In late 1965, a new young family moved into the apartment downstairs:

Kirkpatrick Sale, his wife, Faith (née Apfelbaum), and their young daughter, Rebekah. The couple had attended Cornell with Richard Fariña and Thomas Pynchon (the latter coauthored a never-produced musical called *Minstrel Island* with Sale). Sale focused most of his literary energy on polemics, history, and environmental studies. In later years, he would joke, "One reason that Don could be so spare and exact in his writing . . . was that he was able to get rid of all the unnecessary, cumbersome, undignified, aimless words. The way it worked was this: he would let all the unwanted words fall through his typewriter . . . *downstairs,* to my apartment, in fact to my typewriter—which is why I write these large bulky books and Don's were so small and jewel-like and perfect."

For a while, the Sales frequented the folk scene at Gerde's on Fourth Street, listening to Dave Van Ronk, Bob Dylan, Judy Collins, and Richard Fariña. By 1965, they were parents, ready for nesting. Sale became more serious about his writing. Faith had worked as an editor at J. B. Lippincott and Macmillan—"using the skills I had taught her when we were on the [student] paper at Cornell," Sale says—and now she did freelance editing for publishing companies, literary agents, and authors.

It took a few months for the Sales to get to know Don and Birgit. Don "was a private person," Sale says. "Not distant but private. Nothing personal or intimate. Birgit was a strange one. Quiet, aloof even, and totally unemotional. Pleasant always, but sort of Scandinavian cold. I never once saw her drunk. She would read Kierkegaard—pronounced, she told me, Keergor (and Copenhagen, she said, was Cohnhawn) but I don't think she ever talked philosophically. Or politically. If I think about it, I can't see any reason that Don married Birgit, except that her cool style attracted him—cool, calm, bright, that would be his type, like Lynn Nesbit."

Birgit made her first friendly overture toward Sale after a conversation in the hallway, in which, somehow, Schubert's Trout Quintet came up. Sale said he didn't know it, and Birgit went out and bought him a recording of it. He warmed to Don through their mutual concern for the building. Don "was protective of [it], making sure the super (who slept in the basement, an old black guy that Don thought was so smart he should help him go to college, but Jimmy was in truth a lush, and that idea didn't fly) was content and doing his job," Sale says. "[Once] the woman in the third floor rear apartment, another lush—and that does seem a recurrent theme here, doesn't it?—fell asleep while smoking and set her bed on fire. Nothing serious, but the local firemen came rushing round and a mess was made. Don called a building-wide meeting, for the first time, to discuss what we should do to make the place more fireproof and what we should do in case of a real fire—of particular concern since the couple in the third floor front had an old guy with half a leg and a prosthesis he usually wouldn't wear. Well, no one thought there was much chance of a serious fire in that solid building, which had fire-spray thingies in the hallway, and the old guy said he could make it down the stairs if he had to, but we had a long talk, and Don said that everyone should get a rope fire-ladder. He did. No one else. And I was on the ground floor. But it says something about him that he was basically a regular guy who cared about his neighbors, not a wooly-headed intellectual, and was a subtle man of action."

In time, Don started inviting Sale upstairs for lunch—they were both writing at home during the day. "He'd always serve 'poorboys,' which he said were standard in Houston," Sale says. "Hoagies, I guess we called them up here. Don had a beautiful apartment, kept it sparsely decorated and furnished. Though he knew about modern art, there was very little of it on his walls, which were white. He liked things neat and plain." Sale was impressed by Don's immersion in jazz. "He once said that if he had the choice, he would rather be blind than deaf—and this from a writer and avid reader—because he loved music," Sale recalls. "Though, you know, he never talked much about it, never showed off his knowledge of it." Birgit preferred classical music to jazz, and usually commandeered the record player in the evenings.

After writing in the mornings, Don took long walks around the neighborhood. Almost every day he'd see—usually on the corner of West Eleventh and Sixth—a short, wild-haired, cheerful but determined woman carrying anti-war signs, or handing out leaflets for political rallies, or wearing a makeshift smock painted with the words "Money/Arms/War/Profit." This woman turned out to be his across-the-street neighbor, Grace Paley. Don knew her book *The Little Disturbances of Man,* published in 1959. Since then, she'd written only a handful of new stories. She'd been busy raising her kids, helping with the local PTA, and organizing the Greenwich Village Peace Center, a group composed mostly of women, who helped teachers at P.S. 41 and whose opposition to the Vietnam War was an outgrowth of their concern for children. They'd meet in parks, one another's apartments, or in church basements, mimeographing flyers. Purple stains covered Grace's hands. Her politics were never abstract or ideological; they were rooted in motherhood and the activities of her block. Don admired this about her. As he would say of her later, "[She is] a wonderful writer and troublemaker. We are fortunate to have her in our country."

"I was so interested in my friends," Grace said. "I didn't want to leave them"—meaning that, after her book was published, she didn't want to move into some insulated literary community. "I was very afraid ... and my fear was the fear of loss, loss of my own place and my own people." Besides, her "sphere" of mothers and children and workers "created" her subject matter.

Nevertheless, by the time Don got to know her in 1965, she had begun to teach fiction writing, first at Columbia, where she had once worked as a secretary, then at Sarah Lawrence, located in Bronxville, half an hour's drive north from Manhattan. Her kids, Nora and Danny, were teenagers, and Grace needed family health benefits. Her marriage to Jess Paley, a motion-picture cameraman, was shaky. He often worked away from home. Grace was growing steadily more intimate with a landscape architect and fellow politi-cal activist named Bob Nichols. She had met him in the late fifties when Vil-lage residents protested the city's ban on folk music in Washington Square Park. Nichols would later redesign the park for pedestrian traffic. In 1967, Grace would leave her husband for him (she and Nichols married in 1972).

In Don, Grace saw a fellow worrier. "He was in his life and work a citizen," she wrote. "That means he paid attention to and argued the life of his street, his city (New York or Houston), his country. He never played a game of liter-ary personalities." He became another member of her family, and he cared for her in turn. Briefly, they were lovers, more out of a need for mutual com-fort than passion. "There was sadness in our lightest conversations," she re-called. "He smoked and drank in the manner of American writers (his only untransformed cliché)," and she grieved for him, her neighbor and "true friend," every day.

"He was drinking more when he got back from Copenhagen than he had been when we first started going out in New York," Lynn Nesbit recalls. "De-spite his new circumstances, he assumed we could just continue with our af-fair but it was over for me at that point. Sometimes he'd knock on my door at midnight but I wouldn't let him in. Birgit must have been miserable."

Nesbit continued to represent Don's work because, she says, she "had a professional responsibility to him. And I felt sorry for him."

As he continued to work on *Snow White* during the early part of 1966, readers began to identify him as a *New Yorker* regular. Just as, in the 1830s and 1840s, *The Southern Literary Messenger* and *Godey's Lady's Book* gave Edgar Allan Poe mainstream visibility, *The New Yorker* provided a steady, "respectable" home for Don's radical reinventions of the short story. Not since Poe had anyone brought such ingenuity to the form.

"This Newspaper Here," a monologue by an old man full of "worrywine," appeared in *The New Yorker*'s February 12 issue. "See the Moon?" ran on March 12—with a last-minute addition comparing the care of a baby to the maintenance of a battleship. "The Balloon" was published in the magazine's April 16 issue, around the time, coincidentally, that Andy Warhol's "Silver Clouds" exhibit opened at the Leo Castelli Gallery.

In Don's story, a "free-hanging," "frivolous," and "gentle" balloon expands mysteriously one night over Manhattan, filling most of the "air space" and abutting the buildings. "There were reactions" from citizens, says the balloon's inventor: Some people insisted on knowing the balloon's meaning; others were suspicious because it displayed no advertising and appeared to be without purpose; some felt frustrated that it blocked their daily paths; others accepted its presence.

In the story's final paragraph, the narrator admits that the balloon was a "spontaneous autobiographical disclosure, having to do with the unease" he felt at his lover's absence, and "with sexual deprivation." This strange thing was not randomly conceived, then—longing is its source, and it is appropriately breastlike (or it is an image of pregnancy). Like loneliness, the balloon expands until it seems to fill the world. Paralysis and awe, intimacy and distance from others—reflected, here, is a profound ambivalence about desire.

But to *really* plumb the story's richness, we need to leap briefly from Don's balloon to another famous flying contraption, the one in Edouard Manet's 1862 lithograph *Le Ballon.*

As noted earlier, Paris in the 1850s and 1860s underwent a vast transformation, a historic moment that fascinated Don. Georges-Eugène Haussmann evicted the working class from the center of the city, destroying the artisan guilds, redesigning the streets, and widening them to prevent insurrections.

As a result, every social category—class, gender, neighborhood—fell under increasingly centralized national control. But the process was messy. According to T. J. Clark, Manet saw the new city as a "greasy press of people," with "ladies in crinolines having to come into contact with legless beggar-boys on trolleys."

Le Ballon shows a mixed-class crowd gazing in awe at a hot-air balloon, the kind of public spectacle that could not have occurred in Paris until Haussmann's reordering of the city, when the old social categories broke down. These are people whose routines have dissolved, who have encountered a strange new presence—modernity—in their midst. Manet's balloon vividly embodies that moment.

His model was a hot-air balloon that belonged to the photographer Nadar (Gaspard-Félix Tournachon). Nadar used the balloon to photograph Paris from unique new angles, the city as never before seen.

As a publicity stunt, and to make room for his camera equipment, Nadar built his balloon six times the normal size. As he floated in it, he felt like a "traveler who [had] arrived yesterday in a strange city," a city in which "they have destroyed everything, down to the last *souvenir.*" Nadar's photographs flatten space and collapse the horizon. They reduce the landscape to a sea of signs—cathedrals become merely steeples; homes, chimneys; factories, smokestacks.

The invention of photography was a turning point in modern art, not only by *supplying* new images but by forcing artists to paint images beyond the camera's reach. Similarly, movies would later challenge novelists' authority (Balzac complained that cameras stole his thunder, conjuring more vivid pictures than he could muster in prose).

Manet's paintings mark the historical moment when these revolutionary changes first occurred. But this was just the *beginning* of modernity. Three years after *Le Ballon* (when *Le Ballon* was still very much in the public eye), Manet showed *Olympia* at the Paris Salon, inciting a violent scandal and signaling another turning point in art. T. J. Clark wrote, "The crush of spectators was variously described as terrified, shocked, disgusted, moved to a kind of pity" by the painter's portrait of a nude prostitute, the onlookers "subject to epidemics of mad laughter, 'pressing up to the picture as if to a hanged man.' "

Olympia presented Paris with another image of the modern, the commodification of sex and class, the unadorned power of desire—once more forcing spectators to move beyond their accustomed paths of perception. The 1865 Salon scandal, coming as it did in the midst of the city's physical and social upheaval, is one of the seminal moments of modernism.

"Observations" about the painting "are made out loud," reported the paper *La France.* "Some people are delighted . . . others observe the thing seriously and show their neighbor [how it is] improper."

"There were reactions" to the balloon, says the narrator of Don's story. "Critical opinion was divided." Some engaged in "remarkably detailed fantasies" of delight; others were perturbed, thinking words like "*sullied.*"

Manet's detractors noted the "irregularities" of his work, and its "unfinished" qualities.

Don's narrator speaks of the balloon's "deliberate lack of finish" and of "irregular" areas on its surface.

Le Grand Journal reported that *Olympia*'s body seemed made of "rubber," and *Les Tablettes de Pierrot* described her as shapeless, shape-shifting, "some form or other, blown up like a grotesque in . . . rubber."

Don's balloon is a "vari-shaped" rubberlike mass with a surface "pneumaticity," in contrast to the "city's flat, hard skin."

As many readers have observed, Don's story considers public responses to art. But besides this general theme, he had in mind a specific set of reactions, in a crucial time.

In invoking Manet's balloon and the *Olympia* scandal, Don encoded in his story an early chapter of the art that nourished him throughout his career; an art inseparable from social change, resistant to strict ordering, and opposed to the narrowing of perceptions required by commodification.

"The Balloon" resonates with one more modernist touchstone, Virginia Woolf's *Mrs. Dalloway.* As the novel opens, Mrs. Dalloway is walking the streets of an increasingly "new" London, a city torn by the conflicts of social

class, when she sees a crowd gaping up at an object "coming over the trees"—
an "aeroplane . . . making letters in the sky!" The shapes move and melt; the
crowd disagrees as to the plane's purpose. What are the letters trying to say?
The message turns out to be a toffee ad, but its true meaning, people feel,
"would never be revealed," for the spectacle continues to shift, the figures
now beautiful, now terrible. One observer is moved to consider how "solitary" everyone is.

A common thread ties Baron Haussmann's Paris in the 1860s, Virginia
Woolf's London of the 1920s, and Don's mid-1960s Manhattan: massive social transition, just before capitalism tightened its grip another notch. In
these chaotic intervals, while the signs were still elusive, people remained
free to interpret, create, and act in unpredictable (unspeakable, unnatural)
ways. Far from ignoring history, trashing literary tradition, or practicing
randomness—as some critics later claimed of him—Don chose a particular
battle, and helped to man the barricades.

With the publication of three stories three months in a row, Don erased his
debt to *The New Yorker*—"which is good news for all hands," Angell wrote
him. Belatedly, the magazine sent Don an extra $82.90 for the "battleship"
addition to "See the Moon?"

The flush period didn't last long. With a restless wife and a hungry baby,
Don requested, and was granted, a one-thousand-dollar advance against fu-
ture work. In June, he renewed his agreement with the magazine, allowing it
the right of first refusal. Birgit was homesick. She pressed Don for a trip to
Denmark. He figured the only way they could travel was if he received a
Guggenheim Fellowship. He had been denied one the previous year—Lynn
Nesbit and Herman Gollob had written him letters of support. This time, he
asked Angell for a recommendation.

Angell told the Foundation:

> *I believe that Mr. Barthelme is far and away the most intelligent and the
> most original young writer of fiction in the United States today. As his
> editor at the* New Yorker, *I am in close contact with his work and his
> writing methods, and I can say with assurance that he is an entirely
> dedicated artist, capable of the most severe and admirable self-
> discipline . . . [he is] "courageous" because financial hardship has not
> tempted him to take a job and thus become a part-time writer, nor has it
> forced him to alter his style in the interest of popularity and assured sales.
>   . . . [his stories'] meanings are both poetic and cerebral [and] cannot be
> escaped or forgotten . . . what most distinguishes his apparently avant-
> garde style is its lack of self-consciousness, its absolute inevitability.*

Barthelme writes as he does because no other method could begin to
convey his echoey multiple meanings.
. . . He must be given a chance to complete a longer, more significant
work of fiction. He has no other means of support than his writing, and his
need for money—money that will buy him time to write—is greater than
ever, for he now has a wife and a young baby.

Angell's support at this time was crucial. Letters kept coming to the magazine, complaining about Don's work. More crushingly, S. J. Perelman said he
didn't care for Don's fiction (though, more happily, John Updike admitted he felt
challenged by pieces like "The Balloon" to try more daring formal experiments).

As Don waited for news of the Guggenheim, he shopped for Anne—and decided that the seven little men who lived with Snow White in his novel would
manufacture baby food (with a comical Chinese twist): "BABY BOW YEE
(*chopped pork and Chinese vegetables*) . . . BABY DOW SHEW (*bean curd
stuffed with ground pike*) . . . BABY JAR HAR (*shrimp in batter*) . . . BABY
JING SHAR SHEW BOW (*sweet roast pork and apples*) . . ."

Because of Anne, he could no longer hang around jazz clubs till the early
morning hours. Some evenings, while Anne slept, he slipped away to the
Eighth Street Bookshop, which was open late. It was owned by Eli Wilentz,
whose son Sean would become a well-known historian. The elder Wilentz
looked like "an older Bob Dylan" and could be seen with a "cigarillo stuck between his lips or burning between his fingertips," wrote M. G. Stephens, a
former clerk in the store. The place offered four floors of books, and customers often stood in the aisles discussing poetry or European novels. Don
opened a charge account at the store. Other regular customers included Edward Albee, Anaïs Nin, Albert Murray, Djuna Barnes, and a Mafia don—one of
the Gallos—who one night told Stephens, "I read a lot of Albert Camus."

Susan Sontag's *Against Interpretation* was the most exciting book Don discovered that year. In her celebration and blurring of high and low culture, Don
found a kindred spirit. "Perhaps there are certain ages"—like the present—
"which do not need truth so much as they need a deepening of the sense of reality," Sontag wrote. "An idea which is a distortion may have a greater
intellectual thrust than the truth." In a section of *Snow White,* in typically
playful, aphoristic fashion, Don echoed Sontag: "In the midst of so much that
is true, it is refreshing to shamble across something that is not true."

At times, Don felt as if he were living in Haussmann's Paris: The cost of
living in the United States rose more dramatically in the winter of 1966 than
it had at any time since 1958, people were protesting in the streets against
the federal government, and a construction boom was changing the face of
the city. The grand old Beaux-Arts Pennsylvania Station had been demol-

ished the previous year to make way for a twenty-nine-story building. In August 1966, groundbreaking would begin for the World Trade Center.

In the latter part of the year, Don retreated indoors. He hunkered down with his family, his friends, his novel. He composed a scene in which Snow White writes a four-page poem: "The thought of this immense work . . ."—a joke on him, to keep him on task.

Angell was curious to see this immense new work. Don put him off. He'd write, walk, shop, write some more, sit with Grace Paley on a neighborhood stoop, then go home to soothe the baby and listen to music.

He urged Grace to write more stories. She said she was too busy trying to stop the war. She apologized to Don for her inactivity during the Korean conflict. "We were so unconscious, so unaware of that war," she said. "The whole country was unconscious. . . . [We] just didn't want to pay attention."

Finally, in early October, Don showed Angell the nearly completed manuscript. Angell snapped it up, and convinced his fellow editors that the magazine should publish all of it in a single issue. On October 26, he sent Don a "first" payment for *Snow White.* "This was an exciting day around here," he said. "I am delighted." Earlier, Don had gotten word that he had received a Guggenheim Fellowship. He was happy. His editor was happy. Birgit was happy. Even the baby seemed happy.

"Here's that check. . . . Sending this out makes me feel like God. Or maybe Joseph E. Levine," Angell wrote Don on December 8, 1966. The check raised Don's total payment for *Snow White* to $25,000.

He was busy writing last-minute additions and making cuts, rearranging sections of the novel to "correct poornesses in the storyline." In his version of the tale, Snow White is a modern young woman living in New York with seven little men. The men have communal sex with her in the shower, though she has grown tired of the arrangement (as has Bill, the men's "leader"). The men, born of different mothers but the same father ("a man about whom nothing is known") were reared in national parks. They clean buildings, make baby food, and manufacture plastic buffalo humps ("Heigh-ho"). Snow White is torn: She wants to hear "some words in the world that [are] not the words" she always hears; she is dissatisfied with her education, and with the domestic duties she's forced to perform. She understands that the world is too complex to be contained in romantic myths. Yet the myths' power draws her still. She waits, however skeptically, for a prince. She lowers her hair from an upper window, an erotic invitation, but there is not a man in sight with the gumption to grab it. Modern consumer culture has emasculated them all. "It has made me terribly nervous, that hair," thinks Paul, the book's Hamlet-like prince figure. He knows he is *supposed* to respond to the hair; what stops him is the realization that beyond the hair's sexual symbolism lies daily life, the eventual dullness of habit, practical considerations ("Teeth . . . piano lessons . . ."). Stripped of their ideals, but still yearning for them, men and women circle one another in a wary, frustrating dance. America's "daughters are burning with torpor and a sense of immense wasted potential," Snow White thinks, "like one of those pipes you see in the oil fields, burning off the natural gas that it isn't economically rational to ship somewhere!"

Helen Moore Barthelme has said Don explored "his own love life" in *Snow White*—not that he ever shared one woman, except his mother, with several other men. What she meant was that Don took parts of himself—his romantic expectations and his experiences—and gave them to each of the characters: the little men, the prince figure, the "vile" Hogo de Bergerac, who defiles women, even Snow White herself. This way, Don "could both examine his own feelings and imagine the reactions of the girl," Helen explained.

Helen and others recognized Don's personal history in the book. "During our courtship, Don [had] told me of a group of male graduate students who were part of his first wife's circle of friends at Rice University," Helen wrote. "Years later, one of these friends wrote a note to me in which he said it was possible to identify which 'dwarf' portrayed each of them." Certainly, shards of Don's trajectory—from the Alamo Chile House to New York to Denmark— are traceable in the novel's fragments.

Atheneum published *Snow White* a month after it had appeared, in its entirety, in *The New Yorker,* and it became one of the most talked-about novels of the year—a year in which Susan Sontag said "the beauty of . . . a painting by Jasper Johns, of a film by Jean-Luc Godard, and of the personalities and music of the Beatles is equally accessible" and equally valuable. The "feeling (or sensation) given off by a Rauschenberg painting might be like that of a song by the Supremes." In 1967, the high and the low, the sublime and the ridiculous, danced cheek to jowl.

That year, at the beginning of what *Time* and other newsweeklies called the "Summer of Love," the Beatles released *Sgt. Pepper's Lonely Hearts Club Band.* The group was hailed as more than just rock stars: they were artists. *The New Yorker* quoted a classical music enthusiast, who said of this newest release, "This album is a whole world. It's a musical comedy. It's a film. Only, it's a record."

Here was art as "sensation," a "feeling" not limited to its format.

In *Against Interpretation,* Sontag argued that the blurring of "high" and "low," "popular" and "serious" did not signal the demise of art, but a "transformation of [its] function":

> Art today is a new kind of instrument, an instrument for modifying consciousness and organizing new modes of sensibility . . . artists have had

to become self-conscious aestheticians, continually challenging their means, their materials and methods. . . . Painters no longer feel themselves confined to canvas and paint, but employ hair, photographs, wax, sand, bicycle tires, their own toothbrushes and socks. Musicians have reached beyond the sounds of the traditional instruments to use tampered instruments and (usually on tape) synthetic sounds and industrial noises.

In such an atmosphere, a "literary" novel based on a Walt Disney cartoon (*and* an old fairy tale), containing numerous typefaces and page layouts, wasn't out of place. It was the extremity of Don's imagination, and his metaphysical grounding, that made *Snow White* seem so radical.

"It's not my favorite book," Don later told an interviewer. In another interview, he said, "The thing is loaded with cultural baggage, probably too much so."

Here, Don touched on one of the riskiest aspects of his writing: his use of time-sensitive materials. If a sculptor places a metal pipe in the center of his piece and then it tarnishes over time, darkening, flaking, the new hue and texture will alter the entire structure, and will change the viewer's response. The trick is to choose materials that will change in interesting ways, but this is difficult to predict. (Remember Don's dad wrapping his home in copper sheeting, hoping it would taint attractively, only to be disappointed in its rough discoloration.) "Cultural baggage"—and language—has similar organic properties, which is susceptible to the seasons.

In trying to extend his literary methods to novel length, Don faced other dilemmas. "Writing a novel consists of failing, for me, for a long time . . ." he said. "The problem . . . is that I'm interested in pushing the form, if not forward then at least in some direction."

More than short stories, novels tend toward formula . . . or, at the very least, toward *habitual* structures, steady rhythm, and foreshadowing to keep the reader engaged till the end. The trouble is, habit lacks magic. It cheapens the values of images and words. It's the sudden eruption, the improvised melody or phrase, that tickles our imaginations, and adds wonder to the world.

Up to now, Don's fiction had proceeded by verbal collage. By its very nature, collage depends on brevity, fragility—a kind of once-only quality. *Brevity* because the joy and humor of an unexpected connection wear thin with repetition; *fragility* because the delicacy of an oddly made piece can be strangely moving, even when the piece is silly, gawky, or somehow frightening.

Imagine a spiderweb, an ingenious trap that is, nevertheless, *barely there,* at the mercy of the slightest touch or breath or gust of wind, and all the more beautiful for being both calculated and vulnerable. This is the sort of fragility that characterized Don's gift.

How does one sustain an elegant synthesis beyond a single moment? How long can a balloon sigh in the air before the reader's gaze, weary of the concept, pops it?

Ideally, *brevity at length* is what Don hoped to achieve in the novel—an impossibility on the face of it.

In *Snow White,* he tried to solve the problem by using the fairy tale/movie/bedtime story as a ghost structure, touching on it ever so lightly. He was free, then, to spin a series of vignettes that captured or lampooned America's cultural chaos. "[T]he story of Snow White and the Seven Dwarves is known to all . . . you can play against expectations," Don said.

Additionally, since readers did not expect Snow White to be "realistic," Don was free to use her as an excuse for playing with words. "[A]ll of [the] people in this book are pretexts for being able to encounter certain kinds of language," Don said—metaphysical language, psychological categories (*The Many Faces of Love*), textbook jargon, newspaper headlines, hip phrases: all the grammars that enforce the (often false) expectations by which society tells us to live. "Oh I wish there were some words in the world that were not the words I always hear!"

By playing one idiom off another, in a raucous, Rabelaisian romp, Don created literary noise, a polyphony, a multidirectional conversation that challenged conventional wisdoms and undercut notions of love, heroism, beauty, and literature. Stripped of her fairy tale, Snow White begins to disintegrate, her inner "discourse" a broken mirror:

> Those men hulking hulk in closets and outside . . . I only wanted
> one plain hero . . . parts thought dissembling . . . not enough ever . . .
> mirror custody of the blow scale model I concede that it is to a degree
> instruments . . .

At the end, when her "arse" fails to seduce a prince into action, she "RISES INTO THE SKY," undergoes an "APOTHEOSIS," and becomes a virgin again.

Bill, the men's leader, is hanged for his failures. Paul, the "prince," is dead, a disappointment to all. The little men, manufacturing buffalo humps so they can get in "on the leading edge" of the nation's "trash phenomenon," are left contemplating "Theodicy and Rime." At this point, a bold headline is inserted into the book:

ANATHEMATIZATION OF THE WORLD
IS NOT AN ADEQUATE RESPONSE TO
THE WORLD

Better to accept the contradictions of evil and good (the contemplation of Theodicy) and the paradoxes of language (Rime). Ambiguity is the air we breathe.

Ultimately, like lost children—without a leader or a knowable father, without a romantic ideal—the little men "DEPART IN SEARCH OF A NEW PRINCIPLE HEIGH-HO."

DROWNING

Don dedicated *Snow White* to Birgit. The first printing of five thousand copies vanished from bookstores right away; within four months Atheneum readied a second printing of three thousand copies. Not long after this, Bantam's paperback edition appeared with a cover photo of a woman wrapped in a towel. She stands next to a shower stall filled with men. The book took off. In August 1968, 154,000 copies were shipped. A month later, the publisher ordered ten thousand extra copies, and more than thirty thousand more in the following months. Unlike most of Don's books, it has never gone out of print.

Reviews, some puzzled but most of them laudatory, appeared in all the mainstream venues. Don's old pal Jack Kroll, writing in *Newsweek,* called Don a "splendid writer who knows how to turn spiritual dilemmas into logic, and how to turn that logic into comedy which is the true wised-up story of our time." In *Life,* Webster Schott said that Don was probably "the most perversely gifted writer in the United States. . . . *Snow White* has everything, including William Burroughs cutups, words posing as paintings, ribald social commentary, crazy esthetic experiments, and comedy that smashes." *Time* gushed, "Donald Barthelme's work creates the impression that something miraculous happened to him overnight—as if, blind from birth, he could suddenly see." And in *The New*

Republic, Richard Gilman noted the seriousness beneath Don's humor. He described Don as one of a "handful of American writers who are working to replenish and extend the art of fiction instead of trying to add to the stock of entertainments." Gilman said, "[Barthelme] keeps the very possibility of fiction alive, and by doing that shows us more of the nature of our age and ourselves than all those novels which never recognize the crisis of literature and therefore do nothing but repeat its dead forms."

Despite the book's success, Don and Lynn Nesbit argued with Herman Gollob about Atheneum's "niggardly advertising campaign." Gollob said Nesbit "demanded an extravagant advance, or so I saw it, for Don's next book." She threatened to shop Don to other publishers. "In a phone conversation with Lynn, I exploded," Gollob wrote. "Very unprofessional of me, that little tantrum. I had taken the matter personally, looking upon it not in the spirit of honest competition but as the betrayal of a friendship. . . . I refused to take [Don's] calls and returned his letters unopened."

Throughout 1967 and 1968, Don, Birgit, and Anne split their time between New York and Denmark. They traveled in Europe, in part on the money from Don's Guggenheim Fellowship (though he had spent most of it on a build-it-yourself harpsichord kit, hoping Birgit would play music and become happier, more grounded). Don took some satisfaction in finding his work in translation. *Come Back, Dr. Caligari* had appeared in Germany, Italy, Hungary, and Spain. Suhrkamp Verlag was planning a German edition of *Snow White.* On the move, Don didn't wholly register the shock waves that *Snow White* sent through the world of *New Yorker* subscribers. Hundreds of faithful readers canceled their subscriptions to protest Don's "gibberish." The response of one subscriber, an executive of the Hertz Corporation, was typical:

> [I]t seems to me a frightful waste that bilge of this sort be included in your magazine. I am an English major; my wife is an English major; my son is an English major and I like to think we have some fragmentary knowledge of the English language . . . to sponsor and nurture such pure drivel without any merit must eventually depreciate the value of your otherwise excellent magazine.

Angell replied, "I told Mr. Barthelme about your letter . . . and he (displaying a certain libidinous interest in reality) asked me to inform you that it recently took him one month and numerous telephone calls to recover a $500 deposit he had made after renting an automobile from your company." Howard Cushman, an old classmate of E. B. White, grumbled to White and his wife, Katharine, that *Snow White* was "garbage." In a lengthy letter, Katharine (now seventy-four and no longer actively editing for *The New Yorker*) replied:

> The New Nonsense or Hysteria School of fiction and satire is not my special cup of tea and I sometimes love Barthelme's writing and sometimes don't, but I do think he has great gifts. He is an experimentalist and a modern with a sense of satire and humor. This is what the New Yorker, *if it is to keep up its tradition of innovation, needs and must seek out.*

Don relished stirring up trouble. But on the whole his attention was focused on his travels and on problems more pressing than *New Yorker* readers—Helen's anger, Gollob's disaffection, and, most dreadfully, the fact that, almost from the start, his marriage to Birgit was broken and sad.

Early traces of Huntington's were now unmistakable in Birgit's behavior, and they were getting worse: a block against planning, unpredictable onslaughts of melancholy or anger. These unstable patterns undermined Birgit's attempts to be a good mother. Don's patience with her was wearing thin, and he drank more and more.

"It was tempestuous between them," Anne says. "I don't know if she was bipolar, but mentally . . . she was just *off*. Emotionally, there was a disconnect. You never knew how she was going to react to any given situation. My father was the more emotionally stable of the two."

Constant movement played hell with Don's concentration, but new places offered welcome distractions from the family's sadness. He relished Paris's seasonal beauty and he embraced the California-like weather he encountered almost everywhere. At other times, he couldn't hide his weariness and exasperation: "I'll write a real letter [later] when Anne is not throwing the hotel keys out of a seventh floor window onto a rushing boulevard," he told Angell. In another letter to Angell, he said, "I'm thinking of writing a long long story in the manner of Kleist or somebody, full of bodies discovered in bogs with nooses across their necks. I don't know why I want to do this, particularly, but it's a strong urge."

For his part, Angell urged Don to be "fat and happy" and encouraged him with cash advances. "[Here's a] check that ought to keep you and Brigit [*sic*] in aquavit for some time to come," he wrote.

Don was far from fat and happy, but he enjoyed Birgit's sister and father. Birgit's dad had seen Birgit's mother through *her* battle with Huntington's, and Don admired the man's fortitude. He didn't know if he could provide the same care for Birgit. Birgit's father understood what Don faced—including the self-doubt—and he didn't press Don or judge him. "I wish he had been my father," Don said to friends. Whenever he and Birgit ended a visit, Birgit's dad sent them away with sprays of flowers.

"I feel that I'm writing . . . piecemeal which is a lot of trouble for you," Don told Angell at one point. "Please bear with me." In fact, Angell was delighted with Don's output. In the spring of 1967, Don completed a piece called "Report," an outraged satire on military technology. Angell thought the story "wonderful" and "infinitely more effective" than antiwar editorials because it "makes [its] powerful point entirely in terms of fiction and fantasy . . . strik[ing] at the heart of things without arousing all the predictable built-in reactions and responses that we all have on this subject." He cautioned Don against didacticism in a couple of paragraphs but otherwise left the story alone. It ran in the June 10, 1967, issue of *The New Yorker.* Its opening lines— "Our group is against the war. But the war goes on"—captured the country's growing weariness and uncertainty.

Don addressed his literary anxieties in a story called "Certificate," later titled "The Dolt": "Endings are elusive, middles are nowhere to be found, but worst of all is to begin, to begin, to begin." When a character in the story walks into a room wearing a "serape woven out of two hundred transistor radios" and looms over his parents "like a large blaring building," Don seemed to have found, once again, a succinct image for the noisy mood of the moment, and for the cultural dynamics pulling America in many directions at once.

Angell rewarded him with cost-of-living adjustments. "Buy yourself a Trova toe," he said, a reference to the vaguely human-shaped sculptures of Ernest Trova which were popular in New York art circles. He enticed Don to work faster: "Incidentally, you are three legs up on a fiction bonus, and if we buy another story from you [within two months] it will mean some extra dough."

Don struggled to keep pace, sometimes unsuccessfully. He never compromised his standards for money. In February 1968, he would withdraw a story entitled "Some Trouble Friends Are Having," even though the magazine had accepted it and would have paid him a bonus for it. "While this may not be one of your very best stories, we really did want to publish it, and I'm sorry you no longer like it," Angell wrote to him. "[I]t is certainly a writer's privilege to make the final judgment in these matters, and we will now take the story off our books."

Don seemed rueful, at best, about his achievements. "I assume the Arab-Israeli war (to which I see Renata [Adler] went [as a reporter]) pretty well killed my story," he wrote Angell, referring to the outbreak of the Six-Day War between Israelis and Palestinians in June 1967. Don's story, "Report," had gotten lost amid the urgent news. "I seem to remember another [story of mine]"–"The Indian Uprising"–"that ran the week of Selma when everybody was watching TV. Oh well."

Nor was his confidence improved when Angell rejected a story, particularly one that Don knew was solid. In the summer of 1967, he submitted an enigmatic piece that he had begun two years earlier. Entitled "Robert Kennedy Saved from Drowning," it presented an object of contemplation, as in "The Balloon," only this time the object was an American celebrity, a U.S. senator. A series of verbal portraits akin to Andy Warhol's silk screens of Jackie Kennedy, the story did not attempt to delve beneath the figure's surface, yet its overall effect was remarkably revealing. This was precisely the opposite of what readers expected of characters in fiction, but for that reason it captured the ghostliness of America's celebrity culture.

"He is neither abrupt with nor excessively kind to associates. Or he is both abrupt and kind," the narrator says of Kennedy. These contradictions never sort out—as they never did in life: Kennedy was an extraordinarily wealthy man worried about poverty; an empathetic man with a reputation for ruthlessness; a family man who liked to fool around; a straight arrow who enjoyed naughty parties.

What prevents "Robert Kennedy Saved from Drowning" from being an exercise in futility is the narrator's empathy for K.–a simpatico that extends to the reader—and the real Kennedy's habit, at the time the story was written, of absorbing America's turmoil. In 1965, when Don had begun the story, Kennedy was "impotent and frustrated . . . kind of floundering," wrote Kennedy's friend and biographer Evan Thomas. Alienation, youthful angst, the civil rights movement, and war protests marked this era, and at various moments, Kennedy seemed to embody the nation's pain.

From 1965 to 1967, Don had set his story aside; it's possible he went back to it after learning that *Life* magazine had commissioned Saul Bellow to write a profile of RFK. Bellow always stirred Don's competitive juices. Their old argument about feelings versus meaning was revived in their mutual attempts to pin down Bobby. Bellow never finished his piece—according to Evan Thomas, Bellow viewed Kennedy as a blank screen "upon which others projected their hopes and fears. The true believers wanted him to star in an epic for which he was not yet prepared." This slipperiness, which defeated Bellow, became the core of Don's story, and accounts for its success at limning the meaning of celebrity.

"I never met Robert Kennedy nor did I talk to people who had," Don told Arthur Schlesinger, Jr., in 1977. "[A]ny precision in the piece comes from watching television and reading the *New York Times.* . . . The story was begun while I was living in Denmark in 1965. . . . The only 'true' thing in it was Kennedy's remark about the painter." In the story, K. goes to a gallery where the works of a well-known geometricist are on display. "Well, at least we know he has a ruler," K. says. "I happened to be in the [Pace] gallery when [Kennedy] came in with a group," Don told Schlesinger. "I think the artist was Kenneth Noland. Kennedy made the remark about the ruler—not the newest joke in the world." The rest of the story was whole cloth, woven from Don's sense of the nation's direction—and from his existentialist readings. Near the end of the piece, K. reads the French author Poulet on another writer, Marivaux: "The Marivaudian being is . . . a pastless futureless man, born anew at every instant. . . . The Marivaudian being has in a sense no history. Nothing follows from what has gone before. He is constantly surprised. He cannot predict his own reaction to events." Saul Bellow's conception of character could not accommodate such randomness, but Don's embrace of the instant got him as close to the truth as anything that has ever been written about Kennedy.

So far as we know, RFK never read Poulet—the narrator projects *himself* onto K.'s blank screen. His talent for projection, and K.'s ability to absorb, enables the narrator to "save" K. They have established a bond. K. is drowning in the sea of contradictory images about him: "His flat black hat, his black cape, his sword are on the shore. He retains his mask."

The narrator throws a line, K. grasps it, and he is pulled from the water.

The story's title is a nod to Jean Renoir's 1931 film, *Boudu Saved from Drowning* (*Boudu Sauvé des Eaux*). In the movie, a Parisian tramp insinuates himself into a bourgeois household and, over the course of a few weeks, tears it apart. In the end, having exposed the contradictory nature of "civilized" life, the tramp returns to the water. "It's his destiny—the currents have taken him again," a character says. The film's most remarkable achievement is its refusal to prettify class distinctions and to pass judgment on people. Whatever ultimate meaning the movie may have, the viewer has to project it—a quality Don's story shares with the film.

Roger Angell was on vacation when "Robert Kennedy Saved from Drowning" arrived at *The New Yorker*. William Maxwell read it and discussed it with William Shawn. On August 8, 1967, Maxwell wrote to Angell: "What bothers [Shawn] is attributing immaginary [*sic*] statements to an actual person, and . . . he suggests removing it from Robert Kennedy, to a fictitious person"—a strategy that shows how completely Shawn and Maxwell missed the story's point. No "fictitious person" could be America's blank screen the way RFK was. Don refused to consider the change.

On August 30, Angell notified Lynn Nesbit, "I am afraid we are turning [this story] down. The objection here is not with the writing, which is up to his best, but rather with the form. It just isn't possible for us to run a fictional work about a real person, for a number of complicated reasons. . . . I certainly hate to lose this."

Don was deeply hurt by this particular rejection, and frustrated with *The New Yorker*'s timidity. Nesbit wasted no time in sending the piece to

Ted Solotaroff, the young founder and editor of *The New American Review*.
"Barthelme's reputation was just getting under way," Solotaroff recalled. "I'd
read a few of his things in the *New Yorker* and thought of him as a literary
dandy . . . kind of Frenchified . . . surrealism as cultural fun and games, out of
step with the strenuous late sixties. Despite this prejudice, I was bowled over
and then haunted by his impressionistic portrait of Kennedy." He said:

> "Bobby" was on everyone's mind just then—an exciting, distrusted figure.
> [H]e had emerged from the shadow of his brother's death as a prospective
> leader of the opposition to the war. Shorn of his kid-brother brashness he
> seemed half-ruthless opportunist, half liberal crusader, Joe McCarthy in
> his background and Eugene McCarthy in his foreground.
>
> In Barthelme's hands he was transformed from the banal chameleon
> Bobby to the bemusing, enigmatic "K." . . . he became both more abstract
> and more intriguing: a pure politician in the contemporary American
> mode: an overt and subliminal image-maker.

Solotaroff conceded that he didn't fully grasp the story, but an "editor
doesn't have to understand everything, you just have to trust the feeling of
seeing freshly and also being teased out of thought, as Keats said of Shakespeare." Don's story "made my mind feel like it had been awakened and was
rubbing its eyes," he said.

The New American Review published the piece in April 1968, two months
before Kennedy was shot to death in Los Angeles. "I cannot account for [the]
impulse of the I-character to 'save' [Kennedy] other than by reference to John
Kennedy's death," Don told Arthur Schlesinger, Jr. "[S]till, a second assassination was unthinkable at that time."

In late April, Jack Newfield of *The Village Voice* showed the story to
Kennedy. Kennedy asked him, "Well, is he for me or against me?" Don was
amused by the anecdote—and later haunted by the fact that no one was actually able to save Kennedy.

In another spooky trick of timing, Martin Luther King, Jr., was assassinated just as Don's story appeared in bookstores. King's associates demanded
to know if the FBI was responsible for the murder. Dick Gregory went public
with the fact that the FBI had harassed King. The agency's code name for him
was "Zorro." Don had dressed RFK in a Zorro costume, in the story's final
scene, to mock Kennedy's heroic image. The coincidence unnerved him.

In the summer of 1967, Don wrote to Walker Percy, pleased that Farrar,
Straus and Giroux, Percy's publisher, was now his publisher, as well. Lynn
Nesbit had brokered a deal. Percy was happy for Don but also wary about

sharing his editor, Henry Robbins. At the time, Percy was struggling with a draft of his novel *Love in the Ruins.* He wanted Robbins's full attention, and he told Don, only partly in jest, to stand in line.

Roger Straus had founded his publishing house along with John Farrar in 1945. Straus's mother was Gladys Guggenheim; his father, Roger W. Straus, was chair of the American Smelting and Refining Company. His family also owned Macy's. Farrar, Straus and Company's first title was *Yank, the G. I. Story of War,* selections from the army's weekly publication, *Yank.* Shirley Jackson's *The Lottery,* published in 1949, was among the company's first literary titles. Financially anemic until the 1950s, the firm got its first big boost when Edmund Wilson left Doubleday in a legal dispute and cast his lot with Roger Straus. Wilson remained on the company's list for the rest of his career. In 1955, Robert Giroux, a young editor who had earned his chops at Columbia University's *Columbia Review,* joined the firm, bringing with him from Harcourt, Brace seventeen new authors, including Flannery O' Connor, T. S. Eliot, Bernard Malamud, and John Berryman. This move established the company's reputation for publishing fine literature. (By the mid-eighties, FSG could boast of fifteen National Book Awards and six Pulitzer Prizes; a decade later, it had added ten Nobel laureates to its list, including Isaac Bashevis Singer, Wole Soyinka, Nadine Gordimer, and Seamus Heaney. Each winter, Straus would give a mock groan and say, "Oh my God, I have to go to Stockholm again.") Eventually, Giroux became a managing partner in the firm. Robert Lowell's *For the Union Dead* was the first title under the imprint Farrar, Straus and Giroux, in 1964.

Theatrical, flamboyant, gossipy, gracious but salty, usually clad in an ascot, a double-breasted pinstripe suit, and lilac-colored socks, Straus was the tireless company crusader and its iconic image—the picture of the "gentleman publisher" (when he'd gone into business in the forties, the New York publishing world consisted of about a dozen small houses run by families—for example Knopf, Scribner's; Harcourt, Brace; and Farrar and Rinehart). Straus railed against "huge corporate bullshit" and refused to become a "spaghetti salesman"—his term for bottom-line publishing—or to let FSG become a "division of Kleenex, or whatever."

By the late 1960s, FSG was known for its cheapness as much as for its literary prestige. Straus's favorite boast was that he'd published a "hell of a book" and paid next to nothing for it. Most of his authors didn't mind this arrangement—or the fact that there was no hot water in the bathrooms in FSG's offices at Union Square—because low advances allowed Straus to keep books in print for a long time. His personal loyalty to his writers was charming, flattering, intense.

Henry Robbins, a Harvard graduate two years older than Don, was relatively new to Farrar, Straus and Giroux. For some time, he had kept an eye on

Don. After Herman Gollob's outburst at Lynn Nesbit, she courted Robbins and he responded favorably.

"Robbins was a man who took himself and his literature seriously (he was inclined to confuse them)," wrote editor Michael Korda. "[P]ugnacious, arrogant, opinionated, and self-righteous . . . Robbins [was] a classic type A personality . . . he enjoyed a good fight for its own sake . . . [h]e did not compromise. Reasoning with him, as Churchill complained about de Gaulle, was like trying to reason with Joan of Arc."

One imagines the old editorial board of *Forum* speaking of Don this way. Small wonder Don became attached to the man. "Henry was hot-headed," Lynn Nesbit agrees. "But he was hot-headed about the right things."

Joan Didion, another of Robbins's authors, has stressed his loyalty to writers: "I remember his actual hurt and outrage when any of us, his orphan sisters or brothers, got a bad review or a slighting word or even a letter he imagined capable of marring our most inconsequential moment."

Though Don would rarely pass up a professional opportunity, he also prized loyalty in friendship. When opportunity and friendship clashed, he was anguished. Shortly after signing with FSG, he called Herman Gollob from Europe—at 3:00 A.M. Gollob's time. "I'm not mad at you for not giving me the fucking money," Don said. "Why are you pissed off because I asked for it?"

Gollob, groggy, was disarmed. "End of quarrel," he said later, looking back on the incident.

By now, Don had made up with Helen, too. One night, when he and Birgit were in New York, Helen phoned him. She was returning to Houston from a trip to Boston, and an airline strike had temporarily stranded her in Manhattan. "Don was startled to hear my voice, but after a moment he recovered his equanimity and we talked for a long time," Helen recalled. "I asked about his work, but he was more interested in telling me of his role as 'father of the child.'

" 'I do everything for my daughter—bathe and dress her, feed her, everything,' he said. . . . He was learning to cook as well. And then after the first few minutes, he began to tell me of Birgit's emotional condition and how it had manifested itself in both Copenhagen and now in New York."

Helen remembered that she and Don were "warm and kind to each other." "In fact," she said, "I later realized that I had talked to him with the same endearing language I had used during our marriage. We finally said goodbye, and this was the last time that we talked for several years."

In February 1968, as the number of U.S. Navy and Air Force reservists on active duty in Vietnam topped fifteen thousand; as Americans flocked to *Planet of the Apes,* in which Charlton Heston battled simians who ruled an America in ruins; and as Richard Nixon announced his candidacy for the U.S. presidency by telling voters that "peace and freedom in the world" depended on his election, Farrar, Straus and Giroux published 6,500 copies of Don's latest short story collection, *Unspeakable Practices, Unnatural Acts.*

The title comes from *Hamlet*—the quintessential drama about corrupted power, intergenerational conflicts, and dysfunctional families. Near the end of the play, Horatio says: ". . . And let me speak to the yet unknowing world / How these things came about: so shall you hear / Of carnal, bloody and unnatural acts, / Of accidental judgments, casual slaughters, / Of deaths put by cunning and forced cause, / And, in this upshot, purposes mistook / Fall'n on the inventors' heads: all this can I / Truly deliver."

Don dedicated the book to Herman Gollob—"an unspeakable and unnatural thing for you to do," Gollob told Don on the phone.

"You mean it made you feel guilty? Good!" Don said. "That means you still retain a spark of Hebraism."

"The Indian Uprising," with its images of complete social breakdown, led off the collection; the book ended with "See the Moon?" in which the narrator, with a new "locus of . . . hopes" awaits the birth of his first child. In between, mysterious objects appear in the city ("The Balloon"), couples drift ("Edward and Pia"), the U.S. military perfects the efficiency of killing ("Report"), while politicians remain aloof ("Robert Kennedy Saved from Drowning" and "The President").

Even more than *Snow White,* Don's latest book took readers into a world at once recognizable and unfamiliar. The portrait of Robert Kennedy was spot-on accurate, and yet the story was also a surrealist word machine. RFK dreams of "strange aircraft which resemble kitchen implements, bread boards, cookie sheets, colanders. The shiny aluminum instruments are on their way to complete the bombing of Sidi-Madani."

"Kafka might well be not turning over but grinning in his grave at Donald Barthelme, for here at last is a worthy successor," said Anatole Broyard in the *New York Times Book Review.*

In an extended piece in *The New York Review of Books,* William Gass quoted a line from "The Indian Uprising" and said, "It is impossible to overpraise such a sentence, and it is characteristic" of *Unspeakable Practices, Unnatural Acts.*

Hilary Corke, who had perceptively reviewed Don's first collection, detected a "coarsening and souring" of Don's attitude toward life: "[S]ex . . . which once seemed to Barthelme the one possible real act remaining to us in our conurbations of unreality, is . . . seemingly becoming for him yet another thing to be flicked through, switched on or off, a spectator sport even for its participants." Still, the new book was, she said, "richer in ideas, and in laughs of all colors for that matter, than the combined collections of a dozen ordinary writers."

It was apparent to most reviewers that Don's stories were more powerful than his novel. In a culture that prized the flamboyant over the small and complex, this would become an increasing problem for Don. *Unspeakable Practices, Unnatural Acts* was published just as Norman Mailer released *The Armies of the Night,* his "non-fiction novel" about the march on the Pentagon in October 1967. A "big" book in every way, combining memoir, history, fiction, the personal and the political, Mailer's achievement was rightly praised (by Alan Trachtenberg in *The Nation*) as a "permanent contribution to our literature." This remark was followed in the magazine by Calvin Bedient's claim that "Donald Barthelme [is] relentlessly and entertainingly unmeaningful" in his "brief, bright, breezy stories."

In contrast to this view, Earl Shorris noted a few years later in *Harper's,* "Donald Barthelme has accomplished the work that the New Journalists are not competent to do. In a single story he is able to include more of the taste of the times than there is in the collected works of Wolfe, Breslin, Talese & Co. The difference lies in Barthelme's ability to compress, almost to transistorize the world, and then make his miniatures real again by virtue of his talent for language."

Writing in *Newsweek,* Jack Kroll, who knew how hard Don worked, and what he faced day to day, said simply, "Here is a writer one wishes good health, no tax problems, not too much phony success—this voice must not be allowed to crack."

THE POLITICS OF EXHAUSTION

On May 3, 1968, the Sorbonne's rector called the Paris police to clear the university courtyard of a "disputatious student meeting," igniting protests in the city. Students held hands and marched through the Latin Quarter, as well as the old neighborhoods linked by legend to Manet, Courbet, and Baudelaire. Student rioting had already occurred in Nanterre, a poor Parisian suburb. Beginning May 13, Paris would host the peace talks between the United States and North Vietnam, but in the next few weeks, the May rebellion would swamp all other news from the city. Students and workers, striking together, marching in tandem, erecting barricades, would stun Europe and nearly cripple the French government.

In the Latin Quarter, and on the walls of schools, slogans appeared: "Let's open the gates of nurseries, universities, and other prisons"; "Be a realist, demand the impossible"; "I take my desires for reality, because I believe in the reality of my desires." As with the 1871 Commune, this was an erotic, creative, and playful revolution—and all the more serious for being so. It was a refusal of all authority, "an ever-growing bubble," one observer wrote, "sucking in all that is young against all that is black."

The New Yorker ran regular updates of the events in Paris that May. Several "Letters from Paris" appeared from Janet Flanner (writing under the pseudonym Genet), and over the course of two issues

in September 1968, Mavis Gallant published "Reflections, the Events in May: A Paris Notebook." She talked about tear gas wafting through the windows of fifth-floor apartments, damaged trees, the "extremely moving" faces of boys and girls linking arms in the streets, the middle-aged urban professionals "who must know they are hated now."

During the time between Flanner's reports and Gallant's two-part article, Don slipped two stories into the pages of the magazine. The first, "The Policemen's Ball," ran beside Flanner's assertion, dated June 2, that this "has been the decisive week since France's crisis began."

In Don's story, Horace, a policeman with the "crack of authority" in his voice, takes his girlfriend Margot to a policemen's ball, hoping she will surrender to his force—the "force of the force." At the ball, she is drawn to a fireman named Vercingetorix. Finally, though, she returns home with Horace and gives him what he wants—"his heroism deserves it." All the while, the "horrors" lurk outside Horace's apartment. "Not even policemen and their ladies are safe," the horrors think. "No one is safe. Safety does not exist. Ha ha ha ha ha ha ha ha ha ha!"

The story's smirk at authority is clear. The names Horace and Vercingetorix come to us from Roman history. Vercingetorix was a Gallic rebel noted for building barricades to thwart Roman soldiers. Shortly after vanquishing Vercingetorix, Caesar was assassinated. Horace, an irreverent poet and satirist, fell under Brutus's sway, and joined him in a hopeless attempt to establish a republic.

The historical referents—to a decadent empire and rebellions against it—make Don's story, in the context of the May Days, an extended utopian slogan, as playful, sly, and funny as much of the graffiti in the Latin Quarter.

Meanwhile, students were setting fire to the streets, pouring oil and gasoline into the gutters. Flames soared from the sewers.

As weeks passed, the Paris demonstrators were backed by teachers, philosophers, and historians who lauded their actions and compared their uprising to earlier French revolutions—particularly that of 1871. Sartre, who had settled into near obscurity in Paris, became visible again in the melee. Henri Lefebvre emerged as a powerful voice. In 1947, he had written a book called *Critique de la Vie Quotidienne,* which argued that large-scale social change could occur only after people's "everyday" lives had been revolutionized—after they ditched the yoke of authority and remade their lives as works of art.

By August, just weeks before Jean-Luc Godard's *Weekend* opened in New York, featuring scenes of random violence, surreal horror, attacks on the bourgeoisie by hippie guerillas, Paris was trying to piece itself together again. In *The New Yorker*'s second issue that month (August 17), Don published "Eugénie Grandet," ostensibly a parody of the Balzac novel, or of its synopsis in *The Thesaurus of Book Digests,* which opens the story. The synopsis compresses the novel's plot in the style of *TV Guide.* Don riffs on its disjunc-tures, presenting a confettilike version of Balzac's work, bits and pieces of a tale with no real conclusion. Don's critics, seeing it as a trifle, have virtually overlooked this piece.

The question is, why *this* particular parody at this specific time? Don could have mocked *any* entry from *The Thesaurus.*

Balzac's novel (1833) follows the life of a rich miser, and of a family wrenched by greed and ambition. As Ronnie Butler wrote in *Balzac and the French Revolution,* Balzac was convinced that any "redivision of wealth" in France could only act as "an incentive to the natural cupidity of the masses." He was appalled by workers' calls for economic justice and constitutional government. The "only answer to the Parisian masses," Balzac told a friend, "was the bayonet." "What will become of the country" once power and money have passed into the hands of the people? the narrator asks in *Eugénie Grandet.*

In parodying this particular novel in the context of May 1968, Don com-posed a potent political document. It not only touched on the rebellion's seminal issues, but invoked the reinvigorated Sartre (in *Nausea,* Sartre's ex-istentialist hero reads *Eugénie Grandet*). In essays, Natalie Sarraute was calling for a new kind of novel, a novel that could accurately portray social chaos. As an example of narrative exhaustion, she cited Balzac's fiction.

Don's Eugénie asks, "Mother, have you noticed that this society we're in tends to be a little . . . repressive?" "You'd better sew some more pillow-cases," her mother snaps.

The Bank of France, we're told, "has precise information on all the large fortunes of Paris and the provinces." In the Indies, Eugénie's cousin Charles sells "children," "Chinese," "Negroes."

At the end of the story, "Adolphe des Grassins, an unsuccessful suitor of Eugénie, follows his father to Paris. He becomes a worthless scoundrel there." Don's deliberately flat sentence—like the plainness and understate-ment of a Daumier lithograph—should not blind us to its power. By the time this story appeared, newspapers around the globe had called the Paris demonstrators scoundrels, savages, vandals, agitators.

Elsewhere, Don wrote that vandals have been "grossly misperceived." "Their old practices, which earned them widespread condemnation, were a response to specific historical situations." In particular, in each of the French revolutions, authorities tried to discredit political insurgents by calling them vagabonds and vandals. "Vagabonds [are] always ready to do anything. For a cigar or a glass of eau-de-vie [they] would set fire to all of Paris," one nineteenth-century commentator said.

Between 1830 and 1896, convictions for vagrancy in France, many of them politically motivated, increased sevenfold.

Kristin Ross has reminded us that "Rimbaud's ... resistance to work is well-known." Similarly, throughout the 1950s and 1960s, a group of dissident intellectuals called the Situationist International (who were strongly influenced by Henri Lefebvre) promoted dropping out and turning daily life into a "mobile space of play," seeking chance encounters and random experiences on city streets. And during May 1968, the slogan "Never work!" covered walls all over Paris.

To become a "worthless scoundrel" in Paris meant you were politically dangerous, part of a long tradition of social and artistic dissent. After all, what was Baudelaire's flaneurship if not meditative wandering through city streets, searching for the "chance perspectives" that Haussmann's broad boulevards sought to deny?

Don's "Eugénet Grandet," firmly attached to modernist history, and appearing, as it did, in a mainstream weekly, tucked among ads for glittering cars, watches, and diamonds, is a remarkable American artifact.

Initially, *The New Yorker* rejected it. "Sometimes I wish we were a purely literary magazine—a feeling that usually evaporates on payday," Angell said by way of apology. Convinced of the story's timeliness, Don sent it back to Angell with an "explanatory note" and the slightly scolding admonition, "I thought you might want to look at it again. . . ."

Don remained intrigued by the May Days and their aftermath. In 1972, he wrote a story entitled "Critique de la Vie Quotidienne," which ends with a character studying "Marxist sociology with Lefebvre." In the early 1980s, at the University of Houston, he bought for his students several copies of a special issue of the *Chicago Review* (vol. 32, no. 3, [1981]), which focused on "The French New Philosophers." He didn't say why he'd purchased the journal, but he placed a stack in the center of the student lounge, marked each copy with a rubber stamp—big baroque letters spelling out "Property of the University of Houston: Your Immortal Soul Is in Peril if You Do Not Return It"—and obviously expected students to study the issue.

The journal contained excerpts of writings by Guy Lardreau, Christian Jambet, André Glucksmann, and Bernard-Henri Lévy, philosophers wrestling with, among other things, the failure of the May 1968 uprising. Generally, their meditations involved reevaluations of Freud, Marx, Adorno, Althusser, and Lacan, and looked for ways to reconcile theories of sociology, psychology, and political activism.

The gist of their arguments was this: If sociologists insisted that individuals embody primitive, prelinguistic tendencies that determine their social actions, and literary structuralists argued that language and texts shape human behavior, was there any common ground between the two? Following Lacan, most of these "French New Philosophers" recognized no real boundary between self and society. Language is the foundation of culture's social and political structures, they said, and the individual's psychological states are mediated and symbolized by words. Primitive, prelinguistic tendencies—desire, repression—come to be clothed in language, and in this way, society dwells in us all. Psychoanalysis *is* politics. Freud is Marx.

Wistfully, this view proposed to show why the May 1968 slogans "Everything Is Possible" and "Imagination Is Power" were overly simplistic, though admirable in their utopian thrust.

CITY LIFE (I)

"My father made a wonderful toy for me when I was a child," Anne recalls. "It was a record player, an old Victrola, I think, with a big lid. He painted it funky pink and black on the outside, and he collaged a picture, cut into black-and-white slices with a photograph of my mother, on the turntable part of it. He loved collage and to work with his hands."

Even as a small child Anne understood that her father "looked at writing as a serious job." "He'd get up in the morning, cook breakfast, and write," she says. "Later in the afternoon he'd take a nap. Then he'd write again until dinner. He was incredibly disciplined."

She loved her uncle Rick: "Beard and all, wild hair. He was a goofball." He'd come by the apartment and "he'd walk around with his shirt over his head, or crawl around on the floor with me. A master entertainer. He made me laugh."

On trips to Texas with Birgit and Don, Anne discovered that Don's mother was "pure love." "There was something ethereal about her," Anne says. "She only had good things to say. She was sweet and soft. And incredibly bright."

She took Anne to church. "Because of my parents, I had no relationship to religion whatsoever," Anne says. "But I'd go to Mass with my grandmother. She was faithful without being obnoxious about it."

As for her grandpop: "I liked him. He treated me like an adult. He was hard on my father, mentally and physically, but he changed as he got older. He was never *soft,* don't get me wrong. But softer."

New York's wonders Anne saw through her father's eyes. On the corner of Sixth Avenue and Fifty-fourth Street, Moondog sang and plied strollers for money. His real name was Louis Thomas Hardin; he tagged himself after a favorite old hound of his "who used to howl at the moon more than any dog" he knew. He wore a Viking helmet, sold self-published poetry, and sang madrigals, jazz, blues, and rock.

In "City Life," Don based a character on Moondog. In early drafts of the story, he is linked to Don himself. Don writes that "Moonbelly" came to New York from Texas (Hardin hailed from Kansas).

Moonbelly laments, "This city! If it weren't for the fact that I am a famous musical artist, that I scream and write, that I *need* this city to torture me into that state of rage which, alone among the psychic states, produces a—"

The thought breaks off. Moonbelly then sings a song "about a relationship." The line "This is an unhealthy relationship" appears on the page thirteen times.

The passage did not make it into the story's final draft.

In another excised scene, Moonbelly calls the Poison Control Center. His kid has eaten something. An exchange takes place between father and child:

> —What's in your mouth?
> —I don't know. I found it behind the refrigerator. In a little can.

The streets were scary, but home was just as perilous, so Don walked, often with Anne in tow. Tenth Street, at the Avenue of the Americas, was one of the few places in the city that offered a view of the sunset, its pale rays bathing Patchin Place, the old home of E. E. Cummings and Djuna Barnes. Sometimes, standing there watching the sun go down, Don sang softly Harry Nilsson's "City Life."

One of Don's regular paths took him past the Guggenheim Museum. Outside the museum, Ernest Trova's chrome-plated sculptures, from his *Falling Man* series, overlooked Fifth Avenue: faceless male forms, in various attitudes of distress, adorned with objects (oxygen tanks, shower nozzles, stainless-steel tubes). Don was moved by Trova's work—the figures' status as goods in a world of goods, the loss of their humanity—but he felt the image of the falling man couldn't nourish Trova as an artist much longer.

One day, on one of his walks, Don encountered a dog in a rage, barking at him from an upper-story window. He wondered what would have happened if the dog had jumped on him. Right away, this thought attached itself to Trova: Don imagined a sculptor in "that unhappiest of states, between images." He went home and roughed out on paper a scenario in which a dog leaps on a sculptor from a window. The sculptor—whose previous achievement, the *Yawning Man* series, has played itself out—is seized with a "new image," the falling dog: "I wanted the dog's face. I wanted his expression, falling." The artist's creativity is rekindled, with an accidental gift from the city.

Mad dogs were the least of Gotham's problems. At any moment on the street, in restaurants, behind locked doors, violence might flare. On a Monday afternoon in early June 1968, a frustrated playwright and actress named Valerie Solanas walked into Andy Warhol's Factory on Forty-seventh Street and shot him with a .32-caliber pistol. Before the shooting, she had self-published *The SCUM Manifesto,* a rant against men. "[M]aleness is a deficiency disease," she wrote, "and males are emotional cripples . . . already dead inside [the male] wants to die." She said that SCUM (reportedly an acronym for the Society for Cutting Up Men) "will kill all men" except "those . . . who are working diligently to eliminate themselves."

Two years later, on March 6, 1970, just a block away from Don and Birgit's apartment, members of the Weather Underground accidentally blew up a town house while making bombs.

For most of the country, it was easy to dismiss the Warhol shooting and the town house blast as isolated events. But for many people living in Manhattan, they seemed part of a larger pattern of city life. Valerie Solanas's rage bloomed in soil that then spawned the Stonewall riots, the demonstrations against the exclusive men's bar at the Biltmore Hotel, and the U.S. Women's Strike for Equality, when over ten thousand women marched down Fifth Avenue demanding emancipation. *The SCUM Manifesto* may have been extreme, but even men recognized the truth of statements such as "[T]he kid . . . want[s] Daddy's approval . . . it must respect Daddy, and . . . Daddy can make sure he is respected only by remaining aloof. . . ."

The Weathermen's tactics were repugnant, but opinion polls revealed that most Americans agreed with the anarchists that the government was corrupt, particularly in its handling of the Vietnam War. Even Walter Cronkite, the "most trusted man in America," questioned the president's war policies on the CBS Evening News.

In an environment so shaky, the city dweller must choose between "dignity and hysteria," said Ernest Trova. The choice is difficult because rage is everywhere, and it is hard not to respond with rage of one's own. As Don wrote, in lines he later cut from "City Life," "Now [Moonbelly] will write a song which will destroy the city, which will smash the great city into eighteen miles of broken glass, six inches deep."

• • •

"I'd often hear Don typing while I was still in bed," Kirk Sale recalls. "He would work in brief spells. Then he would go out wandering the neighborhood. He would knock off work at 11:45 precisely to have a vodka and tonic, and then a lunch with another drink at least, and he would take a nap shortly after. When he woke in midafternoon he would usually put on some music. And then he would read, magazines and books, and take a turn or two around the neighborhood, and then cocktail time would come around five, with Scotch being the usual drink as I remember, in which I would sometimes join him, and we'd just talk. Often politics—it was the sixties and seventies, after all."

Don and Birgit seldom gave parties, though Don "came to our dinner parties often enough with wine or Scotch, and he'd be finished, and I mean that near literally, by nine," Sale says. "Oftentimes at one of our parties he would just get up in the middle of dinner or a conversation and say he was going to bed and off he went, drunk but decorous enough, and knowing he shouldn't stay any longer."

Don once told Sale that "morning was the only time for sex—but that's because he would be too drunk at night."

Usually, in his afternoon walks around the neighborhood, Don ran into Grace Paley. He never failed to push her to write more stories. She had recently left her husband, and was now spending most of her time with Bob Nichols. Her life was chaotic, but what really kept her hopping was politics. She told Don the literary world was male-dominated and narcissistic, and that she intended to keep her distance from it.

What does that have to do with the fact that you're not writing? Don asked her. Grace just laughed, smacked her gum, and shook her head.

Occasionally, Don went to gallery shows in the East Village, and he kept up with the East Village poetry scene through Kenneth Koch, who shared with him a few of the neighborhood's "little" magazines: *Trobar, Fuck You, C, Poems from the Floating World,* and *Umbra,* one of whose regular contributors, Lorenzo Thomas, would later move to Houston and become active in *its* literary scene when Don returned to the city in the 1980s.

Aside from Kirk and Faith Sale, the couple with whom Don and Birgit spent the most time was Harrison Starr and his wife, Sally Kempton, recent acquaintances (Don met Starr when they both tried to hail the same cab one afternoon, and wound up sharing the ride). Starr was a film producer. By the time Don met him, he had worked on a number of notable movies, including Arthur Penn's *Mickey One,* starring Warren Beatty, and Paul Newman's *Rachel, Rachel,* with Joanne Woodward. He had begun as an experimental filmmaker. In 1958, he collaborated with Maya Deren on *The Very Eye of*

Night, a fifteen-minute film in which ballet dancers, in photographic negative, appear to rotate in the air against a starry sky.

Don was fascinated by Starr's stories about Deren, about Godard and
Truffaut, with whom he had worked briefly, and about Michelangelo Antonioni, whose movie *Zabriskie Point* Starr would eventually produce. In
"Kierkegaard Unfair to Schlegel," Don wrote of a typical evening with Starr
and Sally Kempton, who had made her name as a journalist: "H. and S. came
for supper. Veal Scaloppine Marsala and very well done, with green noodles
and salad. Buckets of vodka before and buckets of brandy after. The brandy
depressed me. Some talk of the new artists' tenement being made out of an
old warehouse building. H. said, 'I hear it's going to be very classy. I hear it's
going to have white rats.' "

Weekends were mostly for Anne. Don also wrote about this in "Kierkegaard
Unfair to Schlegel":

> Sunday. We took the baby to Central Park. At the Children's Zoo she
> wanted to ride a baby Shetland pony which appeared to be about ten min-
> utes old. Howled when told she could not. Then into a meadow (not a real
> meadow but an excuse for a meadow) for ball-throwing. I slept last night
> on the couch rather than in the bed. The couch is harder and when I can't
> sleep I need a harder surface. Dreamed that my father told me that my
> work was garbage. Mr. Garbage, he told me in the dream. Then, at dawn,
> the baby woke me again. She had taken off her nightclothes and slipped
> into a pillowcase. She was standing by the couch in the pillowcase, as if at
> the starting line of a sack race.

For a period of several months, city rage, professional expectations, growing
marital difficulties, and increased drinking appear to have shattered Don's
concentration. In 1969, Angell rejected a number of stories, including pieces
entitled "Behavior of the Underwriters," "Glut," and "Lying Howard." They
never reappeared. For Angell, these stories only "sort of, partly" worked. Don
lost confidence in a piece called "Blushes," on which he had spent a great
deal of time. Eventually, parts of it wound up in "The Explanation" and
"Kierkegaard Unfair to Schlegel." It is a story about nervousness, "sad fantasies," and "dangerous" city streets.

Birgit was homesick for Denmark, Don was in debt again to *The New
Yorker,* and the pressure to be seen in publishing circles, mingling with the
"right people," was intense. "I . . . enclose an invitation to the upcoming
Paris Review party—a bargain if you feel like laying out fifty bucks to get
close to George Plimpton," Angell wrote Don on May 29.

Domestic life continued to spawn surprises. In "Blushes," Don wrote (in a tone that presaged the more personal turn his writing would take late in his life): "The wax is gone from the floor where the baby urinated, puddle in the shape of Florida. The baby knocks back another flagon of Mott's Apple Juice, thirty-seven cents the quart. She's a tube of finite length, like the mind."

On balance, Angell's notes indicate that, despite the appearance of slippage, Don was, in fact, working furiously and producing steadily; if the pieces were unsuccessful, that was because they were attempting to break through to something new. Don pushed himself harder than ever. This was evident in his revisions of "City Life" and in the multiple drafts of "The Falling Dog."

The version of "The Falling Dog" that appeared in *The New Yorker* begins with a series of contemplations:

> gay dogs falling
> sense in which you would say of a thing
> it's a dog, as you would say, it's a lemon
> rain of dogs like rain of frogs
> or shower of objects dropped to confuse enemy radar

Then the narrator sets the scene: "Well, it was a standoff. I was on the concrete. [The dog] was standing there." This is followed by further meditations, this time on various media available to the artist (Plexiglas, aluminum). Finally the reader learns what has happened: "Yes, a dog jumped on me out of a high window." The narrator, a sculptor, is flooded with thoughts of how to "do" the "falling dog."

As it appeared two years later in *City Life*, the story begins with the explanation ("a dog jumped on me") followed by the "gay dogs" list. The revision provides an immediate context for the reader but loses the dramatic impact of the earlier beginning. In any case, the lists keep the reader off-kilter even in the later version; Don's changes don't make the story any easier to enter. If clarification was his goal, the simplest solution would have been a few extra lines of exposition. Instead, Don rearranged blocks of words, but not in aid of logic or linearity. It's as though the paragraphs were sculptural scraps that Don kept rearranging to see which combination of space, depth, and perspective cast the greatest sparks.

As in all of his stories *about* art, Don stressed that an artist begins not in some rarefied theoretical realm but in the world itself. The sculptor smuggles the world into his studio in the form of the dog. "The world enters [our] work as it enters our ordinary lives," Don once said, "not as world-view or system but in sharp particularity."

His struggles early in 1969, followed by an astonishing period of productivity, suggest the mental preparation he was making in order to create richer work. His domestic woes and the distractions of parenting and drinking were factors in his struggles, but most of all he was deepening his emotional and intellectual knowledge.

He had immersed himself in Anton Ehrenzweig's *The Hidden Order of Art,* which he claimed was the most enlightening book he had ever found about creativity. Ehrenzweig was a psychologist and arts educator from Vienna. Like Freud, he believed that Oedipal tensions form the basis of Western civilization's social structures. The artist uncovers the hidden motivations behind our public behaviors, and finds symbols for them by delving into the "dynamic instability" of the unconscious mind.

Don's study of *The Hidden Order of Art,* and his reacquaintance with Freud in the late 1960s, gave him firm control of his materials and his central themes. (It would be too reductive to read all of Don's early stories as Oedipal tales or to see the characters as dreamlike displacements enacting Freud's view of the central family drama, but this approach helps illuminate some of the emotional resonance in "Me and Miss Mandible," "Florence Green Is 81," "Hiding Man," "The Dolt," "The President," "Game," and many others.)

According to Ehrenzweig, in passages Don pondered intensely, the creator must surrender to the vast, "oceanic" depths of the prerational mind where distinctions weaken, objects and feelings blur—the way opposites frequently displace one another in dreams—and thereby forge "cooperation between several mental levels." The creative thinker links previously disconnected matrices. And these "matrices . . . function according to their different codes."

The rhythm of creativity is the rhythm of labor and birth—expansion and contraction—leading to a creative *rebirth.* The mother is the source of life; she "unites in her . . . image both male and female." In creative work, the "father figure"—the maker of rules—"recedes behind the mother," a reprieve, for the artist, from aggression and rigidity. The artist returns to a pre-Oedipal state, when the mother's body was the world. Eventually, the artist "merges with the mother and incorporates her generative powers." The "boundary between the internal and the external world gives way."

Reading Ehrenzweig sent Don back to Freud's "Dostoevsky and Parricide" (1928), in which Freud discussed the self-destructive leanings of an artist who seeks the "oceanic" state. In longing to be "under the control of his unconscious," the artist tries to reduce himself to "brief periods of absence." Freud speculated that Dostoevsky's epilepsy might have been induced by this desire. Other artists reach absence by drunkenness or various other forms of addiction.

Freud then upped the ante and suggested that Dostoevsky's guilt feelings toward his father lay behind everything he wrote. The old fellow was murdered when Dostoevsky was eighteen; though the young man had nothing to do with it, the killing fulfilled his secret wish that his father be removed from the world. Forever afterward, he felt blameworthy. Dostoevsky's "death-like seizures" became more than just "absences"; they signified "an identification with a dead person, either with someone who is really dead or with someone who is still alive and whom the subject wishes dead" (Freud noted that a "moment of supreme bliss" often precedes an epileptic's blackout).

A "great need for punishment develops in the ego" of a person who feels such rage toward the father, Freud stated. Besides seizures and inebriation, gambling (another of Dostoevsky's afflictions) often manifests as a form of self-punishment—"guilt" taking "tangible shape as a burden of debt."

"[F]ate is, in the last resort, only a . . . father-projection," said Freud.

In the context of these remarks, Don must have wondered about his childhood "fits" and his drinking. "Don would drink himself into some state of inebriation each night," says Karen Kennerly, one of his girlfriends in the early 1970s. "Once he called me from Houston. He was staying in his father's home. He said he'd been drinking and he passed out on his father's drafting board, and had thrown up on it."

After "Dostoevsky and Parricide," Don reread Freud's *The Interpretation of Dreams, The Psychopathology of Everyday Life,* "Errors," *Totem and Taboo,* and Karl Abraham's gloss on Freud's Oedipal theories, "Father-Murder and Father-Rescue in the Fantasies of Neurotics" (1922). Shortly thereafter, he wrote a story called "Views of My Father Weeping," in which the narrator's father is run over by an aristocrat's carriage when the coachman whips his horses into a frenzy. Afterward, after some hesitation, the son tracks down the coachman for reasons not entirely clear, even to himself.

The narrative style recalls Dostoevsky's novels, and a book by his literary descendant, Venyamin Kaverin, *The Unknown Artist* (1931), in which a young man attempts to find his place in society following the Russian Revolution.

In Don's story, the search for the coachman is interrupted by present-tense "views" of the narrator's father as he sits in bed weeping, plays with a ball of knitting or a water pistol, smudges the tops of cupcakes, or indulges in other childlike acts. "Why do I desire with all my heart that this man, my father, cease what he is doing, which is so painful to me?" the narrator asks himself. "Is it only that my position is a familiar one? That I remember, before, desiring with all my heart that this man, my father, cease what he is doing?"

As the critic Michael Zeitlin pointed out, the carriage scene is a replay of *Oedipus Rex:* Oedipus encounters his father's carriage on a road, and winds up attacking and killing the old man. Furthermore, Don's scene is an echo of Abraham's "Father-Murder" essay. Abraham recounts a dream of one of his patients, similar in structure to Oedipus's run-in with Laius. "There can be no doubt that a birth fantasy is contained in the myth" and in the dream, says Abraham. The son must get "his father out of the way in order to be born." The street is the birth canal. The sexual symbolism of horses is well known, and the carriage is a womb symbol: Oedipus's fight with his father is a "contest about the maternal genitals."

In "Views of My Father Weeping," Don reversed the elements of the myth: Oedipus becomes the father, approaching the carriage, and he is killed by an aristocrat's servant (the aristocrat being another father figure.) Don's narrator is merely an observer after the fact. Or is he? In his essay on Dostoevsky, Freud said, "It is a matter of indifference who actually committed the crime; psychology is only concerned to know who desired it emotionally and who welcomed it when it was done." Don's reversals indicate an elaborate screening by the son of a wish so intense, he keeps disguising and displacing it: the desire for his father's demise.

At the scene of the crime, the son leans over his father's body. Blood from the old man's mouth stains the collar of his coat. Later, when the narrator learns the identity of the coachman, Lars Bang, he notes that the name was "not unlike my own name."

Indeed, in early drafts of the story, Don called the coachman Lars Bo. Don's nickname, as a boy, was Bo.

In the story, the son's guilt is so great, he is haunted by views of his father weeping, regressing into childhood. The present-tense verbs give them greater immediacy than the rest of the story. Grammatically, the weeping episodes are endless and halt all psychic progress. As Zeitlin says, "[T]he son kills the father in fantasy but is left to be ravaged forevermore by guilty dreams—or views—of weeping and pathetic fathers (the last word of the story is 'etc.'). After all, who is this dead and weeping father but the father-in-the-son."

Don's version of the myth is "darker even than Sophocles'," says Zeitlin. Don's son is "denied his oedipal victory, dying the thousand deaths of remorse before he gets anywhere close to [his mother] or to solving the mystery of the roots of his own existence."

To date, "Views of My Father Weeping" was Don's most intricate story about fathers and sons, and it helped elucidate some of his earlier work. Its explicit Freudian subtexts (always handled playfully) reminded readers that Don had flirted with Freud before.

In an essay, well known to Don, called "A Special Type of Object Choice Made by Men," Freud wrote, "All [the son's] instincts, those of tenderness, gratitude, lustfulness, defiance and independence, find satisfaction in the single wish to be his own father." Freud continued:

It's as though the boy's defiance were to make him say, "I want nothing from my father; I will give him back all I have cost him." He then forms the phantasy of rescuing his father from danger and saving his life; in this way he puts his account square with him. This phantasy is commonly enough displaced on to the emperor, king or some other great man; after being thus distorted it becomes admissible to consciousness, and may even be made use of by creative writers.

These observations place the ending of "Robert Kennedy Saved from Drowning" in a fresh context. As it turns out, the story is not only a meditation on RFK, politics, and celebrity but also—like many of Don's other early stories—a powerful Oedipal fantasy.

After floundering a bit, trying to discover the right forms for his growing ambitions, Don would produce his strongest collection yet, *City Life.* The stories showed a remarkable range and diversity of shapes, yet they were united in their conscious examination of Oedipal rage. If "The Phantom of the Opera's Friend" was a gentle homage to Gaston Leroux's tale—and to the ability of slight content to transform itself into various media (books, musicals, movies)—it was also an allegory of a son's attempts to please an impossible father. If "On Angels" was an amusing literal take on the notion that "God is dead," it was also a meditation on the emptiness that attends the realization of an unspeakable wish.

On May 24, 1969, *The New Yorker* published "At the Tolstoy Museum," Don's story of an imaginary museum dedicated to the life and works of Leo Tolstoy. "The holdings of the Tolstoy Museum consist principally of some thirty thousand pictures of Count Leo Tolstoy," the narrator says. "More than any other museum, the Tolstoy Museum induces weeping. Even the bare title of a Tolstoy work, with its burden of love, can induce weeping—for example, the article titled, 'Who Should Teach Whom to Write, We the Peasant Children or the Peasant Children Us?'"

The text is accompanied by visual collages. In one, the Great Master's head (one of the museum's exhibits) overwhelms a small Napoleonic figure. A sketch investigating architectural perspective illustrates "The Anna-Vronsky Pavilion"; in the foreground, a top-hatted man holds a swooning woman.

With its deliberately flat prose, the story is at once a parody and a tribute, a denial of the literary past and a longing to return to it. It is another examination by a son of his ambivalent feelings toward the world of his father.

The story's appearance prompted a family in Holly Hill, Florida, to write to the magazine to learn the location of the Tolstoy Museum. Roger Angell replied that while "there is a Tolstoy Museum somewhere in Russia," the one that Mr. Barthelme wrote about "exists only in Mr. Barthelme's marvelous imagination. I hope this does not come as too much of a shock to you."

A more sobering letter arrived on June 9. Countess Alexandra L. Tolstoy, the writer's daughter, wrote to protest "Donald Barthelme's absurd article." She asked, "What is the aim of such an article? To make people laugh? . . . How funny! Ha, ha, ha!"

She concluded: "I wish the so-called writers of now-a-days would have more respect to the memory of my father, Leo Tolstoy, and leave him in peace, and would have a little consideration to me as his daughter while I am still alive." To set the magazine straight, she enclosed a hagiographic brochure she had composed called "The Real Tolstoy."

On June 25, Angell responded: "I can assure you that neither [the author] nor we wished to show the slightest disrespect for [your father] or his immense works. . . . I have shown your letter to Mr. Barthelme and he asks me to apologize deeply for any distress he may have inadvertently caused you."

A difficult, elliptical writer appearing regularly in a popular magazine; a rebellious son with a strong sense of citizenship; a modern father constructing an "old Victrola" for his daughter and a harpsichord for his wife; an avant-gardist in the "hip" sixties reading musty old Freud: Don's paradoxes and uniqueness among his literary contemporaries couldn't be more pronounced.

In an article in the second issue of *Location,* Willem de Kooning said he "reinvent[ed] the harpsichord" in his work. Of this comment, Thomas Hess noted, "One of the most remarkable accomplishments of New York painting has been its simultaneous renewal and defiance of the past. With its radical assumption that anything can become art and that the artist can do anything, the painters proceeded to drag past art up into the present." For de Kooning, the *new* had been achieved by the "daring step of canceling out the whole idea of an avant-garde. . . ."

Don's Oedipal battles—and his increasingly conscious use of them in his fiction—put him in sync with de Kooning, the king, the aristocrat. It was not just a matter of being attracted to the old *and* the new, to the world of our fathers *and* the plains of possibility, but of being unable to escape either one of them.

CITY LIFE (II)

Day to day, Birgit drifted in an unreachable world, leaving Don with most of the child care. She wanted to return to Denmark, and hinted that suicide was a possibility if she didn't get her way. Don's picture of perfect romance had paled considerably, along with much of his optimism about art's revolutionary capacities.

"At the Tolstoy Museum we sat and wept," he had written, longing for the grandeur of the past. "The entire building, viewed from the street, suggests that it is about to fall on you. This the architects refer to as Tolstoy's moral authority."

His irony notwithstanding, Don believed with more conviction now that he had not been born into a moral world. Such a world was lost to him; he inhabited a fallen sphere. In Houston stood the mirror opposite of the Tolstoy Museum, in a sleepy residential neighborhood near Don's old living quarters. The Hyde Park Miniature Museum displayed car parts, arrowheads, shoe buttons, and toilet-paper statues. On his visits back home, whenever Don stumbled upon *this* collection, he saw it as the measure of his world—the only world available to him.

A sign in the window of the Hyde Park Miniature Museum said PLEASE BEAR IN MIND THIS IS A PRIVATE MUSEUM AND WE CANNOT EXPECT TOO MUCH FROM THE EXHIBITS.

• • •

Don published *City Life* in 1970. At the book's center is a pair of complementary stories, "The Explanation" and "Kierkegaard Unfair to Schlegel," featuring dialogues between "Q" and "A."

Q's qualities peg him as Apollonian, a voice of authority invested in order and machinery. A is Dionysian, drawn to dreaming and the arts. Occasionally, Q and A appear to be projections of the same consciousness. At intervals, they switch personalities. Each has a daughter.

"The Explanation" begins with an image of a big black square. The image is repeated three times in the story, and shows up again in "Kierkegaard." Initially, Q refers to the square as a machine. He asks A, "Do you believe that this machine could be helpful in changing the government?" Later, a similar square represents a "picture" of Q's daughter.

According to the critic Jerome Klinkowitz, a "box" inserted into a text is "a common journalistic device used at the stage of laying out a page when the story is already typeset but the accompanying photographs are not yet available." The black square is a place holder for any number of illustrations.

Additionally, the Bauhaus painter Josef Albers did a well-known *Homage to the Square* series, which helped pioneer geometric painting. Mark Rothko's final "spiritual" paintings, designed for a Houston museum, were hard-edged and dark. The artist Tony Smith engaged in a series of black box sculptures.

Perhaps most famously, Kasemir Malevich did a series of all-black paintings in 1913; their notoriety raised the twentieth century's central aesthetic questions: What *is* a work of art? What do we think of a world in which something like this is *seen* as a work of art? These questions are germane to "The Explanation" and to "Kierkegaard." Malevich said his black squares were "pure feeling," and that "pure feeling" was *the* central artistic reality.

In "The Explanation," Q and A discuss whether "purity" is "quantifiable." They agree it is not. It can only be represented abstractly. Each character reads into the black squares whatever most engages him at the moment.

Moreover, the "machinery" of "pure feeling" is bound up with the mechanisms of projection and repression. In Freudian fashion, Q and A project attitudes and desires onto each other to see how an "other" judges them. Between them, Q and A's dialogue unearths several buried fantasies. As they test each other, they debate art and machinery's effects on the soul. (In his now-famous essay, "The Work of Art in the Age of Mechanical Reproduction"—which Don referenced more than once in his fiction—Walter Benjamin argued that technology's ability to mass-produce words and images had compromised art. It is indistinguishable, now, from mechanics. It is soulless and impure.) Throughout the stories, the repeating square simultaneously illustrates and mocks Q and A's debate.

In sum, the stories' dialectics reflect the aesthetic, philosophical, and psychological issues that dominated mid-twentieth-century city life—or Don's experience of it. In 1963, the year he moved to New York, the Jewish Museum held an important show, "Black and White," featuring paintings in the "pure" spirit of Malevich by Pollock, de Kooning, Newman, Hofmann, Kline, Rauschenberg, Johns, and others. Alfred Barr, of the Museum of Modern Art, said that abstract paintings were question-producing machines. He quoted John Graham, whom Don mentioned in "Eugénie Grandet": The question-and-answer format, Graham said, lay behind every true artwork.

In 1967, Michael Fried published an important essay entitled "Art and Objecthood"; in it, he attacked Harold Rosenberg without naming him. He disparaged the idea of the "anxious" object that so excited Rosenberg, Thomas Hess, and Don. In part, Fried's essay focused on Tony Smith's black boxes, featured a Q & A with Smith, and spoke of museumgoers' unavoidable tendency to anthropomorphize abstract art.

Together, Don's stories formed a witty reply to Fried. "I don't like to use anthropomorphic language in talking about these machines," Q remarks in "The Explanation" (*machines*, here, meaning technology *and* art). Still, he insists that these mysterious objects are "brave."

Q and A do not resolve their differences . . . yet, to quote Wallace Stevens, a "relation appears" between them. At one point, A, whose love of chaos has resisted Q's ordering, assumes Q's view. Q asks him, "Now that you've studied [the machine] for a bit, can you explain how it works?"

A answers, "Of course. (Explanation)"

"Kierkegaard Unfair to Schlegel" focuses more explicitly on verbal art. Q and A continue to spar, but here A's mind is more divided. He discusses Kierkegaard's attack on Friedrich Schlegel in *The Concept of Irony*. In 1799, Schlegel published a novel called *Lucinde*. He was a prominent literary theorist, and critics received *Lucinde* as more than just a novel: It was a polemic against conservative thought. The novel was fragmented in form, a gleeful dialectic between nature and man, men and women, spirituality and sexuality.

The Concept of Irony was Kierkegaard's university dissertation in 1841. In it, he went after Schlegel's "very obscene book." He objected to what he perceived to be Schlegel's nihilism and his "artistic voluptuousness," which ignored "chronology," narrative "development," and other literary conventions.

A is torn between Kierkegaard *and* Schlegel, order and disorder. He admits that his ironic frame of mind does nothing to "change" the world. "I love my irony," he says, but he concedes that it gives him only a "poor . . . rather unsatisfactory" pleasure.

Eventually, Q's "imbecile questions leading nowhere" crack A's emotional control. Momentarily, he drops his wry armor. "He has given away his gaiety, and now has nothing," Q says as an aside to the reader.

Bitterly, A recognizes the validity of Q's world. Yet ironies abound. As Don knew, neither Schlegel nor Kierkegaard was quite who he appeared to be. *Lucinde* presented a chaotic surface; in truth, Schlegel longed for a world in which all contradictions were resolved. *The Concept of Irony* seemed to disparage humor, disorganization, and fragmentation; in fact, it was a model of these qualities, as Kierkegaard intended it to be a parody of academic thought. Through fierce sarcasm, *The Concept of Irony* dismantles its own arguments and utterly self-destructs.

Ultimately, "The Explanation" and "Kierkegaard Unfair to Schlegel" solve none of the vexations of city life, but in their demonstration that, in Wallace Stevens's words, "These / Two things are one"–*whatever* the extremes of the dialectic–they urge acceptance of life's stunning abundance.

Don's black square must be considered from one more perspective. His ex-wife Helen had phoned to tell him she was now dating a linguist, a professor at the University of Houston named Sam Southwell. Though Don no longer desired Helen, he experienced an irrational jealousy of her new lover. Don had always dabbled in philosophy, including linguistic theory, but he feared that his failure to earn a college degree exposed him to the charge of dilettantism. Now his ex was seeing a true philosopher.

In light of all this, it seems likely that *one* of the square's referents is the cognitive language theory advanced by Noam Chomsky, a concept with which Don was familiar through Walker Percy's essays on language. At the time, cognitive scientists regularly spoke of the human mind as a black box, and Chomsky used the box as an illustration of what he called a "language acquisition device"–a machinelike part of the mind busy processing words.

Among the subjects Q and A examine are theories and uses of language. At several points, their dialogue falls into repetitive near-nonsense that sounds like examples of syntax formation from linguistics textbooks.

Q runs a series of "error messages" past A: "improper sequence of operators," "improper use of hierarchy," "mixed mode, that one's particularly grave." These could be computer errors, but they could also be the listings of a language acquisition device, sorting through usage. (They also define salient qualities in Don's fiction.)

As he speaks with Q, A entertains fantasies of a woman–apparently a former lover. He imagines her removing her blouse. Combined with these fantasies, the "error messages" sound a Freudian note. Errors in speech, Freud said, are openings in which repressed thoughts break through to the conscious mind.

Late in "The Explanation," A, frustrated by Q's chilly demeanor, raises a formerly suppressed concern of his:

> I called her . . . and told her that I had dreamed about her, that she was naked in the dream, that we were making love. She didn't wish to be dreamed about, she said—not now, not later, not ever, when would I stop. I suggested that it was something over which I had no control. She said that it had all been a long time ago and that she was married to Howard now, as I knew, and that she didn't want . . . irruptions of this kind. Think of Howard, she said.

In both stories, as A's frustration grows, A thinks of striking Q. At one point, he imagines being struck by his father. At the end of "The Explanation," the object of his fantasies, the woman removing her blouse, acquires—in A's mind—a "bruise on her thigh." The repressed thought has finally emerged, through thickets of theorizing, arguing, displacing, fantasizing: A's anger at his former lover.

As in "Views of My Father Weeping," Don explored, in these Q & A pieces, his deepest fears and motivations, his conscious defenses. He did not spare himself. Without being overtly autobiographical or self-indulgent, the stories were highly revealing.

"You seem emotionless," A tells Q.

Q replies, "That's not true."

The reader felt a similar push-pull. On the surface the stories were cold and abstract, but with a lingering and mysterious emotional power.

City Life was released to ecstatic reviews—the best of Don's career so far—including coverage on the front page of *The New York Times Book Review.* The publication of *City Life,* Morris Dickstein said, confirms that "our best writers are doing radically new things" in the wake of traditional fiction's exhaustion, "of which Saul Bellow's novel *Mr. Sammler's Planet* is a current illustration."

"Barthelme comes out of all his books as a complex and enigmatic person," Dickstein said. He "has discovered how crucially books mediate our access to our deepest experience, and he brings to his 'discussions' of literature his own large reserves of fervor and ambiguity." With *City Life,* he "undertakes larger, more positive projects" than before, "which betray him into new risks, new emotional defeats, and the deepest kinds of artistic victories."

"Barthelme's subject in *City Life* is the . . . production of symbols that pretend to clarify more than can be clearly seen," Peter Berek wrote in *The Nation.* "Barthelme's creations help vivify our plight even if they do not clarify its outcome."

Writing in *Harper's,* Richard Schickel declared, "Mr. Barthelme has accepted, with great good cheer, the current cant that art may no longer be possible and has then gone cheerfully about the business of making it anyway, almost, it would seem, for the hell of it." In *Life,* Guy Davenport said that "it will be a while yet before we can tell just what [Barthelme] is up to," but he is "reinventing fiction . . . in a particularly brash and original way." *Time* listed *City Life* as one of the "Year's Best Books"—"Barthelme is a genius," the magazine said; he "knows no peer."

Not all readers agreed. Angell had to defend Don vigorously against accusations by a *New Yorker* subscriber from the Bronx that a consortium of publishers had mounted a fifty-thousand-dollar "campaign" to "put across Donald Barthelme" to the public.

"For all the acclaim [Mr. Barthelme] has received, his books are not the kind that will ever sell in large numbers," Angell replied, "and I doubt that the advertising and promotion budgets for all of his books together would total more than a thousand dollars. Publishers, you see, only spend heavily when they can see an almost guaranteed return; they are businessmen, and can't afford the kind of games you see as accounting for favorable reviews. . . . I'm afraid you'll have to dig a little deeper to explain the diabolical schemes and creeping phoniness that sustains a Barthelme and that keeps you so unhappy."

After another angry barrage from the subscriber, Angell wrote:

> I will . . . tell Mr. Barthelme that I am now on to his sly ways, which have enabled him to take advantage of my deep, underlying streak of phoniness. I will not be tricked again! Mr. Barthelme has been excused, and I will fling him into that corner of oblivion already occupied by such errant fakers as Joyce, Beckett, Picasso, Pollock, and Vivaldi.
>
> Thank you . . . I can honestly say that yours is the most entertaining letter I have seen in months.

City Life opened with the intensely interior "Views of My Father Weeping" and closed with the communal portrait "City Life." In between, Don slipped in meditations on art, friendship, religion, philosophy, social order, and language. The stories were spare and austere. They were funny, obscure, and charming.

In *Come Back, Dr. Caligari* and *Unspeakable Practices, Unnatural Acts,* the persona behind most of the stories was a negative version of the "Marivaudian being": a man who did not know what was happening to him from moment to moment, with no control of his environment, no sense of a foundational past (except for steady shocks of Oedipal guilt). The persona in *City Life* was far more complicated, like the ironist in "Kierkegaard," able to examine his irony and admit its limitations, capable of analyzing his repressive mechanisms and facing his personal history.

Even the book's title, less showy and smartly knowing than its predecessors, suggested a more mature approach to Don's obsessions. Not that he had abandoned his love of wordplay. Far from it. Of "Paraguay," the second story in the collection—a kind of science fiction tale reminiscent of Vonnegut or Borges—Don said:

> What I like about "Paraguay" is the misuse of language and the tone. Mixing bits of this and that from various areas of life to make something that did not exist before is an oddly hopeful endeavor. . . . Every writer in the country can write a beautiful sentence, or a hundred. What I am interested in is the ugly sentence that is also somehow beautiful. I agree that this is a highly specialized enterprise, akin to the manufacture of merkins, say—but it's what I do. Probably I have missed the point of the literature business entirely.

The story "Sentence" ends: "[T]he sentence is . . . a man-made object, not the one we wanted of course, but still a construction of man, a structure to be treasured for its weakness, as opposed to the strength of stones[.]"

These are the words of a writer determined to refresh language, but one who knows the limits of his enterprise. This mix of invention and sweet resignation, the humor and fierce intelligence along with a gift for poetic compression, is what distinguished Don's work from the failed literary experiments that littered the streets around him.

"Elsa and Ramona entered the complicated city," begins the book's final piece. At first, the two young women in "City Life" appear to face a variety of choices—everything an urban environment can offer. But in fact their options are few:

> —Where shall we put the telephone books?
> —Put them over there, by the telephone.
>
> —Where shall we hang [the painting]?
> —How about on the wall?
>
> —What shade of white do you want this apartment painted?
> —How about plain white?

Like Snow White, they discover that they will never get all they've been promised: passionate love, self-fulfillment. The law school they want to attend admits them only grudgingly, and refuses to take them seriously as students.

"Ugh!" Ramona groans.

It is only at the story's end, when Ramona absorbs the "fused glance" of the city's contradictory forces that her future blooms. She is impregnated with creative energy, "dancing little dances of suggestion and fear."

The city that emerges in Don's story is not the congested urban center of nineteenth-century industrialism, nor is it the well-ordered city of suburban pockets that began to develop immediately after World War II. It is a new, de-centered city, barely held together by fading cultural traditions and highways connecting shopping hubs swarming with motion. It is a city first glimpsed, in literature, in Ralph Ellison's *Invisible Man*—a city of wild electrical currents running underground. It is a place, Don wrote, of many "muddy roads," and the only way to live in it is to "accept" its impure muck.

It is *city* as *anxious object.*

Don's story was itself an impure mix of influences, many from the experimental film world that so fascinated him. Around the time Don began "City Life," Andy Warhol, recovering from his gunshot wounds, was editing his movie *Ramona and Julian,* in which a woman named Ramona (played by the actress Viva) is spurned by several potential lovers. Similarly, Don's Ramona is disappointed by love. At the time, Viva was also appearing in an Agnès Varda film called *Lions Love,* in a ménage à trois with two men, a situation touched on in "City Life." In 1960, Varda's husband, Jacques Demy, had made a movie called *Lola,* in which a woman has to choose between three lovers—as Ramona does in Don's story. (Ramona's friend Elsa marries a man named Jacques.) Varda had once made a film called *Elsa la Rose,* about Elsa Triolet, the wife of the surrealist Louis Aragon. Varda's most famous film, *Cléo de 5 à 7,* follows a woman through a day on the streets of Paris—a quintessential portrait of city life.

This name game would be meaningless were it not for the vision of art implied by Don's use of these cinematic materials. All of these films share the spirit of surrealism, the spirit, as André Breton said, of "systematic refusal" of the "whole series of intellectual, moral, and social obligations that continually and from all sides weigh down on man and crush him."

But Don's Ramona *does not refuse.* "I accepted," she says in the story's final paragraph. "What was the alternative?"

By accepting, she swells with new life.

A refusal of surrealism's refusal. A bold new step *beyond* the old avant-garde.

Significantly, Don uses eye imagery to convey Ramona's acceptance: The city's "pupil enlarged to admit more light," Ramona says, "more me." Eye imagery was central to many surrealist works, perhaps most notably Georges Bataille's erotic novels and Luis Buñuel's movie, cowritten with Salvador Dalí, *Un Chien Andalou.*

Finally, readers will recall that the most famous fictional Ramona is Helen Hunt Jackson's heroine. Jackson openly condemned the United States' genocidal policies toward Native Americans, and *Ramona* (1884) was written to spotlight the plight of mission Indians in Southern California. In "City Life," Don's Ramona watches "sun dancers" beat the "ground with sheaves of wheat" in the middle of the city, an echo of Arapaho and Cheyenne ceremonies honoring the sun's life-giving power. In an early draft of "City Life," Moonbelly describes himself as "part Indian," composing songs of rage against a system that "cannot withstand close scrutiny."

"The Indian Uprising" had touched on this theme: Modern urban life exists at the expense of the past, and because of crimes against Native Americans.

And yet . . . what are our alternatives now? Art and its devices cannot "change the government." Far from bringing justice to California's Indians, Helen Hunt Jackson's novel became just another popular entertainment. Two films were made from it, and a stage version . . . ultimately, *Ramona* turned into sludge: best-seller, polemic, trifle. Like *The Phantom of the Opera,* like several classic fairy tales, it was endlessly transformable, endlessly watered-down, especially in an age dominated by the technology of reproduction.

Best to accept the world's "muddy roads." At least therein lay the possibility of something new.

FREAKED OUT

"Donald Barthelme will quit writing and in five years he will commit suicide." This comment was attributed to a "well-known novelist, possibly envious," by Richard Schickel in a lengthy profile of Don entitled "Freaked Out on Barthelme," which appeared in the August 16, 1970, issue of *The New York Times Magazine.* In the article, Herman Gollob confirmed that Don was "one of the great despairers of all time," though he added that Don had a "great sense of camaraderie." Roger Angell said, "There's very little difference between Donald Barthelme the person and Donald Barthelme the writer." Harrison Starr characterized Don as "an extraordinarily gentle and ethical man" with a "very naked eye for pain and a very complex Catholic Christian guilt."

Starr's wife, Sally Kempton, told Schickel, "When he's dissatisfied with his work, he feels it's not good enough because he's not intelligent enough. He thinks of fiction in philosophical terms and I think he thinks that some shift of vision, if he can manage it, will reveal the true nature of our existence to him."

After spending time with Don, Schickel composed this portrait:

> Barthelme is neither tall nor short, neither fat nor thin. He shields
> his blue eyes behind rimless glasses. He has red hair and a beard

and dresses conservatively. He lives quietly in a floor-through walk-up on West 11th Street with his third wife, a Danish girl named Birgit, and his 4-year-old daughter, for whom he has made a most interesting pull-toy out of found objects. He is handy with carpenter's tools. His manuscripts arrive at the *New Yorker* very neatly typed. He works in the morning and is often seen walking around the Village of an afternoon. His social life has been described as "incredibly commonplace." . . . He is known to grow quite restless confronted by the quiet of a country weekend. He is likely to become "aggressively silent" at large gatherings of literary people, but he is also a talkative and loyal intimate.

The article was accompanied by snippets from "Brain Damage"—text and illustrations—and a photograph of Don standing warily in his apartment, hand on hip, in front of a framed Ingres poster. A music stand occupies a corner of the room, and an acoustic guitar sits on a tall dresser (sometimes Birgit tried to play).

"Freaked Out on Barthelme" appeared as *City Life* was earning great praise, and it brought Don as much fame as a literary writer could expect in America. This pleased him and made him nervous. The Book-of-the-Month Club made *City Life* an "alternate" choice one month. In his profile, Schickel said that Henry Robbins phoned to tell him the good news, insisting it would boost book sales. It's not much money, Robbins said, but it's a "chance to speak to a new audience," a more mainstream crowd. A few days later, Don called Robbins back. "Henry, is there some way we can politely turn down the Book-of-the-Month?" Absolutely not, Robbins replied. When Angell called to congratulate Don on the honor, Don was silent, Schickel related. Angell said, "Don, I don't think you want to be discovered." Don agreed.

Of course, matters weren't so simple. It was one thing to refresh the possibilities of art, and to be recognized by one's peers; it was another to become a celebrity, even a minor one.

For "Kierkegaard Unfair to Schlegel," Don had composed a rueful paragraph (later excised) about the artist in a culture that values spectacle over substance:

> It is not true that Kafka wanted Brod to burn his manuscripts after his death. Rather it is the case that Kafka was on fire to be published . . . rushed to the postbox day after day . . . ate with editors . . . intrigued for favorable notices . . . read the *Writer's Digest* . . . consorted with critics . . . autographed napkins . . . made himself available to librarians . . . spoke on the radio . . .

Later, in a speech at the University of Houston, Don returned to these themes:

> I often think not enough attention is paid to dead writers. It was formerly the case that we had a lot of long winter nights with nothing much to do and on these nights dead writers—from Dickens to Conrad to Heinrich von Kleist—received their merited attention. We still have long winter nights but they are filled, for most people, with old movies. I have nothing against old movies, but the trouble with them is that they don't have first sentences, those amazing and wonderful first sentences that grip you, drive you inexorably into the work. . . .

Hip readers "freaked out on Barthelme" would have been surprised to hear their latest cultural hero speaking so conservatively, but that was just the point for Don: He wanted to join the centuries-long literary conversation, not titillate thrill seekers looking for a Book-of-the-Month selection. By now, Don had seen enough of journalists and advertising to know fame's double edge. Schickel's article gave him tremendous visibility, but for most readers it would also freeze him in time. Forevermore, the phrase "freaked out" would link Don with what the media now called the "counterculture." From this point on, virtually everything written about Don, from dashed-off book reviews to more substantial critical examinations, saw him as representative of the anti-Establishment ethos of a particular moment. His aesthetic, psychological, philosophical, and theological investigations were largely ignored. Casual readers came to think of him as a "1960s writer." Academics came to see him as a "postmodernist"—a fancy way of saying a "1960s writer."

It was enough to turn you into a great despairer—if you weren't one already.

To Book-of-the-Month Club members, *City Life* was pitched as a wacky youth-culture statement. Nothing could have been further from Don's intentions. Most of his prepublication correspondence with Robbins concerned page layouts. "I've asked for a new black square," he said with regard to the beginning of "The Explanation." "It solves the problem of having so little type on that page." And he noted that on page 73, he'd "killed a line to get a space which should have been there. I need the space more than the line." In a certain section of "Bone Bubbles," Don wanted exactly "33 lines. A nicety."

These layout problems are the obsessions of an artist worried about every word, every line, every blank. No other prose writer in America thought as much as Don did about the *look* of a page, about the way typeface and spacing would affect the way a reader absorbed the meaning of a sentence. Don's literary project, exacting, exceedingly careful, was hardly countercultural; rather, it was cultural in the highest sense, that of nudging the culture forward. Like all such projects, it was bound to be misunderstood. Despite newspaper profiles and growing critical attention, Don discovered—as he feared he would—little real change in the world resulting from his efforts. Younger writers were beginning to imitate him. Mainstream magazines were publishing "wilder" material than before. But these changes were superficial and left Don dissatisfied.

City Life performed very well, particularly in paperback, but it hardly reached blockbuster status. Bantam printed 110,000 copies of the book; Pocket Books followed this up with 30,000 more. The initial hardcover sales had been modest. In 1972, two years after the book was first published, Farrar, Straus and Giroux notified Don that they needed to reduce their warehouse inventory. They offered him copies of *City Life* at fifty cents apiece. Don bought twenty copies, and sent a note: "Why didn't we think of pricing it at 50 cents in the first place? We would have sold hundreds of thousands." In later years, he joked that books should be sold like paintings: one of each, priced at millions of dollars.

If the machinery of celebrity and success, or the *perception* of success, dropped Don deeper into despair, his old habits of walking the city and of studying art kept him afloat. These pleasures are reflected everywhere in *City Life.* Don had his *own* cultural heroes, who gave him strength: Harold Rosenberg, Thomas Hess—and Willem de Kooning, still for Don the king of romance and artistic dedication. However, by 1970 the art world's publicity machine tended to ignore de Kooning in favor of Clement Greenberg's favorite painters, Morris Louis and Kenneth Noland—and it was harder for Don and his friends, who found Greenberg's enthusiasms soulless, to attain comfort from galleries and musuems.

Still, Don tried to engage the key issues driving contemporary art. Herbert Marcuse, formerly of the Frankfurt School, had recently said that art was dominated by the administrative structures of machinery. For this reason, the protests of May 1968 had failed, Marcuse said: Technological *systems* control everything, including social behavior and thought.

Marcuse's remarks reflected the fact that many artists, including Robert Rauschenberg and Andy Warhol, were working with engineers and scientists; John Chamberlain had accepted a commission from the RAND Corporation. Was art complicit in the horrors of Vietnam?

In this context, "The Explanation" and "Kierkegaard" are of a piece with Don's earlier stories, "Report" and Game," about military gadgetry. "Paraguay," with its futuristic vision of "sheet art," which is "run through heavy steel rollers," controlled by "flip-flop switches" and "dried in smoke," comes straight out of 1960s art-world conversations. "Each citizen is given as much art as his system can tolerate," Don wrote.

Of intense interest to artists and writers was the degree to which individuals were trapped by systems. Words like *variable, feedback,* and *looping* were entering everyday speech as a result of computer research, the space program, and military research and development. Naturally, art absorbed these concepts. In asking, "Why is *this* thing art?" conceptual and minimalist work tried to implicate viewers in the *system* of structuring and authenticating aesthetic experience. In "The Explanation" and in "Kierkegaard," when Q or A gets stuck in a linguistic loop—"How is my car? How is my nail? How is the taste of my potato? How is the cook of my potato?"—language reveals itself as part of a system, self-testing, self-correcting, self-perpetuating.

At stake in these art-world debates are two sobering questions, one social, the other metaphysical: 1. To what degree can art *humanize* an increasingly high-tech society, which is more and more efficient at war? 2. To what degree can an individual in a speeded-up culture live in the moment—and what does it *mean* to "live in the moment"? If nothing else, when confronted by a series of identical black squares, or an eight-hour film of the Empire State Building, you become aware, perhaps excruciatingly so, of each passing second. If nothing else, when confronted by a hard metallic shape where you don't expect to find it, you may begin to question the beneficence, and the purpose, of machines.

In mid-April 1971, Don entered St. Vincent's Hospital so the latest medical technology could be used to remove a basal-cell malignancy from his upper lip.

His hospital stay lasted four days. "In my mind, the basal-cell malignancy resembled a tiny truffle," he wrote in "Departures." " 'Most often occurs in sailors and farmers,' the doctor had told me. 'The sun.' But I, I sit under General Electric light, mostly." In fact, the cancer had been caused by his heavy smoking.

The doctor told Don that most people could lose up to a third of their upper lip "without a bad result." In an autobiographical section of "Departures," Don recounted his exchange with a Franciscan priest employed by St. Vincent's. The priest wanted to know why Don had marked "None" on his medical forms in the space reserved for "Religion." "I rehearsed for him my religious history," Don wrote. "We discussed the distinguishing characteristics of the various religious orders—the Basilians, the Capuchins. Recent outbreaks of enthusiasm among the Dutch Catholics were touched upon."

He was given a local anesthetic and was aware, throughout the procedure, of "[s]omething . . . going on there," above his teeth. "I opened my eyes," he wrote. "The bright light. 'Give me a No. 10 blade,' the doctor said."

His "truffle" was taken to a pathologist for examination. The next day, he was wheeled into surgery, where the "doctors were preparing themselves for the improvement of my face," he said. "I felt the morphine making me happy. I thought: What a beautiful hospital."

He emerged from St. Vincent's without the delicate, full mouth he had inherited from his mother. His upper lip was almost totally gone, leaving a large white space below his nose and a tiny triangle of flesh near the center of the absent lip. His grin was more elfin than ever. In the 1980s, when Phillip Lopate met Don, he thought Don was cultivating an "avant-garde" look by growing a beard without the mustache. Don told him he couldn't grow a mustache because of his cancer surgery. Lopate was abashed.

Don left the hospital with stitches in his face and a lingering morphine high. "I had my pants on and was feeling very dancy," he wrote. " 'Udbye!' I said [to the nurses]. 'Hank you!' "

A piece Don wrote about his surgery was "handsomely done," Roger Angell said, "but somehow it still sounds like someone talking about his operation." The magazine turned it down (until it appeared later as part of "Departures"). Medical, grocery, and other bills piled up, and *The New Yorker*'s accountants continued their arcane practices with all the glee of medieval alchemists. By the beginning of June 1971, Don had once more reached the magazine's "debt ceiling of two thousand dollars." "[W]e are not allowed to exceed" this, Angell told him. Though Don's first-refusal renewal was imminent, *The New Yorker* did not make advance payments against the renewals, nor did it allow "our writers to repay a debt to us out of that particular source of income." Angell added, "I'm sorry to let you down, especially for such complicated reasons."

With the stitches out, Don was free to smile again, but he didn't much feel like smiling. He stuck his new face into the wind and walked.

He passed the Museum of Modern Art. He recalled an exhibition there, a few years before, entitled "The Machine as Seen at the End of the Mechanical Age." It featured work by Jean Tinguely, Nam June Paik, and Kurt Schwitters. Soon, Don would draft a story called "At the End of the Mechanical Age." "It was a good age," he would write. "I was comfortable in it, relatively. Probably I will not enjoy the age to come quite so much. I don't like its look."

These days, it was hard to like the look of the city's West Side; for years, it had endured the nation's largest urban-renewal experiment, overseen by the all-powerful developer Robert Moses. As Don walked to Lincoln Center for music and film festivals, he passed newly dead-ended streets, torn-up avenues reminiscent of Paris under Baron Haussmann. Eventually, Don would write a story about a struggling family called "110 West Sixty-First Street." The setting played no part in the story except as the unspoken context in which it unfolds. But the context said it all. West Sixty-first Street was chopped off right where Don placed his beleaguered couple.

City life.

As he walked, Don felt "freaked out" about many things . . . and harbored a persistent suspicion that he'd missed something important.

"I have reached an age where I am ready to indulge myself in the luxury of not understanding everything, of not having to understand every last motherfucking nuance," he had written in an early draft of "City Life." Eventually, he cut the lines. He didn't mean it. He took a long, ragged breath and kept walking.

SLIGHTLY IRREGULAR

One day, Birgit asked Don if she could initiate an affair with a professor she had met at the New School. Don didn't answer, assuming her whim would pass and that she was trying to provoke him. He worried about his drinking. Sometimes he blacked out in the evenings after several scotches. The following morning, he'd have no memory of the night before. Birgit's scowl told him they had argued.

Eventually, Don forced a separation. His innate restlessness and the increasing difficulties of living with Birgit's disease led him to want "more freedom," Harrison Starr believes. "He didn't want the restraints and the kind of narrowness they had. He got Birgit settled around the corner on Seventh Avenue, where Waverly Place comes across, in an apartment that was kind of triangular because the Waverly intersection was oblique. Birgit began to unravel. I would go to pick Anne up, or I was taking her somewhere, and it'd be thirty degrees out and she'd have a T-shirt on. Birgit became increasingly depressed and had a couple of very self-destructive affairs . . . with Anne in the apartment."

The apartment was "dark, and it had a feeling of transience to it, as if [Birgit] was just passing through . . . which of course she was," says Sandra Leonard, an art historian and gallery director who fell in love with Starr in 1971, after Starr's separation from Sally Kempton. Don introduced Starr to her and the couple spent many evenings with Don

and Birgit. Leonard recalls the Eleventh Street apartment as "immaculate," but after Birgit moved out, it slipped into "complete disarray."

One afternoon, Starr, who had bought a carriage house on Charles Lane, and who had, he said, "always been the practical one for Donald," got a call from Don. He said, " 'Birgit.' I said, 'What is it?' And he said, 'I think she's dead.' And I said, 'I'll be right there.' I could see that she had overdosed about ten or twelve hours earlier, and I could see that she was alive. She wasn't going to die. Now whether she was brain-damaged or not, I couldn't tell. We picked her up . . . and carried her to St. Vincent's, cradling her."

When Birgit recovered, she and Anne returned to the Eleventh Street apartment with Don. Soon thereafter, he took a studio apartment down the block, close to the Hudson River. Anne thought of it as her father's "writing studio." "It wasn't a writing studio," Starr says. "It's where he moved."

Finally, early in 1972, Birgit insisted on returning to Denmark. "I think Dad knew that if he didn't let her go back to Copenhagen, she'd try to kill herself," Anne says. She and her mother flew to Denmark and stayed with one of her mother's friends in a beautiful apartment in the center of Copenhagen. Don moved back to his old place on West Eleventh. Six months later, Birgit and Anne returned to New York, but they did not move in with Don. They took a place on Perry Street. Don and Birgit tried to work things out, but the marriage was damaged beyond repair. Birgit went back to Copenhagen for good. "Anne was locked in to Donald and did not want to go," Starr says. "He and I had a fight about it because [by now] I was kind of a godfather to Anne. She did not want to go, and I told him, 'Absolutely not.' Then there was some psychiatrist who said, 'The daughter must stay with the mother, blah blah blah.' It was bullshit."

"Living with my mother was . . . well, you know . . . you're a kid. I didn't know any different," Anne says. "But I wanted to be with my father. He was more grounded."

Around the time Birgit left with Anne, Don met the Swiss novelist and poet Max Frisch, whose work he greatly admired. Frisch had come to the States with his new young wife, Marianne, for an extended series of lectures and readings. Marianne was translating *City Life* into German, for an edition to be published by Suhrkamp Verlag. Don was charmed by her intelligence, humor, and openness. While Frisch—at sixty, nearly thirty years older than his wife—relished his literary celebrity, and indulged in an affair with a publisher's assistant, Don and Marianne began to spend time together.

"Of the women I knew that [were around] Donald, she was quite different," Sandra Leonard says. "Physically different, first of all. She was *really* a woman. And she was just a delight to be around."

Starr concurs that Marianne was "physically powerful." In the past, Don had tended to be drawn to petite women with rather boyish figures. For him, this new passion was tinged with desperation: He was shaken by his separation from Birgit, though it had long been coming, and by the fear that he might lose his daughter. He had come to feel he couldn't survive without his little girl.

Marianne was drawn to Don's "tense" attentiveness, his "sparkling, cunning, laughing eyes," and his rueful humor. In a remembrance written shortly after his death, she recalled the day she told him she was translating his book. She was standing at a traffic light, waiting to cross the street at Sixth Avenue and Tenth, when she spotted Don. She asked him what he was doing there. In her remembrance piece, Marianne wrote of Don's reply and the conversation that ensued:

> "Intersections interest me. Sometimes cute girls cross. . . . Time for coffee?"
>
> Three meters from the light there was a brightly lit, sad-looking coffee shop.
>
> "Do you always cry on Saturday afternoons?"
>
> "Often."
>
> "Are you crying today because I don't write as well as Samuel Beckett?"
>
> . . . "I'm crying, first, because I'm nervous, second, because it's Saturday, and, third, because I have something difficult I should tell you."
>
> "Something criminal?"
>
> "Possibly . . . I signed a contract some weeks ago."
>
> "You're too young for contracts, much too young."
>
> "But I've signed to translate *City Life*."
>
> "That's no reason for a grown-up girl to cry."
>
> "I'm worried that Donald Barthelme's prose is too difficult for me—untranslatable."
>
> "I will translate him from English into English for you. No problem. That's my specialty. I have translated Tolstoy, Balzac, Kafka, Borges, and many, many others from English into English. I can help you even though my German is non-existent."

As she worked with him, he was a "dinosaur of patience," she recalled, "a true master." He "spoke of music, the music of words that was the most important thing, the rhythm of the sentences."

"Pretty funny, isn't it? Is it crazy enough?" he would ask her about a particular line.

When the book finally appeared in Germany, with the subtitle "Modern Classic," Don just grinned, said Marianne.

As their mutual fascination deepened, they began to meet at the Trattoria da Alfredo on the corner of Bank and Hudson streets. The place was dark inside, painted in cool greens and yellows, with rows of wine bottles on shelves around the walls.

They were genuinely anguished by the intensity of their connection. Don had enormous regard for Frisch. In "Departures," he wrote, with only slight exaggeration, of a man in similar circumstances, phoning a couple's apartment hoping to reach the woman but getting her husband instead: " 'Well . . .' I ask cordially, 'what amazing triumphs have you accomplished today?' "

In another story, "Three," Don writes fancifully of a struggle between an old man and a younger one over the older man's wife. Here, as in "Departures," the young lover is presented as miserable and ineffectual in the shadow of the brilliant elder statesman.

In 1975, Frisch published a short autobiographical novel entitled *Montauk.* Although Don is never named in the book, Frisch wrote candidly of the suspicions he had of his wife's relationship with an American writer, describing in detail the Trattoria da Alfredo and the interior of Don's apartment (with its "INGRES poster"). He quoted a passage from "Departures" ("But where are you today? Probably out with your husband for a walk. . . . Do you think he has noticed? . . . What foolishness! It is as obvious as a bumper sticker. . . .")

Frisch portrayed himself as responsible for his wife's unhappiness ("I had been preoccupied with the world") and accepting of, though saddened by, her friendship with the writer, whom he "admired." He wrote that this writer "is afraid of feelings that are not suited to publication; he takes refuge then in irony; all he perceives is considered from the point of view of whether it is worth describing, and he dislikes experiences that can never be expressed in words. A professional disease that drives many writers to drink."

Elsewhere in the book, Frisch recounted an occasion when, after an evening of eating and drinking at the Frisches' place, the writer suddenly "rose to his feet, went to the door, and disappeared." Worried, Frisch followed the man to his apartment. "Sorry," the writer told him. "I'm drunk."

Don sometimes sought late-night conversations with other women. Renata Adler recalled that at three o'clock one morning she was awakened by her apartment buzzer. "I lived then in . . . a brownstone on East Seventy-Eighth Street," she wrote in her book *Gone.* "Don came up the stairs, sat down in the living room, accepted a scotch, and said, 'All right. Go ahead and say it. I know it. You think García Márquez is a better writer than I am.' " García Márquez's breakthrough novel, *One Hundred Years of Solitude,* had appeared in English in 1970. "I said, Honestly not," Adler wrote. "I had never read García Márquez. [Don] said, 'Come on. You think García Márquez is a better writer than I am, and *A Hundred Years of Solitude* [*sic*] is a better book than I will ever write.' I said that I had truly never read García Márquez. After a while he left."

In the midst of all this, Don began an affair with Karen Kennerly. He met her through Jerome Charyn and Mark Mirsky, writers and teachers at City College with whom he had become friendly. She was putting together an anthology of fables from around the world entitled *Hesitant Wolf and Scrupulous Fox.* Random House had signed to publish it. She had gathered more than a hundred pages of notes for the introduction she needed to write for the book, but the task felt overwhelming to her and she had stalled on it. Don told her, "Write five pages and make every sentence golden." She did as he said, and came up with seven "perfect" pages.

Kennerly says, "Don had the golden ear of all time." In conversation, "every sentence he uttered was stylish, like his work." At the same time, "he didn't lead his life like a major writer who is totally boring in person. Style was simply what he breathed. Maybe his Catholic schooling accounted for his very fine manners and his formality."

She adds, "He was a tortured soul. He had a great darkness inside. And he was heartbreaking. I was very moved by him."

At the time, she was also dating Miles Davis. Naturally, this intrigued Don. "I was with Miles from 1966 to 1979," she says. "Don's story 'The Sandman' is all true. I'm the woman in that story." In the piece, the woman receives a late-night phone call from a man she is seeing. "That's Miles," Kennerly explains, " 'very good, very fast,' as the story says."

"Don always wanted to meet Miles, and Miles was curious about Don, whom he called 'Texas,' " Kennerly says. "I desperately wanted to keep them apart, because I thought Miles would outcool Don, and Don had a very big investment in being cool. One night, Don came over to my apartment and we were about to go to dinner. Miles called and said (hoarse, whispery voice), 'Whatcha doing?' I kept trying to put him off and he said, 'Is he there? Is Texas there? I'm having dinner at Elaine's. Come meet me here.' Don said, 'What is he saying? What is he saying?' I told him and he said, 'We're going.' When we got there—it was very early, about 6:30—Miles was sitting at a table by himself, already halfway through dinner. It wouldn't have occurred to him to wait on anyone. He had on these big sunglasses. Finally, Don said, 'Hey man, why don't you take off your shades?' Miles said, 'Why? It's *all* black.' After that, the conversation was very stiff. Then Miles got up and said, 'Bye. Gotta go. Good to meet you.' Don and I barely got through dinner. It was very painful. That was the only time I ever saw him out of control in a social situation—it's what I feared would happen. We asked for the check and the waiter said Miles had covered it. Don said, 'No, he has not. I am paying for

this meal. Put his money on his tab.' The waiter didn't know what to do, because Miles only came in about twice a year. Finally, I took the boy aside and
said, 'Just consider yourself lucky that you got a big tip tonight.' He kept
Miles's money and let Don pay for the dinner."

Don would tell Kennerly that Miles had a "tin ear, nowhere as good as
Charlie Parker's." Kennerly argued with him, and Don admitted, "Well, he's
great, but he's not *up there.*"

"I think he really thought that, and not just because I had been with this
very sexy man," Kennerly says. "Don always feared that he would be like
Miles, that he wouldn't be considered one of the greats."

In the early days of Kennerly's affair with Don, Anne was around much of the
time, visiting from Denmark. "I had a big mother-daughter crush on her and
had fantasies of her coming to live with me—*screw* mean old Don," Kennerly
says. "In a way, at first, Anne was our glue." In the spring of 1972, Don made
plans with Birgit to send Anne back to Denmark for the summer. When he
told Kennerly he wanted to spend the summer with her, and grow closer, she
was thrilled. He promised he'd find a summer rental for them in Maine. But
after that, whenever she'd ask about the arrangements, he'd put her off, or
say he'd checked into a couple of places but hadn't heard back from them.

"He could be a tough customer," Kennerly says. "Finally, toward the end
of spring, we were drinking somewhere in the Village, and he said the single
cruelest thing a man has ever said to me." He stroked his beard with one
hand while gripping a scotch in the other. He turned to her and said, "So.
What are *you* doing this summer?"

Kennerly was stunned. "But the truth is, we were perfectly matched," she
admits. Suspecting that Don wouldn't follow through with his promise, she
had, in fact, made other plans. She went to Ireland and had a fling with a
young Irish journalist. "Don went to Texas that summer," Kennerly says.

In Houston, Don spent time with Pat Colville, an old friend from his museum days. She and her husband, Bill, had thrown the going-away party for
Don when he first moved to Manhattan. Now she was separated from Bill,
teaching at the University of St. Thomas.

Anne had flown to Houston with Don. They stayed with his parents for a
few days until she was scheduled to travel to Copenhagen. One day, Don's sister, Joan, and her two sons accompanied Don and Anne to AstroWorld, a
Disney-like amusement park. Don tried to enjoy the outing, but all he could
think of was Anne's imminent departure.

One afternoon, Don left her with his mother and drove to Helen's advertising agency on Buffalo Drive, a busy thoroughfare near the places he and
Helen had shared in Montrose. Without warning, he walked into the office.

Helen looked up from her desk and there he stood, grinning at her. After she'd regained her composure, she said simply, "I've thought of you mostly with love and affection." Don replied, "Me, too." Quietly, she told him he'd hurt her feelings when he'd dedicated *Snow White* to Birgit. He said her letter about the dedication hurt him, as well. She stood and kissed him on the cheek. Then they hugged and laughed.

At lunch a few days later, at the Courtlandt Restaurant on Francis Street, close to the first apartment they had rented together, they caught up with each other. In addition to her work with the ad agency, Helen had been taking courses at the University of Texas and writing a Ph.D. dissertation on William Faulkner. She noticed that Don seemed nervous to be back in Houston, "apprehensive of getting too personal or at least wary of becoming nostalgic or sentimental." His boyish look was gone, she says, his red hair noticeably thinning, but he was slender and jaunty. It took her awhile to get used to the indentation in his upper lip, a result of his cancer operation.

"He was as dissatisfied as ever," she recalled. "He was not unhappy with [his] work but with what he felt was limited recognition for it." She was surprised at this, having seen the splendid reviews of *City Life*. Don's desires were contradictory: On the one hand, he wanted only readers he could respect; on the other, he felt his audience was too small, made up only of a few *New Yorker* readers and the literati in Europe.

Mostly, Don talked about Anne, about the anguish he felt because of living much of the year without her. He told Helen he "couldn't have made it" without his daughter. Of Birgit, he simply said that she was ill. She often phoned him from Denmark, seeking help with problems he couldn't assist her with long-distance, like locating her misplaced checkbook.

Helen saw Don frequently that summer at social events where he'd show up with Pat Colville. Helen was still dating Sam Southwell; they were considering marriage. Don told her he no longer expected marriage to provide an "ideal relationship."

Back in New York, he resumed his affair with Karen Kennerly. He told her he had been miserable in Texas, and he seemed distressed that she had enjoyed herself in Ireland. He appeared to doubt his virility around her, though this struck her as silly: "We made love every night. He was in his early forties, and his drinking didn't slow him down," she says. He'd point to young men in the street and tease her, saying, "*He* could be your lover. Or what about *him*?"

When she told him about her Irish fling, "he started hammering away at my self-esteem, telling me I couldn't be happy, [that] I was an anxious, depressed type," she says. "Like many male writers, Don, I think, wanted someone simpler than he was, less complicated."

She says, "He was spooked by a lot of things."

"Donald was extremely fond of women, and it's not gossipy to say that," says the novelist Walter Abish, who met Don around this time. "It was central to him; it was in his makeup. And it was also literary. I mean, read the writing: There is concealment there. . . ." A love of language, games—the flirtations, the obstacles, the *overcoming* of obstacles—that keep things interesting between women and men.

HITHERING THITHERING

In the midst of his domestic churning, Don gathered several copyright-free nineteenth-century illustrations to make a picture book for Anne. He called the book *The Slightly Irregular Fire Engine, or The Hithering Thithering Djinn.* Farrar, Straus and Giroux published it in 1971.

The "book was dictated by the pictures," Don said. The "text was written to fit" them. A knitting pirate becomes one of the central characters, whom the heroine, Mathilda, encounters in a magical Chinese pagoda that appears mysteriously in her yard one day. "The pirate comes from a rather well-known children's book of the period, which had an entirely different story," Don said.

His illustrations are accompanied by legends such as "SLEN-DER-WAISTEDNESS / Corseted Divinities with Waspish Affinities / Worrying, Flurrying" and "BURIED JEWELS / Oceanic Dredging Company." Sometimes, the legends enhance a particular picture. For example, when the pagoda appears out of nowhere in Mathilda's backyard, the phrase "Suburban Disturbance" lines the right-hand margin of the page. In other cases, the legends bear only a peripheral relationship to the story line: Surrealism for children.

The legends "come from a nineteenth-century printer's type-specimen book," Don explained. "It's a catalog from which printers can order type, samples from type specimens, and whoever set the

specimens was wonderfully funny and imaginative. . . . I just took them out of the catalog and used them . . . as a design element to make the pages more interesting. . . ."

The pagoda is stuffed with astonishing surprises—a tumbling elephant, a rainmaker, a "barrel of pickles surmounted by a sour and severe citizen"—none of which satisfies Mathilda. She wants a bright red fire engine. Finally, the pagoda vanishes, leaving in its stead a *green* fire truck. Well, "green is a beautiful color too," Mathilda concedes.

In *The Slightly Irregular Fire Engine,* Don suggested that the world of "CONTENTMENT" is bought at a severe price ("Corseted Divinities . . . Worrying, Flurrying"). "Entertainment" is our only means of escaping worry. Yet there are limits to what we imagine. The adventurous pirate has been reduced to a harmless domestic figure, knitting and rocking in a chair. The truck comes painted in the wrong color. The Victorian illustrations remind children *and* adults of Lewis Carroll, but they locate this remarkable world at an unreachable distance from us.

"I never saw *The Slightly Irregular Fire Engine* in progress," Anne says. Don said he "tried it out" on Anne, on one of her visits to New York, "and she was kind enough to say that she liked it very much."

While he may have discovered the pirate pictures at random, their appeal for him was tied to his childhood delight in Sabatini. He was sharing a cherished personal pleasure with his daughter.

The book ends with a portrait of a "gay and laughing couple," Mathilda's parents, accompanied by the caption "CONTENTMENT." Given Anne's family situation, this was heavily ironic—it was also a poignant recognition of what Anne most desired, just as Mathilda wants a fire engine. Don gave his daughter what she was after . . . but only in fiction. It was the best he could do.

Reviewers were generally respectful of *The Slightly Irregular Fire Engine,* but they were concerned that it might sail over the heads of many children. The book was distinguished by "elegant chatter," but the pictures were "too static" for kids, grumbled *Time*'s reviewer. Writing in *The New York Times Book Review,* Selma G. Lanes praised Don's "felicitous and blithe voice," his "considerable promise as an author for children," but she also worried that kids, lacking a sense of nostalgia, wouldn't enjoy the "wooden" Victorian illustrations. In *The New Yorker,* Jean Stafford effused over this "immensely captivating" book with its "disconcertingly bright" heroine. Roger Straus was pleased enough with the book's reception to offer Don a contract for a second children's volume (which he never attempted).

Don had published two books in two years, one of which, *City Life,* had received extraordinary attention, but he struggled during this period to please Roger Angell. At this point, Angell was the reader Don most trusted; he spi-

raled into a "panic" whenever Angell went on vacation, but these days—
particularly throughout the summer, fall, and winter of 1972—Angell rejected more of Don's stories than he accepted. "Badly strained," "much too
close to Joyce," "familiar and overused irony"—these were Angell's typical responses. To the editor of an anthology seeking to reprint the definitive version of one of Don's stories, Angell said, "Almost everything [Barthelme]
submits these days seems to be in midstage; he keeps revising even the stories we have purchased, right up to the page proof, so one can't be too defi-
nite in advance about the final look of the thing."

"At the End of the Mechanical Age," in retrospect one of Don's funniest,
most charming pieces, elicited an "unhappy opinion" from Angell; "The Educational Experience," a parody of academia, left him "irritated" at its ab-
struseness. He "didn't admire" "Swallowing," Don's satire on the Nixon
administration; he passed on "Three." "Belief," a wry meditation on aging,
he returned without comment.

"I feel especially bad about hitting you with so many rejections in the
midst of a difficult time for you," he told Don. "I'm sure this is only a temporary phenomenon. There is *no* feeling here that we care less for your work,
and I don't think we are judging it in any new way."

A month or so later, on October 10, 1972, Angell wrote to Don, "I'm unhappily aware that a) You are in a slump, or b) We are in a slump, or c) We are
both in a slump. I'm sure it's not much consolation to you when I say that
these bumpy stretches happen to all writers and that they go away of their
own accord. . . . In any case, I hope you know that it distresses me to disap-
point you this way. We can talk about this at any time if you want to."

He also reminded Don that his current indebtedness to the magazine
stood at $1,778.

On the occasions when Angell *was* pleased with the work, Don wasn't
happy. He withdrew a story that the magazine had bought, and was forced to
return the $1,375 advance. On September 9, 1972, *The New Yorker* published
a piece called "Edwards, Amelia." Don didn't like it enough to ever reprint it
in a book. The title character, listless and depressed, feels that her life is
falling apart, but she doesn't have the energy or the will to do much about it.
She wonders, "Am I a standard-issue American alcoholic?"

Despite Angell's assertion that he wasn't judging Don differently now, a mild
peevishness crept into his letters during this period, apparently in the conviction that Don was living recklessly.

Certainly, the drinking was a concern. But Angell seemed just as irked at
Don's hithering and thithering. He was in and out of Houston. In the fall of
1972, he accepted a temporary teaching position at the State University of

New York at Buffalo. John Barth recruited him as a sabbatical replacement. At first, Don didn't relish the idea of teaching creative writing, but he needed the money. He owed *The New Yorker*—perpetually—and he had assumed full financial responsibility for Birgit and Anne.

Angell never said so directly, but he appeared to feel that Don should stay put and concentrate on his fiction. "How was the Buffalo hunt?" he asked rather snidely near the beginning of September. A few weeks later, he complained, "I tried to reach you this morning, but I guess you're back in Buffalo." In mid-October, as he tried to clarify his negative reactions to Don's recent stories, his wording got tangled, and he quipped, "You can ask your students to straighten out that metaphor."

Teaching gave Don a merciful respite from his back-and-forth with the magazine; though he remained aloof and awkward in public, contact with young writers energized him.

In the late 1960s and early 1970s, SUNY Buffalo had the money and the vision to assemble possibly the most astounding English Department in the country. Under the leadership of its chair, Al Cook, the department hired or brought in as visitors Barth, Leslie Fiedler, Charles Olsen, Robert Creeley, Lionel Abel, Hélène Cixous, Michel Foucault, Eugenio Donato, John Logan, J. M. Coetzee, Robert Hass, Dwight Macdonald, and Don—a stellar team of scholars and artists (if disproportionately male). Some of them, including Don, did not have university degrees, but the school recognized their impact on American arts and letters and hired them anyway.

Don's "literary income never kept pace with his literary stature, and he remarked to me . . . that he could remember scarcely a month in his adult life when he hadn't had to worry seriously about paying the bills," Barth recalled. The pay was good at Buffalo and Don's teaching responsibilities "entail[ed] only a pair of once-a-week workshop sessions and conferences with the apprentice writers; he could fly out to the Queen City overnight, do his seminars and conferences, and take his week's worth of manuscripts home to West Eleventh Street for line-editing," Barth said.

Privately, Barth worried that Don's inexperience in the classroom, and his desire to commute from Manhattan, would "short-change" his students. "What Donald did, in fact, was *long*-change them," Barth said. "Word reached me . . . that he and they were publishing the best of the students' work in . . . tabloid format . . . complete with wonderful graphics by Donald himself." Furthermore, "he let them take him after class to Buffalo neighborhood bars, where he instructed them in the perils of alcohol for aspiring American writers."

"The key thing about those years" at SUNY Buffalo "was the war in

Southeast Asia," recalled Bruce Jackson, a young professor in the department then. "It touched nearly everything we did: how we taught our classes, the lives of our students, our conversations. You can't imagine now the antipathy between town and gown. For a time, hundreds of Buffalo policemen in riot gear occupied the Main Street campus. Forty-five faculty were arrested for demonstrating against the war in the administration building one Sunday morning." Tear-gas canisters "were fired into stairwells of the old Norton Union (now part of the School of Dental Medicine) so they would enter the circulating air system of the entire building." Though Don was not involved in antiwar activity on campus (after the killings at Kent State, most people were literally gun-shy), Buffalo's air was tinged with chaos.

"He seemed sad," says Michael Silverblatt, one of Don's students, and now the host of the syndicated radio talk show *Bookworm.* "A friend and I talked about getting him a dog. We gave him a collection of some of our favorite objects and he arranged them into an altar; he really did like making collage. We all began making altars, kept in the corner of the room, or on a shelf. I had a Donald altar."

In class, Don "could be terrifying," Silverblatt recalls. He'd suddenly "toss out a phrase like 'Me pap! Me pap!' and be utterly disappointed that I didn't know it came from [Beckett's] 'Endgame.' It was a pop quiz." Don never questioned the "content of a story, only the language. And he edited word by word." He never "changed a student writer's sense of truth."

He was a "little stern, always noble, very funny—but the funny things he said were a little dour," says Silverblatt. "He advised me several times that 'we were put here on earth to love one another.' I once heard him say, 'You make my life a living hell,' to a dear friend and she answered, right back, 'You make my life a living hell.' I remember that this was said in the friendliest way, while Don fixed barbecued ribs for supper."

On his father's advice, Don started trusting his money—including his earnings from teaching—to an accountant, who told him how much to spend and when.

On Don's frequent visits to Houston, he rented an apartment, a short-term arrangement, on Richmond Avenue in Montrose. For a while, he continued to see Pat Colville, but she disapproved of his drinking. At a party one evening in the fall of 1973, he ran into Helen and Sam Southwell. "I saw him looking closely at Sam and a few days later, when he asked what Sam had said about him, I replied that he thought Don seemed 'noble and graceful,'" Helen recalled. "Clearly satisfied with the description, he said of Sam that he 'looked quite strong.'"

Don had gone to Texas that autumn under the auspices of the Southwest

Writers Conference. He taught a fiction workshop and held individual manuscript conferences with paid participants. Beverly Lowry, who would eventually become a successful novelist but who at that time had published
nothing, recalled her "lesson" with him at the conference. "We [met] at a
table in the middle of a wide and busy hall [at the University of Houston].
Around us, other literary pilgrims met, consulted, and milled about." Don
stood with "[s]pine erect." He "held himself at a tilt, as if to get a bead on whatever action was in the works."

He took her story manuscript and "blue-penciled" it, pragmatically,
straightforwardly. "He ran his pen down a page to these sentences: 'I never
said a word, never asked, never complained. I did the dishes.'

"He peered down his eyebones," Lowry said. " 'You don't have to do this of
course,' [he said]. And he made the one substantial change he was to suggest
that day:

" '*I never said a word, never asked, never complained.* Period, new paragraph. *What I did was the dishes.*'

"In low comedy, I'd have slapped my forehead with the heel of my hand,"
Lowry recalled. "It was like jokes, after all; you had to set up the punchline,
same as Henny Youngman."

During this period, Don's frustrations with Roger Angell were minor compared to his friend Mark Mirsky's fury at the American literary scene. "I had
been trekking over to Donald's [West Village apartment] to listen to his talk
about books and show him my own work," Mirsky wrote in a history of *Fiction*
magazine. "At one moment I . . . angrily threatened to bring out a magazine
in pure spite at the vast conspiracy of indifference" toward quality fiction in
this country. Don took him up on this, and said, "I will do the layout."

In this way, *Fiction* magazine "owed its existence to Donald Barthelme,"
said Mirsky.

Mirsky approached City College for funding, but the school blew "hot
and cold" on the project. Mirsky's hopes flagged, but on his own Don produced a "handsome dummy page which was the basis for the first issue's design and layout"—"three elegant walls of type" enhanced by a whimsical
collage. "I knew that if we never went beyond a single number of *Fiction,* it
would be worth it, whatever the contents, just to hold [Donald's] work . . . in
my hands," Mirsky said.

He begged donations from friends and took money from his savings account to jump-start the first issue. Together, he and Don solicited stories
from Stanley Elkin, John Hawkes, Max Frisch, Jerome Charyn, and John Ashbery (who submitted an excerpt of what would later become *Three Poems*).

Late one afternoon, Don went to the typesetters to supervise the final pasteup. He took a bottle of scotch along with him. In his enthusiasm, he spilled a drink over several of the boards. Mirsky showed up and saw him "holding the wet paste-up, abashed. . . . It was one of those rare moments when I saw him in boyish embarrassment," Mirsky said. In the end, Don and a couple of Mirsky's friends chipped in to cover the redo costs.

One day, as they were editing manuscripts in Don's apartment, Don told Mirsky, "There's a woman downstairs"—Faith Sale—"who is willing to help you with the copy editing."

"[Eventually] many of our most important submissions came through her," Mirsky wrote, adding:

> She was far shrewder than I about commercial fiction but not as sympathetic to surrealism, or the experimental novel. . . . Donald enjoyed arbitrating between us. Faith . . . was more than alert to my tendency to irresponsibility, my desertions of duty at the helm (I was often on [my] motorcycle escaping into the country [and she was] not shy about scolding me). This was just what Donald loved, two editors at daggers with each other—he was the pacifying father. . . .
> The role she fell into with Donald was [one of] motherly concern . . .

"About Faith," says Kirk Sale, "the first thing to know is that after our second daughter was old enough to go to kindergarten, Don one day told me that she should go to work . . . he would ask [a] friend at Dutton to give her a job. She was reluctant—she was working as a freelance copy editor then, and organizing a freelancers' union so they could get reasonable pay—but Don went ahead and got her the job, which she loved, and she moved on and up. She always gave him credit. Their working arrangements were close, and I think he really loved her in his way—love was not something he would ever declare, at least to anyone other than his wives.

"On *Fiction,* Don more or less had his way."

Jerome Charyn, who soon joined the *Fiction* staff, agrees. "He gave it such flair in terms of its design. You felt his absolute seriousness. Everyone had such respect for him. All these writers—Günter Grass, Max Frisch, John Barth—wanted to be in a magazine where he played such a dominant role. No one got paid anything, but we never had trouble getting work from anyone. I even asked John Lennon for a piece and he gave it to us." (Lennon and Yoko Ono lived in the West Village then, on Bank Street).

Finally, the first issue was ready for distribution. For its cover, Don created a hilarious collage: Little Red Riding Hood in bed with the wolf (wearing a bow-tied granny cap); on the golden wallpaper behind the bed was the face of Marcel Proust, repeated dozens of times.

Mirsky believes *Fiction* was born in a "bleak moment" for American

literature, and this accounts for its "noisemaking: the fact that for an instant we were able to get national attention—the back page of *The New York
Times Book Review, New York* magazine's 'Best Bets,' a lot of newspaper coverage" (including notices in *The Washington Post* and the *St. Louis Post-
Dispatch*).

The truth is, quality fiction has always had to fight for notice in America;
Fiction's visibility had to do with Don's growing literary celebrity. NBC's *Today* show called, said Mirsky, and asked if "we could produce one of [*Fiction*'s]
famous writers, they would be interested in having us on television." Mirsky
knew they were "angling" for Don, who refused to appear.

The *Fiction* staff—Mirsky, Jane DeLynn, Penny Blum, Kathy Harman—
arranged to distribute five thousand copies of the magazine across the city.
Quickly, they learned harsh truths about the "wars of . . . newstand deliverers,
the piracy of distributors, the Mafia." Still, within days, five hundred copies
"melted away" at the Eighth Street Bookstore—Ted Wilentz placed issues
prominently next to the cash register. They sold for fifty cents apiece. "We
were never able to collect, however, from the distributors who brought it to the
newstands," Mirsky wrote. Don stored unsold copies in one of his bedrooms.

Six months after the inaugural issue appeared, Tom Wolfe attacked
Mirsky in *Esquire*. "The idea that the novel has a spiritual function of providing a mythic consciousness for the people is . . . popular within the literary community today," Wolfe said. "[In *The New York Times Book Review*]
Mark J. Mirsky writes a manifesto for a new periodical called *Fiction* devoted
to reviving the art [of myth] in the 1970's." But, Wolfe contended, myth
couldn't have been "further from the minds of the realists who established
the novel as the reigning genre over a hundred years ago. As a matter of fact,
they were turning their backs, with a kind of mucker's euphoria, on the idea
of myth and fable."

Wolfe ended by exalting the true to life over fairy tales.

Don took the attack in stride—he had heard Wolfe's howling before. But
Mirsky was furious. *Esquire* refused him reply space. All he could do was
mutter to friends that Wolfe "had amnesia" about the origins of realism. In
the meantime, quietly wounded, he hustled *Fiction* from bookstore to bookstore.

Magazine work and teaching were time-consuming and draining, but also
revitalizing for Don. Briefly, he distracted himself from worries about Anne.
He could work through literary problems unrelated to his own writing
(though he continued to labor diligently on stories), and he was surrounded
by people—students and younger colleagues—who looked to him as a pioneer, a mentor, a father figure.

"I was in every sense his junior and happy to carry his cup of coffee," Mirsky says.

Nationally, Don's profile continued to rise. Leslie Cross, a reporter from the *Milwaukee Journal,* who was visiting New York, called and asked to interview him. Surprised and pleased that a woman from Milwaukee had read his fiction, Don met her at the Cedar Tavern. Immediately, he asked her if she'd seen *Fiction* magazine. He was quite proud of it. "When a magazine like *Harper's Bazaar* announces it isn't buying any more fiction and book publishers cut back on their fiction lists but find money for stuff like *Valley of the Dolls,* that seems to me madness, sheer idiocy. So we're getting out this newspaper," he said. "It's a co-op: the writers don't get paid; the artists don't get paid; the editors get paid, the printers get paid. It's cheap to produce because it's on newsprint and it's done offset. It's printed in a Chinese plant down in Broome Street. This causes some problems because they don't speak much English around there. But it's selling!"

Don was getting ready for another trip to Buffalo. Ms. Cross wondered if writing could really be taught. No, Don said, but it could be encouraged. "I don't lecture," he explained. "Rather than talking about the art of fiction—which I haven't yet understood myself—I read manuscripts. I take a pencil and say, 'This is good' or 'That sentence doesn't do what you want it to do.' All the while I emphasize that this is only one man's opinion—I might be wrong, but consider it. I try to bring up what the student is trying to do, because you don't want to produce little imitations of yourself. I'm fairly rough with their manuscripts, and they appreciate it."

After a couple of drinks, Don said he had to go. The Sales were having plumbing problems, and Don had to let them into his apartment so they could take baths. He helped Ms. Cross hail a cab. With "Texas-sized strides," she said, he walked back up West Eleventh Street. That evening, he was due at Grace Paley's for supper: one last taste of neighborhood comfort before braving the snows of Buffalo.

Along with newspaper reporters, young academic scholars were beginning to notice Don. In December 1972, he was asked to give a formal talk on fiction at the annual meeting of the Modern Language Association, the nation's largest professional organization for English professors. Serious critical articles on Don's work had been published in *The Atlantic Monthly, Harper's, The New Republic,* and *The New York Review of Books,* as well as in academic journals such as *Twentieth Century Literature, The Minnesota Review, Modern Occasions, The Hudson Review,* and the *Western Humanities Review.* Don's stories received lengthy attention in books, including Tony Tanner's *City of Words,* William Peden's *The American Short Story,* Charles B.

Harris's *Contemporary American Novelists of the Absurd,* and Ihab Hassan's *Contemporary American Literature.* Most of these commentators classified Don as a "black humorist" whose "disjunctions" came from the "absurdity" of modern life, or they hailed him as the most successful purveyor of American Surrealism.

A dissenting voice rose from Joyce Carol Oates, who wrote in the June 4, 1972, issue of *The New York Times Book Review* that Don's art was random, antiseptic, unemotional, disengaged from the world, and ultimately irresponsible. "If you refuse to make choices," she said, accusing Don's fiction of lacking clear values, "someone else will make them for you."

In the early 1970s, the most determined scholar pursuing Don was an assistant professor at Northern Illinois University named Jerome Klinkowitz. He taught contemporary literature and, finding Don's work distinctive, wrote to him care of Lynn Nesbit. He asked to do an interview—which eventually appeared in a book called *The New Fiction: Interviews with Innovative American Writers,* edited by Joe David Bellamy and published by the University of Illinois Press in 1974. The book included talks with John Barth, Susan Sontag, Kurt Vonnegut, William Gass, Joyce Carol Oates, and others.

Don told Klinkowitz in a letter, "Usually I don't like to be interviewed, for several reasons, among which Paranoia is probably Paramount. However, your project sounds like a meaningful one, and I would be willing to answer written questions, which would give me an opportunity to think rather than mumble."

Klinkowitz "put together a kit of sorts, with each question typed at the head of a blank page which Barthelme could fill as amply or sparsely as he chose." When a month passed with no reply from Don, Klinkowitz nudged him with a note. Don wrote back, "Dear Mr. Klinkowitz—I know I know I know."

Another month of silence ensued. Klinkowitz was about to write Don again, when the phone rang late one afternoon. "The voice was clipped and mannered in a way that sounded almost British, and I was surprised to hear it was Donald Barthelme calling from New York," Klinkowitz said. He recalled their conversation:

> "I've just put my answers to your questions in the mail," he said, and I remarked that this was good news indeed and thanked him. Yet his tone was anything but happy; in fact, he was apologizing for the material, and urged that I not even open the package when it arrived.
>
> "Are you retracting the interview?" I asked in alarm, but Barthelme assured me that he wasn't, that I could do anything I wanted with his answers. He just felt badly that "they weren't any good," and didn't want me to be bothered with such nonsense.

"I thought of pulling them out of the mailbox," he admitted, "but that would be misunderstood."

In fact, Klinkowitz was delighted with the answers. They were full, funny, and honest, touching on Don's journalistic background, his love of music, and his passion for European literature. "I think fewer people are reading," he said in answer to a question about the "death of the novel." "I invite you to notice that the new opium of the people is opium, or at least morphine. In a situation in which morphine contends with morpheme, the latter loses every time." As for his working methods, Don said, "I do a lot of failing and that keeps me interested."

In preparing the interview for book publication, Klinkowitz arranged the Q & A in *New Yorker*-style columns and type. This distressed Don. "I think it's too cute and also serves to place too much emphasis on the NYer—as if the magazine were in some sense responsible for what I do," he said. Klinkowitz agreed to drop the format.

Don could not resist devising his own question to end the piece: "In your story 'See the Moon?' one of the characters has the line 'Fragments are the only forms I trust.' This has been quoted as a statement of your aesthetic. Is it?"

Don answered Don: "No. It's a statement by a character about what he is feeling at that particular moment. I hope that whatever I think about aesthetics would be a shade more complicated than that. Because that particular line has been richly misunderstood so often (most recently by my colleague J. C. Oates in the *Times*), I have thought of making a public recantation. I can see the story in, say, *Women's Wear Daily:*

"WRITER CONFESSES THAT HE NO LONGER TRUSTS FRAGMENTS

"Trust 'Misplaced,' Author Declares

"DISCUSSED DECISION WITH DAUGHTER, SIX

"Will Seek 'Wholes' in Future, He Says"

"NEW YORK, JUNE 24 (A & P)—Donald Barthelme, 41-year-old writer and well-known fragmentist, said today that he no longer trusted fragments. He added that although he had once been 'very fond' of fragments, he had found them to be 'finally untrustworthy.'

"The author, looking tense and drawn after what was described as 'considerable thought,' made his dramatic late-night announcement at a Sixth Avenue laundromat press conference, from which the press was excluded.

"Sources close to the soap machine said, however, that the agonizing reappraisal, which took place before their eyes, required only four minutes.

" 'Fragments fall apart a lot,' Barthelme said. Use of antelope blood as a bonding agent had not proved . . . ' "

This was not the sort of reply to appease stern critics.

In 1972, Don received the Zabel Award from the American Academy of Arts and Letters, in recognition of his achievement in writing. *The Slightly Irregular Fire Engine* was nominated for a National Book Award.

The NBA was a twenty-two-year-old program in 1972—a series of literary prizes funded by the book industry and administered by a committee composed of a group of editors, sales personnel, publicists, book reviewers, and former prizewinners. Annually, the committee awarded one-thousand-dollar prizes to the authors of the year's "best books," in an effort to promote the "wider and wiser use of books." Initially, the committee considered only fiction, nonfiction, and poetry. By 1972, the number of prize categories had jumped to ten, to include Arts and Letters, Biography, Contemporary Affairs, Fiction, History, Children's Books, Philosophy and Religion, Poetry, the Sciences, and Translation. Literary purists grumbled that the awards had been watered down, publicists were happy to pounce on several new advertising opportunities, and in general the NBA tried to steer an honest course between literary excellence and good business.

The award ceremonies were held in Lincoln Center's Alice Tully Hall in late April. By all accounts, it was a rather melancholy affair. Three of the prizewinners were dead. Flannery O'Connor, who had passed away in 1964, topped the fiction category with her just-published volume of collected stories. The late Frank O'Hara's *Collected Poems* split the poetry prize with Howard Moss's *Selected Poems,* and the history award went to the recently deceased Allan Nevins for the final two volumes of *Ordeal of the Union,* his eight-volume study of the Civil War.

The ceremony was made even gloomier by many of the prizewinners' forecasts about the planet, the subject of several nominated books, such as George L. Small's lament for the vanishing *Blue Whale.* Other speakers warned against creeping commercialism in the book trade; the previous year, businessman Leonard Riggio had bought New York's floundering Barnes & Noble store, sold B & N's publishing division to Harper & Row, and made plans to create a huge discount-bookselling chain, sending tremors of fear through small presses and literary enthusiasts.

And what would an awards show be without controversy? Gary Wills walked out when his fellow judges in Contemporary Affairs chose *The Last Whole Earth Catalogue,* a "non-book," said Wills, put together by a committee. And Lore Segal, a longtime writer of juveniles, protested when her fellow judges awarded a newcomer who had weighed in with a decidedly off-kilter book: Donald Barthelme and *The Slightly Irregular Fire Engine.*

Unlike many of the winners, Don kept his acceptance speech to a graceful minimum. "Writing for children, like talking to them, is full of mysteries," he said, adding:

> I have a child, a six-year-old, and I assure you I approach her with a copy of Mr. Empson's *Seven Types of Ambiguity* held firmly in my right hand. If I ask her which of two types of cereal she prefers for breakfast, I invariably find upon presenting the bowl that I have misread my instructions—that it was the other kind she wanted. In the same way it is quite conceivable to me that I may have written the wrong book—some other book was what was wanted. One does the best one can. I must point out that television has affected the situation enormously. My pictures don't move. What's wrong with them? I went into this with Michael di Capua, my editor [for *this* book] at Farrar, Straus and Giroux, who incidentally improved the book out of all recognition, and he told me sadly that no, he couldn't make the pictures move. I asked my child once what her mother was doing, at a particular moment, and she replied that mother was "watching a book." The difficulty is to manage a book worth watching. The problem, as I say, is full of mysteries, but mysteries are not to be avoided. Rather they are a locus of hope, they enrich and complicate. That is why we have them. That is perhaps one of the reasons why we have children.

SADNESS

Sadness, Don's fourth short story collection, published on September 19, 1972, signaled a more personal turn in his work. Though most of its contents had appeared in *The New Yorker* over the previous three years, the most formally complex pieces, "Traumerei" and "The Sandman," had been rejected by the magazine. Don did not include "The Educational Experience" and "At the End of the Mechanical Age," which Angell had passed on.

The book contained fewer graphics and less typographical play than Don's earlier efforts—Angell had informed him that William Shawn was getting fed up with such stuff, so Don produced less of it. He worked significant changes on "The Flight of Pigeons from the Palace" and "A Film" between magazine and book publication—mostly to avoid repetitions and set pieces that didn't contribute to an overall effect. The order of the stories in prepublication galleys differs widely from that of the finished book. The shuffling indicates that Don was still trying to get a feel for the new directions and registers of the stories—directions implied by the simplicity of the title.

"*Sadness* was a different sort of title [for me]," Don said, "and I thought a long while before using it. And somebody, I think it was Rust Hills of *Esquire,* inquired how the devil I ever got the publishers to accept it, how I got away with it. I'm not sure I did get away

with it in the sense of having it work as a book title, but it's not embarrassing to look at. Of course, it's ironic, as well as being what it is."

Wordplay remains central to his fiction, but more than expressing verbal irony, the title emphasizes a psychological stance toward the world. This is underscored in the one passage in the book that includes the word *sadness*. In the story "The Rise of Capitalism," the narrator says, "The first thing I did was make a mistake. I thought I had understood capitalism, but what I had done was assume an attitude—melancholy sadness—toward it." Don's satire, wit, and erudition are abundant from page to page, but more than his previous collections, the book explores the attitudes of recognizable men and women living under late capitalism in late-twentieth-century America.

Reviewing the collection in the November 5, 1972, issue of *The New York Times Book Review,* Charles Thomas Samuels neatly summarized the shift that had taken place in Don's writing:

> Before *Sadness* . . . most of Barthelme's best stories put you into the problem of art in a world hostile to the continued vitality of imagination . . . [the] stories [in *City Life*] constitute brilliant literary criticism written in fictive form. Anxious parables, they assert that literature, which was once a means of revitalizing the imagination and opposing banality, has itself become exhausted and banal.
>
> The best stories in *Sadness* put us into a different, though related, problem. Not parables so much as monologues spoken by neurasthenics, they throb with distress at what one of them calls "the present era's emphasis on emotional cost control" and "its insistent, almost annoying lucidity."

Oblique literary references energize the stories. As usual, Kierkegaard preoccupied Don. The narrator's self-disgust in "The Party" ("Wonderful elegance! No good at all!") recalls a famous passage in Kierkegaard's journals in which he berates himself for his "witticisms" at a party and feels such emptiness he wants to shoot himself. The ordinary saint in "The Temptation of St. Anthony" is an embodiment of Kierkegaard's "Knight of Faith," as well as a first cousin to Flaubert's St. Anthony.

Passages from Paul Klee's published diary appear, barely transformed, in "Engineer-Private Paul Klee Misplaces an Aircraft Between Milbertshofen and Cambrai, March 1916" (a story equating art to fraud). King Kong's dialogue in "The Party" is a clear homage to Kafka's "A Report to an Academy."

But for all these references, the book is characterized by remarkable straightforwardness and a strong autobiographical strain. In "Critique de la Vie Quotidienne," Don mined details from his marriage to Birgit. "A City of Churches" is a phrase he often used to describe Houston. "The Genius" also tips its hat to Texas: At the end of the story, the Genius receives a gift from the mayor and city council of Houston, a "field of stainless steel tulips." The image may have been suggested by the life-size metal palm tree adorning the lot of Houston's Contemporary Arts Museum. "Perpetua" appears to be a satiric response to a feminist call to action, "Cutting Loose: A Private View of the Women's Uprising," published in *Esquire* by Sally Kempton, Harrison Starr's ex, in which she claimed most men need to marry a child in order to protect their egos. (Don dedicated the book to Starr and his new wife, Sandra). "The Catechist" takes us back to Catholic teaching, and "Departures" touches on many of Don's experiences, not the least of which is his friendship with Marianne Frisch.

A character in "Daumier," sounding very much like Don, thinks, "[Y]ou want nothing so much as a deep-going, fundamental involvement—but this does not seem to happen. Your attachments are measured. . . . What does this say about you—that you move from person to person, a tourist of the emotions? Is this the meaning of failure?"

Perhaps the clearest autobiographical note rings in the depictions of mental effort and its costs. "I always say to myself, 'What is the most important thing I can be thinking about at this minute?' " the Genius says. The narrator of "The Party" muses, "Of course we tried hard, it was intelligent to do so, extraordinary efforts were routine," but he winds up lamenting, "What made us think that we would escape things like bankruptcy, alcoholism, being disappointed . . ." In "Subpoena," the narrator tries to comfort himself: "See, it is possible to live in the world and not change the world."

Don's strengths were best displayed in "The Sandman." It picked up where "Views of My Father Weeping" left off, probing Freud's theories of sexuality with marvelous textual compression, but it presented a more contemporary and forthright surface.

The story grows out of E. T. A. Hoffmann's "The Sandman" (1815) and Freud's "The Uncanny" (1919). Hoffmann's fantastic tale, related partially in a series of letters, concerns a young man named Nathaniel. He is haunted by an evil figure, a friend of his father, who threatens to snatch Nathaniel's eyes. As an adult, Nathaniel continues to be stalked by this presence; he is unable to find romantic fulfillment—unable to distinguish reality from fantasy—and he winds up a suicide, driven to his death by the reappearance of the threatening man.

In "The Uncanny"—in part, an examination of Hoffmann's story—Freud said that, symbolically, Nathaniel's papa and the evil figure were one, representing a child's ambivalence toward his father. The fear of losing one's eyes is "a substitute for the dread of being castrated." Nathaniel's inability to form a mature and stable sexual union is related to his failure to resolve Oedipal tensions.

Don's story is in the form of a letter: A man writes to his girlfriend's "shrink" to challenge the therapist's analysis of the woman. He asks the therapist not to show his letter to his girlfriend. "Please consider this an 'eyes only' letter," he says.

He heaps scorn upon psychoanalytic theory, yet he quotes a variety of sources (Anton Ehrenzweig, Walker Percy, Erwin W. Strauss) to buttress his theoretical arguments. At one point he tells the therapist, "I thought of making a personal visit [to you to discuss Susan, the girlfriend] "but the situation then, as I'm sure you understand, would be completely untenable—I would be *visiting a psychiatrist.*"

Despite his contempt for the doctor, he has made an overture by writing the letter. The Percy passage suggests that reversals by doctors and patients are common maneuvers in psychoanalytic procedures; the narrator's protests might be cries of help. His defensiveness masks some shame. What about? According to Ehrenzweig, Oedipal fears and the role guilt plays in the ego's death wish.

On the other hand, the narrator cites "Shame as a Historiological Problem" by Erwin Strauss. Shame is a healthy impulse, Straus says, protecting whatever is still in the act of "becoming"—a new love affair, a creative project—from the destructiveness of public exposure. Exposure "completes" a process before it is ready to be formed. "Becoming" is thwarted and it shrivels. Hiding and shame can be powerful, positive virtues.

Don's narrator is a man torn between the desire to escape the torments of his shame and his impulse to protect his creative and erotic vitality.

As for the girlfriend's depressions: "I wouldn't do anything," he says. "I'd leave them alone. Put on a record." In a footnote, he recommends George Harrison's song "Wah-Wah" (from Harrison's spiritually pitched album, *All Things Must Pass*). "What I am saying is that Susan is wonderful. *As is,*" he concludes. "There are not so many things around to which that word can be accurately applied. Therefore I must view your efforts to improve her with, let us say, a certain amount of ambivalence."

The narrator asserts, "The world *is* unsatisfactory; only a fool would deny it," but ultimately he affirms things as they are, embracing the ordinary, even run-of-the-mill problems. This was a new note in Don's work, and it would be repeated in work to come.

Sadness received near-unanimous praise from book reviewers. In *The Saturday Review,* John Seelye called Don's stories "serious toys." "The artistic tradition in which Barthelme works originated in the legendary company of magicians, jugglers, tightrope walkers, necromancers, wizards of all sorts," he wrote. Guy Davenport, writing in the *National Review,* said that Don was the "first American writer" to understand and adopt the strategies of the great modernists such as Flaubert, Joyce, and Beckett. "Barthelme's talent is real, authentic, and thoroughly new," he said. Charles Thomas Samuels concluded that Don had written "stories that belong among the finest examples of the art in recent times."

A few years earlier, Don had announced his literary arrival with absurd, combative, and blustery titles such as *Come Back, Dr. Caligari* and *Unspeakable Practices, Unnatural Acts.* Now in his early forties, he was turning toward more documentary impulses; he was more willing to accept the world as it is (though not without complaint). If the stories are any guide, he was less angry than he used to be. As he wrote in "Daumier," "There are always openings, if you can find them, there is always something to do."

MARION

In Copenhagen, Anne found lots to do on her own. "My mother just let me go. I ran wild," she says. "Midnight tree climbing and rooftop hunting with these banshee friends. In that sense, Copenhagen was extraordinary, a magical place to grow up in.

"I saw my dad twice a year, at Christmas and in the summer. Sometimes he'd take me to readings he was giving, and sit me on the stairs of the auditorium and people would say, 'That's Donald Barthelme's daughter.' I ate it up."

New York was gorgeous at Christmas, and there was no school, and Don would take her shopping, just the two of them. She didn't want to leave. "He cooked all my meals for me and he was a great cook. I would miss him so much when I was away that I was probably a little overwhelming once I was back in New York. I would hug him and he would be affectionate in his own way, with words, with how he'd tease you. When I was little we would roughhouse a lot. He didn't understand his own strength with me. I was a child and he was this big guy . . . I would end up in tears. I'd watch a lot of television when I was in New York. I was obsessed. Whenever there was a commercial, I'd go over to his desk. I'd wrap my arms around him from behind. He knew what was going on. He'd scowl and say, 'Commercial?' But he would never go, 'I'm writing; I can't talk to you.' He was *there* the whole time."

After the holidays, back in Denmark, she'd ask herself, "Why isn't my dad coming to rescue me?" Her mother was a ghost. Don would call and tease her: "Well, when you're older and you come back to the States, maybe you'll go to Berkeley." And Anne says she'd think, "I'm never coming. I can never leave her. I'm all she's got. He didn't know. He didn't ask questions, other than just, 'How's your mother?' And I didn't tell him how bad it was. I think I was secretly afraid that if I told him, he wouldn't come anyway. He had terrible constraints. And he didn't know what to do."

Anne found pleasure playing ice hockey and soccer. She told school officials she was older than she was, so she could get into after-school social groups. She linked up with other kids who had troubled home lives. "This was the early seventies; we had parents who grew up in the sixties, very laid-back, sort of loosey-goosey," she says. Even at an early age, she felt that Don's reserve was partially a way of protecting her: "I was never unsure of how he felt about me. He'd tell me he missed me, but I think he thought if I knew how *much* he missed me, it would burden me. Not showing his need. 'Just push it down,' you know. And I matched him, was afraid to show it, but I missed him terribly."

Don sent as much cash as he could to support her mother. He wrote steadily, trying to earn bonus payments from *The New Yorker.* Joe Maranto hired him to write ad copy for *Mobil World.* Don took the job not only to earn money for his family but to prove to his landlord that he had regular work with a steady income, so he could continue to qualify for a rent-controlled apartment.

He remained in debt to *The New Yorker.*

He followed his Buffalo stint with a visiting position at Boston University, another appointment that came to him through John Barth's connections. The writer John Domini, a BU student at the time, recalls after-class gatherings with Don in a bar across Commonwealth Avenue from the campus. One night, some students announced that they had gotten a deal on air fares to Copenhagen and planned a long weekend there. "I lived in Copenhagen once," Don told them. "I was very happy there. It's a good place to live if that's what you want—to be happy."

"In class he went on instinct and taste," says Domini. "Late in the term he shared a first draft of the story 'Nothing: A Preliminary Account' and he made a change based on a student's concern that one phrase was too close an echo of Eliot."

One evening in 1973, Don and Kurt Vonnegut read together in Boston. The university auditorium was "packed and boisterous (marijuana in the air). By far, most of the crowd had come to hear Vonnegut," Domini recalls. He says of the reading:

> He read a piece of *Breakfast of Champions,* then his most recent book. His material pretty much had Don coming across as marginal. Don closed

with "The Indian Uprising" and it had most people squinting and shaking their heads. After the tepid response, the chair of Creative Writing, George Starbuck (a sweet, funny guy) stepped up to the podium and spoke a few extemporaneous words in defense of the story, declaring it one of the few pieces he could think of that effectively responded to the crisis in the arts since World War Two. But alas, in saying that, Starbuck left most people all the more puzzled. That evening in front of two or three hundred folks who just didn't get him certainly must've shaken Don, as galling proof of the special nature of his gifts—of their limits, you could say.

Off and on, Don continued his affair with Karen Kennerly. He stayed busy editing and doing layouts for *Fiction* magazine. One afternoon in the spring of 1972, while shopping for dinner at the Jefferson Market, he ran into a beautiful blond young woman. Her name was Marion Knox. She worked as a researcher-reporter for *Time* magazine, and she lived just up the street from Don, at 274 West 11th. That afternoon, she had popped into the market after playing softball in Central Park. Howard Junker, who worked at *Newsweek* (and who would later found the West Coast literary journal *ZYZZYVA*), had challenged his friend Jose Ferrer at *Time* to put together a team. Marion says she was a "very expendable pitcher but the teams had to have some women."

"Donald always says he stepped on my foot [in the market]," Marion says, "but we just started chatting at the counter and he asked me out. I thought he was very distinguished and nice-looking. I knew who he was because I knew Henry Robbins, one of his Farrar Straus editors, and had read a couple of his short stories ('The Glass Mountain') in the *New Yorker*."

Kennerly remembers the day Don broke the news to her that he had "met someone." He had spent a weekend with Marion and fallen in love. "He dumped me, but I was relieved to be dumped," she says—her affair with him didn't seem to have legs. "I think he wanted me to suffer a little bit and was unhappy when I didn't. We stayed close for three or four months after that, and then, after a time, we became real friends."

Kennerly thought Marion a "Goody Two-shoes" compared to Don's literary pals. "She's a very proper woman, with a strong, healthy ego," Kennerly says.

"It was not to my liking when Marion first came into my father's life," Anne admits. "I wanted him to myself in those days. I was pissed off, but nobody paid much attention to that. I always liked Karen Kennerly because she was enamored of me. Marion was straight and narrow, kind of blue-bloody. . . . Dad called her Marigold, Good as Gold."

"When [she and Donald] first [got] together, they were like freshmen in high school," says Harrison Starr. "I always had a car in New York. Native

Californian, right? I'd thread my way. We went to dinner [one night] at a French restaurant up in the Thirties, East Thirties, and they were in the backseat like little high school children."

Kirk Sale saw that Don's hours were "much warmer and fuller" whenever Marion was around.

"Don had never led a normal life, but he sort of started one with Marion," Kennerly says. It was the "closest he'd come to a steady life."

Marion Knox was born in Baltimore, the middle sister of three. Her father was a general surgeon. She attended Garrison Forest School in Baltimore, then the Masters School in Dobbs Ferry, New York. In 1967, she earned a B.A. in history at the University of Wisconsin. After that, "I went to Paris with a girlfriend intending to backpack around (it was those days)," she says. She "ended up working at different jobs (no green card)," including a several-month stint with *La Jeune Afrique,* a magazine for francophone countries of Africa. The editors paid her "under the table." Eventually, *Time*'s Paris bureau hired her to file newspaper clips and to make telephone calls in French. She had to get stock market quotes from the bourse, "which was horrifying because they were given so fast and I had to secretly call back many times to get them right," she says. During *Les Jours de Mai,* when gasoline was rationed because of student riots and workers' strikes, the office staff asked Marion to fill the tank of her borrowed car so they could siphon the gas off. In 1971, she moved to Manhattan and went to work in the forty-eight-story Time-Life Building on the Avenue of the Americas, at first doing research for other writers, then more and more reporting, primarily on education and women's roles in various professions.

"I am happy and know myself to be happy—a rare state," Don wrote soon after meeting Marion. Other events did not escape his attention: the increasingly nefarious lunacy of the Nixon administration and the opening of the World Trade Center in lower Manhattan, which sucked much of the island's trade its way. Contemplating these developments, in his new happy mood, Don wrote a whimsical letter to George Christian in Houston, proposing that the two of them "form a new government." The "inadequacies of the existing government I need not dwell upon," he said. Don's idea was that "when the former real government does anything *especially* horrible, dull, stupid, or evil, we will issue a press release, stating the position of the new real government. . . . Our statements will be so eloquent, right-on and funny that the press will of course eventually become conditioned to turn naturally to us for comment on the major issues of the day."

Don suggested Norman Mailer for president (sworn in on the steps of the New York Public Library, with his right hand on a copy of *Webster's Unabridged Dictionary*), Lynn Nesbit for chair of the Joint Chiefs of Staff, and for himself, "Gray Eminence." Oh—and one of the Supreme Court seats, he said, should go to "my dear friend Marion Knox."

PEN AND SWORD

A secret White House tape, recorded on June 23, 1972, caught Richard Nixon haranguing his perceived enemies. He ordered the CIA to block investigations of Howard Hunt. Nixon had offered Hunt hush money so he wouldn't reveal the "seamy things he had done" for the president during the Watergate affair. The June 23 tape became known in Washington as the "smoking gun," and led to the final stages of the debacle that ended in Nixon's resignation.

"Watergate sure did get [Don] revved up," wrote Thomas Pynchon, who met Don through Kirk and Faith Sale. By 1972, Pynchon said, Nixon had "mutated into a desperate and impersonal force, no longer your traditionally human-type President, but now some faceless subgod of folly."

Don wrote, "One can attempt to explain this Administration in a variety of ways, but *folie à deux* is perhaps too optimistic, and on the other hand I do not want to believe that we get what we deserve." He could only fall back in "stunned wonder at the fullness and mysteriousness of our political life."

He penned half a dozen satires of Nixon, including this parody of the White House tapes:

> P—What did I do then?
> E—You understood that inaudible had unintelligible.

P—When did I understand that?

E—You understood that on the morning of the unintelligible.

P—Oh, I see. I understood that because inaudible had informed me that unintelligible . . . But won't that look like expletive deleted?

H—It will look like you at least knew that unintelligible before inaudible and had the guts to be unintelligible.

P—I've never been afraid to be unintelligible.

Don published his satires in *The Village Voice,* in *The New Yorker*'s "Notes and Comment" section, and on the op-ed page of *The New York Times.* They were his attempts to "hurl great flaming buckets of Greek fire (rhetoric) at the Government," he said, "not thinking that the Government is paying the slightest attention, but merely for the splendid exercise given the Citizenship muscle."

His ruefulness reveals why his satires were generally more gentle than biting. He was "prevented from becoming a world-class curmudgeon on the order of, say, Ambrose Bierce, by the stubborn counter-rhythms of what kept on being a hopeful and unbitter heart," Pynchon says. A "tenderness and geniality" always "shine through" whenever Don "drops the irony, even for a minute."

During the early seventies, Pynchon lived off and on in the Sales's basement apartment, below Don, when the Sales were away. He wrote parts of *Gravity's Rainbow* there. As he came to know Don, he was impressed by Don's neighborliness. "He disliked being alone, preferring company, however problematical, to no company," Pynchon recalled. The two men hit it off; they shared a quick wit. Karen Kennerly says that one morning, Pynchon called Don and said, "I've just put the cat in the refrigerator. Do you think that's a problem?" On another day, he sent Don a note saying he'd thought he'd spotted Don walking around the Village, but he didn't approach him "on the off-chance it was Solzhenitsyn."

Most Village dwellers cheered Nixon's departure, though local politics consumed them more intensely than national battles. For many in the neighborhood, the demolition of the Women's House of Detention, a twelve-story prison at the corner of Sixth Avenue and West Tenth Street, was a greater source of joy than the fall of the paranoid in chief. The building had been an eyesore; it housed mostly addicts, black and Puerto Rican prostitutes, and antiwar activists. In an era of growing feminist consciousness, it had come to be seen as a shameful reminder of social inequalities.

Grace Paley had been held there for six days in the late 1960s, for sitting in a street and impeding a military parade. In her cell, a tall black woman put her arm on Grace's shoulder. "What's your time, sugar?" she asked.

"Six days," Grace said.

"Six days? What the fuck for?"

When Grace told her, the woman screamed at the guards, "Hear me now, you motherfuckers, you grotty pigs, get this housewife out of here! Six days in this low-down hole for sitting front of a horse!"

When the prison came down under pressure from neighborhood activists, and after large trucks had hauled away all the bricks, Grace was one of the few people sorry to see the place go. "[I]f there are prisons, they ought to be in the neighborhood, near a subway—not way out in distant suburbs . . . and the population that considers itself innocent forgets, denies, chooses to never know that there is a huge country of the bad and the unlucky and the self-hurters," she said.

A group calling itself the Village Committee for the Jefferson Market Area designed and planted a garden on the old site, to "create a verdant blooming oasis in the heart of Greenwich Village," filled with daffodils, tulips, and roses. On his daily walks in the neighborhood, Don watched the garden in progress. "It's going to be pretty," he wrote. "I don't know who the genius responsible for getting this done is, but I take off my hat to her."

Grace's objection to the prison's removal was ideological; Don's approval of its absence was aesthetic. Grace did not want people to forget *how the world is.* Don insisted on considering *how the world should be.*

His privacy and decorum were always at odds with his love of community and his powerful sense of *shouldness.* The more he walked and talked to his neighbors, the more he acknowledged how much he "dearly" loved the Village. "I care for the marvelous dangerous Oz-like city as a whole." Increasingly, his writing reflected this, in the less angry, more personal style of *Sadness.*

For instance, in an unsigned piece in *The New Yorker*'s "Notes and Comment," he wrote of a local street festival, where a high school stage band played jazz standards. The kids in the band copied the attitudes and gestures of professional musicians. When "they played 'Yesterdays,' tears came to my eyes, which I don't much like in public, so I asked this girl if she wanted to dance," Don said. "She wasn't a girl, really, she was a woman, and all the time we were dancing she had this three-year-old child (wearing glasses) clinging to her right leg. I didn't get her name, but I sure did enjoy that dance."

What is remarkable about this passage—and, again, it was new in Don's writing at this time—is the ease with which he conveyed complex emotions and simultaneously painted a social portrait. Central but unspoken in the scene is time's relentlessness: The high school kids strained toward the future, imitating mature gestures, while their performance evoked an embarrassing nostalgia in Don. He tried to recover decorum with a romantic

Don as director of the
Contemporary Arts Museum,
Houston, 1961. *Houston Chronicle*

Don, Houston, circa 1961.
Barthelme Estate

Don's third wife, Birgit
Egelund Peterson, in
Connecticut, 1965.
Courtesy Anne Barthelme

Birgit and Anne, New York,
1965. *Courtesy Anne Barthelme*

Don and Anne, circa 1967. *Courtesy Anne Barthelme*

Don, circa 1964. *Courtesy Anne Barthelme*

Don, Birgit, and Anne
in Connecticut, circa
1967. *Courtesy Anne
Barthelme*

Don and Anne, early 1970s. *Courtesy Anne Barthelme*

Don and Grace Paley in the 8th Street Bookshop, New York, 1972.
Mark Ivins

Don, Birgit, and Anne, circa 1967. *Courtesy Anne Barthelme*

Don's apartment building,
West 11th Street,
New York. *Tracy Daugherty*

Interior of Don's apartment on West 11th Street, New York, 1970. *Barthelme Estate*

Don and his mother (with Marion in the background) in the kitchen of the West 11th Street apartment, New York, early 1970s. *Barthelme Estate*

Don and Marion, New York, early 1970s. *Barthelme Estate*

Don's daughters, Anne
and Katharine, today.
Courtesy Anne Barthelme

Don in front of his Houston home, 1986. *Joel Meyerowitz, Courtesy Edwynn Houk Gallery*

gesture, but the girl he asked to dance was not really a girl (youth was lost to him) and the romance was tarnished by the clinging three-year-old, whose body was already starting to fail (the glasses), and yet, the moment was exquisitely touching, because Don accepted the frailties of everyone present, including himself. For all his utopianism, he never lost his "tenderness and geniality" toward things as they are. As it turns out, nothing is more radical, as a source of political consciousness, than tenderness.

To his fellow writers, Don was by now a potent political force, respected for his modesty and his refusal to promote himself, and admired for his ability to get things done for those whose causes he chose to champion. Since he had moved to New York in 1962, he had been busy bringing people together from various reaches of the literary world. Because he usually worked behind the scenes, rarely pushed overt agendas, and couched his arguments precisely and with common-sense righteousness, he almost never met resistance.

"Don was a very active, astute, literary politician," wrote Renata Adler, who gave an example of this in her book *Gone:*

> Once he enlisted me to block the appointment of a particular candidate for *The New York Times Book Review.* "Why me?" I asked, . . . "You've worked for the *Times,*" he said. "It's your duty." His voice had its note of irony, as his voice always did, . . . but he meant it. In the event, I called Diana Trilling, who spoke to Lionel, who did intervene. The rejected candidate never knew what happened; neither did the man, Harvey Shapiro, who actually got the job.

He took numerous stands on small but crucial issues, including a censorship flap at the Caldwell Parish Library in Louisiana. A librarian there had hand-painted diapers on the illustrations of Mickey, the naked little hero of Maurice Sendak's popular children's book *In the Night Kitchen.* Don signed a letter to the American Library Association objecting to the librarian's handiwork.

Most of his literary politicking came through the international organization for poets, playwrights, essayists, editors, and novelists. P.E.N. was founded in London in 1921 by John Galsworthy and C. A. Dawson Scott. P.E.N. initially had the feel of a private club, but it harbored the ambitions of the League of Nations. Its logo was a quill pen slicing a sword in half. Walt Whitman once wrote, "My dearest dream is for an internationality of poems and poets, binding the lands of the earth closer than all treaties and diplomacy." P.E.N. embraced this sentiment.

PEN American Center sprang to life in New York with the help of the writers and publishers Joseph Anthony, Willa Cather, Carl Van Doren, and John Farrar. A formal dinner in Manhattan's Coffee House Club on April 19, 1922, marked its official beginning. From England, Galsworthy sent words of support: "We writers are . . . trustees for human nature . . . [a]nd the better we know each other . . . the greater the chance for human happiness in a world not, as yet, too happy."

According to Marchette Chute, keeper of PEN's official history, in the 1930s the organization found itself "with less and less space in a world" making room "for the absolute power of the totalitarian state." Hitler became chancellor of Germany the month that Galsworthy died. At International P.E.N.'s 1933 Congress, held in Dubrovnik, Yugoslavia, the delegation of German writers, led by the author of a Hitler hagiography, tried to prevent Ernst Toller, a German Jew living in exile, from speaking. H. G. Wells, the president of the Congress, forced the matter to a vote and Toller got his moment. But the German delegation (which walked out on the speech) had intimidated many other participants. Henry Seidel Canby, the only American delegate at the Congress, felt a "visible fear rising like a cold fire."

This is the moment when PEN *really* became a political organization. At the Congress, Canby read a statement drafted by the Executive Committee of the American Center: ". . . it is the duty of the artist to guard the spirit in its freedom, so that mankind shall not be prey to ignorance, to malice, and to fear . . ."

Under John Farrar's leadership in the fifties, the American Center returned to its private-club atmosphere, holding regular cocktail parties at the Pierre, a Fifth Avenue hotel. In the 1960s, when Don became an active member, the group found office space in a building at Fifth Avenue and Twentieth Street. The cocktail parties continued at the Pierre, though they were stuffy affairs. Don didn't enjoy them much. He preferred to drink at home. "In time, Don developed considerable influence in PEN," says Kirk Sale. "It was he and I who started up chapters in places outside New York—Texas being the first." At the "PEN Board meetings . . . he would habitually come in his cowboy boots, and habitually sit in the back, the *eminence gris* as owl. And he would not talk often, and never long, but what he said was always pithy and appropriate, and usually right. I recall the time he was to present a report to the Board of a PEN all-star reading that we had just put on at the University of Houston. He stood up and, as I remember it, said just, 'Richard Howard took the word *rebarbative* to Texas . . . where it was badly needed,' and sat down."

Don took an energetic role in PEN's letter-writing campaigns to free prisoners of conscience. When Soviet police agents forcibly detained Aleksandr Solzhenitsyn, Don signed a cablegram to Soviet party leader Leonid Brezhnev. It said, in part, "We, his colleagues in the West, call for the immediate cessation of threats and persecution of Aleksandr Solzhenitsyn." He sent a telegram urging then secretary of state Henry Kissinger to condemn the Soviet Union.

On behalf of PEN, Don and others worked to get restrictions lifted on the travel visas of a number of Latin American writers, including Carlos Fuentes and Gabriel García Márquez.

He signed a letter to Poland's prime minister, Gen. Wojciech Jaruzelski, calling for an end to martial law in that country, the release of "imprisoned writers, educators, labor leaders, students and others" and a "speedy restoration of basic human rights in Poland."

For Don, now in his early forties, political conscience was inextricable from a traditional, almost religious, notion of morality that valued generosity and tolerance—values linked to his Catholic schooling and his father's modernist crusade. Late in his life—and despite people like Richard Nixon— Don said, "Democracy is the best idea we have come up with that I know of politically—a Greek-Christian kind of social organization." Any "individual guy or voter (poorly educated or well-educated, it doesn't matter) . . . is going to vote for X who answers his own needs, or he's going to vote for Y because this man seems to be more in tune with him spiritually."

But, he concluded, "I haven't seen a government I liked yet."

GUILTY PLEASURES

Marion kept her apartment at 274 West Eleventh Street, but spent most of her time at Don's place. Her steady daily life with him— bolstered by his acceptance of the position of Distinguished Visiting Professor at the City College of New York—simmered with creative tension. "Living unmarried with an artist/writer wasn't bourgeois convention," Marion says. "I had a solid, middle-class upbringing, and while I wanted a different life-path, [my background] gave me a centeredness and independence that Donald appreciated. I thought he was the most fascinating person I had ever met. He wanted to know everything and he understood everything, even things only women understand. My mother thought he had bewitched me. He had. One of the first mornings I stayed over, he read me all of *Krapp's Last Tape* in bed. That could win a girl over."

Kirk Sale recalls several small "spats" peppering the couple's days, but Marion says, "The only spats we had concerned my long hours at *Time* and Donald's occasional paranoia about my whereabouts." Max Frisch, on a return visit to the city, wrote this fictionalized portrait of an afternoon he spent with the pair:

> He is now divorced, the apartment unchanged though recently painted; the INGRES poster in the same place. When she returns home, he looks at his watch: where has she been all this

time? She is (so others had told me) a brilliant woman. She greets me with unconcealed curiosity, not entirely free of constraint, but with watchful eyes, as if comparing me with a police description. She is blond, her hair combed upward . . . they pretend to be joking with each other. It is three o'clock, she left the house at eleven. I say something or other–about West Berlin and East Berlin, I believe. He really wants to know where she has been since eleven o'clock. She laughs and shows what she has bought– not very much. Four hours for that? She is interested in West Berlin and East Berlin. She knows Paris pretty well. She would be happy to make some coffee. His tone is still joking: when one rings her in the office, she is out shopping or has gone to the library, where one can't telephone her; and when one doesn't ring her in the office, she has been there the whole time. She laughs; he does not.

Like Karen Kennerly, Marion put up with but was more amused by Don's possessiveness and jealousy–his constant teasing about younger men who might be her lovers, remarks designed to test her reactions and provoke sexual tension. "It was a game," Marion says. "I never really worried about it; it just seemed to be one of Donald's personality quirks, and I knew he wasn't a 'regular' guy." Consistently, his stories ("Florence Green Is 81," "Can We Talk," "Three") explored the fear of boring one's lover, or the feeling of inadequacy compared to more vigorous or intelligent men. A real fear, clearly, but also, as Marion says, a game–on the page and in the home–played to keep things snappy. With Marion, Don's stratagems were particularly intense. So was his generosity.

"Right after I met Donald, I went to Stonington, a small town in Maine that had an historic granite quarry whose workers–immigrant quarrymen from Scotland, Ireland, and Italy–were still living with lots of colorful stories about the old days," Marion recalls. "It was my first freelance piece and it ran in *The Maine Times*. Donald gave me a small antique Corona typewriter as a present afterwards."

It pleased him to see her freelance. "He didn't like *Time*," Marion says. "Once, early [in our relationship], I took him up after a dinner to show him my cubicle. Donald felt uncomfortable and never returned. But he was keenly interested in my work and in the office details. When I came home each evening, I would get a glass of wine and he would pull up a chair to his desk and debrief me. Various details ended up in his work. It was a great lesson for me in observation. He was intensely curious about everything."

Among the stories she worked on that caught his fancy was a piece on the Unification Church. "I pretended to be a lost young person so I could infiltrate the church ranks," Marion remembers. "Donald advised me about ponytails or braids–which looked sillier and more 'dazed and confused.'

When I started freelancing, he went out and bought a bunch of magazines on men's fashion, dressed accordingly and then had me describe him, 'pants puddling at the ankles.' The [fashion] story ran in the *Atlantic.* I was learning so much. He gave me books to read. We listened to jazz. We looked at art. We were always fixing up the apartment. One spring he painted the walls and I did the windows. When I quit *Time,* and started freelancing seriously, he took me out to buy a hollow core door desktop, which he set up in the back room on filing cabinets. We had already taken down the kitchen wall and put in a butcher block counter. He loved interior decorating, simple and clean, Japanese. Even when we traveled to a hotel, he'd move the furniture around— I think because of the joy of creating a new space that was unique and beautiful that didn't involve writing."

Their travel together included summer weeks spent in Copenhagen to visit Anne and Birgit. While there, they stayed in an apartment that belonged to Madame Schuman, an elegant equestrian in the Schuman Circus, which overlooked Hans Christian Andersen Boulevard. "The acrobats and performers lived there, too," Marion recalls. "Donald would write in the mornings and then we would have lunch, get Anne, and sightsee. We invested in a cheap badminton set and the three of us played together in the courtyard. Once, when the birdie got stuck on a second floor window sill, I stood on Donald's shoulders and was able to grab it—to the applause of the circus people who, unknown to us, were watching from a window above."

Back in New York, Don and Marion would cook together happily. "People have talked a lot about Donald's melancholy and sadness. It was deep in him, but so was great humor and joy," she says. "We once had a big argument which he wrote about and, to my amazement, there was my point of view perfectly understood and represented. He was, as he said, a double-minded man. The only thing that frightened him was not writing well."

Though they weren't yet married, Don considered Marion his domestic partner. Kirk Sale recalls a conversation with Don in the early 1970s: "Don asked me if I was having an affair because I looked so happy. I said I was. Damn if he didn't tell Marion, and damn if *she* didn't tell Faith, and when I complained to Don, he simply said, 'Men don't have secrets from their wives.'"

It was not his love life but his growing visibility as a literary icon that provoked *genuine* paranoia in Don. In the December 23, 1973, issue of *The New York Times Book Review,* he published the following letter:

> The fall 1973 number of the Carolina Quarterly contains a story called "Divorce" and signed with my name. As it happens, I did not write it. It is quite a worthy effort, as pastiches go, and particularly successful in re-

producing my weaknesses. A second story, "Cannon," also signed with my name, appears in the current issue of Voyages. As a candidate-member of the Scandinavian Institute of Comparative Vandalism, I would rate the second item somewhat inferior to the first, but again, I am not responsible. May I say, as a sort of notice to mariners, that only manuscripts offered to editors by my agent, Lynn Nesbit, are authentic—not good or bad, but at least authentic.

"Divorce" mimics several of Don's stories, including "Philadelphia," "City Life," and "Porcupines at the University." Passive voice, non sequiturs, and absurd imagery predominate, but without the philosophical underpinning or melancholy that give Don's best efforts their gravity and meaning. Don's "golden ear" is nowhere in evidence.

Even clunkier is "Cannon!" which appeared in *Voyages* and in the Winter 1973 issue of *The Georgia Review.* "Cannon!" echoes "Porcupines at the University," but where the language in Don's story is an obvious parody of film Westerns and country music, "Cannon!" and "Divorce" offer deliberately mixed metaphors and abstract phrasing *without* Don's satiric intent.

In the Spring 1974 issue of *The Georgia Review,* Edward Krickel, the editor, apologized to readers and to Don for being duped. "Admittedly, editing a journal easily becomes a kind of celebrity-mongering," he wrote, but he defended his decision to publish the piece on the basis of its "quality." He said he *wasn't* dazzled by the name Barthelme on the manuscript. "Why would anyone mask as anyone else?" he asked. "Specifically, why would anyone other than the real author submit a story under the name of Donald Barthelme, correspond with us on letterhead stationery (and pompously say he was 'glad to help out down there'), correct proofs, submit upon request a social security number so that he might be paid—all of this over a period of six months before the truth came out? For money? We don't pay that much."

He concluded that the hoaxer was a "monster of malice" seeking to "damage" Don's reputation.

One more fake appeared in 1973, "Sentence Passed on the Show of a Nation's Brain Damage, etc., Or, The Autobiography of a Crime," a poor pastiche of Don's visual collages, published by Chicago's December Press.

Don's letter to the *Book Review* effectively silenced the prankster or pranksters.

Meanwhile, Don had published several pieces under pseudonyms. Publicly, he admitted to wearing only one mask, Lily McNeil, which he first used to parody the theatrical style of women's magazine articles. One day, "*Esquire* called up and wanted to know if Lily would be interested in writing a monthly column for them, giving the women's view on things," he said. "Lily . . . didn't feel up to it."

Later, William White was another name he used, in *The New Yorker*'s "Talk of the Town" section, in pieces parodying book reviewers and fashionable new authors.

While he was busy writing, with or without a false face, Don continued to bring other people's work to the attention of readers as one of the invisible editors of *Fiction*. Mark Mirsky had finally talked City College into giving the magazine a small office and a stipend for a graduate student to help with production. Owing to Don's and Marianne Frisch's connections, the magazine published an astonishing array of talent: J. G. Ballard, John Barth, Samuel Beckett, Robert Creeley, Kenneth Koch, Thomas McGuane, Nathalie Sarraute, Leonard Michaels, Russell Banks, Anthony Burgess, Frederick Busch, William Kittredge, Clarence Major, Ronald Sukenick, Raymond Carver, Sallie Bingham, Halldór Laxness, Peter Handke, John Hawkes, and Manuel Puig.

Don solicited a story from Grace Paley, a meditation on racism, which Mirsky found too incendiary, given racial tensions on campus. Grace submitted another piece, "The Immigrant Story," which ran in the magazine's third issue.

Walter Abish recalls getting a call one day from Don, whom he didn't know at the time. "I said, '*Snow White*'? He said yes. He had read some of my work in *New Directions* and *TriQuarterly*. He invited me to be published in *Fiction*. I sent him a couple of pieces and he took one of them, 'Non-Site,' about a Richard Smithson earthwork."

Abish lived in New Jersey, in a cottage built into the cliffs overlooking the Hudson River and Ninety-sixth Street in Manhattan. After Don accepted his story, Don asked him to drop by with a photo to run with the piece. "We got along very well," Abish says. "Unlike most writers I knew, he was very knowledgeable about the arts. My wife's an artist. The seventies was a very exciting period in the art world, and Don and I were both very intrigued by it all."

One thing hampered the men's closeness. "I had a health problem and couldn't drink, and that was a problem for the friendship," Abish says. "In any case, I would see Donald from time to time—we had people in common in the art world. We prioritized literature, prioritized work. He'd come to my book parties. And there were parties at his house. I was the younger writer, you know . . . his early work was very significant to me."

Like Frisch, Abish observed Don's avidity toward Marion. "She was very striking, very nice. I was quite fond of her," he says. "But this possessiveness was something in Donald's makeup. Once, she came home with flowers. Donald was, 'Where have you been, where have you been?' Frisch was the same way toward women. These men from a rigorous home . . . they don't show any pain or mercy . . . in one way, very stoic. . . . I found this fascinating. There was a whole crowd like that: Frisch, Donald, Saul Steinberg. Though I felt a literary kinship with Donald, in the playfulness of our work, finally we were very different. I like to scrutinize things, and *I want it all out.* Donald was about concealment."

Ultimately, Abish felt that, with friends *and* lovers, "Donald was just not prepared to give certain things. In giving them, he would be transformed into someone he was not." The *Fiction* group, and the writing teachers at City College, "belonged to a different world than Donald did," according to Abish. True, "they seemed to satisfy something in him. Jerry Charyn is an incredibly nice guy . . . and Mark Mirsky . . . but like many literary people, Donald inhabited more than one world, and the worlds did not converge."

In part, it "satisfied" Don to serve as a father figure to younger colleagues and students. As for his other partners: From time to time, the creative writing faculty at CCNY included John Hawkes, James Toback (who later made his name as a filmmaker), Ishmael Reed, and Frederick Tuten. Like Charyn and Mirsky, Tuten was younger than Don, but he shared Don's sensibility. "I was taken by the idea of an impersonal fiction, one whose personality was the novel's and not apparently that of its author, an ironic work impervious to irony," Tuten wrote.

One day, Peter J. Rondinone, one of Don's students, got up the gumption to ask Don, "How can I be like you?" Don responded, "How many words do you think I put into print before I sold my first short story?"

He "had no set reading list," says Brian Kitely, another pupil. "He simply said, 'Read all of Western philosophy . . . then read some history, anthropology, history of science.'" Kitely recalls a class at Johns Hopkins: "A student there said, 'But we have to eat and sleep.' 'Give up sleeping,' Barthelme replied; 'that's a good place to start.'"

Outside of class, and apart from *Fiction,* Don advanced American letters. "One day in 1973 he crossed the street to talk to me on my stoop," wrote Grace Paley. "'Grace,' he said, 'you now have enough stories for a book.' (My last book had been published in 1959.) 'Are you sure? I kind of doubt it,' I said. 'No, you do—go on upstairs and see what you can find in your files—I know I'm right.' I spent a week or so extracting stories from folders. He looked at my list at dinner at his house. 'You're missing at least two more,' he said. 'You've got to find them. I'll wait here.'"

At Don's insistence, she pulled the stories together and published her second book, *Enormous Changes at the Last Minute,* with Farrar, Straus and Giroux.

Meanwhile, beneath Don's floor, in Kirk and Faith Sale's apartment, Thomas Pynchon had been typing away at *Gravity's Rainbow.* Faith read several rough pages and blessed them with her editorial hand.

Joseph McElroy recalls having dinner one night with Don and John Barth "down in Baltimore" around this time. McElroy's novel *Lookout Cartridge* had just been published. According to McElroy, "Barthelme said . . . 'Well, the smart money is on you for the National Book Award.' And I was surprised to hear that, but surprised also because he was in a politically rather strong position." (Don was set to serve as one of the NBA judges.)

His plans for McElroy's book—if he'd *had* any plans—changed when the 1974 Pulitzer Prize advisory panel ignored the unanimous recommendation of the fiction jury (Benjamin DeMott, Elizabeth Hardwick, and Alfred Kazin). The jury proclaimed *Gravity's Rainbow* most deserving of the fiction prize. The book was so controversial—dense, challenging, obsessive—the panel overruled the jury and offered no prize that year.

Later that year, in his service as a judge for the National Book Awards, Don joined Truman Capote; Timothy Foote, a book editor at *Time;* James Boatwright, the editor of the literary journal *Shenandoah;* and Cynthia Ozick. The judges were paid $250 apiece to read over 160 books and to sit one after-noon in an empty Broadway theater and argue with one another.

Don was determined to right the Pulitzer wrong—no easy task, given Capote's personal disregard for him (he had once called Don, in print, a "fraudulent" writer) and Ozick's strong opinions. But Don would not be swayed, and he managed to force a split decision. The 1974 NBA in fiction went to Isaac Bashevis Singer's *A Crown of Feathers and Other Short Stories* and *Gravity's Rainbow.*

Pynchon notified the NBA that he was not inclined to accept a literary prize, but he did not wish to offend Isaac Bashevis Singer. Fittingly, the award ceremony at Lincoln Center devolved into chaos. A streaker ran across the stage, and Pynchon's publisher sent the comedian Irwin Corey to accept the prize on his behalf. A somewhat befuddled Ralph Ellison intro-duced Corey, who spouted nonsense for several minutes.

Don's ability to secure recognition for Pynchon was not the only evi-dence, that year, of his political acumen. Benjamin DeMott, a reader in the Philosophy and Religion category, said the winning entry, *Edmund Husserl: Philosopher of Infinite Tasks,* had been brought to the committee's attention by Donald Barthelme, who had arranged to have lunch with another judge, Francine du Plessix Gray, to talk about it. The author of the Husserl book was Don's old mentor and friend, Maurice Natanson, who learned that he had won the prize just as his publisher was going out of business.

On September 11, 1974, Farrar, Straus and Giroux published *Guilty Plea-sures,* Don's first "nonfiction" book, a collection of Nixon satires, graphic collages, and social critiques.

The book's appearance was a victory for FSG: Don's continued alliance with them had been in doubt. In late December 1973, *The New York Times* published a short article announcing that Simon & Schuster had "lured" Henry Robbins away from FSG. This was news to Robbins's authors, including Don. "No announcement has yet been made as to which of the authors Mr. Robbins has already been editing . . . may follow him," the paper said. "The group includes Donald Barthelme, Joan Didion, Marjorie Kellogg, Grace Paley, Walker Percy, Wilfrid Sheed, and Tom Wolfe."

Don found exceedingly depressing the paper's implication that "authors are large striped or spotted animals to be trundled bound and gagged . . . from one game preserve to the next. Editors are not big-game hunters," he wrote in a letter to the *Times*, "they are more like farmers . . . an editor attends to the spring and fall planting, looks at the sky hoping for rain, and pays some slight attention to the compost heap, that is to say, the media."

Quietly, he asked Lynn Nesbit to get him out of his contract with FSG so he could accompany Robbins to Simon & Schuster. Straus, fearing a mass exodus of his best authors, refused to discuss terms. On January 9, 1974, Don wrote Straus, praising the "exemplary fashion" in which FSG had published his books, and thanking the publisher for his extraordinary "patience in the matter of my as-yet unfinished [second] novel."

However, he added, "my association with Henry has been and is extremely close, both professionally and personally, and I would be deeply upset to have it cut off":

> There is the question of a boy's functioning and peace of mind. I have not written this damned book [the long-promised novel] out of malice or (I hope) self-destructiveness, but because I hadn't figured out how to do it; and now, when the thing is on the verge of getting itself written, all of this changing-about-of-editors comes up. I would have much preferred that Henry had stayed with you, but what's done is done. In sum, I would be deeply grateful, and much eased in the mind, if you could see your way clear to letting me go, on such terms as might seem to you appropriate.

Straus replied that Robbins had made "damaging" allegations, implying "to a number of literary agents that we would welcome the return of advances because of our alleged financial condition." Robbins's behavior, Straus stated, "leaves us no recourse except that of counteracting it with a blanket decision" to refuse all authors' requests to renegotiate their contracts. Straus reminded Don that FSG had optioned a novel from him in 1967, and in 1972 had contracted for another children's book and a book of stories. He thanked Don for the "generous tone and spirit" of his letter of January 9 and assured him that in the long run he would be "glad" he had stayed with FSG.

Once more, Don asked him to reconsider: "What remains is an author-editor relationship of years' standing which has been and is very important to me. I am sure that you of all people understand the significance of this."

Straus stood firm. He replied, curtly, that the "more I've thought about our decision and the more I've reconsidered it, the more certain I am that it is right."

Nesbit advised Don that it was best not to contest his contract. Eight months later, *Guilty Pleasures* appeared. FSG paid him a five-thousand-dollar advance for the book. Don's editor was now Pat Strachan, a lively, intelligent woman, with whom Don worked well.

He remained the darling of *Time* and *Newsweek,* whose reviewers praised the new book's charms. They, and other writers, argued that *Guilty Pleasures* lacked the complexity of Don's best fiction but that for this reason it was Don's most accessible book. Some of its humor was "pretty low," one critic remarked, and another said Don risked ephemerality by "draping his motley over perishable structures" like the Nixon scandals. But everyone agreed that Don skewered what needed to be skewered.

In the wake of this cheerful reception, FSG offered Don a contract for another nonfiction book. He devised a tentative title: *Women.* Perhaps he imagined, as the book's center, an expansion of the remarks he had written for an exhibition catalog at the Cordier & Ekstrom Gallery in 1970 for a show called "She," about women in art. ("'The looking at a woman sometimes makes for lust,' says Thomas Aquinas, in one of the great understatements of the 13th century," Don wrote. "Women now demand a presuppositionless regard . . . [but] the disembawdiment of the eye will not be easily achieved.")

In August 1975, FSG advanced him ten thousand dollars on signing for the book, plus another five thousand in December, and one thousand a month for the first six months of 1976. Don would be paid an additional five thousand dollars "on delivery of an acceptable manuscript." Straus worked hard to keep Don happy; besides looking ahead, Don was working to finish the novel he'd owed Straus since 1967.

PEANUT BUTTER

Don's second novel, *The Dead Father,* published in 1975, roughly in the middle of Don's career, is "our representative American minimalist work, an audacious cultural document as well as a dynamic and original fiction," wrote the critic Frederick Karl. In *The Dead Father,* Don constructs a narrative not around a single tale as in *Snow White,* but around all tales—the story is the journey of the hero, the primary subject of myth. Structurally tighter than *Snow White,* the novel does not move by cause and effect so much as by a "process of accretion." Ideas and images cling, barnaclelike, to the book's central action (the Dead Father's trip to his grave), until the center is nearly obscured. At one point, the Dead Father's journey is interrupted by "A Manual for Sons"—a separate text altogether, tucked boldly into the book (it later appeared as a short story in *Sixty Stories*)—which, though charming, arguably has only minor relevance to the novel's core.

The novel is "minimalist" in its effort to "expose" truths by taking as its point of reference "not the line [developed], but the beyond"—what is only hinted at, said Karl. Don had learned this strategy from two of *his* dead fathers: Kafka and Hemingway.

At the end of the book, the Dead Father, who has come to represent traditional literature and Western cultural history as well as the weight of paternity, is buried by bulldozers—but clearly not forever.

Like Tim Finnegan, the hero of the Irish vaudeville song around whom Joyce built *Finnegans Wake,* the Dead Father may reappear at any time, an irrepressible giant.

The Dead Father introduces the extended-dialogue form that largely characterizes Don's remaining novels and several of his late stories. He admitted that these conversations couldn't have been written without the example of Beckett. In *The Dead Father,* the dialogues serve as counterpoints to the main narrative and startle the reader with a flurry of non sequiturs. Here, two women, Julie and Emma, are speaking:

> Hoping this will reach you at a favorable moment.
> Wake up one dark night with a thumb in your eye.
> Women together changing that which can and ought to be changed.
> Dangled his twiddle-diddles in my face.
> More than I can bear.
> No it's not.
> Will it hurt?
> I don't know, I don't know, I don't know.
> He's not bad-looking.
> Haven't made up my mind.
> Groups surrounding us needing direction.

As opposed to traditional male "parley," the women's language is adventurous, pushing the limits of discourse, like Gertrude Stein's "Ladies' Voices," "telling of balls." (Jerome Charyn says that at one point in the early 1970s, Don "was beginning a novel about Gertrude Stein. It was brilliant but he didn't finish it because *The New Yorker* turned part of it down." Julie and Emma's dialogues appear to be salvage from this project.) The women, in spite of their competitiveness with each other, are out to "change" the world and give it "needed direction." They hope the present is a "favorable" historical "moment" for female visions.

In contrast, the men in the book reinforce old, flawed ideas (violence, humiliation of one's enemies and children, war). Early on, the Dead Father and his entourage come upon a man tending bar in an open field. The bartender tells Julie he can't serve unaccompanied women. Exhausted language lies at the heart of his boorishness. "I can talk to you. We understand each other," the bartender says to the Dead Father, the very embodiment of weary tradition. These men use the same vocabulary—the lexicon of fathers, of patriarchy, which perpetuates injustice. Julie and Emma may not always make sense, but they are linguistic explorers, shattering old forms and their cognitive restraints. They are cousins of Sylvia Plath's anguished daughter in the poem "Daddy": "Daddy, Daddy, you bastard, I'm through!"

Earlier, Don's Snow White had longed for "words in the world that [are] not the words [we] always hear," but like the woman in Plath's poem, she had no partner to help create a liberated "grammar." Julie and Emma have each other; though their alliance is often uneasy—and not yet successful—together they have advanced further than the princess. In these passages, *The Dead Father* movingly extends *Snow White*'s themes.

As for the Dead Father's words, they form the rituals behind order and authority. In *Totem and Taboo* (1912), Freud said that at some point in the history of human development, rebellious sons banded together to kill and eat the father, who had been chasing the boys away so as to keep the females to himself. Freud suggested that the guilt for this deed has haunted every subsequent generation, and to atone for it men have created and worshipped totems for the father: animals, symbols, cultural forms—theology, law, aesthetics. The language of these forms has become the words in the world we always hear. They trap us in authority's grip.

Kafka's "Letter to His Father" is a poignant statement of the problem (and an important literary touchstone for Don): "[M]y writing was all about you," Kafka imagines confessing to his father. He speculates that if he had been able to forge a lasting bond with a woman, he could have been a "free, grateful, guiltless, upright son," but then everything that had ever happened between father and son "would have to be undone" and he (Kafka) would be left without a self. When he tried to picture a new self, he could only hear his father's words speaking back at him: "You are unfit for life. . . . You have only proved to me that all my reproaches were justified." There is no escape. The structure of language is the shape of the father's body (corpse equals body; corpus equals the body of literature).

Those who try to escape, like Paul, the prince figure, and Bill, the leader of men in *Snow White,* suffer debilitating neuroses. The psychoanalyst Jane Gallop puts it this way: "If one tries to think at one and the same time about the desire for the father's death and the desire to be in the father's place, one risks facing the desire for one's own death." In *Snow White,* Bill exhibits the classic features of schizophrenia, withdrawing from human relationships—he can't bear to be touched—and Paul flails in his attempts to avoid social conformity (the very glue of fatherly authority).

Thomas, the Dead Father's son, is also caught; he has worn the foolscap forced on him by his father. By the novel's end, it is unclear whether he will step into the father's role and perpetuate patriarchy, or whether he will break his chains—but he seems a step ahead of Paul and Bill, perhaps because of his union with Julie. At least, in conversation with her, he recognizes the challenges he faces.

By the mid-1970s, Michel Foucault had argued that "power has its principle not so much in a person as in . . . an arrangement whose internal mechanisms produce the relation in which individuals are caught up." Jacques Derrida had insisted that "speech" is the "father" while "logos" (writing) is the "son." "The son," he said, "would be destroyed in his very *presence* without the *attendance* of his father." That is, *the act of writing* was a sign of filial devotion.

Don's Dead Father, a purely verbal creation, an abstract, shifting being, half-human, half-mechanical (with a movie house and a confessional lodged in his leg), the progenitor of the "poker chip, the cash register, the juice extractor, the kazoo, the rubber pretzel, the cuckoo clock, the key chain, the dime bank, the pantograph, the bubble pipe, the punching bag both light and heavy, the inkblot, the nose drop, the midget Bible, the slot-machine slug, and many other useful and humane artifacts" is the perfect (non-)image for the grammars of power obsessing Foucault, Derrida, and others. He is Plath's "bastard," Kafka's faceless bureaucrat, and Alfred Jarry's *Père Ubu* rolled into one. He is Freud's totem filtered through Jacques Lacan ("It is through the *name of the father* that we must recognize the . . . symbolic function which, from the dawn of history, has identified . . . the figure of the law," Lacan said).

And for all the symbolic weight the Dead Father carries, he is movingly, even sympathetically, human.

At one point, one of the women, Julie or Emma, asks the other, "What is your totem?" Elsewhere, the characters speculate about eating the Dead Father—all of which indicates Don's familiarity with *Totem and Taboo.* Does he offer expiation for primal guilt?

Perhaps the playfulness of Julie's and Emma's talk—the playfulness of the novel as a whole—suggests a direction. As the critic Peter Schwenger says, play is a release of tensions both conscious and unconscious, a loosening of the patterns and internal mechanisms by which the father governs our every thought. "Patricide is a bad idea," Don wrote. "[I]t proves, beyond a doubt, that the father's every fluted accusation against you was correct: you are a thoroughly bad individual. . . . And it is not necessary. It is not necessary to slay your father, time will slay him, that is a virtual certainty." No, rebellion is not the way. Play, play, and by means of play, "*Fatherhood can be, if not conquered, at least 'turned down' in this generation.*"

Centrally placed, *The Dead Father* refines what has been and anticipates what's to come in Don's writing. It is an enlargement of Oedipal meditations such as "Views of My Father Weeping" and "The Sandman." It is also a deepening of a dialectic that has been present in his work from the start. "For I'm the Boy Whose Only Joy Is Loving You" is perhaps the clearest example of this thread in his fiction—a clash between male and female language, realms of experience, and related other differences (public versus private, aesthetic detachment versus involvement in daily life).

In "For I'm the Boy," Bloomsbury's friendship with Huber and Whittle is rendered in formal terms. It is unsatisfactory: The men know only the merest facts about each other. They long for emotional connection—Huber and Whittle are even willing to pay Bloomsbury "a hundred dollars" for a "feeling"—but this is denied them in the highly postured male sphere.

On the other hand, the language linked to women is free-flowing and playful. The men are enclosed in a car; women fly into the sky. Bloomsbury's friends have no access to his inner life, his private (feminine) language, and in the end can only connect with him by beating him. In Don's work, male encounters often end in violence ("For I'm the Boy," *Snow White,* "Some of Us Had Been Threatening Our Friend Colby").

In *The Dead Father,* the language tied to Thomas is terse and concerned with logistics. If there is any hope for him, it lies with Julie—though without the aid of the father's deep grammar, she, too, will have trouble equating the "kind of life" she has "imagined" with "what [she] is actually doing."

The only character in the novel free of *all* constraints is a drunken bastard named Edmund (an echo of Shakespeare's *Lear?*).

The Dead Father prompted one of the most blistering attacks ever launched against Don, courtesy of Hilton Kramer in *Commentary.* A conservative cultural critic, he accused Don of holding "life itself in contempt, and seek[ing] a redress of . . . grievances in the kind of literary artifice that shuts out all reference to the normal course of human feeling." Don, he said, "adopts an attitude of irony and condescension" toward "nature" and "innocence."

After railing for several paragraphs against Don's "aestheticism," Kramer revealed his true concern—*and* his political agenda: He said Don's work expressed "that hatred of the family that was a hallmark of the ideology of the counterculture of the 60s." Let the culture wars begin.

It's hardly worth noting that there never really existed, in this country, a coherent "counterculture"—and that, if one had existed, Don would not have participated in it. Perhaps Kramer had something like the Beats in mind, whose dominant political ideology was, if anything, more antiwar than antifamily.

Nevertheless, Don's fiction challenged the complacent "truths" of our culture in all its variety. It challenged easy, prevailing notions of literature, politics, and social relations. "His [writing] . . . is the most sophisticated" weapon in the war against traditional cultural values, Kramer said, "because [it] is the most calculated and refined."

Kramer's anger about the decline of American culture might have been aimed more accurately against the greed of commercial publishers. This was the topic of a conference held at the Library of Congress in October 1975, at which Don was invited to speak. The nation's poet laureate at the time, Stanley Kunitz, noted the "state of crisis" in publishing—the fact that major houses were abandoning their poetry lists and quality fiction because literature was not economically viable. "Perhaps much of contemporary literature will go underground and be published in mimeograph for a handful of friends," Kunitz fretted. He convened a group of editors and writers, including Don, Peter Davison, James Laughlin, Grace Schulman, Kathleen Fraser, Larry McMurtry, Ted Solotaroff, Daniel Halpern, and Jonathan Baumbach to discuss this "sad state of affairs." Most of the writers agreed with Baumbach that "we're really a country" of "quasi-literacy" and that the vast quantity of "schlock" that gets published each year "drives out serious fiction."

The editors tried to defend their practices, but most admitted that the business had changed "unimaginably" in recent years. It used to proceed with "considerably more pride and generosity," but now the financial bottom line drove publishing, rather than intellectual rigor or high literary standards.

Don grasped the situation this way:

> The main difficulty with the book business is that a book is two kinds of objects. You have, on the one hand, a thing that a reasonable and prudent man might decide is a book. You have on the other hand an object which looks very much like a book, feels very much like a book, but is in actuality a bucket of peanut butter covered with a thin layer of chocolate sauce. These things are sold in the same way. The latter seems to sell better, for some mysterious reason, than the former. A good example of this that I ran into recently is a book called *The First Time,* which apparently has to do with accounts of initial sexual experiences of either eminent or reasonably well-known people. This, I would say, is a bucket of peanut butter. Actually, they missed. They should have done a book called *The Last Time,* which would not only be funnier but more poignant. The idea is copyrighted, by the way. Take notes.

Don's colleagues at the conference hailed him as a hero, an example of a serious literary artist persisting in his work despite steep odds against him. McMurty said he believed few people were adept at both novels and short stories. "Speaking from my generation of fiction writers in America, I can think of only two: Donald Barthelme . . . and, I suppose, Leonard Michaels," he said. "They have developed principally as short story writers and managed to achieve some reputation and sustain some kind of a career"—this in spite of having "no places to publish what they write."

When an audience member pointed out that short fiction was thriving in Latin America and in other parts of the world, the panelists debated whether there was something in U.S. culture now that resisted this once-robust American form. All agreed that there was less leisure time in Americans' daily lives but that this didn't account for the story's decline. Again, the speakers blamed the commercial market. Publishers could make more money selling peanut butter.

Later that month, Don appeared at a symposium on fiction at Washington and Lee University in Lexington, Virginia, with his old pals William Gass, Grace Paley, and Walker Percy.

Percy was struggling with his fourth novel, *Lancelot.* In March, he had confessed to Don that he was drinking heavily because he was "not very happy." "I keep remembering what Faulkner said: that if a writer doesn't write, he is certain to commit moral outrages," he wrote.

To cheer him up, Don convinced Washington and Lee to invite Percy to speak.

During the panel discussion, Paley clashed with Gass, who said fiction was only about fiction—the "world" was not particularly relevant to what a writer did. What a writer did was illuminate the qualities of his medium. Paley argued that readers always looked for the world in the work. Gass claimed he didn't *want* that kind of reader. "Well, it's tough luck for you," Paley said.

Percy was less contentious, but he insisted that fiction was a "form of knowing" different from any other "form." Fiction, he said, was a cognitive (and moral) exploration of the "forms of feelings."

Don served as moderator, diplomat, provocateur. He goaded Gass into metafictional flights, Percy into abstract meditations, and Paley into praise of "story." "I wonder about our need [for a] linear sense of *what happened then, and then what happened, and what came next.* I wonder to what extent that isn't . . . necessary . . . it seems to me a very honorable business to be a storyteller and to tell stories to people," Paley said.

Don never took sides. He orchestrated the conversation and made sure all views got an airing. He was still worried about the state of publishing. He said, "Publishers are very brave, as brave as the famous diving horses of Atlantic City, but they're increasingly owned by conglomerates, businesses which have nothing to do with publishing and these companies demand a certain profit out of their publishing divisions. They take very few risks. . . ."

He insisted that "one of the funny things about experimentalism in regard to language is that most of it has not been done yet. . . . There's a lot of basic research which hasn't been done because of the enormous resources of the language." He intended to "work more on [the] rather simple-minded principle of putting together more or less random phrases—but not so random as all that. . . . The writer in the twentieth century who went farthest in this direction is of course Gertrude Stein . . . she's a greatly misunderstood writer, and that's where I would locate experimentalism."

As for "truths": "I have heard only one in the last ten years that I thought was any good," he said, "a large statement about life, and this comes from my friend Maurice Natanson who's a philosopher and he was quoting a Hasidic scholar, and the statement is as follows: 'It is forbidden to grow old.' "

A month later, Percy wrote to Don:

> *Thanks for getting me to Va.—it was a good thing to do. . . . It didn't help much [with my depression], but . . .*
>
> *I found the solution in* The D. F. *The only thing to do is hasten senescence by drinking and smoking whereupon . . . all dear [women] will say: you are, you are, you are too old. . . .*
>
> *The reason I know* The D. F. *is a very good book is that when I read it, I feel better, even exhilarated.*

Most reviewers agreed. They had awaited a second novel from Don. Its publication provided an occasion to evaluate his career. "Over the past 10 years Barthelme . . . [has] been getting better and better. So have his sales," noted Jerome Klinkowitz in *The New Republic*. "As with Barthelme's earlier work, the funniest and most effective things in *The Dead Father* are accomplished by language, by the writing itself . . . [it is] essential reading."

The New Yorker praised Don's ability to "flick . . . scenes onto the page with scarcely a breath" and called his body of work "an appropriately slapstick homage to the spirit of anarchy."

Peter Prescott said in *Newsweek* that Don was "always witty, and occasionally beautiful." *The Atlantic* said that "he provides a way of listening to the cacophony around us; he gives comfort."

The New York Times Book Review chose *The Dead Father* as one of its Editor's Choices for 1975. "*The Dead Father* is the author's most sustained, ambitious and successful work," the editors wrote on page one. They commented that it was "deadly serious" and that "most other 'experimental' ventures seem mild compared" to it. "In the Freudian sense, it is a brave book."

Jerome Klinkowitz, now an English professor at the University of Northern Iowa, was still busy compiling a comprehensive bibliography of Don's work. He had proved to be one of Don's most incisive critics. Don told him, "[Y]ou damned critics are pushing us damned writers a little too closely . . . making me uncomfortable. But I was already uncomfortable." The bibliography seemed accurate and complete, he said, and "persuaded me that I've been working too hard these last years and should begin judicious use of lit. contraception."

Still, he was grateful for Klinkowitz's "effort," which, he said, "affirms what I am always in doubt about, that I am a writer. May seem to other people that one is doin' pretty well, but always seems to the midget in question that he has just fucked up again maybe not so badly as the last time but still behind the door when the brains were passed out. I think only very good or really terrible writers have confidence, for the rest of us it is Anxiety City, forever." He invited Klinkowitz to call on him in New York "and let us have a drink or many drinks."

In late October, Klinkowitz responded and made an appointment to drop by. "Don's neighborhood ... was something I hadn't expected," he wrote later. "This didn't seem like the urban mass of Manhattan at all, for as the rumble of the Seventh Avenue subway faded behind me I found myself walking up a tree-shaded sidestreet of two and three storey townhouses, each with its neatly fenced front yard. Strollers waved to friends in windows or sitting on the steps, and up ahead Sixth Avenue offered nothing more imposing than a corner grocery store, a liquor shop, and a pizzeria. I could have been back in Cedar Falls."

At 113, he found a mailbox labeled "Barthelme / Knox"—"taped to it, a scrap of bond paper with the neatly typed message, 'Bell broken. Stand at window and yell.'" He stepped back and shouted, "Don! Oh, Don? Hey, Don!" He felt like a kid calling his buddies to come out to play. Eventually, Don appeared at the window and motioned him into the building.

Inside, Don sat in a "straight-backed cane rocker that made him look very upright and nineteenth-century in a rather stern Scandinavian way," Klinkowitz said. "Yet all was friendly." Don introduced him to Marion and they had a "couple scotches." Then Don suggested they walk to a restaurant called Hopper's, over on Sixth Avenue.

Hopper's was trendy and new. A young man greeted them as soon as they sat down: "Good evening, my name is William and I'm your waiter—"

"No you are *not!*" Don answered with mock severity.

"Sir?" the waiter asked.

In his book *Literary Company: Working with Writers Since the Sixties,* Klinkowitz recounted the scene:

> "I said you are *not* a waiter!" Don repeated. He moved his head from side to side, taking in Marion and myself for the bit of wisdom to come. "This is Greenwich Village, young man. You are really an actor, or a painter. Maybe even a writer struggling for a break. But you are most certainly *not* a *waiter!*"
>
> The restaurant was filling with customers and young William surely had enough to do already. Marion and I had become uncomfortable with

Don's teasing, and I could tell she was about to intercede and ask for more scotch as a way of smoothing the waters.... Thankfully William stood up for himself.

"I'm sorry, sir," he said with firmness, "I *am* a waiter and a damn good one! May I please have your order?"

He wasn't getting one from Don, who reacted with a moody silence and downcast glance that didn't rise 'til William had left. Marion ordered chicken Kiev for Don and lamb for herself.

After dinner, the waiter brought Don a complimentary brandy. Satisfied, Don paid for the meal. For Klinkowitz, the incident illustrated a mannerism of Don's that was also one of his literary strategies: "His very posturing was the sort that set him up for a fall—for a pratfall, in fact, that he seemed to enjoy taking," Klinkowitz said. It was a "style," in life and on the page, "of inevitable deflation."

Of course, Don also knew Sartre's example of "bad faith" in *Being and Nothingness:* a waiter who overidentifies with his role, and is therefore alienated from his true self. Don's story "A Shower of Gold" was all about bad faith, and it was one of the first pieces he worked on when *he* moved to Greenwich Village. Now in midcareer, hosting an enthusiastic critic, Don seemed to want to recapture a bit of the old adventure.

Back in Don's apartment, Marion disappeared into her study to work. "[W]ithout Marion as an audience his penchant for display seemed less keen," Klinkowitz said. Don surprised him by praising a "conservative crowd" of writers: Walker Percy, Joyce Carol Oates, Ivy Compton-Burnett, Anthony Powell. Then he rose and pulled from his shelf Klinkowitz's latest book, *Literary Disruptions,* a discussion of contemporary American writers. "Kurt Vonnegut," Don said, thumbing through the first chapter. "No question about [his importance]—absolutely first-rate! We're friends, you know."

He turned to chapter two. "Now this next fellow, 'Barthelme,' I have no idea whatsoever about him, but for the third one I think you're making a mistake."

"Jerzy Kosinski? Don't you like his work?" Klinkowitz asked.

"*The Painted Bird* is good, but halfway through *Steps* the writing begins to lose substance. And since then he's done absolutely nothing."

Don continued down Klinkowitz's list. "Leroi Jones hasn't written fiction for years. Probably never will. James Park Sloan—a one-book man. Now, Ronald Sukenick. He hasn't done his best work yet, but he's obviously thinking. Sukenick—okay."

"What about Raymond Federman?" Klinkowitz asked.

"Nope."

"Gilbert Sorrentino?"

"Nope." Don closed the book and sat even more upright in his chair. "Now if you want to be the top-dog critic, and you surely do, you're going to have to be right a lot more often than you're wrong."

"Isn't three for eight a good average?" Klinkowitz asked. "That's hitting .375, good enough to lead most leagues!"

"But you're not the hitter," Don said. "We're the hitters. You're the fielder, and you're not going to get anywhere if you keep dropping every other ball."

Klinkowitz wrote of what ensued:

> For this I had no ready answer and Don sat there in satisfied silence. Then we heard Marion's voice from down the hall. "Why, Donald," she was saying, and I could see her coming up behind his chair. From Don's point of view the timing was perfect, and I could see from his smile that he was anticipating some praise, some marvel about himself that his fiancée had just discovered.
>
> "Why, Donald," Marion repeated, now standing just behind his chair. "Your father's is bigger than yours!"
>
> With a lunge forward Don fought not to choke on his drink, from which he'd been taking a pleasurable sip to accompany Marion's expected praise. As his complexion struggled through different shades . . . I could see Marion enjoying her trick on him—and also to what she was referring, for in her hands was the latest edition of *Who's Who,* where she had doubtlessly just compared the entries for Donald Barthelme, Senior and Junior.

In the months ahead, as Klinkowitz got to know Don better, he saw in Don's "posing" a perfect, "classically simple . . . generating force for narrative": the "subject poses, upright and noble, impressed with its own feeling of command. A statue, noble and erect; a veritable monument. But life isn't so static. As language, [life] is all motion and change." What is the Dead Father but a "steadfast object" amid the shifting narrative, particularly the play of women's language?

And what was *The Dead Father* but an astonishing marker in the flow of Don's life? He looked back—"I married. Oh, did I marry. I married and married and married moving from comedy to farce to burlesque with lightsome heart," he wrote. And he looked ahead. He dedicated the book to Marion.

DOWNTOWN

In April 1975, television screens filled with the spectacle of a U.S. military helicopter lifting off the roof of the American embassy in Saigon as several South Vietnamese citizens tried to latch on to the flying machine and be carried away from the chaos on the ground. U.S. Marines were seen wielding rifles against desperate Vietnamese who tried to block the Americans' escape routes. Furious ARVN soldiers, formerly Western allies, fired on departing U.S. personnel for what they saw as a craven betrayal. America's longest, and most ignominious, war had reached an end.

"The greatest dissonance of my adult lifetime was the Vietnam war," Don said. It was the "late twentieth century music." Its strains had shaken American literature. Don had directly addressed the war in only a handful of stories—among them "Report" and "The Indian Uprising"—but his dissonant style was partly an outgrowth of the conflict's effects on every aspect of American life. To some extent, Don's phrase "Fragments are the only forms I trust" was a witty refinement of Hemingway's mistrust of *honor, glory,* and other "patriotic" words, just as Vietnam marked a refinement in military technology since World War I. The twentieth century had become more efficient at killing, and language had become more complicit in covert crimes. Hence the embrace of fragments—little glimpses of authenticity—rather than wholehearted acceptance of grand visions.

Don's prose style, shaped by his dance with philosophy and modernism, may have been outré, but it was not different in spirit from more mainstream writing touched by the war, which stretched the possibilities of American "realism." (Remember Don's comment that the "function of the advance guard . . . is to protect the main body, which translates as the status quo.")

"Vietnam has spawned a jargon of such delicate locutions that it's often impossible to know even remotely the thing being described," Michael Herr said in his dispatches from the war. Long ago, George Orwell had warned readers that when words are used to obfuscate, rather than communicate, narrative breaks down. Meaning is lost. Vietnam was the perfect example. "We tell ourselves stories in order to live," Joan Didion wrote in an essay dealing with the late 1960s. But, she admitted, it was a time "when I began to doubt the premises of all the stories I had ever told myself."

She was not alone. As Don's narrator says in "See the Moon?" his "irregular methods"—as well as those of Tim O'Brien, Michael Herr, Robert Stone, Joan Didion, and others—were a "Distant Early Warning System," signaling troubles ahead . . . at heart, a conservative and deeply sentimental impulse: to warn, to caution, to protect the middle.

In 1976, America's bicentennial year, Don went to the airport to meet his daughter. Anne had flown in from Denmark for her annual summer visit. "I put the United States on a pedestal, because that's where my dad was," Anne says.

"As soon as she stepped off the plane, people began slapping red-white-and-blue Bicentennial stickers on her and she came under fire from three different platoons of Light Infantry, all in authentic period uniforms," Don wrote, only slightly tongue in cheek, in a "Talk of the Town" piece. In it, he related a conversation he had had with Anne about the bicentennial:

> "The Bicentennial means that we have been a nation for two hundred years."
>
> "The Americans got loose from the evil English king," she said.
>
> "Well, he wasn't so evil. Just not too bright. The point was that we got the feeling that the country should belong to the people who lived in it."
>
> "What about the Indians?"
>
> "You're right. I'm just telling you what happened."
>
> "Tell me what's good about the Americans," she said.
>
> "Well, we tried to design a government that would be better for the people than the old governments of Europe."
>
> "Is it?"
>
> "In some ways. There's still a lot wrong with it."

"Like what?"

"It doesn't take good enough care of the poor people, and it takes excessively good care of the rich people."

"Why is that?"

"It's mostly run by the rich people. . . ."

. . . "What's a sex scandal?" She'd been watching television.

Their bicentennial conversation continued throughout the summer as Don took Anne shopping around the West Village. She kept pressing him, asking, "What else? What else is *good* about Americans?"

"We're sensible," Don told her one day. "We're sensible as an old shoe."

New York City was broke that summer, and the federal government refused to come to its aid. The *New York Daily News* ran a headline summing up President Ford's response: FORD TO CITY: DROP DEAD. Crime was commonplace; garbage piled up on the streets. Two years earlier, so many people were living in once-deserted buildings in Lower Manhattan, the city council passed a new law, the Emergency Tenant Protection Act, to regulate illegal occupancy. For a "sensible" father, an old-shoe sort of dad, it was frightening to take his daughter around the streets that summer.

In SoHo, on the Lower East Side, over on Avenue D, and along the old West Side piers, painters, musicians, and performance artists gathered in large numbers—in part because of the abandoned building space—and responded to the city's crisis. "New York in the 1970s was a dark and dangerous place," writes Marvin Taylor, director of the Fales Library and Special Collections at New York University. "The hippie euphoria of the 1960s, with its optimism, free love, and paeans to personal fulfillment, had evaporated. Hippie culture had never really found New York to be fertile ground anyway. . . . If acid had been the mind-expanding substance of the West Coast sixties, heroin was the drug of preference in Gotham." Leadership could not be counted on . . . Watergate, Vietnam, bankruptcy, corruption . . .

One result, in what the press came to call New York's "Downtown" scene, was loud and nihilistic art, with large doses of didacticism and rage. Punk rock led the way in clubs such as CBGB on the Bowery. Television and similar bands dragged glam and glitter through the garbage dump and staged performances that were indistinguishable from assaults on the audience. "[E]veryone was in a band," Taylor says, even those who were really painters and writers. "Downtown works undermined the traditions of art, music, performance, and writing at the most basic structural levels. Artists were also writers, writers developed performance pieces, performers incorporated videos into their work." Influences included the "Symbolists, Beats, New York School, Situationists, Dada, Pop Art, Hippies, Marxists, and Anarchists."

Keith Haring would soon turn graffiti into an art form. Jenny Holzer was already doing the same for billboards. Philip Glass made minimalism the new musical currency. Laurie Anderson brought William Burroughs back into vogue. And by the next decade, Jean-Michel Basquiat would become the new Andy Warhol, famous for being famous.

Downtown writing—much of it self-published or appearing in ephemeral literary tabloids sold in the St. Marks and Spring Street bookshops—was an attack on the "nicey-nicey-clean-ice-cream-TV society," Kathy Acker said. In her work, and the work of other Downtown writers such as Lynne Tillman, Constance DeJong, and Dennis Cooper, the reader finds "language divided against itself," said Robert Siegle, a culture critic. The fiction produced was clearly "related to the generation that preceded it, writers who emerged in the sixties and balanced commercial and critical success with remarkable skill, including . . . Donald Barthelme (whose witty appropriations must have encouraged the more politically engaged forms [of Downtown writing])."

Yet Don was ambivalent about this Downtown stew. In a story called "Visitors," he would write, "Barking art caged in the high white galleries, don't go inside or it'll get you, leap into your lap and cover your face with kisses. Some goes to the other extreme, snarls and shows its brilliant teeth. O art I won't hurt you if you don't hurt me." Later in the same piece, two characters talk:

> "Actually, I can't stand artists. . . ."
> "Like who in particular?"
> "Like that woman who puts chewing gum on her stomach—"
> "She doesn't do that anymore. And the chewing gum was not poorly placed."
> "And that other one who cuts parts off himself, *whittles* on himself, that fries my ass."
> "It's supposed to."

For Don, the problem with the new "barking" art was its lack of subtlety and wit. The battles it waged had been tackled already, and in finer fashion. While Don's generation of American writers—among them, Barth, Pynchon, Paley, Hawkes, and Gass—had attempted to expand modernism's discoveries, to develop *from* and *against* it naturally, this new wave seemed merely repetitive, less cognizant of its roots and deepest aims. Whereas Downtown writing seemed content with polemics, Don had always yearned for transcendence. At the Washington and Lee symposium, he had made a remarkable statement that placed him at a distance from many of the writers who now claimed him as a father. "I would suggest . . . that there is a realm of possible knowledge which can be reached by artists . . . [and] which is true," he said. "This is something spoken of as the ineffable. If there is any word I detest in the language, this would be it, but the fact that it exists, the word ineffable . . . suggests that there might be something that is ineffable. And I believe that's the place artists are trying to get to, and I further believe that when they are successful, they reach it . . . an area somewhere probably between mathematics and religion, in which what may fairly be called truth exists."

When it came to contemporaries, Don's affinities lay with Europeans—and increasingly with Latin Americans, whose "magic realism" was booming.

Since the early sixties, he had kept his eye on the Paris-based journal *Tel Quel,* edited by Philippe Sollers. *Tel Quel*'s literary ideology was founded on the notion that textual structures could be studied "scientifically," and that a systematic approach to reading and writing would dispel literature's *mystique.* Implicit in this project was an attempt to erase humanism, to downplay subjectivity (there was much talk about the "death of the subject," "the death of the author") and to focus on literary production as a politically, historically, and mechanically determined process.

Don was intrigued by *Tel Quel*'s theories, the way one is amused by the rules of a board game. But he was not fully convinced by the program. In the work of Michel Butor, Alain Robbe-Grillet, Sollers, and others, the effort, Don said, is "to get rid of psychologizing the novel, and . . . the effort is considerable. In doing this, it seems to me, [these authors] miss much else, they pay far too little attention to language, although many of them write beautifully."

At an extreme, the *Tel Quel* group (admittedly, the group was inconstant) implied that literature was hermetically sealed, a world unto itself. On the other hand, the Vietnam books appearing then in America suggested that literature was *highly* sensitive to the world. Meanwhile, New York's Downtown writers viewed literature as a blunt political tool.

Like Edgar Allan Poe's intrepid sailor, Don rode the whirlpool of these competing forces, and rejected all attempts to restrict his art.

In 1976, Don's ninth book, *Amateurs,* was published. It was his fourth book in four years and it was a remarkably assured collection—if not Don's most ambitious outing, perhaps his most purely entertaining. It's as though, with *The Dead Father,* he had fulfilled the need to prove himself, to carve a niche in the rock of modernism. As with his last two collections, he chose a simple, noncombative title that suggested a cheerful acceptance of humanity's frailties. In "postmodern" terms, *The Dead Father* followed by *Amateurs* may imply weakness in the shadow of giants, but the title is less narrow than that, noting, instead, human essentials: our dabbling, doodling natures . . . and that other essential, amour. "[O]ne should never cease considering human love, which remains as grisly and golden as ever," Don wrote in "Rebecca."

The book opens and closes with stories about the mechanical flavor of our age. It is temporal, our age, soon to be washed away. In the meantime, we have love, work, and play. "Our Work and Why We Do It" accepts the *Tel Quel* argument that texts are received ideas spit out by machines. But rather than wallow in systematic dullness, Don celebrated human ingenuity. "[A]dmirable volume after admirable volume tumbled from the sweating presses . . ." he began. Then he cataloged machinery's "precious" products: "carefully justified black prose," "Alice Cooper T-shirts," atlases and maps, matchbook covers, the "*Oxford Book of American Grub.*" The narrator boasts, "Our destiny is to accomplish 1.5 million impressions [of print] per day." A meaningless spewing of trash in a self-justifying economic system (the "postmodern condition")? Or an example, to be cherished, of energy and creativity? The work itself is a joy, a purpose for our lives, and the matchbook covers are charming.

"I saw the figure 5 writ in gold," the narrator says, reminding us that mechanization also assists poetry and art. The line was inspired by William Carlos Williams's "The Great Figure," in which the poet described a fire truck moving "tense" and "unheeded" through the "dark city," with the number 5 emblazoned on its side. In an homage to Williams, Charles Demuth painted the figure 5 on a large canvas. Now Don pulled the poem *and* the painting into the mechanics of *his* work.

The story ends with an affectionate nod to Joyce: "Our reputation for excellence is unexcelled, in every part of the world. And will be maintained until the destruction of our art by some other art which is just as good but which, I am happy to say, has not yet been invented." As an epigraph to *A Portrait of the Artist as a Young Man,* Joyce had chosen a line from Ovid: "And he turned his mind to unknown arts." Stephen Dedalus sets out to forge in the smithy of his soul the uncreated conscience of his race; Don's man aspires only to maintain the nuts and bolts of daily "impressions." A falling off from previous generations? Perhaps. An amateur effort. But that is the nature of our age, and, in truth, of *all* ages, as one era sweeps aside another.

The volume's concluding story, "At the End of the Mechanical Age," owes its title, in part, to Walter Benjamin's famous essay "The Work of Art in the Age of Mechanical Reproduction." Benjamin refined Valéry's concern that just as "water, gas, and electricity are brought into our houses from far off to satisfy our needs in response to a minimal effort, so we shall be supplied with visual or auditory images, which will appear and disappear at a simple movement of the hand, hardly more than a sign." With endless reproduction, the "aura" of art—its authenticity—will "wither."

In this story, Don concurs, but he insists that at least for a while "standby generators" will ensure the continued "flow of grace to all of God's creatures at the end of the mechanical age." The artists of our time may not be the great visionaries the world has formerly known—and possibly we "will not enjoy the age to come quite so much"—but in the meantime we can "huddle and cling" in the light from our backup systems.

The story's characters sing songs of "great expectations." And here Don is firm in his belief that, if there is a slide in the quality of our period's art, the fault lies in the world's brute facts. "The end of the mechanical age is in my judgment an actuality straining to become a metaphor," says one of the characters—a rejection of the Aristotelian view that language precedes and shapes facts. Rather, Don insists that the actualities come first. Objects and particularities resist the mechanics of language, as does the "ineffable." But the mechanics are means for scratching away at the things we cannot reach.

And the mechanics are delightful. Several stories in *Amateurs* ("What to Do Next," "The Agreement," "And Then") demonstrate the joy of sentence generation. A simple simile, a faint connotation, makes possible multiple "impressions." Each of these stories is an outgrowth of "Sentence" in *Sadness,* but they are more relaxed, more confident, glorying in their music rather than scoring theoretical points about the nature of language.

Overall, there are fewer fragments in this book, a lightening of the collage effect: Habitual systems *do* have their dangers. Don's story "The Sergeant" points out the problems of mechanized politics. The "military-industrial complex," seeking to perpetuate its enormous profit-making capacity, leads to endless wars and mistakes in war. "Works is what counts, boy, forget about anything else and look to your works, your works tell the story," a chaplain tells the sergeant. The noble aims *behind* the "works" have been lost in the midst of a flatulent bureaucracy.

Huddle and cling: "it will pall, of course, everything palls, in time," says one of Don's characters, but *Amateurs* affirms that the "fear of pall [is] not yet triumphant."

Most reviewers received the book with enthusiasm; the praise, and Don's remarkable productivity, cemented his reputation as a major writer. "The public wants reassurance, and Barthelme, true to his vision, gives it to them," Linda Kuehl wrote in *The Saturday Review.* "He offers gestalts on behalf of the multitude he champions, on behalf of mechanized, betrayed Everyman.... He counters grim, audacious reality with a wry wit, warm heart, and sympathetic—if surreal—eye."

Even those who felt that *Amateurs* was a lesser effort than *Sadness* and *City Life* inadvertently confirmed Don as an important literary presence. Richard Locke, writing in the *New York Times Book Review,* complained that Don's style had become a "mannerism, self-duplicating, an automatic reflex not an act of local intelligence." What this charge ignores is the miracle that Don developed styles at all using literary and cultural detritus, and the further astonishment that these styles could be refined into a "mannerism." In other words, *Amateurs* solidifies a unique American voice.

Locke's review was accompanied by a series of photographs of Don's head, tumbling down the page (it is an age of mechanical reproduction). He is smiling wryly, eyebrows raised.

He was everywhere now.

Specifically, in the summer of 1976, as America buried its war sorrows in bicentennial bluster, he was on the streets of New York with his daughter. There was nothing mechanical in his approach to the role of father—or citizen. "The great task is to make the word 'American' mean what it meant in the beginning—new hope," he told Anne.

"That's going to be a bitch," Anne said.

"I don't know where she gets such language," Don wrote, "but I didn't disagree."

UNCLE DON

"In the mid-1970s I was living in a house in Connecticut with several other people when the phone rang, and it was for me, and it was Donald Barthelme," says Ann Beattie. "I thought, Oh sure, it's Donald Barthelme. He mentioned that he had been reading and liking my stories in the *New Yorker*, and he asked if I ever came to New York."

Occasionally, she *did* go to New York to "sit at Roger Angell's side" as he edited one of her pieces. Don invited her to lunch the next time she was in town, so one day she found herself at his apartment. Don cooked for her. "He had little interest in ingesting food, to my knowledge, except that he *did* care about good ingredients," Beattie says. "If I recall correctly, he made me tortellini in cream sauce that tasted very good, and certainly not like something I ever ate. Can I really have sat on a stool while he busied himself on my behalf? What might I have said? And Don B.?"

Eventually, she moved to New York and settled on Sixteenth Street. Though she didn't see Don often, she always kept a bottle of Teacher's scotch for him in her fridge. She saw that he loved to walk, anticipating the fact that "something ridiculous was bound to happen" on the street whenever he went out. "I always assumed he liked [his neighborhood] because it so clearly was not Houston," she says. He found it "pleasant and reinforcing: casual, short meet-

ings on the street; pleasantries exchanged at the magazine shop. But the refrain to all this surface cheeriness was to increase his sense of isolation (he knew he was passing time), and meanwhile, there was every chance his world within the neighborhood would cave in on him. He was always having to argue with the landlord about his rights as a rent-controlled tenant. Then, as ever, New York has been about money. No one was impressed that he was Mr. Barthelme, long-time tenant."

When she was laid up in Mount Sinai after an appendectomy, and her mother was staying with her, Don was her first visitor. He came into the hospital room carrying a box of chocolates and a "Scandinavian sex magazine with a bare-breasted woman and a snake on the cover." These gifts charmed Beattie's mother. "He was kind" to her, Beattie says, and she "thought he was a gentleman and also very funny."

On another occasion, Beattie was with Don when "a very bad review of his new, very good book appeared in the Sunday *Times,* and being stupider in those days, but in trying to make him feel less bad, I said (of the reviewer) that it was just the 'luck of the draw.' I can still remember the look he gave me, and the quick retort: 'Did it ever occur to you that at some point, it shouldn't be?' "

His sadness aggrieved her. "I was mad at him once, and I asked him what made him happy. He expected excitement. He did think that at its best, writing was fun. Certain music made him happy. Certain pieces of glass. Watching others eat cream-laden tortellini that would make them fat while he had a mere drink (okay: *too* many) made him happy. He was happy for success, when it was earned.

"He knew a lot, and he never bothered to talk about things just because it was expected, or because they were current, or because other people were talking about them. He was genuinely modest," Beattie says. On the other hand, "he could be a snob." One night, Don and Marion went to her apartment for dinner. "How strange that I've never forgotten this detail, but Marion had on a belt buckle that was either Mickey or Minnie Mouse, and Donald was preoccupied with the fact that she was wearing a belt buckle he thought was silly. Not silly in the sense that Marion, of course, knew it was silly, but silly."

Don's first phone call to Beattie is indicative of how he "kept up," as she puts it. "He went out of his way to meet young writers, and to encourage them," she says. "Perhaps more than a bit pessimistic about himself, he was optimistic on other peoples' behalf. He really cared about whether they made it or not. He put in a great deal of time on their work. Vigilance mattered. There was an unstated sense that some of us were fighting the good fight and should stick together to do so."

Don was no longer the young iconoclast. He was an Establishment figure now, much admired, much imitated—if not exactly a father to a younger generation, then at least an uncle. And he competed with *himself.* "The way Roger [Angell] put it was that your stories weren't judged against the stories of other writers, but against your own," Beattie says. "Imagine the mixed blessing (at best) of being involved in that game."

Helping others relieved some of Don's pressures. His brothers Rick and Steve were among the young writers pressing him for advice—as were his students at City College. Oscar Hijuelos recalls, "Even after I had left the CCNY program in writing in 1976 . . . he did not mind keeping in touch with me even though I was not yet a published writer. For all he knew, I would have never published anything, ever, and yet he used to receive me at his Eleventh Street flat as if I were a writer. We'd drink goblets of Scotch on the rocks, chain smoke, and talk about literature, a radio playing jazz in the background. Mostly I remember his encouragements . . . though once when I was deeply impressed by D. M. Thomas's *The White Hotel,* he exploded into a rage: 'Manipulative crap!' "

Hijuelos was awed by the "neat and mysterious stacks of manuscripts" next to the IBM typewriter on Don's desk. "He used to take naps in a small room facing Eleventh Street at about four p.m.—I know this because once, when I got off work early, and showed up at a quarter to five, he was really angry that I had awakened him. He told me that, reaching his forties, naps were quite helpful to him.

"In his living room, facing Eleventh Street, were high shelves featuring many of his own books in European translation. Books were also piled here and there around a coffee table. He had a little bathroom with modern art on the walls, and all kinds of other prints on the walls of his apartment. Once when I visited him, I noticed that he had a snare drum and high hat, stuffed off in the corner. I asked him if he played, and while some piece of music came over his stereo, he showed me how he would play along with songs. I had a group then, and asked if he would like to jam with us, but he declined."

As a teacher, he "circled misspellings and stupidities in my manuscripts with severity," Hijuelos says, "and yet, while reading my work out loud, which was his habit then with students, he always took care to pronounce the Spanish phrases I used correctly, with respect for the language. And he had great patience with silliness ('This word, *snapar,* as in *snapar* your photo, did you make that up?')."

He gave parties to celebrate even the small publishing successes of his students—Ted Mooney, Wesley Brown, Philip Graham, and Michele Wallace, among others. His growing role as uncle-overseer extended to his colleagues and peers. Through his contacts at City College, he helped Susan Sontag and Richard Sennett set up an Institute for the Humanities, which introduced an international coterie of intellectuals to students and writers in Manhattan. Through the institute, Joseph Brodsky taught a seminar on urban studies. Brodsky convinced Derek Walcott and Dennis Altman to participate in the series. Sontag invited, as lecturers, Edmund White and Jorge Luis Borges.

When Sontag fought her first round of cancer in the mid-1970s, Don organized a fund-raiser, along with Robert Silvers, Elizabeth Hardwick, Arthur Miller, Roger Straus, and others, to cover her medical expenses.

He was always two people: the "hiding man," withdrawing from the world to work in the "smithy of his soul," and the citizen, working to better the world for others. When the English Department at the State University of New York at Binghamton offered him a permanent teaching position, he politely declined, saying, "My worries about a possible affiliation are two. First, and most serious, I am not at all sure that fulltime teaching would be compatible with the annual production of X amount of prose. Secondly, I would need some kind of a schedule that would allow me to spend most of my time here, where there are loving friends who cannot endure the evils & perils of the city without me."

PEN remained the focus of his citizenship. In 1978, Karen Kennerly became PEN's executive director. At first, this worried Don. He feared that his personal history with her might interfere with business. Within a short time, Kennerly proved herself to be a marvelously adept director, and Don worked smoothly and productively with her in a professional context.

Ted Solotaroff recalled that the "part of [Don] that was from Houston (the other part . . . seemed anchored somewhere in Northern Europe, Stockholm or Paris) came forward [in PEN meetings] as the consummate politician. He rose to speak in . . . procedurally messy meeting[s] . . . as though he were in the statehouse in Austin and was its most elegant parliamentarian."

According to Solotaroff, Don was an "enigmatic combination of the lordly and the twinkling." He "wore a downtown leather jacket but was very courtly and poised, as though 'Don' should be given its Italian meaning and emphasis. On the other hand, with his scraggly beard and droll eyes looking over his rimless glasses he also brought to mind Doc, the leader of the Seven Dwarfs."

In 1975, the PEN election committee nominated Gay Talese to be the organization's next president. Talese was "a foppy sort of a guy who was on the PEN Board," Kirkpatrick Sale says. "Don was outraged" by the nomination—"this was a second-rate hack, had no literary quality, and was famous then for having done some book about sex."

Don "asked me to send a telegram protesting the candidacy of Gay Talese," Renata Adler recalls. He said that, "among other things, it would seem to European branches of PEN that the American branch lacked any sense of the stature and dignity of the organization, if it were to have as its head the author of *Thy Neighbor's Wife*."

Don "organized an alternate slate, something almost never done, and got support from a whole bunch of people," Sale says. Solotaroff joined him. "Speed is of the essence in mounting an opposition," Don told Solotaroff. "Our candidate should be unexpected and irresistible."

They settled on the poet Muriel Rukeyser. "[We] took her to lunch at Alfredo's in the West Village," Solotaroff said. "At the time, PEN was just emerging from a position of almost total irrelevance to the literary life of New York, and Muriel, a veteran radical, must have thought the scheming of these two young men (we were thirty years her junior) to get her to preside over an organization known mainly for its decorous little cocktail parties . . . was rather bizarre. I certainly did. But Donald made it seem like a part of the ongoing campaign" against the world's "authoritarian" forces.

"There was a lot of drinking . . . in our rump movement," Solotaroff recalled. "As we were walking along Greenwich Avenue after the lunch at Alfredo's, Donald said he might stop for a brandy. Still pretty tight, I wondered why he would want to do that. 'You seem to have missed the point, Ted, that I'm an alcoholic,' he said. He said it in his characteristic dignified way that seemed completely noncommittal except for the light ironic gleam in his eye."

For Solotaroff, this incident defined Don's "essence": that "uniquely formal, accurate, stoned, enigmatic quality of his improvisations and prophecies."

In any event, as president, Rukeyser "turned out to be a dud," Sale says. Later, Don admitted that he'd misjudged Talese, who proved to be a committed and effective member of PEN.

On September 4, 1978, Grace Paley and ten other activists broke free of a White House tour group and raised a banner on the lawn to protest nuclear proliferation. NO NUCLEAR WEAPONS—NO NUCLEAR POWER—U. S. OR U. S. S. R., it read. Their event was timed to coincide with a similar protest in Moscow's Red Square. The Soviet authorities detained the Red Square group for a few hours before letting them go. Paley and her comrades were arrested and convicted of unlawful entry. They faced the possibility of six months in jail.

Bella Abzug, Theodore Weiss, and others held a rally in New York in February 1979 in support of the "White House Eleven." On February 2, on the op-ed page of *The New York Times*, Don pointed out that the PEN American Center kept records of writers imprisoned around the world by oppressive governments. Now the United States was poised to join this "dismal roster."

"Our Government seems to be proceeding in a somewhat ham-handed fashion here," he said. "The demonstrators offered no threat whatsoever to the President, to the White House, to America as an idea, or even to the grass—they walked on it, says Grace Paley, 'softly and carefully, armed only with paper.'"

Prison sentences in this case would be a "considerable miscarriage of justice. The authorities might also bear in mind that getting a message to the authorities is a difficult business, and sometimes *requires* walking on the grass," Don wrote.

On February 12, Paley and her comrades were fined one hundred dollars apiece and given a 180-day suspended sentence and unsupervised probation of three years.

A statesman in the literary world, Don was still a prankster on the page.

In the February 17, 1973, issue of *The New Yorker,* Lis Harris, a young staff writer, contributed an unsigned review of Jack Kerouac's *Visions of Cody.* She praised Kerouac's "descriptions of men or places . . . that in their frozen, melancholic vision bring to mind the paintings of Edward Hopper." However, Harris noted that in the book such "moments are rare," and she dismissed the volume.

Shortly afterward, Don published a story that appears to be part of a playful dialogue with Harris, though it is also filled with details from Don's life with Marion. The story was called "You Are as Brave as Vincent Van Gogh." In it, an unnamed narrator tells a woman, "The three buildings across the street from my apartment—one red, one yellow, one brown—are like a Hopper in the slanting late-afternoon light. See? Like a Hopper."

The woman to whom the narrator addresses his thoughts, in an obvious bid for her attention, "explicate[s] the Torah." Harris was planning a book about her Jewish roots.

The narrator is drawn to the woman's intelligence, although frustrated by her naïveté. "You don't offer to cook dinner for me again today," he tells her. But then: "You telephone to tell me you love me before going out to do something I don't want you to do." One day, he accompanies her to the school "across the street" from his apartment so she can vote, but she is one minute too late. The doors are locked. She cries.

He concludes, "You are as beautiful as twelve Hoppers. You are as brave as Vincent Van Gogh."

Mixing vivid imagination with details from Don's real and invented relationships, the story achieves a resigned, avuncular tone, in the situation of an older man torn between mentorship and lust in his dealings with a young woman.

One day Birgit phoned Don from Denmark to talk about Kierkegaard, and he found himself, once more, in a mentorship role with his ex-wife. In a piece Birgit eventually published in a journal called *Kierkegaardiana,* her musings on irony are identical to Don's summary of it in "Kierkegaard Unfair to Schlegel."

The ironist, Birgit later wrote—possibly thinking of her ex-husband—is a man who "sees everything as possibility and nothing mundane is allowed to drag him down."

To his neighbors, Don was now a familiar presence, his daily appearances on the street another aspect of his sagacious demeanor. The novelist David Markson says, "I lived over near Sixth, and so I'd frequently walk up West Eleventh and we'd run into each other. He was a famous writer, and I had no reputation at all, so I was always kind of quiet around him. He was *the* Donald Barthelme. Once, I was walking with my daughter, who was about sixteen at the time, and we bumped into him. Afterward, she asked me who he was and I told her, and she said, 'Dad! You didn't even introduce me! My friends and I love his work!'

"One time, Faith Sale passed this message on to my wife; she said, 'Donald Barthelme wants you to please tell David Markson that he's not *always* coming out of that liquor store where you frequently see him"—probably Lamanna's, on Sixth. "It was very funny," Markson says. "I, of course, went to a *different* liquor store, and was probably there more often than Don was in his!"

Ann Beattie was now a regular, if infrequent, guest in Don's apartment, or he and Marion would go over to her place for dinner. One night, while Beattie cooked for them, she felt "exorcized," she said, because she'd "just finished [reading] *Poets in Their Youth.*"

Poets in Their Youth is Eileen Simpson's memoir of John Berryman, Randall Jarrell, Robert Lowell, Delmore Schwartz, and others. The book details the heavy drinking and nervous breakdowns that anguished these poets. At the end, Simpson pictures the poets' idea of heaven. They would all be together and they would "recite one another's poems and talk for hours on end, free at last of worldly concerns about where the next advance, the next drink, the next girl or even the next inspiration would come from—free at last to be obsessed with poetry."

"I thought the ending must be meant ironically," Beattie says. Don shot her a pained look. "He despaired of me," she admits.

THE END OF AN AGE

In August 1977, Roger Angell returned a story of Don's called "Tene-brae." Passing on this "was a hard decision," he said. The story con-tained material that would resurface in "Great Days" and "The Farewell Party." It was pure dialogue, without exposition or identi-fiable characters. Angell recognized that "Tenebrae" was "a serious work" and that it was a "new form" for Don. It also had "some long and lovely passages and some short and funny ones that [I] admire extravagantly." But after several readings, the story remained "pri-vate and largely abstract" to Angell, and he felt "let down or simply bored by passages that meant very little and that sometimes al-most appeared to go on just because it was easier for [Don] to con-tinue them than to cut them off."

Angell knew the rejection would be a blow to Don because, as he wrote him, "you told me that this is the direction that your work is taking now and may be taking for some time to come. Well, maybe we'll learn to read you. It won't be the first time *that* happened."

This news came on the heels of some very public attacks on Don's work. Josephine Hendlin, writing in *Harper's,* said that Don felt "such disdain for life he aestheticizes even his depression." In *Matters of Fact and Fiction,* Gore Vidal claimed that Don "writes only about the writing he is writing . . . [and] I [am] put off by the pictures."

Don's new dialogue stories would only embolden his critics. The stories edged toward complete abstraction. Conversations in medias res, they risked, even flirted with, randomness.

In 1978, John Gardner published *On Moral Fiction.* Don described it as a St. Valentine's Day Massacre: "John took all his contemporaries into a garage and machine-gunned us all—with full moral intent, I'm sure." Gardner dismissed his peers on the grounds that their writing stank of moral rot. The ironic laughter in Don's stories was "enfeebled," he said: "He knows what is wrong [with the world] but he has no clear image of, or interest in, how things ought to be."

The Barthelme backlash of the late 1970s occurred for several reasons, obvious in retrospect. First, praise and then scorn is a natural journalistic cycle: switching the poles of a story in order to keep the story "new" (a worm in the apple of celebrity). As a former newspaper man, Don knew the rhythm well.

Second, some writers clear paths for their work by slaying whatever moves (Don had once taken shots at Graham Greene and John Kenneth Galbraith). At the time of *On Moral Fiction,* Gardner was a frustrated novelist who believed his work hadn't received its due; he had published a book on Chaucer whose originality had been questioned by academics. He demanded respectability. Third, the excitement of the linguistic daring that had distinguished Vonnegut, Barth, Pynchon, Don, and others had worn off. Each of these writers was now settling into the style or styles he had forged for himself—an intensely interesting movement, but no longer novel.

Perhaps more than anything else, constriction—of a political nature—had seized the culture. Willie Morris (fired by *Harper's* for publishing "provocative" essays) put it this way: America's "[idealistic] party was pretty much over" and the nation was suffering a hangover.

All along the political scale, the suspicion spread that America had gone too far. We had overindulged in the sixties and early seventies, and now we'd have to pay (there was, the media claimed, a very real "energy crisis"). It is remarkable how often Don's critics worried about his "morals" instead of his literary ability.

Don felt a winding down. "[E]verything in New York City is getting shabbier and rattier and rattier," he said. "My eyes are getting worse. *Everything's* getting worse. My back hurts. *Everybody's* back hurts.

"Aside from that, the physical surround is deteriorating. And beyond that, I feel a deterioration of the world's mental life. I think it's a shared perception; it's brought up in Christopher Lasch's book *The Culture of Narcissism.* Everybody seems to agree that everything is getting worse. Of course the ancient Greeks, the Romans, the Elizabethans also complained that things were falling apart. But I think here everything *is* getting worse."

Thus the dialogues. They were not a turning away from the world but a *turning toward* something, a purer search for transcendence, which had always occupied Don, whatever else he had been up to.

In the past, "I have" often been "a realist, a Dreiserian chronicler of historical time," Don insisted, and as evidence he could point to all the details in his work: student rebellions, the "new music," urbanism. . . .

With the dialogues, Don was seeking "something . . . *beyond* [emphasis added] which I haven't figured out yet. . . . I know it's there and I can't quite get there. . . ." He was drawn to the "poetic" possibilities of dialogue that had opened to him in composing the ladies' voices in *The Dead Father.*

While Marion was still working for *Time,* the magazine began pressuring her to "live and work in other cities/bureaus like other correspondents," she says. She needed to make plans.

She asked Don what he wanted to do. New York City was getting "rattier," but Don didn't want to leave it.

What about marriage? He had written in "Rebecca" that love is "an incredibly dangerous and delicate business" and he had once said that "The Rise of Capitalism" was about "incredibly beautiful and good women who are moving toward a rather terrible destiny and a kind of disenchantment."

If these remarks betrayed hard-earned doubts about marriage, the enthusiast in him felt otherwise: "Show me a man who has not married a hundred times, and I'll show you a wretch who does not deserve God's good world."

Occasionally now, Helen Moore Barthelme spoke to Don on the phone. He told her about Marion. "Although reluctant to marry again, he was considering it," Helen recalled. "He said that Marion wanted marriage and he thought it was the 'right' thing to do."

One day, in June 1978, Steve Barthelme called Helen to tell her that Don was planning to marry. Steve worked for Helen's ad agency now, and he "thought [she] should know" about Don. "A few days later, I called to wish Don well," Helen said. "He was pleased and then laughed because the marriage was to take place that very evening. In fact, he was delighted that his mother and father were in town for the ceremony. He was at that moment 'scrubbing the john' as part of cleaning the apartment for the occasion. He was clearly pleased with his decision."

For the wedding, Elizabeth Fonseca, ex-wife of the sculptor Gonzalo Fonseca, opened her home, just down the street from Don and Marion's place. A judge performed the ceremony, and a jazz band graced the reception.

Herman Gollob recalls standing around, listening to the music, and joking with his wife, Barbara: "Since you and I have been married, we've been to
three weddings. And they've all been Don's!"

Harrison Starr felt Marion's family came to the wedding worrying about
"their darling daughter marrying this writer, this bohemian."

Starr's wife, Sandra, says that "one of [Marion's] relatives came up to me
at the reception and asked, 'Well, what happened to his other wives?' By this
time I'd had a couple of glasses of champagne and I said, 'Oh, he buried them
in the back garden on Eleventh Street!'"

Don and Marion went to Barcelona for their honeymoon. "Some part of
'Overnight to Many Distant Cities' came from that trip, when the lights went
out in the city," Marion says.

In the story, Don writes, "*In Barcelona the lights went out.* At dinner. Candles were produced and the shiny langoustines placed before us. Why do I
love Barcelona above most other cities? Because Barcelona and I share a
passion for walking? I was happy there? You were with me? We were celebrating my hundredth marriage? I'll stand on that."

As he moved toward remarriage, Don had remained in touch with each of his
exes. Birgit phoned him regularly to talk about Anne or Kierkegaard or some
difficulty she couldn't solve. Marilyn says, "Don got back in contact with me.
Gallimard had published some French translations of his work, and he suspected that the translations were not good at all. He wrote to ask if I'd take a
look and give him my opinion. He was entirely correct. There were enormous
bloopers, so bad they obscured the meaning of the stories. He asked me if I'd
be willing to vet any new translation, and I said sure."

In the late 1970s, Gallimard agreed to translate *City Life* and *Sadness.*
With his advance, Don wanted to pay Marilyn to scour the French texts. The
publisher and *their* translator were not happy with the arrangement. "If it's
any consolation to the author, though Gallimard's sales are pretty awful, I do
find French publishers and writers talking about Barthelme with admiration," a foreign rights agent wrote to Maggie Curran, a young agent who
worked with Lynn Nesbit on Don's behalf. Don was *not* consoled, but the publisher was so offended by his insistence that his "friend" vet the manuscripts, Maggie Curran backed off, and Marilyn never saw the drafts.

"I did see Don again, in France—I can't put an exact date on it," Marilyn
says. "I was in Paris and he'd been to Denmark to see his daughter. We had a
very nice lunch in Paris. We talked about this and that, nothing important.

"Of course I'd read him. I thought it was interesting work. I was on a bus
in Paris one day, and a friend of mine started telling me that she was reading

this great new writer. When she'd finished, I said, 'Yes, he was my first hus-band.' I'd been waiting my whole life to say that."

In "The Leap," one of his new dialogue stories, Don made reference to a "wed-ding day" and wrote, "Today we make the leap to faith." Ruefully, Helen re-flected that, at one point in the piece, Don appeared to evoke earlier, failed relationships: ". . . 'the worst torture [is] knowing it could have been other-wise, had we shaped up,' " he wrote.

Marion felt at ease with Don's old friends, and together she and Don social-ized comfortably with a number of people: Roger Angell and his wife, Carol; Saul Steinberg; Richard Sennett and his first wife, Caroline, who worked for *The New York Times;* Elizabeth Fonseca. "Even though Elaine de Kooning had quit drinking, [we always looked forward to] meetings with her," Marion recalls. "The meetings were never awkward. Elaine was so full of stories, humor, and sparkle. She had various teaching gigs outside of New York City, but we always caught up with her when she returned. [One day] she took us to visit Willem in his studio in the Springs. [She was] trying to save [him] from booze . . . she felt [he] was beginning to lose his mind from his constant drinking."

On another occasion, Marion and Don spent a weekend with Roger and Carol Angell in Blue Hill, Maine. While there, they visited Katharine and E. B. White. It was a "very special" day, Marion says. "Mrs. White served us tea and wore a beautiful brooch. Visible in the background were the sites of *Charlotte's Web* and some of White's essays." It was important to Don to keep his friends close.

On July 11, 1978, Harold Rosenberg died of a stroke. Two days later, Tom Hess suffered a fatal heart attack. Like figures swept from a game board, Don's mentors, the men who had brought him to New York, were gone.

"I will think about him for the rest of my life," Don said at Hess's memo-rial service. "He was amazingly generous in all sorts of ways. He helped more people, and more imaginatively, than anyone I've ever known.

A year later, Don would be asked to speak at another memorial service, this one for his old editor, Henry Robbins. Robbins, fifty-one, had died of a heart attack in the Fourteenth Street subway station on his way to work.

The service was held on August 3, 1979, in an auditorium of the Society for Ethical Culture at Sixty-fourth Street and Central Park West. "I think people were always happy to see Henry, to be with him," Don told friends and mourners. "There was a gaiety about him that was consistent, that never seemed to tire." Don had lunched with him just a week before, he said, "at a place on Third Avenue called Entre Nous, which was not quite that. We lunched well into the early afternoon and could have lunched on serenely until suppertime, had we not been responsible citizens of the republic of letters. Henry was delighted . . . by the intellectual freedom which distinguished the life he had chosen."

To Don, Robbins had been "an exemplary figure—very much what an editor and publisher should be," and there were damned few like him now—few who abjured easy choices, easy money, who remained "devoted to good work" for the "permanent enrichment of our literary life." "He was a rare man," Don said, "and he will be sorely missed."

"I've been to more than my share [of funerals] in the last two years," Don told J. D. O'Hara in 1981. "[You] don't go to a funeral . . . without ambiguous feelings. I certainly wish that all the people I have been to funerals for . . . were back here, so [I] could go to lunch with them and keep on with [our] life as we have always lived it. At the same time you notice that this funeral . . . is a social occasion of a certain kind, and it is being well or ill managed."

The loss of friends was bad enough. But a certain *style* was leaking out of life. "I went to one [funeral] in an un-airconditioned hall, and I was sweating like a pig, and so was everybody else, and it was horribly uncomfortable, and one could not concentrate on the business at hand, which was celebrating a dear friend. And I went to another where we were looking around, saying ah, here's so-and-so, he showed up, well, son of a bitch, he *should* show up; and all these other considerations come into this moment. I mean, there are no pure moments."

Life as he had "always lived it" was gone. What little integrity remained in the publishing industry appeared to be evaporating in the desert of corporate invoices. However, Don's induction into the American Academy of Arts and Letters lifted his spirits momentarily. He and Marion were invited to a reception at Ralph Ellison's house before the ceremony. Ellison and his wife were "very avuncular and welcoming," Marion recalls, though at the awards event, Ellison, the master of ceremonies, rambled, ad-libbed his introductions of new members, and did not seem to know who any of them were. It was in this shifting, unpredictable literary climate that Don released his sixth story collection, his tenth book overall, and the last volume he would publish with Farrar, Straus and Giroux, *Great Days*.

The book offered sixteen stories, seven of which were dialogues—"possibility-haunted colloquies," the dust jacket called them, "stripped of everything save voices. . . . Extravagant, profane, and comic, the dialogues are a considerable achievement, testing the possibilities of form and extending our engagement with the world." Don dedicated the book to Thomas Hess.

The dialogues furthered Don's attempts to express the inexpressible—longings and intimations beyond words. In the past, he had employed metaphors ("The Balloon"), myths (*The Dead Father*) and traditional characterization ("110 West Sixty-First Street") to move beyond silence; now, he let rhythm, tone, and counterpoint carry the day. The speakers of the dialogues know the specifics of their lives; the reader does not. We can only eavesdrop; the background remains impenetrable to us, and our attention keeps bobbing toward the surface. ("The periphery is [actually] a way of rendering the core experience," Don told J. D. O'Hara.)

"They're Beckett-y," O'Hara said of the stories. "Are they Beckett-y?"

"Certainly they couldn't exist without the example of Beckett's plays," Don replied. "But I have other fish to fry. The dialogues in *Great Days* are less abstract than those between the two women in *The Dead Father*, which aren't particularly reminiscent of Beckett and preceded them. There's an urge toward abstraction that's very seductive. . . . I'm talking about a pointillist technique, where what you get is not adjacent dots of yellow and blue which optically merge to give you green but merged meanings, whether from words placed side by side in a seemingly arbitrary way or phrases similarly arrayed. . . ."

In a passage later cut from the *Paris Review* interview—apparently because he couldn't think the argument through well enough—Don noted John Ashbery's influence on the dialogues. "There is some sense in which John Ashbery is central to writing at this time, and I couldn't tell you . . . There's a line that goes from Wallace Stevens to Ashbery . . . Ashbery is onto something that I'm quite curious about. If I can figure out why Ashbery is so important . . ."

Three Poems, Ashbery's most recent book, was composed of abstract prose, non sequiturs with little concrete imagery, apparently illustrating the back-and-forth of a mind at war with itself.

In *Great Days,* as in Don's earlier books, the "double-minded" characters recall Kierkegaard's thorny texts. "The Leap" makes explicit reference to *Purity of Heart Is to Will One Thing,* in which Kierkegaard calls "double-mindedness" an "infantile . . . fear of punishment" in one who can't tell if his father is a "loving" or "bad man": Don's old subject, done up in a new style.

In addition to Beckett's plays, Don's dialogues could also be usefully compared to Willem de Kooning's *Woman* paintings, in which there is just an intimation of a figure nearly lost beneath the texture of the brush strokes. In "Great Days" and other stories, Don gives us the barest whisper of characters beneath a busy surface of words:

   —Featherings of ease and bliss.
   —I was preparing myself. Getting ready for the great day.

—Icy day with salt on all the sidewalks.
—Sketching attitudes and forming pretty speeches.
—Pitching pennies at a line scraped in the dust.
—Doing and redoing my lustrous abundant hair.

Aging, loss, and friendship—its warmth ("Belief") and its betrayals ("Cortés and Montezuma")—inform the new stories. Old obsessions reappear: Oedipal confusions, the tyranny of conformity ("On the Steps of the Conservatory"), the limitations of the educational system ("Morning").

In "The Death of Edward Lear," dying is seen as a social occasion, a stylized event. Don appeared to be thinking of the funerals he had recently attended. But "Lear" was an older piece; he had almost included it in *Amateurs.* In fact, the idea for "Lear" may have come from Susan Sontag's "farewell" parties in the mid-1970s, when she feared she was dying of cancer. She invited friends to her place to say good-bye to her in the midst of gaiety and planned performances.

On balance, the reviews were highly respectful; for now, the Barthelme backlash had receded. Like him or not, Don was a major artist, reviewers said. He had to be dealt with, and seriously.

"Literary history shows that the avant-garde of one period is either the norm a few decades later, the way four-letter words are now the norm, or else the highly original writer, his imitators fallen away, is left in the isolation of his special gift—standing, one might say, in the altogether. This sixth collection is bare Barthelme at his best, quite inimitable, with a new kind of calm confidence, a new depth of subject," Diane Johnson wrote in *The New York Times Book Review.* In her opinion, the dialogue stories reflected a "somber mood in Barthelme"; his eye is "on Great Subjects (fear, faith, hope, sexual contention)." The "old-fashioned reader, casually reading for profit and pleasure, will find [contemporary] parables," Johnson said.

Writing in *The Saturday Review,* Denis Donoghue said that Don's "stories are brief for the same reason that . . . sonnets have 14 lines, because that is enough." His "sentences . . . are so much more beautiful than God's version [of the world] that we . . . repudiate the latter as a mere vulgate of experience, a first shot, at best a near-miss."

The Nation's reviewer, James Rawley, was struck by the collection's "muted . . . melancholy." He said, "Barthelme has liberated himself, for good or for ill, from mere funniness," and added, "[It] is the most haunting book anyone ever chuckled over."

Newsweek's Peter Prescott agreed. He considered Don "one of our best and most adventurous writers." If none of the stories in *Great Days* "shows him wholly at his best," that is because "[m]ore than most writers, Barthelme

is willing to make difficulties for himself, discarding the fiction writer's traditional resources to invent new forms with which to mirror our compla-
cency, our discontent." Because the dialogues "are so ambitious," they "are
not all successful." They push "writing to the limit of comprehensibility." It
"may be all we can ask" that *some* of Don's pieces *do* work. "It is in the nature
of the way he writes that his pieces . . . can be no better than the invention,
the controlling metaphor, that he chooses for each," Prescott said, adding,
"If his inventions are sometimes slight, it doesn't matter much, for the least
of Barthelme's stories must make us smile, and over the years he has assembled an impressive body of work."

Were the great days over? In a crepuscular mood, Don imagined growing old
in New York City. "I'll probably hole up in the Gramercy Park Hotel the way
[S. J.] Perelman did . . . a very nice hotel . . ." he mused. "I think Perelman's
solution is an admirable one. It's very pretty over there, by the Gramercy
Park Hotel. And you can still hear the garbage trucks in the morning."

But what to write about, now that the life he had always lived seemed im-
periled? Marion's freelance work offered a subject or two. While researching
a piece on Mexico, she brought home Bernal Díaz del Castillo's book on the
conquest. Don picked it up, and so was born "Cortés and Montezuma." On
another occasion, Marion "accumulated all these things" about "Chinese
culture, Chinese history, Chinatown etc." for a piece she was writing. "I began picking them up" and wrote "The Emperor," Don said.

Roger Angell had finally warmed to a few of the dialogues, but he still rejected many of Don's stories, including a long piece called "The Emerald,"
which Don pared from an aborted novel. "I can see that the story is elegant
and strongly flavored; I just wish I liked it more," Angell said.

In the fall of 1979, Pauline Kael, *The New Yorker*'s film reviewer, took a
hiatus from reviewing. Angell asked Don to fill her place for six weeks. In all,
he wrote seven omnibus reviews between September 10 and October 15,
mostly of foreign features such as Werner Herzog's *Woyzeck,* Paul Verhoe-
ven's *Soldier of Orange,* François Truffaut's *The Green Room,* and Bernardo
Bertolucci's *Luna.*

The reviews were erudite and witty, lessons in craft and art. For instance,
in one review, Don noted, "It's possible that the idea of man-as-victim-of-
society or man-as-victim-of-the-conditions-of-existence has minimum dramatic life left in it. . . . Like the birth trauma, victimization as a given
doesn't take us very far."

Or consider this: "[S]train as we may, we *still* don't have any damn decadence [in our art]."

It seems that for the most part, Don didn't enjoy watching these movies.

He was happiest with the American products, even the dumb, cheesy ones like *Love and Bullets,* a mob movie with Rod Steiger. In Don's pleasure in Charles Bronson, who, he wrote, was "as solid as a tool-pusher on a Texas oil rig," the gleeful young reporter for the *Houston Post* almost reemerged.

What he thought he *should* appreciate—the sophisticated self-reflexiveness of Truffaut—he found "less fun than it used to be." Instead, he responded to "detail" and "ugly knowledge." He liked learning "what things are called" in various walks of life. He especially admired Joseph Wambaugh's *The Onion Field,* which, he felt, thoroughly understood its "milieu."

During these six weeks, Don's best few minutes at the movies occurred in the middle of a short feature by Lawrence Weiner called *Altered to Suit.* It was screened as part of the Whitney Museum's New American Filmmakers Series. Don wrote, "There's a strangely pleasant moment with a man and woman looking out a window, the man's hand caressing the woman's (clothed) back in husbandly fashion; the moment is protracted, goes on and on, the man's hand moves to the cleft of the buttocks, in husbandly fashion—a good and true observation."

For nearly twenty years now, Don had lived in Manhattan, clinging to a fragile way of life during a particularly tumultuous period in American history: civil rights and antiwar marches (barricades in the streets); feminist demands; a bombed-out brownstone down the block. . . .

Now, he watched on his TV screen as Islamic hard-liners burned U.S. flags outside the American embassy in Tehran. On November 4, 1979, militant students—protesting America's support of the former Shah—had stormed the embassy and taken about seventy Americans hostage. The siege would last 444 days, and it would destroy Jimmy Carter's presidency.

Depressed, Don walked. All around him, New York seemed to be selling itself off to pay its debts.

The "government isn't very good and the New York Culture Center is being sold and there is so much pornography around . . . many people are persuaded that these are dark times," Don wrote in a "Notes and Comment" piece for *The New Yorker.* In the midst of the deterioration, he took a cue from his moviegoing and tried to make "good and true observations." At first, he noticed "shrubs—whatever—" but then he looked more closely. In the window of a bakery, he saw the "silverware, cups and saucers, sugarers and creamers, stainless steel pots and pans, and five sets of spun-candy wedding bells in their plastic wrappings." Sadly, the bakery was going out of business. He saw a book, *Graham Greene on Film,* in the open rumble seat of a parked British car. He stopped at the window of the Elephant and Castle on Greenwich Avenue to read the menu: a "Love Omelette (hearts of artichoke, hearts of palm) for $3.05." He studied the bulletin board inside the Perry Street Laundromat: a reading by Nelson Algren, a flyer from the "International Committee to Reunite the Beatles, headquartered in Merrick, N. Y. Send one dollar to Let It Be."

Don's writing began to swell with details. Buoyed by his ability to *observe*—which had never been central to his meditative fiction—he began to relax and become more comfortable with personal comment, personal revelation. He turned to what W. H. Auden had called the "doggy life." From such materials, much of Don's late style would grow.

"In the '70s the sheer glut of consumable culture reached almost oceanic proportions as the media—television, movies, theater, books, records, concerts, opera, dance, radio, the visual arts—poured out an endless stream of beguilement to be soaked up by vast, voracious audiences," says Jack Kroll. For him, the decade's most important cultural development was the "process of blurring the distinctions between serious stuff and pop stuff" (so the "high intelligence, formal brilliance and even mythic aspiration" of a movie like *The Godfather* was inextricable from its "entertainment value"—an example of what "popular culture can produce under optimum conditions").

Also of note was the "attempt to come to terms with the [Vietnam] war" in movies and books, the mentality of "big budgets, big risks, big successes, big failures" in the arts, and the "question of the relationship of art to morals" (not because of John Gardner but because of Aleksandr Solzhenitsyn and his exposure of Soviet gulags).

Of this period, Alfred Kazin wrote that American life had taught especially harsh lessons to city dwellers. "The city arouses us with the same forces by which it defeats us," he said.

Nearly twenty years after setting foot on the island, and despite his literary successes and fresh marriage, Don felt more defeated than aroused by his adopted city. There were too many spirits—of every kind; too many losses. As he walked through the Village, fewer and fewer faces were familiar.

—Will you always remember me?
—Always.
—Will you remember me a year from now?
—Yes, I will.
—Will you remember me two years from now?
—Yes, I will.
—Will you remember me five years from now?
—Yes, I will.
—Knock knock.

—Who's there?
—You see?

So ends "Great Days." And in "Morning," Don concluded:

—Say you're not frightened. Inspire me.
—After a while, darkness, and they give up the search.

This was a far cry from the "Heigh-ho!" that ended Don's first novel, years ago. But that book's final thought remained pertinent to him now—perhaps more so than ever. He craved a "new principle."

PART FIVE

RETURN

MISS PENNYBACKER'S CASTLE

In the fall of 1980, the poet Cynthia Macdonald, then teaching creative writing at the University of Houston, wrote Don, "[People] are tying yellow ribbons round all the oak trees. Guess why?—in honor of the Iranian hostages."

She said, "You are ardently wanted by us all. Saying here what I am too inhibited to gush in person, I think you are an inventive, touching, funny, strong, wonderful writer. And I like you. To have you as a colleague would be special." The coquettish tone, and the joke about the ribbons (no, it's not about *you*, dummy—it's the hostages) was perfect, and perfectly timed. Don was intrigued.

Macdonald had met him in 1971, when she was teaching at Sarah Lawrence College. Don came to give a reading. He presented "On Angels." The story's unusual structure started an on-again, off-again conversation with Macdonald that lasted the rest of his life. The topic was the frontier between fiction and poetry—"a kind of no-man's land," Macdonald wrote, where she and Don felt at home. "Poetry should only be attempted by saints and Villons," Don often quipped. He agreed with Macdonald that poetry and prose offered "different [kinds of] music," but he enjoyed mixing the tunes.

Shortly after meeting Don, Macdonald moved to Houston with her husband. A former opera singer and a trained psychoanalyst, Macdonald was by nature restless. Her marriage didn't last; she

fled Texas, and wound up teaching poetry workshops at Johns Hopkins in Baltimore. But Houston left a lasting impression on her. The city "has a sense of possibility that is very, very different from the Northeast," she said. "The attitude . . . is, 'If you want to do something, well why not?'" This is the same *ah-hell* civic disposition that inspired Don's dad in the 1930s, and Philip Johnson in the 1950s. Macdonald tasted it in the early seventies. She loved the "excitement of the city," so in 1978, when the English Department at the University of Houston called and asked if she'd like to spearhead a new creative-writing program there, the "Joanna Appleseed" in her stirred to life.

Immediately, she thought of Don, but after consulting colleagues she decided to lay a solid foundation in one literary genre at a time. She phoned a fellow poet, Stanley Plumly. He was living in New York and teaching at Princeton. Eventually, Macdonald convinced him that Houston was "on the make." If he agreed to come, the university would need to hire two fiction writers to even out the faculty.

In her mind, the key component—as ribbons adorned Houston's thick and sumptuous trees—was to lure the city's most famous literary son back home.

From 1935 until 1970, creative writing at the University of Houston was Ruth Pennybacker's castle. She was the sole ruler—and a noble figure she was. "She taught by offering the works of great writers as examples. And she kept her ego out of it," said a former student, Glenda Brownback. Another UH graduate, Janet Marks, agreed. "She creat[ed] an environment where [students] all came together. She helped us to help each other. She was very generous with her time, and she gave her all to the students." This was the teaching model Don witnessed when he was Miss Pennybacker's pupil in the 1950s, and he carried it into his classrooms in Buffalo, Boston, and New York.

With Pennybacker's retirement in 1970, Sylvan Karchmer, who had published over one hundred stories and plays, mostly under pseudonyms, took over the creative-writing classes with the help of a younger colleague, James Cleghorn. A few years later, Karchmer fell ill and retired. His departure coincided with the university's procurement of a grant to hire the critic Helen Vendler to study the university's programs and recommend "paths to distinction." She told the school to focus its energy on one area of study and marshal its resources there to achieve a national reputation.

John McNamara, then chair of the English Department, knew that creative-writing programs were inexpensive to maintain—they required no equipment and minimal library additions. Faculty salaries accounted for most of the costs. Terrell Dixon, a UH English professor, said that "the feeling at the time was that . . . we should do something a little different. And when we looked at the city and looked at the department, creative writing looked like a good way to go." Houston was booming financially; nationally, it had finally been recognized as a cultural center. Its visual and performing arts were strong: a writing program, if it could be "*about* Houston," was a natural.

Initially, Cynthia Macdonald refused the program directorship. "I didn't want to isolate myself from the writing world," she said. She agreed to serve as a special consultant to integrate writing into the department's literature curriculum. It was Peter Stitt, a poetry critic and young UH professor, who suggested recruiting Stanley Plumly.

"Houston seemed so foreign to me and it just seemed like an impossible task," Plumly said. But at this point, Macdonald was "captured by the feeling of what a really good creative writing program could do for the city." She began to work on Plumly, and erased his resistance. She met him in New York. "[W]e negotiated this program going back and forth through Central Park," Plumly recalled.

Next, Macdonald set her sights on an off-kilter Texan living in the Village.

Don had come to enjoy teaching on a limited basis. He liked socializing with students, and watching them succeed. Still, he had resisted a full-time position. When Macdonald first approached him about Houston, he refused. But something in their conversation encouraged her not to quit asking him. He shared with her the story about the therapist he'd seen before leaving Houston in the 1960s—the one who'd told him he could return when he'd reached a certain level of achievement. "I think I'm almost ready," Don told Macdonald (she was, after all, an analyst, with a gift for drawing people out).

She asked him again. Money was a factor. So was institutional commitment to the program. But by now, Macdonald knew Don well enough to understand what would really appeal to him: the certainty that his talents were needed. Macdonald saw that Don had a "willingness to work" for others "unusual" in someone "at that level of achievement." She appealed to his generosity.

Her overtures were brilliant—possibly no one else could have swayed him. Of course, she benefited from timing. Roger Angell was still lukewarm about the dialogue stories. The loss of so many close friends in quick succession had left Don reeling. New York City was broke, dark, dangerous. And on the positive side, Don had just started over with a new young wife. Change was in the air.

Despite Marion's steadying influence, Don struck Kirk Sale as enormously sad. The "death of friends" was part of his melancholy. Don "took friendship seriously," Sale says, but he feels there was more to it than this. "I would say the sadness had to do with a sense of failure to have a larger influence on literature, and the culture around him, and an awareness that he had said what he had to say and there wasn't much point in saying it over again. . . . I think that basically [by 1980] he felt he had written himself dry, and that's the reason he agreed to go to Houston. He wouldn't say it, exactly, but I felt he was pushing it, forcing [the work]."

On the other hand, Jerome Charyn feels sure Don "didn't *want* to go to Texas. He wanted to stay in New York. But he couldn't get the kind of job that would have supported him." Anne was in her teens, college expenses were looming, and Don's CCNY salary wasn't much help there.

Marion had gotten profit sharing when she left *Time,* and earned $25,000 the second year she freelanced. Still, Don wanted to take financial pressure off his writing and he turned to his dad for advice.

"The biggest mistake you can make is to *assume* that what exists now will be true [later]," the elder Barthelme said. "So all the determinations based on current facts are suspect."

He told Don that, when it came to financial planning, the one "advantage your mother and I have [is that] we don't expect [to live] another ten years." More than anything else, it may have been this talk of mortality that convinced Don he should return to Texas.

"I felt that he needed to be in Houston again for a while," wrote Helen Moore Barthelme. "He was fifty years old and sad" at the passing of friends. Recently, Mary Ann Hayes, whom Don had known since the 1950s, when they had worked together at the University of Houston, had died of a brain tumor. Don had seen her in New York when she came through on a visit. "Her visit and subsequent death . . . deeply affected" him, Helen said.

So when Cynthia Macdonald called again, putting out another feeler, Don agreed to go to Houston for a year, beginning in September 1981. ("I was furious when [City College] let him go and will never forgive the Chairman at that juncture for not fighting harder [to keep him]," says Mark Mirsky.)

Harrison Starr figured that "going to Texas would be a good thing [for Donald]. Texas would give him a little grounding to do whatever came next." He understood that Don's departure, even on a part-time basis, would be a blow to New York's literary culture. Starr says, "Donald, even though he was an avant-garde writer, was considered in New York by most of the people I knew as one of the best writers in America, if not *the* best—certainly, one of the top three or four writers of any significance. And the *best* writer, word for word, pound for pound—no matter how many commas they tried to put in, in the goddamn *New Yorker.*"

"People I knew used to think that one of the great things about being in New York was Donald," Roger Angell says.

"I thought that moving to Houston would be interesting although it surprised me because Don had kind of fled Houston when he first went to New York," Marion says. "It didn't mean we would pull up stakes because initially it was every other semester. It was nice to have a steady salary and we had happily visited Don's parents a number of times in the past, and Joan and the brothers were around."

Also, Marion had learned she was pregnant. "I was totally content with just about anything," she says.

Don's parents, especially his mother, welcomed the news of Don's return. His father wrote him in April 1981: "Your mother's check-up . . . turned out OK—or so the Doctor said—what does he know? Pete's still in trauma about not being married [anymore]. Joan is wrassling with her job and the background of the kids and a husband. Rick glows even by daylight—let him enjoy it. Steve is—Steve[,] and I guess he is entitled to play the game anyway he wants to. I guess we'll see you this fall."

THE KING

To someone who had been away from Houston for a long time (except for short visits), the city by 1980 must have seemed overbuilt and decentered. In the late 1930s, *Fortune* magazine called Houston "the city the Depression missed"; following World War II, bankers, developers, and Realtors helped Houston enjoy a longer period of economic growth than any other metropolitan area in America. Four hundred and one major office buildings rose in downtown Houston between 1971 and the early 1980s. The boom had been sustained by the early development of a freeway system, cheap land, and the absence of zoning laws. But more than anything, Houston's reputation as the nation's oil capitol spurred its growth. In 1971, a barrel of crude oil cost $3.39. By 1981, the price had risen to $31.77. Money showered onto the city. In no time, there were "too many dollars chasing too few deals," according to one investor—by 1982, this situation would spark a fiscal crisis in the city—but the perception remained that Houston was "hot."

Don's childhood neighborhood once sat out in the country, slightly beyond the western edge of Houston. Now, the Galleria shopping complex dominated the area, along with high-rise buildings and high-end retail outlets. Most of the single-family homes were gone. "I never knew what led the elder Barthelme to sell his house in West Oaks and move to a very banal townhouse develop-

ment several miles farther west," says architectural historian Stephen Fox. "On the one occasion I visited Mr. and Mrs. Barthelme in the mid-eighties, I was disconcerted to see the ordinary surroundings they lived in, knowing how exceptional and insistently singular the architect Donald Barthelme had been about his domestic setting. It was as if they had gone into exile. The house seemed cramped and anonymous."

Traces of the old Houston were hard to find, but on his return, Don loved going to Felix, a family-owned Tex-Mex restaurant on Westheimer, near Montrose. "The food at Felix is really terrible. But everyone I know who grew up in Houston in the 1940s and 50s loves it," Fox says. "It is one of those rare Houston places (and especially a middle-class place) that never changed, and its mediocrity was part of what made it so reassuring. It still exists, and it's still terrible."

In the UH English Department, "there was a feeling among the literature students that their position was being usurped by creative writing students," recalled Tom Cobb, who had been a Ph.D. candidate at the time. "I don't think that's true. The creative writing students were not standing on Cullen Boulevard with baseball bats keeping the lit students" from getting into the English building.

Phillip Lopate, who had just been hired to teach fiction writing, absorbed the fury of certain literature professors who resented the higher salaries given to creative writing teachers. Lopate believed that several of the writers—students *and* faculty—engaged in "high-handed behavior" toward old-timers in the department.

The "writing program ventilated the department and maybe the university in a way it hadn't been before. And opened it to things it wasn't quite sure at the time how it felt about," Plumly commented later.

Cynthia Macdonald dismissed these tensions as the natural growing pains of a department in transition. But clearly the old castle was in tatters, and it wasn't going to straighten up without a firm hand.

Within a month of Don's arrival, a male teacher who was suspected of sometimes teaching his classes drunk infuriated women on the staff by telling a sexist joke in the main office. One day, he stopped Don in the hallway and said, "These tight-ass feminists are taking potshots at me." He laughed, apparently expecting Don to sympathize with his plight. Don replied, "You don't seem to understand. I'm part of the firing squad."

Days later, this particular teacher appeared to be gone from the department.

Word filtered out of Don's classes that he would not brook bad writing. Years later, reflecting on Don's workshops, a former student named Glenn

Blake said, "What he was teaching us, what we were learning, was how to edit our own fiction. . . . He knew that one day we would move on, away from writing classes, away from writing instructors, alone, with only our own mean eyes."

The process was rigorous. "All you had to do was walk to the front of the room, stand, and read your story to the class," Blake said. "And when it was all over, you could not sit down and hide. No. You had to stay up there for as long as it took and listen to the criticism—sometimes, line by line. You could not say a word—that was in the rules—could not defend yourself."

He remembered his first writing class with Don:

> A friend of mine [named Rick] walked to the front of the room and started reading this forty-five-page story about basketball—it seemed he was always writing about basketball—*long* stories. I mean, there wasn't so much as a dribble until the tenth page.
>
> Somewhere about halfway down the third page, Don stopped him and said, "Rick, does it get any better?"
>
> "Yes," Rick said. "Oh yes," Rick said. "Oh hell yes, Don. It gets a *whole* lot better. Just wait."
>
> Don just looked at him and said, "I think not. Have a seat."

Tom Cobb remembered taking the first chapter of his novel into Don's class, a story about a down-and-out country singer. Don asked Cobb what he planned to do with the character. Cobb said the man would "play a couple of bars, get drunk, and take some women back to his room." Don replied, "Well, I think you should pour gasoline on him and set him on fire. The novel's getting nowhere."

To another student, Don advised removing all descriptions of weather from a story. Writing about sunshine and storms, he said, led to "acres and acres of rather ordinary prose." The student protested: "But what would *King Lear* be without weather?" Don responded, "If you write *Lear* again, I'll make an exception in your case."

If a student's work appealed to him, Don stirred from his boredom and became exceedingly generous with his time. Olive Hershey, then writing a novel, later recalled "epic" editing sessions with Don. One day, he called her and said, "I'm coming over, buy a bottle of Scotch." "What kind?" she asked. "Teacher's, of course," Don said.

Off and on, over a period of four days, Don cut more than a hundred pages from her manuscript. He would draw a line though an entire page. "All right?" he'd ask. Hershey would swallow hard and say, "All right." Don would then say, "Good woman."

Padgett Powell recalled, "For our first tutorial . . . Don put a comment in a margin of mine and blotted it out before I saw it." Powell recounted the conversation that ensued:

> What was that? I asked.
> A comment.
> I *suspected* that. What did it say?
> What did it say?
> Yes, sir. *What did it say?*
> I didn't know you. I can see now you can take it.
> All right, I can take it. What did it say?
> That half said *Faulkner.*
> And that half?
> That half?
> *That* half.
> That half said *ersatz.*

Powell sat silently. Don asked him, "You do know what 'ersatz' means?"

"*Of course* I know what *ersatz* means. What is the big deal with *ersatz Faulkner? Of course* it's ersatz Faulkner. *Everybody* does *ersatz Faulkner—*"

"Okay, okay. I said I didn't know you. You can take it."

Powell made Don promise he would never "withhold a comment" from him. "I am not here to *get a degree,*" he said. "I am here to *write a book.*" And then he told Don, "If we have to do *this* anymore, we're not doing it in an office. We are doing it in a bar."

Looking back on this incident, Powell said:

> I was a blustery boy then, and had no idea I'd called for a change of venue so dear to my . . . mentor. Whether he liked my slapping around of the father—insisting on *more* discipline—or the betrayal of my own proclivity to drink, or was reminded that it was time for one himself, I do not know. He was to extend to me . . . a very careful, gingerly fathering and I to him a very careful, blustery obedience, neither of us admitting very much the little tango.

With remarkable swiftness, mediocrity had been banished from the castle. An *actual writing program* took shape. Since Don had never earned a university degree, the department would not let him teach literature courses, but he offered a Fiction Forms class, in which students edited and rewrote Hemingway's *Islands in the Stream.* If Hemingway had lived, Don said, he never would have published such terrible prose. Don set another group of students to writing stories that employed plot devices from the television police drama *Hill Street Blues*—a way of learning to manage many characters at once.

Marion says that despite his strict standards, "He never thought anyone was a hopeless writer."

To his fellow faculty members, Don went out of his way to present himself as part of the group. He was not, he insisted, the program's director. He was firm that all program decisions be made by faculty agreement. But everyone knew who was king. His status as hometown boy gave him clout with the university, and connections to the city's art world.

That first semester, in the fall of 1981, Don lived with his brother Pete in Pete's house at the corner of Bissonnet and Shepard streets, not far from Houston's best bookstore, the Brazos, and the Museum of Fine Arts. Marion stayed in New York. Pete's eighteen-year-old daughter shared the Houston house, which made the place feel crowded and "sort of like a barracks," Don said. But he enjoyed "uncling," picking his niece up from school, driving Pete's big Chevy Ranger; he liked cooking for his brother, and he put a lot of energy into housekeeping.

Occasionally, he lunched with his ex-wife Helen at a restaurant called Ruggles on Westheimer Street. They talked about old friends—Pat Goeters was now practicing architecture in California; Robert Morris was still in Connecticut; Harry Vitemb had been shot to death during a holdup in a doughnut shop. Don seemed happy to be in Houston. Anne was nearly sixteen. He missed her terribly during the year, he told Helen, but he was glad she was going to school in Copenhagen and not in New York City, whose schools were "hell holes." Marion was expecting a child in January; she had "worn [him] down" on the subject of having a baby. He said he was trying to write a novel. Its tentative title was *Ghosts.*

STILL LIFE

"I know that Donald was good for the university and am prepared to believe that the university was good *to* him. Whether academic life was good *for* Donald Barthelme the writer is not for me to speculate," John Barth said.

In Don's late work, wrote Jerome Klinkowitz, "No longer will Kafka or Tolstoy be asked to sit uncomfortably within the . . . confines of our postmodern world . . . nor will there be a cubist disorder of conversations. . . . There will be precious few fragments. . . ."

Did Don, easing into tenured life, lose his edge? Was he stunned into contentment by fine furniture, good food, and the habits of domesticity? His new colleague Phillip Lopate entertained the possibility. "He would often talk to me about new types of VCRs or word-processors, a sportscar he was fantasizing buying," Lopate said. "He was also very interested in food: I would run into him shopping in the supermarket, wicker basket in hand, throwing in a package of tortellini; one time he began talking about the varieties of arugula and radicchio, then added that he could never leave the place without spending a fortune. 'They create these needs and you can't resist. They've figured out a way to hook you,' he said.

"These disquisitions on arugula were not exactly what I had hoped for from Barthelme," Lopate wrote. "I wanted him to stand up and be the staunch intellectual hero-father. Part of me responded

with a line from Ernest Becker's *The Denial of Death:* 'The depressed person enslaves himself to the trivial.' Another part suspected that I, long-time bachelor, was merely envious of his settled . . . family life."

Marion points out that Don had been interested in food and cooking for quite some time. "It was a way for him to both relax and be creative. And it's another form of nourishing people," she says. "He was always in search of that elusive Thai curry from the days in Korea, and an early-memory gumbo that he kept trying to replicate. He'd spend hours cooking it and then would say, 'Nope, it's not right.'

"I liked to cook, too," Marion says. "I had a friend who gave me a couple of lessons when I first lived in New York. She knew Julia Child, so that was my cookbook. Don's was Rombauer [*The Joy of Cooking*]. Our copy still has his annotations on how to [improve] popovers. It's so old and splattered now, you could toss it in water and make soup. He'd make great stews in which there was butter, butter, butter and he always cooked fried chicken for Anne the first night [she'd arrive for a visit]."

As for the writing: Such early eighties stories as "Bishop" and "Visitors," meditations on a middle-aged man's not-so-eventful days, may seem tame after so many years of Don's formal playfulness. But *straightforward narrative* was just one more approach to storytelling that Don had added to his arsenal (and, in any case, narrative wasn't unprecedented in his work). Klinkowitz has suggested that Don's late stories are more "relaxed" and "generous" than his earlier pieces. Don was no longer dueling with tradition; he was drawing from material he had established over time. The late work reveals a "confidence with subject and form equal to almost any previous high point in the development of the American short story."

Then there's this: When Don turned to "realism" in stories like "Bishop," he held in mind a model from the visual arts. His early work thrummed with the spirits of Abstract Expressionism, Pop Art, Dada, and Surrealism. Now, he contemplated American still lifes.

Still lifes depict inanimate objects arranged for aesthetic purposes. Though often viewed as extreme realism—domestic experience in its humblest aspects, fruit on a table, picked flowers—still life is, in fact, "the most artificial of all artistic subjects and the one most concerned with the making of art," wrote John Wilmerding, who had closely studied the subject. "Before actually painting, an artist has crucial preliminary decisions to make regarding his selection and arrangement of forms." Thus, the "foremost concern of still-life painting is pure artistic form. In this regard, it is not accidental that the great cubist breakthrough . . . took place via still-life components,"

Wilmerding said. "[Still life] has always drawn special attention to its inherently abstract and conceptual character."

Wilmerding's insights help us grasp Don's distinctive type of "realism": As ever, he was mostly engaged with formal concerns—juxtapositions, layerings—and the nature of art.

"Bishop" tells the story of a man's day, but every gesture, thought, or activity in which he engages is isolated from the others, sentence by sentence. The story presents a series of moments, arranged the way objects are grouped together (but apart) in a still life. Bishop, an art critic, is writing a biography of the nineteenth-century American painter William Michael Harnett. In the course of his research, he learns about a second artist, the still-life painter John F. Peto, whose work "was discovered when, after his death, his pictures were exhibited with the faked signatures of William Michael Harnett."

Peto and Harnett are actual historical figures. Harnett enjoyed a successful career. His most famous painting is called *After the Hunt,* a phrase appropriate to Bishop's emotional life.

On the other hand, little is known about Peto. According to Wilmerding, he is an "American artist only partially discovered": a hiding man. Like Don, he was born in Philadelphia, and later moved to the East Coast. He "appears to have been a bit of an eccentric," someone who "spent his creative energies alchemizing domestic bric-a-brac." His still lifes "were indexes of his autobiography, and . . . his work was about the mysterious struggle of creation." Peto's later still-life paintings came to resemble collages, shaded with complex buried meanings, and were often "eloquent meditations on the mortality of things." Additionally, Peto was "out of tune" with his age. In his formal constructions, he anticipated such "modern artists as Robert Rauschenberg."

Given all this, it's easy to see why Don was drawn to Peto—his playfulness, his compressed images, his sadness and obscurity.

The American still-life tradition flourished toward the end of the nineteenth century, in the wake of the Civil War. "It borders on oversimplification to [suggest] a change in national life from innocence to complexity and cynicism" at that time, admitted Wilmerding, "yet unquestionably the tone of America's self-perception and of artistic expression was different" from the way it was before the war.

The same mood obtained in post-Vietnam America. Don's Bishop stories focus on an urban, middle-class American in the late twentieth century who is surrounded by material luxuries that fail to fulfill him. The first great American still lifes were created at a time of "great accumulations and expenditures of wealth" in this country; the Bishop stories chronicle another moment of affluence and decadence. They reveal the spiritual and cultural dead ends to which prosperity is prone to lead.

When "Bishop" first appeared in print, Don "began getting calls from friends, some of whom I hadn't heard from in a long time and all of whom were offering Tylenol and bandages," he said. "The assumption was that identification of the author with the character"—a man experiencing "a rather depressing New York day"—was "not only permissible but invited. This astonished me. One uses one's depressions as one uses everything else, but what I was doing was writing a story. Merrily merrily merrily merrily."

In this case, it's impossible to miss the parallels between author and character (in early drafts, Bishop's name was *Plumly*): same age, same physical appearance, same home city, same general profession. When we encounter Bishop again in "Visitors," he has a teenaged daughter who lives apart from him. He begins a desultory affair with a young woman.

"Roger Angell and I went to a reading on the Upper West Side—must have been the Y—in which Don read 'Bishop,'" Ann Beattie recalls. "People who knew Don were rather astonished that with Marion in the audience, this was what he was reading. Years later, I found out that several people assumed *they* were the one he was writing about in that story."

Oscar Hijuelos remembers Don saying around this time that he'd like to write a straightforward book about growing up in Texas but that no one would expect that from him. "Had Don lived to experience the age of memoir, I can only think it would have made him back off from writing about growing up in Texas," Beattie says.

Even at his most autobiographical, Don was more likely to layer material, and to reference works of art, than he was to confess anything. Here, again, John F. Peto provided a model for him. Peto's mature paintings brim with outdated furniture and old tin cups—objects, Wilmerding wrote, that evoke "nostalgia for a lost frontier past: in a sophisticated urban age the simple tin cup is a relic to dream on." In similar fashion, "Bishop" ends with a weary city dweller dreaming about his grandfather's country ranch.

Don's other signature style, late in his career, is the lyrical dialogue, which he continued to write. He included eight of them in his retrospective collection, *Sixty Stories,* which was published just before he returned to teach at the University of Houston. With a new job, a new (old) home, a new baby on the way—and having just turned fifty—the time was right for taking stock.

Reviewers received the collection warmly. Writing in *Newsweek,* Walter Clemons said, "Barthelme isn't easy, and he frequently fails, but he's written some of the best stories of the last twenty years." Clemons had lost patience with critics who claimed the word *story* didn't adequately describe Don's work: "Somerset Maugham didn't believe Chekhov or Katherine Mansfield wrote proper stories either, because theirs weren't like Maupassant's, or like his own."

Clemons said the "tension, gaiety, and exactitude of [Don's] despair" are what give his stories "their eerie energy." His "calm, precise prose requests the most strenuous attention." After all these years, Don was still, according to Clemons, "one of the most adventurous American writers now at work."

In *The New York Times Book Review,* John Romano recalled the "excitement caused among readers" at the appearance of Don's first stories in the 1960s. "There just weren't then, as there aren't now, very many stories published that you wanted to call your friends up and read aloud from; and Barthelme gave us more than a few," wrote Romano.

"[Now] on rereading, [he is] not just witty but extremely funny," Romano said. "[The] will to please us, to make us sit up and laugh with surprise, is greater . . . than the will to disconcert. The chief thing to say about Barthelme, beyond praise for his skill, which seems to me supererogatory, is that he is fiercely committed to showing us a good time . . . although there is an avant-gardist flair, and broken lines and paragraphs, and an air of experiment everywhere in his prose, nothing much is finally challenged. . . . The spirit is: Many things are silly, especially about modern language, and there is much sadness everywhere, but all is roughly well. So let's try and enjoy ourselves, as intelligently as possible."

Romano concluded by saying that Don was "marvelously gifted"; still, he felt that Don's "development [has been] more or less toward the lyric and trivial . . . he is shifting his artistic focus from the true to the beautiful; instead of conjuring, in his fractured, collagiste way, the weirdness of emotional life, he is seeking the unbroken arias of the imaginary." This made for "slicker and slicker prose" but led Don more and more into "trifles."

What no reviewer discussed was that Don's recent works seemed meant for public performance more than for silent reading, as was true of the earlier, denser work. The dialogues, especially, crackled with energy when delivered aloud—a point not lost on director J. Ranelli and the actors at the American Place Theatre in New York, who set about trying to adapt several of them for the stage (a process that took several years).

The dialogues were minimalist Don: a style nevertheless distinct from the fiction being *called* "minimalist" by book reviewers and critics. By the early 1980s, "minimalism" had become the hottest trend in American literary publishing.

"1975 seems to be the year when minimalist fiction first appeared significantly in the 'slick' [magazines], with the publication of [Ann] Beattie's

'Dwarf House' and 'Wanda's' in the *New Yorker* in January and October, respectively, and [Raymond] Carver's 'Collectors' in *Esquire* in August," noted Roland Sodowsky, who studied American magazine fiction during the 1970s and 1980s. "[Mary] Robison's stories began to appear in 1977, followed by [Bobbie Ann] Mason's in 1980. The 'heavy' years in the *New Yorker* began in 1981 . . . when Beattie, Robison, and Mason were joined by Frederick Barthelme and Carver."

Kim Herzinger, Rick Barthelme's former colleague at the University of Southern Mississippi, described minimalist fiction this way: It is "characterized by equanimity of surface, 'ordinary' subjects, recalcitrant narrators and deadpan narratives, slightness of story, and characters who don't think out loud." If most of this list could describe Don's work of the previous twenty years, there were two striking differences between him and the minimalists: Whereas Don's fiction was pervaded by an "experimental spirit," the minimalists pursued an "aggressive lucidity," and, in general, betrayed a "profound uneasiness with irony as a mode of presentation." Minimalist stories were "terse, oblique, realist or hyperrealistic," John Barth wrote. Often, their spare settings were evoked by nothing more than product brand names. Purposely flat, many of the stories were first- or second-person narratives, and many of them (especially those by Carver and Mason) concerned blue-collar lives. Beattie, on the other hand, limned the affairs of white middle-class yuppies.

Arguably, Don had been the most imitated short story writer in the United States in the late 1960s and early 1970s. Raymond Carver could now claim that distinction. Critics advanced various theories as to why minimalism had caught on—some said university writing programs promoted a certain simple style that was easy to teach and learn; others said that in a culture saturated with too much information, readers' minds were no longer attuned to difficult prose; some claimed that in an increasingly ambiguous world, readers longed for clarity, others termed minimalism the literary equivalent of the nation's "energy crisis." Whatever the reasons, by the early 1980s, the "minimalist fad" was so dominant that "nothing else could get through into the light," said the novelist Madison Smartt Bell.

Of the twenty-two pieces in the annual *O. Henry Prize Stories* published just before *Sixty Stories* appeared, all were "realistic" and most matched Herzinger's definition of minimalism. Magazine editors declared the end of the "experimental" era. Daniel Halpern, editor of the prestigious (now defunct) journal *Antaeus,* went so far as to say, "Experimentalism is only the misuse of the language."

Contemplating the state of the American short story in 1980, Anita Shreve said that U.S. fiction remained "surprisingly isolated, for the most part, from current international trends. The best foreign stories—those of

Argentina's Jorge Luis Borges, Colombia's Gabriel García Márquez, Italy's Italo Calvino and Austria's Peter Handke—are surrealistic in style, rent with bizarre invisible seams, unsettling, and sometimes to the uninitiated, even creepy. . . . Most American stories attempt to draw readers in; many of the best foreign stories challenge them."

Readers old enough to recall the first issue of *Location* saw how similar Shreve's observation was to Harold Rosenberg's diagnosis of American fiction in 1963. Despite a brief blip on the screen, "experimental" prose had always been, and remained, an anomaly in American literature. "Donald Barthelme," Shreve said, "[is] often seen as the only American alternative to the naturalistic story."

Released into the context of minimalism's strongest year to date, *Sixty Stories* was a stubborn statement by the nation's "most adventurous writer" as well as a summing up. Walter Clemons reminded readers that the volume wasn't "the late-life 'Collected Stories' of a senior master who may not write many more but an interim selection of a distinctive writer who just turned fifty and is, I hope, in mid-career."

INPRINT

In the fall of 1981, as he was living in Houston with Pete and await-
ing the birth of his second child, Don imagined conversations with
the unborn baby. This unfinished fragment is an example:

It's Wednesday morning, Buttercup.

Got to go out to the university to pick up my check. Unless Uncle Pete
decides to put the truck into the shop to get the muffler fixed. The muffler's wired to the body with coathangers.

The air is clear but hot. I hear you've been kicking your mother in
the stomach and belching. Belching is not polite. The first of
500,000 admonitions . . .

This place has black iron bars on all the windows and doors. The
outside is seen through a IIII or in the case of the bigger doors, a IIIII-
IIIII. If I had the wings of an angel / over these prison walls I would fly.
No, it's really not so bad, an irk here and an irk there but bearable. . . .

Going to put your box under my desk and tickle your stomach with
the toe of my boot. Hurry up, Buttercup, we're tired of waiting. . . .

When fall classes ended, Don flew back to New York. "Katharine
was born January 13, 1982 in the middle of a horrific snowstorm,"
Marion says. "It took what seemed ages to get to New York Hospital
from the Village and I'm not sure how Donald ever snagged the cab

we took but I was Lamaze deep-breathing the whole way up through the deeply whitening city with Donald saying, 'You're not supposed to do that until it's really time,' and me saying, 'It's time!' "

Anne visited in the summer and introduced herself to her good-natured sister. In the fall, Don moved his wife and new child to Doville, in Houston's Montrose area. Doville was named for Dominique de Menil. In the 1960s, she began buying the old bungalows in the area around the University of St. Thomas, where she would also commission the Rothko Chapel to be built in 1969 (followed, nearly twenty years later, by the Menil Museum). The bungalows had been constructed in the teens and twenties, when Montrose was the city's elite residential neighborhood.

Here, de Menil hoped to salvage old Houston charm. Her dream, which she realized over the years, was to rent the houses to artists and patrons of the arts.

Rosellen Brown moved into the neighborhood in the early 1980s, when she was hired to teach fiction writing at UH. She loved the "vernacular 'everyman' feel" of the "little wooden bungalow[s]" with their "cement and brick" front steps. "The light that filtered through our large magnolia and pecan trees was perfectly softened; the temperature of the long [fall and winter] was ideal," she said. "A lovely informal peace prevailed around the loosely controlled space of the Menil 'compound.'" On any given evening, wedding parties might "break ... out through the doors of the Rothko [chapel]"—or funeral crowds, mourning victims of AIDS.

Marion thought her own "little Menil" house was "wonderful." She says it was "fixed up in [Don's] stark minimalist way with some rented furniture, striped wallpaper tacked up for shades in the windows, my kimono which he hung on the wall, a desk he'd made from a hollow core door, a kitchen table he fashioned, a borrowed crib, four forks, four knives, etc. He loved that clean interior design, Knoll look, influenced by his father, I'm sure."

Around a lightbulb hanging from the ceiling in a corner of the living room, Don placed a large, round paper shade, startlingly white. It fascinated Katharine.

One warm mid-September evening, with sunset lingering and cricket song in the air, Don and Marion invited students over for drinks. Whenever Marion walked by carrying Katharine—like her mother, a stunning little blonde—Don's eyes softened. That night, Katharine took some of her first steps toward one of the students in the kitchen. Don looked on, beaming.

"I never really did get over my surprise at Don's institutional energy, his savvy, the sheer kick he seemed to get out of creating an academic program that mattered," said Lois Zamora, a comparative literature teacher in the

English Department at the University of Houston. "His dedication to his students ('They're my new affinity group, Lois'), to English Department and Creative Writing projects, to hiring, fundraising, cheerleading, mentoring, enabling, never ceased to amaze me, in part because I didn't expect him to be so generous with his time but mainly because he was so good at it all. His authority as 'famous writer' was important, but that was only a starting point. Don was, I think, fascinated by the workings of the often unwieldy bureaucracy of our large state university. Its institutional irrationalities and its moments of collective genius coincided with Don's own sense of the world—absurd, mysterious, deeply worthwhile."

Barry Munitz, chancellor of the University of Houston from 1977 to 1982, knew he'd struck gold with Don. "I knew that to build an excellent program in the arts, you had to take some risks and move across dotted lines. In the arts, the student-faculty ratio has to be smaller, and you have to bring in different types of people," he says. "The fact that Don didn't have a university degree made no difference to me. The best places can afford to stretch out. It's the B, B+ institutions that are too tight, too caught up in traditional notions of prestige. If you're serious about being good, you get past that."

Munitz says he asked Don to be the "head of our celebrity dog and pony show as the school raised money throughout the city for the writing program, and set up Inprint, an organization that allowed the program to raise funds independently of the university.

"The key was, we'd have these conversations with potential donors in small groups," Munitz says. "Eloise Cooper, the owner of a Houston café called Ouisie's, hosted events for us. In fact, one of our first terrific fundraisers was built around the movie *Babette's Feast.* We rented the Greenway Plaza movie theater, screened the movie for folks, and Eloise cooked the same meals as in the movie. So people got to see a show, schmooze with writers, and have a wonderful meal."

Don designed a poster for the program featuring silhouettes of a man and woman, dressed in a tux and a flapper-style dress, dancing. The text reads:

> Tried Houston. It was terrible.
> Terrible?
> Terrible in the morning, terrible at night.
> Even in the spring?
> Even in the fall.
> How are their funerals?
> Terrible.
> Even in the rain?
> Especially in the rain.

Their weddings?
Terrible. Jasmine, that sort of thing—
Do they hug and kiss?
Sometimes, but not well. Terribly, in fact.
Why is that?
They're writers.

"At a fund-raiser, we'd host, say, twenty or thirty people at a time," Munitz says. "These were local corporate heads and entrepreneurial people, high-net-worth individuals who were multigenerational or who had built their own companies. And they were extraordinarily generous. At the time, those of us interested in the arts were working to build the opera, the Alley Theatre, the ballet. . . . Our pitch was, none of these could be sustained without a strong public university and a strong writing program.

"In a small group, Donald would sit and draw on place mats or on napkins, saying, 'We can do this in fiction, this in poetry, and let's not forget nonfiction. We can bring in so-and-so to lecture.' We'd tie the writing program to the other arts."

Always, Don's priority was "shoring up student stipends." He worked more on that than on faculty salaries. "Don wanted the very best students. And he was determined to work them hard," Munitz says.

"His commitment to the program was genuine and extraordinary. He made it out of loyalty to the city and to the institution—he wouldn't have felt the same way anywhere else," says Munitz. "But he was also loyal to the type of students he had here. It was counterintuitive—*Houston?* He loved running into people in New York, and they'd ask him, 'What have you been up to?' and he'd say, 'I've been teaching down in Houston,' and they'd say, '*Houston?* Why?' Or he'd meet some academic from Boston who'd tell him how much trouble they were having getting Stephen Spender to come for a talk, and Don would say, 'Oh, he just spent a semester with us in Houston.' He'd tell these stories joyfully. He was proud that we built something out of nothing."

Phillip Lopate also noted Don's commitment to "underdogs." "He attended all the meetings, never missed a class, gave enormous amounts of time to his students. He was incredibly responsible," Lopate says.

Students who spent a lot of time with Don realized it was best to catch him in late afternoon or early evening, when he'd want to slip off to a bar, or—now that Katharine was around—when he'd invite you to bring a manuscript to his house for an editing session, during which he broke out the scotch. Earlier in the day, he was often taciturn and withdrawn. Later in the evening, he'd tend to lose focus, and might repeat something he'd forgotten he'd told you the day before.

A faculty member recalls telling Don that a relative of his had an awful drinking problem. Don asked him, "Is she sober sometimes and then out of it, or a little drunk all the time?"

Then Don admitted, "I'm a little drunk all the time."

His colleague answered, "I know, Don."

"In his distance" from his colleagues and friends, "he seemed to be monitoring some inner uneasiness," Lopate says. "I suppose that was partly his alcoholism . . . [but] I never saw Don falling-down drunk; he held his liquor, put on a good performance of sobriety."

At work and at home, "he was a world-class worrier," says the poet Ed Hirsch, another colleague of Don's. "I picture him like the speaker in his story 'Chablis,' sitting up in the early morning, at the desk. . . . It is five-thirty, and he is 'sipping a glass of Gallo Chablis with an ice cube in it, smoking, worrying.' "

Don was scared that something would happen to his baby girl; scared that the castle would crumble; scared that he possessed neither faith nor fidelity enough to shoulder what he had, in fact, shouldered; scared that he had "done his little thing."

"He may have felt he had done what he could in writing, and then turned to the Houston program to leave a different sort of legacy," Barry Munitz says. "That's a hard thing to do-it's like being a Nobel Prize-winning physicist who gives up research to keep the lab running. There's satisfaction in helping others, but it's hard to know that you're not doing the real work anymore."

"Sometimes he would come to my house late at night, unannounced," says Hirsch. "He'd show up around twelve and ring the bell. He wouldn't talk about what had happened, but clearly something had propelled him out of the house. I'd give him a hug, which made him feel awkward. I'd ask questions and he'd answer them or he wouldn't answer them. He liked that I would fill the space. I'd do the social work when we were together. We'd talk about writing and the literary life and then he'd go home. 'Do you want me to drive you?' I'd ask. He'd answer, 'I've been driving drunk since I was sixteen. I can manage.' On those occasions I saw the depth of his solitude."

Writing had ceased to be pure enjoyment. It was business—and, in tangible terms, not terribly rewarding. Royalty statements show that *Snow White,* the one book that had remained steadily in print, earned Don anywhere from thirty to three hundred dollars a year. For all his other books combined, he was liable to make, in any given year, less than a thousand dollars. For a while, even after taking the Houston job, he remained in debt to *The New Yorker.*

Frustrated with Farrar, Straus and Giroux's penny-pinching, its lack of commercial chutzpah, Don finally jumped ship. He took *Sixty Stories* to his old friend Faith Sale, now an editor at Putnam. He signed a three-book deal, breaking his contract with FSG. He had promised his old publisher a second children's book and another novel. Early in 1982, Maggie Curran, to whom Lynn Nesbit now entrusted much of Don's business, told Don that FSG was demanding 75 percent of everything he earned from *Sixty Stories.* In turn, they would pay him 50 percent of the 75 percent. This was in addition to FSG's demand that the entire advance for *Sixty Stories*—thirty thousand dollars—be paid back, which was a further condition of releasing Don from his contract. As of February 1982, the book had earned only fifteen thousand dollars, so Don was likely to owe FSG for a long time.

He took genuine delight in Katharine and in living with his family. Katharine was becoming more active, and the rental agreement on his Doville house would soon be up. Don looked for another place. He found a stately brick house on South Boulevard, in one of Houston's oldest and most elegant neighborhoods, close to Rice University and the Museum of Fine Arts. It was right across the street from the Edgar Allan Poe Elementary School. The boulevard was distinguished by a fifty-three-foot esplanade down its center, with massive oak trees on either side whose limbs met overhead and provided a leafy canopy.

Don, Marion, and Katharine moved into the shady upper floor of the house. White floor-to-ceiling bookshelves lined one wall of the living room. A framed De Chirico print hung next to the kitchen doorway. Just off the living room, a spacious area with windows all around overlooked the neighborhood's backyard gardens. Don liked to sit there in a wicker rocker. His bedroom doubled as his study. His desk sat before a window above the boulevard. Early in the mornings, Don would rise, heat an El Patio enchilada dinner for breakfast, and write.

Here, he composed "Chablis" and "The Baby," two affectionate pieces about Katharine. He loved to read the stories to audiences. In "The Baby," a hapless father fails to train his infant not to tear pages out of books, and ends up joining her in her mischief. "That is one of the satisfying things about being a parent—you've got a lot of moves," he wrote. Now, "[t]he baby and I sit happily on the floor, side by side, tearing pages out of books, and sometimes, just for fun, we go out on the street and smash a windshield together."

In "Chablis," a gentle father worries that his baby "may jam a kitchen knife into an electrical outlet while she's wet" or that she may wolf down a box of crayons. He worries about money. He worries about the fact that he is "not a more natural person, like [his] wife wants [him] to be." As he sits at his desk, watching runners on the street, "individually or in pairs, running toward rude red health," he remembers his reckless youth. The story ends on a note of wistfulness for his long-ago wildness, but also with love for his child: "I remember the time, thirty years ago, when I put Herman's mother's Buick into a cornfield, on the Beaumont highway. There was another car in my lane, and I didn't hit it. . . . That was when I was a black sheep, years and years ago. That was skillfully done, I think. I get up, congratulate myself in memory, and go in to look at the baby."

MANY DISTANCES

"He was going to settle down and be the family man. And it didn't work," says Phillip Lopate. "[Don's] return to Houston was a kind of defeat, I believe. In stories like 'Chablis,' he tried to put the best face on things, but he was restless. He cared a great deal about the writing program, but his world had shrunk, and I think he knew it, and he tried to cover that up. He'd shut down. He'd stopped taking things in, so there was no more Kierkegaard, no more Cortés and Montezuma. What he was taking in were lifestyle things, new cars, food. I used to tell him, 'You know, Don, just because you haven't heard of something doesn't mean it's not important.' He'd made up his mind a long time ago about things."

Several times, Don told Lopate he'd lost his zest for life. With the deaths of Harold Rosenberg and Tom Hess he'd stopped learning new things. "I'm still working off that old knowledge. What I really want are older men, father-figures who can teach *me* something. I don't want to be people's damn father-figure. I want to be the baby," Don said. "The problem is that the older you get, the harder it is to find these older role models."

In this sad spirit, Don confided to Padgett Powell that he "might retire, that he had done . . . his 'little things.'"

"Well, Don, why not do the *big things?*" Powell asked him one day.

"I have a black heart," Don said.

"Well, *write* a black heart."

"Have a wife and child."

"We are talking *Art,* aren't we? Damn the torpedoes."

"No."

"At times he gave the impression, like a burn victim lying uncomfortably in the hospital, that there was something I was neglecting to do or figure out that might have put him at greater ease," Lopate says. "[I noticed] he liked to be around women, particularly younger women, and grew more relaxed in their company. I don't think this was purely a matter of lechery, though lust no doubt played its classical part. . . . Certainly some of the women in the writing program objected to what they felt was [Donald's] preference for the pretty young females in class."

"Donald was existentially very lonely and by temperament alienated. He liked to be part of something," says Ed Hirsch.

In Don's next book—*Overnight to Many Distant Cities,* published in 1983— one of the stories, "The Palace at Four A.M.," paints an indelible portrait of loneliness. The title alludes to a Giacometti sculpture, a piece the artist made after he'd lost a lover.

In Don's story, a king writes his autobiography. The king's representative implores Hannahbella, a "tiny spirit" with whom the king has had a romance, to read the passages about her: a ploy to get her back. The story ends: "You loved him, he says, he is convinced of it, he exists in a condition of doubt. . . . The palace at four a.m. is silent. Come back, Hannahbella, and speak to him."

The reviews for *Overnight* were among the harshest of Don's career. The book "repels any understanding whatsoever," Jonathan Penner wrote in *The Washington Post.* "What this book says is that nothing can be said. . . . Life means nothing, art is false. . . ." In *The New York Times,* Anatole Broyard bemoaned what had "become a pattern in the late Barthelme work: the promise is grand, but then the author . . . stutters. . . ."

Also in the *Times,* Joel Conarroe remarked on the "curiously vacuous" effect of most of the stories, and concluded, "I don't mean to suggest that the Emperor [has] no clothes. I do, though, increasingly get the impression that his suit [is] threadbare."

Twelve brief interchapters link the stories in *Overnight,* similar to the vignettes in Hemingway's first collection of stories published in the United States, *In Our Time.* Hemingway remarked that his vignettes offered coastline views as seen from a ship. In Don's case, the interchapters offered "overnight" dreams, weirdly transforming the daylight material from the book's companion tales of domesticity and urban life.

One of the interchapters, "I put a name in an envelope . . ." was part of a catalog introduction Don had written for a Joseph Cornell exhibit at the Castelli Gallery in 1976. Cornell's spirit touches all of *Overnight:* Many of the short texts involve the construction of small-scale imaginative worlds ("Holding the ladder I watch you glue . . . chandeliers to . . . [tree] limbs . . .") while a number of the longer stories take place in hotels or in the midst of temporary arrangements, recalling Cornell's celebration of the ephemeral in his work (Cornell made a *Hotel* series of boxes; often, he included stamps and letters in his collages—correspondence blown on the wind).

Don's reviewers missed these echoes and aims. They seemed to have lost patience with learning from a writer how to read him. Instead, they approached *Overnight* with a fixed idea of "story." When the book did not match their preconceptions, they dismissed it. It was one thing to say, as did Anatole Broyard, that *Overnight* did not represent top-drawer Barthelme. It was another to call the book nonsense without taking into account the writer's intentions. One could readily believe that "minimalism" *was* the new literary currency: Anything beyond six-word sentences about fast food and television now seemed beyond the capacities of many readers, even those who read for a living.

Dispirited, Don loped down the halls of the Roy Cullen Building. Fissures had opened up among the faculty. Some of them complained that the best students flocked toward Don—not just because they prized Don's teaching but also because they hoped to use his literary connections. The lunch meetings became more awkward.

"During heated discussions" at these meetings, "Donald would often wait until everyone else had declared a position, and then weigh in with the final word, more like an arbiter than an interested party," Lopate says. "He was good at manipulating consensus through democratic discussion to get his way; and we made it easy for him, since everyone wanted his love and approval. . . . Still, when a vote did go against him, he bowed sportingly to majority will. He often seemed to be holding back from using his full clout; he was like those professional actors who give the impression at social gatherings of saving their real energy for the real performance later."

Only once did Don give in to pleasure at one of these afternoon gatherings. The group was discussing how to update faculty bios for a new promotional poster. Rosellen Brown suggested, "Donald Barthelme—Still Famous." Don leaned back in his chair, put his napkin to his mouth, and roared.

For all his deflation, he soldiered on with a touching almost optimism. Once, he organized a dance in a local art annex, the Lawndale, for students in the creative-writing program and the UH Art Department. He felt that students' teaching and class schedules restricted their social lives. The party space was as big as a warehouse. The young painters, in green-and-red-spattered overalls, huddled on one side of the room, shy as middle school kids, while Don's protégés crowded into the opposite corner. Finally, in an attempt to merge everyone, Don stepped into the center of the floor, wearing (as usual) a striped cotton shirt, khaki pants, and cowboy boots, and asked a scared young art student to dance. No matter—the painters and writers never relaxed with one another that night, to Don's great disappointment. Still, he'd tried.

For a while, he joined a graduate-student band, Moist and the Towlettes. "I used to play the drums, you know," he told his astonished students. The group played ratchety three-chord rock at parties and book signings. *Texas Monthly* called it the "worst band in Houston, if not the universe." Soon enough, the tedious practice sessions bored Don, but at the band's first couple of gigs, he seemed transcendently pleased. At a dance one night in a bookstore parking lot, he beamed and waved his sticks like a sprightly conductor. Midway through the show, the group's backup singers wandered off into the crowd (discipline, like harmony, was not a Towlette virtue). Don laughed, hit a mighty rim shot, and carried the band into the next wild song.

BETWEEN COASTS

Houston was an easier and safer place than New York to raise a child, said Don. But he kept returning to Manhattan with his family, at first for half a year, then only in the summers. Phillip Lopate, who also spent part of his time in Manhattan, said that Don was "slightly more speedy and nervous" in New York.

Around this time—in the spring of 1983—"Donald had this idea to make a dinner in SoHo," says Walter Abish. "A major dinner for a group of writers, and he planned it very, very carefully. It was a strange event. Amusing and intriguing. He invited . . . well, that was the thing of it. The list. I was astounded that he consulted me, but he called and said, 'Should we invite so-and-so?' Naturally, I did the only decent thing and said 'Absolutely' to everyone he mentioned. I pushed for Gaddis. Gass was there, and Coover and Hawkes, Vonnegut and his wife, Jill Krementz, who took photographs, I think. Don's agent, Lynn Nesbit, was there. She was always very friendly. Susan Sontag, the only woman writer invited."

Pynchon couldn't make it. He wrote Don to apologize. He said he was "between coasts, Arkansas or Lubbock or someplace like 'at."

"Donald had picked the restaurant," Abish says:

It was very pricey, and we all had to pay our own way. About seventy-five dollars apiece, very steep back then. There was a fixed menu. It was in a

loft somewhere. Very strange. Sort of monumental. The occasion made me think of Paris, you know, this group of artists. Donald was absolutely in charge of the seating. To my surprise, he seated me across from him. He was sitting with his back to the window. On his right, Coover ... well, Coover selects his own place; you don't tell Coover where to sit. But he was on Don's right. Gaddis was on the other side, with Muriel Murphy nearby. And Donald barely said anything the entire meal. He did not look happy. Very, very dour. Vonnegut was to my left. To my right, Hawkes and Barth, and they were pretty jovial. In all, about twenty-one people. It seemed ... since Donald had put it together, planned it for three or four weeks ... it invited interpretation, and I couldn't figure it out. You couldn't take it at face value. Everyone gave a short little speech about their work and their friendship with the other people there. Hawkes was very eloquent, warm and nice. Gaddis was, as always, very quiet. Donald was both withdrawn and a dynamo. He was the center though he didn't dominate in any way. It was puzzling. I left with questions. . . .

"Donald didn't socialize the way others do—he didn't like small talk," Ed Hirsch explains. In part, the "Postmodern Dinner" may have been Don's way of signaling to friends that his return to Houston didn't imply exile from New York or the literary world. "The thing is, Donald's New York-centric friends felt he was too big a talent to go back to Texas, back to teaching," says Hirsch. "But in Houston he wrote very early in the morning. He got several hours of writing done before he talked to anyone. The place was good for him."

Naturally, his New York friends missed him terribly. "I was afraid he'd get stuck [in Texas], what with the working presence of so much family and his responsibilities at the University of Houston," Grace Paley recalled.

"We were family," says Roger Angell. He missed seeing Don "sitting and smoking in my regular armchair at my place . . . [trying to] keep the evening's sadness at bay. We counted on each other—a great many people felt this way about him. . . ."

When in New York, Don proved to be a "true good neighbor" to Phillip Lopate, helping him move furniture, offering to help him paint his apartment, giving him tips on interior design. One hot summer day, Don helped Lopate carry books and chairs up a flight of stairs into Lopate's new place on Bank Street. "[I]t was ninety-four degrees . . . and several trips were required, and we must have looked a sight, Sancho Panza and the Don with his scraggly beard, pulling boxes roped together on a small dolly," Lopate recalls. "At one point the cart tipped over and spilled half my papers onto the sidewalk. After that, I let Donald carry the lion's share of the weight, he having a broader back and a greater liking (I told myself) for manual labor than I, as well as more steering ability. He was hilarious . . . joking about the indignity of being a beast of burden, and I must admit it tickled me to think of using one of America's major contemporary writers as a drayhorse. But why not take advantage when he seemed so proud of his strength, so indestructible, even in his mid-fifties?"

ANNE

Anne's mother jumped out of a window when Anne was eighteen. "In a way, her death was not a surprise, and it was kind of a relief," Anne says. "It freed me."

Don brought her to Houston. The move—in 1984—is still "kind of hazy," Anne admits. She'd known New York and Copenhagen; Houston was, she says, the "armpit of the nation. It was a serious culture shock. And the weather! I felt I'd crashed these people's lives, Marion's and my father's. I wasn't made to feel unwelcome, but I think Dad and Marion were going through a difficult time.

"Dad gave me a curfew. At eighteen! I said, 'You're joking.' I'd been my own keeper since the age of seven. But he was very protective. It was sweet, really. We all had to adjust to each other. I wanted to go out into the world. I was eighteen. I smoked. I drank. I think I just wanted to live and feel it. I saw how wonderful Dad was with Kate. He had really learned to be more demonstrative and loving. It was the stable home life I had never known."

School was a problem. "I'd been in the gymnasium in Copenhagen, so in the States I had to take the GED, the high school equivalency test. The test was very important to Dad and Marion. I barely got into the University of Houston. I was essentially a foreigner. I had no relationship to sentence composition. I was a voracious reader in English, but I hadn't learned the grammar."

While she studied at home, Don hoisted Katharine onto his shoulders and played "horsie" with her, or took her down the street for an ice-cream cone. Later, he'd try to help Anne study, but she resented the restrictions he'd forced on her. She resisted him.

Yet fairly quickly her steady schedule and the family atmosphere began to appeal to her. "There was a lot of cooking and dinner-table talk. It was exquisite," she says. "Dad and I loved to watch movies together. It was one of our favorite things to do. Especially John Wayne movies. He loved the character of John Wayne. He'd say, 'There's a Duke movie on tonight.' And *Hill Street Blues*. '*Hill Street*'s on tonight,' he'd say. He thought the show was well written and the characters were well-rounded." In these moments with him, she was "made to feel I was his number-one daughter." They didn't talk about Birgit.

Eventually, Anne became comfortable enough to kid her dad. "He'd look out the window and see a woman jogging on the street in a T-shirt and shorts, and he'd say, 'That's a cute girl.' I'd go, 'Dad! You're a dirty old man.'"

On many occasions students sat with Don in his living room while he read their story manuscripts. Anne would bounce through the house, a brunette blur, all motion and smiles. Though she was younger than her father's charges, she gazed at them wryly, as if to say, Trust me, I *know*. He'll give you what he *wants* to give you, and no more. You don't have anything to do with it. "He was inspired by his students," she says now. "They kept his juices flowing. He really wanted to make everything work."

At the university, Anne's composition teachers were often her father's pupils. "I remember, at one point I was flunking English," she says. "Dad tried to help me. There was a rubella outbreak on campus, and we wrote this story together about a character named Rubella (she had red hair). *He* wrote most of it, and it got a *D*. We really got a kick out of that. I wanted to tell this woman, the teaching assistant, that she'd flunked my dad."

Don's new family now expanded to include his daughter from a previous marriage. Occasionally, he ate lunch with his ex-wife Helen. He was building a fresh academic program, but at his old institution. Every morning, in the hallways of the English Department, he ran into another figure from the bygone days, Sam Southwell, his second ex-wife's former lover, who muttered under his breath about "presence" and "absence" in the literary theories of Jacques Derrida.

Presence/Absence was not just a theoretical binary for Don but also his daily paradox. Whenever he went to supper in a filthy student apartment, his students thought he was slumming, but theirs were the neighborhoods, and the types of rooms, he'd lived in when he was first on his own, playing music, writing stories. In dropping in on their lives, he revisited his early self. A myth-minded man, he appreciated the poignancies and ironies of all this: a search for lost youth, potency, reinvigoration; mirroring, doubling, symmetry. Here he witnessed a Kierkegaardian repetition, bound to fail.

So it was that Don invited the art critic Arthur Danto to campus to speak on the end of historical necessity and the new age of pluralism in the arts (a view completely adverse to Don's).

So it was that he invited Hans Magnus Enzensberger to campus to pronounce the death of postmodernism. Don listened ruefully in the back of the auditorium.

So it was that he invited Susan Sontag to campus to defend narrative fiction, a forecast of the traditional turn her novels would take: an unspoken repudiation of the works, including Don's, which she had championed at the start of her career. She bristled when a student suggested that her stories were more cerebral than emotional. Don grinned, enjoying her discomfort and the student's.

He lived a pastiche of old and new lives, birthing the future while often feeling his own moment was over.

Though he tried to shield Anne, she sensed his melancholy: "Once, when I asked him if he was happy, he said, 'Nobody's happy. I just want to go to sleep.' His mind took in so much stuff . . . politically . . . in *every* way . . . it had to be tiring for him. And of course he found relationships very difficult."

Karen Kennerly remembers calling from New York one night to discuss PEN business. "I said, 'Hi. How are you?' He gave out that Barthelme sigh, the sigh of sighs. He said, 'My wife doesn't love me anymore.' He wasn't joking, but I'm sure it wasn't true, either. I said, 'You must have done something to make her stop loving you.' He didn't deny it. He went on about the sorrows of marriage."

Yet his sadness never paralyzed him. Every few weeks, *The New Yorker* carried a new Donald Barthelme story: "Construction," in which the narrator vows to "explore the mystery" of a woman named Helen (Don's ex-wife read this as a nod to their renewed friendship); "Basil from Her Garden," in which a husband admits to adultery; and "Bluebeard," a retelling of the fairy tale.

In the classroom, he was often bemused, especially when a student tried something unusual. One day, the patrician Southern writer Peter Taylor, visiting campus, sat in on a workshop. One of the students read an abstract piece. It involved the ringing of bells. Taylor was startled. "Care to comment?" Don asked him, smiling. Decorously, Taylor declined.

In large public gatherings, Don continued to promote the writing program with astonishing enthusiasm. Phillip Lopate recalled a difficult "letdown" after a fund-raising ball one night. "Donald and Marion, Cynthia [Macdonald] and I drove . . . to [Donald's] house for a nightcap," he said, recounting the evening:

The event had been pretty successful, but not as large a windfall financially as we had fantasized. . . . Instead of sitting around having a post-
mortem, we—began singing songs. . . . Donald had a lovely baritone and a
great memory for lyrics: Cole Porter, musical comedy, jazz ballads. Each
of us alternated proposing songs, and the others joined in . . . Donald
seemed particularly at ease. There was no need to articulate his thoughts,
except in this indirect, song-choosing fashion.

This was the funny/sad atmosphere Anne encountered after nearly two
decades of a long-distance courtship with her father, and after the trauma of
finding her mother dead. "I was messed up, but it *was* good for me in Houston," she says. "I came to see it was amazing, who my mother was, who my
father was. They were extraordinary people, even if they were kind of unusual. And they're the fabric of what I am."

In Houston, her relationship with Don "got better and better," Anne says.
And he "really *did* love the place, despite the ups and downs. He was a total
rock star there."

THE STATE OF THE IMAGINATION

In 1986, Anne left for California. Life in Houston had been good for her, but she craved independence. "Dad would say, 'I'll get you your own apartment nearby.' But I wanted to be away," she says. "I had a friend attending SDSU in California, and I said, 'That's it! I'm going, too!'"

She enrolled in San Diego State and tried her hand at acting. "My father wasn't great at communicating after I left," she recalls. "I wasn't that connected to home. It was sad, because he was getting better with age, or maybe I was just becoming an adult and could understand him more. So much more could have happened with our relationship if he had lived."

Day by day, Don was enmeshed in administrative tasks at the university, while trying to stay active in the larger literary community. The year had begun with the 48th International P.E.N. Congress in Manhattan. Because of fallout from the conference, the year would end with a sad break with his old pal Grace Paley.

"Basically, Don and I put the PEN conference together," Karen Kennerly says. "Norman Mailer raised the money, and he was the most generous man in the world. Don and Richard Howard came up with the conference theme: 'The Imagination of the Writer and the Imagination of the State.' 'The Imagination of the State' is pure Don."

At fund-raising dinners, gala events, and readings (tickets cost one thousand dollars apiece for a series that featured Saul Bellow, Eudora Welty, Arthur Miller, William Styron, Woody Allen, and others), Mailer attracted huge amounts of cash. At one point, he persuaded Saul Steinberg and his wife, Gayfryd, to join the fund-raising efforts. In business circles, Steinberg was known as a "takeover baron"; on behalf of PEN, he opened the wallets of fellow entrepreneurs such as Ivan Boesky, Brooke Astor, Lily Auchincloss, and Leonard Stern. One night, Gayfryd hosted a reception in her thirty-four-room Park Avenue apartment. After a lavish dinner, Saul Steinberg asked Mailer to say a few words about PEN. Then Steinberg plied the guests for money. Some of them contributed up to ten thousand dollars that night. One wealthy old gentleman, an alumnus of the University of Pennsylvania, thought he was donating to Penn. "He probably wondered what part of the campus he'd helped improve," Kennerly says.

Some PEN members, distrustful of big business, grumbled about consorting with "richies" and their "bad money," but Mailer's joviality and ambitions for the International Congress sparked the most successful fund-raising campaign PEN had ever enjoyed.

One day, shortly before the conference began, Kennerly walked to the loft where PEN was headquartered, a spare fourth-floor space on lower Broadway. "So I'm at one end of the loft," Kennerly says, "and I hear that Norman has invited George Shultz, Ronald Reagan's secretary of state, to address the conference. I thought, Oh no. You can't just do that without asking people if it's all right." Mailer admitted he had not consulted the PEN board before issuing the invitation.

Later, Calvin Trillin told Kennerly, "Don't worry. Shultz will be too busy invading some small country to come to our little conference."

"But one day I get a call from Shultz's secretary, saying, 'I've got good news for you,'" Kennerly says. "I thought, Oh shit."

In an op-ed piece published in *The Nation* and *The New York Times,* E. L. Doctorow spoke for many board members when he said, "America is one of the few nations in the world in which writers don't have to ask for the endorsement of the government" but that now "American PEN has put itself in the position of a bunch of obedient hacks . . . gathering to be patted on the head by the Minister of Culture. It is astonishing to me that [PEN would] set up . . . fellow writers as a forum for the Reagan Administration," which, he claimed, was responsible for "killing men and women and children and mutilating their bodies" in Nicaragua, torturing black and white writers in South African prisons, and practicing "ideological exclusion" by refusing to issue an entry visa to Nobel Prize–winning novelist

Gabriel García Márquez—among others—because he was friendly with Castro.

Generally, Kennerly agreed with Doctorow's politics and she was miffed at Mailer for bypassing the board. Still, it rankled her that Doctorow and other PEN critics had not lifted a hand to help plan this enormous and complex conference. It was easy to do nothing and grouse from the wings.

As usual, Don stayed behind the scenes, organizing, orchestrating, setting the tone where he could. Though he felt as Kennerly did about the sniping at Shultz, he kept silent about the controversy, hoping for openings to patch things up quietly.

January 12, the night of Shultz's keynote address in the South Reading Room of the New York Public Library, was bitterly cold. Security was tight; guards at the library's Forty-second Street entrance bullied invited guests. Saul Bellow barely managed to squeeze inside. Mario Vargas Llosa was left standing in the chill wind, as was the 1985 Nobel Prize winner in literature, Claude Simon. One writer quipped, "This is what happens when you invite the state."

"The room was packed and there was an overflow crowd in the next room with a mike feed," Kennerly says. "I was in the overflow room. When Shultz started talking, a big group led by Grace Paley started booing him."

Paley and others had drafted a letter, signed by Susan Sontag, Nadine Gordimer, Richard Howard, Richard Gilman, Russell Banks, Ted Solotaroff, John Irving, Kenneth Koch, Lynne Sharon Schwartz, and over fifty others, declaring it "inappropriate" for a man who had harmed freedom of expression and who supported governments that tortured and imprisoned writers to address PEN. During Mailer's introduction before the keynote address, Paley stood and shouted, "Norman, we would like to have our letter read. Norman, please read the letter."

Mailer refused, then apologized to Shultz for the "silly bad manners" of the "puritanical leftists" in the audience.

Shultz's speech was innocuous and vague. He told the assembled writers, "President Reagan and I are on your side." Kennerly says, "Shultz let people boo. Then he just picked up and went on." A few people walked out on the speech, but that was all. "I was standing in the overflow room with delegates from the GDR, Hungary, Poland, Czechoslovakia, and they felt as if they'd died and gone to heaven. It was like angels had flown down, that this protest could happen and nobody got too upset about it," she recalls.

The ironies were rich: Mailer, long regarded by the press as a radical "bad boy" was suddenly an apologist for the "establishment." And even as Shultz hailed a "liberality of views," his assistant secretary of state for inter-American affairs, Elliot Abrams, was calling for American intervention in Nicaragua.

After Shultz's speech, Mailer defended his decision not to read the protest letter. "I didn't invite Secretary Shultz here in order to be insulted, to be, uh, pussywhipped," he said. Asked by a reporter if public dissent was secondhand to her by now, Paley said no. It felt awful every time, but it had to be done, she explained.

Shultz's appearance was only the beginning of tensions at the International Congress. The conference theme guaranteed debate, as Don surely knew. In a panel discussion, Claude Simon insisted that states lacked imagination and showed a "constant preoccupation for staying the same." For the public at large, he said, "pleasure is only elicited, as with children, by the endless repetition of the same forms, so that the masses and the states which spring from them find they are in spontaneous agreement about condemning and rejecting whatever might disturb the established order."

William Gaddis countered, dryly, that the state is the "grandest fiction to be conceived by man."

On another occasion, Susan Sontag argued that it was the writer's duty to oppose the state, while Mario Vargas Llosa insisted that writers must cooperate with official institutions. "For communal life to exist, given the nature of man, certain rules are required," he said.

One day, Toni Morrison shocked an audience by declaring, "At no moment in my life have I ever felt as though I were an American. At no moment. The whole reason that I am invited here, and the whole reason that I am sitting here, is because some black children got their brains shot out in the streets all over this country. And had the good fortune to be televised. . . . I am a read, as opposed to unread, writer because of those children . . . had I lived the life that the state planned for me from the beginning, I know that if I had the gifts of Homer I would have lived and died in someone else's kitchen on somebody else's land and never written a word. That is what the state always planned for me as a black person and as a female person."

Taking his turn on a panel, Saul Bellow tried to shift the week's focus away from politics. "Language is a spiritual house in which you live, and no one has the right to evict you," he told his fellow writers. "We should get rid of pretentious words like alienation." Americans weren't alienated, he said; they were interested in "common sense desires" like clothing, shelter, and health care. Günter Grass accused Bellow of ignoring realities in his own country: "I would like to hear the echo of your words in the South Bronx, where people don't have shelter, don't have food, and no possibility to live the freedom you have."

Salman Rushdie asked Bellow why so many American writers abdicated the task of examining America's power in the world. "We don't have tasks," Bellow replied. "We have inspirations."

Later in the week, Grass said to a *New York Times* reporter, "Is capitalism better than Gulag communism? I don't think so."

By midweek, newspaper and magazine reporters were denouncing the conference's strident tone. They mocked well-dressed writers eating lavish meals and soaking up booze at the Metropolitan Museum, the National Arts Club, and the Cat Club in Greenwich Village while decrying poverty. A petition condemning U.S. foreign policy, particularly in Nicaragua, made the rounds of the St. Moritz and the Essex House hotels, where most of the events had been scheduled. The Cuban writer Heberto Padilla skimmed the petition and shook his head. "I only sign what I write," he said.

Everywhere she went, Rosario Murillo, a poet and the wife of Nicaragua's president, Daniel Ortega, was treated like royalty.

Cynthia Ozick tried, with little success, to stir interest in a petition critical of the Jewish ex-chancellor of Austria, Bruno Kreisky, for meeting with members of the Palestinian Liberation Organization.

Petitions circulated that chastised the government of Iran for "condemning . . . creative intelligence to death," that of Romania for its "perpetual harassment" of "Hungarian cultures," and those of Turkey, Vietnam, and South Africa for imprisoning writers.

Exhausted, Don and his fellow organizers were near collapse. He was saddened that the conference had not transcended weary Left-Right squabbles. A panel had been assembled to discuss Utopia, but no one rose to the challenge of actually imagining such a place. Famously, Plato had pitted the Republic against poets, but no one mentioned the Greeks or other philosophers. Tired, tense, disappointed, Don drank too much. "I remember meeting Donald Barthelme, whose work I loved, but who was so drunk that I had the feeling of not really having met him," Salman Rushdie says.

Events concluded with yet another major protest, one that seriously wounded Don's friendship with Grace Paley. She and others noted that only seventeen women had been chosen to moderate panels (over ninety panels were scheduled). In response, several female PEN members called a caucus meeting, from which men were excluded. Someone invited Betty Friedan, not at that time a PEN member, to address the caucus. She told the group they should force the conference organizers to apologize "to the women writers of the world." Paley urged caution. It wouldn't help to "point fingers," she said. Cynthia Macdonald agreed. It was best, she said, to forget punishment and focus on redress.

At the final session that week, Macdonald thanked Mailer for the work he had done on behalf of the event, but she pleaded with PEN to take note of its failure to represent women adequately. "Won't we ever do enough to make this boring subject obsolete?" she asked.

Margaret Atwood and Nadine Gordimer concurred, and gently chided Mailer. He responded, "You are all middle-class women, as I am a middle-class man. And in the middle-class, the center of activity is obligatory excellence."

Whatever Mailer was trying to say—and his point was unclear—several of the women regarded his remark as an insult. He made things worse by insisting that not many women were "intellectuals first, poets and novelists second," and this meant there was a limited number of female panelists who could participate.

Thus the week ended.

Karen Kennerly remains bitter at the thought of the women's protest. Like Doctorow, none of the critics helped to plan the International Congress. Before raising their voices, they did not seek to understand the organizing process. "I was very angry over the charge that women were underrepresented at the conference," Kennerly says. "We had invited a lot of women, but many had turned us down for one reason or another. And you have to let delegates from the countries pick whom they want to represent them.

"Later, Margaret Atwood was at a P.E.N. event in Europe. She was the *only* woman at that one, and she didn't say anything about it. And Betty Friedan—what did she ever have to do with PEN? At one point, in a crowd, she was trying to shout out a statement. She started, 'Now, now . . .' and a bunch of people said, 'No, Betty, it's not NOW, it's PEN, PEN!'"

Don and Paley's "sad political parting," as Paley put it, had begun early in the week, when she opposed George Shultz's appearance. Don was no fan of George Shultz, but he felt that his old pal had made too much of the issue. "He considered his position long-term, overriding that year's key speaker," Paley said. By week's end, when she had embarrassed the conference organizers over their treatment of women, Don was furious with her. Like Kennerly, he felt that every effort had been made to include female panelists—it was simply the case that many women, citing other commitments, had turned them down. All Paley would have had to do was ask him, and he would have told her this. Instead, she had gone public, hastily, with a hue and cry. "He thought me disloyal and was angry," she said. "I was never angry at him, partly because political opposition is more natural to me."

For the next year, the two old friends barely spoke to each other.

PARADISE . . .

In 1975, Don had claimed that writing *The Dead Father* taught him how to write his next novel. He was too optimistic. *Paradise* didn't appear for another eleven years. But at least one failure along the way indicates that the secret of *how* was the extended-dialogue form.

He once said that "The Emerald," a story published in 1980, was meant to be a novel, but he couldn't sustain it. "The Emerald" begins:

> Hey buddy what's your name?
> My name is Tope. What's your name?
> My name is Sallywag. You after the emerald?
> Yeah I'm after the emerald you after the emerald too?
> I am. What are you going to do with it if you get it?
> Cut it up into little emeralds. What are you going to do with it?
> I was thinking of solid emerald armchairs. For the rich.

Eventually, the emerald is revealed to be a bastard child (it pees and talks) born of the moon's union with a witch named Moll. Moll and her jewel manage to evade the kidnappers and live in peace.

It's unclear why this material wound up as salvage for a story. Don's tendency to shave chips from bigger blocks of writing suggests

that he didn't distinguish story form from that of the novel—except in one regard: "The Emerald" and his subsequent novels indicate that he'd come to equate long fiction with almost pure dialogue.

In extended dialogue, Don—essentially a nonnarrative writer—had discovered a loose, playful structure, which was suitable for his interests and gifts. It also had a natural narrative drive. Surprising juxtapositions are possible—perhaps even inevitable—whenever characters speak, and the narrative flow is automatic. Further, dialogue is the form of Socratic give-and-take (uncertainty, investigation, open-endedness) and the questing, reflexive consciousness.

At bottom, all written dialogues are questionnaires. The questioner or dominant conversational partner sets the tone, subject, direction, and *push;* the responder adds counterweights, textures, incidentals. This inherent tension powers the prose.

Don's use of dialogue's push-pull is best displayed in his story "Basil from Her Garden," portions of which later appeared in *Paradise.* In the story, the characters, identified familiarly as Q and A, discuss A's adulterous affairs. Q (A's psychiatrist? his conscience?) is genteel, morally rigid, comfortable with his worldview ("Ethics has always been where my heart is"). A is anxious, ethically uncertain.

A's behavior shocks Q, but Q presses him for details. When A *does* recount his affairs, Q recoils: "I don't want to question you too closely on this. I don't want to strain your powers of—"

"Well no," A says. "I don't mind talking about it."

Eventually, Q's squeamishness tips the narrative in A's favor. Q becomes tentative, and no longer runs the conversation.

Don varies the story's pace to maintain rhythmic surprise, inserting monologues by Q and A. Q, vicariously stimulated by A's erotic adventures, admits that he is "content with too little" in life. Once again, the narrative shifts, as the dominant character, the one who has controlled the give-and-take, falters.

By the end, Q's moral position ("Adultery is a sin") feels weak—his ethics have not kept him from feeling depressed, buried in the mundane, while A's confusion, painful as it is, keeps him self-engaged and involved with others. "Transcendence is possible," Q says in one last attempt to assert his ideals. A agrees.

Q—Is it possible?
A—Not out of the question.

Q—Is it really possible?
A—Yes. Believe me.

In this final exchange, the speakers have traded roles: A is confident, even if he is only pretending for Q's sake, and Q's faith has been shaken. Though Q is still the inquisitor, his tone is pleading. A leads the discussion now. He hasn't changed. Adultery is his chosen form of "transcendence"— sex as novelty to distract him from the humdrum of daily life.

By being aware of the power struggles within even the most casual conversations, Don managed to inject this brief comic piece with a forceful narrative drive.

Paradise is a series of "shards and rag ends" that "tend to adhere to the narrator," said Peter Prescott in his warm review of the novel in *Newsweek*. The narrator is a middle-aged architect named Simon, on sabbatical in New York City. He comes to share his apartment with three young unemployed women, former fashion models. Textually, they are verbal abstractions—in their vagueness, reminiscent of Willem de Kooning's *Woman* series (Don dedicated the book to Willem's wife, Elaine). They provide the novel's most extended conversations, which, like the women's repartee in *The Dead Father,* serve as counterpoint to the main narrative: in this case, Simon's thoughts and fears.

Paradise is no fairy tale. It's a mirror image of *Snow White.* Instead of a woman living with a gang of men, we see a man sharing space with several women. Don's first novel was pure fantasy; this one is distinguished by its brutal views of aging, sex, and death.

The women's talk coheres more fully than the exchanges between Julie and Emma in *The Dead Father,* but there are enough gaps between statements to allow humor, confusion, discovery, and surprise. Here, the group discovers that Simon is sleeping with a fourth woman, a poet.

> "Well it's just what I thought would happen what I thought would happen and it happened."
>
> "He's a free human individual not bound to us."
>
> "Maybe we're too much for him maybe he needs more of a one-on-one thing see what I'm saying?"
>
> "It may be just a temporary aberration that won't last very long like when suddenly you see somebody in a crowded Pizza Hut or something and you think, I could abide that."
>
> "But if she's a poet she won't keep him poets burn their candles down to nubs. And then find new candles. That's what they do."

Not only are the lines unimpeded by identifying tags or physical descriptions; the sentences run together for urgency: brevity at length.

The book's other extended dialogues involve Q and A from "Basil from Her Garden," here more clearly identified as Simon and his doctor. Q and A's discussions (or is it one long discussion, interrupted by memories of the women?) occur after Dore, Anne, and Veronica have said good-bye to Simon. The exchanges establish a poignant tension between past and present in the narrative. The past (Simon's life with the women) is conveyed through present-tense verbs, while the present ("After the women had gone") unfolds in the past tense: Simon's life is all but over. His most vivid and immediate moments remain locked in his past. "Today" feels already lived.

Simon calls his time with the women a "series of conversations." This is also an apt description of *The Divine Comedy,* and it points us to the novel's subtext.

Every night, Simon has nightmares—bad dreams sparked by the guilt he feels over the mess he has made of his life (or so his doctor says). He dreams of being trapped in a leper colony. He envisions six-foot boll weevils flirting with one another "with little squirts of Opium behind their ears."

These *Inferno*-like horrors are offset by the calm, even the pleasure, Simon experiences on his sabbatical. "I felt blessed," he tells his doctor, remembering the women, his erotic trinity. In limbo, he has an opportunity to reevaluate his life.

Together, the women also review their pasts. One night, they conduct a raucous purifying ritual. "Hit me," Veronica says to her friends when they accuse her of being "bad." In the end (the novel concludes around Easter), the women leave to find work. Simon finds new personal and professional directions for his life.

Early in the book, his estranged wife accuses him of wallowing in triviality. "You worry about the way [people] say things but you don't worry about what [they] mean," she says. "That's not so," Simon replies. His actions bear him out. In his work, he fusses over gel coats and fiberglass (details that might *appear* to be trivial), but his projects have a rigorous consistency: a school in a "rundown area," a church in a "not-good area." "The more time you put into a job, the less money you make," Simon says. It's no surprise he can't stay solvent.

Ultimately, he rejects standard American business practices and their shoddy shortcuts. He branches out on his own, taking as much time as he needs to design office space for a charity organization. When he is not speaking to the women, he helps a cop on the street, an injured drunk in the vestibule of his apartment building, and a homeless man in his neighborhood.

As Simon's life unfolds, from his dreams of punishment to his expurgation to his recommitment to his art and rebirth as an independent man, we see that, like Dante, he "loves righteousness," however secularly and unsentimentally he defines it in Manhattan, in 1986.

Paradise received a mixed response. Michiko Kakutani groaned about its "very tired theme of the male midlife crisis" and said the female characters were "ciphers—vaguely unpleasant cartoony people." The author's efforts, she said, were "halfhearted and perfunctory."

Conversely, Peter Prescott found the book "charming." Richard Burgin applauded Don's "poignant awareness" of time and the "problem of aging"— an awareness, treated comically, that made the novel the "most moving of [Barthelme's] many brilliant books."

Don himself never warmed to the novel. He simply seemed relieved to have finished it. When Phillip Lopate congratulated him on the book's appearance, Don said he thought it was "pretty weak." Grace Paley wrote to say it was the "cleanest dirty book [she] had ever read . . . it doesn't give up its purity or delicacy despite the nice natural grossness of fucking and sucking. It's as though genitals could dream. . . ."

She closed with a plea: "So—write me a letter, because even though you still think I'm wrong [about PEN] and I still think you're wrong, we do love each other. Right?" Don responded with fondness, but the friendship never quite regained its former footing.

Ed Hirsch says, "I don't find a falling off in Donald's work after he came back to Houston. I like the late work. It's true that the postmodern fireworks can't be found much in the later writing. If what you value most is innovation, then the early work will draw you. But there is a wistfulness and a melancholy in the late stories that I find beautiful. And they're deceptively personal."

In his melancholy, Don sought solace in his friendships with Hirsch and others—like Beverly Lowry, who recalls a car trip with Don and Marion to San Antonio and a "long night in Helen's Majestic Bar [there], listening to Don and [the writer] John Graves swap stories about Spain as the jukebox played 'If I Said You Had a Beautiful Body Would You Hold It Against Me?' Don kept the quarters coming."

On the way back to Houston, "the ladies talked about the rump of a noted poet," Don wrote in "Overnight to Many Distant Cities," in a passage he once admitted was strictly autobiographical. " 'Too big,' they said, 'too big too big too big.' 'Can you imagine going to bed with him?' they said . . . and laughed and laughed. . . .

"I offered to get out and run alongside the car, if that would allow them to converse more freely."

Such trips and other distractions—romping with Kate on the playground at the Edgar Allan Poe school—along with his work, kept Don comfortable, if not wholly content, in Houston. "I think it suited Donald to have one foot in Houston and one in New York," Hirsch says. "There is a gap between the reality of Houston and the way many people perceive it. When we were all there together, it didn't feel like the far margins of anything. It felt like literary life."

Yet New York kept tugging at him. On the one hand, he was loyal to UH's writing program. On the other hand, *The New Yorker* was his home, and increasingly *The New Yorker* came under siege.

William Shawn was in his late seventies now. He had not named an editor to succeed him. The crepuscular tone of his control, combined with the recent deaths of so many regular contributors (Harold Rosenberg, Hannah Arendt, Janet Flanner, John Cheever, S. J. Perelman) had sent the magazine into a funk. To make matters worse, its readership and its advertising revenue had dropped.

In 1985, Samuel I. Newhouse, Jr., bought *The New Yorker* from the magazine's owner, Peter Fleischmann. Fleischmann's health was poor and he had lost patience with Shawn's inability to appoint a younger, more vigorous editor. He was also concerned about estate taxes, so he sold off his stock for two hundred dollars a share. In the end, Newhouse paid about $170 million for the magazine.

Newhouse ran a media conglomerate called Advance Publications, which included the Condé Nast group of magazines (*The New Yorker* had once called him a "rag-picker of second-class newspapers"). Under his guidance, *Vanity Fair,* one of Condé Nast's most venerable publications, had become a gossipy, photo-filled celebrity mag edited by Tina Brown. To allay the fears of *New Yorker* readers and staffers, Newhouse released a press statement saying he had no plans to "seek control of the *New Yorker* or to influence its management"—welcome, if implausible, news.

At first, little changed. Shawn finally appeared to be moving—at his own glacial pace—toward naming Charles McGrath as his successor. Then, on January 13, 1987, the magazine staff received a memo from Newhouse announcing Shawn's retirement, effective March 1. Robert Gottlieb would be the new editor.

In a hastily arranged meeting in the cramped *New Yorker* offices, Shawn, standing in a stairwell so everyone could see him, said he had not agreed to retire, nor had he agreed to Gottlieb's appointment. Outraged, the staff insisted that Roger Angell draft a letter to Gottlieb. The letter should say there was nothing personal here but that the staff of *The New Yorker* would prefer that he not be a party to Newhouse's humiliation of Shawn. He should not accept the job. There were 153 signatories (some names, like Don's, were gathered long-distance).

Gottlieb replied, courteously, that he understood the staff's position but that he intended to take the job. Newhouse moved Gottlieb's starting date up to February 16.

On his last day at the magazine, Shawn posted a letter on the communal bulletin board. It read, in part: "Whatever our individual roles at *The New Yorker,* whether on the eighteenth, nineteenth, or twentieth floor, we have built something quite wonderful together. Love has been the controlling emotion, and love is the essential word. . . . I love all of you, and will love you as long as I live."

These swift and painful developments were twice as excruciating for Don, as he felt unable to help his *New Yorker* family from his outpost in Texas. In addition to his anger at the way Shawn had been treated, Don worried about Newhouse's aims. Would there be a place for Don in a glossy new "television" magazine?

In his usual fashion, he "worked through" his distress. He prepared another retrospective collection, *Forty Stories*—along with *Sixty Stories,* the number amounted to one hundred, summing up his career. This fourth book with Putnam's fulfilled the contract he had signed. Years earlier, Don had promised a second children's book to Farrar, Straus and Giroux. Now, as if responding to some inner symmetry, he published, in collaboration with the artist Seymour Chwast, an illustrated book called *Sam's Bar: An American Landscape,* in which patrons of a pub say things like, "I'm a second-generation artist. My daddy was a chainsaw artist, made sculptures with his chainsaw. You don't see that so much in the East. I do Hair Art. Like what I'm wearing." *Sam's Bar* was a children's book for adults.

Very consciously, Don seemed to be tidying up loose ends.

. . . AND BEYOND

In the end, Don did not abandon Houston. Perhaps the city's child-friendly amenities proved too sweet to leave behind. Maybe a steady paycheck could not be passed up. Perhaps he simply did not have the energy to pack up and move again.

He relished contradiction—Houston's essential quality. He once wrote that among the places he loved there were the "[M]useum areas, including North and South Boulevards, with their great oaks and generous medians," as well as "Westheimer," an unzoned commercial strip. The museum areas embodied standard beauty, symmetry, and common sense; Westheimer, a ramshackle street dotted with porn shops, jazz clubs, palm readers, and funky restaurants heaped together like hurricane remnants, uglied things up.

There was no need to choose Westheimer over the Museum District, or vice versa. The point is, Westheimer's existence posed new possibilities for the *meaning* of the Museum District (after all, years earlier, Don had planned "The Ugly Show" at the Contemporary Arts Museum).

In "Return," one of his last stories, an architect leaves Manhattan for Houston. In the course of his time there, he sketches a proposal

for a "beautiful stainless steel azalea nine hundred feet high." Someday, he says, "God and the Gerald D. Hines Interests willing, you'll see this nine-hundred-foot-high stainless steel azalea taking its place with the city's other great and tall monuments in the garden of the creative imagination."

This enormously interesting sentence insists that any city, even Houston, can be a "garden of the creative imagination." Furthermore, it links spirituality, creativity, and business—God, architecture, and the Gerald D. Hines interests. If we're going to build Paradise, especially in an unlikely spot, it's going to take vision, prayer, money, and spit. But finally, the image implies that, for all our efforts, Paradise will remain elusive. A "nine-hundred-foot stainless steel azalea" is too implausible to exist outside of language.

And yet . . . Don's azalea recalls a sculpture that actually exists in the city: a sharp silver palm tree, several feet tall, on the west side of the Contemporary Arts Museum. It is a tiny spot of magic in the dense urban fabric. Drive by it if you're ever in Houston. It will dazzle you.

Ghosts was the working title of *Paradise.* Time-smudged strollers moving too swiftly for the camera to realize: Don's Eden is graced by the lost, the not-quite-there, the never-was.

Tucked away in Houston, on a pleasant oak-lined boulevard across the street from the Edgar Allan Poe Elementary School, Don moved toward a spare, monastic prose. Like Hans Pfall, Poe's crafty balloonist, he "determined to depart, yet live—to leave the world, yet continue to exist—in short, to drop enigmas."

Late in his life, in a public-television interview with George Plimpton, Don admitted that literary experimentation leads to "dead ends." He said, "I've encountered every one of them and published a few of them." Still, he contended, it was vital to experiment for the "health of the medium."

As the literary thrills of past years dimmed and the medium's health surged and fell, and while a limited strain of "realism" mounted a new attack on American letters, Don withdrew. His personal melancholy deepened, but he understood patience and the usefulness of neglect. He knew that someday historical contingencies would coax new blooms from buried roots, and he had not been unprepared for this sea change. Concealment had always been one of his tools. As the master scoundrel, Vautrin, says in Balzac's *Père Goriot,* "Set yourself a splendid goal, but don't let anyone see what means you adopt and the steps you take to reach it. Lie in wait, lie in ambush in the world of [the city]. . . ."

Don remained as splendidly productive as ever—but quietly, out of earshot of New York's "red hot center."

In 1987, he collaborated with his old friend Jim Love on a mixed-media project entitled *The Rook's Progress* for a show to be held at the Glassell School of Art in Houston. Don had proposed the show—a series of collaborations between visual artists and writers—and organized the exhibit with Janet Landay of the Glassell School. They matched a number of local artists and writers based on "temperament and intuition." To give the event a historical perspective, the curators displayed collaborative books by Juan Gris and Pierre Reverdy, Joan Miró and André Breton, Max Ernst and Georges Ribemont-Dessaignes, Jasper Johns and Samuel Beckett, along with a special edition of John Ashbery's *Self-Portrait in a Convex Mirror,* illustrated by Richard Avedon, Elaine de Kooning, Willem de Kooning, Jim Dine, Jane Freilicher, Alex Katz, R. B. Kitaj, and Larry Rivers.

Once again, Don had come full circle, tackling museum work with artist friends. Of working with Love, he said:

> Jim Love does nothing hastily, except nix a bad idea. . . . But a bad idea is a step on the way toward a better, and gradually a scheme evolved we could both tolerate. We began by writing notes back and forth and ended up in the studio staring at a four-by-eight foot piece of Homosote on which various elements of the composition were moved around, usually in increments of a quarter inch. . . . I miss the grandiosity of our first conception—the work was to have been forty-eight feet high by one hundred and sixty-three feet wide and have its own army, navy, and embassies abroad—but one must leave some things to the future.

The completed piece, 42×78×7½ feet, is fashioned of steel, wood, canvas, and magnesium. A flat, wilted chess rook, caged behind bars, leans toward a female torso made of steel (as if it were armor); a string of wire and double-headed nails, suggesting a barbed-wire fence, separates the torso from a rumpled man's shirt with a hole in the heart. The right sleeve reaches toward the woman's body but is blocked by the wire. Above and below this sleeve, words are etched into brightly reflective rectangular panels.

The top panel reads:

> Everything reflects well on our city
> Our audiences are amazingly perceptive
> The string section has a broken heart
> We cheer it because it is outstanding
> Gulls smash into the great glass windows
> I have never been more optimistic, more sanguine.

The bottom panel is more somber:

> She is riding naked on the catafalque
> We'll to the woods no more my darling
> I am boned, crack-skinned, malapropos
> A chorus of dromedaries humming triumphantly
> Revolves the stage machinery
> Away from me, away from me.

Like the best of Don's fiction, *The Rook's Progress* is both playful and melancholy: the giddiness of the words near the top (and their apparent indifference to the figures around them); the elegiac tone of the bottom words; the visual pun of the word *reflects* shining from a smooth, reflective surface, and the verbal pun of the *Rook* in the title, implying fool as well as chess piece; the reference to Hogarth's *The Rake's Progress* (1734), which Hogarth conceived as a novel in paintings; the sad, impossible reach of the empty shirt.

The viewer's eye goes immediately to the heavily shielded female figure: This torso is not to be trifled with. The rook's resemblance to a softening penis is unmistakable, and the flattened, damaged shirt, like wrinkled skin, lies forever unrequited—a balloon popped on the wire or on the sharp, virile curves of the womanly form. The shirt's shape recalls Matisse's *Icarus* from his *Jazz* series—the right arm straining to grasp what's always out of reach, the void in the heart. Away from me, away from me . . .

One of Don's final collages, *The Rook's Progress* fully marries his visual and verbal skills.

In November 1987, Don joined several other writers, including Grace Paley, William Gaddis, Walter Abish, Robert Coover, Rita Dove, Lisa Alther, and Marilyn French at a festival of American writing in Berlin, billed as "The American Chapter." Heidi Ziegler, a young literary scholar, and Lutz Engelke, then the director of international cultural events for the deputy mayor of West Berlin, arranged the event. Don and Marion flew sixteen hours from Houston and arrived exhausted on a cold and dismal evening. They were whisked to a reception at the American consulate in West Berlin. Don retired into a corner with a drink while Marion served as his "social bridge to the world," Engelke recalled.

The following day, Don and Marion walked around the Reichstag, visited the Bauhaus Museum, and saw the "spy bridge" near the Schloss Glienicke. At the Wall, in the Martin-Gropius-Bau museum, Don became intrigued by a flight simulator that took him through aerial images of war-torn Berlin. "He kept looking into those city scars as if he needed to find an explanation for it," Engelke said later.

From the start, Walter Abish had clashed with the conference organizers. For some reason, the arrangements were not to his liking. He threatened to boycott a panel he was slated to chair; in response, the organizers threatened not to pay him. "Fine," he said. Don tried to mediate the dispute. He called Abish early one morning and said, "I know you're upset, but you don't want to let our side down." Abish exploded, saying, "What side? America? American literature? Fuck our side." On the other hand, Don and Grace Paley treated each other civilly, if coolly—sadly, silently mourning their damaged friendship.

Late in the week, a semiclandestine meeting was planned between the Americans and a group of East German writers. "[A]lthough it was clear that the STASI had somehow heard about the meeting, the level of fear was low enough so that it could take place. All the same, it took place under circumstances of conspiracy," Engelke said. "The group met in an old pottery workshop" on the east side, within walking distance of the Brandenburg Gate, "and because it was unofficial—that is, not reported—we had to use all sorts of little tricks to come together. For instance, everybody from the West had to memorize the address, so that no one's name would be written on a piece of paper, and we had to arrive at intervals. Because of this, Robert Coover didn't get the message right and got there too late! The press had not been informed, although the meeting was of political and cultural significance. For the Westerners, a certain romantic flavor was evident. It was a little like planning, playing, and editing your own black-and-white movie," Engelke wrote.

Don and Paley read stories, translations of which had been provided to the group; then some of the East German writers—among them, Jan Faktor, Helga Königsdorf, and Edmond Hesse—read. In that "brownish, dark East Berlin atmosphere," Don's stories "were all of a sudden more than merely Postmodern," Engelke said. To Western ears, accustomed to *too much language*—a surfeit of meaning—Don's stories sounded merely playful. But to the East Berliners, who in their daily lives scoured "every detail for sense and meaning, although the official metaphors for sense had been reduced to stupid rituals of repetition," Don's absurdities exploded like "Molotov cocktail[s]." Quietly, he had smuggled across the Wall radical devices to scramble and reshape semantics.

Still, he refused to let his fiction be reduced to Cold War polemics. "Politics is something of which literature has to have a disappointed position," he declared to the group. Asked about Texas, he said that Houston and East Berlin were "two poles of the same world."

Don returned to the States. Marion and Grace Paley stayed for a couple of days at Marianne Frisch's apartment in Berlin. A few months later, Robert

Coover reprised Don's Postmodern Dinner. The event, "Unspeakable Practices: A Three-Day Celebration of Iconoclastic American Fiction," honored
John Hawkes upon his retirement from Brown University. Held in Providence, Rhode Island, the festival could not have been more different from
the edgy, romantic gathering in East Germany.

On a panel whose subject was "Traditional Values and Iconoclastic Fiction," the critic Leslie Fiedler called "postmodern" writers "iconoclasts with
tenure." He asked his fellow panelists—Don, William Gass, William Gaddis,
Stanley Elkin—rote questions: Why do you write? Who is your audience? Irritated by Fiedler's superficiality, Gaddis grumbled, "I write to avoid boredom,
which is probably why I came up here today." After that, he slumped into a
torpid silence.

Don said, "I know exactly who I'm writing for. They are extremely intelligent and physically attractive."

Fiedler closed the discussion with this remark: "None of us will be remembered as long or revered as deeply as our contemporary, Stephen King."

The writers filed out of the hall, quietly furious.

On the festival's final night, Coover took everyone to a Portuguese restaurant in East Providence for roast pig and fried calamari. A singer named
Manny, dressed in a maroon jacket, told moronic jokes and sang lounge-
lizard tunes, occasionally shouting to Gaddis or Hawkes, "You're lookin'
good!" Coover loved the camp, and clapped along; he insisted on keeping the
group there through three full sets of the show. Most of the others, including
Don, felt ill at ease.

This was the last full gathering of the leading figures of what had come
to be known as American postmodernism.

Following all these travels, Don seemed, for a while, more at home in Houston. He was the king there, the "one who ironically, gracefully, and profoundly bore the burdens and shouldered the responsibilities," letting out,
now and then, a "lovely sigh—weighty, humorous, world-weary," according to
Ed Hirsch. Don told him, "All writers are really black sheep," and a "writing
community is a whole flock of them." The "black sheep have to stick together and help each other out."

Briefly, he experienced renewed relish at the creative-writing lunches.
"Let's stir up the troops!" he'd goad his colleagues. Or: "Let's have a Dada
happening!" Among the faculty, there were "rivalries for Don's affection,"
Hirsch recalled. "I once asked him about his theory of committee meetings.
'Be the last one to speak,' he said. He preferred not to speak at all, to just let
things unfold. But if the meeting took a dark turn, and there was a risk he
wouldn't get what he wanted, he'd intervene. His reserve gave him tremen-

dous authority. Incidentally, I think that was also his theory of fatherhood—and of teaching."

In the classroom, he challenged a new group of students to rethink narrative. On one occasion, he took a pair of scissors and cut a student's story into several sections. "There's something wrong with this piece. Let's rearrange it," he said. After collaborating with the class to redo the story, he admitted, "No, this doesn't make it any better, does it?"

"The first time I met [Don], I recognized that he was the most intelligent person I'd ever met—not just in terms of knowledge, but also in terms of his perceptions about people," recalled Vikram Chandra, a New Delhi native who had come to Houston via Johns Hopkins. At the time, Chandra was writing his novel *Red Earth and Pouring Rain.* The other students hated his work. "It was 1987 when all the minimalist stuff was in vogue, and suddenly here I am with these Indian gods making pronouncements," Chandra said. "They'd say, 'This is melodramatic!'—and I'd answer, 'I know, but I like melodrama. We Indians do melodrama.'"

Another student, Eric Miles Williamson, says, "One day, after we read a piece by Vikram—I thought it was tedious, but Don loved it—Don said, 'I think Mr. Chandra's work deserves a round of applause.' And he made us clap for this guy. Half of us didn't want to, but Don made us."

In 1995, *Red Earth and Pouring Rain* was published to worldwide acclaim.

Outside of class, Don continued to extend to his students extraordinary generosity. When George Williams and his wife, both enrolled in the program, learned they were going to have a baby, Don called them. "I understand there is a pregnant woman on the premises," he said.

"How did you find out?" Williams asked.

"Jungle drums, jungle drums. Will a thousand do?"

It took Williams a moment to realize Don was offering them money.

"Often, students would end up at Don's house late at night after a reception for some visiting writer," Williams says. "I got the impression we'd go till two or three in the morning if Marion hadn't kicked us out. She was very protective of Don. We were all in our twenties and could stay up all night. Marion knew Don couldn't take it physically. But he wouldn't be the one to throw us out."

One late spring night in a Thai restaurant, Don joined several students to celebrate the end of the school year. A waiter approached the table and asked the group if they wanted something to drink. "A thousand glasses of wine," Don said.

"By the end of the evening [his] guests were out on the sidewalk, flush with the success of the evening, due entirely to [Don's] presence," Williams recalls, "talking and shaking hands and hugging and bumping into one another and promising phone calls and dinners and tennis games and fishing trips that never materialized, while Don tried to break up a party that refused to, by reminding us he didn't enjoy playing father to us. 'Home now,' he said. 'Home now.'"

During the spring semester of 1988, Phillip Lopate noticed that Don's reserve seemed to be growing. At public gatherings, he acted more remote than ever. "I kept having the feeling that Don was becoming cooler toward me," Lopate says. "Interactions that used to take up thirty-five seconds were now clipped to twelve. . . . Had I done something to offend him? I raised the question to Ed Hirsch, who was closer to Donald than I was, and Eddie told me that he had detected the same curtness of late."

At lunches, Helen Moore Barthelme also encountered a more closed-down companion. He looked like an old man, she thought. But he loved being father to Katharine. One day, he admitted to Helen he had been writing one morning, when he realized that Katharine, whom he was supposed to be watching, had disappeared. He scrambled downstairs and found her toddling halfway down the block.

"After we left the restaurant, I drove [us] through two of our old neighborhoods off Montrose Boulevard," Helen said. "The apartment building in which we had lived on Richmond Avenue was still standing, an ugly, imposing interior. Don and I commented on the strangeness of seeing it. . . . We were extremely happy when we had lived there. . . .

"When we returned to his home . . . he looked especially unhappy . . . his demeanor as he walked away was somber and dispirited."

In mid-April, Don's friends and colleagues learned that he had been hospitalized for throat cancer. For a while before that, Marion says, "despite Don's smoking, his doctor hadn't suspected that his long-term sore throat and some weight loss might be cancer, and put him through three rounds of antibiotics." Houston's M. D. Anderson Cancer Center housed one of the world's premier cancer-research facilities, but Don refused to go there. "He had a lot of Houston biases—you know, he liked to eat at that terrible Mexican place, Felix—and maybe the biases extended to hospitals," says Ed Hirsch.

"He was so sure that MDA had nothing over Memorial and Park Plaza," Marion says. "I would have preferred him to go to MDA, and in hindsight I think real follow-up care might have saved his life, but I trusted and respected his choice, especially when he told me he had discussed it with his doctor, who felt Park Plaza could do the job."

Don asked his friends not to visit him in the hospital because he didn't want people to see him looking frail. Eerily, at around the same time, his brother Pete was diagnosed with throat cancer. He was recovering from a similar operation.

The doctors told Don he had squamous cell carcinoma of the pharynx. It had metastasized to the lymph glands in the right side of his neck.

He remained in the hospital for nearly two weeks. A few days after he'd returned home, Phillip Lopate paid him a visit, bringing five jazz albums as a get-well gift. "With his newly shaven chin, Donald looked harshly exposed," Lopate wrote. "His eyes were dazed. He had a tube running from his nose to his mouth like an elephant's proboscis; its purpose was to feed him liquids, as his throat was still too sore to take in solids."

Don set the albums on his lap and patted their covers without looking at them. "I'm tired of sounding like Elmer Fudd," he told Lopate in a pinched, weak voice. But "Demerol is great stuff."

He had no energy, and Lopate felt awkward. Fortunately, their visit was interrupted by a naked and squealing Katharine, who ran into the room dripping water. "Don't look at me!" she shouted. "I've just taken a shower!" Her presence cheered Don and gave Lopate an excuse to slip away.

A week later, Don showed up unexpectedly at the weekly lunch meeting of the creative-writing faculty. "He said he was bored hanging around the house," Lopate said. "He also seemed to be telling us with this visit: I may be sick but it doesn't mean I'm giving up my stake in the program. Perhaps because he was up and about, and therefore one expected an improvement, his pasty, florid appearance shocked me even more than when I had seen him at home." He was beardless and gaunt. "He looked bad. We wanted him to go home and lie down, not sit through our boring agenda."

Don's doctors had forbidden him to drink or smoke, and he passed up his usual white wine. When he left the meeting, one of his colleagues said, "That just wasn't Donald." The others agreed.

Over the next several weeks, he showed up at readings and other public events, his face and neck marked by the blue lines the doctors had drawn on his skin to guide the radiation treatments. "He was a walking art object," one of his students said.

He went to Del Rio, a local rehab center, to kick booze and cigarettes. "He quit drinking for about three months and when he thought he had it under control, he began slowly, occasionally, to take a glass of white wine," Marion says. "He discovered when he was in radiation that he didn't have the stamina to drink, write, and deal with cancer, so he cut out the drinking to protect his writing." On the phone, he told Lynn Nesbit it had been "easy" to kick alcohol. She thought, "For Christ's sake, Donald, if it was easy, why didn't you do it long ago?" Talking to Anne, however, he admitted he worried about writing—what would losing booze do to his imagination?

The news that he had received the thirty-thousand-dollar Rea Award for the Short Story did little to console him. One day, an old pal and former colleague at the *Houston Post,* George Christian, came by the house. Several times that day, Don told Christian he wanted to die. He just wanted to "go to sleep and never wake up." Whenever Marion walked through the room, Don put on a cheerful face for her. But as soon as she went out, Christian said, "Don resumed talking about how miserable he was."

The later medical "follow-up he got from Methodist and Park Plaza Hospital was inadequate," Marion says. But slowly, over the next few months, he appeared to gain strength and seemed to be in remission. He grew back his beard, though it was not as thick as before. He remained thin. In the fall, he resumed teaching part-time, though his classroom duties strained his voice. "He was talking through the blood etchings in his throat, all raspy," says Eric Miles Williamson. "It was scary and amazing."

Little by little, he regained his old pluck. "One day, a student read a story about a woman with a baby, sitting in a trailer house," says George Williams. "Nothing was happening in the piece, and the other students were asking, 'What could make the story interesting?' Don said, 'Kick the baby.'

"In another workshop, there was a student who was one of these therapist types who are now trying to run the world, you know, and he was challenging Don a little, making veiled references to Don's alcoholism. Don turned three shades of red. He was humiliated by this personal attack in the classroom. But afterward he never treated this guy any differently. He just took it."

At a party one night, Williams overheard Don say, "Life is altogether too impoverished without booze."

In the spring of 1989, Don and Marion flew to Rome. He had been awarded a senior fellowship by the American Academy there. He was offered a brief residency and studio space in the Academy's villa atop Janiculum, the tallest, most glorious hill above the city.

Established in 1894, and chartered as a private institution by Congress in 1905, the American Academy awards fellowships in a range of disciplines, among them literature, music, architecture, history, and design. In the spring, Ed Hirsch had also been awarded a Prix de Rome, and Don looked forward to seeing him in Italy. "He didn't like to leave home," Hirsch says, "but having me there helped Marion convince him to go."

Don loved the villa, ten buildings and eleven acres of gardens overlooking Rome's bell towers, stucco walls, and golden domes. Don and Marion's apartment had a huge living room with "shabby old furniture and old paint,"

Don said. A small terrace off the bedroom opened out above the city center. "[J]ust looking [through] the window in the morning is a great joy," Don wrote his parents. Each day, he and Marion breakfasted on the terrace, which offered a stunning view of the hills.

That spring, the Academy was busy replacing old furniture with new birch, plywood, and wire designs by the New York decorator Mark Hampton. Don enjoyed the mix of old and new things in the villa's rooms, and loved overhearing discussions of design. He and Marion relished short trips out of the city. They saw Mount Vesuvius and, with Katharine and Marion's parents, who had arrived for a visit, a "tiny town called Ravello on the Amalfi coast which turned out to be the most beautiful place I've ever been," Don told his folks.

Mostly he spent time working in the villa. He knew the Academy's rich history. Henry James had once been a guest. In the 1950s, architectural post-modernism had gotten a start here, as Robert Venturi stayed in the villa with several other architects, engaging them in lengthy discussions. Marion's great-uncle, Gorham Phillips Stevens, had been a temporary director of the American Academy after World War I. His portrait hung in the entrance hall.

Both Marion and Ed Hirsch attest to the fact that Don was surpassingly happy during his stay in Rome. "He was writing and he was in high spirits," Hirsch says. "It was a good moment for them as a family. Kate was with them. And the setup suited him. He loved the layers of Rome, the way the old and the new came together, contemporary life against the ancient backdrop. He was as relaxed as I'd ever seen him, more spiritually at ease than in either Houston or New York. Part of the pleasure of the experience for him was that his happiness there was so unlikely. Or so he'd thought. He had a flaneur's temperament, and he could indulge it in Rome."

There was no more talk of a desire to die.

"I have neither television nor newspapers," Don wrote in an unfinished "diary" of his time in Rome—remarks found on a computer disc after his death. "[One day] I followed a whistling man down the street for several blocks, just for the music. He was whistling the Marine Corps Hymn and I thought he might be a fellow countryman, but he looked very barbarico, as we say here, and I hesitated to speak to him." On another occasion, Don wrote, "I picked up the *Corriere della Serra* and it told me that BUSH IN-QUISITORE NON PESCARE. Our President menaced by fish, and me six thousand miles from home."

In Italy, Don finished a draft of his novel *The King.* A mythic and rueful med-itation on dead societies and the "worrisome" twentieth century, it would be published in 1990, a year after his death.

The story takes place during World War II. Britain is being pounded by the Axis military powers. In Don's version of history, King Arthur and his Knights of the Round Table share the battlefield with Winston Churchill's army. The legendary figures know they're anachronisms. Contemporary technowarfare, with its tactics of bombing civilians and killing at a distance, has no place for courteous knights who wrestle face-to-face.

The book presages the Cold War's end: A Polish fellow from the "shipyards"—a clear reference to Lech Walesa and the Solidarity movement—agitates for justice as the fighting escalates. (Within months of Don's passing, the Berlin Wall would collapse.)

As he had done so often, Don contrasted old and new. But if, in *The Dead Father,* tradition seems exhausted, it has much to offer in *The King.* (Just as *Paradise* reverses the story of *Snow White, The King* is a mirror image of *The Dead Father.*) Few contemporary commanders in chief would refuse to develop a tactical weapon, but that is precisely what Don's Arthur does out of concern for civilian lives. Knowingly, the King gives away his future: He is bound by the traditions of chivalry, courtliness, and politeness—and though his prolonged existence is the chief irony in a heavily ironic book, he is a dignified figure.

Perhaps the novel's gentle treatment of Arthur can be traced to Don's feelings of loss, his suspicion that this would be his last book. He had witnessed modernism's failure to change the world. He had watched American postmodernism fall from critical favor, and he had grown weary of the concept himself. Safe to say that he—like Daumier in *his* day—felt eerily anachronistic.

In quoting the sad, anti-Semitic ravings of Ezra Pound, *The King* portrays the modernist spirit as blind and mad instead of innovative and hopeful. Contrast the exuberance of the Dead Father's good-bye speech with its playful echoes of *Finnegans Wake*—"I was Papping as best I could like my AndI before me"—with Pound's venom in *The King:* "[T]he Talmud . . . is the dirtiest teaching that any race ever codified."

The King appears to be Don's final argument with himself, a valentine to the ethos that nurtured him as well as recognition of its dark side: its potential for tyranny and "messianic impulses"; its tendency to value aesthetics and technical advancement over human needs.

The argument is conducted through now-familiar dialogues, punctuated by only a little exposition. Many of the chapters start with participial fragments: "Guinevere . . . sitting in a chair buttering an apple"; "Launcelot whanging away at the helm of the Yellow Knight."

These sentences establish an eternal present—the action is ongoing, like the lives of the mythical figures. Yet they (and their humane qualities) belong to the past, and they know it. At one point, Guinevere tells Launcelot that Arthur chants for strength in his sleep. "Always before," she adds, "he's *had* strength, don't you see."

Arthur paces the world, but he's fading. So are his companions. Deftly, Don illustrates their predicament with subtle grammatical twists. The present-participial phrases mix with past-tense verbs to create a simultaneous then and now:

> At the Café Balalaika, Launcelot and Guinevere drinking coffee.
> "All these people who don't know who we are!"
> "Anonymity," said Launcelot, "is something I have always cherished."

The lovers are here and not here: *drinking* continuously in the present, but speaking (*said*) in the past. Linguistically, thematically, these characters are caught in a time warp—like their author, wondering if he'd outlived his historical moment.

Toward the end of the book, the worshipful knights begin to vanish. Their time is finally up. "You, dear Arthur, are a bit at sixes and sevens, in terms of legend. You require, legend requires, a tragic end," Guinevere reminds the king. "No particular hurry, I suppose?" he replies, but he has already doomed himself by refusing to develop the atomic bomb. The age of chivalry is dead.

In the book's final scene, two unidentified speakers, who have served throughout as a chorus, watch Launcelot dream:

> "He is dreaming that there is no war, no Table Round, no Arthur, no Launcelot!"
> "That cannot be! He dreams, rather, of the softness of Guinevere, the sweetness of Guinevere, the brightness of Guinevere, and the sexuality of Guinevere!"
> "How do you know?"
> "I can see into the dream! Now she enters the dream in her own person, wearing a gown wrought of gold bezants over white samite and carrying a bottle of fine wine, Pinot Grigio by the look of it!"
> "What a matchless dream!"
> "Under an apple tree . . ."

And so we return to the garden, and to an ordinary yet marvelous vision of Paradise. *The King* is heavily elegiac—a catalog of wonders about to disappear from the earth. Though the novel echoes Malory's *Le Morte d'Arthur,* this final exchange sounds more like Puck's last speech in *A Midsummer Night's Dream:* "Think . . . / That you have but slumb'red here / While these visions did appear. / And this weak and idle theme, / No more yielding but a dream . . ."

Fragile and brief. The supply of strange ideas is not endless, but in Don's stories and novels—technical and imaginative achievements of the highest order—matchless dreams, with each rereading, continue.

On Don's last day in Rome, Ed Hirsch lunched with him on a terrace at the Academy. Don drank several glasses of wine and smoked a cigarette. "Don't tell Marion about the cigarette," he warned his friend. "If you tell her, I'll never speak to you again." (Marion knew about the cigarettes because she could smell them. "I did not bug him about these things," she says.)

"We had a terrific lunch," Hirsch recalled. "[P]asta in cream sauce . . . We took a long walk, since it was one of those days when the singing sunlight turns you every way but loose. He was going home in the morning. 'So long, see you but not tomorrow,' I said, ever the glib one. 'See you,' [Don said,] 'but not in Paradise.'"

Back in the apartment on West Eleventh Street, Don didn't appear any frailer than he had in Rome, "but he did seem disconnected some of the time, irritated by loud noises," Marion says. "He showed uncharacteristic irritation if Katharine yelled too loudly."

Marion recalls that "the ceiling in the living room had partially fallen—the molding, actually—and we were fixing it." For this reason, Don may have postponed a medical check-up he had scheduled in Houston, but eventually, in late June, he decided to fly to Texas to see the doctor. He asked Marion to stay in New York to finish the ceiling job and other repairs. "I don't think he felt well, but he never said that," she recalls.

In Houston, Don was alone in the house on South Boulevard. One afternoon, he phoned his brother Pete and asked if he would accompany him on a "test drive." Don wanted to see if he could "function as a driver." He was "not really coherent," Pete discovered, and the short drive was "terrifying." Pete forced Don to pull over; he took the wheel and drove them back to the house.

"Some time later, maybe the next day, Donald had the check-up with the internist that he had gone to Houston for. It included blood samples," Marion says. "Following the appointment, Donald went home. I talked to him then and he told me he was going to take a nap. Meanwhile, the lab found his blood electrolytes—I guess calcium, too—to be way out of whack, and telephoned him to go to the hospital. He didn't answer because he was asleep. I got a call from a friend he'd listed as a contact that the hospital was looking for him. I told her to go bang hard on the door because he was asleep. She did and then waited for him to pack a few things which he put into his computer bag. He told her to stop rushing him and she sat quietly until he was ready. She drove him to the hospital."

Shortly afterward, having arrived from New York, Marion moved Don to M. D. Anderson. "Donald's blood stabilized with IVs and we hoped he would be able to start chemo, but he never became strong enough," she says.

Pete had fully recovered from his own bout with throat cancer. He speculated that Don's withdrawal from alcohol had weakened his stamina. Doctors told Marion that "cells from [Don's] original cancer either spilled during the surgery or were already circulating in his system and took up sites in other areas of his body—his heart, head, femur."

Calcium was streaming into his blood, causing him to hallucinate. Doctors met with Don's family in a plush office filled with potted plants and framed pictures of the doctors' children. Calmly, the medical men outlined the seriousness of Don's condition.

Don's mother asked one of the medical men if he had ever "seen a miracle." The doctor said, "Yes, I have."

Eventually, treatments to reduce calcium levels in the bloodstream gave Don some relief. He startled in and out of consciousness and experienced days of vivid lucidity. Some of his students came to see him. He asked about their welfare. Were they writing? How were their finances? What was the latest gossip? He discussed chemotherapy with Marion. He asked her to call the UH English Department and tell them he didn't know when he'd return. Don't be "overly optimistic" with them, he told her.

According to Maggie Maranto, when George Christian came to visit, Don told him "regretfully and with deep feeling that he was afraid he was finally being paid back for all his sins. His Catholicism was always in the background during his lifetime, but [it] must have come back to haunt him in his last moments."

Beverly Lowry stopped by but didn't stay long. He peered at her with "love, sadness, skepticism." He "loved women, you know, and he had his vanity—he didn't really want me there," she says.

The doctors kept him on heavy doses of morphine. He began to have trouble breathing. Within a few days, he slipped into a coma, from which he would not awaken. Helen came to see him, though he was unaware of her presence. There she met Anne for the first time. "I've heard of you all my life," Anne told her. "It was all good."

On Sunday, July 23, 1989, at 5:55 A.M., Don died. He was fifty-eight years old. Days earlier, when he had first been admitted to the hospital, he was groggy, suffering from a surfeit of calcium in the blood. A doctor asked him, "Do you know where you are, Mr. Barthelme?"

Don said, "In the antechamber to Heaven."

He was cremated on July 25. "I remember going to the wake," says George Williams. "It was in some student's backyard—I don't remember whose. We're all drinking J & B, and there are these candles lit all around the yard, nothing ostentatious. At one point I'm aware that there's this white box on the table—Don's ashes. Marion had brought it. I was surprised when I picked it up. It weighed more than I thought it would."

A short time later, a memorial service was held in the Rothko Chapel. Other remembrances took place in New York and on the University of Houston campus.

THE FINAL ASSIGNMENT

After Don's death, his books drifted, one by one, out of print and out of reach. As of this writing, some of them have popped up in new editions: *The Dead Father, Paradise,* and *The King. Sixty Stories* and *Forty Stories* reappeared, featuring appreciations by popular young writers (David Gates and Dave Eggers). Still, Don remains largely hidden.

"The movement of history always takes place *behind one's back*," he wrote. Nothing prepares you for time's changes—even if you've managed to place yourself in the center of modern consciousness.

As if to underscore this point, two days after militants attacked the World Trade Center and the Pentagon on September 11, 2001, Michiko Kakutani wrote, "Language failed this week. . . . In a day when hype and hyperbole have become a staple of cable news, in a day when the word 'reality' has become associated with stage-managed fame-fests . . . words felt devalued and inadequate to capture the disasters at the World Trade Center, the Pentagon and near Pittsburgh."

In part, she blamed the failure of language on American writers who had abandoned the "effort to write about American public life" in the wake of the social upheavals of the 1960s and beyond. She chided certain novelists (Ann Beattie, Harold Brodkey, Philip Roth)

EPILOGUE

for focusing "on the private realm of the self, on the convolutions of the individual psyche. Others, like John Barth and Donald Barthelme, contented themselves with performing postmodern experiments with fable, farce and recycled fairy tales," she said.

A few days later, also in the *Times,* Edward Rothstein argued that September 11 "challeng[ed] the intellectual and ethical perspectives of . . . postmodernism." "In general postmodernists [question] assertions that truth and ethical judgment have any objective validity," he claimed. "But such assertions seem peculiar when trying to account for the recent attack. This destruction seems to cry out for a transcendent ethical perspective."

He concluded that postmodernism was "perverse . . . a form of guilty passivity in the face of ruthless and unyielding opposition."

By implying that "postmodernism" had, figuratively speaking, provided the terrorists with flight plans, he appeared to be marching alongside televangelists Jerry Falwell and Pat Robertson. They insisted that America's secularism, its acceptance of gay rights, abortion, and civil liberties had enraged God to the point that God loosed mass destruction upon the land. So who, according to these views, was to blame for the slaughter of innocents? By implication, Planned Parenthood and the ACLU; Ann Beattie and Donald Barthelme.

It could be argued that, like Hilton Kramer in the 1970s, Rothstein and others seized upon a moment of uncertainty and masked themselves behind aesthetics to advance a political agenda.

"Postmodernism" does not—cannot—denote a single ethos. Nor is it solely the province of artists, writers, and academics; if by "postmodern," we mean style over substance, a blurring of values, and vague historical awareness, then the conditions for it are set by lawyers, real estate developers, money speculators, televangelists, and the nation's professional political class, along with its symbiotic companion, the popular media.

Remember Don's remark: "The disorientation in my stories is not mine. It is what is to be perceived around us."

Far more important than squabbles over postmodernism was the speculation, in the press and on the Internet, about literature's continuing efficacy in the face of modern disasters. Rosellen Brown said, "I don't think people are going to lose interest in telling stories about how people live their lives." When the first plane hit the World Trade Center, she said, "ordinary people were going about their lives, putting cream in their coffee, picking up the phone to start the day; the ordinariness of those lives is what seizes us." But Joan Didion suggested that definitions of the ordinary may have shifted for Americans. She said a "different level of apprehension" would appear in her work from now on, reflecting increased apprehension in daily life.

Writing in a special edition of *The New York Times Magazine,* Richard Ford said, "I remember very well the day my father died. It was in the early morning of a Saturday in 1960," and he told the story of that day in rich and vivid detail. But then he admitted, "Of course, I can tell you about all these events . . . this intimacy . . . because my father didn't die by having a jet airplane fly through his window and obliterate him without a thought. . . . My father died, if there is such a way to die, properly: in his house, in his bed."

He added, "It is an axiom of the novelist's grasp on reality that a death's importance is measured by the significance of the life that has ended. Thus to die, as so many did on Sept[ember] 11–their singular existences briefly obscured–may seem to cloud and invalidate life entirely." And, by extension, may invalidate the novel's "grasp on reality."

In the days following the WTC's collapse, the south side of St. Vincent's Hospital, down the block from Don's old apartment, became a wailing wall where people tacked up pictures and descriptions of individuals lost in the ash and melted steel. Don had once delighted in the children's artwork, advertising, and books on display in the Village's windows. Now, pages and pages of prose covered the neighborhood's walls: physical details, personality profiles, urgent pleas for help–thousands of fragments of stories, stories in the making, stories interrupted. "Fragments are the only forms I trust."

Newspaper and television pundits claimed that humor and irony had died in the attacks. No one felt like laughing. Satire–particularly of politicians–seemed in poor taste. Yet bizarre "disorientations" remained all around us, and begged to be spoofed. For instance, two weeks after the towers fell, while rescue workers continued to dig for bodies, the Aegis Realty Corporation ran a full-page ad in *The New York Times Magazine,* touting "Trump Tower, the World's #1 Address" in mid-Manhattan. "Your clients and customers will be overwhelmed by the luxurious surroundings," read the text, next to a photo of a looming skyscraper.

Postmodernism, anyone?

The Verizon telephone company bought a two-page ad in the September 23, 2001, edition of *The New York Times:* "All of us at Verizon want this message of hope and recovery to ring loud and clear across the world." The ad quoted John Lennon: "Imagine all the people living life in peace," and proclaimed, "Let freedom ring." Multiple ironies blessed this notice. Songs by Lennon, who had been shot to death in New York City some twenty years before, had been virtually banned from certain radio stations after the attacks because programmers felt his utopian lyrics were inappropriate now. Cell phone sales had increased dramatically, as several passengers on the doomed planes contacted their families, using their phones, to say good-bye–good news for Verizon.

The free market, seizing every occasion to sell its products, was part of the "American way of life" under siege on September 11. One way to "let freedom ring" was to purchase a cell phone and invest in America's economy. President George W. Bush called his "war on terrorism" a fight between "freedom" and "fear," and urged Americans to keep on shopping.

In "City Life," Don wrote, "[W]e are locked in the most exquisite mysterious muck. This muck heaves and palpitates. It is multi-directional and has a mayor. To describe it takes many hundreds of thousands of words. Our muck is only part of a much greater muck—the nation-state—which is itself the creation of that muck of mucks, the human consciousness. Of course all these things also have a touch of sublimity. . . ."

Despite tectonic shifts, this "muck" remains the same. *Modernity* hasn't changed, with its struggles between old and new modes of existence, its economic and social conflicts, its urban disruptions. Buildings reach for the sky. Buildings fall.

It's an architectural problem.

The past haunts the present, and the future broods somewhere out of sight.

In "Tradition and the Individual Talent," first published in 1919, T. S. Eliot said, "No poet, no artist of any sort, has his complete meaning alone. His significance, his appreciation is the appreciation of his relation to dead poets and artists. You cannot value him alone; you must set him, for contrast and comparison, among the dead." Extrapolating from Eliot's remarks, we must consider not only individual writers but whole generations, historical moments, literary eras.

So when we notice a line from Georg Büchner's *Woyzeck*—"And the moon looked at him so kindly!"—played upon by Don—"See the moon? It hates us"—the past and the present clasp hands. Büchner feeds Don. Don updates Büchner. Centuries connect and converse. Our understanding of the "modern," and the muck of human consciousness, expands.

In his final novel, mindful of the future's pressure on the past, Don wrote, "Things yet to come will make us sadder still." But the body of his work, with its humor, its delight in the everyday, suggests we'll carry on—like angels, like Snow White's little men, like the ordinary men and women we are—in search of new principles, with the "best will in the world!"

In the summer of 1984, I visited Don in New York. Kirk and Faith Sale were out of town. I stayed in their apartment. Marion and Katharine were away.

That first night, Don followed me down to the Sales's place to make sure I had everything I needed. The shelves were filled with books about Vietnam, Marxism, student protest movements. I said, "Your generation has witnessed so much. Mine is asleep." Don looked at me as if to say, Well then, wake up.

Next morning at seven o'clock, he banged on the door to rouse me. "You're in New York. You don't want to waste your days!" Together, we toured several art galleries in SoHo. At one point, he made a big show of giving money to a street beggar. He walked me down a cobbled alley and pointed to a loft window. "That's where I built a harpsichord," he said. We happened upon a street fair with live music and dancing, and I saw how happy it made Don. In that moment, his life in Houston seemed to me constricted—convenient, perhaps, familiar, easy on the child, but lacking the protein that Don's mind and sensibilities required.

That night, we walked to the Village Vanguard and listened to the Woody Shaw band. Don got very drunk. We both thought the drummer was a showboat; his pretensions and stylistic flair overwhelmed the music. As we left, Don stumbled on the steps leading to the street. He wouldn't let me help him up.

The last time I saw him was in February 1989, six months before he died. I had invited him to give a reading at Oregon State University, where I taught.

His gaunt face startled me. "Corvallis isn't bad for a small town," he said, looking around. "At least it has a Mexican restaurant." The afternoon was mild. "Is anyone here smarter than you?" he asked me.

"Sure. Plenty of folks," I said.

"Good. The only way to keep learning is to surround yourself with people smarter than you are."

The day before, an acquaintance of mine admitted he wouldn't be attending the reading. "I only read dead authors," he'd said.

When I mentioned this to Don, he quipped, "Tell your friend to stick with me."

He insisted I take him to a liquor store so he could buy a bottle of wine. I knew he shouldn't drink, but he was still my teacher and now he was my guest. I couldn't refuse him. He purchased an inexpensive Pinot Grigio. In the parking lot, we glimpsed a small helium balloon floating in the air, advertising Fuji film. "My lovely balloon," Don murmured.

In his motel room, we shared the bottle and talked about colleagues, friends, books; drumming, Houston, the Village Vanguard.

He told me he had sold a new story, "Tickets," to *The New Yorker.* "It's a relief to know I still have some juice," he said. The story is about diminished circumstances, a man making the best of life in a rather provincial city.

"I'm afraid of dying," he said, and we sat quietly.

Later, in a fiction-writing class, one of my students asked him, "What's kept you working for so many years?" He stroked his beard and tapped a booted foot. "All my life I've been interested in intoxication, in dazzling the mind," he said. "Your mind is constantly capable of surprising you if you work it hard enough."

That night, in the small campus auditorium where the reading was to be held, he asked the stage manager to tweak the lighting just so. It took several minutes before Don felt satisfied with the atmosphere. He carried typed copies of his stories and excerpts of his novel in progress, *The King,* in a manila folder with a reproduction of one of Jasper Johns's *Target* paintings on the cover.

During the reading, he modulated his weakened voice perfectly. Now and then I saw him lift his right foot ever so slightly—a subtle dance behind the podium. He didn't challenge listeners with his most difficult pieces. Instead, he offered the funniest, most straightforward work: "Chablis," "The Baby," "Conversations with Goethe," "I Bought a Little City."

During the Q and A portion of the evening, someone asked him if his work was autobiographical. He said, "Don't confuse the monster on the page with the monster here in front of you."

After the reading, Don and I walked to my car. The weather had turned. The sidewalks had iced over. He stumbled and I reached for him. He shrugged me off. "Don't treat me like an invalid," he said.

In a local bar, he settled into a chair with a glass of white wine and talked generously, long into the night, with my students and colleagues. When we were alone once more, on the way to his motel, he turned and asked me, "Did I do okay for you?"

I recalled the end of *The Dead Father.* Just before he's covered in his grave, the Dead Father, speaking of the role he has played, of the life he has lived, asks his son Thomas, "Did I do it well?"

Oh yes. Oh yes. Marvelously well.

The following morning, ice covered western Oregon. The snow was thick as cotton. Don needed to get back to Houston, for which I was still mighty homesick. The airport was ninety miles away. Unexpectedly, planes were still flying. My windshield wipers froze. We slid a few blocks on our way to the freeway. I couldn't see. "I'm afraid this isn't going to work," I said.

"No," Don said. "We don't want to be badly killed."

I called a cab for him, and promised to pay the taxi company the exorbitant fare. Don was grateful. As we placed his bags in the trunk, I thought of his story "Departures": "I cannot imagine the future . . . [you are] sailing away from me!"

"Write a story about a genius," he told me. A teacher's last assignment to his student.

"Okay."

He shook my hand. "Work well," we told each other. "Be well." He was driven away into a blizzard.

CHRONOLOGY

1931	Born April 7 in Philadelphia to Donald (an architect) and Helen Bechtold Barthelme.
1932	Barthelme family moves to Galveston, Texas.
1937	Barthelme family moves to Houston.
1945–1946	Writes for *Eagle*, the St. Thomas High School newspaper.
1948–1949	Wins short story and poetry awards in *Sequoyha*, the Lamar High School literary magazine.
1949	Enrolls at the University of Houston.
1950	Edits the *Cougar*, the University of Houston's newspaper.
1951	Begins writing for *The Houston Post*.
1952	Marries Marilyn Marrs.
1953	Drafted into the U.S. Army. Serves in Korea.
1955	Returns to the University of Houston, resumes writing for the *Houston Post*. Separates from Marilyn Marrs.
1956	Divorced from Marilyn Marrs. Marries Helen Moore. At the University of Houston, he writes speeches for the university president, edits *Acta Diurna*, the faculty newsletter, and founds *Forum*, an interdisciplinary intellectual journal.
1959	Joins board of directors, Contemporary Arts Museum, Houston.
1961–1962	Director, Contemporary Arts Museum, Houston.
1962	Moves to New York City, becomes managing editor of *Location*, an arts magazine founded by Harold Rosenberg and Thomas B. Hess. Separates from Helen Moore.
1963	First appearance in *The New Yorker*, with short story "L'Lapse."
1964	*Come Back, Dr. Caligari* is published.
1965	Lives in Denmark. Divorced from Helen Moore. Marries Birgit Egelund-Peterson and returns with her to New York. Their daughter, Anne, born in New York.
1966	Awarded Guggenheim Fellowship.
1967	*Snow White* is published.
1968	*Unspeakable Practices, Unnatural Acts* is published.
1970	*City Life* is published.

1971   *The Slightly Irregular Fire Engine, or the Hithering Thithering Djinn* (children's book) is published.

1972   *Sadness* is published. Receives National Book Award for *The Slightly Irregular Fire Engine*. Receives the Mortin Dauwen Zabel Award from the National Institute of Arts and Letters. Teaches writing at the State University of New York at Buffalo.

1973   Teaches writing at Boston University. Divorced from Birgit Egelund-Peterson.

1974   *Guilty Pleasures* is published. Becomes Distinguished Visiting Professor of English at City College of New York.

1975   *The Dead Father* is published.

1976   *Amateurs* is published.

1978   Marries Marion Knox. Inducted into the American Academy of Arts and Letters. *Here in the Village* (limited edition) is published.

1979   *Great Days* is published.

1980   *Presents* (limited edition) and *The Emerald* (limited edition) are published.

1981   *Sixty Stories* is published. Becomes Cullen Distinguished Professor of English, University of Houston; begins living half the year in Houston, half the year in New York.

1982   Daughter Katharine born in New York.

1983   *Overnight to Many Distant Cities* is published.

1986   *Paradise* is published.

1987   *Forty Stories* and *Sam's Bar* (latter with Seymour Chwast) are published.

1988   Receives Rea Award for the Short Story. Diagnosed with throat cancer; undergoes surgery and radiation treatments.

1989   Receives senior fellowship from the American Academy in Rome; spends the spring in Rome. Dies of throat cancer in Houston on July 23.

1990   *The King* is published posthumously.

1992   *The Teachings of Don B.: Satires, Parodies, Fables, Illustrated Stories, and Plays,* edited by Kim Herzinger, is published.

1997   *Not-Knowing: The Essays and Interviews,* edited by Kim Herzinger, is published.

2007   *Flying to America: 45 More Stories,* edited by Kim Herzinger, is published.

NOTES

Introduction: The Lost Teacher

page 3 *"At this time of life"; "From the outset":* John Ashbery, *Three Poems,* in *Selected Poems* (New York: Penguin, 1986), 123, 125.

page 3 *"managed to place himself in the center of modern consciousness":* William Gass, *Fiction and the Figures of Life* (New York: Vintage, 1972), 100.

page 4 *"unfortunate discontinuance":* Amazon .com.

page 4 *"Oh, I think they want me to go away":* "Interview with Charles Ruas and Judith Sherman, 1975," in *Not-Knowing: The Essays and Interviews,* ed. Kim Herzinger (New York: Random House, 1997), 236.

page 4 *"Neglect is useful":* Donald Barthelme, "Culture, Etc.," in ibid., 135.

page 5 *"political and social contamination":* Donald Barthelme, "Not-Knowing," in ibid., 14-15.

page 5 *the relationship of his fiction "to political writing":* Lois Zamora, "The Long Sonata of the Dead," *Gulf Coast* 4, no. 1 (1991): 183.

page 5 *"lowered expectations in terms of life":* "Interview with Bobbie Roe, 1988," in *Not-Knowing,* ed. Herzinger, 319.

page 5 *Baudelaire's "pitiful" acrobats:* Charles Baudelaire, *The Parisian Prowler,* trans. Edward K. Kaplan (Athens: University of Georgia Press, 1989), 29.

page 6 *"Art is not difficult because it wishes to be difficult":* Barthelme, "Not-Knowing," in *Not-Knowing,* ed. Herzinger, 15.

page 6 *"The point of my career":* Donald Barthelme, *Forty Stories* (New York: Putnam, 1987), 256.

page 7 *The "irruption of accident":* Donald Barthelme, "Nudes: An Introduction to *Exquisite Creatures,*" in *Not-Knowing,* ed. Herzinger, 182.

page 7 *"What is magical [about art]":* Barthelme, "Not-Knowing," in *Not-Knowing,* ed. Herzinger, 20.

page 7 *"It [is not] easy to conjure up a man":* Phillip Lopate, *Getting Personal* (New York: Basic Books, 2003), 357.

page 7 *"There's not a strong autobiographical strain":* J. D. O'Hara "Donald Barthelme: The Art of Fiction LXVI," *Paris Review* 80 (1981): 274.

pages 7-8 *"I will never write an autobiography"; would not "sustain a person's attention"; "biography is always interesting"; his work had "not perhaps [been] adequately" commented upon:* Donald Barthelme and J. D. O' Hara, "Rough Draft #1" of the *Paris Review* interview, Special Collections and Archives, University of Houston Libraries.

page 8 *"Time works on fiction as it does on us":* The Writer in Society: Donald Barthelme (Houston: KUHT-TV, 1984). This recording is of an interview with George Plimpton.

page 8 *"I remember Donald well":* Roger Angell, in conversation with the author, May 27, 2004.

page 8 *"I don't mind trying"; "When I reflect how many cells":* Kirkpatrick Sale, in E-mails to the author, May 20 and 25, 2004.

1. Tools

page 11 *"I Bought a Little City":* Donald Barthelme, *Sixty Stories* (New York: Putnam, 1981), 296.

page 12 *"wasn't going to be able to just stand there":* Frederick Barthelme and Steven Barthelme, *Double Down: Reflections on Gambling and Loss* (Boston: Houghton Mifflin, 1999), 133.

page 12 *"world was a place that needed fixing":* ibid., 192.

page 12 *"for some indiscretion in the school newspaper":* ibid., 16.

page 12 *"tall, dark, and handsome one":* Helen Moore Barthelme, *Donald Barthelme: The Genesis of a Cool Sound* (College Station: Texas A & M University Press, 2001), 7.

page 12 *"He was a fortunate man":* Barthelme and Barthelme, *Double Down,* 16.

pages 12-13 *"What else happened in 1931?":* Donald Barthelme, draft of "Kierkegaard Unfair to Schlegel," Special Collections and Archives, University of Houston Libraries.

page 13 *"beloved mother":* Barthelme and Barthelme, *Double Down,* 35.

page 13 *Philadelphia Savings Fund Society building:* See www.publ.gsfa.upenn.edu.

page 13 *"Where did you get this idea?"; People "laughed at him":* Barthelme and Barthelme, *Double Down,* 65, 186.

page 13 *Paul Philippe Cret:* For background information on Cret and the Beaux-Arts style, I have drawn upon Lisa and Donald Sclare, *Beaux-Arts Estates: A Guide to the Architecture of Long Island* (New York: Viking, 1980), and Marcus Whiffen and Frederick Koeper, *American Architecture, 1607-1976* (Cambridge: MIT Press, 1981).

page 14 *He could "cut through" the politics:* Elizabeth Greenwall Grossman, *The Civic Architecture of Paul Cret* (Cambridge: Cambridge University Press, 1996), 10.

page 14 *the "excesses" of his profession:* Donald Barthelme, *Paradise* (New York: Putnam, 1986), 79-80.

page 15 *"Together let us conceive and create the new building":* Quoted in Kenneth Frampton, *Modern Architecture: A Critical History* (New York: Oxford University Press, 1980), 123.

page 15 *"house machines":* ibid., 153.

page 15 *"The maximum effect with the minimum expenditure of means":* ibid., 163. Like the Bauhaus members, Le Corbusier and Mies saw themselves as apostles of a better world through art. Le Corbusier's image of the "City of Tomorrow" included cruciform towers—he called them "Cartesian skyscrapers"—whose glass and reinforced concrete would, he said, express thought. Idealism of this magnitude can be ominous, especially when applied to the improvement of others. Early on, modern architecture's potentially tyrannical aspects were frequently overlooked, but they were apparent. For example, Le Corbusier's plan for an ideal city in France called for a strict separation of workers and administrators, a blinkered, class-mired vision of utopia. The Communist newspaper *L'Humanité* called the project "reactionary" and asked, "Which better world do we want? Who decides?"

Mies often seemed to want to leave the world altogether to attend to the soul. What is the task of architecture? he asked again and again. What is the truth? Thomas Aquinas gave him one answer he liked: "Truth is the significance of fact." From this statement, Mies said, the idea of a "clear construction came to me"—that is, repeating fundamental building elements from the smallest to the grandest details, thus stressing the essential facts. Structure, he insisted, is a metaphysical notion, and architecture the "will of the age expressed in spatial terms." In 1921, when he proposed an all-glass office complex for the Friedrichstrasse in Berlin, he noted that light and shadow did not guide his design; instead, the important thing to him was the play of reflections on the glass. This suggests that his eye was not on human needs, or the will of the age, but on the beyond (see ibid., 103, 155, 161).

page 15 *the "country of timid people":* John Burchard and Albert Bush-Brown, *The Architecture of America: A Social and Cultural History* (Boston: Little, Brown, 1966), 361.

page 15 *A "tendency toward Oedipal overthrow":* Herbert Muschamp, "A Building with a Song in Its Heart," *New York Times,* October 2, 2003.

page 15 *"Mr. Barthelme, I find that I can make things beautiful":* Barthelme and Barthelme, *Double Down,* 132.

page 16 *U.S. Department of Justice building:* For details on this building, see the National Register of Historic Places Travel Itinerary at www.hps.gov/history/NR/travel/wash/text.htm.

page 16 *"We had told Mr. Wright"; "little or no closet space":* Stanley Marcus, *Minding the Store* (Boston: Little, Brown, 1974), 91-95. See also "House for Stanley Marcus, Dallas, Texas," *Architectural Forum,* December 1939, 461-467.

page 16 *"I couldn't understand [Wright's] plans":* Donald Barthelme, Sr., quoted in Stephen Fox, "Donald Barthelme, 1917-1996," *Cite* 35 (1996): 9.

page 17 *The result was too conventional:* Marcus, *Minding the Store.*

page 17 *the Hall of State:* For details on this building in Dallas's Fair Park, see www .dallascityhall.com and www.bluffton.edu/ ~sullivanm/texas/dallas/fairpark/hallofstate.

page 17 *"I told [Staub]":* Stephen Fox and Janet M. O'Brien, "An Interview with Donald Barthelme," typewritten transcript, Special Collections and Archives, University of Houston Libraries.

page 17 *"the qualifications of which":* *Architectural Forum,* July 1939, 7.

page 18 *"wonderful to live in but strange to see on the Texas prairie":* "Interview with Jerome Klinkowitz, 1971-72," in *Not-Knowing: The Essays and Interviews,* ed. Kim Herzinger (New York: Random House, 1997), 200.

page 18 *"The furniture...wasn't like other people's furniture":* Steven Barthelme, "It Used to Be Right Here," *Texas Magazine, Houston Chronicle,* May 20, 2000, 4.

page 18 *"The atmosphere of the house was peculiar":* "Interview with Jerome Klinkowitz, 1971-72," in *Not-Knowing,* ed. Herzinger, 200.

page 18 *"sheer literary talent and output of the Barthelme family":* Don Graham, "book review,"

Texas Monthly, August 2001; posted at www .texasmonthly.com.

page 18 *"a cigar box with a cracker box on top"; "an ever-ready work force"; "He was prone to handing":* Steven Barthelme, "It Used to Be Right Here," 4.

page 18 *his kids liked the warps and ripples in it:* Marion Barthelme recalls, "I once asked Donald how he'd gotten such strong shoulders, and he said that as a young boy, under his father's direction, he'd spent a summer rolling a Coke bottle across the copper to give it that warp and ripple."

page 18 *"There was one thing that . . . affect[ed] my childhood":* Barthelme and O'Hara, "Rough Draft #1."

page 20 *In the 1970s, he told a friend:* Karen Kennerly, in a conversation with the author, May 29, 2004.

page 20 *"moonstruck":* Barthelme, *Sixty Stories,* 103.

page 20 *"Ever been subject to epilepsy?":* Barthelme, *Paradise,* 15.

page 20 *"Modernist architecture was a crusade"; "It took a month or so":* Steven Barthelme, "It Used to Be Right Here," 4.

page 20 *a "magical" part of the house:* Steven Barthelme, "Tools That Fit Just So," *Texas Magazine, Houston Chronicle,* October 21, 1990, 4.

page 20 *"a designer is responsible"; "everything good ever done"; "Walk alone":* Donald Barthelme, Sr., quoted in Fox, "Donald Barthelme, 1917-1996," 9, 10.

2. The Educational Experience

pages 21-22 *"half school and half circus"; "Barthelme [has] made a lot out of a little"* to *"Barthelme is a liberated man":* "Wirework School: Simplicity + Ingenuity = Low Cost and High Value," *Architectural Forum,* October 1952, 103-106.

page 23 *Their mother shows up as a drunken barmaid:* Frederick Barthelme and Steven Barthelme, *Double Down: Reflections on Gambling and Loss* (Boston: Houghton Mifflin, 1999) 20-21.

page 23 *Helen threw herself into housework and child rearing:* Steven Barthelme, "And Off to Work We Go," *Texas Magazine, Houston Chronicle,* March 29, 1998, 3.

page 23 *Rafael Sabatini's:* Steven Barthelme, "Fancy Girl in a Fancy Car," *Texas Magazine, Houston Chronicle,* November 3, 1999, 3.

page 23 *cruised down Highway 6:* Steven Barthelme, "Just Being Out There and Loose," *Texas Magazine, Houston Chronicle,* September 1, 1991, 4.

page 23 *"stack of saddles in a corner"; "rifles on pegs":* Donald Barthelme. *Sixty Stories* (New York: Putnam, 1981), 449.

page 23 *"wonderful place to ride and hunt":* J. D. O'Hara, "Donald Barthelme: The Art of Fiction LXVI," *Paris Review* 80 (1981): 275.

page 23 *"terrain studded with caliche"; "[H]is grandfather points"; "walking in the water":* Barthelme, *Sixty Stories,* 449.

page 24 *"skill of editing":* Barthelme and Barthelme, *Double Down,* 6.

pages 24-25 *"Dr. Trump . . . has pushed a door ajar"; "The Barthelme scheme"; "I never understood":* "Three Ace Schools for the Trump

Plan," *Architectural Forum,* March 1960, 119, 124.

page 25 *"programs his direction"; "preparation of source material"; "Whereas previously it was the teacher's problem":* "Three Ace Schools for the Trump Plan."

page 25 *"It was an attitude toward his work":* Jo Brans, "Interview with J. Brans: 'Embracing the World, 1981'" in *Not-Knowing,* ed. Kim Herzinger (New York: Random House, 1997), 293-294.

page 26 *"I was aware that he was studying me":* Gallatin quoted in Helen Moore Barthelme, *Donald Barthelme: The Genesis of a Cool Sound* (College Station: Texas A & M University Press, 2007), 11.

page 26 *"actually talked to each other":* Brans, "Embracing the World," 294.

page 26 *"in their dash and glitter"; "tendencies [in any given art]":* Sigfried Giedion, *Space, Time and Architecture* (Cambridge: Harvard University Press, 1941), 19. It's intriguing to compare certain passages in *Space, Time and Architecture* with Don's story "The Balloon," published in 1966, at a time when many writers Don admired, including the architect Robert Venturi, Susan Sontag, and Marshall McLuhan, were citing Giedion's ideas. Giedion devoted a section of his book to "balloon frame construction," the "substitution of thin plates and studs" for "mortised and tenoned joints"—an "industrialized" and "revolutionary" concept in house building. Many carpenters resisted it at first. The term *balloon frame* was derisory, referring to the lightness of the construction.

In an allegorical fashion, Don's story relates a similar set of events. In the piece, an odd industrial object, a massive but elegant balloon, appears overnight in Manhattan., initiating outrage, concern, and resistance among citizens. Eventually, people come to accept its presence, just as people grew accustomed to balloon-frame housing. "'The Balloon Frame belongs to no one person,'" Giedion says. He quoted architect George Woodward as saying, "'[N]obody claims it as an invention.'" The unnamed maker of Don's balloon stakes *his* claim incompletely, revealing himself only briefly at the end of the story. (For Giedion's discussion of the balloon frame, see Giedion, *Space, Time, and Architecture,* 269-276.)

page 27 *Don related to one of his students a dream he'd had:* See Brian Kitely interview with Sandra Descheune at www.du.edu/~bkitely.

page 27 *"a number of men [were] competing":* "Interview with Charles Ruas and Judith Sherman, 1975," in *Not-Knowing: The Essays and Interviews,* ed. Kim Herzinger (New York: Random House, 1997), 256.

3. Soul

page 28 *"education within the [Catholic] church's mission of evangelism":* See archives at www.basilian.org.

page 28 *"Catholic boys cannot be built":* ibid.

page 28 *random distension:* Stephen Fox, *Houston Architectural Guide* (Houston: American Institute of Architects, Houston Chapter, and Herring Press, 1990), 254.

page 29 *"Teachers enjoy bright students":* Gallatin quoted in Helen Moore Barthelme, *Donald Barthelme: The Genesis of a Cool Sound* (College Station: Texas A & M University Press, 2001), 11-12.

page 29 *"We were schooled in guilt":* Frederick Barthelme and Steven Barthelme, *Double Down: Reflections on Gambling and Loss* (Boston: Houghton Mifflin, 1999), 6.

page 30 *"Members of [our] community":* See www.sths.org (Web site of St. Thomas Catholic High School, Houston).

page 30 *housing defense-industry workers:* For more details on defense housing in the early 1940s, see *Architectural Record,* November 1941, 56-59.

page 30 *Avion Village:* For more details on Avion Village, see *Architectural Forum,* October 1941, 240-242.

page 31 *"'Good evening, fellow Englishmen,' the radio said":* Donald Barthelme, *The King* (New York: Harper & Row, 1990), 3.

page 31 WORKS OF MASTERS OF MANY AGES: Marguerite Johnston, *Houston: The Unknown City, 1836-1946* (College Station: Texas A & M University Press, 1991), 342. Subsequent statistics regarding Houston are taken from page 310.

page 32 *"getting connected":* Donald Barthelme, "Return," in *Liquid City: Houston Writers on Houston,* ed. Rita Saylors (San Antonio: Corona Publishing Company, 1987), 35.

page 32 *"to go to the establishment and support and maintenance of hospitals":* Johnston, *Houston,* 307-308.

page 32 *"A verbal bully":* Helen Moore Barthelme, *Donald Barthelme,* 54.

page 32 *"let him be":* ibid., 60.

page 32 *"You had some kind of a nervous disorder":* Donald Barthelme, *Sixty Stories* (New York: Putnam, 1981), 99-100.

page 32 *He would "distance" himself:* Helen Moore Barthelme, *Donald Barthelme,* 58.

page 33 *Don was "fully formed":* Joe Maranto quoted in ibid., 5.

4. High and Low

page 34 *"[My father] gave me":* J. D. O'Hara, "Donald Barthelme: The Art of Fiction LXVI," *Pans Review* 80 (1981): 274.

page 34 *DILIGITE IUSTITIAM QUI IUDICATIS TERRAM:* Dante Alighieri, *The Divine Comedy,* trans. John Ciardi (New York: New American Library, 2003), 754.

page 34 *an "anti-image":* ibid., 585-586.

page 35 *not the "name of the city":* Donald Barthelme, *Overnight to Many Distant Cities* (New York: Putnam, 1983), 10.

page 35 *"I can do no more":* See www.newadvent.org.

page 35 *"I don't know what value":* Donald Barthelme, *Forty Stories* (New York: Putnam, 1987), 256.

page 36 *"What is man?":* Quotes from the *Baltimore Catechism* and *An Explanation of the Baltimore Catechism* can be found at www.Catholic.net/Rec/Catechism.

page 36 *"weekly magazine most educated Americans grew up on":* Ben Yagoda, *About*

Town: The New Yorker and the World It Made (New York: Scribner's, 2000), 32.

page 37 *"Sweden announces"; "Meat and poultry":* Howard Brubaker, "Of All Things," The *New Yorker,* May 1, 1943, 43; and May 8, 1943, 32.

page 37 *"Everybody must know by this time":* James Thurber, "1776-And All That," *The New Yorker,* April 24, 1943, 15.

page 37 *"The American people have swallowed a lot":* Donald Barthelme, *Guilty Pleasures* (New York: Farrar, Straus and Giroux, 1974), p. 65.

page 38 *"little man"; "matter-of-factly positing":* Yagoda, *About Town,* 88.

page 38 *"A man must have some reading matter with him in the subway":* "Talk of the Town," *The New Yorker,* April 13, 1946, 23.

page 39 *"I hope I am not being stupid about this book":* Edmund Wilson, in a review of Carson McCullers's *The Heart Is a Lonely Hunter, The New Yorker,* March 30, 1946, 87.

page 39 *"first writer Don imitated":* Helen Moore Barthelme, *Donald Barthelme: The Genesis of a Cool Sound* (College Station: Texas A & M University Press, 2001), 14.

page 39 *"Perelman ... could do ... amazing things in prose":* "Interview with Larry McCaffery, 1980," in *Not-Knowing: The Essays and Interviews,* ed. Kim Herzinger (New York: Random House, 1997), 263.

page 39 *"I think you ought to decide when you write a piece":* Yagoda, *About Town,* 114.

page 39 *Perelman's stories:* Perelman quotes are from "Stringing Up Father" and "Methinks He Doth Protest Too Much," *The New Yorker,* January 1, 1949, 16; November 27, 1948, 29.

page 40 *Mr. Arbuthnot, the "Cliché Expert":* Frank Sullivan, *A Pearl in Every Oyster* (Boston: Little, Brown, 1938), 15.

page 40 *"You realize, of course":* Frank Sullivan, "The Cliché Expert Testifies on the Atom," *The New Yorker,* November 17, 1945, 27.

page 41 *"I started to get out a light magazine":* Yagoda, *About Town,* 193.

page 41 *"Style is not much a matter of choice":* Barthelme, "Not-Knowing," in *Not-Knowing,* ed. Herzinger, 22.

page 41 *"Peter Blood, bachelor of medicine and several other things besides":* Rafael Sabatini, *Captain Blood: His Odyssey* (Washington, D.C.: Gateway/Regnery, 1998), 1.

page 41 *"Kevin said a lot more garbage to Clem":* Donald Barthelme, *Snow White* (New York: Atheneum, 1967), 66.

page 41 *"The countryside. Flowers":* Donald Barthelme, *The Dead Father* (New York: Farrar, Straus and Giroux, 1975), 13.

page 42 *In reading "[my] Captain Blood":* J. D. O'Hara, "Donald Barthelme: The Art of Fiction LXVI," *Paris Review* 80 (1981): 277.

page 42 *"fitted with life jackets under their dresses"; "The favorite dance of Captain Blood":* Donald Barthelme, *Forty Stories* (New York: Putnam, 1987), 197, 202.

page 42 *"Why Errol Flynn?":* J. D. O' Hara, "Donald Barthelme," 277.

page 42 *"I had counted upon going home":* Sabatini, *Captain Blood,* 362.

page 43 *"What a matchless dream!":* Donald Barthelme, *The King* (New York: Harper & Row, 1990), 158.

page 43 *"taught us all"; "wonderful things about":* Jo Brans, "Embracing the World," in *Not-Knowing,* ed. Herzinger, 299-300.

page 43 *"It was getting hot":* Ernest Hemingway, *The Nick Adams Stories* (New York: Scribner's, 1972), 233.

page 44 *"surrounded by oak trees":* Pat Goeters, in an E-mail to the author, July 8, 2007.

page 44 *"I started dating Don":* Beverly Arnold, in an interview with the author, May 11, 2004.

page 44 *"I was going to First Methodist Church":* Beverly Arnold, in a letter to the author, July 11, 2004.

page 44 *"Baby":* Donald Barthelme, letter to Beverly Arnold (née Bintliff), April 6, 1947; courtesy, Beverly Arnold.

page 45 *"We ran around in a little crowd":* Alafair Kane, in an interview with the author, May 11, 2004.

page 45 *"Recruiting writers among a school full of testosterone-crazed boys":* Pat Goeters, in an E-mail to the author, July 8, 2007.

page 45 *"Damon Runyan ripoff":* Pat Goeters, "Pulitzer Parable," an unpublished essay, in an E-mail to the author, April 22, 2004.

page 45 *"Bo–that's what we called him back then":* Carter Rochelle, in an E-mail to the author, May 22, 2004.

page 45 *"I found him slouched":* This and subsequent Goeters quotes are from an E-mail to the author, July 8, 2007.

page 46 "In Mexico City we lay with the gorgeous daughter of the American ambassador": Donald Barthelme, *Forty Stories,* 219.

page 47 *"My friend Herman and I"; "After the second border checkpoint":* Donald Barthelme, *Sadness* (New York: Farrar, Straus and Giroux, 1972), 99-100.

page 48 *His parents finally agreed to let him transfer to Lamar High School:* Helen Moore Barthelme, *Donald Barthelme,* 13.

5. The New Music

page 49 *"I do believe this was my idea":* "Interview with Charles Ruas and Judith Sherman, 1975," in *Not-Knowing: The Essays and Interviews,* ed. Kim Herzinger (New York: Random House, 1997), 209.

page 49 *"an Allegory":* See *Pilgrim's Progress* at www.sacredtexts.com.

page 50 *"an impressive array of state barges"; "a parody, to be completely effective"; "Disingenuous though it is":* Robert Murray Davis, "Donald Barthelme in Houston," *The Houston Review: History and Culture of the Gulf Coast* 2, (1980): 96–97.

page 51 *" 'The Rover Boys at School' has been written":* See Edward Stratemeyer, *The Rover Boys at School,* at www.ftp.ibiblio.org/pub/docs/books/gutenberg/etext. Stratemeyer later founded a publishing syndicate that produced the Hardy Boys and Nancy Drew series for young readers.

page 51 *"In the fall of 1948,":* Carter Rochelle, in an E-mail to the author, May 22, 2004.

page 52 *"I remember the time"; "There were five children in my family":* Donald Barthelme, *Forty Stories:* (New York: Putnam, 1987), 11–13. The Goeters comment about the crash is in an E-mail to the author, July 8, 2007.

page 53 *"my older brothers had raced and wrecked the three earlier Corvettes":* Steven Barthelme, "Fancy Girl in a Fancy Car," *Texas Magazine, Houston Chronicle,* November 3, 1999, 3.

page 53 *"Seventeen is a wild age":* Donald Barthelme, *Sixty Stories* (New York: Putnam, 1981), 456.

page 53 *"Though we felt a fierce tribal loyalty"*

to *"for the most part excused himself":* Frederick Barthelme and Steven Barthelme, *Double Down: Reflections on Gambling and Loss* (Boston: Houghton Mifflin, 1999), 17–18.

page 53 *"very much like his mother"* to *"kept his own counsel":* Elise Hopkins Stephens, in an E-mail to the author, February 2, 2007.

page 53 Lamar Lancer: Jerome Klinkowitz, Asa B. Pieratt, Jr., and Robert Murray Davis, *Donald Barthelme: A Comprehensive Bibliography* (Hamden, Connecticut: Shoestring Press/Archon Books, 1977), 101.

page 54 *"in his aerie":* Pat Goeters, in an E-mail to the author, July 8, 2007.

page 54 *went to "black clubs"; "something about making a statement":* J. D. O'Hara, "Donald Barthelme: The Art of Fiction LXVI," *Paris Review* 80 (1981): 275–276.

page 54 *"it was strictly an African-American establishment":* Carter Rochelle, in an E-mail to the author, May 22, 2004.

page 55 *"Some say drums have no part of the melody":* Sid Catlett quoted on Big Bands Database at www.nfo.net.

page 56 *"Whereas in the days when it was necessary to swing a band":* Buddy Rich quoted in an excerpt from *Metronome Magazine,* March/April 1956; interview conducted by Willis Conover for Voice of America Radio, copyright Shawn C. Martin; posted at www.drummerman.net/buddy.html.

page 56 *a series of engagements in southeast Texas:* Helen Moore Barthelme, *Donald Barthelme: The Genesis of a Cool Sound* (College Station: Texas A & M University Press, 2001), 14.

6. From Baudelaire to Rosenberg

page 57 *"If you imitate a writer's style, always choose the best":* Helen Moore Barthelme, *Donald Barthelme: The Genesis of a Cool Sound* (College Station: Texas A & M University Press, 2001), 52.

page 57 *He laments his "advanced age"; "I see the robbers":* François Rabelais, *Five Books of the Lives, Heroic Deeds, and Sayings of Gargantua and His Son Pantagruel,* trans. Sir Thomas Urquhart and Peter Motteux (London: A. H. Bullen, 1904), 13, 15.

page 57 *It traces a consistent artistic line rooted in romanticism:* Marcel Raymond, *From Baudelaire to Surrealism* (New York: Wittenborn, Schultz, 1950), 6–7.

pages 57–58 *"[T]he word with its vowels and diphthongs":* ibid., 26.

page 58 *"Did you ever realize":* Donald Barthelme, Sr., quoted in Stephen Fox, "Donald Barthelme, 1917–1996," *Cite* 35 (1996): 11.

page 58 *Eventually, he designed a course called Concepts:* ibid., 8–9.

page 59 *the one "important" nugget he'd gotten from Frank Lloyd Wright:* ibid., 9.

page 59 *"rip [everything] out":* ibid., 9. Barthelme had specified 9/16" glass, the minimum required for safety. To save money, the contractor used ½" glass. When Barthelme discovered this, he required the contractor to replace it with the glass that was specified for safety.

page 59 *"been working on transforming an old armory":* Donald Barthelme, *Paradise* (New York: Putnam, 1986), 34.

page 59 *"I really quit practicing":* Donald Barthelme, Sr., quoted in Fox, "Donald Barthelme, 1917-1996," 11.

page 59 *"forc[ing] . . . the gates of Paradise":* Raymond, *From Baudelaire to Surrealism,* 8.

page 59 *"[A] mysterious shift":* Donald Barthelme, "After Joyce," in *Not-Knowing: The Essays and Interviews,* ed. Kim Herzinger (New York: Random House, 1997), 3.

page 60 *"obscurity":* Raymond, *From Baudelaire to Surrealism,* 8.

page 60 *"However much the writer":* Donald Barthelme, "Not-Knowing," in *Not-Knowing,* ed. Herzinger, 15.

page 60 *"whisper . . . close to silence":* ibid., 16.

page 60 *In the end, Raymond admitted:* Raymond, *From Baudelaire to Surrealism,* 39.

page 60 *"[S]ince romanticism":* ibid., 355-356.

pages 60-61 *"The best French poetry since Baudelaire"* to *"the acid of poetry":* Harold Rosenberg, in the introduction to Raymond, *From Baudelaire to Surrealism,* not paginated.

7. Bardley

page 62 *"It was a bright shy white new university":* Donald Barthelme, *Sixty Stories* (New York: Putnam, 1981), 101.

page 63 *Don attracted people "like a magnet":* Joe Maranto quoted in Helen Moore Barthelme, *Donald Barthelme: The Genesis of a Cool Sound* (College Station: Texas A & M University Press, 2001), 5.

page 63 *his "striding, almost jaunty walk"; "handsome girl":* Helen Moore Barthelme, *Donald Barthelme,* 3.

page 64 *"would quote Dorothy Parker":* Maranto quoted in ibid., 5.

page 64 *a course of study in creative writing:* For the history of creative writing, I have drawn upon D. G. Myers, *The Elephants Teach: Creative Writing Since 1880* (Englewood Cliffs, New Jersey: Prentice Hall, 1996), 31, 66-67, 123-128.

page 64 *"we study literature today":* Allen Tate quoted in Myers, *The Elephants Teach,* 127.

page 65 *"irony, humility, introspection, reverence":* Allen Tate, *The Poetry Reviews of Allen Tate,* ed. Ashley Brown and Frances Cheney (Baton Rouge: Louisiana State University Press, 1983), 107.

page 65 *"by selecting fathers":* "Interview with Charles Ruas and Judith Sherman, 1975," in *Not-Knowing: The Essays and Interviews,* ed. Kim Herzinger (New York: Random House, 1997), 211.

page 66 *"Poetry wants to be pure":* Robert Penn Warren, "Pure and Impure Poetry," cited in *The New Criticism and Contemporary Literary Theory,* ed. William I. Spurlin and Michael Fischer (New York: Garland Press, 1995), 21.

page 66 *"If any one person is to be singled out":* Lee Pryor quoted in Suzanne Shumway, *University of Houston Magazine* (winter 1992); posted at www.uh.edu/collegium/fall97.

page 66 *"[Because] Hemingway had been a newspaperman":* "Interview with Charles Ruas and Judith Sherman, 1975," in *Not-Knowing,* ed. Herzinger, 211.

page 66 *"Tiger in the Garden [was] once regarded as the cream":* Paul West, *Master Class: Scenes from a Fiction Workshop* (New York: Harcourt, 2001), 150.

page 66 *"as emotion-charged as a telephone's dial tone":* Robert Murray Davis, "Donald Barthelme in Houston," *The Houston Review: History and Culture of the Gulf Coast* 2 (1980): 97.

page 67 *Don's Cougar columns:* For details and certain excerpts from Donald Barthelme's *Cougar* writings, I have drawn upon Jerome Klinkowitz, Asa B. Pieratt, Jr., and Robert Murray Davis, *Donald Barthelme: A Comprehensive Bibliography* (Hamden, Connecticut: Shoestring Press/Archon Books, 1977).

page 67 *"created [a] homely":* Maggie Maranto, in an E-mail to the author, February 15, 2005.

page 67 *"Yes, I'll take credit":* Pat Goeters, in an E-mail to the author, July 8, 2007.

page 68 *Years later, he was appalled at himself:* Jerome Klinkowitz, *Keeping Literary Company: Working with Writers Since the Sixties* (Albany: State University of New York Press, 1998), 125-126.

page 68 *"Jane was one of the younger wicked old witches":* Donald Barthelme, "Grimm Revisited," *Daily Cougar* (University of Houston), July 13, 1951, 2.

page 68 *"I originally began writing":* The *Writer in Society: Donald Barthelme* (Houston: KUHT-TV, 1984).

page 69 *"think of religion":* Donald Barthelme, *Forty Stories* (New York: Putnam, 1987), 248.

page 69 *"[Barthelme], a 20-year-old sophomore journalism major":* Klinkowitz, Pieratt, and Davis, *Donald Barthelme,* 101.

page 69 *"Don seemed so young":* Helen Moore Barthelme, *Donald Barthelme,* 3, 18.

8. Let's Take a Walk

page 72 *"[A]s a raw youth"*: Donald Barthelme, "Return," in *Liquid City: Houston Writers on Houston*, ed. Rita Saylors (San Antonio: Corona Publishing Company, 1987), 38-39.

page 72 *"Well, thank you, sir"*: Gerald Langford, *Alias O. Henry: A Biography of William Sidney Porter* (New York: Macmillan, 1957), 95-96. For a nearly complete collection of Porter's writing for the *Houston Post,* see O. Henry, *Postscripts* (New York: Harper and Brothers, 1923).

page 72 *"Thank you," Kennedy says:* Donald Barthelme, *Sixty Stories* (New York: Putnam, 1981), 85.

page 73 *"[N]ewspaper work didn't teach me all that much about writing"*: "Interview with Charles Ruas and Judith Sherman, 1975," in *Not-Knowing: The Essays and Interviews,* ed. Kim Herzinger (New York: Random House, 1997), 211.

page 73 *"I worked for newspapers at a time when I was not competent to do so"*: Donald Barthelme, *City Life* (New York: Farrar, Straus and Giroux, 1970), 138.

page 73 *"I used to be in the government service"*: Fyodor Dostoevsky, *Notes from Underground,* in *Three Short Novels of Dostoevsky,* trans. Constance Garnett (Garden City, New York: Doubleday Anchor, 1960), 179-181.

page 73 *"George is editing my copy"; Don "always wanted to write tight, short sentences"*: Helen Moore Barthelme, *Donald Barthelme: The Genesis of a Cool Sound* (College Station: Texas A & M University Press, 2001), 19.

page 73 *"The newspaper building was populated with terrifying city editors"*: Barthelme, in *Liquid City,* ed. Saylors, 38.

page 74 *Don imagines a chamber orchestra:* Donald Barthelme, *Overnight to Many Distant Cities* (New York: Putnam, 1983), 25.

page 74 *"We crouch in empty cups"*: Barthelme quoted in Helen Moore Barthelme, *Donald Barthelme,* 6.

page 74 *"horses are considered valuable"*: This and subsequent quotes from "Eros in Archer County" are from Larry McMurtry, *In a Narrow Grave: Essays on Texas* (New York: Touchstone Books, 1968), 55-74.

page 75 *"His demeanor, especially with women"*: Helen Moore Barthelme, *Donald Barthelme,* 16-17.

page 75 *"If you were a female person"*: Grace Paley, "Some Nearly Personal Notes," in *Gulf Coast: A Journal of Literature and Art* 4, no. 1 (1991): 161.

page 75 *"going with"; "Poor Don"*: Maggie Maranto, in an E-mail to the author, June 18, 2004.

page 75 *she should "take a walk"*: Helen Moore Barthelme, *Donald Barthelme,* 16.

page 76 *"Miss Maggie was a sexy creature"*: Herman Gollob, *Me and Shakespeare: Adventures with the Bard* (New York: Doubleday, 2002), 167.

page 76 *Don had an argument with his father:* Helen Moore Barthelme, *Donald Barthelme,* 20.

pages 76-77 *"custard affair"* to *"Don was a man's man"*: Maggie Maranto, in an E-mail to the author, June 18, 2004.

9. Feverish

page 78 *"One or more of them would drop by our apartment"*: Maggie Maranto, in an E-mail to the author, April 20, 2004.

page 79 *Goeters was "eccentric and individualistic"*: Maggie Maranto, in an E-mail to the author, April 20, 2004.

page 79 *"one needed a decoder ring to read and understand"* to *"I shared with him"*: Pat Goeters, "Pulitzer Parable," an unpublished essay, in an E-mail to the author, April 22, 2004.

page 79 *"They weren't getting married in a church"*: Pat Goeters, in an E-mail to the author, July 8, 2007.

page 80 *"Joe and I were not impressed with her"*: Maggie Maranto, in an E-mail to the author, April 20, 2004.

page 80 *"When I'd go out with my Rice friends"; "At the time, very few people"*: Marilyn Gillet, in a conversation with the author, November 17, 2004.

page 80 *"We didn't see much"*: Maggie Maranto, in an E-mail to the author, April 20, 2004.

page 80 *"hear[ing] about Don occasionally"*: Helen Moore Barthelme, *Donald Barthelme: The Genesis of a Cool Sound* (College Station: Texas A & M University Press, 2001), 22.

page 81 *"[Hubert] Roussel went to all of the interesting shows"*: Marilyn Gillet, in a conversation with the author, November 17, 2004.

page 81 *"Disney's horniest animated feature"*: See Jeremy Heilman at www.moviemartyr.com.

page 82 *his "nastiness"*: Jerome Klinkowitz, Asa B. Pieratt, Jr., and Robert Murray Davis, *Donald Barthelme: A Comprehensive Bibliography*

(Hamden, Connecticut: Shoestring Press/Archon Books, 1977), 88.

page 82 *"I am persuaded that Surrealism first existed in the cinema":* Langlois quoted in Colin MacCabe, *Godard: A Portrait of the Artist at Seventy* (New York: Farrar, Straus and Giroux, 2003), 48. For background information on *Cahiers du Cinéma,* I have drawn upon MacCabe's book.

page 84 *"packed with color, spectacle, and glamour"; "cracks the fraternity-sorority*

question wide open": Robert Murray Davis, "Donald Barthelme in Houston," *The Houston Review: History and Culture of the Gulf Coast* 2 (1980): 99.

page 84 *"a deeply disturbing novel of the South":* This and subsequent quotes from *Amanda Feverish* are from Davis, "Donald Barthelme in Houston," 98.

page 85 *"Less than three months after":* Davis, "Donald Barthelme in Houston," 98.

10. Basic Training

page 89 *Don was assigned to Company M:* Helen Moore Barthelme, *Donald Barthelme: The Genesis of a Cool Sound* (College Station: Texas A & M University Press, 2001), 22.

page 89 *Camp Polk:* For information on Camp Polk, see "Louisiana Maneuver Camps and Bases" at www.crt.state.la.us/tourism/lawwii/Maneuvers/Robertson/Camps.htm. E. J. Kahn, *The Army Life* (New York: Simon & Schuster, 1942) provided a useful source of general information on basic training.

page 91 *"a lieutenant [or] some other higher animal":* Donald Barthelme quoted in Helen Moore Barthelme, *Donald Barthelme,* 22.

page 91 *"In the number of books circulated":* Edward Frank Allen, with Raymond B. Fosdick, *Keeping Our Fighters Fit for War and After* (New York: The Century Company, 1918), 90.

page 92 *the certainty that he'd have to do it all again:* Intermittently, for the rest of his life, Don suffered nightmares about having to return to the army, a trauma he wrote about in "The Sergeant." Just as the army never seemed to end for him, "The Sergeant" resisted closure. In the story's first appearance, in *Fiction* magazine, the recycled recruit refuses a command to "harm" a civilian with his M16. As punishment, he is ordered to stuff onions into olives for a martini-guzzling general. Anguished, he cries, "Father!" A shout for help? A curse? A prayer? A year later, when the story resurfaced in *Amateurs,* Don had changed the sergeant's cry to "Andromache!" The reference is to Euripides' play and to the aftermath of the Trojan War. The play ends with an explicit statement of Don's theme: "Many a thing . . . [comes] to pass contrary to our expectations," the chorus intones. "[That] which we thought would be is not accomplished."

The epitome of a faithful wife, Andromache appears briefly in the *Iliad,* holding her baby, crying for her husband, Hector, as he stomps off to battle. Eventually, Achilles slays Hector and the baby is killed. Andromache, carted to

Sparta, becomes a concubine of Achilles' son. She endures indignities and threats, and is the only self-controlled person in a society rent by jealousies, suspicions, and a hunger for war.

Like Euripides' play, Don's story, written in the 1970s, as U.S. involvement in Vietnam staggered to its sloppy end, depicts a corrupt, confused, and bloated authoritarian system. As the Greek chorus chants, "Better it is not to win a discreditable victory, than to make justice miscarry by an invidious exercise of power. . . ." Many Americans saw Vietnam as a repeat of the Korean mistake ("Look, I've already done this"). In the mid-seventies, readers of "The Sergeant," forced to contemplate harming a civilian, would naturally be reminded of the My Lai massacre. The sergeant's plea to Andromache serves as a bond with her suffering as well as a confession that he has fallen short of her dignity.

What has he done to call such trouble on himself ("Of course it's what I deserve," he says)? The story doesn't spell things out, but if Andromache is a model of fidelity, we can assume the opposite of the sergeant (just as he reverses her image in losing his dignity). "O marriage, marriage, woe to thee! thou bane of my home, thou destroyer of my city!" the warrior Peleus shouts in the middle of Euripides' play, lamenting the intimate duplicities, reflected in public power, that have ruined his culture. By the time Don wrote the story, he was thrice divorced. His second wife—from whom his split had been especially painful—was named Helen. On one level, the cry of "Andromache!" is an in joke, for in the play, Andromache blames Helen of Troy for the war that wrecked her family. In her final years, she marries a man named Helenus, and finds happiness. (Helen Moore Barthelme recalls that "Don's friends gave us as a wedding gift a painted golden apple along with a poem alluding to the mythological tale of the winning of Helen of Troy by Paris of Greece.")

Don's separation from Marilyn Marrs during

his Korean sojourn certainly hastened the end of his first marriage, a marriage his bond with Helen was supposed to erase. In any case, "Andromache!" makes clear his conviction that, in private as well as in public, "discreditable" behavior leads to a "stain on a house."

But Don wasn't yet done with "The Sergeant." In its third appearance, in *Sixty Stories* in 1981, he changed the story's final plea to "Penelope!" Penelope is another model wife. She is better known to most readers than Andromache—a possible reason for the change. She is also a less woeful figure, celebrated for her strength, cunning, and guile, qualities that make her example a greater rebuke to the sergeant (who is a wanderer like Odysseus, like Leopold Bloom) and a more poignant target for his longing. The loss of Andromache softens the story's social critique—less a sign of mellowing on Don's part than

recognition that, as Vietnam fell further into the past, the story's power lay more in its portrait of individual psychology.

For the various versions of the ending of "The Sergeant," see *Fiction* 3, nos. 2-3 (1975): 25; Donald Barthelme, *Amateurs* (New York: Farrar, Straus and Giroux, 1976), 77; and Donald Barthelme, *Sixty Stories* (New York: Putnam, 1981), 308. All quotes from *Andromache* are taken from Euripides, *Andromache,* trans. E. P. Coleridge, posted at www.classics.mit.edu/ Euripides/Andromache.

page 92 *Fort Lewis:* For information on Fort Lewis, see "I Corps and Fort Lewis" at www.lewis .army.mil/CampLewis.shtml.

page 93 *"You could write for a week":* Ernest Hemingway, "Voyage to Victory," in *Hemingway on War,* ed. Sean Hemingway (New York: Scribner's, 2003), 326.

11. The Thirty-eighth Parallel

page 94 *"I've crossed . . . the Pacific twice":* Donald Barthelme, *Paradise* (New York: Putnam, 1986), 151.

page 94 *"[I sailed] over the pearly Pacific":* Donald Barthelme, *Sixty Stories* (New York: Putnam, 1981), 102.

page 94 *"grimy hills of Korea":* Helen Moore Barthelme, *Donald Barthelme: The Genesis of a Cool Sound* (College Station: Texas A & M University Press, 2001), 23.

page 95 *"Walking down the road wearing green clothes":* Barthelme, *Sixty Stories,* 101.

page 95 *it's a "sour" feeling:* James Brady, *The Coldest War: A Memoir of Korea* (New York: Orion Books, 1990), 1.

page 95 *"waving Korean, American, and United Nations flags":* W. H. Lawrence quoted in Lloyd C. Gardner, ed., *The Korean War* (New York: Quadrangle Books, 1972), 100-101.

page 95 *"At 10:00 p.m. on 27 July [1953]":* Cal-

lum A. Macdonald, *Korea: The War Before Vietnam* (New York: The Free Press, 1986), 249.

page 96 *making reveille in "an offhand way":* Helen Moore Barthelme *Donald Barthelme,* 23.

page 96 *"not, of course, deliriously happy":* This and subsequent quotes from Don's letters home to Joe Maranto and to his family are from Helen Moore Barthelme, *Donald Barthelme,* 22-34.

page 97 *The army had not prepared:* For details on the conditions along the thirty-eighth parallel, I have drawn from descriptions in James Brady, *The Coldest War.*

page 99 *"Krian war":* This and subsequent quotes from "Thailand" are from Barthelme, *Sixty Stories,* 433-436.

page 100 *"style of the age":* Erich Auerbach, "Philology and Weltliteratur," trans. by Edward and Maria Said, in *Centennial Review* 13 (1969): 1.

12. No Butterfly

page 102 *"THE GREAT AMERICAN NOVEL":* This and subsequent quotes from Don's letters to Joe Maranto or to his immediate family are from Helen Moore Barthelme, *Donald Barthelme: The Genesis of a Cool Sound* (College Station: Texas A & M University Press, 2001), 22-34.

page 103 *"[I] am working on a major fiction project"; "[W]e're short-handed":* Donald Barthelme, letter to Mr. and Mrs. George Marrs, February 1954; courtesy, Marilyn Gillet.

page 103 *"[In] Tokyo . . . [h]e was once in bed":* Donald Barthelme, *Forty Stories* (New York: Putnam, 1987), 108.

page 104 *"Don described the experience later":* Helen Moore Barthelme, *Donald Barthelme,* 28.

page 104 *"The transformation of everyday reality":* Barthelme, "Parachutes in the Trees," in *Not-Knowing: The Essays and Interviews,* ed. Kim Herzinger (New York: Random House, 1997), 109.

page 104 *admired it "more than any other building":* Helen Moore Barthelme, *Donald Barthelme,* 27.

page 104 *"worthy tradition":* Frank Lloyd Wright, *Sixty Years of Living Architecture: The Work of Frank Lloyd Wright* (Los Angeles: Municipal Art Patrons and Art Commission of Los Angeles, 1953), 8-9.

page 104 *"There were little terraces and little courts":* Peter Blake, *Frank Lloyd Wright: Architecture and Space* (Baltimore: Penguin Books, 1960), 69, 72. For more information on the Imperial Hotel, see Frank Lloyd Wright, *An American Architecture* (New York: Horizon Press, 1955), 149-159; and Robert King Reitherman. "Frank Lloyd Wright's Imperial Hotel: A Seismic Re-evaluation," posted at www.nisee.berkeley.edu/kanto/kanto.html.

page 105 *A pair of Japanese jazz drummers:* For more information on Japanese jazz, see Mathew Gregory, "Jazz Kissa Radicals: Tokyo Free Jazz and the Anti Appo Uprising," posted at www
.newschool.edu/gf/historymatters/papers/confo3_mathewgregory_free%jazz.pdf.

page 105 *"Tell me, is the Tennessee Tea Room still the top jazz place":* Donald Barthelme, *Sixty Stories* (New York: Putnam, 1981), 355.

page 106 *tiny bars, overpriced liquor; "love hotels":* Rick Chernitzer, "Tokyo's Hardy Barracks Was Home Away from Home for U. S. Soldiers in 1950s," in *Stripes Sunday Magazine* (*Stars and Stripes*), November 10, 2002; posted at www.estripes.com/article.asp?section=126&article=11528&archive=true.

page 106 *"only concerned [itself] with customers' yen":* ibid.

page 107 *"At 2200 hours":* Donald Barthelme quoted in Helen Moore Barthelme, *Donald Barthelme,* 30-31.

page 108 *"most nerve shattering"* to *"browbeating the poor devil":* ibid., 30.

page 109 *"[I sat] in the bow fifty miles out":* Barthelme, *Sixty Stories,* 102.

13. Cockypap

page 110 *"I got a card from the Apache Distributing Company":* See www.americanradiowork.publicradio.org/features/korea/archive/index homecomingtrans.php#jackson.

page 111 *his son's "veteran face"; "My clothes looked old and wrong": "city looked new":* Donald Barthelme, *Sixty Stories* (New York: Putnam, 1981), 102.

page 111 *"There just wasn't much to Houston":* Philip Johnson quoted in Frank D. Welch, *Philip Johnson and Texas* (Austin: University of Texas Press, 2000), 42.

page 111 *"What is coming will be of more value":* Stephen Fox, *Houston Architectural Guide* (Houston: American Institute of Architects, Houston Chapter, and Herring Press, 1990), v. 21.

page 111 *"full of the 'nothing' to which Mies":* ibid., 105.

page 112 *"We have to have cheerleaders":* Barthelme, *Sixty Stories,* 102.

page 112 *"Tiny Diva Warms Shamrock"; "John Wayne Goes to the Bottom":* Jerome Klinkowitz, Asa B. Pierrat, Jr., and Robert Murray Davis, *Donald Barthelme: A Comprehensive Bibliography* (Hamden, Connecticut: Shoestring Press/Archon Books, 1977), 94, 96.

page 113 *"the cops decided to show":* Barthelme, *Sixty Stories,* 194.

page 113 *"[Pete and I] were always together"; "I began to realize he was an attractive man":* Helen Moore Barthelme, *Donald Barthelme: The*
Genesis of a Cool Sound (College Station: Texas A & M University Press, 2001), 35.

page 113 *"Talk to Farris Block":* ibid., 36.

page 113 *"old school":* This and subsequent quotes from "See the Moon?" are from Barthelme, *Sixty Stories,* 103.

page 114 *"I had never . . . [worked] in the daytime before":* Donald Barthelme, *Forty Stories* (New York: Putnam, 1987), 28.

page 114 *"I'd read his [movie] reviews":* This and subsequent Gollob quotes, except those noted hereafter, are from Herman Gollob, *Me and Shakespeare: Adventures with the Bard* (New York: Doubleday, 2002), 166-168.

page 115 *"Ah Martha coom now":* Barthelme, *Sixty Stories,* 37-38.

page 115 *"I've never been a good drinker":* Marilyn Gillet, in a conversation with the author, November 17, 2004.

page 115 *"She wasn't relaxed or natural"; "We were all drinking":* Herman Gollob, in a conversation with the author, April 19, 2007.

page 116 *it was Maggie who "no longer wanted to be married":* Helen Moore Barthelme, *Donald Barthelme,* 36.

page 116 *"By the time Don came back from Korea"; "I think Donald always wanted":* Marilyn Gillet, in a conversation with the author, November 17, 2004.

page 116 *"too scared to unboard":* Helen Moore Barthelme, *Donald Barthelme,* 36-37.

page 117 *"[You] go to college":* "Interview with Charles Ruas and Judith Sherman, 1975," in *Not-Knowing: The Essays and Interviews,* ed. Kim Herzinger (New York; Random House, 1997), 208.

page 118 *"He was a lovely man":* Eileen Pollock, in a conversation with the author, June 5, 2005.

page 118 *"Purity of heart is to will one thing":* Barthelme, *Sixty Stories,* 384.

14. The Object

page 119 *"But that's more than some of our male faculty members earn!":* Helen Moore Barthelme, *Donald Barthelme: The Genesis of a Cool Sound* (College Station: Texas A & M University Press, 2001), 44.

page 120 *"I felt quite alone in my marriage":* ibid., 37-38.

page 120 In her memoir, Helen claims that she started the newsletter: ibid., 71.

page 120 Lee Pryor, a UH English professor: Suzanne Shumway, "Creative Writing Program: A Haven for Future Literati," *Collegium Online* (University of Houston): Winter 1997.

page 120 Acta Diurna's *format should be revised:* Donald Barthelme, memo to Douglas McClaury, Special Collections and Archives, University of Houston Libraries.

page 120 *"As to material used":* Donald Barthelme, letter to Pat Nicholson, Special Collections and Archives, University of Houston Libraries.

page 120 *"as part of our public relations program":* Donald Barthelme, public relations announcement, Special Collections and Archives, University of Houston Libraries.

page 120 *"The level of readership we are aiming at":* Donald Barthelme, letter to Dr. Richard A. Younger, Special Collections and Archives, University of Houston Libraries.

page 121 *"Kierkegaard is Hegel's punishment":* Maurice Natanson, *A Critique of Jean-Paul Sartre's Ontology* (Lincoln: University of Nebraska Press, 1951), 5.

page 121 *"[After] Sartre":* Maurice Natanson, *Edmund Husserl: Philosopher of Infinite Tasks* (Evanston, Illinois: Northwestern University Press, 1973), 3.

page 121 *"Although it has always been known":* ibid.

page 121 *"the story of . . . philosophy":* Natanson, *A Critique of Jean-Paul Sartre's Ontology,* 5.

page 121 *"Kierkegaard found his novelist":* ibid., 7.

page 121 *"I was conscious every moment":* Fyodor Dostoevsky, *Notes from Underground,* trans. Richard Pevear and Larissa Volokhonsky (New York: Vintage Books, 1993), 5.

page 122 *"chain of thought [that was] stated with agonizing force by Kierkegaard":* Natanson, *A Critique of Jean-Paul Sartre's Ontology,* 9.

page 122 *"a means of blending"; "insignificant-seeming details":* Ronald Hayman, *Sartre: A Biography* (New York: Simon & Schuster, 1987), 97-98.

page 122 *"the leaves of the tree"; "The waiter poured":* Ernest Hemingway, *The Snows of Kilimanjaro and Other Stories* (New York: Scribner's, 1961), 29, 30.

page 123 *"pressed itself against my eyes":* Jean-Paul Sartre, *Nausea,* trans. Lloyd Alexander (New York: New Directions, 1964), 127-128.

page 123 *"A man is involved in life":* Jean-Paul Sartre, *Existentialism,* trans. Bernard Frechtman (New York: Philosophical Library, 1947), 20.

pages 123-124 *"With scarcely a pause in our conversation"; "I never imagined falling in love with him":* Helen Moore Barthelme, *Donald Barthelme,* 38.

page 124 *"romantic and often expensive"; "excited and happy":* ibid., 39.

page 124 *"liked Helen a lot":* Pat Goeters, in an E-mail to the author, April 16, 2004.

page 124 *"earth mother"; on the "rebound":* Maggie Maranto, in an E-mail to the author, May 9, 2004.

page 124 *"lavish social events":* Helen Moore Barthelme, *Donald Barthelme,* 39.

page 125 *"uneasy"; "possibility of perfection"; "being with Don was so intensely romantic":* ibid., 40.

15. The Many Faces of Love

page 126 *"Then wear the gold hat":* F. Scott Fitzgerald, *The Great Gatsby* (New York: Scribner's, 1953), epigraph.

page 126 *"What the hell is [this poem] all about?":* F. Scott Fitzgerald, *This Side of Paradise,* ed. James L. W. West III (Cambridge: Cambridge University Press, 1995), 50-51.

page 126 *"[They're] not producing among 'em one story or novel":* F. Scott Fitzgerald, *This Side of Paradise* (New York: Scribner's, 1960), 217.

page 126 *"exquisite, anachronistic, and decadent":* Jeffrey Meyers, *Scott Fitzgerald: A Biography* (New York: HarperCollins, 1994), 25.

page 127 *"incredibly delicate and dangerous business":* Donald Barthelme, *Sixty Stories* (New York: Putnam, 1981), 281.

page 127 *"[He] desired both the beauty":* Helen Moore Barthelme, *Donald Barthelme: The Genesis of a Cool Sound* (College Station: Texas A & M University Press, 2001), 41.

page 127 *"snares and often lead us into error":* Hubert Benoit, *The Many Faces of Love,* trans. P. Mairet (London: Routledge and Kegan Paul, 1955), 1. A number of Don's stories seem to echo—and improve upon—passages in Benoit. For example, at one point, Benoit said that "people like shame." "In the name of love," he wrote, "human beings humiliate and injure one another in interminable conflicts." In "The Leap," Don wrote, "Love ... enables us to see each other without clothes on ... in lust and shame. . . . [It] allows us to say wounding things to each other which would not be kosher under the ordinary rules of civilized discourse. . . . [It] allows us to live together male and female in small grubby apartments that would only hold one sane person, normally."

Benoit spoke at length of "adoring" the lover: "The word 'adore' implies an idea of 'divinity,' of the perception of the holy, of the infinite, of something beyond this world." This was a powerful concept for Don. In "The Indian Uprising," he quoted Valéry on the subject: "The ardor aroused in men by the beauty of women can only be satisfied by God."

For Benoit, "intense adoration" is akin to "inebriation." It arises from what Jung called images of the "ideal other" in every person's psyche. The "essential behavior of the lover" consists "in a pure, static contemplation" of the imagined ideal. The ideal is "projected" onto the "object" of the beloved, who becomes so "necessary to my inner state of adoration ... so deeply associated with my condition that I depend on her existence and tremble at any threat to it." Don examined Jungian archetypes in a number of stories, most wittily in "Daumier," where he looked at Jungian projection in reverse. Additionally, many of his stories are examples of "pure, static contemplation" of an ideal. For example, "Nakedness ... is a delight," he wrote in *Presents.* "[T]hat is why we are considering all these different ways in which naked young women may be conceptualized, in the privacy of our studies. . . ." Benoit pointed out that fidelity is "incompatible with sexuality upon the plane of images."

Cited above: *"people like shame":* Benoit, *The Many Faces of Love,* 149; *"Love ... enables us":* Barthelme, *Sixty Stories,* 384; *"The ardor aroused in men":* Barthelme, *Sixty Stories,* 111; *"intense adoration"* to *"pure, static contemplation":* Benoit, *The Many Faces of Love,* 11, 16; *"necessary to my inner state of adoration":* Benoit, *The Many Faces of Love,* 10; *"Nakedness ... is a delight":* Donald Barthelme, *Presents* (Dallas: Pressworks, 1980), 21; *"incompatible with sexuality":* Benoit, *The Many Faces of Love,* 299.

page 127 *"As soon as I am in erotic love":* Benoit, *The Many Faces of Love,* 150.

page 127 *"without coming into collision"; "intellectual recognition"; "plain language":* ibid., 99.

page 127 *"By bypassing":* Donald Barthelme, "Interview with Charles Ruas and Judith Sherman," *Not-Knowing: The Essays and Interviews,* ed. Kim Herzinger (New York: Random House, 1997), 221.

page 128 *"He really wanted nothing less":* Helen Moore Barthelme, *Donald Barthelme,* 40.

pages 128-129 *"prosperous, empty, uninspiring uniformity":* This and subsequent quotes from "The Glamour of Delinquency" are from Pauline Kael, *I Lost It at the Movies* (Boston: Atlantic Monthly Press / Little, Brown, 1965), 46.

page 129 *"I found it exciting":* Helen Moore Barthelme, *Donald Barthelme,* 46.

page 129 *"The problem is":* "Interview with Charles Ruas and Judith Sherman, 1975," in *Not-Knowing: The Essays and Interviews,* ed. Kim Herzinger (New York: Random House, 1997), 225.

page 129 *"Nothing to be done":* Samuel Beckett, *Waiting for Godot* (New York: Grove Press, 1982), 2.

page 129 *"don't seem to be able to depart":* ibid., 50.

page 130 *"That's the idea":* ibid., 70.

page 130 *"essential"; "the extra-temporal":* Samuel Beckett, *Proust* (London: John Calder, 1999), 75.

page 130 *"I sometimes wonder":* Beckett, *Waiting for Godot,* 58-59.

16. Forum

page 131 *his philosophical studies:* Don's line "Fragments are the only forms I trust" from "See the Moon?" pulses with Kierkegaard. In 1844, Kierkegaard published *Philosophical*

Fragments. In it, he wrote, "What is offered here is only a pamphlet." It "is impossible for anyone to dream of attributing . . . importance to a pamphlet." In fact, Kierkegaard intended his fragments to be an important alternative to Hegel's weighty volumes, which had proposed nothing less than a history of the universe. Kierkegaard's "modest" work mocks such grandiose ambitions: A pamphlet by a self-doubting author is far more trustworthy than the man who claims to know it all.

After over a hundred pages investigating what can and cannot be known, Kierkegaard ended by saying, ". . . how shall we ever manage to begin?" In "The Dolt," Don would write, "Endings are elusive, middles are nowhere to be found, but worst of all is to begin, to begin, to begin."

As Kierkegaard stands to German philosophy, Don would stake himself (in more modest fashion) with regard to Western fiction; as Kierkegaard questioned rational and systematic thought, Don would prod a suspicious finger at omniscience and realism . . . not to deny the strength of traditional forms (Kierkegaard didn't doubt Hegel's greatness), just to offer a polite or humorous "But," a quiet "Or."

Cited above: *"Fragments are the only forms I trust":* Donald Barthelme, *Sixty Stories* (New York: Putnam, 1981), 98; *"What is offered here is only a pamphlet"; "how shall we ever manage to begin?":* Søren Kierkegaard, *Philosophical Fragments / Johannes Climacus,* ed. and trans. Howard V. Hong and Edna H. Hong (Princeton, New Jersey: Princeton University Press, 1985), 5, 110; *"Endings are elusive":* Barthelme, *Sixty Stories,* 96.

page 131 *"today refers to faddism":* Maurice Natanson, *A Critique of Jean-Paul Sartre's Ontology* (Lincoln: University of Nebraska Press, 1951), 5.

page 131 *"in spite of every imaginable obstacle":* Helen Moore Barthelme, *Donald Barthelme: The Genesis of a Cool Sound* (College Station: Texas A & M University Press, 2001), 70.

page 132 *"Don was concerned that his mother should understand":* ibid., 41.

page 132 *"Don had filled the entire apartment":* ibid., 42.

page 133 *In the French Quarter:* For Helen's account of their honeymoon, see ibid., 42-43.

page 133 *her "authority":* This and subsequent quotes regarding the early days of Helen's marriage to Don are from ibid., 45, 48-55.

page 135 *"at present a circulation of 3,000":* Donald Barthelme, template for advertising solicitation letter for *Forum,* 1957, Special Collections and Archives, University of Houston Libraries.

page 135 *"The magazine is, in a sense, experimental":* Donald Barthelme, letter to Dr. William J. Handy, March 13, 1957, Special Collections and Archives, University of Houston Libraries.

page 136 *unfettered emotions:* This and subsequent quotes from this essay are from Donald Barthelme, "A Note on Elia Kazan," in *Not-Knowing: The Essays and Interviews,* ed. Kim Herzinger (New York, Random House, 1997), 99. This essay was originally published in *Forum* 1 (1956).

page 136 *"given forty-five minutes, they could master anything":* Helen Moore Barthelme, *Donald Barthelme,* 20.

page 136 *"Your recent articles in* Partisan Review*":* Donald Barthelme quoted in Helen Moore Barthelme, *Donald Barthelme,* 72.

page 137 *"Forum is most attractive":* Walker Percy quoted in Helen Moore Barthelme, *Donald Barthelme,* 72.

page 137 *"in Houston, a city ordinance":* Helen Moore Barthelme, *Donald Barthelme,* 51.

17. The Psychology of Angels

page 138 *"old piece of junk":* Helen Moore Barthelme, *Donald Barthelme: The Genesis of a Cool Sound* (College Station: Texas A & M University Press, 2001), 49. All subsequent quotes from Helen regarding the early years of her marriage to Don are from ibid., 46-69.

page 138 *He enjoyed working with his hands:* Don's narrator in "The Indian Uprising" also enjoys working with his hands. Throughout the story, he repeatedly makes tables out of hollow-core doors. Simon, the narrator in *Paradise,* remarks that there is "[n]othing more fun than buying furniture." See Donald Barthelme, *Paradise* (New York: Putnam, 1986), 138, 188.

page 139 *"issue would be closed out by the end of the month"; would "interest both the scientifically minded":* Barthelme and Percy letters quoted in Helen Moore Barthelme, *Donald Barthelme,* 72-73.

page 139 *"that being in the world":* Walker Percy, *The Message in the Bottle: How Queer Man Is, How Queer Language Is, and What One Has to Do with the Other* (New York: Picador, 2000), 150-158.

page 139 *"very good-looking job":* Percy quoted in Helen Moore Barthelme, *Donald Barthelme,* 73.

page 140 *"aim of literature . . . is the creation of a strange object covered with fur":* Donald Barthelme, *Come Back, Dr. Caligari* (Boston: Little, Brown, 1964), 14.

page 140 *She found the time spent on type fonts:* In a 1972 interview, Don said, "I enjoy . . . problems of design. I could very cheerfully be a typographer." See "Interview with Jerome Klinkowitz, 1971-72," in *Not-Knowing: The Essays and Interviews,* ed. Kim Herzinger (New York: Random House, 1997), 201.

page 141 *"evolved a new type dress":* Donald Barthelme, letter to Maurice Natanson, October 17, 1957, Special Collections and Archives, University of Houston Libraries.

page 141 *"Our idea . . . [is to] . . . catch the dancers":* Donald Barthelme, letter to Gene Gaines, October 2, 1957, Special Collections and Archives, University of Houston Libraries.

page 141 *"It is difficult to know where to publish short stories":* Donald Barthelme, letter to David Riesman, November 8, 1957, Special Collections and Archives, University of Houston Libraries.

page 141 *"[W]e would . . . like to pay not more than $16.00 per page":* Donald Barthelme, letter to Wayne Taylor, April 17, 1958, Special Collections and Archives, University of Houston Libraries.

page 141 *"[H]ow come a U. of Houston publication isn't paying":* Percy quoted in Helen Moore Barthelme, *Donald Barthelme,* 73.

page 142 a *"very nasty letter":* Donald Barthelme quoted in ibid, 77.

page 142 *"pale new critic[ism]":* ibid, 84.

page 142 *"You are absolutely right":* ibid.

page 143 *"As to your sympathy with the 'existential-phenomenological movement'":* James Boyer May, letter to Donald Barthelme, September 24, 1959, Special Collections and Archives, University of Houston Libraries.

page 144 *"Paul and Eugenie went to a film":* Donald Barthelme quoted in Helen Moore Barthelme, *Donald Barthelme,* 62.

page 144 *"working in a vacuum":* ibid., 79.

page 145 *"I'll pay for it":* ibid., 83.

page 145 *"I've been reading and enjoying your Partisan pieces":* Donald Barthelme, letter to Diana Trilling, undated (1957), Special Collections and Archives, University of Houston Libraries.

page 145 *One of his favorite contributors to* Forum: In all, Joseph Lyons published four essays in *Forum,* including a phenomenological study of a rock and a meditation on tarot cards and magic. In the latter piece, he mentions a (probably fictional) astrologer named Madame Cherokee, whom Don resurrected at least twice in his own writing, including a story entitled "Affection" (where she is renamed Madame Olympia and takes on added echoes of Sosostris from Eliot's *The Waste Land*). "Affection" was collected in *Overnight to Many Distant Cities.*

page 145 *"The response from our readers":* Donald Barthelme, fund-raising letter for *Forum,* July 22, 1958, Special Collections and Archives, University of Houston Libraries.

18. The Mechanical Bride

page 147 *"recommend some young fiction writers":* Donald Barthelme, letter to Martha Foley, September 25, 1959, Special Collections and Archives, University of Houston Libraries.

page 147 *"wrassling with a piece of fiction"; "ingenious young moviegoer"; "Yes, Knopf did option my book"; "Glad you wish to use as much as you do":* Percy quoted in Helen Moore Barthelme, *Donald Barthelme: The Genesis of a Cool Sound* (College Station: Texas A & M University Press, 2001), 73-74.

page 148 *"[N]ot publishing this story"; "Joyce, Pound, Eliot, Lawrence, Stein":* Donald Barthelme quoted in ibid., 86.

page 148 *"Any ethics that does not roundly condemn":* William Gass, "The Case of the Obliging Stranger," *Forum* 3, no. 4 (1960), draft in Special Collections and Archives, University of Houston Libraries.

page 148 *"I . . . undoubtedly . . . have [a] different audience in mind":* Howard F. McGraw, letter to Donald Barthelme, October 30, 1959, Special Collections and Archives, University of Houston Libraries.

page 149 *"I wouldn't say it was sadness":* Marilyn Gillet, in a conversation with the author, November 17, 2004.

page 150 *"I could see and feel an abating of his exuberance for life"* to *"had a responsibility to live out his life":* Helen Moore Barthelme, *Donald Barthelme,* 66.

page 150 *Natanson "alluded to Don's penchant for fast cars"* to *"driving a Jaguar":* ibid., 67.

page 150 *"Don saw it as the need to confront the choice"; "inappropriate for a serious writing career":* ibid., 66.

page 151 *"strange and beautiful" pieces:* "Interview with Jerome Klinkowitz, 1971-72," in *Not-Knowing: The Essays and Interviews,* ed. Kim Herzinger (New York: Random House, 1997), 201.

page 151 *"It looks as if I might receive better than full value":* Norman Mailer, letter to Donald

Barthelme, quoted in Donald Barthelme, letter to Dr. Patrick J. Nicholson, January 9, 1959, Special Collections and Archives, University of Houston Libraries.

page 151 *"[W]e thought you might be interested":* Donald Barthelme, letter to Ima Hogg, July 7, 1958, Special Collections and Archives, University of Houston Libraries.

page 151 *"drudge work":* Helen Moore Barthelme, *Donald Barthelme,* 89.

page 151 *"Because* Forum *has now published"; "Educational television, engineering education":* Donald Barthelme, letter to Dr. Patrick J. Nicholson, January 9, 1959, Special Collections and Archives, University of Houston Libraries.

page 152 *"get inside the . . . collective mind":* This and subsequent quotes from *The Mechanical Bride,* including citations from Edgar Allan Poe's "A Descent into the Maelstrom," are from Marshall McLuhan, *The Mechanical Bride: Folklore of Industrial Man* (London: Routledge and Kegan Paul, 1967), v-vi.

page 152 *"We read signs as promises":* Donald Barthelme, *Sixty Stories* (New York: Putnam, 1981), 33-34.

page 153 "[s]kiing along on the soft surface of brain damage": Donald Barthelme, *City Life* (New York: Farrar, Straus, and Giroux, 1970), 149.

page 153 *McLuhan provided some of the earliest:* By 1970, McLuhan's theories were wildly popular, upsetting traditionalists in many fields, from science to art to business. Don commented, wryly, on this development in "Brain Damage": *"The humanist position is not to plug in . . . flowers—to let them alone. Humanists believe in letting everything alone to be what it is, insofar as possible. The new electric awareness, however, requires that the flowers be plugged in, right away. . . . My own idea about whether or not to plug in the flowers is somewhere between these ideas, in that gray area where nothing is done, really, but you vacillate for a while, thinking about it. The blue of the flowers is extremely handsome against the gray of that area."* (See Barthelme, *City Life,* 136.)

page 153 *". . . try an experiment in reading [McLuhan]":* Andreas Huyssen, "In the Shadow of McLuhan: Jean Baudrillard's Theory of Simulation," *Assemblage* 10 (1989): 7.

page 153 *"RUB and FAB and TUB"; "huddle[s] and cling[s]"; "God . . . stand[s] in the basement":* Barthelme, *Sixty Stories,* 272, 279.

page 153 *"Don wanted 'to see the interior' "; "After we moved [in]":* Helen Moore Barthelme, *Donald Barthelme,* 67-69.

page 154 a doctor *"down in Texas":* Barthelme, *Sixty Stories,* 193-194.

page 154 *"washing . . . hands between hours":* Donald Barthelme, *Come Back, Dr. Caligari* (Boston: Little, Brown, 1964), 4.

page 154 *"that when he had achieved certain things in life and in himself":* Tim Fleck, "Burying the Dead Father," *Houston Press,* February 8, 1990.

page 155 *"ordinary shrink could have said to me":* Donald Barthelme, "Return," in *Liquid City: Houston Writers on Houston,* ed. Rita Saylors (San Antonio: Corona Publishing Company, 1987), 39.

page 155 *elected destiny:* Henri F. Ellenberger, "The Psychology of Destiny," *Forum* 3, no. 1 (1959); draft in Special Collections and Archives, University of Houston Libraries.

page 155 *"some of them four feet tall":* This and subsequent quotes from "Pages from the Annual Report" are from Donald Barthelme, "Pages from the Annual Report," *Forum* 3, no. 1 (1959): 13-18.

page 156 *"his work has sought out the clutter":* Harold Rosenberg, "The Audience as Subject," *Forum* 3, no. 3 (1959); draft in Special Collections and Archives, University of Houston Libraries.

page 156 *"It's my hope that these . . . souvenirs":* Barthelme, *Sixty Stories,* 98.

page 156 *"full of pep":* Rosenberg, "The Audience as Subject."

page 156 *Among the last pieces Don published in* Forum: Don published an essay on architecture by his friend Pat Goeters. Many of Goeters's ideas came from classes he had taken with Don's father. In editing the piece, Don may have felt he was editing his father. The "public *does not like* houses which are designed by architects," Goeters wrote. "[The] consumer's idea of a house is not the architect's idea of a house. The architect is not in some sense *ahead* of the public in this respect; he is, rather, in a different world." Shades of the old man shine through here.

Goeters tended to be wordy. Don's edits aimed for severe compression and rhythmic grace. He changed the phrase "Avant-garde work . . . needs time to become accepted" to "avant-garde work will be accepted only with time." At one point in the article, Goeters spoke of the kitsch in many American houses. He imagined a "green china dog that whistles 'My Old Kentucky Home.' " Don changed the song to "Elmer's Tune." (See Pat Goeters, "Poetry and Pragmatism," rough essay draft prepared for *Forum* 3, no. 4 [1960], Special Collections and Archives, University of Houston Libraries.

page 156 *"world of objects":* This and subsequent quotes from "Sartre and Literature" are from Maurice Natanson, "Sartre and Litera-ture," *Forum* 3, no. 3 (1959): 4-11.

page 157 *"[T]here is apparently a fundamental disagreement":* Helen Moore Barthelme, *Donald Barthelme,* 87.

page 157 *"very nebulous":* Donald Barthelme, letter to Herman Gollob, undated (probably late 1959), Special Collections, University of Delaware Library, Newark, Delaware.

19. Darling Duckling

page 158 *"This is your big chance":* Herman Gollob quoted in Helen Moore Barthelme, *Donald Barthelme: The Genesis of a Cool Sound* (College Station: Texas A & M University Press, 2001), 87-88.

page 158 *a rigorous writing routine:* In discussing Don's writing routine, I have drawn upon the chapter entitled "The Creation of a Strange Object" in Helen Moore Barthelme, *Donald Barthelme,* 90-101.

page 159 *"The customer is never right in archi-tecture":* This and subsequent statements by Donald Barthelme, Sr., are from "Construction and Conformity: Architect-Professor Barthelme Talks," *Houston Post,* January 10, 1960; Special Collections and Archives, University of Houston Libraries.

page 160 *"I . . . sit in this too-small seat":* This and subsequent quotes from "Me and Miss Mandible" (originally titled "The Darling Duck-ling at School") are from Donald Barthelme, *Sixty Stories* (New York: Putnam, 1981), 24-35.

page 161 *"Well, Babe, are you ready for this?":* Helen Moore Barthelme, *Donald Barthelme,* xiii.

page 161 *"stark"; "fearlessly obscene"; "speak to the present":* Jonathan Vaitch, *American Su-perrealism: Nathanael West and the Politics of Representation in the 1930s* (Madison: University of Wisconsin Press, 1997), 48.

page 162 *"much like Guillaume Apollinaire":* ibid., 16.

page 162 *curators translated the word* Surreal-ism *as "Super-Realism":* ibid., 15.

'**page 163** *In payment for his story:* Evan S. Con-nell and his coeditors struggled for seven years, beginning in 1958, to keep *Contact* alive. "We'd hear from everyone about how important the magazine was, how beautiful it looked, and so on," Connell recalled. "And then we'd have to beg in order to insure survival. We'd write to founda-tions, but most of them wouldn't even answer." Finally, in 1965, the journal gave up the ghost. In 1932, as its second incarnation ended, William Carlos Williams had said, "When an-other of the little reviews . . . died, I thought it was a shame. But now I think differently. Now I understand that all those little reviews ought by necessity to have a short life, the shorter the better. When they live too long they begin to dry

up. But they have had at least one excuse for their existence—they have given birth to at least one excellent writer who would not otherwise have had the means to develop. *Contact* has pub-lished N. West. Now it can die."

Cited above: *"We'd hear from everyone":* Con-nell quoted in Gerald Shapiro, "Evan S. Con-nell: A Profile," *Ploughshares,* Fall 1987; posted at www.pshares.org. *"When another of the little re-views":* William quoted in Vaitch, *American Su-perrealism,* 66.

page 163 *"Don observed that he felt a bit like he was starting a new life":* Helen Moore Barthelme, *Donald Barthelme,* 93.

page 163 *"did not enjoy writing such material":* ibid., 98-99.

page 163 *"In a work of literature form and con-tent":* ibid., 99-100.

page 163 *"everything is different"; "What I write has to be in the present":* ibid., 96.

page 163 *"have been suggested by an article that had appeared in* Time *magazine":* ibid., 93.

page 163 *"speak of cinema as of a religion":* "New Wave," *Time,* November 16, 1959, 119.

page 164 *It is a McLuhan-like exercise in read-ing American culture:* The story also owes some-thing to the literary theories of Kenneth Burke. The main character, Burlingame (Burke literary game?) interprets his situation according to some of the terms (*agent, agency, purpose*) in Burke's Pentad, a method of dissecting literary structures. In the 1950s, Burke was especially in-terested in how *symbols* could provoke *physio-logical responses* (for example, the way a stage play—a symbolic activity—can induce weeping or laughter in a viewer). Don was well aware of Burke's work. (See, for example, the opening paragraphs of Don's essay "After Joyce," in *Not-Knowing: The Essays and Interviews,* ed. Kim Herzinger [New York: Random House., 1997], 3.) At one point in "The Hiding Man," a character starts sobbing and the theater's "cooling system switches on." This incident parallels numerous examples, in Burke's writing, of physiological re-actions as a form of "communication" directly af-fecting the environment. Burke was fond of using movie theaters to illustrate his theory: "[C]onsider the operations of air conditioning equipment in a movie house," he wrote. If "a thriller is being played, this mechanism must work much harder than if the plot is of a milder sort because of the effects which the excitement of the audience has upon the conditions of the atmosphere in the theatre. Such bodily responses as increased warmth and accelerated respiration place a greater burden upon the air conditioning device, which is equipped with mechanical 'sensors' that register change in conditions and 'behave' accordingly." (See Kenneth Burke, "(Nonsymbolic) Motion / (Symbolic) Action," *Critical Inquiry* 4, no. 4 [1978]: 834. This particular statement, though made after Don's "The Hiding Man" was published, is a succinct example of the kinds of illustrations Burke used throughout the 1950s to animate his theories.)

page 164 *"People think these things are jokes"; "Most people don't have the wit to be afraid":* Donald Barthelme, *Come Back, Dr. Caligari* (Boston: Little, Brown, 1964), 37.

page 164 *"As Don wrote his first stories":* Helen Moore Barthelme, *Donald Barthelme,* 99.

page 164 *"Though Don was an essentially post–World War II product":* Maggie Maranto, in an E-mail to the author, August 9, 2004.

page 165 *"[his] vision is too ghastly":* "Waiting for Oblivion," *Time,* June 1, 1959, 92.

page 165 *nihilism and absurd laughter; reactions to the war in Korea:* See Hamlin Hill, "Black Humor: Its Cause and Cure," *Colorado Quarterly* 17, no. 1 (1968): 57.

pages 165–166 *"if you are alive today"; The "New York Times … is the source and fountain":* Bruce Jay Friedman, *Black Humor* (New York: Bantam Books, 1969), viii.

page 166 *"Lenny Bruce seems concerned [only] with"; "direction in which I was going"; "clearly the equivalents of the brief but corny 'quotes'":* Frank Kofsky, *Lenny Bruce: The Comedian as Social Critic and Secular Moralist* (New York: Monad Press, 1974), 22–27, 93–97.

page 166 *West related these disasters in Alger's cheerful style:* Even more than this, West lifted several passages, in their entirety, from Alger's books. Gary Scharnhorst is the scholar who discovered West's extensive "quoting" of Alger. The results of Scharnhorst's scholarship are discussed at length in Robert Emmet Long, *Nathanael West* (New York: Frederick Ungar, 1985) 84–108.

page 166 *"[H]umor [lay in] distinguishing":* Kofsky, *Lenny Bruce,* 97.

20. The Ugly Show

page 167 *"Composing a great or even near-great bookshop":* Larry McMurtry, *Walter Benjamin at the Dairy Queen* (New York: Simon & Schuster, 1999), 158–159.

page 167 *"elegant"; "heart, all along":* ibid., 162.

page 168 *"My book hunting":* ibid., 163.

page 168 *"powered by eight mighty Weed-Eaters":* Donald Barthelme, "Return," in *Liquid City: Houston Writers on Houston,* ed. Rita Saylors (San Antonio: Corona Publishing Company, 1987), 35.

page 169 *"You sure are an illiterate bastard":* Helen Moore Barthelme, *Donald Barthelme: The Genesis of a Cool Sound* (College Station: Texas A & M University Press, 2001), 181.

page 169 *Don "worked in even greater isolation":* ibid., 102.

page 169 *Early in 1960:* ibid., 110.

page 170 *Accounts vary as to when Jean and Dominique de Menil got involved:* See Frank D. Welch, *Philip Johnson and Texas* (Austin: University of Texas Press, 2000), 53. For much of the background information on the Menils' involvement with the CAA, I have drawn upon Welch's account. See also "Contemporary Arts Museum" at the *Handbook of Texas Online* (www..tsha .online.org/handbook/online/articles).

page 170 *"traveling through Europe on 'business trips' ":* Welch, *Philip Johnson and Texas,* 39.

page 170 *"just loved things American and Texan!":* ibid.

page 170 *"Houstonians [think] nothing about spending thousands":* ibid., 53.

page 170 *"[Jean] and Dominique wanted to set an example":* Marguerite Barnes quoted in ibid., 41, 43.

page 171 *the first International Style house built in Houston:* Welch, *Philip Johnson and Texas,* 45.

page 171 *"controversy over … MacAgy's radical ideas"; "Menil grip":* ibid., 66.

page 171 *"The city … may be seen as a texture of signs":* This and subsequent quotes from the catalog are from Donald Barthelme, "Architectural Graphics: An Introduction," in *Not-Knowing: The Essays and Interviews,* ed. Kim Herzinger (New York: Random House, 1997), 165–167.

page 172 *"The public demands new wonders piled on new wonders":* Donald Barthelme, *Sadness* (New York: Farrar, Straus and Giroux, 1972), 139.

pages 172–173 *"cultural artifacts of ambivalent status"; "A baby blue styrofoam chrysanthemum":* Cited in Kevin Cunningham, "L'Eclat du Hazard," *Gulf Coast: A Journal of Literature and Art,* vol. 4, no. 1 (1991): 73.

page 173 *"belong in the show":* ibid.

21. Dangling Man

pages 174-175 *"myth that every Texan is in some sense a cowboy"; "ritual demands of the [cowboy]":* Donald Barthelme, "Culture, Etc.," in *Not-Knowing: The Essays and Interviews,* ed. Kim Herzinger (New York: Random House, 1997), 132-135.

page 175 *"tiny, vaguely Southern American republic":* Helen Moore Barthelme, *Donald Barthelme: The Genesis of a Cool Sound* (College Station: Texas A & M University Press, 2001), 98.

page 175 *"establishment of a perfect state"* to *"One of the disadvantages of being the richest man in the country":* Donald Barthelme, "Mr. Hunt's Wooly Utopia," in *Not-Knowing,* ed. Herzinger, 83-85.

page 176 *Don submitted his formal application:* For the full text of the application, see *Gulf Coast: A Journal of Literature and Art,* 4, no. 1 (1991): 38.

page 176 *"Don relished the challenge of it":* Helen Moore Barthelme, *Donald Barthelme,* 112.

page 176 *"Every year something almost takes me to Texas":* Harold Rosenberg, letter to Donald Barthelme, April 5, 1961, Research Library, Getty Research Institute, Los Angeles, California.

page 176 *"The life-style in Texas":* This and subsequent quotes from these two articles are in John Bainbridge, "The Super-American State," *The New Yorker,* March 11, 1961, 47-80, and March 18, 1961, 79.

page 176 *"It's cheering to find that you're not intimidated":* Donald Barthelme, letter to Harold Rosenberg, April 13, 1961, Research Library, Getty Research Institute, Los Angeles, California.

page 177 *"free associate[s], brilliantly, brilliantly":* This and subsequent quotes from "Florence Green Is 81" are from Donald Barthelme, *Come Back, Dr. Caligari* (Boston: Little, Brown, 1964), 3-16.

page 177 *"several prominent Houstonians":* Helen Moore Barthelme, *Donald Barthelme,* 94.

page 177 *"Bloomsbury could now play"; "word would frequently disclose":* Barthelme, *Come Back, Dr. Caligari,* 67-81.

page 178 *"hotel and its setting were bleak"; "treat":* Helen Moore Barthelme, *Donald Barthelme,* 113.

page 178 *"miserable . . . slipshod, shambling piers":* Melville quoted in Phillip Lopate, *Waterfront: A Journey Around Manhattan* (New York: Crown Publishers, 2004), 21.

page 179 *"This was Don's first intimate contact"; "uncomfortable in the role of student":* Helen Moore Barthelme, *Donald Barthelme,* 114-115.

page 179 *"heart wasn't in it"* to *"106 degrees":* James Atlas, *Bellow* (New York: Random House, 2000), 309-310.

page 179 *"saw him as the major American novelist of our time":* Helen Moore Barthelme, *Donald Barthelme,* 114.

page 179 *"[T]hat summer, no one in the world mattered more":* This and subsequent Dworkin quotes are from Susan Dworkin, "The 'Great Man' Syndrome: Saul Bellow and Me," *Ms.,* March, 1977, 72-73.

page 179 *"I've lived in dirt":* Atlas, *Bellow,* 311.

page 179 *" 'The Big Broadcast' and Don's reading of it":* Helen Moore Barthelme, *Donald Barthelme,* 113.

page 179 *"Do you really believe":* Atlas, *Bellow,* 311.

page 180 *"I myself have often been indignant":* ibid.

page 180 *women writers who "wore their ovaries":* ibid.

page 180 *"Don might have had":* Helen Moore Barthelme, *Donald Barthelme,* 115.

page 180 *"filled with anguish":* ibid., 116. In a letter to Elizabeth Bishop, Lowell described his conference experience: "Saul Bellow goes off for a long killing fiction-discussion meeting with the conference nymphomaniac, leaving me with the conference leech, who invites me to dinner. Supper: at six, after two minutes for drinks—more laundered food. . . . From the next room belonging to my other colleague, Edward Albee, a playwright—the low endless Tennessee voice of the conference nymphomaniac reading aloud a play. At about four-thirty, all is quiet." (See Robert Lowell to Elizabeth Bishop, August 7, 1961, in *The Letters of Robert Lowell,* ed. Saskia Hamilton [New York: Farrar, Straus and Giroux, 2005], 387.)

page 181 *"I saw Don as more insecure":* ibid., 114.

page 181 *"alluded to our marriage":* ibid., 113-114.

page 181 *"I don't believe Sterling":* Lynn Nesbit, in an E-mail to the author, September 9, 2004.

page 181 *"recommended Don":* Helen Moore Barthelme, *Donald Barthelme,* 115.

page 181 *"had just been promoted by Sterling":* Lynn Nesbit, in an E-mail to the author, September 9, 2004.

pages 181-182 *"I was awed by the controlled madness"; "summon up the courage to publish";*

"radically different approach": Herman Gollob, Me and Shakespeare: Adventures with the Bard (New York: Doubleday, 2002), 169.

page 182 "sounds of intimacy, outrage and drinking": Robert Lowell to Elizabeth Bishop, August 7, 1961, in The Letters of Robert Lowell, ed. Hamilton, 387.

page 182 "alcoholic's attention span": Pat Goeters, "Pulitzer Parable," an unpublished essay, in an E-mail to the author, April 22, 2004.

page 182 "tendencies"; "serious"; "had more possibilities to do what he wanted": Marilyn Gillet, in a conversation with the author, November 17, 2004.

page 182 "was addicted, as was I": Gollob, Me and Shakespeare, 167.

page 183 "insight into the New York literary world"; "I could see that": Helen Moore Barthelme, Donald Barthelme, 116.

22. The Emerging Figure

page 184 "in the work of the children of the de Kooning generation": This and subsequent quotes from the catalog's introduction are from Donald Barthelme, "The Emerging Figure," in Not-Knowing: The Essays and Interviews, ed. Kim Herzinger (New York: Random House, 1997), 168-169.

page 185 "barbaric yawp of American painting": Mark Stevens and Annalyn Swan, De Kooning: An American Master (New York: Alfred A. Knopf, 2004), 338.

page 186 "A remarkable number of advertisements": This and subsequent quotes from "The Case of the Vanishing Product" are from Donald Barthelme, "The Case of the Vanishing Product," in Not-Knowing, ed. Herzinger, 136-139.

page 186 "flew by the seat of [his] pants": Marion Knox Barthelme, in an E-mail to the author, October 13, 2004.

page 186 "structural katzenjammer": Hubert Roussell quoted in Helen Moore Barthelme, Donald Barthelme: The Genesis of a Cool Sound (College Station: Texas A & M University Press, 2001), 120.

page 187 "Don had a nice bunch of friends": Kenneth Koch, "Getting to Know Donald Barthelme," Gulf Coast: A Journal of Literature and Art, 4, no. 1 (1991): 142.

page 187 "This job at the museum": Barthelme quoted in Herman Gollob, Me and Shakespeare: Adventures with the Bard (New York: Doubleday, 2002), 169.

page 187 He was "serious, older": Helen Moore Barthelme, Donald Barthelme, 124.

page 187 "[Don and I] spent a lot of time in the car": Koch, "Getting to Know Donald Barthelme," 142-143.

page 188 "[We] were severely strained": Helen Moore Barthelme, Donald Barthelme, 126.

page 188 "pick up the check"; to "Now you have something you can tell our grandchildren": ibid., 124.

page 188 "The E. de Kooning idea sounds fine": Donald Barthelme, letter to Harold Rosenberg, March 28, 1962, Research Library, Getty Research Institute, Los Angeles, California.

page 188 "Congenial and a good teacher": Helen Moore Barthelme, Donald Barthelme, 112.

pages 188-189 "Elaine was vivacious" to "sometimes looked like a boorish drunk": Stevens and Swan, De Kooning, 213, 229, 277, 576-577.

page 189 "I love Texans": Elaine de Kooning quoted in Lee Hall, Elaine and Bill: Portrait of a Marriage (New York: HarperCollins, 1993), 235.

page 190 "In regard to working on the Longview magazine": Donald Barthelme, letter to Harold Rosenberg, March 28, 1962, Research Library, Getty Research Institute, Los Angeles, California.

page 191 "found his absence disquieting": Helen Moore Barthelme, Donald Barthelme, 127.

page 191 "How good you look" to "Uncertain of our future": ibid., 127-129.

page 192 Bayles told him "it was time to get out of town": Cited in Tim Fleck, "Burying the Dead Father," Houston Press, February 8, 1990.

page 192 "I'll need you in New York"; "Don accepted": Helen Moore Barthelme, Donald Barthelme, 129.

page 192 "with about seven prominent creative types": Pat Goeters, in an E-mail to the author, April 26, 2004.

pages 192-193 "I don't believe [Don] ever understood" to "stay [in Houston] and build a home like this": Helen Moore Barthelme, Donald Barthelme, 129-131.

page 193 "When he recalled his work [there]": ibid., 130.

page 193 "I know Don thought that working as the CAM director": Marion Knox Barthelme, in an E-mail to the author, October 13, 2004.

page 193 "I don't think he felt as good about himself": Helen Moore Barthelme, Donald Barthelme, 130.

page 194 "compartmentalize[d] the people he knew" to "extraordinary ability to challenge another person": ibid., 130-131.

23. Location

page 197 *"On this worst of anniversaries":* Helen Moore Barthelme, *Donald Barthelme: The Genesis of a Cool Sound* (College Station: Texas A & M University Press, 2001), 135.

page 198 *"Once, Don took Joe to a party":* Maggie Maranto, in an E-mail to the author, June 18, 2004.

page 199 a *"teeny" bit in love:* Lee Hall, *Elaine and Bill: Portrait of a Marriage* (New York: HarperCollins, 1993), 230.

page 199 *"I spent the first several years of our friendship":* Donald Barthelme, "Thomas B. Hess, 1920-1978," *Art in America*, November/December, 1978, 8-9.

page 199 *"were not worried about putting the magazine out on time":* Donald Barthelme, "Interview with Larry McCaffery, 1980," in *Not-Knowing: The Essays and Interviews*, ed. Kim Herzinger (New York: Random House, 1997), 264.

page 199 *"The only adequate criticism of a work of art is another work of art":* J. D. O'Hara, "Donald Barthelme: The Art of Fiction LXVI," *Pari Review* 80 (1981): 186.

page 199 *"frauds, freaks, charlatans, and worse":* Cited in Florence Rubenfeld, *Clement Greenberg: A Life* (Minneapolis: University of Minnesota Press, 1997), 231.

page 200 *"I heard you were talking at the Guggenheim":* ibid., 232-233.

page 200 *"abstract . . . officer in Kafka's* The Penal Colony*":* Harold Rosenberg. "The Trial and Eichmann," *Commentary* 32, no. 5 (1961): 379.

page 200 *"[The] situation has changed":* Robert Alexander, letter to Harold Rosenberg, October 17, 1961, Research Library, Getty Research Institute, Los Angeles, California.

page 201 *"Dear Harold: Hear you are committing the final sin":* Walter Lowenfels, letter to Harold Rosenberg, December 17, 1963, Research Library, Getty Research Institute, Los Angeles, California.

page 201 *"expression and thinking in art and literature"; "overcome the intellectual isolation"; "endeavor to maintain":* Harold Rosenberg, "Proposal for a Magazine to Be Published by Longview Foundation, Inc.," February 1960, Research Library, Getty Research Institute, Los Angeles, California.

page 201 *initial budget for the magazine:* Harold Rosenberg, "Tentative Budget: Locations," Research Library, Getty Research Institute, Los Angeles, California.

pages 201-202 *"of persons not of pieces"* to *"very few 'new' people":* Harold Rosenberg, "Notes on Location" (undated), Research Library Getty Research Institute, Los Angeles, California.

page 202 *"a stranger"; "attitude was unfriendly, cavalier":* Meyer Liben, letter to Harold Rosenberg, August 3, 1963, Research Library, Getty Research Institute, Los Angeles, California.

page 202 *"[In] vigor and orginality"; "experience of painters and sculptors":* Rosenberg, "Proposal for a Magazine to be Published by Longview Foundation, Inc."

page 202 *"The art world thronged to the opening":* Mark Stevens and Annalyn Swan, *De Kooning: An American Master* (New York: Alfred A. Knopf, 2004), 441.

page 203 *"is a collage":* Donald Barthelme, "Interview with Jerome Klinkowitz, 1971-72," in *Not-Knowing*, ed. Herzinger, 204.

page 203 *"all the filth on the streets":* O'Hara, "Donald Barthelme," 202.

page 203 *"you'd go to see":* Donald Barthelme. Jo Brans, "Embracing the World: in *Not-Knowing*, ed. Herzinger, 306.

page 203 *"Yesterday in the typewriter":* Donald Barthelme, *Sixty Stories* (New York: Putnam, 1981), 22.

page 203 *"After that, it was every two or three days"; "At that point Don called":* Helen Moore Barthelme, *Donald Barthelme*, 133-134.

page 204 *"Gothic [pride]"; a "condition never to be reconciled":* Henry James, *The American Scene* (New York: Scribner's, 1946), 76-78.

page 204 *"The precious stretch of space":* ibid., 87.

page 204 *"New York . . . languishes and palpitates":* ibid., 116.

page 204 *"This muck heaves and palpitates":* Donald Barthelme, *Sixty Stories*, 158.

page 204 the hotel's *"illusions about itself":* This and James's subsequent comments about the Waldorf-Astoria Hotel are from James, *The American Scene*, 101-106. During the Depression, Langston Hughes also famously wrote about the hotel's ostentation and superficiality in his poem "Advertisement for the Waldorf-Astoria."

page 205 *"Carola Mitt":* Donald Barthelme, *Come Back, Dr. Caligari* (Boston: Little, Brown, 1964), 85-86.

page 205 *"leaders in the new wave"; "Marola Witt":* "The Bones Have Names," *Time,* December 22, 1961, 30-31.

page 205 *"Man practices metaphysics":* Barthelme, *Come Back, Dr. Caligari,* 93 (translated from the French).

page 206 *"Mr. Henry James writes fiction":* Barthelme, ibid., 11.

24. Lovely Old Picturesque Dirty Buildings

page 207 *"learned to impersonate a Texan well enough"*: Interview with Jerome Klinkowitz, 1971-72," in *Not-Knowing: The Essays and Interviews*, ed. Kim Herzinger (New York: Random House, 1997), 205.

page 207 *"New York is ... our Paris"*; *"I was one night congratulated by a prominent poet"*: Donald Barthelme, "Terms of Estrangement," in *Taking Stock: A Larry McMurtry Casebook*, ed. Clay Reynolds (Dallas: Southern Methodist University Press, 1989), 104.

page 207 *"I could hear [his] loneliness as well"*: Helen Moore Barthelme, *Donald Barthelme: The Genesis of a Cool Sound* (College Station: Texas A & M University Press, 2001), 133.

pages 207-208 *"walked around for days"* to *"Sweetheart, I look forward eagerly"*: Helen Moore Barthelme, *Donald Barthelme*, 135.

page 208 *"I really had no idea"*: This and subsequent comments about Helen's time in New York are from ibid., 133-144.

page 212 *"Pop art was flowering"*: Phillip Lopate, in a conversation with the author, October 29, 2004.

page 212 *"was just assumed"*: Lee Hall, *Elaine and Bill: Portrait of a Marriage* (New York: HarperCollins, 1993), 99.

page 212 *"We used to drink until all of the booze was gone"*: ibid.

page 212 *"Openings in galleries had bars"*: ibid.

page 212 *"no matter how much he drank"*: ibid., 117.

page 212 *"darkening, becoming a sloppy drunk"*: Mark Stevens and Annalyn Swan, *De Kooning: An American Master* (New York: Alfred A. Knopf, 2004), 432.

page 213 *"She absolutely insisted on being the center of attention"*: Hall, *Elaine and Bill*, 181.

page 213 Pollock *"would glower into his drink"*: Stevens and Swan, *De Kooning*, 364.

page 213 *"that tampon painter"*: ibid., 345.

page 213 *"together with Rosenberg's habit"*: ibid., 365.

page 214 *"loony command center"*: Hall, *Elaine and Bill*, 179.

page 214 *"acting like a stallion"*: ibid., 199.

page 214 *"seemed to flaunt with renewed vigor"*: ibid., 187.

page 214 *"She was this kind of daredevil"*: ibid., 188, 190-191.

page 214 *"Despite the immediacy and the vivacity"*: John Ashbery quoted in Stevens and Swan, *De Kooning*, 577.

page 214 *"Just take care of the luxuries"*: Hall, *Elaine and Bill*, 189.

25. Up, Aloft in the Air

page 216 *"[T]he fact is that I want to live alone"*; *"remain apart for now"*: Helen Moore Barthelme, *Donald Barthelme: The Genesis of a Cool Sound* (College Station: Texas A & M University Press, 2001), 144.

page 216 Kenneth Koch *"came over"*; Jack Kroll: ibid., 144-145.

page 217 *"[N]o other stories have been sold"*: ibid., 144.

page 217 *"further extends the line of attack"*: ibid., 147.

page 217 *"easy ... to approach"*: Michael Korda, *Another Life* (New York: Dell, 2000), 174.

page 217 *"Donald and I had instant chemistry"*: Lynn Nesbit, in a conversation with the author, July 30, 2007.

page 217 *"They'd go to the beach"*: Maggie Maranto, in an E-mail to the author, June 12, 2004.

page 217 *"a really courageous book publisher"*; *"swaggering"*; *"part of Don's posture"*: Helen Moore Barthelme, *Donald Barthelme*, 147.

page 218 *"[Robert] Bly reacted so violently"*: ibid., 145.

page 218 *"uneasy collection"*; *"brief chapters"*; *"fantastically poor"*: ibid., 145, 148.

page 218 *"In 1963, I made new friends"*: This and subsequent Helen Barthelme quotes in this chapter, as well as Don's comments relative to them, are from Helen Moore Barthelme, *Donald Barthelme*, 141-151.

page 219 *"Tell [the pilots]"*: Donald Barthelme, *Come Back, Dr. Caligari* (Boston: Little, Brown, 1964), 138.

page 219 *"Helen would have hung on forever"*: Herman Gollob, in a conversation with the author, April 19, 2007.

page 220 *"these nuts that call[ed] themselves artists"*: Edmund T. Delaney, *New York's Greenwich Village* (Barre, Massachusetts: Barre Publishers, 1968), 104.

pages 220-221 *"frequent contact with a wide circle of people"*; *"humble"*: Jane Jacobs, *The Death and Life of Great American Cities* (1961;

reprint, New York: Modern American Library, 1993), 89, 156.

page 221 *"[O]nce in a while when I was low on cash":* Donald Barthelme, "Interview with Larry McCaffery, 1980," in *Not-Knowing: The Essays*

and Interviews, ed. Kim Herzinger (New York: Random House, 1997), 264.

page 221 *"Ford Foundation overcoat"; "Guggen-heim-applicant feeling":* Michael Houston [Donald Barthelme], "The Ontological Basis of Two," *Cavalier,* June 1963, 22.

26. For I'm the Boy

page 222 *Don was not happy with the issue:* One has the impression that he had chosen a kind of self-exile in New York to remake himself, and that his new magazine work wound up being too much like the old editing he had done. This is not, of course, the only way to view his move to Manhattan (he had moved for excitement and for the sake of his career). But self-banishment appealed to him on some level—recall his remark that a therapist had told him to stay out of town until he was satisfied with his achievements. Though he maintained ties with his family, these bonds were easier to cope with from a distance as he pursued his independence. His strongest literary models at the time, Joyce, Eliot, and Beckett, had remade themselves far from their mother countries. "The feeling of being out of date, of having been born into too late an epoch, or of surviving unnaturally beyond one's term, is all over Eliot's early poetry," says the novelist J. M. Coetzee. This feeling of displacement, which Don shared, is part of what drew him to Eliot in the first place. It is a common feeling among provincials, Coetzee says: They "blame their [home] environment for not living up to art," for falling short of the ideals imposed on, but denied, them by authority, so they seek the "high culture of the metropolis . . . [and] powerful experiences which cannot, however, be embedded in their lives in any obvious way." (See J. M. Coetzee, *Stranger Shores: Literary Essays, 1986-1999* [New York: Viking Penguin, 2001], 6-7.)

Don's long-standing ambition to get to New York (and his willingness to sacrifice his marriage to stay there) is part and parcel of the "Ivy League" dress he adopted early on (according to Herman Gollob) and the careful speaking style he "willed" himself into. He spoke, as he wrote, aphoristically—sometimes, like Eliot, with a faintly British-sounding accent (for example, he stressed the first, rather than the second, syllable of the word *pejorative;* he pronounced the name Beethoven "*Bet*-of-en"). Don remade himself in an attempt to overcome the disorientation forced on him by Houston's provincialism and his father's impossible modernism (impossible because it belonged to another era and because it belonged to his father). The elder Barthelme inhabited Don's thinking—thus, the

simultaneous yearning for tradition and a hunger for the new: embracing *and* escaping the old man. That it was vain to try to erase his confused feelings is clear in the persistence of mislocation in Don's fiction, even in his last novel, *The King,* in which King Arthur survives "unnaturally beyond [his] term."

page 222 *"certain aspects of [an] artist's work":* Thomas B. Hess, "Ideas in Search of Words," *Location* 1, no. 1 (1963): 6-7.

page 222 *"At last there is a place'"; "For twenty years poetry and fiction":* Harold Rosenberg, "The Stockade Syndrome," *Location* 1, no. 1 (1963): 4-5.

page 223 *It should be noted that Rosenberg's literary sensibility:* In 1935, the shock of Stalinist horror forced the *Partisan Review* into a deep identity crisis. The impossible strain in its nature had been clear from the start—most notably in the editors' desire to support high art while imagining a world devoid of social hierarchies. In 1936, the magazine ceased publication. A year later, after intense self-examination, it rose from the ashes with a new outlook. Said *PR:* The personal is political. This formulation, so familiar to us now, arose in the 1930s only after long, exhaustive battles over the meanings of art, politics, and individuality. Clement Greenberg's landmark essay, "Avant-Garde and Kitsch," published in the Fall 1939 issue of *PR* echoed Trotsky's view that "art can become a strong ally of the [socialist] revolution only insofar as it remains faithful to itself." Greenberg argued that painting could be faithful to itself only if it expunged representational content and focused exclusively on its plasticity. Thus, an individual artistic style—freed from received subject matter—was socially revolutionary. Rosenberg agreed (a rare moment of consensus between the two).

In essays that often appeared in the *Partisan Review,* Greenberg and Rosenberg refined their arguments about style and politics by examining the work of Willem de Kooning, Jackson Pollock, and others. Their essays helped turn Abstract Expressionism into the cultural phenomenon it became in the 1940s and 1950s—and crucially, as James D. Herbert has pointed out, Greenberg and Rosenberg "worked to find a safe haven for radical progress within the realm of individualistic culture." Abstract work, they insisted, could not be co-opted to promote the state the way "realistic" imagery had been manipulated by Stalinists and others with political agendas.

Ten years after Greenberg first pitched his ideas in the pages of *PR,* Jackson Pollock posed for a *Life* magazine cover. In his dark jacket, and puffing on a cigarette, Pollock presents the image of a proletariat tough guy, irascibly charming. But the black painting behind him, with its vibrant drips and scrawls, announces a new force in American culture. Meanwhile, Greenberg had become the *Nation's* regular art critic; Rosenberg eventually joined the staff of *The New Yorker.* Both writers continued to move away from hard-line Marxism (tainted now with spectral images of mass death and anonymous prisons). Greenberg hardened his stance that art must eschew all external references, and Rosenberg insisted that literature follow painting's self-reflexive path.

(With the benefit of more than fifty years' hindsight, we know that Abstract Expressionism did not escape co-optation any more than social realism had. MoMA let the CIA exhibit abstract paintings from its collection overseas as a way of asserting America's "social freedom" and "cultural superiority" to Communist countries. Unwittingly, abstract art became a Cold War weapon.)

In its heyday, *PR* was defined by one other cultural thread—Judaism—that would have a strong impact on Don. Phillip Lopate says, "Don was very comfortable in Jewish intellectual circles. Judaism gave him a kind of ethical spine, I think—I mean the secular, politically active Judaism." Don attended a few *PR* gatherings in the early 1960s, where Phillips tried to revive the heady intellectual atmosphere of the old days. Of one such "soiree," *The New York Times* reported, "Donald Barthelme attacked [one of] Lionel Trilling's novel[s] and Diana Trilling retorted by savaging Barthelme." Afterward, Phillips sighed and said, "I was trying to mate lambs and wolves."

Cited above: *"art can become a strong ally of the [socialist] revolution":* Leon Trotsky, "Letter to Dwight Macdonald," cited in *Pollock and After,* ed. Francis Frascina (New York: Harper & Row, 1985), 170; *"worked to find a safe haven for radical progress":* James D. Herbert, *The Political Origins of Abstract Expressionist Art Criticism* (Stanford, California: Stanford Honors Essay in the Humanities, 1985), 2; *"social freedom"* and *"cultural superiority":* Eva Cockcroft. "Abstract Expressionism, Weapon of the Cold War," in *Pollock and After,* ed. Frascina, 125-133; *"Don was very comfortable":* Phillip Lopate, in a conversa-

tion with the author, October 29, 2004. *"Donald Barthelme attacked":* Joseph Berger, "William Phillips, Co-Founder and Soul of *Partisan Review,* Dies at 94," *New York Times,* September 14, 2002.

page 223 *"noticed that the windows overlooking Broadway":* Donald Barthelme, "Being Bad," in *Not-Knowing: The Essays and Interviews,* ed. Kim Herzinger (New York: Random House, 1997), 185.

page 223 *"[The] New York State Court of Appeals":* Barney Rosset, letter to Harold Rosenberg, July 19, 1963, Research Library, Getty Research Institute, Los Angeles, California.

page 224 "The New York Times . . . *received an unprecedented number of poems":* Erwin A. Glickes and Paul Schweber, letter to Harold Rosenberg, February 6, 1964: Research Library, Getty Research Institute, Los Angeles, California.

page 224 *"social and historical happenings":* Harold Rosenberg, "Form and Despair," *Location* 1, no. 2 (1964): 7-9.

page 224 *"A literature which is exclusively about itself?":* Saul Bellow, "A Comment on 'Form and Despair,' " *Location* 1, no. 2 (1964): 10-12.

page 224 *"mysterious shift":* This and subsequent quotes from the essay are from Donald Barthelme, "After Joyce," *Location* 1, no. 2 (1964): 13-16.

page 225 *"[H]e was a talker":* Saul Bellow, *Him With His Foot in His Mouth and Other Stories* (New York: Harper & Row, 1984), 76-77.

page 226 *"Let me confess now":* This and subsequent quotes from the memorandum to Hess and Rosenberg are from Donald Barthelme, "Memorandum on *Location* Prospectus and Prospects," undated, Research Library, Getty Research Institute, Los Angeles, California.

page 227 *"friends of the family":* This and subsequent quotes from the story are from Donald Barthelme, "For I'm the Boy," *Location* 1, no. 2 (1964): 91-93.

page 228 *"soul anguish":* Søren Kierkegaard, *Fear and Trembling / Repetition,* ed. and trans. Howard V. Hong and Edna H. Hong (Princeton, New Jersey: Princeton University Press, 1983), 204-213.

page 228 *"The only way to determine the value":* Jean-Paul Sartre, *Existentialism and Human Emotions* (New York: Citadel Press, 1985), 57.

page 228 *"The artist must . . . above all retain his private vision":* Duncan Grant, cited at www.walrus.com.

page 229 *"contrive somehow to avoid":* Saul Bellow, "Deep Readers of the World, Beware," *New York Times Book Review,* February 15, 1959, 34.

27. Come Back, Dr. Caligari

page 230 The Cabinet of Dr. Caligari: *Come Back, Dr. Caligari,* the title of Don's first book, is taken from the 1919 German expressionist film, *The Cabinet of Dr. Caligari,* directed by Robert Wiene and starring Conrad Veidt. The film's dizzying, oddly angled sets, as well as its stories within stories, challenge mundane perceptions. The "modern reappearance" of an old "myth" (a magician and his victim) forms the film's core. The central showman, Dr. Caligari, promises audiences, "Wonders! Marvels! Miracles!"

Before settling on the title, Don jokingly offered his publisher *Horse Feathers* and *Ned Bobkoff and the Incredible Garbage Cans.*

page 230 *"To be young and in love with films":* This and subsequent Lopate quotes about New York film culture from his book *Totally, Tenderly, Tragically* are posted at nytimes.com/books/first/lopate-totally.html.

page 232 *"a jet black smallish creature"; "fanatical about proper projection":* Rudy Franci's comments are posted at cinematreasures.org/theater/6016.

page 232 *"The themes of [Warhol's] films"; "if the cinemagoer really concentrated":* Klaus Honnef, *Andy Warhol, 1928–1987: Commerce into Art* (Köln, West Germany: Benedikt Taschen, 1990), 75-77.

page 233 *"the look, the editorial and graphic components":* Ben Yagoda, *About Town: The New Yorker and the World It Made* (New York: Scribner's, 2000), 42.

page 233 *"not only partitions":* Robert Coates quoted in ibid., 44.

page 233 *"commas in the* New Yorker*":* E. B. White quoted in ibid., 206-207.

page 233 *"twenty year" war: The Writer in Society: Donald Barthelme* (Houston: KUHT-TV, 1984).

page 233 *"fully comprehended . . . the magazine's commitment":* Yagoda, *About Town,* 244.

page 233 *"combined the best qualities of Napoleon and St. Francis of Assisi":* Harold Brodkey quoted in ibid., 257.

page 233 *"hobbled"* and *"capricious":* John Cheever quoted in ibid., 293.

page 234 *"inhibition[s] led to an "ethic of silence"; "There began to be a feeling"; "physical structure of the office":* Renata Adler, *Gone: The Last Days of The New Yorker* (New York: Simon & Schuster, 1999), 23-24.

page 234 *"The* New Yorker *had an air of complete privacy"; "The offices of editors, writers, artists":* Ved Mehta, *Remembering Mr. Shawn's New Yorker: The Invisible Art of Editing* (Wood-

stock and New York: Overlook Press, 1998), 110-111.

page 234 *"under the pressureless pressures":* ibid., 278.

page 234 *"I've always felt that there was a connection between* The New Yorker *and depression":* Phillip Lopate, in a conversation with the author, October 29, 2004.

page 235 *"amazingly bad"; "obscene and extremely violent":* Adler, *Gone,* 18-19.

page 235 *"At the time I didn't have an agent": The Writer in Society.*

page 235 *"Donald Barthelme has rewritten 'L'Lapse'":* Roger Angell, letter to Lynn Nesbit, January 25, 1963, Manuscripts and Archives Division, New York Public Library.

page 235 *"wealthy film critic":* This and subsequent quotes from "L'Lapse" are from Donald Barthelme, *Guilty Pleasures* (New York: Farrar, Straus and Giroux, 1974), 45-51.

page 236 *"[The novelist] Niccolo Tucci asked me to convey my congratulations to you":* Roger Angell, letter to Donald Barthelme, March 5, 1963, Manuscripts and Archives Division, New York Public Library.

page 237 *"I can only assume":* E. B. White, *Letters of E. B. White,* ed. Dorothy Lobrano Guth (New York: Harper & Row, 1976), 189.

page 237 *"Although he is a member of the family":* ibid., 244.

page 237 *"established an overt"; "The fiction editors themselves":* Adler, *Gone,* 65-66.

page 237 *"cold and irascible"; "a sine qua non for the job":* Mehta, *Remembering Mr. Shawn's New Yorker,* 332.

page 237 *"my lifeline to the literary world":* Roger Angell, in a conversation with the author, May 27, 2004.

page 237 *"vague and obscure":* Roger Angell, letter to Donald Barthelme, March 13, 1963, Manuscripts and Archives Division, New York Public Library.

page 238 *"This strikes us as being highly artificial and entirely unconvincing":* Roger Angell, letter to Lynn Nesbit, April 16, 1963, Manuscripts and Archives Division, New York Public Library.

page 238 *"I do hope that you will not be discouraged":* Roger Angell, letter to Donald Barthelme, May 6, 1963, Manuscripts and Archives Division, New York Public Library.

page 238 *"I showed the stories to my boss":* This and subsequent quotes regarding Gollob's conversation with Ned Bradford are from Herman Gollob, *Me and Shakespeare: Adventures with the Bard* (New York: Doubleday, 2002), 169-170.

When Gollob informed Don of Little, Brown's decision, Don wrote him back: "Montressor: Needless to say, I am ill with GLADNESS at being taken under the Little, Brown wing. I feel I have a home now. You will doubtless find me in your anteroom, before very long, ill-dressed, unshaven, but warm and happy, tugging at your sleeve. . . ." (Donald Barthelme, letter to Herman Gollob, undated [1963], Special Collections, University of Delaware Library, Newark, Delaware.)

page 238 *"That did the trick":* Herman Gollob, in a conversation with the author, April 19, 2007.

page 239 *"John Cheever in a fun-house mirror":* David P. Young, in a review of *Come Back, Dr. Caligari, Studies in Short Fiction* 3, no. 3 (1966): 388.

page 239 *"[Mr. Barthelme] seemed most interested in the offer":* Roger Angell, letter to Lynn Nesbit, July 22, 1963, Manuscripts and Archives Division, New York Public Library.

page 239 *"breathtaking":* Roger Angell, in a conversation with the author, May 27, 2004.

page 239 *"baffled" many staffers:* Yagoda, *About Town,* 346.

page 239 *"was on to Barthelme before anyone else":* Roger Angell quoted in ibid., 346.

page 239 *"I enthusiastically admired":* Roger Angell, in a conversation with the author, December 6, 2006.

page 240 *"Donald Barthelme's book of short stories":* "New Faces, New Forces," *Harper's Bazaar,* June 1963.

page 240 *"It is almost impossible, of course":* Roger Angell, letter to Donald Barthelme, August 1, 1963, Manuscripts and Archives Division, New York Public Library.

page 240 *"best story of his that we have seen":* Roger Angell, letter to Lynn Nesbit, September 9, 1963, Manuscripts and Archives Division, New York Public Library.

page 240 *"Dear Don":* Roger Angell, letter to Donald Barthelme, September 3, 1963, Manuscripts and Archives Division, New York Public Library.

page 240 *"cost of living adjustment":* Roger Angell, letter to Lynn Nesbit, October 14, 1963, Manuscripts and Archives Division, New York Public Library.

page 241 *"more customary" paragraphs* to *"The people who liked it didn't write":* Roger Angell, letter to Donald Barthelme, October 18, 1963, Manuscripts and Archives Division, New York Public Library.

page 241 *"new purchase[s]":* Roger Angell, letter to Lynn Nesbit, December 11, 1963, Manuscripts and Archives Division, New York Public Library.

page 241 *"[I]t just adds up to a nice bundle":* Roger Angell, letter to Donald Barthelme, December 11, 1963, Manuscripts and Archives Division, New York Public Library.

page 241 *"startling and perfect" Christmas gift:* Roger Angell, letter to Donald Barthelme, December 23, 1963, Manuscripts and Archives Division, New York Public Library.

page 241 *"current bonus cycle":* Roger Angell, letter to Lynn Nesbit, January 16, 1964, Manuscripts and Archives Division, New York Public Library.

page 242 *"[P]lease don't start worrying about this":* Roger Angell, letter to Donald Barthelme, June 9, 1964, Manuscripts and Archives Division, New York Public Library.

page 242 *"a mighty strange and disturbing piece":* Roger Angell, letter to Donald Barthelme, June 28, 1964, Manuscripts and Archives Division, New York Public Library.

page 242 *"I spent a happy fifteen minutes":* Roger Angell, letter to Donald Barthelme, August 18, 1964, Manuscripts and Archives Division, New York Public Library.

page 242 *"Dear Reader":* Herman Gollob, letter accompanying the "Advance Preview" of *Come Back, Dr. Caligari,* published by Little, Brown, April 1, 1964.

page 243 *The book jacket, designed by Milton Glaser:* "Milt baby is the best," Don had written to Herman Gollob in an undated letter (1963); Special Collections, University of Delaware, Morris Library, Newark, Delaware.

page 243 *Each story came densely layered:* Don had taken care to arrange the collection for "[c]ontinuity of . . . mood and attack," for "tempo and change of pace and similar glittering abstractions." He joked with Gollob, saying, "I . . . majored in English" (letter to Herman Gollob, July 16, 1963, Special Collections, University of Delaware, Morris Library, Newark, Delaware).

page 243 *mere "entertainment"; "regiment . . . people"; whatever "is not physiologically necessary":* Henry Flynt, cited at henryflynt.org/aesthetics.

page 244 *"MAN DIES!":* This and subsequent quotes from "Marie, Marie, Hold on Tight" are from Donald Barthelme, *Come Back, Dr. Caligari* (Boston: Little, Brown, 1964), 115-122.

page 244 *"minor artist":* This and subsequent quotes from "A Shower of Gold" are from Donald Barthelme, *Come Back, Dr. Caligari,* 173-183.

28. Old Fogey

page 246 The New York Review of Books *debuted:* A useful source regarding New York-related cultural history is James Trager's *The New York Chronology* (New York: HarperResource, 2003).

page 247 *"very talented young writer":* Renata Adler, in an unsigned review of *Come Back, Dr. Caligari, The New Yorker,* June 13, 1964, 141.

page 247 *"cratered landscape of the broken heart":* Jack Kroll (unsigned), "Peers and Mutations," *Newsweek,* April 13, 1964, 97-98.

page 247 *"existentialism [into] as popular an American institution":* R. V. Cassill, "Don't Ignore a Vision," *New York Times Book Review,* April 12, 1964, 36.

page 247 *Robert M. Adams . . . claimed:* Robert M. Adams, "New Short Stories," *The New York Review of Books* 2, no. 6 (1964).

page 247 *"a member of the advance guard":* Granville Hicks, "Sad Secrets and Absurdities," *The Saturday Review,* April 4, 1964, 23-24.

page 247 *"Mr. Barthelme has regarded each construction":* Hilary Corke, "Come Back, Mr. Barthelme," *The New Republic,* May 2, 1964, 18-19.

page 247 *"sold well enough to earn out its modest advance":* Herman Gollob, *Me and Shakespeare: Adventures with the Bard* (New York: Doubleday, 2002), 170.

page 247 *"so personal and so elusive":* Roger Angell, letter to Donald Barthelme, August 18, 1964, Manuscripts and Archives Division, New York Public Library.

page 247 *"With* The New Yorker, *Don found himself playing in the big leagues":* Phillip Lopate, in a conversation with the author, October 29, 2004.

page 248 *"What helped Don the most hurt him the most":* Jerome Charyn, in a conversation with the author, June 14, 2004.

page 248 *"Barthelme was a good example":* Jerome Klinkowitz, *Keeping Literary Company: Working with Writers Since the Sixties* (Albany: State University of New York Press, 1998), 196.

page 248 *Don "sold out by publishing in* The New Yorker*":* Roger Angell, in a conversation with the author, May 27, 2004.

page 248 *"Don was very aware of celebrity":* Phillip Lopate, in a conversation with the author, October 29, 2004.

page 248 *"Q. Is purity quantifiable?":* Donald Barthelme, *City Life* (New York: Farrar, Straus and Giroux, 1970), 77.

page 249 *"Don perfectly matched* The New Yorker *tradition":* Phillip Lopate, in a conversation with the author, October 29, 2004.

page 249 *"[The popular] notion of the avant-garde":* J. D. O'Hara, "Donald Barthelme: The Art of Fiction LXVI," *Paris Review* 80 (1981): 187.

page 249 *"Roger was (and still is)":* Mark Mirsky, in his remembrance of Robert Creeley, posted at conjunctions.com/creeleytribute.htm.

29. Copenhagen

page 250 *"get [his] money for the day":* This and subsequent quotes from "Can We Talk" are from Donald Barthelme, *Unspeakable Practices, Unnatural Acts* (New York: Farrar, Straus and Giroux, 1968), 103-106.

pages 250-251 *"Now I would know better"* to *"One of the things that makes good fiction":* Lynn Nesbit, in a conversation with the author, July 30, 2007.

page 251 *"He called and invited me for a drink"* to *"Either he would cook":* Renata Adler, *Gone: The Last Days of The New Yorker* (New York: Simon & Schuster, 1999), 78.

page 251 *"triumph":* This and subsequent quotes from "The Police Band" are from Barthelme, *Unspeakable Practices, Unnatural Acts,* 73-76.

page 252 *"gigantic with gin":* This and subsequent quotes from "A Picture History of the War" are from ibid., 131-144.

page 252 *"an angry man dragg[ing] his father along the ground":* Gertrude Stein, *The Making of Americans,* in *Selected Writings of Gertrude Stein,* ed. Carl Van Vechten (New York: Vintage Books, 1972), 261.

page 253 *commas that "tiptoed into 'The Police Band'":* Roger Angell, letter to Donald Barthelme, August 26, 1964, Manuscripts and Archive Division, New York Public Library.

page 253 *"travel because he 'had not been anywhere'":* Helen Moore Barthelme, *Donald Barthelme: The Genesis of a Cool Sound* (College Station: Texas A & M University Press, 2001), 151.

page 253 *"get away from Lynn":* Roger Angell, in a conversation with the author, December 6, 2006.

page 253 *"I was ready to have children"* to *"Anyway, he and my friend Carol":* Lynn Nesbit, in a conversation with the author, July 30, 2007.

page 254 *"He was vacationing in Europe":* Anne Barthelme, in a conversation with the author, June 19, 2004.

pages 254–255 *"small but pleasant flat"* to *"a girl named Birgit":* Helen Moore Barthelme, *Donald Barthelme,* 153–155.

page 255 *"I've met this crazy Danish lady"* to *"ethereal, she was beautiful":* Anne Barthelme,

in a conversation with the author, June 19, 2004.

page 256 *"I got letters from him":* Lynn Nesbit, in a conversation with the author, July 30, 2007.

30. Uprisings

page 257 *"Edward put his hands on Pia's breasts":* This and subsequent quotes from "Edward and Pia" are from Donald Barthelme, *Unspeakable Practices, Unnatural Acts* (New York: Farrar, Straus and Giroux, 1968), 77–88.

page 257 *"Please do not confuse my fiction with my life":* This and all subsequent quotes in this chapter from the correspondence between Donald Barthelme and Roger Angell in December 1964 and during 1965 are from the letters in the Manuscripts and Archives Division, New York Public Library.

page 257 *"gray and dismal"; "hordes of Indians and Frenchmen and Italians":* Helen Moore Barthelme, *Donald Barthelme: The Genesis of a Cool Sound* (College Station: Texas A & M University Press, 2001), 154.

pages 258–259 *"soft-footed in"* to *"no other Intelligence":* ibid.

page 261 *"long struggles":* Roger Angell, letter to Lynn Nesbit, February 10, 1965, Manuscripts and Archives Division, New York Public Library.

page 262 *"emotionally important":* "Interview with Charles Ruas and Judith Sherman, 1975," in *Not-Knowing: The Essays and Interviews,* ed. Kim Herzinger (New York: Random House, 1997), 231.

page 262 *"We defended the city as best we could":* This and subsequent quotes from the "The Indian Uprising" are from Barthelme, *Unspeakable Practices, Unnatural Acts,* 3–12.

page 263 *"civilization" fighting "savages":* See, for example, Walter Evans, "Comanches and Civilization in Donald Barthelme's 'The Indian Uprising,'" *Arizona Quarterly* 42, no. 1 (1986): 45.

page 263 *Other critics read the story:* See, for example, Maclin Bocock, "'The Indian Uprising' or Donald Barthelme's Strange Object Covered with Fur," *Fiction International* 4, no. 5 (1975): 134–145.

page 263 *Other readers have noted:* See, for example, John Domini, "Donald Barthelme: The Modernist Uprising," *Southwest Review* 75, no. 2 (1990): 95–112.

page 264 *"meant . . . disembowelling"* the old city: Baron Georges-Eugène Haussmann quoted in T. J. Clark, *The Painting of Modern Life* (Princeton, New Jersey: Princeton University Press, 1984), 39.

page 264 *"The Savages of Cooper":* Paul Feval quoted in Shelley Rice, *Parisian Views* (Cambridge, Massachusetts: MIT Press, 1997), 75.

page 264 *"without turnings, without chance perspectives":* Clark, *The Painting of Modern Life,* 35.

page 265 *"poisonous breath of civilization":* Paul Lafargue, *The Right to Be Lazy* (1883; reprint, Chicago: Charles H. Kerr Publishing Company, 1975), 31.

page 265 *"The white men are landing!":* Arthur Rimbaud, "Mauvais Sang," in *A Season in Hell and the Drunken Boat,* trans. Louise Varèse (New York: New Directions, 1961), 19.

page 265 *"Oh that clown band":* Donald Barthelme, *Forty Stories* (New York: Putnam, 1987), 232.

pages 265–266 *"overturned carriages,"; "prevent enemy forces from circulating":* Gustave Paul Cluseret, *Memoires du général Cluseret,* volume 2 (Paris: Jules Lévy, 1887), 274, 287.

page 266 *"make conscious the unconscious tendencies":* Kristin Ross, *The Emergence of Social Space: Rimbaud and the Paris Commune* (Minneapolis: University of Minnesota Press, 1988), 38–39.

page 266 *"drawing-room fictions"* to *"in command of the situation":* Philip Rahv, *Essays on Literature and Politics,* ed. Arabel J. Porter and Andrew J. Drosin (Boston: Houghton Mifflin, 1978), 3–5. Rahv's essay "Paleface and Redskin" first appeared in *The Kenyon Review* 1, no. 3 (1939).

page 267 *"vanguard writer":* Harold Rosenberg, "The Stockade Syndrome" in *Location* 1, no. 1 (1963): 5.

page 267 *Don's grammatical battles:* At one point in the story, Don's narrator "nonevaluate[s]" language "as "Korzybski instructed." This reference grounds the story, in part, in a specific theory of grammar that is linked to military violence.

Alfred Korzybski (pronounced *Kashibski*) was born in Poland in 1879. In World War I, he joined the Russian army, where he served as a battlefield intelligence officer. Later, he claimed that his theory of language was an outgrowth of his experience of war. "My military experiences gave me a very serious insight into . . . those endless historical disasters which have beset mankind . . . and sharpened my awareness of the helplessness of the old evaluations . . . of the 'nature of man,' " he said.

According to Korzybski, our "old evaluations" are based on false assumptions enforced by language, whose grammatical structures are too limited to encompass reality's complexities. The human nervous system is multidimensional, multidirectional, and involves emotional, neurological, semantic, and behavioral responses to the world. Yet language is stuck in the limited cause and effect of the subject-predicate form; thus, it reduces the world to artificial categories.

The gap between reality and our false linguistic view of it creates "semantic phantoms" with a "savage magic" to confound and disrupt our lives, and add to our "fears and worries." Korzybski said that "many symptoms such as some . . . 'sex' disorders . . . migraines, [and] alcoholism . . . have a neuro-semantic and neuro-linguistic origin."

The only way to ward off these "phantoms" is to "reject cause and effect." Cause and effect is "unnatural" and not at all "similar to the structure of the world." We must learn to embrace the "un-speakable." (Don included "The Indian Uprising" in a collection entitled *Unspeakable Practices, Unnatural Acts.* This title echoes a speech in Shakespeare's *Hamlet,* as well as Korzybski.)

If we do not "part company" with cause and effect, we will "continue in the prevailing chaos," Korzybski said. We must "non-evaluate" the old standards, and appreciate the world's "asymmetrical relations." We must adopt a new language that embraces the "infinite velocity of nervous impulses [which] . . . spread instantaneously in no time."

Accepting Korzybski's challenge, Don wrote, "Strings of language extend in every direction to bind the world into a rushing, ribald whole."

Korzybski noted that, more than other peoples, the "white race" will have trouble accepting this new language, because it has invested so much in falsely "logical" structures.

At the end of "The Indian Uprising," Don's narrator stares into the "savage black eyes" of phantomlike Comanches as an apocalyptic rain falls over "neat rows of houses in the subdivisions" (an image reminiscent of the storm that ends *The Waste Land*).

See Alfred Korzybski, *Manhood of Humanity* (Lakeville, Connecticut: International Non-Aristotelian Library Publishing Company, 1929), v-vi; *Science and Sanity* (1933; reprint, Lakeville, Connecticut: International Non-Aristotelian Library Publishing Company, 1958), 198-199, xxxvii; *Time-Binding* (Lakeville, Connecticut: Institute of General Semantics, 1949), 1; *Science and Sanity,* 218, 59, xxxvi, 192.

page 269 only *"promising young writer":* Tom Wolfe, *Hooking Up* (New York: Farrar, Straus and Giroux, 2000), 278.

page 269 *"I am not well":* This and subsequent quotes from "The Game" are from Donald Barthelme, *Unspeakable Practices, Unnatural Acts,* 109-115.

31. A Village Homecoming

page 272 *"lease is up on the apartment":* This and subsequent quotes from Don's letters to Helen Barthelme and the Barthelme family are from Helen Moore Barthelme, *Donald Barthelme: The Genesis of a Cool Sound* (College Station: Texas A & M University Press, 2001), 156-159.

page 273 *"wrong, wrong, wrong"; "I don't think you have to do this":* Helen Moore Barthelme, *Donald Barthelme,* 157.

page 273 *"I am tired of tiny stories however beautiful":* Donald Barthelme, letter to Roger Angell, undated (1965), Manuscripts and Archives Division, New York Public Library.

page 273 *"I told him to get rid of the kid":* Herman Gollob, in a conversation with the author, April 19, 2007.

page 273 *"We are now in a three-way snit":* Donald Barthelme, letter to Roger Angell, undated (1965), Manuscripts and Archives Division, New York Public Library.

page 273 *"I am going to be 45"; "You are writing so much and so well":* Roger Angell, letter to Donald Barthelme, June 1, 1965, Manuscripts and Archives Division, New York Public Library.

page 274 *"If you don't like the laparotomy":* Donald Barthelme, letter to William Maxwell, August 11, 1965, Manuscripts and Archives Division, New York Public Library.

page 274 *"against future work"; "[Don's] indebtedness":* Roger Angell, letter to Lynn Nesbit, October 4, 1965, Manuscripts and Archives Division, New York Public Library.

page 274 *"manner was like that of a child"; "may suddenly step into the street"; " 'something' happened to her in Denmark":* Helen Moore Barthelme, *Donald Barthelme,* 161, 172.

page 274 *"Edward walked out of the room":* Donald Barthelme, *Unspeakable Practices, Unnatural Acts* (New York: Farrar, Straus and Giroux, 1968), 80-81.

page 275 *"I am sorry that I did not treat"* to *"house is out of the question, really":* Helen Moore Barthelme, *Donald Barthelme,* 158.

page 275 *"I feel [happy] about nothing":* Donald Barthelme, letter to Lynn Nesbit, undated (1965); letter courtesy of Lynn Nesbit.

page 276 *"Otherwise I will have to adopt it later":* Helen Moore Barthelme, *Donald Barthelme,* 159.

page 276 *"We both were reluctant":* ibid.

page 276 *"You'll see that it's not* Indian Uprising*"* to *"I gave him the honorarium":* Herman Gollob, *Me and Shakespeare: Adventures with the Bard* (New York: Doubleday, 2002), 170.

page 276 *Birgit was about to pop:* Herman Gollob, in a conversation with the author, April 19, 2007.

page 276 *The Manhattan to which Don returned:* For details regarding events in New York at this time, I have drawn upon information in James Trager, *The New York Chronology* (New York: HarperResource, 2003), 657–662.

pages 276–277 *"quiet block"* to *"The war had come home":* Roger Angell, "New York, 1967," *The New Yorker,* June 12, 2006, 54.

page 277 *"When a child is born":* This and subsequent quotes from "See the Moon?" are from

Donald Barthelme, *Unspeakable Practices, Unnatural Acts,* 160–170.

page 278 *"there would be no doubt how electric technology shapes":* Marshall McLuhan, "McLuhan: A Dialogue," in *McLuhan: Hot and Cool,* ed. Gerald Emanuel Stearn (Toronto: Signet Books, 1969), 272.

page 278 *"could have been an artist's idea":* Billy Klüver, cited in Catherine Morris, *9 Evenings Reconsidered: Art, Theatre and Engineering, 1966* (Cambridge, Massachusetts: *MIT List Visual Center,* 2006), 32.

page 278 *"fused glance":* This and subsequent quotes from "City Life" are from Donald Barthelme, *Sixty Stories* (New York: Putnam, 1981), 158–159.

page 279 *"The more you create village conditions":* McLuhan, in *McLuhan,* ed. Stearn, 272.

page 279 *"golden time of freedom":* Robert Lowell, cited in Jonathan Raban, "September 11: The View from the West," *The New York Review of Books* 52, no. 14 (2005): 4.

page 279 *"You have a lovely baby":* Roger Angell, letter to Donald Barthelme, January or late December [1965], Manuscripts and Archives Division, New York Public Library.

32. *Snow White* and the Summer of Love

page 284 *"She is a tall dark beauty":* Donald Barthelme, "Snow White," *The New Yorker,* February 18, 1967, 38.

page 285 *The city felt livelier:* For background detail, I have drawn on information in James Trager, *The New York Chronology* (New York: HarperResource, 2003), 665–670.

page 286 *"One reason that Don could be so spare":* Kirkpatrick Sale, "A Tribute to Donald Barthelme," *Poets and Writers Magazine,* March/April 1990, 10.

page 286 *"using the skills I had taught her":* This and subsequent Kirkpatrick Sale quotes are from E-mails to the author, May 16 and May 25, 2004.

page 287 *"[She is] a wonderful writer and troublemaker":* Donald Barthelme, quoted on the book jacket of Grace Paley, *Later the Same Day* (New York: Farrar, Straus and Giroux, 1985).

page 287 *"I was so interested in my friends":* Grace Paley quoted in Judith Arcana, *Grace Paley's Life Stories* (Urbana and Chicago: University of Illinois Press, 1993), 92.

page 288 *"He was in his life and work a citizen":* Grace Paley, *Just As I Thought* (New York: Farrar, Straus and Giroux, 1998), 235.

page 288 *"He was drinking":* Lynn Nesbit, in a conversation with the author, July 30, 2007.

page 288 *"free-hanging," "frivolous," and "gentle":* This and subsequent quotes from "The Balloon" are from Donald Barthelme, *Unspeakable Practices, Unnatural Acts* (New York: Farrar, Straus and Giroux, 1968), 15–22.

Don's balloon is perhaps the most charming and intriguing ekphrastic article since Keats's Grecian urn. Ekphrasis is a verbal description of visual art, an attempt to convey one artistic experience in terms of another. An anomaly like this, placed unexpectedly in our path, has the power to "mislocate" us, releasing us from routine—one of art's intended effects. Objects of contemplation also focus our intellect and emotion, and help us fully experience the immediate moment. In Western literature, Keats's urn and Achilles' shield are the most famous examples of ekphrasis. Just as Don's balloon nudges the edges of skyscrapers, he sets his story bouncing off literary cornerstones: the epic, Romanticism, and Poe's Gothic tales, such as "The Balloon-Hoax." But ekphrasis has its enemies, as Don well knew. Writers "should not regard the limitations of painting"—mere depictions of objects—"as beauties in their own art," Gotthold

Lessing wrote in *Laocoön* (1766), consigning ekphrasis minor status, at best, in literature's toolbox. By embracing ekphrasis, Don elevated a single, arguably secondary literary strategy to the very center of "The Balloon." Like Daumier, who pursued the rather odd practice of lithography while his peers whipped out battle paintings, Don—perversely and obstinately—appears to tinker with trifles. But if we pay heed, we begin to see the usefulness of the "mere," the marginal, and the unexpected as a way of refreshing art, looking askance, viewing things anew.

page 289 *"greasy press of people"*: T. J. Clark, *The Painting of Modern Life* (Princeton, New Jersey: Princeton University Press, 1984), 64-65.

page 289 *"traveler who [had] arrived yesterday"*: Nadar, "Le Dessus et le dessous de Paris," in *Paris Guide,* ed. Corrine Verdet (Paris: Editions La Découverte, 1983), 171-172.

page 290 *"The crush of spectators"*: Clark, *The Painting of Modern Life,* 83.

page 290 *"Observations" about the painting*: This and subsequent quotes about *Olympia* are cited in ibid., 83, 94, 118.

page 291 an object *"coming over the trees"* to *"solitary"*: Virginia Woolf, *Mrs. Dalloway* (1925; reprints, New York: Harcourt Brace Jovanavich, 1953), 29-33.

page 291 *"which is good news for all hands"*: Roger Angell, letter to Donald Barthelme, January 28, 1966, Manuscripts and Archives Division, New York Public Library.

page 291 *"I believe that Mr. Barthelme is far and away the most intelligent"*: Roger Angell, letter to the John Simon Guggenheim Foundation, undated (probably fall 1965), Manuscripts and Archives Division, New York Public Library.

page 292 *"BABY BOW YEE"*: Donald Barthelme, *Snow White* (New York: Atheneum, 1967), 18.

page 292 *"an older Bob Dylan"*; *"I read a lot of Albert Camus"*: M. G. Stephens, "Conrad's List," *Boston Review,* December 2003/January 2004; posted at www.bostonreview.net/BR28.6/stephens.html.

page 292 *"Perhaps there are certain ages"*: Susan Sontag, *Against Interpretation* (New York: Dell, 1966), 50.

page 292 *"In the midst of so much that is true"*: Barthelme, *Snow White,* 62.

page 293 *"The thought of this immense work"*: ibid., 11.

page 293 *"We were so unconscious, so unaware of that war"*: Grace Paley quoted in Arcana, *Grace Paley's Life Stories,* 60.

page 293 *"This was an exciting day around here"*: Roger Angell, letter to Donald Barthelme, October 26, 1966, Manuscripts and Archives Division, New York Public Library.

page 293 *"Here's that check"*: Roger Angell, letter to Donald Barthelme, December 8, 1966, Manuscripts and Archives Division, New York Public Library.

page 293 *"correct poornesses in the storyline"*: Donald Barthelme, letter to Roger Angell, undated (December 1965), Manuscripts and Archives Division, New York Public Library.

page 293 *"a man about whom nothing is known"*: This and subsequent quotes from the novel are from Barthelme, *Snow White,* 13, 19, 31, 178-181.

page 294 *"his own love life"* to *"Years later, one of these friends"*: Helen Moore Barthelme, *Donald Barthelme: The Genesis of a Cool Sound* (College Station: Texas A & M University Press, 2001), 164-165.

page 294 *"the beauty of . . . a painting by Jasper Johns"*; *"feeling (or sensation)"*: Sontag, *Against Interpretation,* 293.

page 294 *"This album is a whole world"*: See "Talk of the Town," *The New Yorker,* June 24, 1967, 22-23.

page 294 *"transformation of [its] function"*; *"Art today is a new kind of instrument"*: Sontag, *Against Interpretation,* 293.

page 295 *"It's not my favorite book"*: Donald Barthelme. Jo Brans, " 'Embracing the World," in *Not-Knowing: The Essays and Interviews,* ed. Kim Herzinger (New York: Random House, 1997), 296.

pages 295-296 *"Writing a novel consists of failing, for me"*; *[T]he story of Snow White and the Seven Dwarves"*; *"[A]ll of [the] people in this book"*: "Interview with Charles Ruas and Judith Sherman, 1975," in *Not-Knowing: The Essays and Interviews,* ed. Herzinger, 224, 255-257.

33. Drowning

page 298 *"splendid writer"*: Jack Kroll, "Wising Up," *Newsweek,* May 22, 1967, 106.

page 298 *"the most perversely gifted writer"*: Webster Schott, "A Sludge-Pump Novel: Fractured Fiction," *Life,* May 26, 1967, 6.

page 298 *"Donald Barthelme's work creates the impression"*: Unsigned article, "Come Back, Brothers Grimm," *Time,* May 26, 1967, 96.

page 299 *"handful of American writers"*: Richard Gilman, "Barthelme's Fairy Tale," *The New Republic,* June 3, 1967, 30.

page 299 *"niggardly advertising campaign"*; *"demanded an extravagant advance"*: Herman Gollob, *Me and Shakespeare: Adventures with the Bard* (New York: Doubleday, 2002), 170.

page 299 *"[I]t seems to me a frightful waste":* Hubert Ryan, letter to Roger Angell, December 2, 1968, Manuscripts and Archives Division, New York Public Library.

page 299 *"I told Mr. Barthelme about your letter":* Roger Angell, letter to Hubert Ryan, January 3, 1969, Manuscripts and Archives Division, New York Public Library.

page 300 *"garbage"; "The New Nonsense or Hysteria School":* Scott Elledge, *E. B. White: A Biography* (New York: W. W. Norton, 1984), 343-344.

page 300 *"It was tempestuous between them":* Anne Barthelme, in a conversation with the author, June 19, 2004.

page 300 *"I'll write a real letter":* Donald Barthelme, letter to Roger Angell, undated (1967), Manuscripts and Archives Division, New York Public Library.

page 300 *"I'm thinking of writing a long long story":* Donald Barthelme, letter to Roger Angell, June 19, 1967, Manuscripts and Archives Division, New York Public Library.

page 300 *"fat and happy"; "[Here's a] check":* Roger Angell, letter to Donald Barthelme, June 20, 1967, Manuscripts and Archives Division, New York Public Library.

pages 300-301 *"I wish he had been my father":* Helen Moore Barthelme, *Donald Barthelme,* 172.

page 301 *"I feel that I'm writing . . . piecemeal":* Donald Barthelme, letter to Roger Angell, undated (1968), Manuscripts and Archives Division, New York Public Library.

page 301 *"wonderful"; "infinitely more effective"; "makes [its] powerful point":* Roger Angell, letter to Donald Barthelme, March 15, 1967, Manuscripts and Archives Division, New York Public Library.

page 301 *"Our group is against the war":* Donald Barthelme, *Unspeakable Practices, Unnatural Acts* (New York: Farrar, Straus and Giroux, 1968), 51.

page 301 *"Endings are elusive"* to *"like a large blaring building":* Barthelme, ibid., 69.

page 301 *"Buy yourself a Trova toe"; "Incidentally, you are three legs up":* Roger Angell, letter to Donald Barthelme, January 25, 1967, Manuscripts and Archives Division, New York Public Library.

page 301 *"While this may not be one of your very best stories":* Roger Angell, letter to Donald Barthelme, February 28, 1968, Manuscripts and Archives Division, New York Public Library.

page 301 *"I assume the Arab-Israeli war":* Donald Barthelme, letter to Roger Angell, June 19, 1967, Manuscripts and Archives Division, New York Public Library.

page 302 *"He is neither abrupt":* This and subsequent quotes from "Robert Kennedy Saved from Drowning" are from Barthelme, *Unspeakable Practices, Unnatural Acts,* 35-47.

page 302 *"impotent and frustrated"; "upon which others projected their hopes and fears":* Evan Thomas, *Robert Kennedy: His Life* (New York: Simon & Schuster, 2000), 309, 343-344.

page 302 *"I never met Robert Kennedy":* Donald Barthelme, letter to Arthur Schlesinger, Jr., July 16, 1977, cited in Arthur Schlesinger, Jr., *Robert Kennedy and His Times* (Boston: Houghton Mifflin, 1978), 816.

page 303 *"What bothers [Shawn]":* William Maxwell, letter to Roger Angell, August 8, 1967, Manuscripts and Archives Division, New York Public Library.

page 303 *"I am afraid we are turning [this story] down":* Roger Angell, letter to Lynn Nesbit, August 30, 1967, Manuscripts and Archives Division, New York Public Library.

page 304 *"Barthelme's reputation was just getting underway"* to *"made my mind feel like it had been awakened":* Ted Solotaroff, "Don Barthelme," *Gulf Coast: A Journal of Literature and Art,* vol. 4, no. 1 (1991): 169-171.

page 304 *"I cannot account for [the] impulse":* Donald Barthelme, letter to Arthur Schlesinger, Jr., cited in Schlesinger, *Robert Kennedy and His Times,* 816.

page 304 *Jack Newfield: The Writer in Society: Donald Barthelme* (Houston: KUHT-TV, 1984).

page 305 *He wanted Robbins's full attention:* Patrick Samway, S. J., *Walker Percy: A Life* (Chicago: Loyola Press, 1999), 267.

page 305 *"gentleman publisher":* This and subsequent Roger Straus quotes are from Ian Parker, "Showboat," *The New Yorker,* April 8, 2002, 55-65.

page 306 *"Robbins was a man":* Michael Korda, *Another Life* (New York: Dell, 2000), 368-369.

page 306 *"Henry was hot-headed":* Lynn Nesbit, in a conversation with the author, August 14, 2007.

page 306 *"I remember his actual hurt and outrage":* Joan Didion, *After Henry* (New York: Simon & Schuster, 1992), 19.

page 306 *"I'm not mad at you"; "End of quarrel":* Gollob, *Me and Shakespeare,* 171.

page 306 *"Don was startled to hear my voice"* to *"In fact, I later realized":* Helen Moore Barthelme, *Donald Barthelme,* 160-161.

page 306 *In February 1968:* In the previous year, many artists and writers in New York had mobilized against the war. In the *New York Times* of January 29, 1967, a full-page ad announced the "[W]eek of the Angry Arts Against the War in Vietnam." Below the heading, smaller print explained that the "artists of New York [would] speak through their . . . work [this week] to dissociate themselves from U.S. policy." Scheduled events included a jazz concert "dedicated to draft-age boys"; "16-mm Earrings," a "Dance Protest" featuring Meredith Monk; "Broadway Dissents" by Alan Alda, Ruby Dee, and John Henry Faulk; shows by folk-rockers, filmmakers, and photographers; and literary readings by Grace Paley, Susan Sontag, and others. Among the Angry Arts sponsors, said the ad, were Philip Roth, Allen Ginsberg, and Donald Barthelme. The Week of the Angry Arts was the largest cultural protest in America since the antiwar parades of the 1940s. Poets moved in caravans across Manhattan, shouting their outraged lyrics; postering brigades plastered buildings with copies of *Guernica*-like lithographs; and a conductorless performance of Beethoven's *Eroica* was held at Town Hall to "symbolize the individual's responsibility for the brutality in Vietnam." Among the week's central events was one organized by Dore Ashton and Max Kozloff at New York University's Loeb Student Center to exhibit the *Collage of Indignation.* One hundred and fifty artists created this piece over a five-day period. Its contents included a coil of barbed wire, a draft card, and a rusty metal slab engraved with the words "Johnson Is a Murderer."

page 307 *"And let me speak to the yet unknowing world":* William Shakespeare, *Hamlet* (New York: Dover, 1992), 119.

page 307 *"an unspeakable and unnatural thing"; "You mean it made you feel guilty?":* Gollob, *Me and Shakespeare,* 171.

page 307 *"Kafka might well be":* Anatole Broyard, "Metaphors for Madnesses," *New York Times Book Review,* May 12, 1968, 7.

page 307 *"It is impossible to overpraise":* William Gass, "The Leading Edge of the Trash Phenomenon," *The New York Review of Books,* April 25, 1968, 6.

page 307 *"coarsening and souring":* Hilary Corke, "Whistling in a Gale," *The New Republic,* June 1, 1968, 35.

page 308 *"permanent contribution to our literature":* Alan Trachtenberg, "Mailer on the Steps of the Pentagon," *The Nation,* May 27, 1968, 701.

page 308 *"Donald Barthelme [is] relentlessly":* Calvin Bedient," No Pretense to Coherency," *The Nation,* May 27, 1968, 702–703.

page 308 *"Donald Barthelme has accomplished the work":* Earl Shorris, "Donald Barthelme's Illustrated Wordy-Gurdy," *Harper's,* January 1973, 92.

page 308 *"Here is a writer one wishes":* Jack Kroll, "The Comanches Are Here," *Newsweek,* May 6, 1968, 112.

34. The Politics of Exhaustion

page 309 *"disputatious student meeting":* Genêt [Janet Flanner], "Letter from Paris," *The New Yorker,* May 25, 1968, 77.

page 309 *slogans appeared; "an ever-growing bubble":* Angelo Quattrocchi and Tom Nairn, *The Beginning of the End* (1968; reprint, London: Verso Books, 1998), 17.

page 310 *tear gas wafting through the windows:* Mavis Gallant, "Reflections, the Events in May: A Paris Notebook," *The New Yorker,* September 14, 1968, 58–59.

page 310 *"has been the decisive week":* Genêt [Janet Flanner], "Letter from Paris, "*The New Yorker,* June 2, 1968,.

page 310 *"crack of authority":* This and subsequent quotes from "The Policemen's Ball" are from Donald Barthelme, *Sixty Stories* (New York: Putnam, 1981), 175–177.

page 310 *people's "everyday" lives:* See Henri Lefebvre, *Critique of Everyday Life,* trans. John Moore (London: Verso Books, 1991), xx. Don admitted suffering from an "American lack-of-languages," though he taught himself some French while stationed with the army in Korea. Lefebvre's book did not appear in English until 1991, but translated excerpts were widely avail-

able before that, as were parts of the Situationist International's writings.

page 311 *As Ronnie Butler wrote:* Ronnie Butler, *Balzac and the French Revolution* (London: Crown Helm, 1983), 242–248.

page 311 *"Mother, have you noticed":* This and subsequent quotes from "Eugénie Grandet" are from Barthelme, *Sixty Stories,* 236–242.

page 311 *"grossly misperceived":* Donald Barthelme, *Forty Stories* (New York: Putnam, 1987), 211.

page 311 *"Vagabonds [are] always ready":* Theodore Homburg, *Études sur la Vagabondage* (Paris: Forestier, 1880), 243.

page 312 *"Rimbaud's ... resistance to work":* Kristin Ross, *The Emergence of Social Space: Rimbaud and the Paris Commune* (Minneapolis: University of Minnesota Press, 1988), 20, 59.

page 312 *a group of dissident intellectuals called the Situationist International:* The group called themselves, first, the Lettrists, then the Situationist International. On principle, they refused steady jobs and sought to turn daily life into a "mobile space of play." From the mid-1950s until the 1970s, they published a series of newsletters— *Potlatch, Situationist International*—in which they outlined their views of the "spectacle" and offered strategies for puncturing its facade. The spectacle was the vision created by the combined apparatus of the media, schools, economics, and urban planning, which, hand in hand with governments, allowed producers of commercial products to control citizen's desires. In *The Society of the Spectacle,* published in 1967, Guy Debord laid out the Situationist argument that life no longer holds "free choices" and "is subject, no longer to the natural order, but to a pseudo-nature constructed by means of alienated labor." The individual must resist this rigid ordering, must seek chance perspectives, must pursue what Rimbaud called the "rational disordering of all the senses."

Debord worked with Henri Lefebvre on an appreciation of the 1871 Paris Commune. In a coauthored article, they praised the communards for reseizing Paris after the corrosive effects of Haussmannization. Debord and Lefebvre said that everyday life—what they also called "social space"—fell firmly under capital's control during the nineteenth century in Europe, when workers migrated to urban areas, and city planners arranged work centers and living quarters in ways that made these areas easy to manage. This involved eliminating chance perspectives, turning the avenues into straight lines, and, above all, separating industrial labor and domesticity, fracturing communities to make them dependent on centralized government.

Lefebvre and the Situationists proposed reorganizing social space as a way of resisting the spectacle: taking trips "with no destination, diverted arbitrarily," breaking free "from routes imposed" by traffic patterns, zoning laws, work routines. Debord saw the city as a carnival, loosed from "functionalism" and the "immediately useful"—to him, the urban environment was a "terrain of participatory games." When function falls away, and people find beauty in the everyday, the spectacle can be shaken. This was the vision, passed from Lefebvre to the Situationist International, that erupted in the streets of Paris in May 1968. As Harold Rosenberg put it, in May 1968 a "trumpet blast" of hope based in imagination and "aroused desire" broke the "power trance." Art tumbled into the streets.

Cited above: *"free choices"; "is subject no longer"*: Guy Debord, *The Society of the Spectacle,* trans. Donald Nicholson-Smith (1967; reprint, New York: Zone Books, 1994), 110–111; *taking trips "with no destination"*: The ideas are Guy Debord's, but the wording here is from Michele Bernstein, "Derive by the Mile" in *Potlatch* 9 (August 31, 1954): 11; *a "trumpet blast" of "hope"*: Harold Rosenberg, *The De-Definition of Art* (Chicago: University of Chicago Press, 1972), 53.

page 312 *"Sometimes I wish we were a purely literary magazine"*: Roger Angell, letter to Donald Barthelme, May 7, 1968, Manuscripts and Archives Division, New York Public Library.

page 312 *"explanatory note"; "I thought you might want to look at it again"*: Donald Barthelme, letter to Roger Angell, undated (May 1968), Manuscripts and Archives Division, New York Public Library.

35. City Life (I)

page 314 *"My father made a wonderful toy"*: This and subsequent Anne Barthelme quotes are from a conversation with the author, June 19, 2004.

page 315 *"used to howl at the moon"*: See "Moondog Biography," posted at www.geocities .com/moondogmadness/biography.html.

page 315 *"This city!"*: This and subsequent quotes from early drafts of "City Life" are from Donald Barthelme, "City Life," drafts, Special Collections and Archives, University of Houston Libraries.

page 315 *one of the few places in the city that offered a view of the sunset*: Noted in Grace Paley, "Life and Literature in a City That Speaks Volumes," *New York Times Book Review,* September 25, 1998, back page.

page 316 *"new image"; "I wanted the dog's face"*: Donald Barthelme, *Sixty Stories* (New York: Putnam, 1981), 166–167.

page 316 *On a Monday afternoon in early June 1968*: For more on the Andy Warhol shooting, see Ultra Violet [Isabella Collin Dufresne], *Famous for Fifteen Minutes: My Years with Andy Warhol* (San Diego and New York: Harcourt, Brace, Jovanovich, 1988), 168, 179.

page 316 *"[M]aleness is a deficiency disease"*: Valerie Solanas, *SCUM Manifesto* (London: Verso, 2004), 35–36, 66.

page 316 *"[T]he kid . . . want[s] Daddy's approval"*: ibid., 43–44.

page 316 *"dignity and hysteria"*: Ernest Trova quoted in "The Uses of Ingenuity," *Time,* January 6, 1967, 76.

page 317 *"I'd often hear Don typing"*: This and subsequent Sale quotes are from an E-mail to the author, May 16, 2004.

page 318 *"H. and S. came for supper"*: Barthelme, *Sixty Stories,* 160.

page 318 *"Sunday. We took the baby"*: Barthelme, *Sixty Stories,* 161.

page 318 *"sort of, partly":* Roger Angell, letter to Donald Barthelme, January 14, 1969, Manuscripts and Archives Division, New York Public Library.

page 318 *"I . . . enclose an invitation":* Roger Angell, letter to Donald Barthelme, May 29, 1969, Manuscripts and Archives Division, New York Public Library.

page 319 *"The wax is gone from the floor":* Donald Barthelme, "Blushes," Manuscripts and Archivess Division, New York Public Library.

page 319 *The version of "The Falling Dog":* All quotes from the first version of the story are from Donald Barthelme, "The Falling Dog," *The New Yorker,* August 3, 1968, 28-29.

page 319 *As it appeared two years later:* Quotes from the revised version of "The Falling Dog" are from Donald Barthelme, *City Life* (New York: Farrar, Straus and Giroux, 1970), 41-48.

pages 319-320 *"The world enters [our] work":* Donald Barthelme, "Not-Knowing," in *Not-Knowing: The Essays and Interviews,* ed. Kim Herzinger (New York: Random House, 1997), 21.

page 320 *"dynamic instability":* This and subsequent Ehrenzweig quotes are from Anton Ehrenzweig, *The Hidden Order of Art* (Berkeley: University of California Press, 1967), 59, 102-103, 172-173, 179, 182, 186, 260.

page 320 *"under the control of his unconscious":* This and subsequent quotes from "Dostoevsky and Parricide" are from Sigmund Freud, *Character and Culture,* ed. Philip Rieff (New York: Collier, 1963), 274-293.

page 321 *"Don would drink himself into some state of inebriation":* Karen Kennerly, in a conversation with the author, May 29, 2004.

page 321 *"Why do I desire with all my heart":* Barthelme, *Sixty Stories,* 114-115.

page 321 *As the critic Michael Zeitlin points*

out: Michael Zeitlin, "Father-Murder and Father-Rescue: The Post-Freudian Allegories of Donald Barthelme," posted at www.jessamyn .com/barth/freud.html.

page 322 *"There can be no doubt that a birth fantasy":* Karl Abraham, "Father-Murder and Father-Rescue in the Fantasies of Neurotics," in *The Psychoanalytic Reader: An Anthology of Essential Papers with Critical Introductions,* ed. Robert Fleiss (London: Hogarth Press, 1950), 303-304.

page 322 *"not unlike my own name":* Barthelme, *Sixty Stories,* 115.

page 322 *"[T]he son kills the father in fantasy":* Zeitlin, "Father-Murder and Father-Rescue."

page 322 *"All [the son's] instincts":* Sigmund Freud, "A Special Type of Object Choice Made By Men," in *The Standard Edition of the Complete Psychological Works of Sigmund Freud,* trans. and ed. James Strachey, vol. 11 (London: Hogarth Press, 1957), 173.

page 323 *"The holdings of the Tolstoy Museum":* Donald Barthelme, *Forty Stories* (New York: Putnam, 1987), 109.

page 324 *"there is a Tolstoy Museum somewhere in Russia":* Roger Angell, letter to Mrs. William McCutcheon, June 11, 1969, Manuscripts and Archives Division, New York Public Library.

page 324 *"Donald Barthelme's absurd article":* Alexandra L. Tolstoy, letter to *The New Yorker,* June 9, 1969, Manuscripts and Archives Division, New York Public Library.

page 324 *"I can assure you":* Roger Angell, letter to Alexandra L. Tolstoy, June 25, 1969, Manuscripts and Archives Division, New York Public Library.

page 324 *"reinvent[ed] the harpsichord"; "One of the most remarkable accomplishments":* Thomas Hess, "A Tale of Two Cities," *Location* 1, no. 2 (1964): 40.

36. City Life (II)

page 325 *"At the Tolstoy Museum we sat and wept":* Donald Barthelme, *City Life* (New York: Farrar, Straus, and Giroux, 1970), 49.

page 326 *"Do you believe that this machine":* This and subsequent quotes from "The Explanation" are from ibid., 75-87.

page 326 *"a common journalistic device":* Jerome Klinkowitz, *Donald Barthelme: An Exhibition* (Durham, North Carolina: Duke University Press, 1991), 62.

page 326 *"pure feeling":* Kasemir Malevich quoted in David S. Rubin, *Black and White Are Colors: Paintings of the 1950s-1970s* (Claremont, California: Galleries of the Claremont Colleges, 1979), 8.

page 327 *"relation appears":* Wallace Stevens, *The Collected Poems of Wallace Stevens* (New York: Alfred A. Knopf, 1975), 215.

page 327 *Schlegel's "very obscene book":* This and subsequent Kierkegaard quotes are from Søren Kierkegaard, *The Concept of Irony,* trans. Lee M. Capel (Bloomington: Indiana University Press, 1965), 302-316.

page 327 *"I love my irony":* This and subsequent quotes from "Kierkegaard Unfair to Schlegel" are from Barthelme, *City Life,* 89-100.

page 328 *"These / Two things are one":* Stevens, *The Collected Poems of Wallace Stevens,* 215.

page 329 *a lingering and mysterious emotional power:* In the early 1970s, Harrison Starr tried to make a film of "The Explanation." Roger Angell, dressed in a suit, represented the "voice" of order, and Starr represented the forces of freedom. Trestles were laid beneath the surface of a small boat pond in Central Park. Angell and Starr rowed out to the trestles, where they shot a scene in which they appeared to be walking on water. Angell recalls being spotted by Lillian Ross, who called out to him, "Roger? Is that you? I didn't know you had a film career!" Afterward, Starr proclaimed the film a failure, and tucked the footage away in a box.

page 329 *"our best writers"* to *he "undertakes larger, more positive projects":* Morris Dickstein, review of *City Life, New York Times Book Review,* April 27, 1970, 1.

page 330 *"Barthelme's subject in* City Life*":* Peter Berek, "Disenchanted Symbols," *The Nation,* May 25, 1970, 630.

page 330 *"Mr. Barthelme has accepted":* Richard Schickel, review of *City Life, Harper's,* May 1970, 130.

page 330 *"it will be a while yet":* Guy Davenport, "A Master of Unstuck Prose," *Life,* May 8, 1970, 19.

page 330 *"Year's Best books": Time,* January 4, 1971, 76.

page 330 *"Barthelme is a genius":* Unsigned article, *Time,* May 25, 1970, 108.

page 330 *"campaign"; "For all the acclaim"; "I will . . . tell Mr. Barthelme":* Roger Angell, letters to Henry T. Blasso, July 11, 1969, and July 28, 1969, Manuscripts and Archives Division, New York Public Library.

page 331 *"What I like about 'Paraguay'":* Donald Barthelme, "On 'Paraguay,'" in *Not-Knowing: The Essays and Interviews,* ed. Kim Herzinger (New York: Random House, 1997), 56-57.

page 331 *"[T]he sentence is":* Barthelme, *City Life,* 118.

page 331 *"Elsa and Ramona entered the complicated city":* This and subsequent quotes from "City Life" are from ibid., 151-173.

page 332 *"systematic refusal":* See André Breton's texts on Surrealism in Charles Harrison and Paul Wood, ed., *Art in Theory: 1900-1990* (Oxford: Blackwell, 1992), 432-439, 440-450, 526-529.

37. Freaked Out

page 334 *"Donald Barthelme will quit writing":* This and subsequent quotes from Schickel's article are from Richard Schickel, "Freaked Out on Barthelme," *New York Times Magazine,* August 16, 1970, 14.

page 335 *"It is not true that Kafka wanted Brod":* Donald Barthelme, draft of "Kierkegaard Unfair to Schlegel," Special Collections and Archives, University of Houston Libraries.

page 336 *"I often think not enough attention is paid to dead writers":* Donald Barthelme, untitled speech, 1974, Special Collections and Archives, University of Houston Libraries.

page 336 *"I've asked for a new black square"* to *"33 lines":* Donald Barthelme, note to Henry Robbins, undated, Farrar, Straus and Giroux records, Manuscripts and Archives Division, New York Public Library.

page 337 *"Why didn't we think of pricing it at 50 cents":* Donald Barthelme, note to Farrar, Straus and Giroux, undated Farrar, Straus and Giroux records, Manuscripts and Archives Division, New York Public Library.

page 337 *"sheet art":* Donald Barthelme, *City Life* (New York: Farrar, Straus and Giroux, 1970), 23.

page 338 *"How is my car?":* ibid., 86.

page 338 *"In my mind, the basal-cell malignancy":* This and subsequent quotes from "Departures" are from Donald Barthelme, *Forty Stories* (New York: Putnam, 1987), 88-95.

page 339 *"handsomely done":* Roger Angell, letter to Donald Barthelme, May 20, 1971, Manuscripts and Archives Division, New York Public Library.

page 339 *"debt ceiling":* Roger Angell, letter to Donald Barthelme, June 2, 1971, Manuscripts and Archives Division, New York Public Library.

page 339 *"It was a good age":* Donald Barthelme, *Sixty Stories* (New York: Putnam, 1981), 267.

page 340 *"I have reached an age":* Donald Barthelme, draft of "City Life," Special Collections and Archives, University of Houston Libraries.

38. Slightly Irregular

page 341 *"more freedom":* This and subsequent comments by Harrison Starr and by his wife, Sandra, are from a conversation with the author, December 29, 2006.

page 342 *"I think Dad knew":* This and subsequent Anne Barthelme quotes are from a conversation with the author, June 19, 2004.

page 343 *"tense":* This and subsequent Marianne Frisch quotes are from Marianne Frisch, "What to Do Next, Donald Barthelme," trans. Tom Reiss, *Gulf Coast: A Journal of Literature and Art,* vol. 4, no. 1 (1991): 114-115.

page 344 *"'Well...' I ask cordially":* Donald Barthelme, *Forty Stories* (New York: Putnam, 1987), 94.

page 344 *"INGRES poster":* Max Frisch, *Montauk* (New York: Harvest/HBJ, 1976), 138.

page 344 *"But where are you today?":* ibid., 113.

page 344 *"I had been preoccupied with the world":* ibid., 37.

page 344 *"admired":* ibid., 83.

page 344 *"is afraid of feelings":* ibid., 9.

page 344 *"rose to his feet":* ibid., 85.

page 344 *"I lived then in ... a brownstone":* Renata Adler, *Gone: The Last Days of The New Yorker* (New York: Simon & Schuster, 1999), 79.

page 345 *"Write five pages and make every sentence golden":* Karen Kennerly, in a conversation with the author, December 3, 2005.

page 345 *"Don had the golden ear of all time":* This and subsequent Karen Kennerly quotes are from conversations with the author, May 29, 2004, and June 19, 2004.

page 347 *"I've thought of you mostly with love and affection":* This and subsequent quotes regarding the time Helen and Don spent together in Houston are from Helen Moore Barthelme, *Donald Barthelme: The Genesis of a Cool Sound* (College Station: Texas A & M University Press, 2001), 166-171.

page 348 *"Donald was extremely fond of women":* Walter Abish, in a conversation with the author, February 16, 2005.

39. Hithering Thithering

page 349 *The "book was dictated by the pictures":* This and subsequent Barthelme quotes about the book are from Donald Barthelme, "Interview with Charles Ruas and Judith Sherman, 1975," in *Not-Knowing: The Essays and Interviews,* ed. Kim Herzinger (New York: Random House, 1997), 245-247.

page 349 *"SLENDER-WAISTEDNESS":* This and subsequent quotes from the book are from Donald Barthelme, *The Slightly Irregular Fire Engine, or The Hithering Thithering Djinn* (New York: Farrar, Straus and Giroux, 1972), not paginated.

page 350 *"I never saw The Slightly Irregular Fire Engine in progress":* Anne Barthelme, in a conversation with the author, June 19, 2004.

page 350 *"elegant chatter"; "too static":* Timothy Foote, "Caboose Thoughts and Celebrities," *Time,* December 27, 1971, 61.

page 350 *"felicitous and blithe voice"; "considerable promise":* Selma G. Lanes, "Once Upon a Time, Three Famous Men Came into the Nursery," *New York Times Book Review,* November 7, 1971, 36-37.

page 350 *"immensely captivating"; "disconcertingly bright":* Jean Stafford, "Children's Books for Christmas," *The New Yorker,* December 4, 1971, 181-182.

page 351 *"Badly strained"* to *"Almost everything [Barthelme] submits":* Roger Angell, undated letters (1969-1970), Manuscripts and Archives Division, New York Public Library.

page 351 *"unhappy opinion"; "irritated"; "didn't admire":* Roger Angell, letters to Donald Barthelme, August 15, 1972, September 6, 1972, and October 10, 1972, Manuscripts and Archives Division, New York Public Library.

page 351 *"I feel especially bad":* Roger Angell, letter to Donald Barthelme, September 6, 1972, Manuscripts and Archives Division, New York Public Library.

page 351 *"I'm unhappily aware":* Roger Angell, letter to Donald Barthelme, September 6, 1972, Manuscripts and Archives Division, New York Public Library.

page 351 *"Am I a standard-issue American alcoholic?":* Donald Barthelme, "Edwards, Amelia," *The New Yorker,* September 9, 1972, 36.

page 352 *"How was the Buffalo hunt?":* Roger Angell, letter to Donald Barthelme, September 6, 1972, Manuscripts and Archives Division, New York Public Library.

page 352 *"I tried to reach you this morning":* Roger Angell, letter to Donald Barthelme, October 10, 1972, Manuscripts and Archives Division, New York Public Library.

page 352 *"You can ask your students":* Roger Angell, letter to Donald Barthelme, October 10, 1972, Manuscripts and Archives Division, New York Public Library.

page 352 *Don's "literary income":* This and subsequent Barth quotes are from John Barth, "Professor Barthelme," *Gulf Coast: A Journal of Literature and Art,* 4, no. 1 (1991): 17-18.

page 352 *"The key thing about those years":* Bruce Jackson, "Buffalo English: Literary Glory Days at UB," *Buffalo Beat,* February 26, 1999; posted at www.acsu.buffalo.edu/~bjackson/englishdept.html.

page 353 *"He seemed sad":* This and subsequent Michael Silverblatt quotes are from Dave Eggers's introduction to Donald Barthelme, *Forty Stories* (New York: Penguin Books, 2005), xix-xxii.

page 353 *"I saw him looking closely at Sam":* Helen Moore Barthelme, *Donald Barthelme: The Genesis of a Cool Sound* (College Station: Texas A & M University Press, 2001), 174.

page 354 *"We [met] at a table":* This and subsequent Lowry quotes are from Beverly Lowry, "The Writing Lesson," *The Gettysburg Review* 2, no. 4 (1989): 559.

page 354 *"I had been trekking over to Donald's":* This and subsequent Mirsky quotes, except those noted below, are from Mark Mirsky, "On *Fiction,*" *Triquarterly* 43 (1978): 515-523, and Mark Mirsky, "About the Magazine," posted at www.fictioninc.com/about.html.

page 355 *"About Faith":* Kirk Sale, in an E-mail to the author, May 16, 2004.

page 355 *"He gave it such flair":* Jerome Charyn, in an E-mail to the author, June 14, 2004.

page 357 *"I was in every sense his junior":* Mark Mirsky, in an exchange with Vincent Standley, posted at www.fictioninc.com/msgboard/messages/7.html.

page 357 "When a magazine like Harper's Bazaar": This and subsequent quotes from the conversation between Barthelme and Leslie Cross are from Leslie Cross, "Down in the Village with Donald Barthelme," *Milwaukee Journal,* February 4, 1973.

page 357 *Serious critical articles on Don's work:* For a comprehensive listing of the early critical work on Barthelme, see Jerome Klinkowitz, Asa B. Pieratt, Jr., and Robert Murray Davis, *A Comprehensive Bibliography* (Hamden, Connecticut: Shoestring Press/Archon Books, 1977), 107-116. The brief quotes I have used to summarize these works appear in this work.

page 358 *"If you refuse to make choices":* Joyce Carol Oates, "Whose Side Are You On?" *New York Times Book Review,* June 4, 1972, 63.

page 358 *"Usually I don't like to be interviewed":* Donald Barthelme, letter to Jerome Klinkowitz, September 7, 1971, Special Collections, Morris Library, University of Delaware, Newark, Delaware.

page 358 *"put together a kit of sorts":* This and subsequent Klinkowitz quotes are from Jerome Klinkowitz, *Keeping Literary Company: Working with Writers Since the Sixties* (Albany: State University of New York Press, 1998), 105-108.

page 358 *"I know I know I know":* Donald Barthelme, letter to Jerome Klinkowitz, undated (1972), Special Collections, Morris Library, University of Delaware, Newark, Delaware.

page 359 *"I think fewer people are reading":* This and subsequent quotes from the Barthelme interview with Klinkowitz are from "Interview with Jerome Klinkowitz, 1971-72," in *Not-Knowing,* ed. Herzinger, 199-206.

page 359 *"I think it's too cute":* Donald Barthelme, letter to Jerome Klinkowitz, May 30, 1972, Special Collections, Morris Library, University of Delaware, Newark, Delaware.

page 361 *"non-book":* Wells's comment cited in unsigned article, "Pangs and Prizes," *Time,* April 24, 1972, 88.

page 361 *"Writing for children":* Donald Barthelme, "Acceptance Speech: National Book Award for Children's Literature," in *Not-Knowing,* ed. Herzinger, 55.

40. Sadness

page 362 *"Sadness was a different sort of title":* "Interview with Charles Ruas and Judith Sherman, 1975," in *Not-Knowing: The Essays and Interviews,* ed. Kim Herzinger (New York: Random House, 1997), 234.

page 363 *"The first thing I did was make a mistake":* Donald Barthelme, *Sadness* (New York: Farrar, Straus and Giroux, 1972), 143.

page 363 "Before Sadness": Charles Thomas Samuels, "Sadness," *New York Times Book Review,* November 5, 1972, 27.

page 363 *"Wonderful elegance! No good at all!":* Barthelme, *Sadness,* 62.

page 363 *"witticisms":* Søren Kierkegaard, *Papers and Journals,* trans. Alastair Hannay (New York: Penguin, 1996), 50.

page 364 a *"field of stainless steel tulips":* Barthelme, *Sadness,* 33.

page 364 *"[Y]ou want nothing so much as a deep-going, fundamental involvement":* ibid., 179.

page 364 *"I always say to myself":* ibid., 30.

page 364 *"Of course we tried hard"; "What made us think":* ibid., 58, 62.

page 364 *"See, it is possible to live in the world and not change the world":* ibid., 116.

page 364 *"a substitute for the dread of being castrated":* Sigmund Freud, "The Uncanny," in *The Standard Edition of the Complete Psychological Works of Sigmund Freud,* trans. and ed. James Strachey, vol. 17 (London: Hogarth Press, 1964), 227-233.

page 365 *"Please consider this an 'eyes only' letter":* This and subsequent quotes from "The Sandman" are from Barthelme, *Sadness,* 87-96.

page 365 *"serious toys":* John Seelye, "Serious Toys," *The Saturday Review,* November 25, 1972, 66.

page 366 *"first American writer":* Guy Davenport, "Temptations," *National Review,* December 22, 1972, 1413.

page 366 *"stories that belong among the finest examples":* Samuels, "Sadness," 31.

page 366 *"There are always openings, if you can find them":* Barthelme, *Sadness,* 183.

41. Marion

page 367 *"My mother just let me go":* This and subsequent Anne Barthelme quotes are from conversations with the author, June 19, 2004, and May 19, 2005.

page 368 *"I lived in Copenhagen once":* This and subsequent quotes regarding Don's time in Boston are from John Domini, in an E-mail to the author, June 11, 2007.

page 369 *"very expendable pitcher":* This and subsequent Marion Knox Barthelme quotes are from an E-mail to the author, January 31, 2006.

page 369 *"met someone":* This and subsequent Karen Kennerly quotes are from conversations with the author, May 29, 2004, June 19, 2004, and December 3, 2005.

page 369 *"When [she and Donald] first [got] together":* This and subsequent Harrison Starr quotes are from a conversation with the author, December 24, 2006.

page 370 *"much warmer and fuller":* Kirk Sale, in an E-mail to the author, May 16, 2004.

page 370 *"I am happy and know myself to be happy":* Donald Barthelme, *Here in the Village* (Northridge, California and Archives: Lord John Press, 1978), 52.

pages 370-371 *"form a new government"* to *"my dear friend Marion Knox":* Donald Barthelme, letter to George Christian, November 22, 1975, Special Collections and Archives, University of Houston Libraries.

42. Pen and Sword

page 372 *"seamy things he had done"; "smoking gun":* Daniel Ellsberg, *Secrets: A Memoir of Vietnam and the Pentagon Papers* (New York: Viking, 2002), 456-457.

page 372 *"Watergate sure did get [Don] revved up":* This and subsequent Thomas Pynchon quotes are from his introduction to *The Teachings of Don B.,* ed. Kim Herzinger (New York: Turtle Bay Books, 1992), xv-xxii.

page 372 *"One can attempt to explain this Administration":* Donald Barthelme, *Here in the Village* (Northridge, California: Lord John Press, 1978), 9-10.

page 372 *"P—What did I do then?":* Donald Barthelme, *Guilty Pleasures* (New York: Farrar, Straus and Giroux, 1974), 93-94.

page 373 *"hurl great flaming buckets":* Barthelme, *Here in the Village,* 9-10.

page 373 *"I've just put the cat in the refrigerator":* Karen Kennerly, in a conversation with the author, June 19, 2004.

page 373 *"on the off-chance it was Solzhenitsyn":* Thomas Pynchon, undated note to Donald Barthelme, Special Collections and Archives, University of Houston Libraries.

pages 373-374 *"What's your time, sugar"; "[I]f there are prisons":* Grace Paley, *Just As I Thought* (New York: Farrar, Straus and Giroux, 1998), 24-30.

page 374 *"It's going to be pretty"* to *"She wasn't a girl, really":* Barthelme, *Here in the Village,* 11-15.

page 375 *"Don was a very active, astute, literary politician"; "Once he enlisted me":* Renata Adler, *Gone: The Last Days of The New Yorker* (New York: Simon & Schuster, 1999), 80.

page 375 *"My dearest dream": A Companion to Walt Whitman.* Donald D. Kummings, ed. (Hoboken, NJ: Wiley-Blackwell, 2006).

page 376 *"We writers . . . are trustees":* This and subsequent quotes detailing the history of PEN are from "Historical Sketch," cited on the "PEN American Center Archives" page at www.libweb.princeton.edu/libraries/firestone/rbsc/aids/pen.html.

page 376 *"Don developed considerable influence in PEN":* Kirk Sale, in an E-mail to the author, May 16, 2004.

page 376 *"At the PEN Board meetings":* Kirk Sale, "A Tribute to Donald Barthelme," *Poets and Writers,* March/April 1990, 9-10.

page 377 *"We, his colleagues in the West":* Donald Barthelme, telegram to Leonid Brezhnev, cited in *The New York Times,* February 13, 1974.

page **377** *"imprisoned writers":* Donald Barthelme, letter to Gen. Wojciech Jaruzelski, cited in the *New York Times,* February 9, 1982.

page **377** *"Democracy is the best idea"* to *"I*

haven't seen a government I liked": Heidi Ziegler, *The Radical Imagination and the Liberal Tradition: Interviews with English and American Novelists* (London: Junction Books, 1982), 48, 44.

43. Guilty Pleasures

page **378** *"Living unmarried"* and all subsequent quotes from Marion Barthelme are from an E-mail to the author on June 6, 2008.

page **378** *"spats":* Kirk Sale, in an E-mail to the author, May 16, 2004.

page **378** *"[He] is now divorced":* Max Frisch, *Montauk* (New York: Harvest/HBJ, 1976), 138-139.

page **380** *"Don asked me if I was having an affair":* Kirk Sale, in an E-mail to the author, May 16, 2004.

page **380** *"The fall 1973 number of the Carolina Quarterly":* Donald Barthelme, letter in the *New York Times Book Review,* December 23, 1973, 17.

page **381** *"Admittedly, editing a journal"; "monster of malice"; "damage":* Edward Krickel, "'O wha is this has done this deid, this ill deid done to me?: A Correction and Commentary" in *The Georgia Review* 28, no. 1 (1974): 5.

page **381** *"Esquire called up":* "Interview with Charles Ruas and Judith Sherman, 1975," in *Not-Knowing: The Essays and Interviews,* ed. Kim Herzinger (New York: Random House, 1997), 240.

page **382** *"I said, 'Snow White'?":* This and subsequent Walter Abish quotes are from a conversation with the author, February 16, 2005.

page **383** *"I was taken by the idea of an impersonal fiction":* Frederick Tuten, "Twenty-Five Years After: The Adventures of Mao on the Long March," *Archipelago* 1, no. 1 (1997); posted at www.archipelago.org/vol1-1/tuten.htm.

page **383** *"How can I be like you?":* Peter J. Rondinone, cited at www1.cuny.edu.portal_ur/news/cuny_matters/july_2003/festival.html.

page **383** *He "had no set reading list":* Brian Kitely, "Some Questions about Donald Barthelme," posted at www.du.edu/~bkitely/barthelme.htm.

page **383** *"One day in 1973 he crossed the street to talk to me":* Grace Paley, *Just As I Thought* (New York: Farrar, Straus and Giroux, 1998), 235-236.

page **383** *"down in Baltimore":* Marc Chénetier et al., "Some Bridge of Meaning: A Conversational Interview with Joseph McElroy," *Révues d'études Anglophones* (Université d'Orléans), Autumn 2001, 13.

page **384** *Corey, who spouted nonsense for several minutes:* See Irwin Corey's acceptance speech, posted at www.ottosell.de/pynchon/corey.htm.

page **384** *Benjamin DeMott . . . said the winning entry:* See Benjamin DeMott, "Anatomy of a National Book Award," *The Atlantic Monthly,* June 1974, 98.

page **384** *"lured":* This and subsequent quotes from the *New York Times* are from Eric Pace, "Simon and Schuster Elated Over an Editorial Coup," *New York Times,* December 24, 1973.

page **385** *"authors are large striped or spotted animals":* Donald Barthelme, letter to the *New York Times,* September 30, 1974.

page **385** *"exemplary fashion":* Donald Barthelme, letter to Roger Straus, January 9, 1974, Special Collections and Archives, University of Houston Libraries.

page **385** *"damaging" allegations:* Roger Straus, letter to Donald Barthelme, January 11, 1974, Special Collections and Archives, University of Houston Libraries.

page **385** *"What remains":* Donald Barthelme, letter to Roger Straus, January 16, 1974, Special Collections and Archives, University of Houston Libraries.

page **386** *the "more I've thought about our decision":* Roger Straus, letter to Donald Barthelme, January 18, 1974, Special Collections and Archives, University of Houston Libraries.

page **386** *"pretty low":* Peter S. Prescott, "The Repairman," *Newsweek,* November 25, 1974, 118.

page **386** *"draping his motley":* Unsigned article, "Notable," *Time,* November 11, 1974, 112.

page **386** *"'The looking at a woman sometimes makes for lust'":* Donald Barthelme, catalog introduction for an exhibition at the Cordier & Ekstrom Gallery, reprinted in *Here in the Village* (Northridge, California: Lord John Press, 1978), 42.

page **386** *"on delivery of an acceptable manuscript":* In-house memo from Roger Straus, July 24, 1975, Farrar, Straus and Giroux records, Manuscripts and Archives Division, New York Public Library.

44. Peanut Butter

page 387 *"our representative American minimalist work":* This and subsequent Karl quotes are from Frederick Karl, *American Fictions: 1940-1980* (New York: Harper Colophon, 1981), 385.

page 387 *the story is the journey of the hero:* See, for example, Joseph Campbell, *The Hero with a Thousand Faces* (Princeton, New Jersey: Princeton University Press, 1972), or Otto Rank et al., *In the Quest of the Hero* (Princeton, New Jersey: Princeton University Press, 1990).

page 387 *"process of accretion":* "Interview with Larry McCaffery: 1980," in *Not-Knowing*, ed. Kim Herzinger (New York: Random House, 1997), 262.

page 388 *"Hoping this will reach you at a favorable moment":* Donald Barthelme, *The Dead Father* (New York: Farrar, Straus and Giroux, 1975), 24.

page 388 *"parley":* ibid., 30.

page 388 *"telling of balls":* Gertrude Stein, "Ladies' Voices," in *A Stein Reader*, ed. Ulla E. Dydo (Evanston, Illinois: Northwestern University Press, 1993), 307.

page 388 *"was beginning a novel about Gertrude Stein":* Jerome Charyn, in an E-mail to the author, June 14, 2004.

page 388 *"change" the world and give it "needed direction"; "favorable" historical "moment":* Barthelme, *The Dead Father*, 23-24.

page 388 *"I can talk to you":* ibid., 29-30.

page 388 *"Daddy, Daddy, you bastard, I'm through!":* Sylvia Plath, *Ariel* (New York: Harper & Row, 1966), 51.

page 389 *"words in the world that [are] not the words [we] always hear":* Donald Barthelme, *Snow White* (New York: Atheneum, 1967), 6.

page 389 *"[M]y writing was all about you":* Franz Kafka, "Letter to His Father," in *Dearest Father: Stories and Other Writings*, trans. and ed. Ernst Kaiser and Eithne Wilkins (New York: Schocken Books, 1954), 138-196.

page 389 *"If one tries to think at one and the same time":* Jane Gallop quoted in Kelly Anspaugh, "Who Killed James Joyce?" posted at www.centerforbookculture.org/casebooks/casebook_swim/anspaugh.html.

pages 389-390 *Michel Foucault; Jacques Derrida:* See Peter Schwenger, "Barthelme, Freud, and the Killing of Kafka's Father," in *Fictions of Masculinity: Crossing Cultures, Crossing Sexualities*, ed. Peter Murphy (Albany: State University of New York Press, 1994), 57-73.

page 390 *"poker chip":* Barthelme, *The Dead Father*, 36.

page 390 *"It is through the* name of the father": Jacques Lacan quoted in Anspaugh, "Who Killed James Joyce?"

page 390 *"What is your totem?"; eating the Dead Father:* Barthelme, *The Dead Father*, 150; 74.

page 390 *"Patricide is a bad idea":* ibid., 145.

page 391 *"a hundred dollars" for a "feeling":* Donald Barthelme, *Come Back, Dr. Caligari* (Boston: Little, Brown, 1964), 63.

page 391 *the "kind of life" she has "imagined":* Barthelme, *The Dead Father*, 169.

page 391 *"life itself in contempt":* This and subsequent Kramer quotes are from Hilton Kramer, "Barthelme's Comedy of Patricide," *Commentary* 62 (1976): 56.

page 392 *"state of crisis":* This and subsequent quotes from the conference at the Library of Congress are from *The Publication of Poetry and Fiction: A Conference (October 20 and 21, 1975)* (Washington, D. C.: Library of Congress, 1977).

page 393 *"not very happy"; "I keep remembering what Faulkner said":* Walker Percy, letter to Donald Barthelme, March 14, 1975, Special Collections and Archives, University of Houston Libraries.

page 393 *"Well, it's tough luck for you":* This and subsequent quotes from the symposium on fiction are from "A Symposium on Fiction," in *Not-Knowing*, ed. Herzinger, 58-82.

page 394 *"Thanks for getting me to Va.":* Walker Percy, letter to Donald Barthelme, November 5, 1975, Special Collections and Archives, University of Houston Libraries.

page 394 *"Over the past 10 years":* Jerome Klinkowitz, "The Dead Father," *The New Republic*, November 29, 1975, 35-36.

page 394 *"flick...scenes onto the page":* Unsigned book review, *The New Yorker*, November 24, 1975, 194.

page 394 *"always witty, and occasionally beautiful":* Peter S. Prescott, "Pater Noster," *Newsweek*, November 3, 1975, 90.

page 394 *"he provides a way of listening":* Richard Todd, "Daddy, you're perfectly swell!" *The Atlantic Monthly* (December 1975): 112.

page 394 "The Dead Father *is the author's most sustained, ambitious and successful work":* New York Times Book Review, December 28, 1975, 1.

pages 394-395 *"[Y]ou damned critics" to "and let us have a drink":* Donald Barthelme, letter to Jerome Klinkowitz, May 5, 1975, Special Collections, University of Delaware Library, Newark, Delaware.

page 395 *"Don's neighborhood":* This and subsequent Klinkowitz quotes are from Jerome Klinkowitz, *Keeping Literary Company: Working with Writers Since the Sixties* (Albany: State University of New York Press, 1998), 103-133.

page 397 *"I married. Oh, did I marry":* Barthelme, *The Dead Father,* 57.

45. Downtown

page 398 *America's longest, and most ignominious, war:* For an incisive short account of the Vietnam War, see George C. Herring, *America's Longest War: The United States and Vietnam, 1950-1975* (New York: Alfred A. Knopf, 1986).

page 398 *"The greatest dissonance of my adult lifetime was the Vietnam war":* Heidi Ziegler, "Donald Barthelme," in *The Radical Imagination and the Liberal Tradition: Interviews with American and English Novelists,* ed. Heidi Ziegler and Christopher Bigley (London: Junction Books, 1982), 44.

page 398 *"Fragments are the only forms I trust":* Donald Barthelme, *Sixty Stories* (New York: Putnam, 1981), 98.

page 399 *"function of the advance guard":* J. D. O'Hara, "Donald Barthelme: The Art of Fiction LXVI," *Paris Review* 80 (1981): 187.

page 399 *"Vietnam has spawned a jargon":* Michael Herr, *Dispatches* (New York: Avon Books, 1968), 97.

page 399 *"We tell ourselves stories in order to live":* Joan Didion, *The White Album* (New York: Simon & Schuster, 1979), 11.

page 399 *"Distant Early Warning System":* Barthelme, *Sixty Stories,* 107.

page 399 *"I put the United States on a pedestal":* Anne Barthelme, in an E-mail to the author, June 19, 2004.

page 399 *"As soon as she stepped off the plane":* Donald Barthelme, "My ten-year-old daughter . . ." in *Not-Knowing: The Essays and Interviews,* ed. Kim Herzinger (New York: Random House, 1997), 151-153.

page 400 *"New York in the 1970s"; "[E]veryone was in a band":* Marvin J. Taylor, "Playing the Field: The Downtown Scene and Cultural Production, An Introduction," in *The Downtown Book: The New York Art Scene 1974-1984,* ed. Marvin J. Taylor (Princeton, New Jersey: Princeton University Press, 2006), 19-20.

page 401 *"nicey-nicey-clean-ice-cream-TV society":* Kathy Acker, *Blood and Guts in High School* (New York: Grove Press, 1984), 94.

page 401 *"language divided against itself"; "related to the generation that preceded it":* Robert Siegle, *Suburban Ambush: Downtown Writing and the Fiction of Insurgency* (Baltimore: Johns Hopkins University Press, 1989), 4, 393-394.

page 401 *"Barking art"; "Actually, I can't stand artists":* Donald Barthelme, *Forty Stories* (New York: Putnam, 1987), 109, 111.

page 401 *"I would suggest":* "A Symposium on Fiction," in *Not-Knowing,* ed. Herzinger, 65.

page 401 *"to get rid of psychologizing the novel":* ibid., 64.

pages 402-403 *"[O]ne should never cease considering human love":* Donald Barthelme, *Amateurs* (New York: Farrar, Straus and Giroux, 1976), 144.

page 403 *"[A]dmirable volume after admirable volume":* This and subsequent quotes from "Our Work and Why We Do It" are from ibid., 3-9.

page 403 *"water, gas, and electricity"; "aura" . . . will "wither":* Walter Benjamin, "The Work of Art in the Age of Mechanical Reproduction," in *Illuminations,* ed. Hannah Arendt, trans. Harry Zahn (1968; reprint New York: Schocken Books, 1978), 219, 221.

page 403 *"flow of grace to all of God's creatures":* This and subsequent quotes from "At the End of the Mechanical Age" are from Barthelme, *Amateurs,* 175-184.

page 404 *"Works is what counts, boy":* Barthelme, *Amateurs,* 74.

page 404 *"it will pall, of course":* ibid., 176.

page 404 *"The public wants reassurance":* Linda Kuehl, "Amateurs," *The Saturday Review,* December 11, 1976, 68-69.

page 404 *"mannerism, self-duplicating":* Richard Locke, "Amateurs," *New York Times Book Review,* December 19, 1976, 16.

page 405 *"The great task"* to *"I don't know where she gets such language":* Barthelme, "My ten-year-old daughter . . ." in *Not-Knowing,* ed. Herzinger, 153.

46. Uncle Don

page 406 *"In the mid-1970s I was living in a house in Connecticut":* This and subsequent Ann Beattie quotes are from a letter to the author, July 23, 2004.

page 408 *"Even after I had left the CCNY pro-gram":* This and subsequent Oscar Hijuelos quotes, except those noted below, are from an E-mail to the author, March 24, 2005.

page 408 *"circled misspellings and stupidi-ties":* Oscar Hijuelos, "Beautiful," *Gulf Coast: A Journal of Literature and Art,* 4, no. 1 (1999): 133-135.

page 409 *"My worries about a possible affilia-tion are two":* Donald Barthelme, letter to Bernard Rosenthal, December 17, 1977, letter in possession of the author.

page 409 the *"part of [Don] that was from Hous-ton":* This and subsequent Ted Solotaroff quotes are from Ted Solotaroff, "Don Barthelme," in *Gulf Coast: A Journal of Literature and Art,* volume 4, no. 1 (1991): 169-171.

page 409 *"a foppy sort of a guy":* This and sub-sequent Kirkpatrick Sale quotes are from an E-mail to the author, May 16, 2004.

page 409 *"asked me to send a telegram":* Re-nata Adler, *Gone: The Last Days of The New Yorker* (New York: Simon & Schuster, 1999), 80.

pages 410-411 *"dismal roster"* to *"considerable miscarriage of justice":* Donald Barthelme, "As

Grace Paley Faces Jail with Three Other Writ-ers," in *Not-Knowing: The Essays and Inter-views,* ed. Kim Herzinger (New York: Random House, 1997), 154-155 (originally published on the *New York Times* op-ed page, February 2, 1979).

page 411 *Kerouac's "descriptions of men or places":* Unsigned review of *Visions of Cody, The New Yorker,* February 17, 1973, 110.

page 411 *"The three buildings across the street":* This and subsequent quotes from "You Are as Brave as Vincent Van Gogh" are from Donald Barthelme, *Amateurs* (New York: Farrar, Straus and Giroux, 1976), 167-171.

page 412 *"sees everything as possibility":* Bir-git Barthelme, "A View of Julien Sorel, the Pro-tagonist of 'The Red and the Black,' with Reference to Søren Kierkegaard's 'The Concept of Irony,' " *Kierkegaardiana* 10 (1977): 249.

page 412 *"I lived over near Sixth":* David Mark-son, in a conversation with the author, July 22, 2004.

page 412 *"recite one another's poems":* Eileen Simpson, *Poets in Their Youth* (New York: Ran-dom House, 1982), 256.

47. The End of an Age

page 413 *"was a hard decision"* to *"you told me that this is the direction":* Roger Angell, letter to Donald Barthelme, August 8, 1977, Manu-scripts and Archives Division, New York Public Library.

page 413 *"such disdain for life":* Josephine Hendlin, "Angries: S-M as a Literary Style," *Harper's,* February 1974, 89.

page 413 *"writes only about the writing he is writing":* Gore Vidal, *Matters of Fact and Fiction* (New York: Vintage Books, 1977), 102, 104.

page 414 *"John took all his contemporaries into a garage": The Writer in Society: Donald Barthelme* (Houston: KUHT-TV, 1984).

page 414 *"enfeebled":* John Gardner, *On Moral Fiction* (New York: Basic Books, 1978), 80.

page 414 *"[idealistic] party was pretty much over":* Willie Morris, *New York Days* (Boston: Little, Brown, 1993), 347.

pages 414-415 *"[E]verything in New York City is getting shabbier"* to *"something . . . beyond":* Donald Barthelme and J. D. O'Hara, "Rough Draft #1" of the *Paris Review* interview, Special Collec-tions and Archives, University of Houston Li-braries.

page 415 *"live and work in other cities":* Marion Barthelme, in an E-mail to the author, January 31, 2006.

page 415 *"an incredibly dangerous and delicate business":* Donald Barthelme, *Sixty Stories* (New York: Putnam, 1981), 281.

page 415 *"incredibly beautiful and good women":* Barthelme and O'Hara, "Rough Draft #1," Special Collections and Archives, University of Houston Libraries.

page 415 *"Show me a man who has not married a hundred times":* Donald Barthelme, *Forty Sto-ries* (New York: Putnam, 1987), 220.

page 415 *"Although reluctant to marry again":* This and subsequent Helen Barthelme quotes are from Helen Moore Barthelme, *Donald Barthelme: The Genesis of a Cool Sound* (Col-lege Station: Texas A & M University Press, 2001), 176-177.

page 416 *"Since you and I have been married":* Herman Gollob, in a conversation with the au-thor, April 19, 2007.

page 416 *"their darling daughter":* Harrison Starr, in a conversation with the author, Decem-ber 29, 2006.

page 416 *"one of [Marion's] relatives":* Sandra Starr, in a conversation with the author, Decem-ber 29, 2006.

page 416 *"Some part of 'Overnight to Many Dis-tant Cities' ":* Marion Barthelme, in an E-mail to the author, January 31, 2006.

page 416 "In Barcelona the lights went out": Barthelme, *Forty Stories,* 220.

page 416 *"Don got back in contact with me":* This and subsequent Marilyn Gillet quotes are from a conversation with the author, November 17, 2004.

page 416 *"If it's any consolation":* Maggie Curran, in a letter to Donald Barthelme, March 6, 1970.

page 417 *"Today we make the leap to faith"; "the worst torture":* Barthelme, *Sixty Stories,* 379, 385.

page 417 *"Even though Elaine de Kooning had quit drinking"* to *"very special":* Marion Barthelme, in an E-mail to the author, June 6, 2008.

page 417 *"I will think about him for the rest of my life":* Donald Barthelme, "Eulogy for Thomas Hess," Special Collections and Archives, University of Houston Libraries.

page 417 *"I think people were always happy to see Henry":* This and subsequent quotes from Robbins's memorial service are from Donald Barthelme, "Eulogy for Henry Robbins," Special Collections and Archives, University of Houston Libraries.

page 418 *"I've been to more than my share [of funerals]":* Barthelme and O'Hara, "Rough Draft" #1.

page 419 *They're Beckett-y:* J. D. O'Hara, "Donald Barthelme: The Art of Fiction LXVI," *Paris Review* 80 (1981): 197.

page 419 *"very avuncular and welcoming":* Marion Knox Barthelme, in an E-mail to the author, June 6, 2008.

page 419 *"There is some sense in which John Ashbery is central":* Barthelme and O'Hara, "Rough Draft #1."

page 419 *"double-mindedness":* Søren Kierkegaard, *Purity of Heart Is to Will One Thing,* trans. Douglas V. Steere (New York: Harper and Brothers, 1948), 87.

page 419 *"Featherings of ease and bliss":* Donald Barthelme, *Great Days* (New York: Farrar, Straus and Giroux, 1979), 157.

page 420 *"Literary history shows that the avant-garde of one period":* Diane Johnson, "Possibly Parables," *New York Times Book Review,* February 4, 1979, 1.

page 420 *"stories are brief":* Denis Donaghue, "For Brevity's Sake," *The Saturday Review,* March 3, 1979, 50.

page 420 *"muted ... melancholy":* James Rawley, "The New Music," *The Nation,* April 7, 1979, 374.

page 420 *"one of our best and most adventurous writers":* Peter S. Prescott, "Sound of Music," *Newsweek,* February 5, 1979, 78.

page 421 *"I'll probably hole up in the Gramercy Park Hotel"; "accumulated all these things":* Barthelme and O'Hara, "Rough Draft #1."

page 421 *"I can see that the story is elegant and strongly flavored":* Roger Angell, letter to Donald Barthelme, April 11, 1979, Manuscripts and Archives Division, New York Public Library.

page 421 *"It's possible that the idea of man-as-victim-of-society":* Donald Barthelme, "The Earth as An Overturned Bowl," in *Not-Knowing: The Essays and Interviews,* ed. Kim Herzinger (New York: Random House, 1997), 106.

page 421 *"[S]train as we may":* Donald Barthelme, "Dead Men Comin' Through," in *Not-Knowing,* ed. Herzinger, 119.

page 422 *"as solid as a tool-pusher on a Texas oil rig":* Donald Barthelme, "Special Devotions," in *Not-Knowing,* ed. Herzinger, 114.

page 422 *"less fun than it used to be":* ibid., 113.

page 422 *"detail"; "ugly knowledge"; "what things are called"; "milieu":* Barthelme, "Dead Men Comin' Through," 115–117.

page 422 *"There's a strangely pleasant moment":* Donald Barthelme, "Three Festivals," in *Not-Knowing,* ed. Herzinger, 124.

page 423 *"The government isn't very good":* This and Barthelme's subsequent observations about New York are from Donald Barthelme, "Spring in the Village!" in *Not-Knowing,* ed. Herzinger, 50–52.

page 423 *"In the '70s the sheer glut of consumable culture"* to *"question of the relationship of art":* Jack Kroll, "Culture Goes Pop," *Newsweek,* November 19, 1979, 112.

page 423 *"The city arouses us":* Alfred Kazin quoted in Morris, *New York Days,* 353.

page 423 *"Will you always remember me?":* Barthelme, *Great Days,* 172. According to Marion Barthelme, "The knock knock joke is something that Roger Angell's son, John Henry, brought home." Perhaps for this reason, she reads the end of *Great Days* as more upbeat than I have presented it here.

page 424 *"Say you're not frightened":* ibid., 129.

48. Miss Pennybacker's Castle

Except for those passages noted below, the information and all quotes in this chapter come from two detailed and invaluable sources: Suzanne Shumway, "Creative Writing Program: A Haven for Future Literati," in *Collegium Online* (University of Houston), Winter 1987; and Tim Fleck, "Burying the Dead Father," *Houston Press*, February 8, 1990.

page 427 *"[People] are tying yellow ribbons"; "You are ardently wanted":* Cynthia Macdonald, letter to Donald Barthelme, undated (1980), Special Collections and Archives, University of Houston Libraries.

page 427 *"a kind of no-man's land"; "Poetry should only be attempted":* Cynthia Macdonald, "Tributaries: Collage for Donald," *Gulf Coast: A Journal of Literature and Art*, vol. 4, no. 1 (1991): 145-150.

page 429 *"death of friends":* This and subsequent Kirk Sale quotes are from an E-mail to the author, May 16, 2004.

page 430 *"didn't want to go to Texas":* Jerome Charyn, in a conversation with the author, June 14, 2004.

page 430 *Marion had gotten profit sharing:* Marion Barthelme, in an E-mail to the author, June 6, 2008.

page 430 *"The biggest mistake you can make":* Donald Barthelme, Sr., letter to Donald Barthelme, April 2, 1982, Special Collections and Archives, University of Houston Libraries.

page 430 *"I felt that he needed to be in Houston"; "Her visit and subsequent death":* Helen Moore Barthelme, *Donald Barthelme: The Genesis of a Cool Sound* (College Station: Texas A & M University Press, 2001), 179.

page 430 *"I was furious when [City College] let him go":* Mark Mirsky, in an E-mail to the author, May 17, 2004.

page 430 *"going to Texas would be a good thing":* Harrison Starr, in a conversation with the author, December 29, 2006.

page 430 *"People I knew":* Roger Angell, in a conversation with the author, December 6, 2006.

page 430 *"I thought that moving to Houston would be interesting":* Marion Barthelme, in an E-mail to the author, April 19, 2006.

page 431 *"Your mother's check-up":* Donald Barthelme, Sr., letter to Donald Barthelme, April 29, 1981, Special Collections and Archives, University of Houston Libraries.

49. The King

page 432 *"the city the Depression missed"; "too many dollars chasing too few deals":* Joe R. Feagin, "Irrationality in Real Estate Investment: The Case of Houston," *Monthly Review*, March 1987; posted at www.findarticles.com/p/articles/mi_m1132/is_v38/ai_4855896.

pages 432-433 *"I never knew what led the elder Barthelme to sell his house"* to *"It is one of those rare Houston places":* Stephen Fox, in an E-mail to the author, June 4, 2006.

page 433 *"there was a feeling among the literature students"; "high-handed behavior"; The "writing program ventilated the department":* Tim Fleck, "Burying the Dead Father": *Houston Press*, February 8, 1990.

page 433 *"These tight-ass feminists":* Overheard by the author.

page 434 *"What he was teaching us":* This and subsequent Blake quotes are from Glenn Blake,

"Memorial Service Remarks," in *Gulf Coast: A Journal of Literature and Art*, 4, no. 1 (1991): 63-64.

page 434 *Tom Cobb remembered:* Fleck, "Burying the Dead Father."

page 434 *Olive Hershey, then writing a novel:* ibid.

page 434 *Padgett Powell recalled:* Padgett Powell, "The Living Father," *Gulf Coast: A Journal of Literature and Art*, 4, no. 1 (1991): 164-165.

page 436 *"He never thought anyone was a hopeless writer":* Marion Barthelme, in an E-mail to the author, August 23, 2004.

page 436 *"sort of like a barracks"; "uncling"; "hell holes"; "worn [him] down":* Helen Moore Barthelme, *Donald Barthelme: The Genesis of a Cool Sound* (College Station: Texas A & M University Press, 2001), 178-183.

50. Still Life

page 437 *"I know that Donald was good for the university":* John Barth, "Professor Barthelme,"

Gulf Coast: A Journal of Literature and Art, 4, no. 1 (1991): 17-18.

page 437 *"No longer will Kafka or Tolstoy be asked to sit":* Jerome Klinkowitz, *Donald Barthelme: An Exhibition* (Durham, North Carolina: Duke University Press, 1991), 109.

page 437 *"He would often talk to me about new types of VCRs":* Phillip Lopate, "The Dead Father: A Remembrance of Donald Barthelme," *Threepenny Review* (Summer 1991): 9.

page 438 *Marion points out that Don had been interested in food:* Marion Knox Barthelme, in an E-mail to the author, June 6, 2008.

page 438 *"relaxed"; "generous"; a "confidence with subject and form":* Jerome Klinkowitz, "Fiction: The 1960s to the Present," *American Literary Scholarship* (als.dukejournals.org/cgi/reprint/2005/1/351).

page 438 *"the most artificial of all artistic subjects":* This and subsequent Wilmerding quotes are from John Wilmerding, *Important Information Inside: The Art of John F. Peto and the Idea of Still-Life Painting in Nineteenth-Century America* (Washington, DC: National Gallery of Art/Harper & Row, 1983), 11–113.

page 439 *"was discovered when":* Donald Barthelme, *Sixty Stories* (New York: Putnam, 1981), 445.

page 440 *"began getting calls from friends":* J. D. O'Hara, "Donald Barthelme: The Art of Fiction LXVI," *Paris Review* 80 (1981): 184.

page 440 *"Roger Angell and I went to a reading"; "Had Don lived to experience the age of memoir":* Ann Beattie, in an E-mail to the author, April 4, 2006.

pages 440–441 *"Barthelme isn't easy"* to *"one of the most adventurous American writers":* Walter Clemons, "Barthelme the Scrivener," *Newsweek,* October 12, 1981, 100.

page 441 *"excitement caused among readers"* to *"trifles":* John Romano, "Working Like a Stand-Up Comic," *New York Times Book Review,* October 4, 1981, 9.

page 441 *"1975 seems to be the year when minimalist fiction first appeared":* Roland Sodowsky, "1970s AD—Decade," *Studies in Short Fiction,* Fall 1996; posted at www.findarticles.com/p/articles/mi_m2455/is_n4_v33/ai_20906637. The statements by Kim Herzinger, John Barth, and Madison Smartt Bell come from this Sodowsky article.

page 442 *"Experimentalism is only the misuse of the language":* Daniel Halpern quoted in Anita Shreve, "The American Short Story: An Untold Tale," *New York Times Magazine,* November 30, 1980, 136.

pages 442-443 *"surprisingly isolated"; "Donald Barthelme [is] often seen":* Shreve, "The American Short Story," 136.

page 443 *"the late-life 'Collected Stories' ":* Clemons, "Barthelme the Scrivener," 100.

51. Inprint

page 444 *"It's Wednesday morning, Buttercup":* Donald Barthelme, "Dear Buttercup," *Gulf Coast: A Journal of Literature and Art,* 4, no. 1 (1991): 41-42.

page 444 *"Katharine was born":* Marion Knox Barthelme, in an E-mail to the author, June 15, 2006.

page 445 *"vernacular 'everyman' feel":* Rosellen Brown, "On Leaving Texas," *Cite* 39 (1997).

page 445 *"little Menil"; "wonderful"; "fixed up in [Don's] stark minimalist way":* Marion Barthelme, in an E-mail to the author, April 19, 2006.

pages 445-446 *"I never really did get over my surprise"; "His dedication to his students":* Lois Parkinson Zamora, "The Long Sonata of the Dead," *Gulf Coast: A Journal of Literature and Art* vol. 4, no. 1 (1991): 180-181.

page 446 *"I knew that to build an excellent program in the arts":* This and subsequent Barry Munitz quotes are from a conversation with the author, September 2, 2004.

page 447 *Don's commitment to "underdogs":* Phillip Lopate, in a conversation with the author, October 29, 2004.

page 447 *A faculty member recalls telling Don:* Tim Fleck, "Burying the Dead Father," *Houston Press,* February 8, 1990.

page 448 *"In his distance":* Phillip Lopate, "The Dead Father: A Remembrance of Donald Barthelme," *Threepenny Review* (Summer 1991), 8.

page 448 *"he was a world-class worrier":* Edward Hirsch, "Donald Barthelme: Doubting It," in *Responsive Reading,* ed. Edward Hirsch (Ann Arbor: University of Michigan Press, 1999), 156.

page 448 *"Sometimes he would come to my house":* Edward Hirsch, in a conversation with the author, December 5, 2006.

page 448 *It was business—and in tangible terms, not terribly rewarding:* Marion Barthelme points out that Don "just didn't live long enough to see the larger royalties come in."

page 449 *FSG was demanding:* Maggie Curran, letter to Donald Barthelme, February 24, 1982, Special Collections and Archives, University of Houston Libraries.

page 449 *"That is one of the satisfying things about being a parent":* Donald Barthelme, *Forty Stories* (New York: Putnam, 1987), 236.

page 449 *"may jam a kitchen knife":* This and subsequent quotes from "Chablis" are from Barthelme, *Forty Stories,* 3.

52. Many Distances

page 451 *"He was going to settle down and be the family man":* Phillip Lopate, in a conversation with the author, October 29, 2004.

page 451 *"I'm still working off that old knowledge":* Phillip Lopate, "The Dead Father: A Remembrance of Donald Barthelme," *Threepenny Review* (Summer 1991): 7.

page 451 *"might retire":* Padgett Powell, "The Living Father," *Gulf Coast: A Journal of Literature and Art,* 4, no. 1 (1991): 165.

page 452 *"At times he gave the impression":* Lopate, "The Dead Father," 8.

page 452 *"Donald was existentially very lonely":* Edward Hirsch, in a conversation with the author, December 5, 2006.

page 452 *"You loved him, he says":* Donald Barthelme, *Overnight to Many Distant Cities* (New York: Putnam, 1983), 161.

page 452 *"repels any understanding whatsoever":* Jonathan Penner, "Donald Barthelme's Just-Not Stories," *Washington Post Book World,* November 27, 1983, 3.

page 452 *"become a pattern":* Anatole Broyard, "Books of the Times," *New York Times,* December 9, 1983.

page 452 *"curiously vacuous":* Joel Conarroe, "Some Tame, Some Wild," *New York Times Book Review,* December 18, 1983.

page 453 *"Holding the ladder":* Barthelme, *Overnight to Many Distant Cities,* 163.

page 453 *"During heated discussions":* This and subsequent Phillip Lopate quotes are from a conversation with the author, October 29, 2004.

53. Between Coasts

page 455 *"slightly more speedy and nervous":* Phillip Lopate, "The Dead Father: A Remembrance of Donald Barthelme," *Threepenny Review* (Summer 1991): 9.

page 455 *"Donald had this idea to make a dinner in SoHo":* This and subsequent Walter Abish quotes are from a conversation with the author, February 16, 2005.

page 456 *"Donald didn't socialize the way others do":* Edward Hirsch, in a conversation with the author, December 5, 2006.

page 456 *"I was afraid he'd get stuck":* Grace Paley, *Just As I Thought* (New York: Farrar, Straus and Giroux, 1998), 234.

page 456 *"We were family":* Roger Angell, in a conversation with the author, December 6, 2006.

page 456 *"true good neighbor"* to *"At one point the cart":* Lopate, "The Dead Father," 10.

54. Anne

page 458 *"In a way, her death":* This and subsequent Anne Barthelme quotes are from a conversation with the author, June 19, 2004.

page 460 *"I said, 'Hi. How are you?'":* Karen Kennerly, in a conversation with the author, May 29, 2004.

pages 460–461 *"letdown"; "The event had been pretty successful":* Phillip Lopate, "The Dead Father: A Remembrance of Donald Barthelme," *Threepenny Review* (Summer 1991): 11.

55. The State of the Imagination

page 462 *"Dad would say":* This and subsequent Anne Barthelme quotes are from a conversation with the author, June 19, 2004.

page 462 *the 48th International P.E.N. Congress:* Details about PEN and the conference, including quotes other than those of Karen Kennerly, have been gathered from numerous contemporaneous sources. See E. L. Doctorow, "Schultz and PEN," *The Nation,* January 18, 1986, 37; Maria Margaronis and Elizabeth Pochoda, "Bad Manners and Bad Faith," *The Nation,* February 1, 1986, 116-119; "PEN Fiasco,"

National Review, February 14, 1986, 18–19. See also Celia McGee, "PEN's New Script," *The Nation,* March 17, 1997, 31–34. For the most part, however, I have depended on the detailed report on the conference, which was compiled by various PEN members (Special Collections and Archives, University of Houston Libraries).

page 462 *"Basically, Don and I put the PEN conference together":* This and subsequent

Karen Kennerly quotes are from a conversation with the author, May 29, 2004.

page 466 *"I remember meeting Donald Barthelme":* Salman Rushdie, "The PEN and the Sword," *New York Times Book Review,* April 17, 2005, back page.

page 467 *"sad political parting":* Grace Paley, *Just As I Thought* (New York: Farrar, Straus and Giroux, 1998), 236.

56. Paradise . . .

page 468 *"Hey buddy what's your name?":* Donald Barthelme, *Sixty Stories* (New York: Putnam, 1981), 389.

page 469 *"Ethics has always been where my heart is":* This and subsequent quotes from this story are from Donald Barthelme, "Basil from Her Garden," *The New Yorker,* October 21, 1985, 36–39.

page 470 *"shards and rag ends":* Peter Prescott, "Hog Heaven," *Newsweek,* November 3, 1986, 76.

page 470 *"Well it's just what I thought would happen":* Donald Barthelme, *Paradise* (New York: Putnam, 1986), 158.

page 471 *"After the women had gone":* ibid., 9.

page 471 *"series of conversations":* This and subsequent quotes from this novel are from ibid., 30, 52, 78, 98, 152, 135.

page 472 *"very tired theme of the male midlife crisis":* Michiko Kakutani, "Books of the Times," *New York Times,* October 22, 1986.

page 472 *"charming":* Prescott, "Hog Heaven," 76.

page 472 *"poignant awareness":* Richard Burgin, "A Poignant Paradise," *St. Petersbug Times,* January 4, 1987.

page 472 *"pretty weak":* Phillip Lopate, "The Dead Father: A Remembrance of Donald Barthelme," *Threepenny Review* (Summer 1991): 8.

page 472 *"cleanest dirty book":* Grace Paley, letter to Donald Barthelme, undated, Special Collections and Archives, University of Houston Libraries.

page 472 *"I don't find a falling off in Donald's work":* Edward Hirsch, in a conversation with the author, December 5, 2006.

page 472 *"long night in Helen's Majestic Bar":* Beverly Lowry, "The Writing Lesson," *The Gettysburg Review* 2, no. 4 (1989): 560–561.

page 472 *"the ladies talked about the rump":* This and subsequent quotes from "Overnight to Many Distant Cities" are from Donald Barthelme, *Forty Stories* (New York: Putnam, 1987), 208.

page 473 *"I think it suited Don":* Edward Hirsch, in a conversation with the author, December 5, 2006.

page 473 *had sent the magazine into a funk:* This and subsequent details about Newhouse's takeover of *The New Yorker* are from Ben Yagoda, *About Town: The New Yorker and the World It Made* (New York: Scribner, 2000), 406–416.

page 474 *"I'm a second-generation artist":* Donald Barthelme (with Seymour Chwast), *Sam's Bar: An American Landscape* (Garden City, New York: Doubleday, 1987), not paginated.

57. . . . And Beyond

page 475 *"[m]useum areas":* Donald Barthelme, "Synergy," in *Not-Knowing: The Essays and Interviews,* ed. Kim Herzinger (New York: Random House, 1997), 146.

page 476 *"beautiful stainless steel azalea":* Donald Barthelme, "Return," in *The Teachings of Don B.,* ed. Kim Herzinger (New York: Turtle Bay Books, 1992), 53–57.

page 476 *"determined to depart, yet live":* Edgar Allan Poe, *Complete Stories and Poems of Edgar Allan Poe* (Garden City, New York: Doubleday, 1966), 528.

page 476 *"dead ends":* The Writer in Society: Donald Barthelme (Houston: KUHT-TV, 1984).

page 476 *"Set yourself a splendid goal":* Balzac, *Père Goriot,* trans. Jane Minot Sedgwick (New York: Rinehart, 1950), 128.

page 477 *"Jim Love does nothing hastily":* Donald Barthelme, untitled piece, *Gulf Coast: A Journal of Literature and Art,* 4, no. 1 (1991): 189.

page 478 *"The American Chapter":* Details of the festival (except those noted below) and all Lutz Engelke quotes are from Lutz Engelke,

"Barthelme, Berlin—No Author, No Text, No Wall," *Gulf Coast: A Journal of Literature and Art,* 4, no. 1 (1991): 96-100.

page 479 *"Fine":* This and other quotes concerning Walter Abish's clash with the organizers are from a conversation with the author, February 16, 2005.

page 480 *"Unspeakable Practices":* Details about this event and all quotes concerning it are from Caryn James, "The Avant-Garde Ex Post Facto," *New York Times,* April 9, 1988.

page 480 the *"one who ironically, gracefully, and profoundly bore the burdens":* Edward Hirsch, "Donald Barthelme: Doubting It," in *Responsive Reading,* ed. Edward Hirsch (Ann Arbor: University of Michigan Press, 1999), 164. All subsequent Hirsch quotes, except those noted below, are from a conversation with the author, December 5, 2006.

page 481 *"The first time I met [Don]"; "It was 1987":* Vikram Chandra, quoted in Kathleen Morris, "Area Writer Introduces First Novel," *This Week,* July 26, 1995, and in an unsigned article in *UC Berekeley News,* posted at www .berkeley.edu/news/media/releases/2005/12/07/ hungry.html.

page 481 *"One day, after we read a piece":* This and subsequent Eric Miles Williamson quotes are from a conversation with the author, November 1, 2006.

page 481 *"I understand there is a pregnant woman"* and *"By the end of the evening":* George Williams, "A Thousand Glasses of Wine," *Gulf Coast: A Journal of Literature and Art,* 4, no. 1 (1991): 175-177.

page 481 *"Often, students would end up at Don's house":* This and subsequent George Williams quotes are from a conversation with the author, November 18, 2006.

page 482 *"I kept having the feeling that Don was becoming cooler toward me":* This and subsequent Lopate quotes are from Phillip Lopate, "The Dead Father: A Remembrance of Donald Barthelme," *Threepenny Review* (Summer 1991): 10-11.

page 482 *"After we left the restaurant"* to *"When we returned to his home":* Helen Moore Barthelme, *Donald Barthelme: The Genesis of a Cool Sound* (College Station: Texas A & M University Press, 2001), 185-186.

page 482 *"despite Don's smoking":* Marion Barthelme, in an E-mail to the author, June 6, 2008.

page 482 *"He was so sure":* This and subsequent Marion Barthelme quotes are from an E-mail to the author, April 19, 2006.

page 483 *"He quit drinking":* Marion Barthelme, in an E-mail to the author, June 6, 2008.

page 483 *"For Christ's sake, Donald":* Lynn Nesbit, in a conversation with the author, July 26, 2007.

page 484 *Rea Award:* For details, see www .reaaward.org.html/donald_barthelme.html.

page 484 *"He just wanted to "go to sleep and never wake up":* Helen Moore Barthelme, *Donald Barthelme,* 187.

pages 484-485 *"shabby old furniture and old paint"; "[I]just looking [through] the window"; "tiny town called Ravello":* Helen Moore Barthelme, *Donald Barthelme,* 187-188.

page 485 *"I have neither television nor newspapers"; "I picked up the* Corriere della Serra*":* Donald Barthelme, "Rome Diary," in *Not-Knowing,* ed. Herzinger, 160-161.

page 485 *"worrisome" twentieth century:* Paul Pintarich, "Writer Barthelme Wraps Erratic Tales in Understated and Homey Brilliance," *Oregonian,* February 9, 1989.

page 486 *"I was Papping as best I could":* Donald Barthelme, *The Dead Father* (New York: Farrar, Straus and Giroux, 1975), 172.

page 486 *"[T]he Talmud . . . is the dirtiest teaching":* Donald Barthelme, *The King* (New York: Harper & Row, 1990), 7. Subsequent quotes from *The King* are taken from the following pages: 29-30, 103, 156, 158.

page 487 *Though the novel echoes Malory's* Le Morte d'Arthur: Echoes of Apollinaire also ring throughout the novel: Apollinaire once wrote a fantasy about King Arthur set in a futuristic London. His novella, *The Poet Assassinated,* ends with an elegy for a hero beneath a tree (". . . he was lover of the queen / He was King . . ."), and "The Poet Resurrected" depicts a future when hero poets are ignored by an increasingly chaotic world (see Guillaume Apollinaire, *The Poet Assassinated and Other Stories,* trans. Ron Padgett [Manchester, England: Carcanet Press Limited, 1985], 68).

page 487 *"Think . . . / That you have but slumb'red here":* William Shakespeare, *A Midsummer Night's Dream,* in *The Riverside Shakespeare,* ed. G. Blakemore Evans (Boston: Houghton Mifflin, 1974), 246.

page 488 *"I did not bug him":* Marion Barthelme, in an E-mail in the author, June 6, 2008.

page 488 *"We had a terrific lunch":* Hirsch, "Donald Barthelme," 168.

page 488 *"but he did seem disconnected"* to *"I don't think he felt well":* Marion Barthelme, in an E-mail to the author, June 6, 2008.

page 488 *"test drive"* to *"terrifying":* Helen Moore Barthelme, *Donald Barthelme,* 188-191.

pages 488-489 *"Some time later"* to *"cells, from [Don's] original cancer":* Marion Barthelme, in an E-mail to the author, June 6, 2008.

page **489** *"seen a miracle":* Helen Moore Barthelme, *Donald Barthelme,* 19.

page **489** *"regretfully and with deep feeling":* Maggie Maranto, in an E-mail to the author, November 2, 2004.

page **489** *"love, sadness, skepticism"; "loved women, you know":* Beverly Lowry, in an E-mail to the author, August 27, 2007.

page **489** *"I've heard of you all my life":* Helen Moore Barthelme, *Donald Barthelme,* 189.

page **489** *"In the antechamber to Heaven":* Cynthia Macdonald, "Tributaries: A Collage for Donald," *Gulf Coast: A Journal of Literature and Art,* vol. 4, no. 1 (1991): 149.

Epilogue: The Final Assignment

page **491** *"The movement of history":* Donald Barthelme, *Guilty Pleasures* (New York: Farrar, Straus and Giroux, 1974), 44.

page **491** *"Language failed this week":* Michiko Kakutani, "Struggling to Find Words for a Horror Beyond Words," *New York Times,* September 13, 2001.

page **492** *"challeng[ed] the intellectual and ethical perspectives":* Edward Rothstein, "Attacks on U.S. Challenge the Perspectives of Postmodern True Believers," *New York Times,* September 22, 2001.

page **492** *"The disorientation in my stories":* Donald Barthelme, *Six Interviews,* Tapes for Readers (Washington, D.C., 1978), audio recording.

page **492** *"I don't think people are going to lose interest"; "different level of apprehension":* Dinitia Smith, "Novelists Reassess Their Subject Matter and Role," *New York Times,* September 20, 2001.

page **493** *"I remember very well the day my father died":* Richard Ford, "Love Lost," *New York Times Magazine,* September 23, 2001, 17-18.

page **493** *"Fragments are the only forms I trust":* Donald Barthelme, *Sixty Stories* (New York: Putnam, 1981), 98.

page **493** *"Trump Tower, the World's #1 Address":* *New York Times Sunday Magazine,* September 23, 2001, 7.

page **493** *"All of us at Verizon":* *New York Times,* September 23, 2001.

page **494** *"[W]e are locked in the most exquisite mysterious muck":* Barthelme, *Sixty Stories,* 158.

page **494** *"No poet, no artist of any sort":* T. S. Eliot, *The Sacred Wood: Essays on Poetry and Criticism* (London: Methuen, 1920), 49.

page **494** *"And the moon looked at him so kindly!":* Georg Büchner, *The Plays of Georg Büchner,* Victor Price (London: Oxford University Press, 1971), 128.

page **494** *"See the moon?":* Barthelme, *Sixty Stories,* 97.

page **494** *"Things yet to come will make us sadder still"; "best will in the world!":* Donald Barthelme, *The King* (New York: Harper & Row, 1990), 102, 125.

page **496** *"Did I do it well?":* Donald Barthelme, *The Dead Father* (New York: Farrar, Straus and Giroux, 1975), 176.

page **496** *"I cannot imagine the future":* Donald Barthelme, *Sadness* (New York: Farrar, Straus and Giroux, 1972), 109.

BIBLIOGRAPHY

Books by Donald Barthelme

Come Back, Dr. Caligari. Boston: Little, Brown, 1964.

Snow White. New York: Atheneum, 1967.

Unspeakable Practices, Unnatural Acts. New York: Farrar, Straus and Giroux, 1968.

City Life. New York: Farrar, Straus and Giroux, 1970.

The Slightly Irregular Fire Engine, or the Hithering Thithering Djinn. New York: Farrar, Straus and Giroux, 1971.

Sadness. New York: Farrar, Straus and Giroux, 1972.

Guilty Pleasures. New York: Farrar, Straus and Giroux, 1974.

The Dead Father. New York: Farrar, Straus, and Giroux, 1975.

Amateurs. New York: Farrar, Straus and Giroux, 1976.

Great Days. New York: Farrar, Straus and Giroux, 1979.

Sixty Stories. New York: Putnam, 1981.

Overnight to Many Distant Cities. New York: Putnam, 1983.

Paradise. New York: Putnam, 1986.

Forty Stories. New York: Putnam, 1987.

Sam's Bar (with Seymour Chwast). New York: Doubleday, 1987.

The King. New York: Harper & Row, 1990.

The Teachings of Don B. Edited by Kim Herzinger. New York: Turtle Bay, 1992.

Flying to America: 45 More Stories. Edited by Kim Herzinger. Emeryville, California: Shoemaker & Hoard, 2007.

Essays by Donald Barthelme and Interviews with Him

Not-Knowing: The Essays and Interviews. Edited by Kim Herzinger. New York: Random House, 1997.

Limited Editions of Books by Donald Barthelme

Here in the Village. Northridge, California: Lord John Press, 1978.

The Emerald. Los Angeles: Sylvester & Orphanos, 1980.

Presents. Dallas: Pressworks, 1980.

Young Oriental Bride (broadside). Northridge, California: Lord John Press, 1980.

Uncollected Stories by Donald Barthelme

"The Ontological Basis of Two" (written under the pseudonym Michael Houston). *Cavalier,* June 1963, 22.

"Then." *Mother* 3 (1964): 22-23.

"The Affront." *Harper's Bazaar,* November 1965, 229-230.

"Seven Garlic Tales." *Paris Review* 37 (1966): 62-67.

"Blue Flower Problem." *Harvest,* May 1967, 29.

"Philadelphia." *The New Yorker,* November 30, 1968, 56-58.

"Momma." *The New Yorker,* October 2, 1978, 32-33.

"Simon." *The New Yorker,* September 24, 1984, 44-45.

Audio and Video Recordings About Donald Barthelme and His Work

New Sounds in Fiction. Menlo Park, California: New Sounds, 1969. Audio recording.

Come Back, Dr. Caligari. Deland, Florida: Everett/Edwards, 1970. Audio recording.

Donald Barthelme (four-tape set). San Francisco: Pacifica Tape Library, 1976. Audio recording.

"Donald Barthelme." From *Six Interviews.* Washington, D.C.: Tapes for Readers, 1978. Audio recording.

The Writer in Society: Donald Barthelme (television interview with George Plimpton). Houston: KUHT-TV, 1984. Video recording.

Selected Shorts: A Celebration of the Short Story (cassette number 2). New York: National Public Radio, 1989. Audio recording.

Memoirs About Donald Barthelme or the Barthelme Family

Barthelme, Frederick, and Steven Barthelme. *Double Down: Reflections on Gambling and Loss.* Boston: Houghton Mifflin, 1999.

Barthelme, Helen Moore. *Donald Barthelme: The Genesis of a Cool Sound.* College Station, Texas: Texas A & M University Press, 2001.

Critical Books About Donald Barthelme

Couturier, Maurice, and Regis Durand. *Donald Barthelme.* London: Methuen, 1982.

Gordon, Lois. *Donald Barthelme.* Boston: Twayne, 1981.

Hudgens, Michael Thomas. *Donald Barthelme, Postmodernist American Writer.* Lewiston, New York: Edwin Mellen Press, 2001.

Klinkowitz, Jerome. *Donald Barthelme: An Exhibition.* Durham, North Carolina: Duke University Press, 1991.

Molesworth, Charles. *Donald Barthelme's Fiction: The Ironist Saved from Drowning*. Columbia: University of Missouri Press, 1982.

Patteson, Richard F., ed. *Critical Essays on Donald Barthelme*. New York: G. K. Hall, 1992.

Roe, Barbara. *Donald Barthelme: A Study of the Short Fiction*. New York: Twayne/Macmillan, 1992.

Stengel, Wayne B. *The Shape of Art in the Short Stories of Donald Barthelme*. Baton Rouge: Louisiana State University Press, 1985.

Trachtenberg, Stanley. *Understanding Donald Barthelme*. Columbia: University of South Carolina Press, 1990.

Critical Books with Chapters on Donald Barthelme

Aldridge, John. *The Devil in the Fire: Retrospective Essays on American Literature and Culture*. New York: Harper's Magazine Press, 1972.

Baxter, Charles. *Burning Down the House: Essays on Fiction*. St. Paul, Minnesota: Graywolf, 1997.

Bruss, Paul. *Textual Strategies in Recent American Fiction*. Lewisburg, Pennsylvania: Bucknell University Press, 1981.

Dickstein, Morris. *Gates of Eden: American Culture in the 1960s*. New York: Basic Books, 1977.

Fasching, Darrell. *Narrative Theology after Auschwitz: From Alienation to Ethics*. St. Paul, Minnesota: Augsburg Fortress Press, 1992.

Gardner, John. *On Moral Fiction*. New York: Basic Books, 1978.

Gass, William. *Fiction and the Figures of Life*. New York: Vintage, 1972.

Giles, Paul. *American Catholic Arts and Fictions*. Cambridge: Cambridge University Press, 1992.

Gilman, Richard. *The Confusion of Realms*. New York: Random House, 1969.

Graff, Gerald. *Literature Against Itself*. Chicago: University of Chicago Press, 1979.

Harris, Charles B. *Contemporary American Novelists of the Absurd*. New Haven: College and University Press, 1971.

Hassan, Ihab. *Contemporary American Literature*. New York: Frederick Ungar, 1973.

——. *Paracriticisms*. Urbana: University of Illinois Press, 1975.

——. *The Postmodern Turn*. Columbus: Ohio State University Press, 1987.

Hendin, Josephine. *Vulnerable People: A View of American Fiction Since 1945*. New York: Oxford University Press, 1978.

Hicks, Jack. *In the Singer's Temple*. Chapel Hill: University of North Carolina Press, 1981.

Hirsch, Edward, ed. *Responsive Reading*. Ann Arbor: University of Michigan Press, 1999.

Kazin, Alfred. *Bright Book of Life: American Novelists and Storytellers from Hemingway to Mailer.* Boston: Atlantic/Little, Brown, 1973.

Karl, Frederick. *American Fictions 1940-1980.* New York: Harper & Row, 1983.

Klinkowitz, Jerome. *Keeping Literary Company: Working with Writers Since the Sixties.* Albany: State University of New York Press, 1998.

——. *Literary Disruptions: The Making of a Post-Contemporary American Fiction.* Urbana: University of Illinois Press, 1975.

Kuehl, John. *Alternate Worlds: A Study of Postmodern Antirealistic American Fiction.* New York: New York University Press, 1989.

Lasch, Christopher. *The Minimal Self: Psychic Survival in Troubled Times.* New York: W. W. Norton, 1984.

Maltby, Paul. *Dissident Postmodernists: Barthelme, Coover, Pynchon.* Philadelphia: University of Pennsylvania Press, 1991.

McCaffery, Larry. *The Metafictional Muse: The Works of Robert Coover, Donald Barthelme, and William H. Gass.* Pittsburgh: University of Pittsburgh Press, 1982.

Newman, Charles. *The Postmodern Aura: The Act of Fiction in an Age of Inflation.* Evanston, Illinois: Northwestern University Press, 1985.

Olderman, Raymond M. *Beyond the Waste Land: The American Novel in the 1960s.* New Haven: Yale University Press, 1972.

Olsen, Lance. *Circus of the Mind in Motion: Postmodernism and the Comic Vision.* Detroit: Wayne State University Press, 1990.

Porush, David. *The Soft Machine: Cybernetic Fiction.* London: Methuen, 1985.

Spacks, Patricia Ann Meyer. *Boredom: The Literary History of a State of Mind.* Chicago: University of Chicago Press, 1995.

Strehle, Susan. *Fiction in the Quantum Universe.* Chapel Hill: University of North Carolina Press, 1992.

Tanner, Tony. *City of Words: American Fiction 1950-1970.* New York: Harper & Row, 1971.

Werner, Craig Hansen. *Paradoxical Resolutions: American Fiction Since James Joyce.* Urbana: University of Illinois Press, 1982.

Wilde, Alan. *Horizons of Assent: Modernism, Postmodernism, and the Ironic Imagination.* Baltimore: Johns Hopkins University Press, 1981.

——. *Middle Grounds: Studies in Contemporary American Fiction.* Philadelphia: University of Pennsylvania Press, 1987.

Special Issues of Journals Devoted to Donald Barthelme

Stewart, James, and Randall Watson, eds. *Gulf Coast: A Journal of Literature and Art* 4, no. 1 (1991).

Olsen, Lance, ed. *Review of Contemporary Fiction* 11, no. 2 (1991).

Taylor, Justin, ed. *McSweeney's Quarterly Concern* 24 (2007).

Bibliographies

Klinkowitz, Jerome. "Donald Barthelme." In *Literary Disruptions,* 2nd ed. Urbana: University of Illinois Press, 1980: 252-262.

——, Asa B. Pieratt, Jr., and Robert Murray Davis. *Donald Barthelme: A Comprehensive Bibliography.* Hamden, Connecticut: Shoestring Press/Archon Books, 1977.

Weisenburger, Steven. "Donald Barthelme: A Bibliography." *Review of Contemporary Fiction* 11, no. 2 (1991).

Selected Critical Studies

Achilles, Jochen. "Donald Barthelme's Aesthetic of Inversion: Caligari's Come-Back as Caligari's Leave-Taking." *Journal of Narrative Technique* 12, no. 2 (1982): 105-120.

Balden, Judith. "Barthelme's *Snow White:* The Making of a Modern Fairy Tale." *Southern Folklore Quarterly* 45 (1981): 145-153.

Bawer, Bruce. "Donald Barthelme and 'la vie quotidienne.' " *The New Criterion* 9, no. 1 (1991): 22-30.

Berman, Jaye. "Parody as Cultural Criticism in *The Dead Father.*" *Dutch Quarterly Review of Anglo-American Letters* 17, no. 1 (1987): 15-22.

Bocock, Maclin. " 'The Indian Uprising,' or Donald Barthelme's Strange Object Covered with Fur." *Fiction International* 4-5 (1975): 124-146.

Clark, Beverly Lyon. "In Search of Barthelme's Weeping Father." *Philological Quarterly* 62 (1983): 419-433.

Culler, Jonathan. "Junk and Rubbish: A Semiotic Approach." *Diacritics* 15, no. 3 (1985): 2-13.

Davis, Robert Murray. "Donald Barthelme's Textual Revisions." *Resources for American Literary Study* 7 (1977): 182-191.

Ditsky, John M. "With Ingenuity and Hard Work, Distracted: The Narrative Style of Donald Barthelme." *Style* 9, no. 3 (1975): 388-400.

Domini, John. "Donald Barthelme's Modernist Uprising." *Southwest Review* 75, no. 1 (1990): 95-112.

Doxey, W. S. "Donald Barthelme's 'Views of My Father Weeping': A Modern View of Oedipus." *Notes on Contemporary Literature* 3, no. 2 (1973): 14-15.

Durand, Regis. "On the Pertinaciousness of the Father, the Son, and the Subject: The Case of Donald Barthelme." In *Critical Angles: European Views of Contemporary American Literature,* edited by Marc Chénetier, 153-163. Carbondale: Southern Illinois University Press, 1986.

Evans, Walter. "Comanches and Civilization in Donald Barthelme's 'The Indian Uprising.'" *Arizona Quarterly* 42, no. 1 (1986): 45-52.

Flowers, Betty. "Barthelme's *Snow White:* The Reader-Patient Relationship." *Critique* 16, no. 3 (1975): 33-43.

Gillen, Francis. "Donald Barthelme's City: A Guide." *Twentieth Century Literature* 18 (1972): 37-44.

Guerard, Albert J. "Notes on the Rhetoric of Anti-Realistic Fiction." *Triquarterly* 30 (1974): 3-50.

Hallissy, Margaret. "Barthelme's 'Views of My Father Weeping' and Dostoevsky's *Crime and Punishment.*" *Studies in Short Fiction* 18, no. 1 (1981): 77-79.

Herr, Cheryl. "Fathers, Daughters, Anxiety, and Fiction." In *Discontented Discourses: Feminism/Textual Intervention/Psychoanalysis,* edited by Marleen S. Barr and Richard Feldstein, 173-207. Urbana: University of Illinois Press, 1989.

Herrscher, Walter. "Names in Donald Barthelme's Short Stories." *Names: Journal of the American Name Society* 34, no. 2 (1986): 125-133.

Horvath, Brooke: "Fool's Paradise?" *Denver Quarterly* 22, no. 2 (1987): 98-102.

Ishiwi, Takayoshi. "The Body That Speaks." Posted at www.asahi-net.or.jp/~kp7t -iswr/btsintro.html.

Johnson, R. E. "Bees Barking in the Night: The End and the Beginning of Donald Barthelme's Narrative." *Boundary* 2, no. 5 (1976): 71-92.

Juan-Navarro, Santiago. "About the Pointlessness of Patricide: A Lacanian Reading of Donald Barthelme's *The Dead Father.*" *Estudos Anglo-Americans* 14-15 (1991-1992): 88-103.

Kane, Thomas H. "The Death of Authors: Literary Celebrity and Automortography in Acker, Barthelme, Bukowski, and Carver's Last Acts." *Literary Interpretive Theory* 15 (2004): 409-443.

Kreutzer, Eberhard. "City Spectacles as Artistic Acts: Donald Barthelme's 'The Balloon' and 'The Glass Mountain.'" *Anglistik und Englischunterricht* 13 (1981): 43-55.

Krupnick, Mark C. "Notes from the Funhouse." *Modern Occasions* 1 (1970): 108-112.

Leitch, Thomas M. "Donald Barthelme and the End of the Road." *Modern Fiction Studies* 26, no. 1 (1982): 129-143.

Leland, John. "Remarks Re-Marked: What Curios of Signs!" *Boundary* 2, no. 5 (1977): 796-811.

Longleigh, Peter L., Jr. "Donald Barthelme's *Snow White.*" *Critique* 11, no. 3 (1969): 30-34.

Malmgren, Carl. "Barthes's *S/Z* and Barthelme's 'The Zombies': A Cacographic Interruption of a Text." *PTL* 3 (1978): 209-221.

Maloy, Barbara. "Barthelme's *The Dead Father:* Analysis of an Allegory." *Linguistics in Literature* 2, no. 2 (1977): 42-119.

Martin, Carter. "A Fantastic Pairing: Edward Taylor and Donald Barthelme." In *The Scope of the Fantastic,* edited by Robert Collins, Howard D. Pearce, and Eric S. Rabkin, 183-190. Westport, Connecticut: Greenwood Press, 1985.

Mathis, Andrew E. "*The King* and the Death of the Text." *Massachusetts Studies in English* 2, nos. 3-4 (2004): 58-71.

Meisel, Perry. "Mapping Barthelme's 'Paraguay.'" *New York Literary Forum* 8-9 (1981): 129-138.

Miller, Ellen Votaw. "Seeing the Sights: Donald Barthelme." *South Dakota Review* 23, no. 1 (1985): 11-14.

Montresor, Jaye Berman. "Sanitation and Its Discontents: Refuse and Refusal in Donald Barthelme's *Snow White.*" Posted at www.compedit.com/montress.html.

Morace, Robert A. "Donald Barthelme's *Snow White:* The Novel, the Critics, and the Culture." *Critique* 26, no. 1 (1984): 1-10.

Moran, Charles. "Barthelme the Trash-Man: The Uses of Junk." *CEA Critic* 36 (1974): 32-33.

Olsen, Lance. "Linguistic Pratfalls in Barthelme." *South Atlantic Review* 51, no. 4 (1986): 69-77.

Owens, Clarke. "Donald Barthelme's Existential Acts of Art." In *Since Flannery O'Connor: Essays on the Contemporary American Short Story,* edited by Loren Logsdon and Charles W. Mayer, 72-82. Macomb: Western Illinois University Press, 1987.

Phillips, K. J. "Ladies' Voices in Donald Barthelme's *The Dead Father* and Gertrude Stein's Dialogues." *International Fiction Review* 12, no. 1 (1985): 34-37.

Piwinski, David J. "Country-Western Music and the Bible: An Allusion in Donald Barthelme's 'Rebecca.'" *Notes on Contemporary Literature* 21, no. 1 (1991): 3-4.

Pizer, John. "The Disenchantment of *Snow White:* Robert Walser, Donald Barthelme, and the Modern/Postmodern Anti-Fairy Tale." *Canadian Review of Comparative Literature* 17, nos. 3-4 (1990): 330-347.

Rother, James. "Parafiction: The Adjacent Universe of Barth, Barthelme, Pynchon, and Nabokov." *Boundary* 2, no. 5 (1976): 21-44.

Samuels, Charles Thomas. "Moving Through 'The Indian Uprising.'" In *The Process of Fiction,* 2nd ed., edited by Barbara Mackenzie, 529-537. New York: Harcourt Brace Jovanovich, 1974.

Schmitz, Neil. "Donald Barthelme and the Emergence of Modern Satire." *Minnesota Review* 1, no. 4 (1972): 109-118.

——. "What Irony Unravels." *Partisan Review* 40, no. 3 (1973): 482-490.

Scholes, Robert. "Metafiction." *Iowa Review* 1 (1970): 100-115.

Schwenger, Peter. "Barthelme, Freud, and the Killing of Kafka's Father." In *Fictions of Masculinity: Crossing Cultures, Crossing Sexualities,* edited by Peter Murphy, 57-73. Albany: State University of New York Press, 1994.

Sloboda, Nicholas. "Heteroglossia and Collage: Donald Barthelme's *Snow White.*" *Mosaic* 30, no. 4 (1997): 109-124.

Springer, Mary Doyle. "Aristotle in Contemporary Literature: Barthelme's 'Views of My Father Weeping.' " In *Narrative Poetics: Innovations, Limits, Challenges,* edited by James Phelan, 93-102. Columbus, Ohio: Center for Comparative Studies in the Humanities, 1987.

Stevick, Philip. "Lies, Fiction, and Mock Facts." *Western Humanities Review* 30 (1976): 1-12.

——. "Ridiculous Words." *The Gettysburg Review* 3, no. 4 (1990): 738-741.

Stewart, Melissa. "Roads of 'Exquisite Mysterious Muck': The Magical Journey Through the City of William Kennedy's *Ironweed,* John Cheever's 'The Enormous Radio,' and Donald Barthelme's 'City Life.' " In *Magical Realism: Theory, History, Community,* edited by Wendy Faris and Lois Parkinson Zamora, 477-496. Durham, North Carolina: Duke University Press, 1995.

Stott, William. "Donald Barthelme and the Death of Fiction." *Prospects* 1 (1975): 369-386.

Upton, Lee. "Failed Artists in Donald Barthelme's *Sixty Stories.*" *Critique: Studies in Modern Fiction* 26, no. 1 (1984): 58-64.

Warde, William B. "Barthelme's 'The Piano Player': Surrreal and Mock Tragic." *Xavier Review* 1, nos. 1-2 (1980-1981): 58-64.

——. "A Collage Approach: Donald Barthelme's Literary Fragments." *Journal of American Culture* 8, no. 1 (1985): 51-56.

Whalen, Tom. "Wonderful Elegance: Barthelme's 'The Party.' " *Critique* 16, no. 3 (1975): 45-48.

Zeitlin, Michael. "Father-Murder and Father-Rescue: The Post-Freudian Allegories of Donald Barthelme." *Contemporary Literature* 34, no. 2 (1993): 182-204.

ACKNOWLEDGMENTS

I wish to acknowledge the Barthelme family, particularly Anne, Frederick, Marion, and Steven, for their forbearance, graciousness, and scrupulousness about accuracy. Whatever errors of fact and/or interpretation may remain on these pages, I am solely responsible.

Kim Herzinger, who has been, since Donald Barthelme's death, the faithful disseminator of Barthelme's previously uncollected work, gave me courage to proceed.

A research fellowship from the Oregon State University Center for the Humanities supported the initial stages of this project. A fellowship from the John Simon Guggenheim Memorial Foundation enabled me to complete the book. I am grateful to the center and its director, David Robinson, and to the foundation and its president, Ed Hirsch.

Julie Grob, of the University of Houston Library, was enormously patient in allowing me to study the Donald Barthelme papers even before she and her staff had completed the cataloging. For access to crucial papers and other archival materials, I am also indebted to Raynelda Calderon and the rest of the staff at the Manuscripts and Archives Division of the New York Public Library, to Mark Henderson of the Special Collections and Visual Resources Division of the Getty Research Library, and to the staff of the Morris Library's Special Collections at the University of Delaware. Jo Gutierrez of the *Houston Chronicle* Library and Linda Salitros of Texas A & M University Press were immensely helpful to me as I pursued my research.

Marjorie Sandor, Rosellen Brown, and Ehud Havazelet encouraged this book from the start, and their insightful readings of the manuscript in the various stages of its progress helped keep the writing on track. Ted Leeson's keen eye improved the manuscript beyond my fondest hopes. Martha Lewis provided crucial help with the photographs. Kerry Ahearn's love of teaching *The Dead Father* to generations of university students inspired me. For their support of the biography, I am also grateful to Charles Baxter, Brooks Haxton, and Phillip Lopate.

I cannot repay the generosity of the many people who kindly shared with me memories and thoughts about Donald Barthelme, who replied to my inquiries about architecture, culture, and literature, or who pointed me toward other useful sources of information: Walter Abish, Roger Angell, Beverly Arnold, John Barth, Anne Barthelme, Frederick Barthelme, Marion Barthelme, Steven Barthelme, Ann Beattie, Glenn Blake, Rosellen Brown, Joan Barthelme Bugbee, Jerome Charyn, Marc Chénetier, Thomas Cobb, Arthur Danto, John

Domini, Jean Dunbar, Stephen Fox, Marianne Frisch, William Gass, Marilyn Gillet, Pat Goeters, Herman Gollob, Kim Herzinger, Oscar Hijuelos, Ed Hirsch, Alifair Kane, Karen Kennerly, Jerome Klinkowitz, Ben Koush, Phillip Lopate, Beverly Lowry, Maggie Maranto, David Markson, Victoria Meyer, Mark Mirsky, Barry Munitz, Lynn Nesbit, J. D. O'Hara, Grace Paley, Eileen Pollock, Padgett Powell, Carter Rochelle, Kirkpatrick Sale, Harrison and Sandra Starr, and Elise Hopkins Stephens.

Old friends accompanied me, in spirit, during the writing: Tom Bernatchez, Terrell Dixon, Jeff Greene, Olive Hershey, Carl Lindahl, Martha Grace Low, George Manner, John McNamara, Gary Myers, Randy Mott, Teri Ruch, Cynthia Santos, Marilyn Stablein, and Gail Storey.

To Brian Kellow, for the use of his apartment in New York during a crucial period of research, I owe my thanks. To Anita Helle, Karen Holmberg, and Keith Scribner, I owe my gratitude for their collegiality and friendship, and to all of my colleagues in the Oregon State University English Department, I owe my appreciation for their goodwill and good spirit. To Ann Leen, office manager extraordinaire, who helped me keep the English Department on an even keel as I wrote and tried to serve as department chair, I owe what remains of my health.

The excitement and, most important, the trust that Kit Ward, my agent, and Michael Homler, my editor at St. Martin's Press, have invested in this project have meant more to me than I can say; they are largely responsible for this book (in all its best aspects) and I will always cherish the opportunity I have had to work with them. Michael's editorial acumen and gentle, informed guidance have been steadying and invaluable.

My admiration goes to Carol Edwards for her heroic copyediting, to production editor John Morrone, and to Diana Frost and Mark A. Fowler for their genial legal advice.

Finally, for their steadfastness, long friendships, and love, which make any and all work possible, I thank my family in Texas and Oklahoma, Michelle and Anna Boisseau, Rosellen Brown, Jerry and Joyce Bryan, Elizabeth Campbell, Hannah Crum, Kris and Rich Daniels, Ehud Havazelet, Kathie Lang, Ted Leeson, Creighton and Deborah Lindsey, Jeff and Pam Mull, Tom Stroik, Marshall Terry, and the greatest of partners, my love, Marjorie Sandor.

INDEX

DB stands for Donald Barthelme. Writings are by DB unless otherwise stated.